Politics and Public Policy in the
Contemporary American West

UNIVERSITY OF NEW MEXICO PRESS

Albuquerque

POLITICS and PUBLIC POLICY in the CONTEMPORARY AMERICAN WEST ★★★

Clive S. Thomas, Editor

UNIVERSITY OF NEW MEXICO PUBLIC POLICY SERIES

Hank Jenkins-Smith, Series Editor

Library of Congress Cataloging-in-Publication Data

Politics and public policy in the contemporary American West / Clive S. Thomas, editor.
  — 1st ed.
        p.   cm. — (University of New Mexico public policy series)
    Includes bibliographical references and index.
    ISBN 0–8263–1250–0. — ISBN 0–8263–1251–9 (pbk.)
      1. West (U.S.)—Politics and government.   2. State governments—West (U.S.)
  3. Local government—West (U.S.)   4. Political participation—West (U.S.)   5. Federal
  government—West (U.S.)
  I. Thomas, Clive S.   II. Series.
  JK2687.P65   1991
  320.978—dc20   90–15473
                                                                                      CIP

Design by Susan Gutnik.

Quotation on p. 399 is from Terry Sanford, *Storm over the States* © 1967, McGraw-Hill
and is reproduced by permission.

This book is dedicated
to my wife
Susan Ann Burke

CONTENTS

PREFACE

W ALK INTO A LIBRARY OR BOOKSTORE ALMOST ANY-
where in the United States and you'll find shelf after shelf of books
on the American West. Besides the standard western pulp novels by
Zane Grey, Louis L'Amour and many others, you'll also run across
picture books on the Old "Wild" West; histories of the settlement of
the region, and biographies of its pioneers, its heroes and its many
colorful characters. You'll also find books on western Indians and
their culture, on western art and artists, tourist guides, and those
large glossy picture books of the magnificent scenery of the West that
people often give as birthday and Christmas gifts.

But if you try to find a book on the West that explains the region's
politics and how they have been affected by the major changes of the
last three decades, you'll probably search long and in vain. If you're
lucky, you may find a book or two on the politics of individual western
states and maybe Frank Jonas's edited books on western politics published way back in 1961 and 1969. But that will be the extent of it.

It was this need that many of us who teach American government
and state and local politics at western universities saw for an up-to-
date comprehensive analysis of western politics that provided the
impetus for this book. When we first conceived the idea of the book,
three types of readers were foremost in our minds. First were those
teaching American government, state and local government, and public policy courses at western universities and the students taking those
courses. This book will provide them with a regional perspective. It
will give more meaning and relevance to the general statements and
theories in the standard textbooks, and also will provide a regional
context in a course on the politics of a particular state such as California, New Mexico or Wyoming.

Second, we wanted to provide a resource book for teachers and
scholars interested in the American West, be they political scientists,
public administration specialists, historians, sociologists, economists,

1

THE WEST AND ITS BRAND OF POLITICS

Clive S. Thomas

*M*OST OF US TRACE OUR FASCINATION WITH THE American West back to our childhood when we were thrilled by stories and movies of the Old West. The "Wild West," as we knew it back then, was a place of high adventure, of manly heroes and of breathtaking beauty. There was the U.S. cavalry and its clashes with proud Indians like Crazy Horse, Geronimo and Sitting Bull; there was the carefree and independent life of the cowboys, and there were the wild frontier towns with the gunfighters, gamblers, dance-hall girls, lawmen, outlaws and vigilantes. There were the wagon trains wending slowly across vast, seemingly endless plains and deserts, fording wide, fast-flowing rivers, and crossing huge snow-capped mountain ranges, while heading for romantic-sounding places like Oregon, Sacramento, Santa Fe and the Comstock. There were the colorful ranchers, farmers, miners and traders. And there was the railroad, with its puffing locomotives with their haunting whistle and clanging bell, built by tough and tireless crews and hardheaded businessmen.

What we probably didn't realize back then, as we re-enacted the gunfight at the O.K. Corral or the battle of the Little Big Horn in our back yard, was that there was another side to this seemingly romantic life of the West. This was the side of stark reality. When we strip away the romance the Old West was much like any other society—it was ridden with conflicts arising out of how to deal with the problems faced by its inhabitants. In essence, these conflicts were rooted in disagreements over varying ways of life and how best to secure and protect them. In all societies, the never-ending existence of such conflicts and the resulting continuous efforts to resolve them lead to politics and politicking. Thus the West was as political a society as any other. And perhaps even more so, as it struggled to deal with the urgent needs and special problems that arise in any developing area.

Many of these problems and conflicts are familiar to us from years of watching western movies. As a result we usually know much more about western politics, both past and present, than we perhaps realize. There was the struggle to bring law and order to the wild western towns. There were sometimes bitter conflicts between those colorful ranchers, farmers, miners and traders over water rights and land use. Those beautiful vistas with their big skies, huge mountains and endless open spaces were often cursed by westerners for increasing the cost of getting supplies and of shipping out cattle, sheep, farm products and ore. As the settlements advanced, the blame for such high shipping costs was increasingly placed on unfair practices by those hardheaded and sometimes heavy-handed railroad pioneers whose transportation monopoly held the power of life and death over most western towns, businesses, ranches, farms and mines.

These numerous problems and conflicts demanded attention and solution. How to resolve them often became the subject of public debate—sometimes very heated debate. This debate, and the power struggle between groups and interests that resulted, formed the core of politics in the Old West. Over the years, while some issues have either been resolved or ceased to be significant, other problems have arisen. Conflict between developers and environmentalists and the desire for bilingual education supported by some minority groups and strongly opposed by other groups are examples. The public debate and power struggle resulting from these and similar issues is an essential element of politics in the contemporary West.

In this first chapter we identify some of the major political threads in both the Old and the New West and provide an overview of the enduring characteristics of western politics. We also raise a question that is a major theme of the entire book: In what ways can the western brand of politics and the resulting governmental processes and public policies be considered distinctive? Taken together these two primary purposes of the chapter provide a basis for comparing and contrasting the politics, government and public policy of the West with other regions of the nation. But first we need to define exactly what we mean by *the West* and to identify its distinguishing features.

The Contemporary West Defined

In this book we define the West strictly in terms of geography. Yet perhaps most of us tend to define places, particularly well-known places, more in terms of mental images: stereotypes of their inhabitants, their culture and their physical environment. Often these images have a great influence on the geographical definition—or *definitions*—of a place. This is particularly true of places shrouded in romance in popular lore, such as the Orient, the South Seas, and the American West. In fact, in the popular mind there have been many perceptions of the location of this "West." These perceptions, or mental maps, have varied over time and according to where a person lives.[1]

In colonial times and in the early years after the Revolution, when settlements hugged the eastern seaboard, anything beyond the westerly limits of a community was considered the *West*. Most often the West was seen as synonymous with the frontier. Until the Louisiana Purchase in 1803 the western boundary of the United States was the Mississippi River. As the nation expanded toward the Pacific Ocean during the nineteenth century, and the frontier kept moving, so did the location of the West change in the popular mind. New terms like *Midwest, Southwest, Northwest* and *Far West* entered the language.

Even today, a person's perception of the West will often depend on where he or she lives. A New Yorker, for example, may consider people living in Kansas City or Omaha to be westerners. Whereas residents of these cities usually consider themselves as midwesterners and reserve the term "westerner" for those living beyond the Rockies. On the other hand, people who live in Alaska and Hawaii do not usually look upon themselves as westerners, but simply as Alaskans or Hawaiians.

Yet another, and perhaps for many the most compelling, mental map of the West is that associated with the Old or Wild West and with the evocative term *western*, as in western wear, and country and western music. This mental map centers on the past and present exploits of that most celebrated of American folk heroes—the cowboy. The West according to this view would include the Plains states from the Dakotas through Nebraska, Kansas, Oklahoma and Texas. Missouri might also be included. It would include the Rocky Mountain states from Idaho and Montana through Wyoming, Nevada, Utah and Colorado to New Mexico and Arizona. Some might include California; but most would not include Oregon, Washington or Alaska. And even though one of the largest cattle ranches in the United States is in Hawaii, most of us consider that state about as western as Florida![2]

These mental maps have certainly influenced geographical definitions of the West. While its western limits are not in dispute, including Hawaii and Alaska, its eastern boundary certainly is a subject of disagreement. Some would argue that every state west of the Mississippi should qualify as the West. Yet states like Iowa and Missouri have quite different economies and population mixes from New Mexico, Idaho or California. To be sure, the Southwest states of Texas and Oklahoma appear to have much in common with the West, but they also have strong ties with the South. Oklahoma also has ties with the farm states of the Midwest.[3]

Thus Richard Lamm, a former governor of Colorado, argues that "a new Mason-Dixon line is being drawn at the 100th meridian."[4] A strong case can be made for using this as a geographical boundary for defining the eastern limits of the West. This line of longitude, which passes through the middle of the Plains states from Bismarck, North Dakota, to Laredo, Texas, marks a very important division. East of this line rainfall is plentiful. Consequently there is a plentiful supply of water. West of this line it is a much different story. Except in Alaska, Hawaii, and a strip along the Pacific Coast, rainfall is less than twenty inches a year and water is scarce—in some places very scarce.

Therefore, one working definition of the West used by many physical geographers is based upon lack of water west of the 100th meridian—a shortage that has a great impact on the life-styles and thus the politics in this region. Thirteen states lie west of this line. Listed in alphabetical order they are: Alaska, Arizona, California, Colorado,

Hawaii, Idaho, Montana, Nevada, New Mexico, Oregon, Utah, Washington, and Wyoming. With noted exceptions, this is the definition of the West that we will use in this book.[5] This is also the definition of the West used by the Bureau of the Census.[6] Map 1.1 shows the political geography of the region.

Prominent Regional Characteristics
of the West

The West is a vast and for the most part sparsely populated region. It accounts for almost half of the land area of the nation, or 1.8 million of the 3.6 million square miles for the fifty states as whole.[7] Alaska alone accounts for 14% of the nation's land area. Nine of the ten largest states in area in the Union are located in the West; and only one, Hawaii (ranked forty-seventh), does not place in the top twenty. But the West contains only 20% of the nation's population. Only two western states rank in the top twenty most populous states, while five rank among the bottom ten. Only California and Hawaii have a population density above the national average of sixty-nine per square mile; seven western states have twenty people or less per square mile. However, contrary to what this might lead us to believe, the West is not a rural society but a highly urbanized region. Projections for 1990 are that about 85% of westerners will be living in urban areas as compared with a national average of 75% and a regional low of 70% for the South.[8]

A closer scrutiny of the West reveals a host of contrasts and differences between its states and subregions. Geographically, it is a region with one state (Hawaii) separated from the others by thousands of miles of ocean and another (Alaska) set apart by a foreign country. It contains the rain-laden coastal area of the northern Pacific as well as the parched great basin between the Rockies and the Sierras. With over 28 million people, of whom 92% live in urban areas, California is the nation's most populous and most urbanized state. But the West also contains the nation's least populous state, Wyoming (pop. 490,000), and one of the least urbanized states, Montana (ranked fortieth with only 53% of its population living in urban areas). Culturally, the region contains states with significant populations of Asian and Hispanic descent as well as major groups of American Indians. California, and to a lesser extent Arizona and New Mexico, are culturally as diverse as any states in the nation.

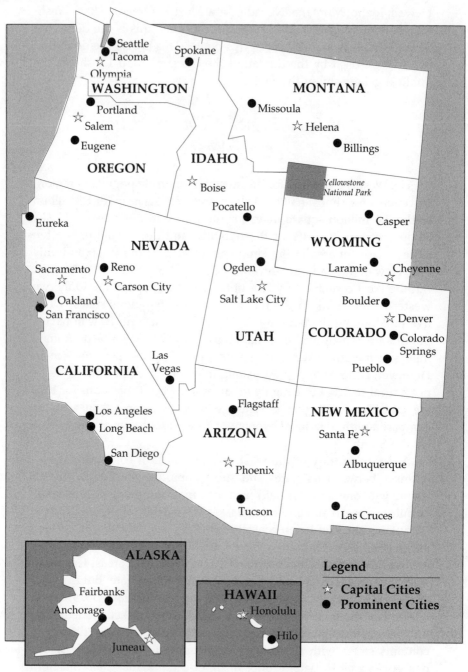

Map 1.1 The Thirteen Western States

Economically, there are also considerable contrasts. California has probably the most diverse economy of any state and leads the nation in both manufacturing and agricultural output. In contrast, Alaska, Wyoming and Nevada rank among the least industrialized and least diverse economies in the nation; while states like Washington, Colorado and Arizona fall somewhere in between. In terms of per capita income, similar diversities are evident. The range is from Alaska, ranked first in the nation for most of the 1980s at over $17,000, to Utah at around $9,700, ranked forty-eighth for most of that period, just above Mississippi and West Virginia. California and Colorado are also among the top ten states, while Idaho, Montana and New Mexico are in the bottom ten with Utah.

Despite these contrasts and differences the thirteen western states share many experiences and attributes. Historically, they share experiences of development from colonization by Euro-Americans to territorial status to statehood. This common history includes: (1) the frontier and the influence of the frontier ethos; (2) colonial status and external dependency, including considerable dependence on the federal government; (3) the power of the railroads and other dominant economic forces that helped fuel the populist and progressive movements; and (4) an economy based on agriculture and natural resource extraction and a consequent lack of industry.

These western states still share several common elements. Although their economic diversity has increased, many are still dependent upon agriculture and natural resource extraction. The federal government is a major landholder in all western states and exerts tremendous influence throughout the region. The vast and difficult terrain and the sparse population of most western states also produce common problems. So it is not just the lack of water and the Census Bureau's classification that warrants consideration of these thirteen states as a separate region that we have defined as the contemporary West. These common experiences and elements, both historical and contemporary, have affected the politics of the region. But what exactly are the common characteristics of western politics that these experiences have produced? And to what extent have they made the West a distinct region politically?

The Enduring Characteristics of Western Politics

Here we identify and briefly explore ten enduring characteristics of western policits. We label these *enduring* characteristics because they have for the most part been a feature of western politics since Euro-Americans first settled the West. They have given certain features and a particular tone to the political debate and the power struggle between groups and interests in the West. In turn, these characteristics have affected the form and operation of government and the public policies it develops.

Before we identify these enduring characteristics we need to be aware that they may manifest themselves at various levels of politics and government. They will likely display themselves in any political arena in which western politicians and governments are involved. At the national or federal level the characteristics of western politics manifest themselves through the region's elected officials in the U.S. Congress, as well as through elected and/or appointed state and local officials and the organizations and individuals dealing with the three branches of the national government. These characteristics are seen in state and local politics and government, as well as in interstate relations and relations between various levels of government. Some characteristics will be more evident in one or two arenas, while others will be present in all arenas of western politics.

The ten enduring characteristics of western politics are identified here and discussed below.

1. Strong emphasis on political pragmatism and de-emphasis of ideology
2. Strong strain of political individualism
3. Significant use of methods of direct democracy
4. Regionalism and sectionalism
5. Candidate-oriented election campaigns
6. Weak political parties and strong interest groups
7. Weak political institutions and a fragmented policymaking process
8. The dominance of the issue of economic development
9. An all-pervasive dependence on government
10. The western political paradox: the political manifestation of the myth and reality of western development

1. STRONG EMPHASIS ON POLITICAL PRAGMATISM
AND DE-EMPHASIS OF IDEOLOGY

In contrast to Western Europe, political pragmatism has always been an important aspect of American political life and is certainly not unique to politics in the American West. However, several factors unique to the environment of the West have placed a particular emphasis on pragmatism in western politics. Therefore, the West has probably been the least ideological and the most politically pragmatic of all the regions of the nation.

Here we are using *pragmatism* to denote an approach to everyday life that uses whatever means are available to achieve a given end. The pragmatist rejects ideology and dogma, and even cherished principles if these stand in the way of getting the job done.[9] In politics this de-emphasizes and undermines adherence to theoretical political ideals and doctrines that are achieved through prescribed, and often undeviating, courses of action. Political pragmatism emphasizes a flexible approach to dealing with political issues and problems. The paramount concern is advancing the interests of some individual or group or solving the problem at hand by the most appropriate means available.

This is not to say that western politics have been devoid of ideology or dogmatism. Conservatism, classical liberalism (*laissez faire*), New Deal liberalism, libertarianism, and even socialism have all been part of the western political mind-set. But, in general, western politics have been marked by flexibility of approach, *ad hoc* solutions, and a willingness to experiment and reform. Westerners tend to borrow bits and pieces from various schools of thought as suits their needs. A positive way to describe this is that westerners have a flexible approach to politics and public policy. This approach can, however, be alternatively viewed as utilitarian, instrumental or expedient.

2. STRONG STRAIN OF POLITICAL INDIVIDUALISM

Western politics have coupled political pragmatism with a strong strain of political individualism. Western political individualism rejects a slavish adherence to ideologies, political creeds, and party labels. Less emphasis is placed on promoting specific ideals for the society as a whole. This political individualism emphasizes the interests of the individual and the group, independence of political choice at the polls, and a pragmatic approach to dealing with political issues and problems. Hence political pragmatism and political individualism are inextricably bound together in western politics. The two do not always exist together, however. For example, nations often attempt to achieve the realization of ideologies such as communism and socialism through pragmatic means, especially when the prescribed theoretical methods have failed.

What has fused political pragmatism and political individualism together in the West is a combination of factors—some of them unique to the region while others were influences from the rest of the nation. Once again, we do not claim that political individualism is a unique western phenomenon. Like political pragmatism, it is very much a part of American political life in general. What can be demonstrated, however, is that political individualism in the West is more extensive than in other regions of the country. As with political pragmatism, and for similar reason, this characteristic of western politics can be viewed either negatively or positively. Judgments aside, throughout this book we will offer various explanations for the prominence of political individualism and political pragmatism in western politics.

3. THE SIGNIFICANT USE OF METHODS OF DIRECT DEMOCRACY

No region makes use of the initiative, the referendum and the recall more than does the West, and these provisions have shaped the brand of politics that exists in the region. At the state level eleven of the twenty states allowing a public initiative for enacting statutory laws are in the West. Twelve of twenty-five states allowing a public referendum (a yes or no vote) on state legislation, are in the West. And nine of fourteen states allowing a recall election of both state and local officials are also located in the West. Of all the fifty states, Oregon and California are the two that, over the years, have made the most use of methods of direct democracy.[10]

4. REGIONALISM AND SECTIONALISM

Regionalism and *sectionalism* are two terms that are subject to various interpretations and are sometimes used interchangeably. They will be specifically defined later in this chapter. For our immediate purposes, however, we will use them to denote political competition, at various levels of intensity, between two or more geographic areas. This competition is rooted in a feeling of distinctiveness on the part of each area, and usually results from economic interests but sometimes also from cultural differences.[11]

The sheer size of the West, its physical geography, its sparse population in many areas, and the uneven distribution of natural resources have produced many manifestations of regionalism. There are, in fact, three levels at which regionalism has manifested itself in western politics. There is the West as a whole in competition with the other regions at the national level. Then there is the competition between subregions in the West as well as interstate rivalries. Finally, there are regional rivalries within states.

Subregional and interstate rivalries manifest themselves in conflicts over resources such as water. The Northwest and the Southwest have many opposing interests in this regard. California and Arizona fought a twenty-year battle over their rights to Colorado River water. With the exception of Hawaii, all the western states exhibit varying degrees of regionalism in state politics and policymaking. For example, California and New Mexico have the division between north and south; Washington, Oregon, Montana and Colorado between the eastern and western parts of their states; and Alaska has divisions between southeast, south-central (Anchorage) and the interior. Perhaps the most regionally divided of all states in the West—and perhaps in the nation—is Idaho. Its three distinct regions of southeast, southwest and north might lead a cynic to suggest that the state motto should be changed from the "Gem State" to the "Sectional State."[12] It is a fact of life that in many western states the regional loyalties of politicians and voters often take precedence over party, state or other interests.

5. CANDIDATE-ORIENTED ELECTION CAMPAIGNS

Western elections have generally focused on the personality and attributes of the candidate and thus have relegated issues to a secondary place and political party to an even lower level of concern. In the last decade or so the nation as a whole has also come to give prominence to the candidate over issues and party affiliation in elections. Whether a blessing or a curse for democracy, this is a characteristic of western politics that has worked its way east.

The long-standing tradition of candidate-oriented elections in the West is due to a combination of factors. Most important among these is the weakness of political parties and the strength of interest groups, which we will discuss in more detail below. This is especially the case when the parties provide little or no campaign funds to a candidate, and interest groups rush in to fill the funding gap. Other factors include the characteristics of western politics as discussed above: the emphasis on political pragmatism and individualism and the de-emphasis of strong ideological commitments, and sectionalism and localism.

One other contributing factor to the origin and continuing prominence of candidate-oriented elections is the fact that in the early years, politics could be and was conducted on a "friends and neighbors" basis. Thus, before World War II the small populations in all the western states except California enabled politics at all levels to be conducted on a very personal level. The candidates running for or holding local, state and even national office were easily accessible to individuals and groups. Many people were on a first-name basis with the politicians. Such a situation was in strong contrast to the political campaigns in large urban states such as New York and Pennsylvania, or even in medium-sized states like Ohio, Michigan and Missouri.

However, the increase in western population and especially the increased urbanization that has taken place since 1945, and particularly since the 1960s, have changed this situation somewhat. California has virtually no traces of personalized politics left, and Washington State, Colorado and Arizona are not far behind. Nevertheless, personalized politics still remains a feature of states with small populations, such as Alaska, Idaho, Hawaii, Montana, Nevada and Wyoming. While difficult to quantify, it does appear that this relative ease of access and feeling of personal political effectiveness has had an important influence on western politics. For example, the existence of personalized politics has contributed to the weakness of political parties and the concomitant strength of interest groups, as well as to the fragmentation of the policymaking process in most of the state capitals.

6. WEAK POLITICAL PARTIES AND STRONG INTEREST GROUPS

Over the years, as compared to many eastern and midwestern states, political parties in the West have been relatively weak. In essence, a weak party is one that has little control over setting the political agenda and consequently little influence over what policies are enacted. In 1981 political scientist Sarah McCally Morehouse classified only two western states (Colorado and Arizona) as having strong parties, eight as moderate, and three as weak (Oregon, New Mexico and Alaska).[13] The trend of the last ten years has been toward even weaker parties.

The long tradition of relatively weak parties in the West is due in part to the five enduring characteristics of western politics that were treated above. Also there are three important historical reasons. One is the fact that the raw material of party strength in the East, i.e., massive numbers of immigrants, was not available in the West. The second factor was the progressives' legacy of de-emphasizing partisanship and replacing it with "administrative expertise." Third was the early establishment of strong interest groups.

While it is far from a simple situation, there appears to be an inverse relationship between the strength of political parties and the strength of interest groups.[14] When parties are strong, groups tend to be weak, and vice versa. Beginning with the mining companies, the railroads and agricultural organizations, interest groups have always had great influence in the western states. In 1981, Morehouse classified six western states as having strong interest group systems. Another six fell into the moderate category. This meant that only one western state, Colorado, had a weak interest group system.[15] The trend in the last ten years, however, has been toward the strong category.

7. WEAK POLITICAL INSTITUTIONS AND A FRAGMENTED POLICYMAKING PROCESS

The legislative and executive branches of government in western states have long manifested a tradition of weakness as regards their ability to control and coordinate the making of public policy. The reasons for this are to be found in a combination of the enduring characteristics that we have so far identified. This situation is exacerbated by the fact that in all but Alaska and Hawaii several top-level executive officers, ranging from attorney general to insurance commissioner, are separately elected or are out of the purview of gubernatorial appointment. Add to this the progressives' legacy of establishing independent state boards and commissions. The result is a multitude of power bases in western political systems. The resulting fragmented policymaking process is the bane of the political leaders, but a boon for interest groups.

8. THE DOMINANCE OF THE ISSUE OF ECONOMIC DEVELOPMENT

Pick up a current or even back copy of a major newspaper in any western state and you will find some aspect of economic development featured as a major issue. More than likely you will find several stories concerned with economic development issues. Before the mid-1960s the issues revolved around economic development of any kind. Today the emphasis is more on economic diversification and its positive or negative effects.

Four factors have kept the issue of economic development at the forefront of state politics in the West. The first has been the need to develop the area and realize the benefits of economic opportunity. Second is the unbalanced nature of most western state economies with their dependence on natural resources, agriculture and government, and the fact that world prices and decisions in Washington often determine the economic well-being of the West. This has led to a search for economic diversification and independence in order to insulate the western states from these external influences. The third factor is that, due to their remoteness from markets, lack of a trained labor force and other factors, some western states are simply not attractive locations for many businesses. Consequently, the issue of economic development, diversified or otherwise, is never satisfactorily dealt with and the search is a continual one. The fourth factor, and one that has become increasingly important in the last twenty years, is that many groups and individuals now question the value of economic development when it is at the expense of the physical environment. As a result, this conflict between developers and environmentalists is becoming an increasingly significant theme of western politics.

Over the years, this preoccupation with economic development, plus the size and terrain of most western states, has led western politicians to emphasize policies relating to the development of natural resources, transportation and, in many parts of the region, water resources. To be sure, like most other states, western states spend a high proportion of their state funds on education. But by various ways of assessing state spending on roads, ten of the top twenty spenders among the states are in the West.[16] Transportation is of course very closely linked to natural-resource development. This in turn is the basis of many aspects of western economies ranging from employment in resource extraction to tourism to the government revenues from sales, corporate and severance taxes. And of course without adequate water there can be no agriculture, no tourism and, indeed, no settlement.

9. AN ALL-PERVASIVE DEPENDENCE ON GOVERNMENT

The West has long relied on federal, state and local government aid not only for development purposes but also for economic well-being in general. It has been used particularly as a source of employment. Today this reliance is more important than ever. Government employment accounts for between 25% (Alaska) and 12.5% (California) of the labor force in the thirteen western states. In fact, seven of the ten states in the Union most dependent on government employment are located in the West.[17] With this reliance on government employment and aid being so crucial, the role of government has come to assume a central role in the politics of western states— a role that is far more significant than in most states in other regions of the country.

10. THE WESTERN POLITICAL PARADOX: THE POLITICAL MANIFESTATION
OF THE MYTH AND REALITY OF WESTERN DEVELOPMENT

Despite or perhaps because of this dependence, the crucial role of the government often goes unrecognized, is frequently ignored and sometimes even is denied in the various arenas of the western political debate. Furthermore, there is a strong antipathy to certain aspects of government in many parts of the West, and even an antipathy to government in general. This seeming inconsistency which we call the "western political paradox" is the political manifestation of the contradictions between the myth and reality of western development.

The Myth of the West, promoted by countless western novels and movies and perpetuated down the years by many western politicians, is that both the Old and the New West were won by westerners alone through self-help, vision, determination and resourcefulness. The reality, of course, is that all the individual and private business effort in the world could not alone have provided all the capital investment and the jobs that were needed to overcome the physical and economic impediments to development and realize the dream of the West. Even in the early days, westerners needed a helping hand to reach their goals. The hand they reached out to grab was that of the government, in those days primarily the federal government. This need for help developed into a state of dependency on government as westerners worked to develop the Old West into the New West. Despite lip service to the contrary, the West was won largely through federal government aid.

While other regions tend to manifest similar inconsistencies, the intensity of these appears to be much greater in the West. It would be a mistake, however, to conclude that this western political paradox is a simple phenomenon based entirely on inconsistency and self-deception or that all westerners are its champions. It is also an ambiguous and elusive phenomenon that is hard to quantify and treat in any definitive way. Nevertheless, it is such an important aspect of the western political mind-set that we will try to explain its nuances and manifestations at appropriate points in this book.

Is the West a Distinct Region or Section Politically?

Having identified the characteristics of western politics we now move to assess these and the West's political interest in the context of the nation as a whole. The essence of our task can best be expressed by posing the following questions: Does the West have a common and distinct interest that distinguishes it from the other regions and states, and a distinct style of politics that sets it apart from the rest of the nation? Or does it simply have *some* distinct interests and *some* unique elements in its politics, government and public policy? And what are the explanations for and consequences of this situation?

To give these questions a more specific focus, we need to define more clearly what we mean by the terms *region* and *section* as used in a political context. The problem is that these two terms have meant different things at different times and have often been used synonymously. For our purposes, however, we must distinguish between them.

Earlier we noted that regionalism is rooted in a feeling of identity with a place based upon interest, usually economic but often also cultural. This reveals itself in political rivalries with other areas or regions over public priorities and the dividing-up of public funds. Political scientist Richard Franklin Bensel has argued that in most nations where regionalism exists it is most often grounded in ethnic identity and religious rivalry and only rarely in economic competition. He goes on to argue that the reverse is the case in the United States. There the relatively low level of ethnic and religious rivalry between regions has meant that regional conflicts have been grounded in economic rivalries. "It is a rivalry rooted in a struggle for control of the national political economy."[18]

Another way to look at this is to say that regionalism in America is rooted primarily in economic geography. According to this view, "differentiation in the distribution of natural resources gives rise to economic specialization and divergent interests among the various regions."[19] Divergent economic interests lead to political competition. The degree of intensity of regional feeling and internal cohesiveness, and thus the distinctiveness of the region politically, will depend in part on how divergent these economic interests are or how much these divergencies threaten the social and political institutions that sustain the economy and the life-style.[20]

Sectionalism is an extreme form of regionalism. It is characterized by very divergent interests between one region and other regions. This usually arises because the beleaguered region sees its economic, social and political systems threatened by the rest of the nation. The consequence is a high degree of cohesiveness and an intense feeling of separateness within the beleaguered region which is manifested in a united front at the national level in dealing with the rest of the country. This intense rivalry may produce a separate political party and a distinct supporting ideology to further the cause of the beleaguered section. Often this intense feeling of distinctiveness expresses itself in the demand for some form of regional autonomy, as in the championing by many southerners before the Civil War of John C. Calhoun's principle of the concurrent majority.[21] The ultimate expression of sectionalism is, of course, secession.[22] Unlike the South, the West has never been sectional in the way defined here.

As we noted in an earlier section, at first glance the apparent economic, social and geographical diversity of the West may lead us to question the degree to which the West is a region at all. There is a great distance in both miles and time from bush (rural) Alaska to the sophisticated living of San Francisco. The Wyoming rancher would appear to have little in common with the high-tech scientist in Colorado or Arizona. And areas like western Washington State and Oregon with more than adequate rainfall would appear to have different interests from the desert areas of New Mexico and Nevada. But a geographical area does not have to have *everything* in common in order to have *some* common interest and thus to exhibit regionalism.

As we have noted throughout this chapter, many elements that the thirteen states of the West share produce manifestations of a separate or distinct political identity. These common interests and elements can express themselves in four ways: (1) at the national level through the region's representatives; (2) in interstate cooperation and interstate compacts; (3) in a distinctive political style involving political and governmental processes; and (4) through public policies. We will be concerned with all four elements of regional distinctiveness in this book, but emphasis will be placed on the third and fourth elements.

So the questions becomes: How distinctive is the West in these four manifestations of regionalism? In all four respects the short, if rather unsatisfactory, answer is that in some cases the West is distinctive and in other cases it is not. For example, the congressional delegations of all thirteen states have never voted as a bloc on any issue, including water or natural resource policy. Often there are keen rivalries between subregions and states for federal dollars. But on many issues, such as tariff policy and transportation, western congressional delegations do exhibit considerable cohesiveness. A similar situation exists when it comes to interstate cooperation. The interest that exists between the western states is evidenced by their creating several interstate compacts to deal with issues of common concern. The establishment of the Western Governors' Policy Office (now the Western Governors' Association) to discuss common concerns and provide a regional voice is evidence of some common interests; as are other western interstate organizations such as WICHE—the Western Interstate Commission for Higher Education. Finally, we have already mentioned several commonalities and differences in political style, politics, government and policies of the region.

Efforts to establish a region as a political community presumably rest on shared values or shared experiences, since no formal political institutional structure exists for a region. This book is based on the recognition that the thirteen western states are thirteen distinctive political communities. However, it is also our contention that there is a set of political experiences and perspectives common to the region that have shaped how westerners understand politics and still influence their actions in the political arena. The extent of the various aspects of western political regionalism, the degree to which they affect politics, power, government and public policy, and the ways in which these regional characteristics are becoming more or less pronounced will be important points of consideration throughout this book.

Notes

1. For an interesting discussion of the interplay between psychology and geography see Peter Gould and Rodney White, *Mental Maps* (London: Penguin Books, 1974).

2. For further discussion of various designations of *the West*, see Frank H. Jonas, ed., *Politics in the American West* (Salt Lake City: University of Utah Press, 1969), 1–2; and Gerald D. Nash, "Where's the West?" *Historian* 49 (November 1986), 1–9. An extensive consideration of the problems of defining regions, including the West, is found in Ira Sharkansky, *Regionalism in American Politics* (Indianapolis: Bobbs-Merrill, 1970), esp. chap. 2.

3. See Ronald J. Hrebenar and Clive S. Thomas, eds., *Interest Group Politics in the American West* (Salt Lake City: University of Utah Press, 1987), 3; and Thomas and Hrebenar, "Comparative Interest Groups in the American West," *The Journal of State Government* 59, 3 (September/October 1986), 125.

4. *Newsweek*, September 17, 1979, 31.

5. One exception to this definition is found in Chapter 8, "The Politics of Women and Ethnic Minorities." Here the authors include Texas in their

definition of the West. Their argument is that in order to fully understand the political role of Mexican-Americans in the West, Texas must be included.

6. See U.S. Department of Commerce, Bureau of the Census, *Statistical Abstract of the United States, 1988*, 108th ed. (Washington, D.C.: U.S. Government Printing Office, 1987).

7. The statistical information in this section was taken from various tables in *Statistical Abstract of the United States, 1988*, 108th ed.; *The Book of the States, 1988–89* (Lexington, Ky.: The Council of State Governments, 1988); Alfred N. Garwood, ed., *Almanac of the Fifty States* (Wellesley Hills, Mass.: Information Publications, 1987); *State Policy Data Book* (McConnellsburg, Pa.: Brizius and Foster, 1988); and Philip M. Burgess, Jack A. Brizius and Susan E. Foster, eds., *Profile of the West* (Denver: Western States' Strategy Center, 1987). For a good overview of current developments and major trends in the West see Katherine M. Albert, William B. Hull and Daniel M. Sprague, *The Dynamic West: A Region in Transition* (Lexington, Ky.: The Council of State Governments, 1989).

8. The Census Bureau defines an urban area as a community with 2,500 or more residents.

9. The term *pragmatism* is also used in a more formal sense to describe a philosophy that developed in America in the period after the Civil War. See Chapter 2, note 11, for a brief description of philosophical pragmatism and its links with practical politics.

10. Michael J. Ross, *State and Local Politics and Policy* (Englewood Cliffs, N.J.: Prentice Hall, 1986), 69–76.

11. Richard Franklin Bensel, *Sectionalism and American Political Development, 1880–1980* (Madison: University of Wisconsin Press, 1984), 3–5. In this book Bensel uses regionalism and sectionalism interchangeably. In our book, however, we make a distinction between them.

12. Two short studies of Idaho politics have, in fact, identified sectionalism as the dominant factor in state politics. See Boyd A. Martin, "Idaho: The Sectional State," in Jonas, *Politics in the American West*, 180–200; and Gary Moncrief, "Idaho: The Interests of Sectionalism," in Hrebenar and Thomas, *Interest Group Politics in the American West*, 67–74.

13. Sarah McCally Morehouse, *State Politics, Party and Policy* (New York: Holt, Rinehart and Winston, 1981), 117.

14. *Ibid.*, 95, 119.

15. *Ibid.*, 108–11.

16. *State Policy Data Book 1987* (McConnellsburg, Pa.: Brizius and Foster, 1987), Tables K-10, K-11, K-12 and K-15.

17. *Ibid.*, Tables B-47 and B-50.

18. Bensel, *Sectionalism and American Political Development*, 3–4.

19. *Ibid.*, 11; see also V. O. Key, Jr., *Parties, Politics and Pressure Groups* (New York: Thomas Y. Crowell, 1964), 238.

20. Bensel, *Sectionalism and American Political Development*, 3–4, 11. For

other perspectives on American regionalism see Merrill Jensen, ed., *Regionalism in America* (Madison: University of Wisconsin Press, 1965) especially Part 1; and Ann R. Markusen, *Regions: The Economics and Politics of Territory* (Totowa, N.J.: Rowman and Littlefield, 1987), esp. chaps. 1 and 3.

21. The doctrine of the concurrent majority holds that democratic decisions should only be made with the concurrence of all major segments of society. Without such concurrence, Calhoun argued, a simple majority decision should not be binding on the group whose interests it violates. See Jack C. Plano and Milton Greenberg, *The American Political Dictionary*, 5th ed. (New York: Holt, Rinehart and Winston, 1979), 4.

22. Bensel, *Sectionalism and American Political Development*, 4–5.

I

Influences on Western Politics

2

INFLUENCES ON WESTERN POLITICAL CULTURE

John G. Francis and
Clive S. Thomas

C HAPTER 1 IDENTIFIED TEN ENDURING CHARACTER-
istics of western politics. But why does the West exhibit these particular characteristics as opposed to others? And when it shares characteristics with other parts of the nation, as in the case of political
pragmatism and individualism, how do we account for the particular
brand of these characteristics existing in the West? In short, what are
the factors, unique and otherwise, that influence politics, power, government and public policy in the American West? It is this question
that will occupy us in this first section of the book.

This chapter examines twelve of these major factors in overview.
Then in chapters 3 and 4 we explore two particularly significant in-

fluences in more depth: the nature and impact of the western economy, and the role of the federal government.

The twelve influences on western politics to be considered in this chapter are as follows:

1. National forces, past and present
2. The components of the frontier ethos
3. The physical environment
4. Demographic factors, including the presence of minority populations
5. The dominant presence of the federal government
6. The dependence of the West on external forces
7. The boom and bust economy
8. The importance of government
9. The populist and progressive traditions
10. The state constitutions
11. Subregional factors
12. Western political culture and subcultures

The first eleven of these influences have, in varying degrees, helped to shape the twelfth factor of the western political culture and subcultures. Understanding what has shaped these political cultures of the West will tell us much about the nature of politics, power, government and public policy in the region. Therefore, before we examine these various influences we will briefly explain the concept of political culture and its values and limitations in studying politics.

The Concept of Political Culture: An Overview

Since the time of Aristotle in ancient Greece, political observers have recognized that the general culture in a nation, region, state or locality has an important impact on politics. In this respect we can define the culture of the American West as the particular values, attitudes, beliefs and life-style of those living in the region. In turn, the general culture of a society will shape that society's *political culture*, which in essence is a shared set of knowledge, attitudes and symbols that help to define the procedures and goals of politics.

A major reason why countries, and often political subdivisions within countries, have different forms of government and produce different types of policy is because of variations in political culture. As a consequence, political scientists have paid considerable attention to the study of political culture in recent years. Like many concepts in social science, however, it exhibits problems of definition and measurement. Despite these limitations, political culture can tell us much about the nature of political attitudes and processes.

Over the past thirty years several definitions of political culture have been used by political scientists.[1] Probably the two most often used are those developed by Daniel Elazar and Joseph Zikmund, and by Sidney Verba. Elazar and Zikmund define political culture as "the particular pattern of orientation for political action in which each political system is imbedded."[2] Verba defines the concept as "the system of empirical beliefs, expressive symbols and values which defines the situation in which broader action takes place."[3] Both definitions share the idea of political culture as identifying values that orient people in a fundamental way to politics.

There are two principal levels of analysis in political cultural studies. One level focuses on the individual's orientations; while studies on the other level consider the political culture of a system, organization, or society.[4] Here we employ political culture to mean orientations found at the level of the individual westerner.

Political culture at the level of the individual has a psychological focus. Such studies often focus on three sets of orientations: toward governmental institutions, toward others in the political system, and toward one's own competence and efficacy in politics. Researchers such as Almond and Verba, Huntington, and Inglehart have argued that societies with wide support for governmental institutions, significant levels of trust in other members of the society, and a strong feeling that political participation is effective for the individual citizen, are likely to possess a stable democracy.[5]

Discussions of political culture lead to two important questions. First, once a political culture has been described, what are the limits to generalization? Are there segments of the population who do not share at all or share only partially in the core values of the culture? Second, political culture is by definition a set of values that endures, yet politics is often concerned with change. How, therefore, do students of political culture account for political change?

LIMITS TO GENERALIZATION

As to the limits to generalization, several studies in comparative politics report on countries that have two or more cultures existing within their borders. Canada is often described as having two cultures: Francophone Quebec and the Anglophone provinces to the west and east of Quebec.[6] Other studies describe a political culture that has a number of significant variations within one nation, variations that are described as subcultures. Subcultures are defined as a segment of the population that possesses important differences in outlook from the majority's viewpoint and in which both the majority and the subculture are conscious of these differences in outlook. The United States is often described as having a national political culture with a number of important subcultures.

Perhaps the best-known description of American political culture and its subcultures is that by Elazar.[7] He argues that the American political culture is rooted in two contrasting conceptions—those of marketplace and commonwealth. The marketplace orientation views public relationships as products of bargaining among individuals and groups acting out of self-interest. In contrast, the commonwealth orientation understands government as realizing certain shared moral principles.

Three distinctive types of subcultures result from the tension between these conceptions. The *individualistic* subculture emphasizes that the American democratic order is a marketplace and government is instituted for strictly utilitarian reasons. Government should play a restricted role that encourages private initiative and widespread access to the marketplace. In contrast, *traditionalistic* political culture is rooted in a mixed view about the marketplace linked with an elitist conception of the commonwealth. Popular participation in government is not widespread. Good government is that which maintains traditional patterns of social relationships. Finally, *moralistic* political cultures stress the value of political participation for the betterment of the commonwealth. Good government is measured in terms of the degree to which it promotes the public good. Principled political participation rather than party loyalty is valued in moralistic political culture. No state has a pure subculture of any one type, but Elazar argues that one type or a combination of two types will predominate in each state.[8]

There is also a close correlation between these subcultures and political ideologies based on a conservative–liberal scale. Traditionalistic states, which until very recently included most southern states, tend to be more conservative and have less activist governments. These also tend to allow more freedom of action to groups and individuals in pursuing their goals, which may extend to bribery and corruption. At the other end of the scale, predominantly moralistic states like North Dakota, Minnesota, Oregon and Michigan often have more activist governments, and place greater strictures on what are and what are not acceptable political tactics. Predominantly individualistic states like Connecticut, Nevada, Illinois and Pennsylvania, and those manifesting a significant individualistic element like California, Montana, Kansas and Iowa, fall somewhere in between.

Elazar's critical working assumption is that culture is rooted in the historical experience of the people, and that once rooted it will survive migrations to quite different parts of the country. In certain sections of the country, a particular subculture will be dominant, which reflects the streams and currents of migration that have carried people of different origins and backgrounds across the continent in more or less orderly patterns.[9]

THE PROBLEM OF POLITICAL CHANGE

The second question is the problem of political change. Inglehart makes a number of important claims about political culture and political change. He argues that political culture is the crucial link between economic development and democracy. Cultural patterns once established influence subsequent political and economic events. "But culture is not a constant. It is a system through which society adapts to its environment. Given a changing environment, in the long run culture is likely to change."[10] Inglehart argues that postwar prosperity in North America and Europe engendered a cultural shift toward post-materialist values that has led to less emphasis on economic growth. In sum, political culture helps shape political institutions and economic objectives, and in turn is responsive to the changing political and economic environment.

With this basic knowledge of the concept of political culture we can move to examine the particular influences that have shaped the political culture and subcultures of the West and thus the politics, governmental institutions and public policies of the region. Then we will be able to pose the question of the extent to which there is a distinct political culture in the West.

National and Traditional American Influences

The West has undergone considerable change since World War II and particularly since the 1960s. Some of these changes are peculiar to the West itself, but most are the result of national trends. To understand recent changes in western politics we need to be aware of these major national trends and influences. Here we list ten of the most significant national developments since the 1960s:

1. Population has increased. The growth was 11.4% for the nation as a whole during the period of 1970–80.
2. Increasing urbanization continues. This has been partly responsible for a power shift from rural to urban areas.
3. Despite the message that we often get from the media, both the standard of living and the level of education have been rising for the United States as a whole. This has largely been due to major advances in technology, especially in computers.
4. The national economy continues to diversify, and some states and regions have made great progress in this regard.
5. Since the early 1970s there has been an increasing national trend toward conservatism. Two manifestations of this have been a decline in union membership and the rise of the Republican party in many areas at the expense of the Democrats.
6. Political parties, however, have experienced a decline in membership and effectiveness since the 1960s.
7. The power vacuum left by the parties has been filled to a large extent by interest groups. This includes the rise of so-called "single issue" groups and political action committees (PACs).
8. Government has increased its role considerably since the mid-1960s. This has led to an increasing reliance on government for funds and employment in some areas of the nation. Intergovernmental cooperation at all levels has also increased.
9. There has been a marked increase in the level of professionalism of elected and appointed government officials as well as of lobbyists.
10. Probably the most significant political development of the last twenty-five years is an expansion in political pluralism. That is, despite what we often read in the papers, hard evidence demonstrates that there are more people and groups participating at all levels of the American political process than ever before.

It is, of course, not just the last twenty-five years that the nation as a whole has had an impact on western politics. From the time of the early pioneers the political debate in the West has been influenced by traditional American values and the national political heritage. Those who came to the West brought with them not only economic and social values but also a set of political values that had been molded back in the East or even in Europe. In other words, these settlers brought with them a political culture—or more precisely, a set of political subcultures. A major aspect of this political culture and its subcultures was a commitment to representative and responsible government. Such values were reinforced by the fact that Congress vetted each state's constitution before approving its admission to the Union, and rejected any constitution that deviated too much from national norms.

So it was that national political traditions and values came to make a lasting mark on western politics. However, as these political traditions and values were applied to local circumstances, needs and conflicts, they underwent some modifications. Westerners adapted them, as far as they felt appropriate and possible, to meet their own needs. Similarly today, national attitudes and trends, like the ten identified above, will be modified or adapted in the West as the result of a host of regional factors, including historical, social, cultural, economic and political needs and realities.

The Frontier Ethos

The various aspects of the frontier ethos have given a particular complexion to western culture and thus to the political culture and subcultures of the region. The idea of a frontier ethos or spirit is an ambiguous and elusive concept. Nevertheless, both academic and popular writers have long recognized that there was a difference in attitude between those who lived in the relative security of long-established settlements back East and in Europe, and those who ventured west and to the frontier. We can identify six major elements in this ethos: progress, optimism, individualism, laissez faire, pragmatism, and a qualified egalitarianism. All were part of the general American culture, but were interpreted and adapted to meet the needs of westerners.

As products of the Enlightenment of the late eighteenth century, the ideas of progress and optimism center on the belief that human beings can affect their environment to improve the human condition; and that they have control over the rate of progress. This contrasted with previously held beliefs that human beings were subject to conditions over which they had no control. A fervent belief in progress and its concomitant optimism has always been part of the American ethos. It was particularly important in the birth and early development of the nation. And nowhere was it a more prominent part of the culture than among western pioneers and settlers. Few people would have ventured west if they had not strongly believed that it was in *their* power to create a better life for themselves; and that it was *their* own efforts that would determine the extent of their success.

The American version of individualism mainly emphasized freedom from government control in all aspects of life and especially in the political sphere. It also lauded self-reliance and private initiative as keys to both personal and national success. Those who came west not only exemplified this creed (at least in theory) but enhanced it with such laudable traits as courage, tenacity and endurance to produce their own unique brand of individualism—*rugged* individualism.

Closely associated with individualism is *laissez faire*. This is the concept that the role of government should be limited to providing law and order and national defense, a concept that dominated nineteenth- and early twentieth-century America. It became, and in many respects remains, a hallmark of American capitalism and political conservatism. The frontier's and later the developing West's espousal of *laissez faire* has been tempered perhaps more than in any other region by practical necessity. While rarely, if ever, openly admitted, in essence this means that many westerners do not want to pay taxes or have their activities controlled and regulated by the government. Yet they certainly want—and actively seek—government aid and support not only to enhance their lives, but in many cases to make existence possible in the first place.

Pragmatism and egalitarianism were largely a product of the environment and conditions of the West. Pragmatism is a major characteristic of the American ethos in general, but it became an even more integral part of life out West and on the frontier. Here a person had to adapt his or her old ways of thinking and acting in order to meet new challenges and conditions. A person's life and his or her acceptance by other westerners often depended on the willingness to adapt—to be pragmatic.[11]

The harsh physical conditions and the premium placed on adaptability and survival had a socially leveling effect on frontier society. Certainly, American society was known for its lack of a class structure, but there were still social stratifications in large cities and particularly in the South. The frontier and the West could not afford these to the same degree. It did not matter who one had been or what one had done back in the East or in Europe. The important question was: What can you contribute here? As with most frontier societies, that was how people were judged. As a result, the frontier and the West emphasized social and political equality to a greater degree than did the rest of the country. The West was, on the surface at least, more egalitarian.

This, however, was a qualified egalitarianism reserved for white only. Western white society was no more tolerant of racial minorities than was the rest of the nation. In fact, in many ways it was less tolerant as will be seen below. Furthermore, the West's pioneering of the extension of the franchise to women (beginning in Wyoming in 1890), which is often cited as evidence of the region's egalitarianism and toleration, was more the result of necessity than of any philosophical commitment to equality. So, as a result, the West had a particular brand of egalitarianism that was essentially the product of pragmatism. Like the frontier ethos in general, it contained both ambiguities and contradictions.

The Physical Environment

We know from western movies that the physical environment had a tremendous effect on the life-style and attitudes of westerners. Despite the advent of modern technology, this physical environment continues to exert a great influence on the life-style and politics of the West today. Map 2.1 illustrates the physical geography of the region. Five key aspects of the physical nature of the West have worked their effects on western politics and public policies.

First, there is the sheer physical size of the West. As noted in Chapter 1, the region contains over half of the nation's land area, but only 20% of the national population. Size and distance push up the costs of roads, the exploitation of natural resources, and the costs of consumer goods and services. This situation is exacerbated by the second factor—the nature of the terrain. Mountain ranges in particular increase the costs of building roads and power lines. The third factor is the climate, which in itself affects the terrain. The West, of course, contains an array of climates from frigid arctic cold in interior Alaska to rain forests on the Pacific Coast to hot deserts in the Southwest. Coping with problems of climate and terrain often requires the expenditure of massive public resources. The fourth factor is very much the product of climate. The vast area of the West receives only 20% of the nation's rainfall, so there are vast arid lands or deserts resulting from lack of moisture. Consequently, the effect of aridity and the need for water has been and remains a central theme in western politics. Fifth, this vastness, terrain, climate and to some extent aridity, have affected decisions about where people have chosen to live in the West.

Map 2.1 Western United States Physical Geography

Demographic Factors Including the
Presence of Minority Populations

The composition and distribution of the population affects western politics in a number of ways. The size of the population will partly determine the tax base. Size will also have an effect on campaign styles: the larger the population the less personal the electioneering process. The age distribution will affect the demand for services such as education, health care, and family services. The density and geographical distribution of the population will affect the type and cost of services. Population growth and decline also affects politics. On the one hand, rapid growth can bring a demand for new and costly services; on the other hand it may bring a demand for limits on suburban and industrial growth and an attempt to protect the environment more carefully. Population decline lowers the tax base and makes for problems in attracting businesses and creating jobs. The racial and ethnic composition will impact the political culture and the policy focus of governments.

Table 2.1 sets out the major characteristics of the population of the thirteen western states, the region as a whole, and compares this with the nation. The table confirms that the West is very sparsely populated and that most people are clustered in a number of what has been termed "urban oases."[12] Over 55% of westerners live in California, and almost another 30% live in Arizona, Colorado, Oregon and Washington. In the 1970s, the West experienced a population growth almost three times that for the nation as a whole, 32.8% compared with 11.4%. This has slowed down considerably in the 1980s; but it is still twice the national average.

The table also shows that one in five westerners is nonwhite and therefore of non-European extraction. The oldest non-European communities are the American Indian communities found throughout the West, but in significant numbers in Alaska, Arizona and New Mexico. Asian communities have long been dominant in Hawaii, and they are significant components of California's present-day population. In some areas Hispanic communities antedate the migrations from the East, but throughout the West, notably in the Southwest, these communities have greatly expanded both by successive immigrations and by natural increase. After World War II, black migration westward paralleled white migration. Today, significant black populations are found in the San Francisco Bay area, Los Angeles, Las Vegas and

Table 2.1   Population Characteristics of the Western States

State	Total Pop. (1987)	Rank in		Persons Per Sq. Mile	Percentage				Percent Increase	
		U.S.	West		of U.S.	West	Urbanized[a]	Nonwhite[a]	1970–80	1980–87
Alaska	525,000	49	12	1	0.22%	1.1%	64.0%	23.7%	32.4%	30.7%
Arizona	3,386,000	25	3	30	1.39	6.8	84.0	25.4	53.1	24.6
California	27,663,000	1	1	177	11.37	55.7	93.0	33.0	18.5	16.9
Colorado	3,296,000	26	4	32	1.35	6.6	81.0	17.1	30.7	14.1
Hawaii	1,083,000	39	8	168	0.45	2.2	87.0	67.7	25.3	12.2
Idaho	998,000	42	10	12	0.41	2.0	54.0	6.0	32.4	5.8
Montana	809,000	44	11	6	0.33	1.6	53.0	6.4	13.3	2.9
Nevada	1,007,000	41	9	9	0.41	2.0	85.0	16.7	63.5	25.8
Oregon	2,724,000	30	5	28	1.12	5.5	68.0	6.6	25.9	3.4
New Mexico	1,500,000	37	7	12	0.62	3.1	72.0	47.0	27.8	15.1
Utah	1,680,000	35	6	20	0.69	3.3	84.0	7.5	37.9	15.0
Washington	4,538,000	18	2	68	1.87	9.1	73.0	9.6	21.0	9.8
Wyoming	490,000	50	13	5	0.20	1.0	63.0	8.1	44.6	4.4
West	49,700,000	—	—	43.7	20.43	100	74.0	21.1	32.8	13.9
United States	243,400,000	—	—	69	—	—	74.0	20.3	11.4	7.4

Note: Percentages have been rounded off.

[a]Based on 1980 Census Bureau figures.

Sources: Compiled by the authors from: *Statistical Abstract of the United States, 1988*, 108th ed. (Washington, D.C.: U.S. Government Printing Office, 1987); *Statistical Abstract of the United States, 1981*, 102nd ed. (Washington, D.C.: U.S. Government Printing Office, 1981); Edith R. Hornor, ed., *Almanac of the Fifty States: Basic Data Profiles with Comparative Tables*, 1989 ed. (Palo Alto, Calif.: Information Publications, 1989); *State Policy Data Book* (McConnellsburg, Pa.: Brizius and Foster, 1988); and Philip M. Burgess, Jack A. Brizius and Susan E. Foster, eds., *Profile of the West* (Denver: Western States' Strategy Center, 1987).

Denver. Over the years, the existence of these various minority populations has had a significant influence on western politics and policy.

The term *minority* has two distinct but often interrelated meanings in American politics. One is that of a numerical minority in relation to the total population of the nation, a region, a state or a locality, such as the non-European groups considered above. The second meaning is that of a group which does not enjoy the same political, civil and legal rights and opportunities as other Americans. In this latter sense a group may actually constitute a majority of the population—as is the case with women, a numerical majority who are often referred to as a "minority."

In both senses of the term, minorities have always had an important influence on American public policy. Until recently, however, it has been the *existence* of minorities, rather than the direct political activities of minorities *themselves*, that has brought about this influence. Until the 1960s the existence of minorities tended to unite the dominant political element in America—white males—in order to exclude these groups from an equal share of the political and economic benefits of American life. This was the dark side of American pluralism and of the American dream.

From the first years of the settlement of the West, minorities in the region were very much subject to such exclusion. The western states, in fact, were at the forefront of the movement to exclude minorities from many of the benefits of American society. California, for example, began to restrict the civil and legal rights of the Chinese in 1852—just two years after achieving statehood. Later the Chinese Exclusion Act of 1882 (extended in 1892 and 1902) was pushed through Congress after anti–Chinese sentiments on the Pacific Coast spilled over into violence. The Act itself was not repealed until 1943. The Japanese also suffered discrimination, particularly through the policy of internment during World War II.

As has been the case in the rest of the country, since the 1960s minorities in the West have been brought more into the mainstream of American society. Minorities themselves have begun to exert direct influence on western public policy, as we shall see in Chapter 8. Table 8.1 also provides a breakdown of the percentage of the population of each major minority groups in the western states.

Dominant Federal Presence

The federal government has always played and continues to play a dominant and crucial role in the West's development and particu-

larly its economic development. One particularly significant aspect
of the federal presence in the West is its ownership of land. The
western states rank one through thirteen of the fifty states in the
percentage of their land area that is federally owned. This ranges from
85.1% in Nevada to 19.9% in Hawaii. In ten of the states at least a
third or more of the land is in federal hands. Only one other state in
the Union, New Hampshire with 12.2%, even reaches double digits
in this respect.[13]

When we combine the factors of development and land ownership, it becomes obvious how dominant the federal presence has been
and continues to be in the West. Add to this the prime importance
of land to much of the West in terms of its natural resource extraction,
its agricultural and its tourist economy, and the federal influence on
western politics becomes even more obvious.

Dependence on External Forces

Because of the tremendous amounts of capital required to develop
the West, of which very little was available in the region itself, plus
the natural resource extraction and agriculturally based economy, the
West has long been dependent on external forces for its well-being. There
have been three such forces in particular: the federal government,
investors and banks from back East and from abroad, and world
markets and the world economy in general.

Capitalists from back East, as well as some foreign capitalists,
financed and controlled many western railroads, mines, banks and
businesses. These groups often made decisions that were not in the
interests of many westerners. Consequently, to westerners it appeared that their region was a colony that the rest of the nation used
to supply important natural resources, and that was to be exploited
for profits regardless of the welfare of its inhabitants. Such was the
feeling regarding discriminatory railroad freight rates levied on many
western communities. Also the West has always been at the mercy
of world markets for the prices of its raw materials and agricultural
goods. Because these prices were and remain subject to supply and
demand forces outside the region, low prices engendered a feeling
of helplessness and anger against these faceless forces.

The Boom and Bust Economy

This feeling of frustration was exacerbated by the fact that so many
western state economies have been based almost entirely on natural

resource extraction and agriculture. So when world prices are high these economies boom; but when prices fall, slumps and sometimes depressions afflict the region. To be sure, California has broken this cycle and Arizona, Colorado, Washington State and Hawaii are moving in that direction. But this boom and bust cycle still afflicts many western states. Over the years, their reacting to and trying to break out of this state of dependence and its volatile economy has profoundly influenced western politics, government and public policy.

The Role and Significance of Government

In the early years government aid took the form of the U.S. Cavalry used in subduing the Indians, and the huge land grants to the railroads to subsidize the development of the first major western transportation lifeline. Later came massive federal funds for water and irrigation projects, hydroelectric systems and roads. In World War II came major military installations and federal research facilities like Los Alamos National Laboratories in New Mexico. After the war came more military installations; more federal scientists; space engineers; workers for a host of federal agencies, ranging from the Bureau of Land Management to the National Weather Service; and major federal defense contracts for companies like Boeing of Seattle. The result is that today a lot of business profits and many a payroll would not have become a reality if it were not for past or present federal aid and, increasingly these days, state government spending.

This heavy dependence upon government in the West has been primarily a consequence of necessity and not of choice. As noted above, it has resulted largely from need—primarily economic need—rather than any philosophical belief in the intrinsic value of government in promoting social goals. Indeed, the antigovernment attitudes and strong strain of political individualism and conservatism that exist in many parts of the West, particularly the Mountain states, opposes such an intrinsic role.

This tension between dependence on government and political individualism and conservatism has produced the western political paradox identified as a characteristic of western politics in Chapter 1. Over the years many of the most successful western politicians have built their careers on the two seemingly contradictory practices of securing huge amounts of federal funds while vocalizing anti–federal government sentiments. In particular, former U.S. Senator Barry Goldwater espoused *laissez faire* at the same time as he was securing millions of federal dollars for the Central Arizona Project and similar federal programs to develop water and other resources. As regards the policy process itself, a political culture that champions the pioneer while spurning the government is likely to affect both policy formulation and implementation.

Heavy dependence on government has other more direct and more easily measurable impacts on western politics. One of these is that even slight changes in government budgets can seriously impact the economy of the region, a subregion or a state. This is particularly the case with federal spending cuts. But it is becoming increasingly important with reductions in state spending, and even local government spending, which is impacted by federal and state cutbacks. The fact that state and local governments are the major employers in many states means that budget cutbacks often lead to major layoffs of public employees. Because public payrolls are a greater percentage of the income of most western states than of states in the rest of the nation, this reverberates throughout their economies in a much more damaging way than it would in states like Pennsylvania or Indiana, which are much less dependent on government employment.

Both western voters and politicians are, of course, very aware of the devastating effects this economic dependence on government can unleash. That is part of the reason why western politicians have an obsession with economic development and diversification, noted as another characteristic of western politics in Chapter 1. The irony, however, is that in order to advance development and diversification, government aid and investment—in the form of roads and other transport facilities, business loans and tax incentives—are often required. In addition, the fact that large numbers of voters are public employees is not lost on western politicians. Neither is the fact that many of the major campaign contributors and the most effective interest groups in the region are public sector unions, such as schoolteachers and state employee associations. All these and other factors work to reinforce another characteristic of western politics among the public and politicians alike—that of political pragmatism.

So within the context of political individualism and conservatism that predominates in many parts of the West, what this all-pervasive role of government has produced, in effect, is a nonideological equivalent of Western European statism. That is, the recognition, if only tacitly and reluctantly in the West, that the transformation or development of society, and particularly its economic welfare, is impossible without the active and constant participation of government.

The Populist and Progressive Traditions

Populism and progressivism were reform movements of the period from the 1880s to around 1920. The origin, development, influence and complexity of these movements, as well as the debate over the degree of cohesiveness of their ideas, have been the subject of many books and articles.[14] In essence, what they had in common was a deep concern about some aspects of America's economic, social and political development and particularly the effects of industrialization. But whereas populism was essentially a rural protest movement of the West, Midwest and South, progressivism was urban, middle class and national in its base of support.

Like populist movements in other countries, American populism sought to wrestle political and economic power from the "urban-oriented oligarchy" or "interests" (banks, trusts, monopolies, railroads, etc.), and return it to the "common people," mainly those living in rural areas. These rural residents were seen as embodying a simpler, more desirable way of life based on traditional practices. Underlying the populist psychology was a belief in a conspiracy of the "monied interests" against common folk and a suspicion of the immigrant hordes flooding into American cities.[15]

As Beitzinger has pointed out, the populists were the first modern movement of any significance in America to insist that the federal government (and, in fact, government in general) has a prime responsibility to provide for the common good. Populists sought to use government to regulate the railroads, control trusts and monopolies, expand the money supply and enact social and economic programs to aid farmers. They also favored several political reforms such as the direct election of U.S. senators. At the same time populists were intensely individualistic and often intolerant of new ideas, of social diversity and racial and ethnic minorities. They sought to use radical means for very conservative ends.

The progressive movement with which populism merged after 1900 was more moderate. Progressives sought to deal with the twin problems of an emerging plutocracy and an increasing number of poor people. Accordingly, they favored reforms to control monopolies and trusts and restore competition, aid small businessmen and farmers, protect labor and enhance its rewards, conserve the nation's resources and protect the environment, and protect consumers through such means as the regulation of the manufacture and sale of food and drugs.

It was on the political reform front, however, that progressivism probably had its greatest impact. Progressives championed an extension of democracy through such devices as the direct primary election, the initiative, referendum and recall. Like many populists, they favored the direct election of U.S. senators. Many progressives also championed replacing "politics" with "administrative expertise." This was to be achieved through the short ballot, the commission and manager form of municipal government, and regulatory commissions. All these measures were aimed at eliminating corruption from politics, especially corrupt city bosses; taking control from political party oligarchies; and giving citizens greater control over government as it expanded its role.[16]

Populism and progressivism have been enormously influential on both the form and operation of American government, especially at the state and local levels, and on the political attitudes of politicians and public alike. As we shall see throughout this book, nowhere were these ideas more influential than in the West. And their legacy lives on. This is in part due to the fact that seven of the thirteen western states wrote constitutions and achieved statehood during the populist-progressive period. Moreover, the other four western states in existence at the time (Oregon, California, Nevada and Colorado) were profoundly affected by these movements. And the late-comers to the Union—Alaska and Hawaii—have also been very much affected by the populist-progressive legacy. One major legacy of populism and progressivism was the incorporation of methods of direct democracy into western state constitutions as well as municipal and county charters.[17] This is but one example of the way in which these creeds have had a profound influence on the political culture of the region and its states.

The Characteristics and Influence of Western State Constitutions

Because a constitution is the fundamental document of a state or nation, its structure and substance have a significant impact on politics, political power, and policy. The constitutions of the western states, like those of the other thirty-seven states, are modeled after the U.S. Constitution. Each contains a preservation of individual rights and the basic structuring of a representative government. Like the federal system, all western state governments are composed of three branches: legislative, executive, and judicial. A comparison of structure alone is deceptive, however. This is because each state's constitution places differing emphases on the role of these branches, thus modifying the federal prototype.

These differences are primarily visible in two areas: executive policymaking and legislative lawmaking authority. The governor, as the executive head of state government, sets the policy for his or her administration. This is a formidable task, as the governor is subject to the checks and balances exerted by the other two branches. In most western states there is another obstacle encountered by governors—the fragmentation of power within their own branch. This fragmentation results in what is known as the "weak executive" model and is characterized by there being several elected officers within the executive branch. These constitutionally mandated officers have their own power base and agenda, and sometimes use these to contravene the governor's policy. In a highly fragmented executive branch, like that in the State of Washington, with eight separately elected top officials, the scope of authority a governor can exercise is severely limited.

The second difference between the federal and western constitutions affects the lawmaking ability of the legislature. As we have previously noted, all western states except Hawaii give the electorate direct power to enact law through initiative or referendum. The ability to make statutory or constitutional changes to state law gives the electorate added power over their designated representatives. Highly publicized initiatives, such as California's Proposition 13, have caught the nation's attention because they typify the saga of "people vs. big government." When combined with the existence of weak political parties and strong interest groups, these constitutional constraints on governors and the legislatures contribute to the fragmentation of policymaking noted in Chapter 1 as another characteristic of western politics.

Besides their collective heritage of populist and progressive ideas, there are several other common features of western state constitutions. One significant area of similarity is their specific treatment of natural resources, reflecting the importance placed on the bountiful material wealth found throughout the West. As we saw above, a great concern of western states has been the exploitation of this wealth by outside interests, particularly the East. Thus many western states use constitutional protections to thwart exploitative uses of their natural resources.

Though the West as a region displays significant similarities, the western states as individual entities have their own peculiarities reflected in their constitutions. New Mexico, with its rich Spanish and Native American heritage, has specific constitutional provisions regarding the protection of this cultural background. Article II of the state's constitution provides that the rights granted to indigenous peoples by the Treaty of Guadalupe Hidalgo shall be preserved. As a further protection, it takes a super-majority (75% of the voting electorate) to adopt changes regarding voting and educational privileges. California, with its long Pacific shoreline, has specific protections in its constitution regarding coastal areas. Colorado's constitution has a special article dealing with nuclear detonations. The other states show their uniqueness in other areas, such as Alaska with its provision against the use of fish traps, and Utah with its prohibition of polygamy.

Most western state constitutions are commensurate in length with their counterparts in the East. Utah's constitution, with about 11,000 words, is one of the shortest; the constitutions of Wyoming and California, with over 30,000 words, are comparable to some of the longer constitutions in the East and South. Since the West is a younger region than the East or South, its need for total constitutional replacement has been less. Of the thirteen western states, only California and Montana have had more than one constitution.

Though most western states have not found it necessary to replace their constitutions, there has been significant activity in the form of amendments—additions to a constitution that alter or replace specific items. California, which leads the nation as well as the western states in amendments, has had over 450 alterations to its constitution. Montana, whose second constitution was adopted in 1972, has had only 21 proposed revisions, of which 13 have been ratified. The other western states range from 20 (Alaska) to 183 (Oregon) successful amendments, with the mean being around 100 revisions.

Subregional Factors in Western Politics

We have noted on several occasions that while the West displays common elements in its politics, government and policy preferences, it also exhibits much diversity. This diversity stems from many sources including historical experience; economic factors, cultural, racial and ethnic differences; and adaptation to the physical environment. When these are combined with geographical location they have often produced a subregional perspective on various aspects of life including politics. These subregional political perspectives—which reflect variations in political culture—influence the nature of politics and policy-making. This is the case, for example, when regional associations or coalitions are formed around some common interest. These differing political perspectives also provide insights into understanding political variations within the West.

Various subregions have been identified over the years. The exact boundaries of these are, like those of the West itself, subject to dispute, and consequently they often overlap. Probably the best-known of these subregions are those based upon clusters of states such as the Southwest, the Northwest, the Pacific states subregion, and the Mountain states subregion. Sometimes a distinction is made within this Mountain subregion between the northern Rocky Mountain and the southern Rocky Mountain states.

Two recently developed subregional divisions transcend political boundaries. One is between the Sunbelt area of the Southwest, Hawaii and parts of the coastal area of the three contiguous Pacific states, and the Snowbelt (sometimes referred to as the Frostbelt), which covers most of the rest of the West. The other is Joel Garreau's division of North America based on economics, culture and political interest. Here the West falls into four of his nine regions, which he describes as "nations." "Ecotopia" is a "nation" dominated by concerns about ecology. It includes the coastal strip from southeast Alaska to around San Francisco. "MexAmerica," where Spanish-American culture is pervasive, embraces much of the Southwest and southern California. The "Empty Quarter," where population is relatively sparse, includes much of the Mountain states and most of Alaska. The fourth "nation" is the "Breadbasket," which includes the eastern portions of Montana, Wyoming, Colorado and New Mexico. Hawaii, according to Garreau, is difficult to classify. It is as much an Asian aberration as it is a North American aberration. He sees Hawaii as a place of Ecotopian possibilities, with MexAmerican growth values and limits, run by Asians.[18]

While both of these subregional divisions certainly have important implications for the present, the Sunbelt–Snowbelt division and the one developed by Garreau are more futuristic and both have broader implications than just the political life of the region. As far as politics is concerned, over the years and particularly in the last two decades, several observers have noticed significant differences between the Pacific states (Alaska, California, Hawaii, Oregon and Washington) and the Mountain states (Arizona, Colorado, Idaho, Montana, Nevada, New Mexico, Utah and Wyoming).[19]

A study on cultural regionalism conducted as long ago as the 1930s drew attention to the relatively high level of prosperity in California and to a lesser extent in Oregon and Washington State in comparison with other sections of the nation and certainly in comparison with the low incomes of people living in the Mountain states.[20] The relative wealth of the West Coast still stands in contrast to the boom and bust economies of many of the Mountain states. Other differences between these two subregions include an increasing conservatism and support of the Republican party in the Mountain states, plus a stronger anti-government attitude in that subregion. Several of the chapters in this book draw a comparison between these two subregions as a means for understanding contemporary variations in western politics and policy.[21]

Western Political Culture and Subcultures

Do all the influences that we have considered above produce a distinctive political culture or subculture that distinguishes the western states from the rest of the nation? Expressed another way, have the various aspects of western culture produced a unique orientation toward politics in the West?

The answer to those questions at present is a qualified no. It is a qualified negative because there is very little survey information of either popular or elite attitudes that can be used to identify a distinctive political subculture in the western states. The surveys that have been conducted suggest that westerners' orientations to politics share much with those found in other regions of the nation. Nevertheless, as with our consideration of the frontier ethos, there is enough evidence of the existence of certain distinctive features of western political culture to justify our separate focus on the politics of the western states.

Earlier we indicated the appeal of Elazar's three subcultures to many scholars who are seeking to understand American politics. In fact, a number of the contributors to this volume rely on Elazar's formulation. Elazar concludes that the individualistic, the traditionalistic, and the moralistic subcultures are all to be found in western states. Elazar argues, for example, that the South being the center of traditionalistic culture, migrants from that region carried its political subculture values with them as they moved west to parts of New

Mexico and California. Those from New England and the upper Midwest carried the moralistic culture to parts of Oregon, Washington State, Idaho and Montana. And those from the Mid-Atlantic and lower Midwest carried the individualistic subculture to all parts of the region. Elazar's assumption that as people move westward they carry their political values along with their possessions seems to make intuitive sense and is supported by studies of other migrations.

This conception of cultural transfer is reinforced by the relatively young age of western political communities. Much of the West only began to attract major migration in the last century and in many areas only during the past forty years. Many westerners were born elsewhere, or their parents were born elsewhere. Maps 2.2 and 2.3 depict the political culture of the western states according to Elazar's classification. Map 2.2 shows the combination of dominant subcultures in each state, and Map 2.3 shows the variation of subcultures in different parts of each western state.

The Elazar classification of subcultures certainly has some explanatory value. For example, Ira Sharkansky found some limited success in utilizing the classification to predict public policy outcomes, but expressed reservations about the reliability of the subcultural designations as applied to some states.[22] We also see considerable value in Elazar's classification for understanding western politics. At the same time, like Sharkansky, we have concerns about the explanatory value of Elazar's theory. Three of these concerns, as they affect the western states, are considered below.

NON–EUROPEAN POLITICAL CULTURAL INFLUENCES

First, significant numbers of westerners do not have their familial origins in the European settlements of the east coast: most significantly the Hispanic, Asian, black and American Indian communities. These communities are not explored as well as they might be in Elazar's work. In the case of all four, we simply lack the knowledge to offer generalizations about the attitudes of individual members. It may be that further investigation will require the formulation of several additional subcultures in addition to the ones advanced by Elazar. Indeed, as some commentators have observed, there may be grounds for believing that there is a quite distinct Mexican-American culture.[23] It is highly likely that we are witnessing in the western states new patterns in political participation and in political relationships. Such increased participation by what are now described as minority groups, which might some day be the majority at least in California, could lead to a new era of politics in the western states.

Map 2.2   Dominant Political Subcultures in the Western States

Source: Adapted by the authors from Daniel J. Elazar, *American Federalism: A View From the States*, 3rd ed. (New York: Harper & Row, 1984), 124 - 25, Figure 5.2. Reprinted with permission.

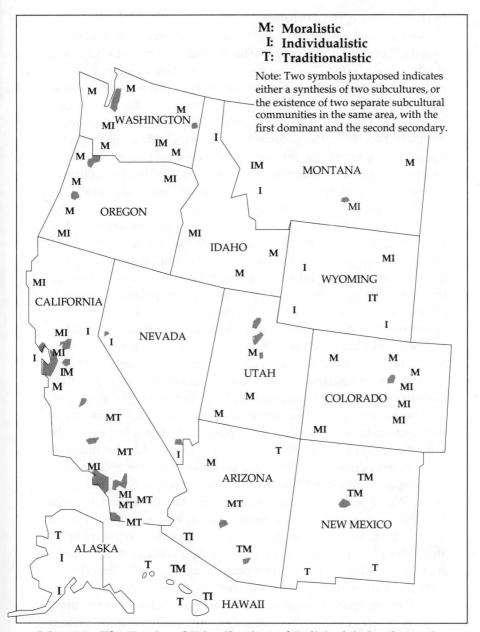

M: **Moralistic**
I: **Individualistic**
T: **Traditionalistic**

Note: Two symbols juxtaposed indicates either a synthesis of two subcultures, or the existence of two separate subcultural communities in the same area, with the first dominant and the second secondary.

Map 2.3   The Regional Distribution of Political Subcultures in the Western States

Source: Adapted by the authors from Daniel J. Elazar,   *American Federalism: A View From the States,*   3rd ed. (New York: Harper & Row, 1984), 124-25, Figure 5.2. Reprinted with permission.

CULTURE AND THE ENVIRONMENT

Second, as Inglehart contends, there is a complex interplay between culture and environment. This is another area that Elazar does not treat extensively. We contend, however, that political attitudes and institutions, particularly governmental institutions in the West, have been strongly influenced by the environment. Take, for example, a recent study of Idaho political culture by Robert Blank. By using the three aspects of the political culture of individuals described at the beginning of the chapter—orientations to government, to others, and toward one's own activities—Blank took Elazar's subculture of individualism and epxlored how it had developed in the state.[24] He found that people in Idaho hold fast to the values of self-reliance that were reinforced by the conditions of the frontier experience. This supports Elazar's theory. But Blank argues that commitment to self-reliance produced an orientation of distrust and suspicion of those persons and groups who were different. Blank also draws attention to what, in effect, is the existence of the western political paradox in Idaho: That is, the seemingly ambivalent attitude toward the federal government. Indeed, Blank describes it as a love-hate relationship. Idahoans, like many other westerners, apparently combine deeply felt patriotism with deep suspicion of federal intervention. Yet they favor and even demand certain sorts of federal financial support for infrastructure developments such as irrigation and highways.

Another example of the relationship of culture and environment that appears to be particularly important in the West, but cannot be explained within the Elazar scheme, has to do with the interplay between economic well-being and policy change. We noted earlier that Inglehart observed that the sustained prosperity of the post–World War II period produced an economic climate that contributed to what he describes as post-industrial values—a concern for the quality of life notably in the area of the environment.[25] What we know about the western states gives us some appreciation of Inglehart's analysis. Conflicts over environmental politics are to be found in all sections of the nation. But in the western states, conflicts over the goals of environmental regulation are front-page news. These conflicts are very much a clash of the contending orientations that are present in every western town and city. Such clashes not only reflect a very deep division among westerners over their respective orientations as to what they want out of politics, but may also reveal the powerful force that the landscape has had on the people living in the West.

Public opinion surveys during the past twenty years have indicated significantly greater support for environmentalist positions at both the mass and the elite level in California than is reported for the Mountain states. In recent years, however, there has been growing support, particularly in the urban areas of the Mountain states, for environmentalist positions. But opposition to restrictions on economic development continues to remain relatively high in the rural areas of this subregion.

FLUIDITY OF POLITICAL LOYALTIES

Our third concern with the explanatory value of Elazar's theory of political culture as it relates to the West is the greater willingness of westerners to change their partisan loyalities and policy views than appears to be the case in other sections of the country. Miller and others have remarked on the magnitude and rapidity of what they regard as realignment in the Mountain states from being one of the most Democratic regions in the nation to being one of the most Republican regions in the country.[26] What is important to note about realignment, occurring in the late 1960s, is that both migrants and residents who were born in the region shifted partisan loyalties. On the basis of survey findings DeGrazia observed in the early 1950s the relative weakness of party loyalties in the West.[27] Kleppner believes that westerners carried their party attachments as they moved west, but that the policy content of party attachment simply made less sense in a frontier that generated a very different set of problems.[28] The widespread use of initiative and referendum weakened the power of parties and legislatures in shaping the political agendas of western states. Westerners became more inclined to look to issues and personalities, and the force of an issue or a striking personality seemed to bring about frequent shifts in party attachment.

The Connection Between Influences and Enduring Characteristics

In this chapter we have attempted to explain how various influences in the West have resulted in the ten enduring characteristics of western politics that were identified in Chapter 1. In summary, we can make five observations about the relationship between these influences and the characteristics that they have produced.

First, each characteristic of western politics is not the result of one influence, but of several. For example, the fragmented policy process is not just the result of weak political parties and strong interest groups, but in part also results from political pragmatism, individualism and regionalism. Likewise, political pragmatism is the result, in part, of the frontier ethos, the physical environment, the nature of the western economy, and the influences of the general American ethos.

Second, while we can show a cause and effect relationship between influences and characteristics as Robert Blank demonstrated in his study of individualism in Idaho, we cannot definitively measure the extent to which each influence contributed to each characteristic of western politics. We cannot say, for example, that the western political paradox is due 50% to the role of the federal government, 20% to the spirit of individualism, and so on. What we *can* say with some degree of certainty about this and other characteristics of western politics is that they are shaped by a complex set of factors. What makes the situation even more complicated is that not only do the influences we identified shape the characteristics of western politics, but one characteristic will often impact another. The characteristic of candidate-oriented elections, for example, will constantly help to undermine the influence of parties and help bolster the power of interest groups. In turn, the characteristic of candidate-oriented elections will be reinforced by weak parties and strong interest groups.

Third, despite the difficulty in measurement and the complexities of relationships, the combination of influences that constitute the western political culture has established a particular context of political life in the West. That is to say, while some of the characteristics of western politics may not be unique to the region, the way in which they manifest themselves in the West is usually distinctive. For instance, the use of methods of direct democracy is certainly not unique to the West. But no region makes more use of these devices, and nowhere is their impact in terms of public policy formulation and the way that they affect the attitudes of government and governed alike more significant than in the West. Similarly, all regions of the nation exhibit antigovernment sentiments and a skepticism toward the federal government. But the nature of the western experience with federal authority has given a particular orientation to the antigovernment feelings of the West.

Fourth, while all thirteen states will exhibit to some extent the ten characteristics of western politics identified in the first chapter, the importance of these will vary from state to state. This is largely due to the fact that some influences are more important in some states than in others. In other words, the political cultural make-up of the states differ. We noted in Chapter 1 that because of physical geography, sectionalism and regionalism are very significant characteristics in the politics of Idaho and Alaska, but are an insignificant characteristic of Hawaiian politics. And because of its diversified economy, California is much less preoccupied with issues relating to economic development than are states like Montana and Wyoming.

This brings us to our fifth and final observation. If the impact of various influences varies from state to state and results in some characteristics of politics being more important in some states than in others, will a significant change in one or more influences result in changing characteristics of western politics? The answer is obviously yes. We alluded to this in the sections on political change in our consideration of political culture, especially comparing the Pacific and Mountain subregions. So the ten enduring characteristics we identifed in Chapter 1 may not be so enduring after all. But we will leave a consideration of this point until the concluding chapter.

Our immediate purpose is to examine in more detail two important influences on western political culture and thus on western politics, political power and public policy. First we will consider the western economy, and then in Chapter 4 we will consider the federal government and the West.

Notes

1. Discussions of the concept of political culture and its value and evolution in political science are found in: Gabriel A. Almond, "The Intellectual History of the Civic Culture Concept," in Gabriel A. Almond and Sidney Verba, eds., *The Civic Culture Revisited* (Boston: Little, Brown, 1980); Samuel C. Patterson, "The Political Cultures of the American States," in Daniel J. Elazar and Joseph Zikmund II, eds., *The Ecology of American Political Culture* (New York: Thomas Y. Crowell, 1975); Alan I. Abramowitz, "The United States Political Culture Under Stress," in Almond and Verba, eds., *The Civic Culture Revisited;* David J. Elkins and Richard E. B. Simeon, "A Cause in Search of Its Effect or Does Political Culture Explain?" *Comparative Politics* (January 1979), 127–65.

2. Elazar and Zikmund II, eds., Introduction to *The Ecology of American Political Culture.*

3. Sidney Verba, "Comparative Political Culture," in Lucian Pye and Sid-

ney Verba, eds., *Political Culture and Political Development* (Princeton: Princeton University Press, 1963), 513.

4. Walter A. Rosenblum, *Political Culture* (New York: Praeger, 1975).

5. Gabriel A. Almond and Sydney Verba, *The Civic Culture: Political Attitudes and Democracy in Five Nations* (Princeton: Princeton University Press, 1963); Samuel P. Huntington, "Will More Countries Become More Democratic?" *Political Science Quarterly* 99, 2 (Summer 1984), 193–218; and Ronald Inglehart, "The Renaissance of Political Culture," *American Political Science Review* 82, 4 (December 1988), 1203–30.

6. David V. J. Bell, "Political Culture in Canada," in Michael S. Whittington and Glen Williams, eds., *Canadian Politics in the 1980's*, 2nd ed. (Toronto: Methuen, 1980), 155–74.

7. Daniel J. Elazar, *American Federalism: A View from the States*, 3rd ed. (New York: Harper & Row, 1984), esp. chap. 5, "The States and the Political Setting."

8. *Ibid.*, 134–37.

9. *Ibid.*, 128–29, for a map showing the transfer of political subcultures across the nation.

10. Inglehart, "The Renaissance of Political Culture," 1223.

11. Perhaps coincidentally rather than intentionally, the West exemplified the philosophy of pragmatism developed by C. S. Peirce (1839–1914), William James (1842–1910) and John Dewey (1859–1952). This was a home-grown American philosophy that attempted to explain the meaning and justification of beliefs through the practical effects of holding them. In large part this philosophy was an attempt to explain and justify the uniqueness of the development and the underlying characteristics of the American economic, social and political system. It has been very influential on the course and methods of American politics. It was philosophical pragmatism that provided the justification and methods for achieving many populist, progressive, and later, New Deal reforms. For a fuller explanation of philosophical pragmatism and its interrelationshps with practical politics see A. J. Beitzinger, *A History of American Political Thought* (New York: Dodd, Mead, 1972), chap. 20; and David W. Minar, *Ideas and Politics: The American Experience* (Homewood, Ill.: The Dorsey Press, 1964), chap. 11.

12. Gerald D. Nash, *The American West in the Twentieth Century: A Short History of an Urban Oasis* (Englewood Cliffs, N.J.: Prentice Hall, 1973; University of New Mexico Press, 1977).

13. Alfred N. Garwood, ed., *Almanac of the Fifty States* (Wellesley Hills, Mass.: Information Publications, 1987), 421.

It is important to note that the specific percentages of federal land in each state varies according to which federal agency's data one consults. This accounts for the variations in percentages in the various chapters of this volume. While such variations may be a serious point of conflict for policymakers, as the differences are only one or two percent, they do not affect the points regarding federal land ownership being made in this book.

14. For a comprehensive treatment of both populism and progressivism see A. J. Beitzinger, *A History of American Political Thought*, chaps. 20 and 21; David W. Minar, *Ideas and Politics*, chaps. 10 and 11; Norman Pollock, *The Populist Response to Industrial America* (New York: W. W. Norton, 1962); Richard Hofstadter, *The Age of Reform: From Bryan to F.D.R.* (New York: Knopf, 1955); and Eric F. Goldman, *Rendezvous with Destiny: A History of Modern American Reform* (New York: Knopf, 1952).

Specific to the West, the checkered history of populism and progressivism is traced by William D. Rowley, "The West as Laboratory and Mirror of Reform," in Gerald D. Nash and Richard W. Etulain, eds., *The Twentieth Century West: Historical Interpretations* (Albuquerque: University of New Mexico Press, 1989), 339–57.

15. Beitzinger, *A History of American Political Thought*, 461.

16. *Ibid.*

17. *Ibid.*, 462.

18. Joel Garreau, *The Nine Nations of North America* (Boston: Houghton Mifflin, 1981), 117–18, and maps of the "Nine Nations" following p. 204.

19. John G. Francis, "The Political Landscape of the Mountain West," in *The Politics of Realignment: Party Change in the Mountain West*, Peter Galderisi, Michael Lyons, Randy T. Simmons and John G. Francis, eds. (Boulder, Colo.: Westview Press, 1986).

20. Howard W. Odum and Harry E. Moore, *American Regionalism: A Cultural Historical Approach to National Integration* (New York: Holt, 1938).

21. For another perspective on western regionalism, see the interesting new regional division of America in Michael Barone and Grant Ujifusa, *Almanac of American Politics, 1988* (Washington, D.C.: National Journal, 1987).

22. Ira Sharkansky, "The Utility of Elazar's Political Culture: A Research Note," in Daniel Elazar and Joseph Zikmund II, eds., *The American Cultural Matrix* (New York: Thomas Y. Crowell, 1975), 262.

23. See Rodolfo O. de la Garza, *Ignored Voices and Public Opinion Polls and the Latino Community* (Austin, Texas: The Center for Mexican American Studies, The University of Texas, 1978).

24. Robert H. Blank, *Individualism in Idaho: The Territorial Foundations* (Pullman, Wash.: Washington State University Press, 1988).

25. Inglehart, "The Renaissance of Political Culture," 1225–30.

26. Arthur Miller, "Public Opinion and Regional Political Realignment," in Galderisi *et al.*, eds., *The Politics of Realignment: Party Change in the Mountain States*.

27. Alfred DeGrazia, *The Western Public, 1952 and Beyond* (Stanford: Stanford University Press, 1954). Other older standard works make the same point: Thomas Donnelly, ed., *Rocky Mountain Politics* (Albuquerque: University of New Mexico Press, 1940); Frank Jonas, eds., *Western Politics* (Salt Lake City: University of Utah Press, 1961); Frank Jonas, ed., *Politics in the American West* (Salt Lake City: University of Utah Press, 1969).

28. Paul Kleppner, "Voters and Parties in the Western States, 1876–1900," *Western Historical Quarterly*, 14 (January 1983), 49–68.

3

THE ECONOMIC ENVIRONMENT

Eric B. Herzik

OF THE NUMEROUS FACTORS THAT AFFECT POLITICS and public policy, those relating to the economic aspects of life are always of great significance and often the most important factors of all. The economic base of a nation, state, locality or region determines the material well-being of its people. Consequently, many aspects of the quality of life, such as secure employment, health care, educational and recreational opportunities, and the provision of basic public services will be greatly influenced by the strengths and weaknesses of the economy. These and many other issues are of crucial importance in the day-to-day life of each citizen, and thus promoting economic well-being becomes a central concern of every society. Exactly how to achieve this economic well-being is often the subject of considerable disagreement among the various groups and interests that make up the society. For all these reasons, economics and politics become inextricably bound together. Therefore, to fully appreciate the nature of western politics we need to understand the unique economic environment that has shaped much of the political debate in the region both in the past and in the present and which will continue to influence that debate for many years to come.

From the days of the first Euro-Americans to arrive in the region, the American West has beckoned as a land of unlimited economic opportunity. The image of abundant resources and available land, along with a general sense of "openness"—meaning both space and a lack of societal restrictions—continues to attract people to the region. Once sparsely settled and mostly agricultural, the West is now in the forefront of technological development. Major metropolitan areas are scattered throughout the region and serve as magnets for business and residential development. Economic growth has also spawned new political clout, with western states and communities leading the so-called "power shift" away from traditional industrial centers in the Midwest and Northeast regions of the United States.[1] The emergence of Japan as a world economic power only solidifies the basic optimistic belief found in western states that a "Pacific Century" is coming for the world economy and that western states will be in the forefront of this economic leadership.

This image of unfettered, indomitable and advancing economic and political power distinguishes the region, but the myth is greater than the reality, however. Certainly, western states have grown in population and diversified their economies, but the region still lags behind established power centers in the Midwest and Northeast. The western image of high-tech leader and economic entrepreneur rests squarely on a foundation of federal government largesse and publicly provided infrastructure—particularly in the case of roads, water systems, airports, parks and government buildings. Natural resources and agriculture, though diminishing somewhat in overall importance, still drive many western state economies. The boom-bust cycles accompanying mineral finds and played-out mines make many western state economies subject to larger national and international economic forces. Indeed, western state economies reflect the basic factors and themes that dominate policy and politics in the region: i.e., a resource-rich base with an individualistic outlook that is dependent upon governmental spending and external economic forces.

This chapter will analyze the western economy and its impact on politics and policy in the region. It specifically will address the myths and realities of regional economic development, with an emphasis on the factors that drive western state economies. The first section outlines the contours of the western economy. The next section discusses the pervasive influence of the federal government in promoting and steering the region's development. The third section explains and discusses the continuing vulnerability of western state economies to cyclical booms and busts, and notes ongoing efforts to diversify economic development. The final section links economic development policymaking to other basic (and often competing) concerns within the region.

The Contours of Western State Economies

Prior to World War II, the West was sparsely populated and economically underdeveloped. Population growth and economic development following the war, and especially in the period since 1965, has propelled the West into a more equal economic and demographic position vis-à-vis other regions in the United States. Even with significant growth in the past two decades, however, the West as a region lags behind most of the United States in several key areas of economic development. For example, only six of the thirteen western states currently exceed the national average per capita income level.[2] Since 1980, income growth has slowed in the West to the point where only two states (Colorado and Alaska) have experienced income growth above the national average and several western states now have income growth rates well below the national average.[3] Furthermore, western states tend to be more dependent on government and service employment than the nation as a whole, and lag well behind in manufacturing employment (Table 3.1).

The data presented in Table 3.1 indicate that western states are not the self-sustaining economic leaders of business promotion literature or regional public opinion. It is true that the gap between the West and other regions in the United States in economic development, employment and income levels has narrowed in recent years. However, reversals in energy, mineral, and agricultural markets, combined with decreases in federal aid, have slowed this regional economic development. At the same time, industrial sectors in the Northeast and Midwest are being revitalized, leaving most western states in a

Table 3.1 Nonagricultural Employment Sectors (Percentage of Workforce by Region)

Region	Construction	Manufacturing	Economic Sector					
			Transport and Utilities	Wholesale and Retail Trade	Finance Insurance Real Estate	Service	Government
U.S.	4.9	19.0	5.2	23.6	6.3	23.1	16.7
Northeast	4.3	20.5	4.6	22.9	7.2	25.0	14.6
Midwest	3.8	21.5	5.3	24.3	5.8	22.3	16.8
South	5.5	18.8	5.3	23.8	5.2	21.4	18.4
West	5.5	14.2	5.6	24.1	6.3	24.3	18.4

Note: Percentage may be less than or greater than 100 due to rounding.

Source: U.S. Bureau of Labor Statistics, 1986.

vulnerable position in terms of achieving economic equality with the nation as a whole.

The uneven pattern and process of economic development in the West, with the boom of the 1970s followed by a relative bust in the 1980s, reflect the basic factors that drive western state economies. Three factors form the base of these economies—agriculture, natural resources, and government spending. Each of these contributes directly to western state economies as a sector of employment and in production value. But equally important are the indirect or interactive effects spawned by activity in each economic sector. For example, tourism and its associated service employment are linked to natural resource attractions in virtually all the western states. Development of tourist centers, especially providing them with adequate water supplies and transportation routes, rests squarely on federal funding of key infrastructure. The region's growing high-tech microelectronics and aerospace industries are also substantially supported by government rather than private market contracts.

The importance of agriculture, natural resources and government spending is clearly shown by analyzing manufacturing output in western states. Table 3.2 lists the leading industry groups (by value added to manufacturing) in western states. In seven of the thirteen states either natural resources or agriculture (food processing) is the leading contributor to manufacturing values. By contrast, either natural resources or agriculture is the leading contributor to manufacturing values in only nine of the remaining thirty-seven states, with six of these states being located in the South. Either natural resources or agriculture is ranked in the top three industry groups for value added to manufacturing in all but two western states (California and Arizona). Ironically, California is the overall leader in the country in agricultural production, and Arizona is a leading producer of fruits and vegetables. The observed lack of importance of agriculture and natural resources in these two states reflects the larger size and diversity of their economies. As shown in Table 3.2, the leading manufacturing groups in western states not related to natural resources and agriculture—especially transportation and electrical equipment—are linked to federal government spending.

This reliance on natural resources, agriculture, and government spending has other ramifications for western state economies. The average annual pay for nonagricultural workers is below the 1986 U.S. average of $19,966 in ten of the thirteen western states. Significantly, the three western states above the U.S. average wage (Ari-

Table 3.2   Leading Industry Groups in Western States (Ranked by Value Added to Manufacture, 1982)

State	Industry Groups
Alaska	Food; petroleum and coal; lumber
Arizona	Electronics; machinery (excluding electronics); transportation equipment
California	Electronics; transportation equipment; machinery (excluding electronics)
Colorado	Machinery (excluding electronics); instruments; food
Hawaii	Food; textiles; stone, clay, glass products
Idaho	Food; machinery (excluding electronics); chemicals
Montana	Lumber; food; petroleum and coal
Nevada	Food; printing and publishing; metals
New Mexico	Petroleum and coal; electronics; food
Oregon	Lumber; food; instruments
Utah	Machinery (excluding electronics); transportation equipment; food
Washington	Transportation equipment; food; lumber
Wyoming	Chemicals; machinery (excluding electronics); food
U.S.	Machinery (excluding electronics); food, transportation equipment

Source: U.S. Bureau of the Census, *Census of Manufactures, 1977 and 1982.*

zona, California, Colorado) are the least dependent upon natural resource extraction, agriculture and agribusiness.

Production and employment in industries related to natural resources tend to be more subject to cycles of boom and bust. Prospering from world oil shortages and inflation, several western states, especially those in the Mountain West, recorded significant income gains. However, downturns in the mid-1980s have caused reversals in these same states with accompanying unemployment and fiscal crises. These problems have been especially severe in Alaska, Montana, New Mexico, and Wyoming. The effects of this boom-bust cycle on economic development will be discussed in more detail below.

The economic structure of western states makes the region more dependent on national and international markets. Centers of decision-making external to the region—these can be congressional leaders determining federal aid expenditures, commodity futures trading in

Chicago and New York, or production-level control efforts by OPEC—often influence economic growth and vitality in the region. In extreme cases this has caused the West to be treated "like a Third World country," with resources mined or harvested in the region and exported for processing elsewhere. For example, while the West is the overall leader in the production of most nonferrous minerals, only 10 of the 505 nonferrous metals processing plants in the U.S. are located in the West. The West is also a leader in the production and export of lumber, but boasts few finished wood products industries.[4]

This failure to develop regional resources has had multiple causes. A major element in this is the pattern of ownership of western resources. Since initial settlement, mining, timber, and agricultural production in the West have often been owned and operated by corporations outside the region. Huge tracts of land, and their associated mineral rights, are controlled by the federal government. Western states also have limited internal financial resources to fund local development. Also, the commercial banks in the region are generally small and the per capita assets controlled by them are limited. Only one western state (Hawaii) has per capita deposits above the U.S. average. Six of the thirteen western states rank in the bottom ten of all states in terms of total assets, and seven of the thirteen states rank in the bottom ten nationwide on the basis of per capita assets.[5]

INTRAREGIONAL DISTINCTIONS

The preceding discussion indicates that the West is economically far less important than popular visions of regional vitality suggest. Overall, the region still lags behind most of the rest of the nation in measures of wealth and wages. The basic economic sectors that drive western state economies also make the region highly subject to external sources of political and economic decision-making. Within the region, however, there are fairly significant differences in the vitality and independence of the individual state economies.

On most measures of wealth and development there is a distinction between the states of the Mountain West and Pacific Coast. The Mountain West tends to be relatively poorer in per capita terms and more dependent on natural resource production and government employment, and it lags far behind the Pacific Coast states (and the nation as a whole) in overall industrial output and employment (see Table 3.3). Personal income per capita in the Mountain states (measured for 1986 in constant 1962 dollars) is nearly $3,000 less than that

Table 3.3   Nonagricultural Employment Sectors, Western States and Subregions (Percentage of Workforce by Region)

Region	Construction	Manufacturing	Transport and Utilities	Wholesale and Retail Trade	Finance Insurance Real Estate	Service	Government
MOUNTAIN STATES							
Arizona	8.5	13.7	4.9	24.2	6.6	24.3	16.8
Colorado	5.4	13.1	6.2	24.8	6.9	23.1	18.1
Idaho	4.4	15.5	5.6	25.0	7.1	20.2	21.2
Montana	3.6	7.6	7.2	26.4	4.7	22.4	25.3
Nevada	5.7	4.6	5.7	20.2	4.9	44.1	13.2
New Mexico	6.6	7.1	5.4	24.0	5.1	22.3	26.1
Utah	5.2	14.5	5.9	24.1	5.2	21.7	22.2
Wyoming	8.5	4.0	7.0	23.1	4.0	16.5	26.6
Mountain States' Avg.	6.3	11.6	5.8	24.1	6.0	24.6	19.5
PACIFIC STATES							
Alaska	5.8	5.4	8.1	19.8	5.8	19.8	29.7
California	4.6	18.3	5.1	24.0	6.7	24.4	16.2
Hawaii	4.3	5.0	7.7	26.7	7.5	27.3	21.5
Oregon	3.2	18.6	5.3	25.3	6.6	21.7	18.8
Washington	4.8	17.1	5.4	24.5	5.9	22.2	19.7
Pacific States' Avg.	4.6	16.9	5.3	24.2	6.5	24.0	17.2
U.S.	4.9	19.0	5.2	23.6	6.3	23.1	16.7

Note: Percentage may be less than or greater than 100 due to rounding.

Source: U.S. Bureau of Labor Statistics, 1986.

in the Pacific Coast states ($11,571 vs. $14,330). Even with Alaska removed from the Pacific Coast state average, the intraregional disparity for personal income exceeds $1,600 dollars ($11,571 vs. $13,174).[6]

There are, however, notable exceptions within this Mountain West vs. Pacific Coast distinction. Colorado and Arizona have more diverse economies than do their Mountain state counterparts. Per capita income in Colorado is exceeded only by those of California and Alaska in the Pacific Coast states. The level of overall employment in nonagricultural jobs in California, Washington, Colorado, Arizona, and Oregon dwarfs similar levels in the remaining western states. In part, this reflects basic differences in population levels between western states. It is also related, however, to the differing levels of economic development and diversity found in these states (see Table 3.2). Within the Pacific Coast states, the small and resource-based economy of Alaska makes it far more similar to Mountain state economies than to its Pacific Coast counterparts.

Two of these states, however, are exceptions to any convenient or simple economic grouping of western states. The California economy is larger, in terms of overall employment, production output, and value of production output, than all other western state economies combined. California is the home base of more major corporate headquarters than the rest of the region, and it has access to internal financial resources that also exceed the totals for the rest of the region. On a per capita basis and in terms of the distribution of economic activity, however, the California economy can be compared to the smaller economies of its regional counterparts—Arizona, Colorado, Washington, and to a lesser extent Oregon.

The Nevada economy is comparable to its Mountain state counterparts in terms of overall size, but the driving force of the state's economy is quite different from the rest of the region. The tourism and gaming base of the Nevada economy dwarfs any competing economic sector. This dependence on tourism and gaming leads to an employment profile in which 44% of nonagricultural workers are in the service sector. The Nevada per capita personal income also exceeds that of all other Mountain West states. However, Nevada shares two elements of economic dependence with the rest of the region. Tourism and gaming receipts can be subject to external shocks, such as the oil and energy shortages of 1974 and 1978. Government spending and decision-making also has tremendous sway in the Nevada economy. The federal government owns more than 85% of all land in Nevada. The only employment sector close to rivaling tourism and gaming is government employment and contracting, particularly in southern Nevada where it is linked to nuclear weapons testing and defense-related industries.

The Influence of the Federal Government

A basic theme of this book is the crucial role played by the federal government in developing the West. The federal government maintains a larger presence—through land ownership, contract awards, employment, and spending on infrastructure—in the West than in any other region of the country. The scope and magnitude of the federal presence has been a constant throughout the history of economic development in the West, and it pervades nearly every sector of economic activity in the region.

The primary vehicle of federal dominance of western state economic development is the ownership of vast tracts of land. With the ownership of land comes control over resources, development, and land use. Federal auctions of timber and mineral rights can flood existing markets and depress the prices of commodities produced in the region. Federal decisions on land use can also run counter to state desires or regulations, such as the selling of offshore oil leases in California and the placement of nuclear waste facilities in New Mexico and Nevada.

While the federal government maintains a massive and independent presence in the West through its land holdings, western states have also benefited from and actively sought federal funding for the development of basic infrastructure. In an earlier volume on the politics of the West, Neil Maxwell concluded that "Water continues to be the 'leitmotiv' of western politics."[7] While the region contains vast tracts of land, water is relatively scarce. Collecting water and delivering water to urban areas has made population increases and economic growth in the West possible. Provision of water has also turned previously arid regions of the West into top producers of fruits, vegetables and forage crops. But this moving of water throughout the West entails enormous costs—costs that the individual states are both unable and unwilling to absorb. Thus the region's water supply, even with recent declines in federal outlays, depends crucially on the federal dollars spent on dams, aqueducts, and other reclamation projects.

Federal dollars spent on water multiply in almost every other aspect of western states' development. Moving water from northern California and the Colorado River transformed Los Angeles, Orange

County, and San Diego into massive centers of population, production and trade. A series of dams stabilized the Salt River and led to the development of Phoenix and central Arizona. Hydroelectric facilities, such as Bonneville Dam in Washington State and Hoover Dam in Nevada, provide relatively cheap energy for economic development throughout the region. As noted, available energy and water supplies allow for the development of natural resource–related industries such as tourism and the agricultural "miracles" that make the deserts of California and Arizona bloom.

Federal spending has also contributed heavily to the development of the western state transportation systems. For example, the western states receive more than 21% of all federal highway trust funds. Average federal spending per capita for highways in the West is nearly double the average expenditures for the nation as a whole ($105.31 vs. $54.62). Federal transportation spending in the West is concentrated on road construction. Urban Mass Transit Administration (UMTA) funding is far less important to the region. Only two western states (California and Oregon) exceed the national per capita average UMTA expenditure, although four other states (Colorado, Washington, Hawaii and Utah) are relatively near the national norm.[8] Thus the interstate transportation system links most western urban areas and keys western trade to the trucking industry.

Data presented earlier in Tables 3.1 and 3.3 show that government employment levels are generally higher in western states than for the nation as a whole. Even though states in the region (especially Montana, Wyoming and Alaska) have relatively small populations, the massive size of western states requires a fairly extensive base of government employees. The federal government's land-holding presence in the region also leads to higher levels of government employment. The ratio of federal government civilian employees is higher in the West than any other region. The average ratio for the region, 134 federal employees per 10,000 population, is exceeded only in five southern states—Maryland, Virginia, Georgia, Alabama and Oklahoma.[9]

Western states also receive a disproportionate share of federal aid dollars. While the West's share of direct federal spending has decreased as a result of changes during the Reagan administration, the region still receives more dollars per capita than any other part of the U.S. The nature of federal spending in the West is also significantly different from that for other regions. Federal aid to western states is less likely to be targeted in the form of direct payments to individuals and has relatively larger percentages spent on defense and procurement than in other regions (Table 3.4).

The West also has the fewest federal dollars sent directly to state and local governments, with larger shares in the form of procurements going to private contracting firms. This has profound ramifications for the structure of the region's industrial output. As noted earlier (see Table 3.2), the West has a relatively underdeveloped manufacturing core and is dominated by production related to natural resources and agriculture. Industrial production in the region is highly dependent upon federal contract awards, especially those related to national defense. The West receives nearly 28% of all Department of Defense (DOD) contract award dollars. Indeed, the four most industrialized states in the region (Arizona, California, Colorado and Washington) receive 25% of DOD contract dollars. As Table 3.5 indicates, DOD contract awards make up a significant portion of total production values of manufacturing concerns in western states. While such contract awards cover the full range of DOD activities, the figures presented show the relative impact of defense spending in the region in relation to manufacturing effort. In addition, dollars for nuclear testing, storage, and development, generally awarded through the Department of Energy and critical to the state economies of Nevada, New Mexico, and Washington, add to the total federal defense-related impact on the region's industrial effort.

An additional area of federal government contribution to the economic development of the West is the support of agriculture. As noted, major water projects have made previously arid regions of the West agriculturally productive. In addition, states in the Mountain West receive over 10% of federal government payments made in support of agriculture. These federal government payments are made generally in support of cattle and forage crops. The average size of ranches in the Mountain West states is nearly four times the U.S. average size of farms. Lands for western agricultural interests are further augmented by subsidized leases of federal grazing rights, money that is not recouped from western agricultural tenants.[10]

A number of consequences for western economic development result from the massive presence of the federal government. Given federal land holdings, autonomous land use and development decisions within western states are inhibited. Federal control of mineral and grazing rights makes related economic activities dependent on federal—rather than individual, regional or local—decision-making. Manufacturing in the region also follows the lead of federal decision-

Table 3.4 Distribution of Federal Funds by Regions (in Millions of Dollars)

Region	Total	Per Capita	Defense	Nondefense	Payments to Individuals	Procurement	Grants to State/Local Government	Salaries and Wages
Northeast	169,004	3,379	40,937	128,066	81,257	38,455	28,015	16,827
Midwest	173,156	2,919	32,854	140,302	86,816	31,497	26,122	18,348
South	281,738	3,395	79,529	202,211	125,125	61,089	33,135	55,005
West	179,069	3,673	61,505	117,563	64,477	55,784	21,679	29,469

Source: U.S. Bureau of the Census, *Federal Expenditures by State for 1986.*

Table 3.5   Department of Defense Contract Dollars as a Percentage of Value Added by Manufacturing, 1986

State	Percent
Alaska	66.0
Arizona	33.1
California	24.9
Colorado	18.7
Hawaii	47.1
Idaho	2.4
Montana	7.1
Nevada	13.6
New Mexico	35.7
Oregon	3.5
Utah	14.7
Washington	17.0
Wyoming	19.7
U.S. Average	13.6

Source: U.S. Department of Defense and U.S. Census of Manufacturers.

making, particularly as related to defense spending. Indeed, John Mollenkopf argues that the bulk of post–World War II urban growth in the West is linked to defense contracting. The continuing input of federal procurement dollars, joined to a generally receptive political and economic climate for such expenditures, provided the basic foundation for growth in the West.[11] Examples of such interaction among defense spending, local support, major firm development, and continuing growth include the centering of the nation's aerospace industry in southern California, the development of the Nuclear Test Site in southern Nevada, the rise of Motorola as the leading private employer in Arizona, and the explosion of the microelectronics industry in northern California. Indeed, the Nuclear Test Site (NTS) in Nevada may be the quintessential example of the federal government's role in western development. NTS brought more than 4,000 jobs directly to the region (and an estimated 15,000 site-related jobs), while placing the entire site on federal lands. Even with the risk associated with testing and transporting nuclear materials, acceptance of NTS was unchallenged in the 1950s and remains strong to this day even though federal spending is generally a favorite target for criticism by Nevada politicians.[12]

Booms, Busts, and Efforts to Diversify

The lack of diversity or autonomy in western state economies makes them dependent on external events and centers of decision-making. Chapter 2 introduced the key problem that such dependence and economic structuring breeds: the boom and bust nature of most western state economies. The region generally lacks vertical integration (control of the various phases of the production process) and the capacity to diversify employment and production patterns. Thus, as world prices and demand for the raw materials produced in the West vary, so do western state economies. Dependence on defense expenditures exacerbates the boom-bust potential of western economies by linking much of the region's manufacturing capacity to a single source of contracts—the federal government.

The most recent case of a boom turning to bust is the collapse of world oil prices. The economic consequences of the oil collapse, particularly on state government revenues and expenditures, are outlined in Chapter 16. But oil is merely the most recent example of such economic woes linked to boom and bust. Similar economic cycles have occurred in the price and production of every mineral and natural resource produced in significant quantities in western states. Falling forest product prices have kept Oregon in the economic doldrums for more than a decade. The collapse of copper prices, due to expansion of production in South America, virtually wiped out whole towns in Arizona and New Mexico. Environmental policy concerns and falling demand lessened the value of western soft coal. A general downturn in agricultural prices affects a wide variety of products produced in the West.

The causes for economic downturns in products produced in the West vary. Expanded world production is often a key factor. Changing technologies (for example, the shift from copper to plastic pipes) can lessen demand. Transportation costs associated with the relative isolation of the West from production centers often make western states' products more expensive than competitors either domestically or internationally. While each of these causes may explain a boom or bust in the production of a particular resource or material, the vulnerability of the West to such external shocks results from the failure to integrate vertically and to diversify state economies.

For western state economies to become vertically integrated would require linking the mining or harvesting of resources with manufacturing of finished products. The West produces many resources, but the processing and transformation of these resources into finished products generally occur outside the region.[13] If alternative sources of materials are developed, and especially if those sources have the key comparative advantages of lower wage or transportation costs, western state production and economies suffer. Without regional outlets that can convert the raw materials into finished products, western state economies will always remain dependent on external (and often international) patterns of supply and demand. With regional manufacturing outlets, these external patterns of supply and demand would still exist, but their effect on natural resource production and prices would be lessened due to the comparative advantages resulting from proximity to the key points of manufacturing.

Integration of the production process is also a means of increasing diversity of economic activity. A jolt to raw material production is lessened in terms of its overall economic effect if a smaller portion of the workforce is directly related to production of raw materials. If prices for a raw material are depressed, manufactured goods utilizing that material may flourish. Thus, if western state economies actively increased manufacturing capacity, losses in the raw materials sector might be offset (either wholly or partially) by increases in manufacturing. At present, few western states (California, Colorado, Arizona and Washington are exceptions) have even this limtied version of economic diversity. True economic diversification comes when multiple production components are vertically integrated. In effect, no one production base (whether it be agriculture or some natural resource such as oil, copper, or forest products) will so dominate a state's economic profile that a collapse of that sector plunges the state into recession. California offers a clear case of the advantages of a diversified economy: the collapse of oil prices did not seriously impair state and local revenues in California or its overall economic output, despite its being the fourth largest oil producer in the U.S. Alaska's experience with the collapse of oil prices is an example of a state economy overwhelmingly dependent on a single resource. With falling oil prices, state revenues have plunged and unemployment reached double digits while national unemployment levels decline. Colorado, New Mexico and Wyoming all fall between these two endpoints of economic diversity and sensitivity to the collapse of oil prices.

PURSUING DIVERSITY

The dependence of western state economies on external events and centers of decision-making has not gone unnoticed by politicians or development planners within the region. States in the region are aggressively pursuing new sectors of economic growth, development, and expansion of trade. The two dominant themes in this pursuit of economic growth are high technology and expanded international trade, particularly with Asian countries.

Several western states are recognized leaders in the production of high-tech electronic, aerospace and transportation equipment. California's "Silicon Valley" and the North County area of San Diego, Seattle, and Phoenix are all areas with established high-tech industrial bases. High-tech industries are actively pursued by community leaders and economic planners because such industries are thought to be environmentally clean, relatively immune from recession and slumps, and sources of higher paying employment. This type of economic development also fits into the region's basic outlook of being in the forefront and thus not tied to the decaying "Rustbelt" of middle America.

The policy of chasing "short stack" rather than "smoke stack" industries does have advantages. Yet the image of high-tech industries and the reality for economic development are not as closely linked as many planners and political leaders have assumed. High-tech industries have particular infrastructure and personnel needs. Pollution problems linked to the use of hazardous chemicals in the production of microelectronic components abound, although of a different nature than the visible air and water contamination of more basic industrial concerns. Even the wage scale needs to be closely scrutinized. While headquarters and development firms employ highly paid engineers, assembly workers for high-tech firms are paid at rates generally lower than the rates paid at the more commonly unionized industrial plants.[14] Increasingly, high-tech centers also need to be associated with top-flight institutions of higher education, particularly institutions with recognized programs in microelectronics or engineering. As so many states are pursuing high-tech firms, local and state governments must also be prepared to give considerable tax and facility concessions to lure such firms. A recent example of competition for a high-tech giant was the multistate bidding for the electronics consortium SEMATEC. Sites in a number of states, including Arizona, Colorado, Texas, and North Carolina, were given serious consideration. The final choice of Austin, Texas, was linked to the provision of building and office space by the state and the existence of a recognized center of educational excellence at the University of Texas.

Building the educational base and providing economic incentives are direct costs associated with the pursuit of high-tech firms. Governors and state development offices now actively package incentives and assorted giveaways to attract major industries. Among the incentives are free or low-cost land, facilities, tax abatements, job training, and direct financial assistance.[15] But such aggressive pursuit of particular industries threatens the competitive position of existing or untargeted firms. The competition for high-tech firms is particularly costly, and many western states are at a comparative disadvantage as their existing educational and infrastructure bases are relatively underdeveloped. Hence, existing centers of urban commerce, education, transportation and development such as Boston thrive in the pursuit of high-tech firms. Such prior investment and development may well prove to be too much for the raw optimism of western states to overcome.

Western states are also active in developing increased Asian and other international trade. Trade with "Pacific Rim" countries exceeds three trillion dollars and is rapidly expanding. To capitalize on their strategic position on the Pacific Rim, governors in western states have sought to develop trade and industrial packages with Asian nations. Toward this end, seven western states maintain trade offices in the Far East.[16]

Developing international markets reaps advantages for western states as the number of outlets for the region's products is expanded. However, if international trade focuses merely on the export of raw materials, the region does little to achieve expanded vertical integration or product expansion. Attraction of foreign production facilities is a more extensive and critical avenue of economic development than simple market outlet expansion.

A type of regional integration of production and marketing is also developing along the West's border with Mexico. The "Maquiladoras" or "twin plant" system combines advantages for both western and Mexican border states. Lower labor costs in Mexico are utilized for the assembly of finished products, the components of which are manufactured in the United States. The finished products are then imported through western states. Western state economies, to the extent that they produce the components used in production and have control over import transportation, achieve direct benefits from this type of production system. Personal computers, consumer electronics and sportswear from firms such as Zenith, Sony, General Electric and Farrah are prime examples of Mexican assembly of goods whose parts are largely produced in western states. As wages for Mexican workers increase, border towns also benefit indirectly through increased retail sales. The potential downside of the system is the export of assembly and manufacturing jobs to Mexico from western states. While the "twin plant" system is rapidly expanding, there is presently no definitive evidence concerning its effects on western state economies.

Growth, Development and Western Culture

One of the distinguishing features of western states has been their rapid growth during the past two decades. Economic growth has also expanded, but the basic structure of western state economies makes them highly dependent on external sources that either utilize the region's raw materials or fund specific production such as that linked to national defense. This basic dependence has tended to limit public input or control over economic development policies. Economic policymaking has generally been dominated by the major economic concerns that exist within each state. With vast underdeveloped sections of land, the bias of most western states has been actively to pursue population and economic growth.

Expansion of the population and economic base of a state or community has historically been a highly prized goal in the West. Existing residents tend to link growth with higher land values, more or better jobs, and improved shopping, cultural and recreational opportunities. For rural areas growth becomes a way to achieve a baseline of community support facilities and a means by which young people remain in or are attracted to the community. State and local government officials often consider growth to be a way of raising additional revenues without increasing taxes.[17]

Unfortunately, the expected benefits of growth do not always materialize in practice. For example, a new plant may provide jobs and increase wages, but infrastructure costs provided for the plant (transportation, water and sewer improvements) may exceed the revenues generated. As states and localities offer incentives to attract economic development, demands for infrastructure will increase but sources of revenues to pay for such demands may be foreclosed. The real irony of such incentive plans suggested by some recent research is that the enticements offered have little effect on business development. Companies considering relocation are more likely to be influenced by factors involving the quality of life for employees and more diffuse economic factors such as labor force productivity and proximity to markets rather than by tax or credit differentials.[18]

The pursuit of growth simply for the sake of growth is increasingly being challenged in many western states. The focus on high-tech firm recruitment is an example of a policy attempt at directing or controlling growth. Chasing businesses in an attempt to lure them from one locale to another has also lost some appeal. Part of the reason for the decline in interest is the realization that competition over industrial relocation is largely a zero sum game. Moving businesses from place to place means that some states and localities win while others lose. Little if anything is added to overall economic development in the larger sense (nation, state or even metropolitan area). Indeed, as noted above, the incentives used to lure companies from place to place may leave state and local governments worse off in terms of raising revenues for increased service demands. In response, many state development agencies are now directing their efforts to nurturing indigenous businesses and industries rather than resting their hopes on relocation inducements. Such a policy shift gives states and localities more control over the timing and structure of growth within their jurisdictions. It also allows for the strengthening of local workforce quality, business competitiveness and general improvement of key quality of life factors within jurisdictions.[19]

Moves to encourage locally based growth factors are consonant with the populist spirit that has helped shape the West. Espousal of individual initiative and economic growth continues to motivate many current economic policies—a link to the frontier ethos of the region. However, these same policies also blend the pragmatic concerns of limiting tax burdens by ensuring that growth essentially "pays its own way." This blending of the individualistic ethos with the pragmatic is a distinguishing feature of western politics—a feature that continues to influence economic and regional development policy.

Economic development policies in western states are also increasingly being shaped by concerns with environmental quality. Western state economies depend critically on the natural resources of the region. But the impact of the physical environment goes beyond simple mining, harvesting or production concerns. The physical environment plays a critical role in defining the quality of life enjoyed by westerners. Excessive or uncontrolled growth places fragile water and ecological systems at risk. Thus, a number of states and localities have responded to popular sentiment and political initiative to balance, at least partially, environmental and growth policies. Oregon has taken perhaps the most aggressive stance, with extensive zoning and development restrictions. Coastal zoning plans in Oregon resulted from public sentiment desiring to protect the state's coastal areas from the type of massive development found in California. However, California, the longtime champion of growth, has also developed policies in an attempt to gain control over growth-related transportation, water, waste, and educational problems. Communities in Colorado (e.g., Boulder) have enacted restrictive growth and development ordinances, and Arizona has recently funded a major study aimed at developing a comprehensive growth management policy for the state.[20]

Economic development policy in western states is thus firmly linked to the larger cultural and historical factors that have shaped the region. When considering western state economies, these basic factors of politics and development cannot be ignored. While popular images of economic leadership, unfettered growth and independence abound, the reality of western state economic performance and development offers a different image. The region has made spectacular gains in recent years to achieve rough parity with other parts of the United States. Still, the basic structure of western state economies makes them vulnerable to external forces, liable to continuing cycles of boom and bust, and dependent on federal government contracting and decision-making. However, the sheer size and potential of western state economies can be adapted into development policies that should bring the popular image of increasing economic growth and power closer to reality in the next two decades.

Notes

1. See Kirkpatrick Sale, *Power Shift* (New York: Random House, 1975).

2. *Book of the States: 1987–88* (Lexington, Ky.: Council of State Governments, 1987), p. 439. See also Chapter 12.

3. See chapter 12, this volume.

4. David Birch, Address to the Annual Meeting of the Western Governors' Conference, Seattle, Wash., July 11, 1988.

5. Board of Governors of the Federal Reserve System, *Annual Statistical Digest* (Washington, D.C.: Federal Reserve System, 1987); and Federal Deposit Insurance Corporation, unpublished data.

6. U.S. Bureau of Economic Analysis, *Survey of Current Business* (Washington, D.C., August 1987).

7. Neal A. Maxwell, "The West on Capitol Hill," in Frank H. Jonas, ed., *Politics in the American West* (Salt Lake City: University of Utah Press, 1969), 486.

8. U.S. Bureau of the Census, *Federal Expenditures by State for Fiscal Year 1986* (Washington, D.C.: U.S. Government Printing Office, March 1987).

9. U.S. Office of Personnel Management, *Biennial Report of Employment by Geographic Area* (Washington, D.C.: U.S. Government Printing Office, 1987).

10. See U.S. General Accounting Office, *Rangeland Management* (GAO/RCED-88-80), June 10, 1988; and U.S. General Accounting Office, *Farm Programs: An Overview of Price and Income Support, and Storage Programs* (GAO/RCED-88-84 BR), June 29, 1987.

11. See John H. Mollenkopf, *The Contested City* (Princeton: Princeton University Press, 1983).

12. See Costandina A. Titus, *Bombs in the Backyard: Atomic Testing and American Politics* (Reno: University of Nevada Press, 1986).

13. Birch, Western Governors' Address.

14. See Gregory Daneke, "Revitalizing U.S. Technology?" *Public Administration Review* 46, 6 (November/December 1986), 668–72; and Lenny Siegel and John Markoff, *The High Cost of High Tech* (New York: Harper & Row, 1985).

15. See Dennis Grady, "Economic Development and Administrative Power Theory: A Comparative Analysis of State Development Agencies," *Policy Studies Review* 8, 2 (1989); and M. K. Clarke, *Revitalizing State Economies: A Review of State Economic Development Policies and Programs* (Washington, D.C.: National Governors Association, 1986).

16. George Deukmejian, Address before the Annual Meeting of the Western Governors' Conference, Seattle, Wash., 1988.

17. See Eric B. Herzik, "Projecting the Fiscal Impact of Municipal Annexation," *Municipal Management* 7, 2 (Fall 1984), 47–53.

18. M. Dubnick, "American States in the Industrial Policy Debate," *Policy Studies Review* 4, 1 (1984); I. Grossman, "States Battle to Attract Jobs," *State Government News* (December 1987); M. L. Clarke, *Revitalizing State Economies*.

19. See David Berman, "Growth Management," in Rob Melnick and Deborah Roepke, eds., *Urban Growth in Arizona* (Tempe, Ariz.: Morrison Institute, 1988).

20. See Jerry Medler, "Governors and Environmental Policy," *Policy Studies Journal* 17, 4 (June 1989).

4

THE FEDERAL
GOVERNMENT
AND THE WEST

Richard H. Foster

THE CENTRAL THESIS OF THIS CHAPTER IS THAT THE federal government's relationship with the states of the West has been so pervasive as to spawn a "politics of symbolism," in opposition to federal influence, within those states. Western politicians invoke symbols that serve mainly to produce conflict between their states and the federal government. That resulting conflict is politically unproductive and better serves the interests of western politicians than the interests of the states or their people.

To illustrate the nature of this politics of symbolism, this chapter is organized into five parts. The first section consists of a brief discussion of an issue that illustrates conflict between the states of the

West and the federal government. This issue, which is primarily symbolic, is the "Sagebrush Rebellion" of the late 1970s and early 1980s. The second section reviews the role of symbolism in politics. The Western Myth that forms the basis for much of this political symbolism is discussed as well. The third section considers the development of the federal relationship with the western states and whether western states share common interests within the federal framework. The fourth section identifies some of the major political issues common to western states. The emphasis is on those issues that are shared by most of the western states rather than issues that are particular to only a very few states or even a single state. In the final section, the politics of the western relationship with the federal government is put in the context of the federal structure as it has evolved in the 1980s and as it will likely continue to evolve during the last decade of the twentieth century. Based on that analysis, it is argued that western politicians, and the interests they represent, would benefit from a "reality check" about the nature of the federal system.

Sagebrush and Symbolism: The Public Lands Issue in the Western States

Every revolution or rebellion has its opening salvo—its "shot heard around the world." The political lines that are irrevocably drawn at the time of this "shot" have of course been building for a long time. By the time British troops marched on Lexington and Concord and exchanged shots with American Minutemen that day in April 1775, the American Revolution probably could not have been stopped even with the best efforts of people with goodwill. The action of that spring day merely ratified the beginning of a rebellion. So it is with all revolts. The "shot heard around the West" came from Carson City, Nevada, in 1979. The Nevada legislature passed, and the governor signed, a bill to require the U.S. government to turn forty-nine million acres of federal land holdings in Nevada over to the state. This included all federal public lands except those held by the Department of Defense, the Department of Energy, and the Bureau of Reclamation; the national forests and parks; and Indian reservations. In short, it took forty-nine million acres from the federal government and gave them to the state. Of course, this law has not yet been, and probably can never be, enforced. (Also, it cannot be compared in importance to the American Revolution.) Nevertheless, it has had immense symbolic importance for the West. This "Sagebrush Rebellion" is a pow-erful symbol of the widespread feeling in much of the western portion of the United States that it has been for too long controlled by the federal government.

This was only the most recent of rebellions in the West over the issue of public lands and it is very unlikely that it will be the last one. A transfer of public lands to the states was suggested as early as during the administration of Herbert Hoover. Nearly two decades later, in the immediate post–World War II era, the leaders of western livestock associations proposed legislation that would transfer public land to the states so it could be sold—preferably to the livestock operators already in possession of grazing leases. Similar proposals were made in 1951 and 1967.[1]

The high point of the rebellion of 1979 probably came in 1980 as Ronald Reagan was pursing the presidency. As a westerner he pre-sumably understood the West and its peculiar needs and the griev-ances against the federal government that are so much a part of its politics. Many in the West felt that the administration of President Carter was a perfect example of how the rest of the nation, and the federal government in particular, simply did not understand or chose not to understand the West and its problems. That administration's attempt to stop or reduce federal spending for water projects in the West and its attempt to impose a racetrack of 4,600 horizontal shelters for 200 MX missiles in the Nevada–Utah Great Basin are cases in point. From the outset, then, the Sagebrush Rebellion was a political issue—one that might easily have been taken advantage of by a presidential aspirant who was both a westerner and running for the presidency by running against the federal government. In Anchorage, Alaska, in December 1979 Ronald Reagan said that the federal government was "land greedy, holding on to land that it was never intended to hold on to." In Salt Lake City some months later he declared, "I happen to be one who cheers and supports the Sagebrush Rebellion. Count me in as a rebel." His subsequent election and with him a new Con-gress seemed a great boon to the rebels. In the new Congress a bill was introduced by Senator Orrin Hatch, a Republican from Utah, to transfer the land managed by the Bureau of Land Management and the U.S. Forest Service to the states. It did not pass, of course, and by the spring and summer of 1981 the rebellion seemed to be dying out. Its demise was in part due to its own success. Some of the rebels became part of the Establishment. The federal government was in their hands and the view became increasingly dominant that now they guided the federal bureaucracy, so there was no real need for state control.[2]

The Sagebrush Rebellion drew both support and opposition from a variety of quarters in the West and in the rest of the country. In a very general way the arguments in favor of the rebellion were three.

First and foremost was the view that too much land in the West is in public ownership. This means that it cannot be developed to its fullest and best use, which, in turn, means that the states and the region cannot be fully developed economically. In short, there is too much potentially productive land just sitting there. The solution is to transfer all of the land, or at least those portions that have productive potential, to the states. The states, in turn, can transfer some of it to private ownership. Private ownership will increase the chances that the land will be utilized at its highest and best use and that the use will be an economic boon to the state and the entire region.

The second major argument of the rebels was the traditional one that democracy works best in those circumstances where the government is at a local level. The government closest to the people is the one that can best turn the wishes of the people into actual policy. From this point of view, state governments are closer to the people and would likely do a better job of managing western land in a manner that would conform to the wishes of the West. This rather academic argument represents only a small portion of western resentment.

In the Native villages of Alaska, on Hawaii Island, among the fishing fleets of California, and in the mining districts of Idaho, there is a deeply held view that the primary role of the federal government has historically been one that favors eastern over western interests. The relationships is seen as one of exploitation. The West and its resources are seen as being exploited for the benefits of eastern interests. To the westerner it is irrelevant that these interests are private financial ones, which can be represented by the private purchase of mining operations in Kellogg, Idaho, only to close down the operation for tax reasons. That action might make sense to corporate accountants in air-conditioned skyscrapers in Houston, Texas, but it does not make sense to a community economically destroyed by the decision made two thousand miles away for reasons they simply do not understand and about which they were not consulted. It is just as irrelevant to the westerner whether exploitation is achieved through federal government policy or by private business. Policies leading to more wilderness and the prohibition of roads in areas so designated are also viewed as threats to local economies based on timber and mining. The West is uncomfortable with suggestions that it could be an energy park for the nation. As an energy park the West would be home to coal fired and nuclear electrical plants serving population centers elsewhere. It also does not want the nation's waste; especially and most emphatically, it does not want the nation's nuclear waste. Western tuna fishers are not impressed by the federal government's reluctance to back forcefully their claims to fisheries claimed as territorial waters by nations in Latin America. To these westerners the federal government seems both far away and out of touch with their concerns. Their respective state governments, on the other hand, seem more responsive to these concerns and less exploitative.

The third major argument is simply that too much emphasis has been given to the protection of wildlife and of the environment in recent years.[3] This is a very strong economic argument as well as an emotive one. To the sheep interests in Wyoming, the ban on the use of certain poisons to control the predator population, especially coyotes, imposes unacceptable costs on their operations in the form of lamb mortality. To lumber interests in states such as Oregon, Washington, Idaho, and Montana, every acre of wilderness area is an acre forever locked away and a further threat to that hard-pressed industry. Westerners are keenly aware that while there is a seemingly inexhaustible supply of land in the West, in reality only a small part of that land is economically viable and exploitable. There is real resentment when some of the best lands are locked away from possible development. While this may seem a short-sighted argument, it is a very powerful one to people who recognize that these federal government policies present a threat to their way of life in the short run.

Those who oppose the Sagebrush Rebellion—and there are many in the West who do—counter the rebels' arguments with ones that emphasize the maintenance of western life-style by conserving and protecting the uniqueness of the West. From this point of view, the land in public ownership ensures that the public will always have access to it for a variety of uses including both economic and recreational ones. Transfer of these public lands to the states would threaten this policy of public trust. Each state would be able to determine the future of the former public lands within its borders. It is likely that much of the land would be sold to private interests and would therefore no longer be available for use by the public. It would also not be protected from activities that would despoil it. Many who oppose the Sagebrush Rebellion argue that private ownership of lands is the "ultimate lock-up."

In their view it is only in recent years and as a result of new laws that there has been a balance of consideration to wildlife, recreation, water quality, and conservation values. To the extent that this new balance is a fact, the Sagebrush Rebellion is a threat to its continuance. Specifically, their view is that commercial interests such as grazing, timber, mining, and energy have dominated federal land management policies in the past. The Sagebrush Rebellion is nothing more than the most recent move on the part of these commercial interests to regain domination over the public's lands at the expense of other users.[4]

In addition to Nevada's law claiming much of the federal land for the state, bills with similar intent were passed in Washington, Wyoming, Utah, New Mexico, and Arizona. The law in Washington State was voided by a referendum of the state's voters. Another law was passed in Colorado only to be vetoed by that state's governor. The same fate awaited a 1981 law passed by the California legislature. Proposals spawned by the Sagebrush Rebellion failed after passing one house of the legislatures of Oregon, Montana, and Idaho. The voters in Alaska passed an initiative claiming ownership for that state of all lands not previously appropriated within its borders.[5] This "Tundra Rebellion" by the voters was in response to the failure by the 1981 legislature to join the rebellion in the lower forty-eight states. The Hawaii legislature, although that state does not have large areas of public land, did unsuccessfully consider support for the rebellion.

The Sagebrush Rebellion is now over. It was unsuccessful in reaching its goals. Yet it played an essential role in that it provided a vehicle for expressing the frustrations many in the West felt, and feel, about their relationship with the federal government.

Symbols in Politics

The states and people of the western United States are not easily categorized. They are urban and rural, liberal and conservative and sometimes radical. They hold values and pursue interests that are in constant conflict. In Murray Edelman's important book on the uses of symbols in politics, he made a critical point: "For everyone the political scene is a pastiche of several patterns, but always there are threatening ones. That one man's reassurance is another's threat guarantees that threat will always be present for all men. It may be imminent or it may be a potentiality to brood about, but the threatening trends naturally loom larger than the reassuring ones."[6]

Table 4.1   State Action on the "Sagebrush Rebellion"

State	Year	Lower House	Upper House	Final Outcome
Nevada	1979	passed	passed	enacted
Washington[a]	1980	passed	passed	voided by referendum
Wyoming[b]	1980	passed	passed	enacted
Utah[a]	1980	passed	passed	enacted
New Mexico[a]	1980	passed	passed	enacted
Arizona[a]	1980	passed	passed	governor's veto overridden
Idaho[a]	1981	passed	blocked in committee	failed
Colorado[a]	1981	passed	passed	vetoed
Montana[a]	1981	blocked in committee	passed	failed
California[c]	1981	passed	passed	vetoed
Oregon[a]	1981	passed	not considered	failed
Alaska	1982			passed by initiative
Hawaii	(Resolution in support of the rebellion was unsuccessful.)			

[a]The Washington, Utah, New Mexico, Arizona, Idaho, Colorado and Montana laws (or proposals) were all based on the Nevada law claiming public lands as state property.
[b]The Wyoming bill was similar but included U.S. Forest Service lands.
[c]The California bill required the state to continue payments in lieu of taxes to local governments if public land was transferred to State of California.
[d]Oregon's was a bill establishing a commission to consider reduction of federal landholdings in Oregon.
Sources: John G. Francis, "Environmental Values, Intergovernmental Politics, and the Sagebrush Rebellion" in John G. Francis and Richard Ganzel, eds., *Western Public Lands: The Management of Natural Resources in a Time of Declining Federalism* (Totowa, N.J.: Rowman and Allanheld), 37.
Janice Adair, "Federal Frustration: A Review of the Nevada Sagebrush and Alaska Tunda Rebellions," unpublished manuscript, University of Alaska, Juneau, 1983, 5.

The conflicting interests in the West, and the inevitable involvement of the federal government in these conflicts means that on some issues and to some people the federal government will be viewed as an ally, on other issues and to the same or other people the federal government will be viewed as an intrusive and overbearing enemy. Either way, much of the politics of the West is the politics of symbolism.

Symbols and myths in the West are written larger than life. The West is big and so are its symbols and its myths. An essential part of the myths is that the West, if it were left alone by the federal government, would rapidly develop economically and in a manner compatible with the life-style and values of westerners. A companion part of the myth is that the West has been held back in its development by interference from the federal government. Part of this view is the fear that the West might be forever condemned to be a colonial dependency of the East. The reality, according to Wallace Stegner, is much different. According to Stegner, the West "has instead become an empire and gotten the East to pay most of its bills."[7]

Westerners view themselves as fundamentally different from other Americans. Although much of the population of the West is urban, westerners think of themselves as free of the shackles of civilization. The preferred myth is that of westerners as independent and individualistic sojourners in the vast expanse of western land and opportunity. The reality is much different: the West is an oasis society. Because of the arid nature of much of the region, westerners have become concentrated in places that have either natural or humanly engineered access to water.

Because many of the western states have a small population, the myth that the region is rural continues as part of the lore of the West. A more accurate portrayal of western space and population would highlight the fact that a great deal of the West is sparsely populated. Instead of dealing with the issues that divide the participants, the discussion is usually couched in the language of symbolism. This, of course, requires the invocation of the Western Myth.

The Sagebrush (and Tundra) Rebellion is not the only issue that divides people in the West and sets the West against the federal government. It probably is not even the most important issue. To the westerners federal government seems at once far away and remote and their closest neighbor. The remoteness of Washington to many westerners means that the federal government and its representatives cannot truly understand or empathize with western problems and concerns. The federal government, paradoxically, is also a neighbor to westerners—a big neighbor and one with a heavy hand. It maintains a massive presence in the West as it does in other regions of the country. Its presence in the West is simply more visible, as our discussion of the Sagebrush Rebellion demonstrates. Public lands constitute a bit more than one-fourth of the total United States lands, or about 2.3 billion acres. Most of this public land is found in the eleven continental western states and Alaska. In the early 1980s the Bureau of Land Management managed 174 million acres in the continental

United States and that much again in Alaska. The Forest Service managed 187.5 million acres, mostly in the West. Over 100 million additional acres are included in lands managed by the National Park Service and the U.S. Fish and Wildlife Service.[8] As we saw in Chapter 1, and as Table 4.2 more fully demonstrates, in several western states over 50% of the land is owned by the federal government and other western states have substantial portions of the land within their boundaries under federal ownership and control. In contrast, even Washington, D.C.—the federal district—has only about 28 percent of its land under federal ownership! Because the federal government is such a big neighbor it is also a big target. Much of what does or does not happen in the West can conveniently be blamed on federal government action or inaction. This is a convenience that has been enthusiastically indulged in by populist politicians of both the right and the left in the West.

To many westerners the federal government seems like a great feather bed that changes shape very little no matter how much it is pushed, pulled, kicked or punched. The fact is that the federal government is very big, especially in comparison with many of the western states where its presence looms so large. It also has a variety of dimensions. For most westerners it is personified by its bureaucracies: the Internal Revenue Service, Forest Service, Bureau of Reclamation, Park Service, and so on. Yet it also includes the courts, which have a lot to say in legal disputes in the West over water, land and tribal and native rights. The elected leaders of the federal government, members of Congress and the president are also part of this mix. Members of Congress are particularly important in the operation of federalism. They are part of the federal government while they directly represent states (in the case of senators) or districts within states (in the case of House members). As a consequence of the federal government's many dimensions, western politicians and their constituents in the West hold a variety of views of the federal government, views that may depend on their state itself or upon the issue being considered. To people in Utah, for example, the federal government is ordinarily viewed as a protector against external threats, but as a threat to their way of life when a major missile field is proposed for part of southern Utah. In Hawaii, the attitude to the federal government has been one of detachment and isolation. Yet there does not seem to be any really strong current of Hawaiian resentment toward the federal government.[9] Idaho gratefully accepts federal government spending at the Idaho Nuclear Engineering Laboratory, but many in

Table 4.2   Federally Owned Land and Total Acreage of States—Fiscal Year 1985

	Federal Acreage	Total Acreage of State	% Owned by Federal Government
WESTERN STATES			
Alaska	313,589,184.4	365,481,600	85.8 (55.0)[a]
Arizona	32,106,785.8	72,688,000	44.1
California	48,008,587.9	100,206,720	47.9
Colorado	24,164,537.1	66,485,760	36.1
Hawaii	711,699.7	4,105,600	17.3
Idaho	33,747,005.8	52,933,120	63.7
Montana	27,616,818.8	93,271,040	29.6
Nevada	59,995,621.0	70,264,320	85.4
New Mexico	26,474,417.0	77,766,400	34.0
Oregon	30,110,211.6	61,598,720	48.9
Utah	32,333,994.7	52,696,960	61.4
Washington	13,123,043.7	42,693,760	30.7
Wyoming	31,386,797.9	62,343,040	50.4
REPRESENTATIVE STATES (AND WASHINGTON, D.C.) FROM OTHER REGIONS FOR COMPARISON			
Alabama	1,213,950.1	32,678,400	3.7
District of Columbia	10,922.9	39,040	27.9
Illinois	660,146.9	35,795,200	1.84
Nebraska	717,441.5	49,031,680	1.5
New York	286,716.1	30,680,960	.94
Ohio	378,132.5	26,222,080	1.4
Texas	3,825,463.6	168,217,600	2.3

[a]While as of 1986, 85% of Alaska lands were still technically under federal control, within the next twenty years this will be reduced to 55% as the state government and the Native population receive the full transfer of land guaranteed to them by the Statehood Act of 1959 and the Alaska Native Claims Settlement Act of 1971 respectively.

Source: U.S. Dept. of Interior, Bureau of Land Management, *Public Land Statistics 1986*, vol. 171, 5.

the state chafe under the environmental regulations imposed by Washington. Western politicians are very careful to make distinctions between federal policies that benefit their states and those that are an inconvenience, when they engage in federal government bashing.

It is well to remember that over twenty years ago, Edelman pointed out that the mass public ignores issues and facts "until political actions and speeches make them symbolically threatening or reassuring, and it then responds to the cues furnished by the actions and the speeches, not to direct knowledge of the facts."[10] To understand this fundamental point is to understand a great deal about politics in the West, and particularly about the relationship of western states with the federal government.

The West and the Developing Federal Structure

American history textbooks have been rich in their descriptions of two major tendencies in nineteenth-century America. The first is the spreading out of population from the original thirteen states into the western wilderness. The net effect of this dispersal was the westward movement of the population center of the nation.

The second tendency was the increasingly strong issues of regional identity and regional interests that threatened the very fabric of our nationhood. The federal structure has always been based upon a delicate balance of federal and state interests. This balance was in constant jeopardy from regional coalitions of interests. This conflict of regional interests reached its most threatening and most dramatic denouement in 1861 with the secession of the southern states from the Union and the subsequent Civil War. Nathan Rosenberg has pointed out that "if, for simplicity, we consider the three major, well-defined antebellum regions—a manufacturing North, an agricultural West, and a cotton-producing South—we could show that, on the four great economic issues of the tariff, internal improvements, alienation of public lands and banking and credit policy, calculations of anticipated regional incidence dominated the pattern of congressional voting behavior."[11]

The first tendency noted above—the westward expansion of population—continues to this day. The population of the United States has grown enormously in the last two hundred years and it has continued its westward shift. In fact, in the last two decades, many of the major urban areas of the Northeast have recorded absolute declines in population, while many similar areas in the West have grown at extraordinary rates. The growth of cities such as Tucson, Phoenix and Las Vegas, for example, has proceeded on a scale that is hard to comprehend and has served to intensify conflict over land, water, and urban services. The second tendency—regionalism—is probably less of a factor in national politics now than it was in the nineteenth century. In the case of the western states, the westward expansion of population has made a more cosmopolitan and less parochial populace. Twentieth-century advances in the technologies of communication and transportation have meant that the West has become less isolated and more subject to a variety of national, rather than regional, influences.

Like the countries of Africa whose boundary lines were established for the convenience of the colonial powers rather than on the basis of natural division, the western state boundaries are artificial and thus are a continuing source of controversy. The boundary lines were not drawn to reflect geography, settlement or culture. Rather, they were drawn for administrative convenience and sometimes by the accident of a survey team's blunder. The eastern states are relatively small and are defined by boundaries that, on the flat surface of a map, seem to wander with no purpose. In fact, they follow nature— the creeks, rivers and mountains that do divide people and determine their relationships with one another. Few straight lines exist in nature. Simply put, the boundaries of western states were established in a more or less arbitrary manner. Their borders are violated by much less precise forces, such as climate, geography, religion, natural resources, history, and population. All of this, of course, is a legacy of the federal government's involvement in the development of the West.

Since the late nineteenth century, westerners have vociferously protested their presumed colonial relationship with the rest of the country. They have noted the domination of western financial institutions by those in the East and have worried about the squandering of western natural resources by easterners for the benefit of the East. This perception and the tradition of this kind of protest are rooted deep in the western psyche and in western politics as evidenced by the Free Coinage of Silver movement and the populist and progressive political traditions in the West. Yet none of those traditions have been effective or successful on a national basis. In short, the West has been politically impotent. It has been impotent because it did not have a large population. In presidential elections the West has been largely ignored. With the possible exception of the Pacific Coast states of California, Oregon and Washington, it still is ignored. National candidates may make token trips to the West, where usually in an airport news-conference they let fly with some generalities about the beauty of the West before climbing back on board their jet for a trip to more populated parts of the country.[12] It just may be that this aspect of the impotence of the West is beginning to change, at least for the heavily populated coastal and southwestern portion of the region. The western states continue to have a high birthrate in comparison to the rest of the nation and simultaneously are the recipients of high net migration.[13] Map 4.1 illustrates the National Planning Association's projection of population growth in the West in the fifteen years between 1985 and the year 2000.

While the number of western senators remains steady at twenty-six, the number of members of the House of Representatives from the West, and the West's percent of total House members, will likely increase. To be sure, it is not wise to assume a direct correlation between the number of members from the West and its influence in the House of Representatives. Nevertheless, Table 4.3 provides a vivid illustration of the changes in western population (as reflected in representation in Congress) relative to the rest of the country in the last half-century. The representation of the West in the House has climbed from just under 10% in 1933 to just under 20% in 1983. It will climb to over 20% as a result of the 1990 census.

The argument can be reasonably made that the West with its resources, its increasing population, and its new economic strength, can have a bright future. Yet for that future to be realized the West must balance its goals against those of the region's most influential force—the federal government. That will require a regional approach, and such an approach, given the Western Myth, is just what we would not expect.[14]

Current Federal–State Political Issues in the West

For all the states in the West, with the exception of Hawaii, the issue of ownership and utilization of natural resources is the most contentious political issue. The problem of natural resources, of course, really includes a host of issues rather than a single one. These include water; the uses of the land for agriculture, grazing and mining, as

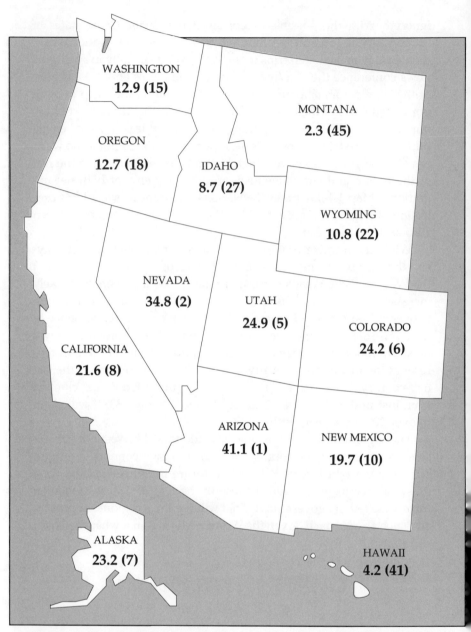

Map 4.1   Predicted Population Growth in Western U.S., 1985-2000 (Percentage, followed by projected growth ranking nationwide)

Source: Philip M. Burgess, Jack A. Brizius, and Susan E. Foster, eds., *Profile of the West* (Denver: Western States Strategy Center), 1987, 15.

Table 4.3   Changes in Representation of the West in the House of Representatives, 1933–1983

Representatives from the West	Percent of Total
43	9.9
49	11.3
57	13.1
69	15.9
76	17.5
85	19.5

Source: Frank H. Jonas, ed., Politics in the American West (Salt Lake City: University of Utah Press, 1969), 471; and Congressional Quarterly Almanac (Washington, D.C.: Congressional Quarterly), vol. 29 (1973) and 39 (1983).

well as for timber and oil; a variety of recreational values, including backpacking, hunting and fishing; and the entire bundle of conservation issues.

Two issues that best represent the entire natural resources debate in terms of both complexity and intensity are those of water and energy. To the arid and semiarid regions of the West, water has always had a special mystique. The idea that water can make the desert bloom seemed confirmed in the early years of the twentieth century as a result of water projects constructed in the Imperial Valley of California, the Magic Valley of Idaho, and the Salt River in Arizona. It really was a "magic" resource, and its provision was deemed critical for the development of large parts of the West for both agriculture and increased population. Its value was so obvious that western interests were able to convince the federal government to invest large sums of money in water projects. These soon revealed the basic problem with water throughout the West, which is that in spite of all the federal, state and local water storage and delivery projects there is only so much water to be allocated. As more and more water is used to reclaim the western desert for agriculture, and as the West undergoes rapid urban expansion, water becomes an ever more rare and valuable commodity. It is increasingly clear that the available supply of water to wet the desert and quench the thirst of the growing cities is unlikely to increase. Many of the best dam sites have already been used, and there is growing environmental objection to many of the new proposed water projects. In addition, the federal government, ever mindful of the cost of domestic programs, seems unwilling to issue a blank check for the construction of future western water projects. "Yet, Westerners believe that where water is allocated, prosperity occurs, and where water is withheld, opportunity vanishes."[15] Tim De Young notes that water projects in the West will face increasingly heavy opposition because of the rising national debt, increasing environmental concerns, and concern about the economic benefits of these programs relative to their costs.[16] Opposition to western water programs is effectively expressed to the Congress and the federal bureaucracies by a variety of groups in the West and from other parts of the country.

The energy issue in the West is quite similar to the water issue in that it leads to strongly held political positions and emotionally charged debates. It is also similar in that, like water issues, energy issues affect the entirety of the natural resources debate. The West has large amounts of untapped energy resources, and the energy shortages brought on by the oil boycott subsequent to the 1973 October War in the Middle East placed a premium on their development. The most widely known and discussed energy projects, of course, were the North Slope discoveries in Alaska and the oil pipeline there. The federal government's leasing program continues to be controversial so far as it relates to leases off the California coast. Less well known is the development of oil reserves in Wyoming. The federal government's synthetic fuels program has been hotly debated in both the West and the rest of the country. Coal fields in Montana and development of oil shale deposits in Colorado and Utah are further issues of contention. It is interesting to note that the development of energy and water resources profoundly affect one another. Dams to store and allocate water, for example, may be used to generate relatively inexpensive electricity. On the other hand, exploitation of oil shale deposits would have taken place using a technology that is highly water consumptive.

Agriculture is a mainstay of western economies. It is as varied as the dryland wheat of Colorado, the potatoes grown on the irrigated Snake River plain in Idaho, the pineapples of Hawaii and the grapes and the wine of California as well as of Oregon, Washington and Idaho. Many of these crops are grown with the aid of water supplied from the vast projects already described or pumped from the ground utilizing cheap electricity generated as part of those projects. Yet throughout the West, as in other regions of the country, agriculture is engaged in a profound transformation as the small operator is being forced off the land because of depressed prices and high debt. This transformation has led to a major debate about the responsibility of the federal government for the "farm crisis." It is an issue that will continue to pit many in the western states against federal government policies. It is also complicated by the concern of smaller farmers that federal policies and practices favor their large competitors and make it even more likely that the small operator will go out of business.

The West is a vast area; much of it is underpopulated and some of it is uninhabited. Its economic development has always been hindered by its remoteness. The issue of transportation is, as a result, a critical one for the West. And that goes double for those areas of the West that remain off the beaten path. For these regions economic development—or even economic survival in some cases—is dependent on the establishment and maintenance of viable transportation linkages. It is within this context that the negative reaction to the fifty-five-mile-an-hour speed limit must be understood. It was seen as a further limitation on the westerner's ability to travel across large expanses of land rapidly. While it was seldom enforced with great rigor in much of the West, until its repeal it remained a serious symbolic irritant to western sensibilities.

For some of the western states and for many communities in the West, tourism continues to be a major asset and contributor to the economy. The example of Hawaii is most obvious, but virtually all the states in the West enjoy the benefits of tourism. Continued stewardship of the national parks by the federal government is a requirement for healthy economic conditions in the park environs. Conflict between federal bureaucracies charged with management of the parks and wildlife therein and the local interests of the citizens will continue. An excellent example of this ongoing conflict occurs in the area of Yellowstone National Park between ranchers and other local residents and the Park Service over the problem of the grizzly bear. Grizzly bears do not recognize artificial boundaries between federal park land and nearby private land. As they wander onto these private lands, they are often viewed as a threat to livestock and to people by the residents of the adjacent parts of Montana, Wyoming, and Idaho.

Associated with the issue of tourism is concern about accessibility. One critical issue relating to transportation which has serious implications for large sections of the West is that of deregulation of airlines and trucking companies. Deregulation means that airlines, for example, are encouraged to compete with one another on the high-volume routes between major cities. To do so they are forced to discontinue or significantly reduce service to smaller communities in order to free airplanes and staff for the more lucrative routes. The result has been a progressive and rapid abandonment of the smaller communities by the major air carriers. To the degree that these abandoned communities are served by regularly scheduled airlines at all, it has been by a variety of commuter airlines. Without the economies of scale of the larger airlines, these carriers fly small airplanes, often have more or less irregular schedules, and are generally very expensive. The cost of a round-trip ticket for a 200-mile flight from a small community to a regional airline hub may well rival the cost for a round-trip ticket from Los Angeles to New York. Certainly, this is a major impediment to tourism as well as to the prospects for future economic development. In much of the West this is seen as the "centralizing" of America. It means that the more rural and underpopulated parts of the western United States will remain that way.

This has served to reinforce a trend that Neal R. Peirce has identified and called the "oasis population" in the Mountain West.[17] He is referring to the fact that while the population of even the Mountain states of the West is growing, that very growth tends to mask significant demographic shifts within the states. It is a population shift that is really part of the centralization of America we have already mentioned. What is actually happening is that the number of people in many of the rural ranching and mining communities is rapidly declining, while there are significant increases in population in and around the cities. The increases in the cities are due both to the rural-to-urban shift and to the external migration to the West from other regions of the country—the new arrivals typically settling in western urban places.

In our consideration of the Sagebrush Rebellion we discussed the nature of the relationship between the western states and the federal government and how that relationship provided an impetus for the rebellion. Many states in the West remain dependent on the federal government. Peirce points out that, for the Mountain states of the West at least, when one adds up the billions of dollars the federal government spends in the West each year, it turns out that the West is receiving much more in services than it pays back in taxes. Without the federal government these states might even be less viable than they are at present.[18] These federal monies often take the form of management costs for the large public-land states, such as Nevada, New Mexico, Wyoming, Utah, Alaska and Idaho. They are more likely to be related to defense expenditures in the defense-related economies of Hawaii, California and Washington. Map 4.2 presents two measures of the impact of federal spending in the western states. This

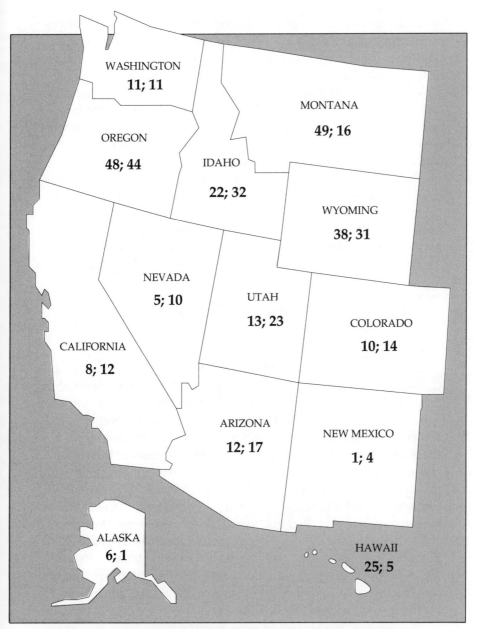

Map 4.2   The Impact of Federal Spending in the West
(National Ranking on Per Capita Value of total Federal Procurement
Contracts, Followed by Ranking in Total Federal Expenditure Per Capita)

dependence on the federal government contributes mightily to political schizophrenia in the West. It is both a necessity to the functioning of the sometimes shaky western economies and at the same
time a constant irritant to western plans and sensibilities.

When President Ronald Reagan took office in 1981, he viewed the
financial relationship between the states and the federal government
as being in need of reform. He called for a "new federalism," which
would be a return to a system of "dual" federalism where the federal
and state government would have distinct spheres of authority and
responsibility rather than overlapping ones. The outcome of Reagan's
new federalism and his general budget cuts was to lower federal aid
to state and local governments. The end of revenue sharing for states
in 1980 and the decision by Congress to allow the program for local
governments to lapse in 1986 were dramatic indications of change in
the national fiscal relationship to state and local governments.

The Western States and the
Federal Government: A Reality Check

In their 1981 book *The New Federalism*, Michael D. Reagan and John
G. Sanzone gave the name "permissive federalism" to the relationship
they perceived between state and federal governments. By "permissive federalism," they meant that while "there is a sharing of power
and authority between the national and state governments, the state's
share rests upon the permission and permissiveness of the national
government."[19] While many citizens in the West might agree with
this description of federalism in the last two decades of the twentieth
century, it is not a formula for state and federal relations with which
they are comfortable. It is one that, at least at some symbolic level,
was to be addressed by both the Sagebrush Rebellion and by President
Reagan's new federalism. Authors Reagan and Sanzone recognized
the importance of symbolism and suggested that people commonly
accept substantive changes they may not like if they are allowed to
continue using the old labels. If we are going to continue to use the
word *federalism*, we should be sure to understand what it does *not*
mean in the present context. It does not mean a constitutionally determined distribution of functions between the two levels of government, and it does not mean that there are certain spheres of authority
for the states that cannot be touched by the national government, or
that there is financial independence on the part of the states. It does

not mean that there is a relationship of equality between the states and the federal government, or that there is any obstacle inherent in the Tenth Amendment to further extension of authority by the federal government.[20]

If Reagan and Sanzone's concept of permissive federalism accurately depicts federal-state relations—and there are many who believe it does—then to engage in constant political battles denying the reality is surely symbolic politics. Certainly, we ought not to be too surprised that westerners are uncomfortable with this reality. It is a reality that challenges their self-image of independence, self-sufficiency, and local control. As such, it requires that the public posture of westerners be in constant opposition to the federal government and its policies. The Western Myth demands no less. The public and symbolic opposition to the federal government almost becomes a test of faith for western politicians, whatever their political party or ideology. The cynic might suggest that this peculiar political posture serves mainly to divert the attention of the politically unsophisticated from the very real issues facing the West. In short, such cynics would continue, it reassures the people of their own superiority, while calling into question the values and intentions of the federal government. The obvious parallel to the manner in which southern politicians used the race issue for so many years cannot be wholly ignored.

Westerners have always been a bit selective about western history and a little too willing to accept the Western Myth as if it were truth. Like all myths, of course, it contains some truth, some exaggeration, and some outright falsehood. Westerners can rightly be faulted for failing to make distinctions between the truth, the exaggerations, and the falsehoods. As a result, citizens of the West have fallen victim to their own creation. They have been unwilling to accept the world as they find it—preferring, instead, to strike out at the federal government in spasms that waste both energy and political capital and that might better be used in adjusting to the political realities of the day. Westerners' reality, in short, has become the symbols themselves.

And yet this is the politics of symbolism. While the West seems perpetually in rebellion against the federal government, it continues its profitable participation in the federal system. As a region, the West continues to receive more money from the federal government than it sends to Washington. The Rocky Mountain states, for example, averaged a return of $1.20 for every dollar sent to the federal government in 1980. The Midwest, by way of comparison, received 79¢ for each dollar sent to the federal government.[21] The West should not be too surprised if there is a notable lack of sympathy for its cries of unfair treatment. The symbolism in rebellion is more useful for local western consumption than it is as a political argument in or with the rest of the country.

The West is a diverse region affected by population increases, economic changes, and changes in its regional identity. These changes mean that the region is maturing. They mean that the West can spend more of its energies developing ties to other regions of the country and of the world. For parts of the West, the Pacific states in particular, the view must become a cosmopolitan one rather than an inward-looking one. For these states, the Pacific and the countries of the Pacific Rim are critical to their future prosperity. For the rural inland states, the view increasingly must be one of trying to resolve the very real problems of water for irrigation, recreation, and domestic use. The growth of cities of the Southwest and the continued viability of an agriculture dependent on water depend on resolving this issue—or at least addressing it. The politics of symbolism no longer has any legitimate place in the politics of the West. It is partly for that reason that the Sagebrush Rebellion is a dead issue today. There was probably no true support for selling the public lands, and the state governments of the West were always lukewarm about the prospect of inheriting the federal role. As Frank J. Popper put it: "The Rebellion had become an abstract ideological cause—a libertarian fantasy—with few practical economic or political possibilities. To most Western conservatives the impulse was attractive, the reality prohibitive."[22] The politicians of the western states can no longer indulge the Western Myth. The politics of symbolism is no longer appropriate. States and localities in the West that persist in holding onto the myth will succeed only in resigning their people to be left behind as the rest of the region accepts reality, adjusts to it and moves on.

Notes

1. Ken Robison, *The Sagebrush Rebellion: A Bid for Control* (Blackfoot, Idaho: Save Our Public Lands, 1981), 16–17.

2. Richard D. Lamm and Michael McGarthy, *The Angry West: A Vulnerable Land and Its Future* (Boston: Houghton Mifflin, 1982), 318–19.

3. Robison, *The Sagebrush Rebellion*, 4.

4. Robison, *The Sagebrush Rebellion*, 4–5.

5. Janice Adair, "Federal Frustration: A Review of the Nevada Sagebrush and Alaska Tundra Rebellions," unpublished manuscript, University of Alaska, Juneau, 1983, 5.

6. Murray Edelman, *The Symbolic Uses of Politics* (Urbana: University of Illinois Press, 1964), 13.

7. Wallace Stegner, *The American West as Living Space* (Ann Arbor: University of Michigan Press, 1987), 56.

8. Robison, *The Sagebrush Rebellion*, 1–2.

9. Clive S. Thomas and Anne F. Lee, "Alaska and Hawaii in the Federal System: A Comparison of Problems, Perceptions and Perspectives," paper presented at the Western Political Science Association meeting, 1986, 17–18.

10. Edelman, *The Symbolic Uses of Politics*, 172.

11. Nathan Rosenberg, "History and Perspective," in Kent A. Price, ed., *Regional Conflict and National Policy* (Washington, D.C.: Resources for the Future, June 1982), 20.

12. Gene M. Gressley, "Regionalism and the Twentieth-Century West," in Jerome O. Steffen, ed., *The American West: New Perspectives, New Dimensions* (Norman: University of Oklahoma Press, 1979), 198.

13. Philip M. Burgess, Jack A. Brizius, and Susan E. Foster, eds., *Profile of the West* (Denver: Western States Strategy Center, 1987), 16–17.

14. Gressley, "Regionalism in the Twentieth-Century American West," 222–24.

15. Helen M. Ingram, Nancy K. Laney and John R. McCain, *A Policy Approach to Political Representation: Lessons from the Four Corners States* (Baltimore: Resources for the Future, Johns Hopkins University Press, 1980), 132.

16. Tim De Young, "Intergovernmental Relations and Water Policy in the West," chap. 18, this volume.

17. Neal R. Peirce, *The Mountain States of America: People, Politics, and Power in the Eight Rocky Mountain States* (New York: W. W. Norton, 1972), 19–20.

18. Neal R. Peirce, *The Mountain States of America*, 25–26.

19. Michael D. Reagan and John G. Sanzone, *The New Federalism* (New York: Oxford University Press, 1981), 175.

20. Reagan and Sanzone, *The New Federalism*, 168–69.

21. Lamm and McCarthy, *The Angry West*, 320.

22. Frank J. Popper, "The Timely End of the Sagebrush Rebellion," *The Public Interest* 76 (Summer 1984), 70.

II
_____

Political Participation in the West

5

POLITICAL PARTIES, ELECTIONS AND CAMPAIGNS, I: THE LEGAL AND POLITICAL SETTING

*Robert C. Benedict and
Ronald J. Hrebenar*

*I*N A LIBERAL DEMOCRACY LIKE THE UNITED STATES, maximizing citizen participation in government decision-making is one of the fundamental principles of the political and governmental system. Therefore, questions relating to the methods, level and effectiveness of political participation are central to both an understanding and an evaluation of the system of government.

When political scientists study political participation they are interested in several questions: What are the ways or avenues through which citizens and groups can participate in politics, and how effective are these? What determines the overall level of political participation? And perhaps most important of all, why does this level vary among different socioeconomic groups, from region to region, from state to state, and often within states? The answer to this last question has important implications for understanding where political power lies and how it is distributed in a nation, state or community.

Other than serving as an elected representative or as an appointed public servant, individual citizens have several channels open to them for participating in the public policymaking process. According to political scientist Thomas R. Dye, the most widely used of these channels is the ballot box. Depending upon the type of election (local, state or federal), between 30% and 55% of the population vote. Next comes talking to others about politics, an activity in which about a third of the public engage on a regular basis. The third channel comes from belonging to organizations involved in trying to influence public policy. About one in every three Americans belongs to these so-called interest groups. Then comes writing or calling a public official (17%–20%); wearing a campaign button or displaying a bumper sticker (15%); making campaign contributions (10%); and actively working for a political party and being involved in an election campaign, whether a general election or a special state or local election (4%–5%).[1]

In this and the following chapter we look at political participation through elections, campaigns and political parties. This chapter focuses on the laws and political factors that influence the structure and roles of political parties, campaigns, and provisions for direct democracy in the West. Chapter 6 provides an evaluation of the impact of parties and elections and considers some recent trends, particularly that of party competition and party realignment in the West.

Our treatment of the subject of western campaigns and elections will have two themes. The first is that in the West, as compared to other regions, greater controversy exists over the question of representation—that is, the best means to link the attitudes and policy views of citizens to their government. Advocates of strong political parties argue that the parties provide the best mechanism for conveying citizen attitudes to elected officials. Yet the West also strongly reflects a heritage of populist and progressive ideas. These two groups believe that citizens should be allowed greater participation in the selection of candidates, and should have direct control over lawmaking through the mechanisms of the initiative process. This tension over the best means of representation underlies the discussion of topics ranging from election laws to the structure of political parties.

The second theme is that politics in the West display diversity as well as commonality. Since the 1960s there has been a shift in the preference of Mountain state voters from Democratic to Republican candidates, and a less pronounced shift in the Pacific states.[2] The reasons for the shift can be traced to the political challenge resulting from the attempt of the West to maintain federal financial support for economic growth without acquiescing to other federal redistributive or regulatory policies. A useful distinction, therefore, is to separate the area into two subregions: the Pacific states (Alaska, California, Hawaii, Oregon, Washington) and the Mountain states (Arizona, Colorado, Idaho, Montana, Nevada, New Mexico, Utah and Wyoming).[3]

Role and Functions of
Political Parties and Elections

It is now widely accepted that parties are essential to the effective operation of modern democratic societies. As one scholar has argued, "Political parties created democracy and . . . modern democracy is unthinkable save in terms of parties."[4] But what do parties contribute to American-style democracy on the state level? First, by structuring campaigns and elections, they help legitimize the entire democratic process in the eyes of the citizenry. Second, by defining and managing the nomination process, parties simplify the election process and make it manageable and understandable to the average voter. Third, advocates of strong parties argue that they provide perhaps the best medium of representation between the mass public and government.[5] Parties share this duty with other institutions that facilitate the flow of communication within American society, such as the mass media and interest groups. Parties have the potential, however, to perform this linkage function more effectively because of the narrow interests of their competitors. Political scientists discuss this very significant function in terms of the two A words: Aggregation and Articulation. Parties aggregate the various and often competing demands of their supporters, sort them out and then articulate the selected policies within the appropriate decision-making arenas, and participate in the implementation of the approved policies.

The preceding discussion highlights the various ways in which parties are viewed in our society. They are viewed in three different ways: (1) in the electorate; (2) as organizations or structures and (3) as governments.[6] Parties are made up of the millions of citizens who identify with one or the other of our parties. This is the psychological dimension of parties. Parties also make up the various party organizations on the national, state and local levels of our federal system. Finally, parties govern the nation, from the White House to the state capitols and the county seats across the nation.

Similarly, in America campaigns and elections serve as important vehicles of political participation in two major ways. First, elections serve as the legal mechanism linking citizens and the government. Second, they allow voters to express their preferences on policies and to hold officials responsible if government does not enact those policies. Yet, with candidates vacillating on the issues and voter turnout on the decline, it becomes increasingly difficult for campaigns and elections to serve the function of holding elected officials responsible for their actions. With these factors in mind, we now move to explain the "rules of the game" for campaigns and elections in the West.

Election and Ballot Proposition Rules

VOTER REGISTRATION

Due to federal court challenges and congressional legislative mandates, requirements for voter registration in all states are fairly standardized.[7] On those issues where the states retain sufficient freedom to act, no "western" pattern emerges. Twenty-two states maintain a residency requirement of twenty-nine to thirty-two days before a citizen can register to vote. Eight of these are western states—Alaska, California, Colorado, Idaho, Montana, Nevada, Utah and Washington. Twenty states have abolished minimum residence requirements, but only Hawaii, New Mexico and Wyoming have followed this path in the West. States also establish a closing date—that is, the number of days before the election that citizens must be registered. The majority of states, twenty-seven in this instance, have closing dates of twenty-eight to thirty-two days before the election. Western states that follow this pattern are: Alaska, California, Colorado, Hawaii, Montana, Nevada, Washington and Wyoming. Registration for voting by mail is permitted in twenty-one states. In the West, Alaska, California, Montana, Oregon, and Utah have adopted this practice.

Combining the three elements of residence requirement, closing date and mail registration in the western states, Arizona's residence requirement and closing date of fifty days before the election are the most rigorous. Conversely, Oregon and Utah place the least burden on potential voters. Oregon imposes only a twenty-day residence and registration requirement.[8] Utah, which stipulates thirty-day residence and five-day closing date, approximates Oregon's ease of registration.

TYPES OF PRIMARY ELECTIONS

A primary election is an election held to nominate party candidates for various public offices—U.S. senator, governor, state representative and so on. These candidates then appear on the ballot at the general election.

Thirty-six states use a closed primary to determine party candidates. In such states voters are required to declare their party affiliation and then can vote only in that party's primary unless they officially change their affiliation within a given period of time before the primary. The six states in the West using a closed primary are Arizona, California, Colorado, Nevada, New Mexico and Oregon.[9] The period to change party affiliation (or for newly registered voters to declare a party) ranges from fifty days in Arizona to twenty days in Oregon. The philosophy behind a closed primary is that the political party should act as a link between the citizens and government. Therefore, only those who are willing to declare their affiliation before the election should take part in choosing the party's nominees. Thus Independent voters can participate only in the general election.

In contrast, the populists and later the progressives sought to decrease the control of perceived corrupt party "machines" and economic influences. Two types of primaries were devised in an attempt to achieve this: the "open" and the "blanket" primary. The first type allows voters to decide on Election Day from which party's candidates they wish to make their selection. Participation should increase because independents are not barred, and voters can "cross over" and take part in the opposition party races if they prove more alluring. The blanket primary operates much as the general election. For example: a Republican voter could choose from his or her own party's candidates for the office of governor, but then select among Democratic candidates for other offices, such as secretary of state and state representative. This system provides for the maximum amount of voter influence over candidate selection, and greatly lessens the influence of the political parties.

Thus, one distinguishing feature of western elections is that seven out of the thirteen states employ either an open or a blanket primary. Five states—Hawaii, Idaho, Montana, Utah and Wyoming—rely on an open primary. In all but Wyoming the voters receive the ballot of all parties participating, and then in the privacy of the voting booth they can determine in which party's primary they will participate.[10] As the blanket primary most fully reflects populist and progressive ideas, it is not surprising that the only two states in the nation to employ it are in the West. Washington State voters used the initiative process in 1936 to establish a blanket primary system, while Alaska has utilized this type of primary since gaining statehood in 1959. A blanket primary is one reason why Washington State in its formative years displayed a "lusty, gutsy politics."[11] This system allows political mavericks, who lack wide support among the party faithful but have public support, to enter the primary and gain the party's nomination for state or national office. The election of combative Dixie Lee Ray to the governorship of Washington (1976–80) provides one example.

Although each state has the responsibility for determining its own type of primary, national influences do affect state practices. The likely impact of a recent U.S. Supreme Court decision will be to require states with closed primaries to modify their systems. In *Tashjian v. Republican Party of Connecticut*, 1986, the Court ruled "independents" (who were defined as those who "declined to state" a party preference when registering) could choose to vote in either the Connecticut Republican or Democratic primary. However, a party in a closed primary state could only allow declared "independents," and not members of the opposition party, to take part in its primary. Examining the number of self-proclaimed independents in closed primary states, Malcolm Jewell does not see many states where the minority party would seek to change the law.[12] Yet pollster Mervin Field believes that the Court decision could lead to a successful challenge of California's closed primary.[13] The "declined to state" status could not only appeal to the state's independents, but also cause weak Republicans and Democrats to change their registration.

THE INITIATIVE AND THE REFERENDUM

One distinct characteristic of western politics is the heavy reliance placed upon direct legislation as a policymaking vehicle. As Table 5.1 indicates, the only state in the region that does not permit any form of direct legislation is Hawaii. Initiatives may take two forms: direct and indirect. The direct initiative allows a statute or a constitutional amendment to be placed before the voters if the requisite number of signatures are obtained on a petition. If adopted, the initiative has the force of a statute or constitutional amendment. The indirect initiative follows a more circuitous route. The petition is first presented

Table 5.1   Direct Legislation Signature Requirements and Usage in Western States

State	Referendum Type(s)	Initiative Type(s)	Percent of Votes Cast[a]	Multidistrict Requirement
Alaska	C[b]	D[c]	10	Yes
Arizona	C	D	10 (gov)	
	L			
California	C	D	5 (gov)	
Colorado	C	D	5 (sec-state)	
	L			
Idaho	C	D	10 (gov)	
Montana	C	D	5	Yes
	L			
Nevada	C	I	10	Yes
New Mexico	C	—	—	—
Oregon	C	D	6	
Utah	C	D	10 (gov)	Yes
		I	5 (gov)	Yes
Washington	C	D	8 (gov)	
	L	I	8 (gov)	
Wyoming	C	D	15	Yes

[a]In last general election; or for office of governor or secretary of state.
[b]C is a citizen referendum, L refers to a legislative referendum.
[c]D is a direct initiative, I refers to an indirect initiative.

Source: The Book of the States, 1988–89 (Lexington, Ky.: Council of State Governments, 1988), 217.

to a regular session of the legislature, which has a specified period in which to enact the proposal. If the legislature alters the proposal or does not act within that period, the proposition is then submitted to the electorate for its consideration.

In similar fashion referenda are divided into two types—citizen and legislative. In the first type, citizens sign a petition to require that a statute enacted by the legislature be submitted for a popular vote. Petitioners have a specific period after legislative adjournment to obtain the required number of signatures, and the statute in question does not go into effect unless it is approved by the electorate. In a legislative referendum a statute is voluntarily submitted to the voters for their approval.

Charles Price suggests several reasons for the adoption of methods of direct legislation in the West.[14] For most of the region's states, statehood was achieved only a few decades before the progressive movement swept the region. Progressives argued that the electorate should have the ability to decide measures referred to them by the legislature through a referendum, and to place measures on the ballot for the citizens to decide through an initiative. Moreover, political institutions were less firmly entrenched in the West than in other regions. Thus it is not surprising that of the nineteen states adopting the initiative process from 1898 to 1918, all but four were west of the Mississippi River. In the region itself, Utah became the first state to adopt the initiative (1902), followed shortly after by Oregon and Montana. More recently, two western states have adopted direct legislation provisions. Alaska entered the Union in 1959 with a constitutional provision for direct legislation, and Wyoming adopted the process in 1968.

Outside the West, however, the use of the process is much more limited. In the 1970s two states, Illinois (1970) and Florida (1978), selected a very restrictive form which permits only initiatives that would amend the state constitution. Rhode Island voters rejected a constitutional amendment to establish the direct initiative in 1986.

Table 5.1 lists the number of signatures required on citizen petitions. Some states also include multidistrict requirements—that is, signatures must be gathered from a percentage of all the electoral districts. The latter provision is to ensure that the proposal has widespread support and is not a product of sectional conflict, such as east versus west or urban versus rural. When a high signature requirement is combined with a multidistrict requirement, the result can be burdensome for signature gatherers. Wyoming, for example, not only requires the signatures of 15% of the qualified vote cast in the last election, but further requires that the signatures must come from at least two-thirds of the counties of the state. The Wyoming signature provisions are the most stringent in the West, and they help to explain why no initiative has qualified for the ballot since adoption of the process.[15] On paper Colorado and California signature requirements—5% of the total vote for the offices of secretary of state and governor respectively—offer the greatest opportunity for proponents of the process. Yet for the 1990 election to qualify a petition in California, 595,479 signatures were necessary for constitutional initiatives and 372,175 for direct initiatives. As a result, a booming state industry has developed around the qualifying of petitions. Citizens still circulate petitions, but reliance upon organizations paid to gather signatures is the most commonly used method.[16] The newest tactic, as reported by Fairbanks and Smith, is for groups to send out petitions to members, asking not only that the member gather signatures but that the petition be returned along with a contribution to the group.[17] In this manner the costs of financing the process of qualifying the petition and of the subsequent campaign to secure its passage are shared by group members. The use of paid organizations and contributions by groups raises the important value question of whether the initiative process benefits the status quo, thereby undermining populist and progressive assumptions about the process.

PUBLIC DISCLOSURE LAWS

Public disclosure laws also trace their roots back to populist and progressive thought. Money in the form of campaign contributions is believed to be the most important way that large corporations, labor unions, and other "special interests" influence both who is elected to public office, and the kinds of policy decisions that are made. The belief that the corrupting power of money allows groups to "buy" officials or elections fueled the enactment of national disclosure laws and a myriad of state regulations as well.[18] Most state regulations were adopted in the period from 1973 to 1978, largely as a response to Watergate and national campaign reporting laws.

Most states require both the reporting of campaign expenditures by candidates (forty-five states) and political committees designated by candidates (forty-four states). Among western states only Utah does not require direct reporting by candidates; while Alaska, Nevada and Wyoming do not demand an accounting by candidates' political committees.[19]

Table 5.2 also provides information on whether various individuals or groups must file reports or are limited in campaign contributions. As the national totals indicate, few states place limits on contributions either by political parties or by candidates to their own campaign. For the other categories the table indicates that approximately one-third to one-half of the states have filing or reporting requirements. Ironically, before 1986 western states did not respond positively to the populist premises about the role of money in campaigns, and preferred less government regulation. However, with the passage of campaign finance measures in Arizona and California in 1986 and 1988 respectively, the region now resembles the rest of the nation.

Depending upon the category in Table 5.2, from one-fifth to one-third of the region's states mandate reports or limits. Colorado, New Mexico, Oregon, and Utah have no current regulation, and are not

Table 5.2 Western States with Campaign Reporting Requirements

	Filing of Expenses by:		Limits on Campaign Contributions by:					
State	Political Parties	PACs and Interest Groups	Corporations	Labor Unions	PACs	Political Parties	Individuals	Candidate's Own Contribution
Alaska	X	X	X	X	X		X	
Arizona	X	X	X[a]	X[a]	X	X	X	X
California	X	X	X	X	X	X		
Hawaii	X		X	X	X	X	X	X
Idaho		X						
Montana			X[a]	X	X	X	X	
Nevada	X	X						
Washington			[b]	[b]	[b]	[b]	[b]	[b]
Wyoming	X	X	X[a]	X	X	X	X	
U.S. Total	23	18	25	26	22	14	27	7

[a]Contributions are prohibited by law.
[b]Unlimited, except aggregate contributions of more than $5,000 cannot be made to a candidate or political committee within 21 days of a general election.

Sources: James A. Palmer and Edward D. Feigenbaum, *Campaign Finance Law 86* (Washington, D.C.: Federal Election Commission, 1986); interviews with appropriate election officers in each state.

listed in the table. In contrast, Arizona, California, Hawaii, Montana and Wyoming mandate substantial reporting or strict contribution limits. Of these highly regulated states, Montana undertook a major revision of its constitution during the Watergate period and the spill-over influenced the passage of legislation on campaign financing. In 1988 California voters passed Proposition 73 which limits political donations in state and local races to $1,000 per fiscal year from individuals and up to $5,000 per fiscal year from political committees. Wyoming and Arizona provide excellent examples of how the general antiregulatory mood can be deflected at times by an equally wide-spread antiestablishment populism. Wyoming passed regulations before Watergate based largely on opposition to entrenched economic interests. When the Arizona legislature killed a sweeping campaign reform bill, a maverick conservative state legislator qualified the measure as an initiative in 1986. Placed in the context of controlling special interests, the measure passed by a prodigious 65% of the votes cast.

Throughout the nation twenty states have public financing and tax-assisted funding of state elections. In this category western states are proportionately represented with six states providing such assistance. Until 1987 Alaska had the most unusual system: contributors received a tax refund instead of reduced tax liability. In that year, however, because of a sharp drop in state revenues due to the fall in world oil prices, the program was suspended until January 1, 1993.[20]

Comparative Uses of Direct Democracy

Table 5.3 provides figures on the number of proposals and rates of adoption of initiatives in the West. Comparisons between this region and the nation yield few dividends, as the West provides the bulk of the measures considered. Concentrating on the total initiatives proposed within the region, the four states of Oregon, California, Colorado and Arizona fall in the "high use" category. Yet voters in these states have been discerning, approving only about one-third of both statutes and constitutional amendments proposed. Conversely, with the exception of Utah, states that have historically used the process to a lesser extent have enacted a significantly higher proportion of initiatives.

As constitutional amendments propose changes in the basic law of the state, a reasonable assumption is that they are less likely to be proposed and approved than statutes. Both aspects of this assumption are borne out by Table 5.3. Disregarding the three states that do not

Table 5.3   Statutes and Constitutional Initiatives in the West, 1902–88

State	Statutes			Constitutional Amendments			Total Initiatives		
	Number Proposed	Number Approved	Percentage Approved	Number Proposed	Number Approved	Percentage Approved	Number Proposed	Number Approved	Percentage Approved
Oregon	148	53	36	111	32	29	259	85	33
California	100	36	36	102	31	30	202	67	33
Colorado	58	25	43	83	25	30	141	50	35
Arizona	72	25	35	48	20	42	120	45	38
Washington	87	43	49	—	—	—	87	43	49
Montana	47	28	60	5	2	40	52	30	58
Nevada	15	7	47	9	5	56	24	12	50
Alaska	19	9	47	—	—	—	19	9	47
Idaho	16	10	63	—	—	—	16	10	63
Utah	14	2	14	0	0	0	14	2	14
Wyoming	0	0	0	0	0	0	0	0	0
The West	576	238	41	358	115	32	934	353	38

Sources: Data for 1902 to 1978 adapted from David Magleby, *Direct Legislation: Voting on Ballot Propositions in the United States* (Baltimore: Johns Hopkins University Press, 1984); data for 1980–88 were obtained from the official election returns of each state. New Mexico and Hawaii are the only states that do not employ any type of initiative.

Table 5.4 Turnout in Western Elections 1960–86

Regions and Western States	Presidential Elections		U.S. House Elections	
	1960–72	1976–84	1962–72	1974–86
Pacific States	62.9	51.7	52.3	39.5
Alaska	46.2	55.0	42.9	41.8
California	63.0	49.7	53.0	38.7
Hawaii	51.0	44.8	48.0	41.0
Oregon	67.4	61.4	54.5	49.0
Washington	68.2	58.4	50.3	38.1
Mountain States	63.8	54.2	52.3	41.0
Arizona	51.1	45.3	39.9	33.7
Colorado	65.4	55.1	52.2	42.2
Idaho	73.4	63.0	62.4	48.6
Montana	68.8	64.5	62.3	52.8
Nevada	53.6	42.4	45.1	36.7
New Mexico	60.5	52.0	51.1	38.9
Utah	75.7	64.8	61.8	47.3
Wyoming	69.8	55.1	62.6	46.2
Regions				
Western States	63.1	52.4	52.3	39.9
Northeast	65.0	54.2	51.7	36.6
Midwest	67.8	59.5	51.6	40.9
South	47.6	47.8	28.7	25.4
U.S.	60.2	53.1	45.2	34.7

Sources: U.S. Bureau of the Census; 1986 data from U.S. Bureau of the Census press release (CB 86-65) and "Returns for Governor, Senate and House," *Congressional Quarterly Weekly Reports* (November 8, 1986), 2864–71.

allow constitutional initiatives, westerners have proposed far more statutes than constitutional amendments. Moreover, the approval rate for statutes is 10% higher than for amendments. Proponents will continue to seek approval for amendments, however, as many of the region's state constitutions are long and detailed, making amendments the only way to obtain change in many areas of public policy.

Voter Turnout in Western States

In this chapter "voter turnout" refers to the percentage of the voting-age population that votes in a specific election. Table 5.4 averages the electoral turnout for presidential and nonpresidential years for two time periods. Averages have been used to reduce the effect of idiosyncratic elections. The year 1960 was chosen as the starting point both because it allows the inclusion of Alaska and Hawaii, and because it marks the beginning of a steady decline in national participation levels. The 1974–86 period documents the further decline after Watergate to the present.

The national trend toward less voter participation has been noted by many observers, and it is clearly evident in Table 5.4. If the four regions are compared, one must first take into account some unique aspects of the South. That region clearly has the lowest turnout, and the percentages remain relatively steady both for presidential and for House elections in the two periods studied. As national participation continues to decline, the figures from the South stand out less during the 1974–86 period, when the region was about 5% and 9% below the national averages for the presidential and House elections respectively.

A comparison of the western states with the Midwest and Northeast regions reveals some distinct patterns. For presidential elections from 1960 to 1984 the midwestern states have the greatest turnout, followed by the northeastern states and western states. Yet for House elections during the 1962–72 period the West ranks first, and the region was barely edged out by the Midwest for the 1974–86 period.

Within the West, the differences in participation levels between the Mountain and Pacific states are small. The greatest differential was 2.5% in the presidential election period of 1976–84. Much more variation, however, is evident among the states in the region. High turnout states are defined as those which are consistently 7% above the national average for both presidential and House elections for the two periods studied.[21] The high-turnout states are Oregon, Idaho, Montana, Utah and Wyoming. Turnout in Arizona has regularly been below the national average for both presidential and House elections. Hawaii, Nevada and New Mexico show low turnout for presidential elections, but are at or above the national average for House races. Perhaps the most interesting trend has occurred in Alaska. In the earlier period of 1960–72 fewer Alaskans were attracted to the polls, particularly to the presidential contests. Yet in the most recent period participation has been 2% and 7% above the national average for the presidential and House contests respectively.

Among the factors that are associated with levels of turnout are state registration requirements, socioeconomic and cultural differences, and political factors. Restrictive registration requirements,

Richard Niemi and Herbert Weisberg suggest, may reduce voter turnout by as much as 10%.[22] One western state where registration appears to be a factor is Arizona. As noted previously, the requirements are among the toughest in the nation, and the state consistently has one of the lowest turnout figures as well. Conversely, Utah and Oregon, with the most lenient registration laws, are among the states with the highest rates of participation.

At the national level socioeconomic status and cultural variations influence turnout levels. Differences in race, age, income and educational level account for a substantial amount of the variety in state voter participation. Young adults, for example, tend to vote less. Extending the vote to those between eighteen and twenty through the Twenty-sixth Amendment to the U.S. Constitution, ratified in 1971, reduced turnout.[23] Similarly, the level of education is important. College graduates have maintained about the same level of participation from the postwar period through 1984. Yet turnout has dropped among all other educational categories.[24]

Political culture is also related to voter turnout. In states with a moralistic culture, individuals strongly believe that they can accomplish something positive by engaging in politics and that political authority should be used to promote the public good. On the other hand, those residing within individualistic political cultures are convinced that political structures and policies should be limited in scope and designed to enhance the interests of the economic marketplace.[25] In Montana, Idaho and Washington the relationship between political culture and turnout is strong. These states display a moralistic culture and have some of the highest participation levels in the nation. In the West a merging of moralistic and individualistic cultures is common. Utah, Wyoming and Oregon are states displaying this mixture of political cultures and high turnout. This combination of political cultures in California, however, is not associated with high turnout.

Two other key political factors influencing turnout are the level of competition between political parties and the importance of issues in the election. Turnout is greatest in those states with strong two-party competition. Alaska is the most dramatic example of the importance of issues leading to an increase in participation. Turnout soared to approximately 60% of registered voters in 1980, 1982 and 1984. Alaskans perceived that national, and especially state issues (including a 1982 referendum on funding the move of the capitol), would have a very great impact on their future and they went to the polls accordingly.[26]

Campaign Methods and Practices

In the western states, campaign methods and practices have a symbiotic relationship with those of the rest of the nation. California continues to be an originator and exporter of campaign techniques, while other states in the region are avid consumers of national campaign practices. Here we will divide the topic into two discussions. The first concerns the campaign strategy of how to get the message across to voters; the second deals with the substance of the message—that is, the changes in the most important issues in western campaigns.

GETTING THE MESSAGE ACROSS TO VOTERS IN THE WEST

With a weak party tradition, western candidates have long believed that individual appeal to voters is the most important factor in gaining election, with their stand on the issues second, and political party affiliation a distant third. In recent years this ranking has also spread to the nation as a whole. Here we explore one problem unique to western politicians in reaching voters, as well as the region's reaction to several national trends.

Western politicians face unique problems of geography and distance in campaigning. For U.S. House races in the Mountain states, Alaska, and eastern Oregon, the combination of low population density and large geographical size results in the greatest disparity of district size of any region in the country. Of the twenty-five largest congressional districts (area in square miles and low density per square mile) eighteen are in the West.[27] In contrast, only two of the smallest geographical districts are located in the region, both of them in California.

As Henry Kenski notes, not only does campaigning in large districts require more time and energy, but it is also likely to be more expensive.[28] Incumbents certainly have their work cut out in retaining these seats, but an even more forbidding task awaits challengers. The costs of campaigning will be determined to a large extent by access to major media markets. One method of measuring how difficult it is for candidates to get their message across to voters is to look at the major television markets they must cover.[29] The problems this causes for congressional candidates can best be illustrated by the state of Wyoming. Candidates here must determine how to reach voters in two major markets—the Casper–Riverton and Salt Lake viewing areas. In addition, they must reach constituents in five secondary markets, because a portion of their constituents are closest to television stations in South Dakota, Montana, Colorado and Idaho. In Utah, however, despite two large geographical districts for the U.S. House of Representatives, candidates can get their message across more cost-effectively, as the Salt Lake television stations cover all counties in the state.

As to national trends affecting the region's candidates, a major development is the use of computer technology to identify and reach specific groups ranging from racial groups to economic interests. Groups can be identified by geographic area, and more precisely by ZIP Code to receive mailings. Even large rural districts are using this technology, as one Montana congressman declared he "can 'target' members of the Blackfeet Indian tribe who have written to him about the equal rights amendment. And he can run those Indians out alphabetically, by ZIP Code, and by which side of the street they live on."[30] Moreover, the polling of the electorate has become so refined that daily "tracking" polls can measure slight shifts in the reaction of voters to the candidate or campaign themes. Not only is computer technology a prerequisite to candidates for national office but its use in state races is common as well. Greater use of computers has uniformly increased campaign costs around the country.

Another national trend with regional impact is the use of negative campaign tactics—that is, making the opponent's character, inconsistent stands on the issues and so forth the major "issue" in the campaign. While the practice has always existed, its use has increased in recent years, and the West has not been spared. Experts disagree about whether the emphasis on negative campaigns is effective enough to become a permanent part of campaigning or if it is merely a political cycle that will run its course. By the late 1980s it was clear that most western candidates could not win solely through negative tactics; instead, they had to tell voters what they stood *for* as well as what, or whom, they were running *against*.

The most effective use of negative campaigning combined these tactics with humor. In the 1986 California senatorial race, incumbent Democratic Senator Alan Cranston defeated Republican Ed Zshau by a narrow margin. Early polling showed the state's voters lined up with Zshau on a majority of the issues. Cranston's media advisers responded by creating the instant classic "Ed Zshau Flip–Flop" television commercial. Produced in the style of a late night commercial for a "golden oldies" album, the "hit song" titles alleged Zshau had reversed his stance on the issues. In a Los Angeles *Times* exit poll those voting for Cranston cited as their main reason Zshau's "flip-flops on the issues."[31]

THE CHANGING SUBSTANCE OF THE CAMPAIGN MESSAGE IN THE WEST

The substance of political campaigns in the West is also affected by what was described in Chapter 1 as the western political paradox. This results from the tension between economic and political dependence as seen in the need for continuing government infusion of funds, and rhetorical declarations of independence through support of the ideology of less government regulation. This enduring characteristic of western politics must be integrated with changes in the issues emphasized by the national political parties.

From 1945 through the early 1970s key elements of the Democratic party's national platform were a strong national defense and development of western resources including land and water. Western Democrats formed the mainstream of the party, and their campaigns could "point with pride" to public works projects and the economic impact of scores of military bases. The party's officeholders often deferred to constituent preferences on an issue like gun control, which was not central to the national party. Some western Republicans were elected on the basis of opposing "wasteful" government spending on social programs, but the region's GOP members provided near-unanimity for resource development projects such as dams and irrigation systems and military and federal government research facilities. In the mid-1960s, however, reflecting such events as the Vietnam War, protests by minorities, and the movement toward protecting the environment and limiting public works projects, the national Democratic party began to respond to other constituencies.

In the Mountain West, two of the most powerful symbols are the notions of the cowboy and the freedom associated with the frontier. In Wyoming, Republican Senate challenger Malcolm Wallop not only evoked the myth, but dramatically illustrated the dilemma posed by the costs of industrialization. In a classic example of television advertising, as the camera focused on a cowboy adjusting his horse's saddle straps on the wide open range, the announcer exclaims, "Everywhere you look these days the federal government is there. . . . Setting up rules you can't follow." As the cowboy rides off with a portable toilet strapped to a horse, the ad proclaims, "We need someone to tell them about Wyoming!"

Political Parties: Legal and Political Definitions

Political parties function in a political system over which they may exercise varying degrees of control. The "rules of the party game" in the United States are almost always written on the state level, and on that level the state legislatures, courts, and popular democratic processes, such as initiatives and referenda, are the key decision-making mechanisms. The U.S. Constitution and the history of American federalism have given the states the primary administrative responsibility for elections and political parties. Each state sets its own rules for defining parties, party access to ballots, candidate selection devices, the timing of nomination events, organizational structures, finances, and reporting requirements.[32]

The states' legal definitions of a political party almost always center on the concept of an organizational label that is able to attract a certain minimum number of votes for its nominees for public office in a general election held within a state. Some states have categorized political parties into various classes based on the criterion of electoral support. California law, for example, accords access to the ballot for any party that receives 2% of the vote in any statewide race or registers 1% of the entire statewide vote. California law also provides that if party registration drops to one-fifteenth of 1% of the total state registration, it ceases to be considered as a party.

New or minor parties can be recognized by the state and allowed access to the ballot after they secure a sufficient number of petition signatures or by winning a minimum number of votes in the preceding general election. In California the requirements are rather stringent. Such parties can gain access to the ballot by submitting a petition with the signatures of registered voters equal to 10% of the statewide registration. In contrast, most western states have made it very easy for minor or new parties to qualify for the ballot. In Washington State they need less than 1% of the primary election vote, and major party status is given to any party that can gain 5% of the total vote in the last general election in whatever political arena it chooses to contest within the state.[33] The various independent campaigns of the last two decades on the presidential level (Wallace, McCarthy, Anderson) have resulted in a series of court decisions that have liberalized the state requirements for gaining access to the ballot.

In the 1986 elections, one minor party—the Libertarians—was

very active in the West. In Utah, for example, Libertarian party candidates contested many state legislative races. In some legislative districts, a Libertarian was the only alternative for voters who did not want to vote for the incumbent Republican. Libertarian presidential candidate David Bergland collected almost a quarter of a million votes nationally in his 1984 campaign, many of which came from western states. Libertarian legislative candidates won three seats in the Alaska state legislature during the 1980s. Ed Clark, the Libertarian candidate for president in the 1980 elections, won 12% of Alaska's total presidential vote, and in some districts ran ahead of the incumbent Democratic candidate, Jimmy Carter. Again in Alaska, the 1982 Libertarian gubernatorial candidate, Dick Randolph, won 15% of the vote. Another minor party candidate in that election, Joe Vogler of the Alaska Independent party, collected 6% of the vote in a contest in which the winner secured only 47% for a four-percentage-point win.

Among registered voters in California, some 2% (245,000) are registered members of minor parties including the Peace and Freedom party, the Libertarians, and various left-wing parties. Significant numbers of votes in California were cast for Libertarian party (52,628), Peace and Freedom (51,995) and American Independent party gubernatorial candidates in 1986. Among the other western states, minor parties won some votes in 1986 statewide contests in Nevada, Utah, and Washington State.[34]

Party Organizational Strength in the West

Party organizational charts in most of the western states are very similar. Almost all states have legal provisions for a state central committee led by a state party chair. These state-level leaders are responsible to state conventions composed of delegates elected or selected at the county or legislative district level. Usually, county-level committees or conventions exist with party county chairs. Dye states that the 6,000 Republican and Democratic county chairs constitute "the most important building blocks in party organization in America."[35] At the lowest level, there are precinct or voting district organizations with several elected officials and meetings scheduled in election years. These levels of party organization are quite autonomous, and *hierarchy* does not well describe the power divisions found within state parties. Perhaps the term that best fits them is *stratarchy,* a word coined by

Samuel Eldersveld. The idea is that party power is exercised at various levels or "strata."[36]

The most powerful party organizations that have ever existed in America were the party machines of the last half of the nineteenth and the first half of the twentieth centuries. These urban-based political machines held sway over many American cities and counties—mostly in the eastern half of the nation. The political machines, thriving on graft and corruption, patronage and preferments, exchanged their governmental benefits with the lower classes for their votes and with the business community for political contributions. In the West, it was not necessary to build party machines to provide political representation for the lower classes or to force government to provide essential services. Both necessity and to a lesser extent western political culture defined the providing of these basic services as normal roles of government. Consequently, in most of the major cities of the West, no party machines or strong party organizations developed. Only in San Francisco, under the administrations of Abe "Curly" Reuf, did machine politics develop in the region.[37]

In fact, the parties in California were so completely dominated by business interests that they hardly existed as independent entities for much of the period from the late 1880s to World War I. It was probably more accurate to call the situation in California "the Southern Pacific Railroad Machine." As one scholar summarized California politics: "It made little difference which party was in power, the railroad still ruled. . . . In 1900, the Republican Party ran California and the Southern Pacific Railroad ran the Republican Party."[38] In fact, the Southern Pacific Railroad functioned as the real party of California by its recruiting of candidates, raising of campaign funds, and direction of the legislators who were elected.

When the progressive reform wave swept California in 1910, many laws were passed that attempted to destroy California's parties as effective tools of business interests. The reformers established nonpartisan elections in local contests, forced the parties to adopt certain organizational structures, and stripped the parties of many of their key functions, such as endorsing and nominating candidates. The direct primary was adopted, and when it was coupled with other mandated organizational devices, political parties were left in such a condition that they were unable to function in a strong manner in contrast to parties in many eastern states.

Modern party supporters have been battling the reforms of the 1910s for years in an effort to make California parties more responsive to the challenges of the latter half of the twentieth century. They seek to free the state's parties from the excessive restriction of mandated state laws that require state chairs to rotate between northern and southern California in alternate terms, and construct party machinery seemingly guaranteed to ensure its ineffectiveness. Only recently has the state law that prohibited party endorsements of candidates in primaries been repealed. One expert on California party organization noted that they resemble a "pyramid in shape—and something as lifeless."[39]

In the rest of the West, the reformers generally enacted their programs not in reaction to strong party organizations, but in the western traditions of maximizing individual freedoms and making politics as responsive to the public as possible. In states such as Utah and Idaho, which were states without any strong party traditions, the primary motivation was to maintain the honesty and responsiveness of the status quo. In states such as Washington and Alaska, as previously noted, the reformers enacted blanket primaries to prevent strong parties from emerging. But, unlike the eastern and midwestern states, the need to break the back of strong party organizations never existed in any of the western states.

Most political scientists continue to suggest that state party organizations bear little resemblance to the power of the old machines. David Mayhew studied party organizations in the fifty states and has developed a "traditional party organization score" (TPO) for each state.[40] The scores range from 1 (low) to 5 (high) and reflect Mayhew's evaluation of the conditions of party organizations in the late 1960s. He notes that outside the Northeast, "the rest of the country produces scarcely any traditional organizations or machines, little party hierarchy, [and] only a few states with routines of publicized slating or endorsing."[41] What Mayhew found was organizations "softer" than the traditional kinds of party organizations found in the Northeast. He notes that "politics in the northern mountain states is largely rural. In the southwest and on the Pacific periphery, it is largely urban. Neither setting has generated much in the way of party organization."[42] In state after state in the West, the lack of effective party organizations along with the significance of personal or individualized politics is repeatedly noted. Of the thirteen western states, only New Mexico with its combination of the three traditions of southern-style politics, Hispanic "machines," and nonpartisan urban politics, warrants a score higher than the minimum of 1.

In another study, James L. Gibson has evaluated city and county party organizations in the fifty states.[43] Local Democratic party organizations in Hawaii, Idaho and Washington, and Republican organizations in Arizona, California and New Mexico were the strongest. It is interesting to note that in the Pacific states, both the Democratic and Republican local party organizations average a rank of 20 out of 50 (with 1 representing the strongest organization and 50 the weakest); while among the eight Mountain states, the average Democratic rank of 29 was surpassed by the Republican rank of 23. Clearly, in much of the West, party organizations are too weak to have a strong impact on nominations, campaigns, legislative organization, policy guidance, and the other significant functions once played by parties in the United States.

Parties in State Legislatures

Among the fifty states, there is great variety in the patterns of party influence in state legislatures. Only in nonpartisan Nebraska are parties formally excluded. Yet in other states one can scarcely detect the existence of a "legislative party" organization. No western state falls into the southern tradition of being dominated by one-party legislatures where intraparty factional conflict substitutes for interparty competition. Probably Utah, Idaho and Hawaii come closest to this one-party-dominated pattern, but except in Hawaii these have not been long-term patterns, and in the Mountain states the minority party plays a significant role in the legislative process. Utah may be the most Republican state in the nation, but as recently as 1974 the Democratic party controlled both houses of the state legislature.

Utah is also a perfect example of another western characteristic, which tends to reduce party influence in state legislatures as well— the "citizen legislature." Most western states, with California being the major exception, tend toward such "citizen legislatures." These legislatures are part-time (often meeting for only a couple of months a year), poorly paid, relatively poorly staffed, and filled with "nonprofessional" legislators. In this setting, there are few incentives or motivations for party discipline or party cohesiveness. As Sorauf and Beck have argued, disciplined, cohesive legislative parties tend to be found in the more urban northern states.[44] In some states with especially weak traditions of legislative party discipline and loyalty, bipartisan coalitions rise and control the chamber. Among the western states in which such bipartisan groups have wielded power in the 1980s have been New Mexico, Alaska and California.[45]

Yet, as Sorauf and Beck have also noted, parties can dominate the legislative process through the power of party caucuses.[46] While such caucuses do not have such influence as in several eastern states, in many western state legislatures the party caucuses do perform important functions. Jewell and Olson have concluded that party caucuses in Idaho, Utah and Hawaii contribute significantly to policymaking; while caucuses in Washington, Arizona, Nevada, Wyoming, Colorado and California contribute significantly to party cohesion.[47] None of the seven states identified by Jewell and Olson as having a nearly nonexistent role in running the legislature were western states.

The frequency of unified or divided party control over the legislative and executive branches of state government is yet another important indicator of party power. The "American style" constitutionally based separation of powers among the executive, legislative and judicial branches makes party government more difficult to achieve. Divided government is usually associated with considerable interparty conflict and tension and in its worst instances, can result in "deadlock or protracted deals in enactment of such crucial legislation as the state budget, and executive appointments."[48] Not only may such deadlocks exist between executive and legislative branches controlled by different parties, but they can also be the result of different parties controlling the two houses of a legislature. Jewell and Olson discovered that between 1965 and 1988, all but three states in the nation had a divided government. The only consistently unified states were Hawaii, Mississippi, and Georgia. Oregon, Washington, and California usually have Democratic legislatures and Republican governors; while Idaho, Utah, Arizona, Colorado, Wyoming, and Montana have the reverse pattern. Finally, Nevada and New Mexico show a mixed pattern of party control of the governorship and the legislature. Divided government is often a result of ticket splitting by the state's voters and of districting patterns and gerrymandering by the legislatures.[49] Regardless of the cause, the result is often much slower policy deliberations and deadlocked political institutions. These outcomes apparently do not cause excessive concern to many voters, who may worry more about their state government causing additional problems than about the possibility of the state government solving existing concerns.

Conclusion

Under the influence of populist and progressive notions, the legal framework of citizen representation in the West has tilted toward participation through the mechanisms of open and blanket primaries, and the ability to influence public policy directly through the use of the initiative and the referendum. Despite the legal provisions favoring individual participation, in general citizens turn out to vote in greater numbers only in those states with either a moralistic or individualistic political culture. In many areas of the West office-seekers are faced with large geographical districts to cover. This factor, combined with the presence of media experts in California, has been instrumental in helping to mold campaign styles not only in the region but also throughout the country.

On the other hand, emphasis on individual participation has meant that western political parties, while modernizing, still remain relatively weak political institutions, especially when compared to some of the powerful interest groups operating in the West. Minor parties often garner more votes than in other regions of the country. Legislative politics in the West is in many states characterized by "citizen legislatures" that tend to have low levels of partisanship and can result in policy stalemate.

Many of the political trends emerging throughout the nation in political participation during the 1970s and 1980s had forerunners in earlier periods of western politics, including relatively open access to the policymaking process, issue- and candidate-oriented voters, weak formal party organizations, and heavy use of media-style campaigns. All of these patterns stem from the longstanding western tradition of independent politics and the laws enacted to implement and protect it.

Notes

1. Thomas R. Dye, *Politics in States and Communities,* 6th ed. (Englewood Cliffs, N.J.: Prentice Hall, 1988), 82.

2. Cal Clark and B. Oliver Walter, "Rising Republicanism in the West: A Regional Ride on Harmonic State Waves," *Social Science Journal* 18 (1981), 1–6.

3. Frank Jonas, ed., *Politics in the American West* (Salt Lake City: University of Utah Press, 1969); Joel Garreau, *The Nine Nations of North America* (Boston: Houghton Mifflin, 1981); Everett Ladd, "Opinion Roundup," *Public Opinion* (March 6, 1983), 26–31; Leonard Ritt, "Must Democrats Sell Their Ideological Souls to Win the West?" paper delivered at the Annual Meeting of the Western Social Science Association, Reno, Nevada, April 1986.

4. E. E. Schattschneider, *Party Government* (New York: Rinehart, 1942), 1.

5. Ruth K. Scott and Ronald J. Hrebenar, *Parties in Crisis* (New York: John Wiley and Sons, 1982), 5–6.

6. *Ibid.*

7. The Federal Voting Assistance Act of 1955 and the Voting Rights Act of 1965 were the two major federal acts accomplishing this task. In 1987 Senator Alan Cranston (D-Cal) introduced the "Universal Voter Registration Act," which would further reduce differences between the states. The act proposed massive distribution of mail-in registration forms and follow-up, along with Election Day voter registration.

8. Until 1986 Oregon had the region's most lenient registration requirement, with a closing date of General Election Day. The stricter standards came about through a citizen initiative.

9. Even in the closed primary state of California, some slack in the system was evident until the late 1950s when candidates could "cross-list," thereby appearing on the ballots of both parties.

10. States differ in the extent to which their primaries are open or closed, making distinctions difficult. As Wyoming permits voters to change party registration on Election Day, and members of one party can vote in the other's primary, the state is listed as having an open primary.

11. Hugh A. Bone, "The Political Setting," in *Political Life in Washington: Governing the Evergreen State*, ed. Thor Swanson *et al.* (Pullman, Wash.: Washington State University Press, 1985), 7.

12. Malcolm E. Jewell, "Whither the Closed Primary?" in *State Government: CQ's Guide to Current Issues and Activities 1987–88*, ed. Thad L. Beyle (Washington, D.C.: Congressional Quarterly Press, 1987), 46.

13. Mervin Field, "Will Independents Vote in Partisan Primaries?" *California Journal* 18 (February 1987), 103–4.

14. Charles M. Price, "The Initiative: A Comparative State Analysis and Reassessment of a Western Phenomenon," *Western Political Quarterly* 28 (June 1975), 248.

15. An even more forbidding requirement is that the affirmative vote on an initiative be equal to at least 50% of the total vote in the preceding general election.

16. California firms have also qualified petitions in Arizona, Montana, and Oregon. Of the western states, only Colorado, Idaho and Washington restrict paid signature collection.

17. Robert Fairbanks and Martin Smith, "There's Gold in Them Thar Campaigns," *California Journal* 15 (December 1984), 468–71.

18. David Broder points out that in a pluralistic society other factors such as size of staff and ideas may exert just as much influence on candidates and policymaking as money. However, those who organize aspects of campaigns or write position papers for candidates are viewed as performing a public service. "Things Other Than $$$ Can Influence Politics," *Salt Lake Tribune*, July 22, 1987.

19. In Utah personal loans obtained by the candidate to finance his or her campaign are included in the report filed by the campaign committee.

20. In addition to Alaska, the states of California, Hawaii, Idaho, Montana and Utah have enacted public finance laws. Oregon enacted legislation for public financing, but its program has been discontinued. See Herbert Alexander and Mike Eberts, *Public Financing of State Elections: A Data Book on Tax-Assisted Funding of Political Parties and Candidates in Twenty States* (Los Angeles: Citizens' Research Foundation, 1986).

21. The 7% figure has been chosen because turnout in the Midwest has ranged from an average of 6.2% above the national figure in the House elections for the 1974–86 period to 7.6% above in the presidential elections between 1960 and 1972. Western states that equal or exceed the standard set by midwestern states are accorded the high-turnout designation.

22. Richard G. Niemi and Herbert Weisberg, *Controversies in Voting Behavior*, 2nd ed.(Washington, D.C.: Congressional Quarterly Press, 1984), 26.

23. Raymond E. Wolfinger and Steven J. Rosenstone, *Who Votes?* (New Haven: Yale University Press, 1980), 58.

24. Paul Abramson *et al.*, *Change and Continuity in the 1984 Elections* (Washington, D.C.: Congressional Quarterly Press, 1986), 114.

25. Daniel J. Elazar, *American Federalism: A View from the States*, 3rd ed. (New York: Harper & Row, 1984), 152–53.

26. Thomas A. Morehouse, "Alaska's Elections," in *Alaska State Government and Politics*, ed. Gerald A. McBeth and Thomas A. Morehouse (Fairbanks: University of Alaska Press, 1987), 121.

27. The list includes at-large districts in Alaska and Wyoming, where the state has only one House member. The districts in other states are Nevada (District 2), Montana (1 and 2), Oregon (2), New Mexico (2 and 3), Arizona (3 and 4), Colorado (3 and 4), Utah (1 and 3), Idaho (1 and 2) and California (14 and 35). See *Congressional Districts in the 1980s* (Washington, D.C.: Congressional Quarterly, Inc., 1983), x–xi.

28. Henry Kenski, "Campaigns and Elections in the Mountain States, 1984" in *The Politics of Realignment: Party Change in the Mountain West*, ed. Peter F. Galderisi *et al.* (Boulder: Westview Press, 1987), 179.

29. The television marketing firm Arbitron Company categorizes television viewing markets by Area of Dominant Interest (ADI). An ADI is defined as all counties in which a particular station is viewed to a significant extent, including via cable. Each county in the continental United States is allocated exclusively to one ADI.

30. "The Election Process" in *We the People of Montana . . . The Workings of a Popular Government*, ed. James J. Lopach (Missoula: Mountain Press Publishing Company, 1983), 49.

31. George Skelton, "Experience Aided Governor, Cranston," *Los Angeles Times*, November 5, 1986.

32. Scott and Hrebenar, *Parties in Crisis*, chap. 3.

33. *Ibid.* For the complete listing of the legal requirements for access to the ballot in each of the thirteen western states, see the first edition of Scott and Hrebenar, 63–65.

34. Richard Scammon and Alice V. McGillivray, *America Votes, 17* (Washington, D.C.: Congressional Quarterly Press, 1987), Michael Barone and Grant Ujifusa, *Almanac of American Politics, 1988* (Washington, D.C.: National Journal, 1987); and Richard A. Diamond, *Guide to U.S. Elections* (Washington, D.C.: Congressional Quarterly Press, 1975).

35. Thomas R. Dye, *Politics in States and Communities*, 134.

36. Samuel J. Eldersveld, *Political Parties: A Behavioral Analysis* (Chicago: Rand McNally, 1964).

37. See Alfred Steinberg, *The Bosses* (New York: Signet, 1972); and Theodore J. Lowi, "Machine Politics—Old and New," *The Public Interest* 9 (Fall 1967), 83–84.

38. John R. Owen, Edmond Costanti and Louis F. Weschler, *California Politics and Parties* (New York: Macmillan, 1970), 32–33.

39. Winston W. Crouch, John C. Bollins and Stanley Scott, *California: Government and Politics*, 5th ed. (Englewood Cliffs, N.J.: Prentice Hall, 1972), 42.

40. David R. Mayhew, *Placing Parties in American Politics: Organization, Electoral Settings, and Government Activity in the Twentieth Century* (Princeton, N.J.: Princeton University Press, 1986).

41. *Ibid.*, 143.

42. *Ibid.*, 173.

43. James L. Gibson *et al.*, "Whither the Local Parties?" *American Journal of Political Science* 29 (February 1985), 154–55.

44. Frank Sorauf and Paul Beck, *Party Politics in America*, 6th ed. (Glenview, Ill.: Scott, Foresman, 1988), 410.

45. Malcolm E. Jewell and David M. Olson, *Political Parties and Elections in American States*, 3rd ed. (Chicago, Ill.: The Dorsey Press, 1988), 232–35.

46. Sorauf and Beck, *Party Politics in America*, 397.

47. Jewell and Olson, *Political Parties and Elections in American States*, 237.

48. John F. Bibby, Cornelius P. Cotter, James L. Gibson, and Robert J. Huckshorn, "Parties in State Politics," in Virginia Gray, Herbert Jacob, and Kenneth N. Vines, eds., *Politics in the American States: A Comparative Analysis*, 4th ed. (Boston: Little, Brown, 1983), 91.

49. Jewell and Olson, *Political Parties and Elections in American States*, 226–30.

6

POLITICAL PARTIES, ELECTIONS AND CAMPAIGNS, II: EVALUATION AND TRENDS

Ronald J. Hrebenar and Robert C. Benedict

*T*HIS CHAPTER EVALUATES THE EFFECTIVENESS OF THE vehicles of political participation described in Chapter 5—initiatives, referenda, elections and political parties—and considers some recent trends associated with them. The most important concerns will be the impact of these methods of participation on public policy in the western states, as well as the changing fortunes of political parties over the last twenty-five years. In this latter regard, we will consider the question of party competition and the extent to which there has been a party realignment in the West.

Evaluating the Direct Legislation Process

Given the emphasis upon direct legislation in western politics, this section focuses on levels of voter participation in such elections and the public policies that result. It should be mentioned at the outset, however, that conclusions about the effectiveness of the initiative and the referendum vary according to how the purpose of these devices is viewed.

The populists and progressives assumed that if citizens decided laws directly, the result would be greater trust in government, higher levels of participation, and added legitimacy to public policy decisions. Direct legislation could also serve as a safety valve. The threat of an initiative or its enactment would "send the legislature a message" about the depth of citizens' concern. Given these premises, the direct legislation process in the West falls short of its stated goals.

An alternate view based on current political trends and the value of direct democracy in increasing voter interest is advocated by Eugene C. Lee:

> The initiative and referendum must be tested not against a theoretical model of democratic institutions but the real world of declining electoral participation, weakened political parties, partisan legislative districting, and television-dominated election campaigns funded by massive contributions from special interests that also dominate legislative lobbying—all set in the context of an economic, social, and political environment of frightening complexity.[1]

If the process is viewed as encouraging participation by sectors of the electorate including the "issue public" (voters who are aware of and concerned about issues), then a more optimistic conclusion about the process can be reached.

EVALUATING LEVELS OF VOTER PARTICIPATION:
THE POPULIST–PROGRESSIVE PERSPECTIVE

Concerning the populist and progressive premise of increased control over government through direct legislation, polls in western states find that citizens overwhelmingly believe that the process should be available to act as a check on the legislative and executive branches. Yet its presence does not directly translate into perceptions of increased input into government. For example, one study of voters' feelings of control over government in thirteen states found no differences between states that employ the direct legislation process and those that do not.[2]

Evaluation of the relationship between ballot propositions and voter participation requires a consideration of many factors that influence whether or not citizens cast a ballot. Closely contested candidate races and the presence of prominent national or state issues obviously play a role. Several indicators could be used to determine the importance of ballot propositions in the decision to vote. The most direct approach—asking voters about the importance of ballot measures—is the least utilized. The only survey information comes from polls conducted in California in 1962 and 1978. The 1962 poll found that less than 2% named a proposition as an important reason for voting, while 75% cited the governor's race. In the 1978 poll only 7% said they would not have shown up at the polls if Proposition 13, the controversial tax limitation measure, had not been on the ballot.[3]

An indirect method of determining the importance of propositions would be to compare voter turnout rates in western states with those of the rest of the nation. Is higher use of direct legislation and higher participation rates in this region evidence of the drawing power of ballot propositions, or is any correlation spurious? Much depends upon how the analyst treats the southern states, a region where initiatives are rare and turnout is lower than average. David Everson argues that southern states should be omitted; on this basis participation in "northern" states (which includes the West) utilizing direct legislation is compared with states that do not use this mechanism.[4] From 1960 to 1980 no difference is found in average turnout in presidential and nonpresidential years.

Comparing the number of votes cast for candidates and ballot propositions within a state provides another indirect indicator of the importance of propositions. Only in rare instances do western ballot propositions draw more general election voters than do statewide candidate races for governor or U.S. senator. However, between 1976 and 1986 this situation has occurred at least once in Oregon, California, Alaska, Montana and Nevada.[5] A more suitable overall measure of participation is the drop-off rate—the proportion of voters who cast ballots for one race (such as the presidential contest) but "drop off" and do not vote on another race (such as a U.S. House seat or a particular ballot proposition). Comparing California and Washington State from 1970 to 1982, David Magleby found the drop-off, or nonparticipation, rate by voters on initiatives to be 8% and 11% respectively, while for propositions submitted by the legislature the figures were 16% and 17% respectively.[6] These rates are higher than the drop-off rate for key candidate races such as governor (2% in California and 3% in Washington State), U.S. senator (4%) or member of Congress (7% and 8% respectively). Only in Washington State do initiatives routinely out-poll such races as treasurer or auditor. Because few voters pass up the governor's race in western states, and because ten of the thirteen states in the region choose governors in nonpresidential years, Magleby suggests that candidates provide the impetus for voter turnout.[7] Given this record, the hope of the populists and progressives that the presence of direct legislation would motivate greater numbers of citizens to electoral participation is not fulfilled.

EVALUATING LEVELS OF VOTER PARTICIPATION:
THE "ISSUE PUBLIC" PERSPECTIVE

If direct legislation has not increased the number of western voters at the polls, a second interpretation of the process argues that it has enhanced the *quality* of participation by allowing further participation by the citizens who are the most interested in issues—that is, the "issue public."

This view focuses on the relatively high levels of voting on many ballot measures, despite the presence of numerous roadblocks not found in voting for candidates. First, voters often face a difficult struggle in simply locating the propositions on the ballot. Candidates are listed first with propositions following. Most western states place citizen initiatives after legislative propositions. The result of long ballots and numerous propositions in such states as California, Oregon and Washington is voter fatigue—the last measures tend to have the least participation. Thus the surprising element is the extreme diligence voters exhibit when a proposition outpolls a major statewide race. For example, in the 1970–82 study cited above, the drop-off for all initiatives compared to the governor's race was only 6% in California, and 8% in Washington State.

A second factor cited by the "issue public" interpretation is that citizens prefer to vote on initiatives as compared to referenda. Measures proposed by the public are generally more controversial, and thus receive greater media attention. Consequently, for referenda voluntarily referred by the legislature it is not surprising to find high drop-off rates in California and Washington State.

Participation on ballot measures is definitely influenced by perceptions of the importance of the issue under consideration. Propositions dealing with moral questions, rates of taxation, or environmental issues (including nuclear power) have appeared frequently on western ballots and are very significant to voters. They will go out of their way to find these issues on the ballot, passing over previously listed issues to do so.

Finally, viewing direct legislation as a vehicle for the issue public transforms citizen participation from a unidirectional view (candidate races draw voters to ballot propositions) to a relationship of mutual reinforcement. In the western states the combination of attractive candidates and ballot propositions often reinforces the decision to participate. The 1986 election, lacking a presidential race or critical national issues, set record low levels of national participation. Yet Idaho posted one of the highest turnout levels. A plausible argument is that the combination of closely contested races for governor (2.5% drop-off), U.S. senator (3% drop-off), and a controversial measure concerning retention of the right-to-work law (2% drop-off) brought voters to the polls.

A similar combination of propositions and candidates not only interested Pacific state Democrats in 1986 but also influenced their decisions as well. A *New York Times* exit poll found the most important issue to Democrats in deciding the vote in U.S. House races was the category of nuclear or hazardous waste, while Republicans cited it as the third most important. Although this issue was not stressed by many candidates, the overlap from propositions in California, Washington and Oregon is evident among the Democratic voters.[8] A question on the issues determining Senate voting was not asked by the *Times* poll, as only one-third of the seats were decided. Yet for Senate contests the connection between candidates and propositions among Pacific state voters was even clearer. In Washington State Democratic challenger Brock Adams charged that Republican Slade Gorton did not fight hard enough to protect the state's interests in the siting of the nuclear waste repository. Adams gained a narrow victory, while polls showed the nuclear issue was one of two where voters sided decisively with Adams.[9] Similarly, in the California U.S. Senate race, the hazardous waste issue was the only substantive one where voters favored incumbent Democrat Allan Cranston over challenger Ed Zshau.[10]

EVALUATING THE DIRECT DEMOCRACY PROCESS
AS A PUBLIC POLICY MECHANISM

To assess the public policy that is made through the direct legislation process, let us consider the roles of special interest groups, voters, and state legislatures. Populists and progressives claimed that allowing the people to decide legislation directly would reduce the role of special interests, while critics believed voters would be more susceptible to the influence of organized groups.

At first, direct legislation was used as a weapon against special interests. Arizona voters enacted a women's suffrage law, Oregon passed legislation to protect workers, California balanced the influence of the Southen Pacific Railroad, and Washington State obtained reapportionment, the blanket primary, and repeal of the poll tax. In recent years, however, interest group penetration of all aspects of the public policymaking process has become a central fact of political life. Therefore, direct legislation is another weapon in the arsenal of all organized interests in the West, including public officials. John Shockley's study of ballot measures in Colorado in 1976 found that all measures that had strong corporate opposition were defeated.[11] Business groups, however, are most often on the defensive in attempting to block measures they perceive to be harmful. Environmental groups in the West are increasingly successful in putting measures on the ballot, with issues ranging from deposits on beverage containers to the development of nonnuclear energy resources. Even public officials resort to the initiative process in attempting to bypass reluctant legislatures. Two California governors, Ronald Reagan and George Deukmejian, unsuccessfully sponsored initiatives on property tax limitation and legislative redistricting.

Yet another factor that ensures the participation of interest groups is the cost of direct legislation campaigning. In 1988 California provided the most vivid example of the cost factor. Contributions to the campaigns for twenty-nine statewide propositions were over $130 million, and over one-half of that amount was spent on five initiatives that dealt with insurance rates.[12]

Thus today it is unrealistic to assert that direct legislation reduces the role of special interests. The more important question is whether a wide range of interest groups is able to take advantage of direct legislation. In theory, of course, any group is free to utilize this device to promote its interests. In practice, however, the cost of mounting such campaigns excludes groups that lack resources—especially money. Consequently, while a variety of groups in the West does resort to ballot propositions, the major bias is the lack of their use by minority groups of all types.

A second question concerns voter decision-making capability in terms of knowledge and recognition of issues. The populists and progressives operated upon three assumptions about voters: (1) they would be informed on ballot measures; (2) they would consider both the individual's and society's needs in making their decision; and (3) they would avoid propositions that were constitutionally suspect.

To assess the extent of citizen knowledge about ballot propositions, a useful distinction is the division between "hard" and "easy" issues.[13] The easy issues are symbolic, deal with policy ends, and go unresolved over long periods of time. Examples are abortion, busing, the death penalty, and environmental protection. Voters have little difficulty making up their minds on these issues, even if publicity is lacking before the election.[14] Hard issues are technical and are concerned with means rather than policy ends. Complex governmental reform propositions, budgetary issues and scientific and technical decisions fall into this category. A lack of direction from political parties, political leaders and civic groups creates an information vacuum. Between 1976 and 1980, for example, voters in six western states decided nearly identical measures proposing a moratorium on the development of nuclear power plants. With scientists divided over the issue, many voters said they had difficulty in understanding the arguments and making a decision.[15] Thus the issue public is disproportionately represented in voting on the hard issues.

"Proposition 13 fever," the combination of tax limitations and dramatic cuts in state government spending imposed by direct legislation on thirteen states throughout the nation in 1978, can be viewed as the most vivid example of placing individual desires ahead of community needs. The fever did spread, as twenty-three major tax and spending limit initiatives or referenda qualified for the ballot in western states from 1980 to 1986. The rate of passage was 39%—about the same rate of passage noted earlier for statutory initiatives. Thus, voters gave careful scrutiny to the proposals and in general rejected those which would impose draconian tax limits or cuts.

Like the legislative branch, voters do pass measures that the courts later declare unconstitutional. California courts, for example, struck down parts of 1978's Proposition 13, and a Washington State anti-school busing initiative was invalidated. One area in which courts act as a check is when ballot propositions attempt to place illegal requirements upon the legislative branch. California courts declared a 1983 legislative reapportionment initiative unconstitutional before it was placed on the ballot, and struck down Proposition 24, an initiative to cut the legislature's budget by 30% and to redistribute power within the legislature toward the Republican party.

The central issue regarding legislative responsiveness is whether the electorate's greater accessibility to ballot measures in the region acts to make state legislatures more attentive to citizen concerns. Certainly, the availability of this vehicle to the public often forces legislatures to act when they would prefer not to do so. One example of this is the passage of campaign finance reform and conflict of interest provisions in Alaska. As the result of a groundswell of support for such measures, two initiative petitions were qualified for the ballot for the 1974 elections. In response the legislature enacted its own provisions before the initiatives came up for a vote.[16]

On the other hand, constitutional provisions for direct legislation allow state legislatures to abdicate responsibility when political costs are perceived to be too high. Recent examples include such issues as development of nuclear power, limits on abortion, and housing for the poor and elderly. Legislatures can refer these to the direct legislation process on the grounds that "the voters should have the right to decide" such "significant" issues. Thus the western public has often determined issues that legislatures preferred not to deal with or have ignored.

Parties and Policymaking in the Western States

One of the continuing questions in political science is, do parties make a difference? According to theory, political parties should aggregate the demands of their followers, articulate those demands in the policymaking institutions and then assist, through the executive branch, in the implementation of the laws that result.

There certainly are some ideological and policy differences separating the Republican and Democratic parties in the West, which we will discuss later in this chapter. Yet the translation of those differences into policy outcomes is much more difficult to evaluate. Most experts agree, however, that party positions and platforms drive policymaking in only a few, and often not the most significant, areas of public concern.[17]

Four generalizations have been made regarding the factors that affect party influence in state legislatures. First, stronger party influence is likely to be found in urbanized, industrialized northeastern states and not in the more sparsely populated western states. Second, party voting in the legislature is also higher in states with very competitive party systems. Third, extra-party coalitions, such as the conservative coalition found in Congress, are not prevalent on the state level. Fourth, if there is to be any evidence of party programmatic leadership, it should be discovered on issues such as social welfare, legislative organization and party-related issues such as reapportionment. Thomas Dye investigated party systems and welfare spending over a thirty-year period and discovered that twenty states had "policy relevant party systems" during that period.[18] However, the party systems in the other thirty states did not exhibit welfare-spending policy patterns. That is, welfare expenditures did not always increase under Democratic party leadership, or necessarily decrease under Republican party leadership. Dye found that in key competitive states, such as New York, Illinois and Connecticut, policy directions were not significantly affected by changes in party control. Eight of the western states were identified as having policy-relevant party systems. These were California, Hawaii and Oregon from the Pacific states; and Wyoming, Idaho, Montana, Nevada and Utah among the Mountain states. Dye argues that these states tend to mirror the policy divisions of the national-level parties, especially where the parties represent separate socioeconomic constituencies.[19]

One of the prerequisites for party rule is the existence of party government. Yet American state governmental structures, based as they are on the principle of separation of powers, allow and facilitate divided government as the norm in most states. With the governor's mansion in one party's hands and the legislature in the other's (as has been the case in California in recent years), the ability of a party to carry out its policy agenda is severely impaired.

There is great variation among the fifty state legislatures in terms of the role played by party leadership in attempting to enact platforms or policy programs. In his study of party influence in state legislatures Wayne Francis concluded that committees were more important than parties as regards which institutions made the most significant legislative decisions. Actually, party leaders dominated only five chambers and shared power with party caucuses in a dozen more of the ninety-nine state legislative chambers. A majority of these party-dominated chambers were found in states with strong traditional party organizations.[20]

Factors that tend to undermine party control in state legislatures, especially those in many western states, include the low levels of professionalism in state legislatures, the lack of strong party organizations, the greater significance of personal ideology or interest group ties and the low levels of financial and political support that the average state legislator needs to secure his or her seat. All of these factors combine to limit severely the impact of political parties on public policy deliberations in most western state legislatures. In earlier research done by LeBlanc, the rate of party voting in western states ranged from a low of 17% in California to a high of 50% in Washington State. As a region, the West had the lowest level of party voting.[21]

Political Party Competition in the West: An Alternative Perspective

Previous studies of party competition have shown very competitive party politics in the West. Focusing on the period of 1962–73, Ranney placed six of the western states in the two-party category; two in the Modified One Party Democratic category (Hawaii and New Mexico); and three in the Modified One Party Republican category (Idaho, Colorado and Wyoming).[22] We believe that the Ranney study and others, such as that by Bibby *et al.*, exhibit two major methodological problems in the assessment of party competition in general and in the West in particular.[23]

The first problem is the use of a wide two-party classification. This blurs the significance of overwhelming party dominance within a state. A party that controls more than 60% of the seats in the legislature can usually effectively control that body. To say, as Ranney did, that until a party almost reaches the 90% mark it does not have one-party control of a state is an example of caution, but does little to illuminate the degree of party control in the western states. The second problem with these competition indexes is that their methods of calculation do not reflect possible significant differences among the various levels and types of elective offices at both the state and federal levels.

Besides dealing with these problems, any comprehensive assessment of party competition in the West needs to take into account two other factors. First, election results from a single election are but a "snapshot" in time and may hide more durable patterns of partisan behavior. Take, for example, the results of the 1986 elections in the West. These were very successful from the perspective of the Democratic party. After November 1986, the Democrats held 53% of the U.S. House of Representatives seats from the region, 38% of the U.S. Senate seats, 62% of the governorships, 46% of the state senate seats and 49.6% of the state house seats. Thus, of these five categories the Democrats held majorities in two, earned a near dead heat in two others and conceded only the U.S. Senate category to the Republicans. From this "snapshot," the West could be considered a well-balanced region in terms of party competition. Because of its snapshot characteristic, however, one needs to view these results over a period of time to determine if 1986 was indicative of party election fortunes in the 1980s.

Second, considering election results in the West as a whole—either for a single election or for a series of elections—obscures some important differences between the subregions of the West. As noted in previous chapters, several observers have argued that the five Pacific states (California, Oregon, Washington, Alaska and Hawaii) are sufficiently different from the eight Mountain states to warrant separate examination of these subregions as well as of the West as a whole.[24]

Therefore, we suggest that any analysis of western party competition needs to take into account: (1) specific offices, such as governor, state representative, etc.; (2) electoral levels, particularly elections for federal and state offices; (3) subregional differences; (4) the fact that the more elections included in the analysis, the more accurate the picture of competition and the trends in competition, and (5) the fact that previous assessments of two-party competition have been too broad.

THE METHOD OF INVESTIGATION

To measure party competition in the West, its subregions and its states we use an indexing method. The index employed is the percentages of seats or offices won by Democratic party candidates. State-level contests have been subdivided into three categories: gubernatorial, statewide elected offices, and legislatures. Federal-level data are also grouped into three subcategories: presidential, U.S. Senate and U.S. House of Representatives.[25] The data for each of the thirteen western states, the subregions, and the West are presented in Tables 6.1 and 6.2. These indexes have been calculated for the 1970–80 period and in order to identify recent trends they have also been calculated for the period 1982–86. We will begin by examining state-level offices.

STATE LEGISLATIVE COMPETITION

The grass-roots of state-level party competition is found in the thousands of battles for state legislature seats. Often on this level party loyalty is a much more significant factor in the voter's decision-

Table 6.1 Major Party Competition in Western States in State and Federal Contests, 1970–80, by Success of Democratic Party

	State-Level					Federal			
	Governor[a]	Statewide[b]	State Leg[c]	State M[d]	Pres[e]	USS[f]	Cong[g]	Fed M[h]	Overall[i]
PACIFIC STATES									
Alaska	45.6	66.5	60.0	57.3	37.5	38.2	33.0	36.2	46.8
California	53.0	55.3	61.7	56.7	46.0	56.5	58.1	53.5	55.1
Hawaii	56.0	100.0	73.3	76.4	46.6	71.5	100.0	72.7	74.6
Oregon	49.0	25.0	58.8	44.3	46.3	43.8	79.2	56.4	50.4
Washington	48.0	46.7	56.0	50.2	43.7	67.0	83.5	64.7	57.5
Pacific Mean	50.3	58.7	62.0	57.0	44.0	55.4	70.8	56.7	56.9
MOUNTAIN STATES									
Arizona	51.0	52.6	40.3	47.9	35.3	47.0	38.8	40.4	44.2
Colorado	53.3	46.7	43.7	47.9	38.6	50.5	55.0	48.0	48.0
Idaho	61.7	60.7	34.2	52.2	31.7	48.5	0.0	26.7	39.5
Montana	57.3	69.0	53.8	60.0	40.7	58.3	58.3	52.4	56.2
Nevada	57.3	69.0	70.0	64.3	38.0	53.5	83.3	58.3	61.3
New Mexico	51.7	100.0	67.3	73.0	42.3	47.3	41.7	43.8	58.4
Utah	59.3	46.7	41.7	49.2	28.3	44.0	58.3	43.5	46.4
Wyoming	48.0	22.0	38.7	36.2	34.0	42.0	66.7	47.6	41.9
Mountain Mean	55.0	58.0	48.7	53.8	36.1	48.9	50.3	45.1	49.5
West Mean	53.2	58.2	53.8	55.8	38.9	51.4	58.1	49.6	52.3

[a] Democratic (Dem) mean percentage of gubernatorial vote.
[b] Dem mean percentage of state-level, statewide elected officers.
[c] Dem mean percentage of state legislature seats.
[d] Dem mean percentage of columns 1, 2 and 3.
[e] Dem mean percentage of two-party presidential vote.
[f] Dem mean percentage of two-party U.S. Senate vote.
[g] Dem mean percentage of congressional seats.
[h] Dem mean percentage of columns 5, 6 and 7.
[i] Dem mean percentage of columns 1, 2, 3, 5, 6 and 7.

Source: Compiled by the authors from election data provided by state and federal governments.

Table 6.2   Major Party Competition in Western States in State and Federal Contests, 1982–86, by Success of Democratic Party

	State-Level				Federal				Overall[i]	Index Change (1970–80 to 1982–86)
	Governor[a]	Statewide[b]	State Leg[c]	State M[d]	Pres[e]	USS[f]	Cong[g]	Fed M[h]		
PACIFIC STATES										
Alaska	54	100	50	68.0	31	37	0	22.7	45.4	−1.4
California	44	83	59	62.0	42	49	61	50.7	56.4	+1.3
Hawaii	58	100	78	78.7	44	79	83	68.7	73.7	−.9
Oregon	45	25	58	42.7	44	35	60	46.3	44.5	−5.1
Washington	53	40	55	49.3	43	57	63	54.3	51.8	−5.7
Pacific Mean	51	70	60	60.0	41	51	53	48.5	54.4	−2.6
MOUNTAIN STATES										
Arizona	57	38	38	44.3	33	50	20	34.3	39.3	−4.9
Colorado	64	60	34	52.7	36	43	48	42.3	47.5	−.5
Idaho	51	40	31	40.7	27	38	33	32.7	36.7	−2.8
Montana	73	75	49	65.7	39	58	50	49.0	57.4	+1.2
Nevada	65	33	57	51.7	33	51	50	44.7	48.2	−13.1
New Mexico	50	70	59	60.0	40	41	33	38.0	49.0	−9.4
Utah	50	25	25	33.3	25	35	11	23.7	28.5	−17.9
Wyoming	59	50	35	48.0	29	33	0	20.6	34.3	+.7
Mountain Mean	59	49	41	50.0	33	44	31	35.7	42.6	−6.9
West Mean	56	57	48	53.6	36	47	39	40.6	47.1	−5.2

[a] Democratic (Dem) mean percentage of gubernatorial vote.
[b] Dem mean percentage of state-level, statewide elected officers.
[c] Dem mean percentage of state legislature seats.
[d] Dem mean percentage of columns 1, 2 and 3.
[e] Dem mean percentage of two-party presidential vote.
[f] Dem mean percentage of two-party U.S. Senate vote.
[g] Dem mean percentage of congressional seats.
[h] Dem mean percentage of columns 5, 6 and 7.
[i] Dem mean percentage of columns 1, 2, 3, 5, 6 and 7.

Source: Compiled by the authors from election data provided by state and federal governments.

Table 6.3   State Legislative Seats by Party, 1978–86

Region	Democratic	Republican	Democratic Percent of Seats
Mountain	1,706	2,412	41.4
Pacific	1,476	982	60.0
West	3,182	3,394	48.4
U.S.A.	22,621	14,352	61.2

Source: Compiled by the authors from election statistics provided by the states.

making than it is for higher offices. Frequently, the only information a voter may have about a legislative candidate is his or her party label. On this most basic level of state party competition, the differences between the two subregions become clear. As the figures in Table 6.3 indicate, while the Democratic party is still the state legislative majority party nationally and in the Pacific states, it has been a minority party overall in the West since 1978 and has lost almost 60% of the legislative elections in the Mountain states.

Using a scale on which 100 indicates the Democrats controlled all the legislative seats up for election during the period and 0 indicates all seats controlled by the Republicans, the West's legislative index for the 1970s is 53.8, while the regional indexes are 62.0 for the Pacific states and 48.7 for the Mountain states. Comparable data for the 1980s indicates the maintenance of strong Democratic index scores (60) in the Pacific states, a strong surge to Republican control in the Mountain states (41), and a Republican edge in the West's overall index of 48.3.

STATEWIDE OFFICES

The second state-level index involves statewide elected offices.[26] Of the six office-level indexes we examine in this chapter, the Democrats do best at the statewide executive office level. The West, Pacific and Mountain indexes during the 1970s are all about 58, indicating strong levels of Democratic success in these elections. The short-term trends of the 1980s follow the legislative patterns, with a decline in the Mountain index to 49, a rise in the Pacific index to 70, and almost no change in the West's overall index (57).

GUBERNATORIAL COMPETITION

The highest and also most visible state-level partisan office is that of governor. In fact, Jewell and Olson argue that control of the governorship is the single most important measure of party competition.[27]

A slight majority (79 out of 151 or 52.3%) of western gubernatorial elections in the postwar era have been won by Democratic candidates. During the 1970s, however, the regional index for gubernatorial elections is a well-balanced 53.2 with almost no difference between the subregions. A pattern quite the reverse of what was discovered in the legislative and statewide offices is detected in the early 1980s gubernatorial index scores. The Pacific gubernatorial index declines slightly to 51, while the Mountain states index rises to 59. This means that the Democratic candidates actually won more frequently in gubernatorial races in the Mountain states during the 1980s.

STATE-LEVEL COMPETITION: A SUMMARY

Summarizing the combined state-level competition index, the 1970s' West index was 55.8. During the 1980s, it was 53.6, showing a slight Democratic edge in state-level politics. Of the two subregions, the Pacific states were only slightly more Democratic than the Mountain states in the 1970s (57.0 to 53.8). Yet, by the 1980s, the regional difference had become quite pronounced, with the Democrats rising to a 60 index in the Pacific states and dropping to around 50 in the Mountain region. Still, the Democrats did not lose a single one of these comparisons. Clearly, on the state level of politics, the West continues to be a Democratic party bastion.

FEDERAL-LEVEL COMPETITION: THE PRESIDENT

Walter Dean Burnham's suggestion of separating presidential contests from the congressional elections in examining party competition reveals some significant trends when the federal competition indexes are examined.[28] No western state shows a pro–Democratic party presidential index during either the 1970s or 1980s. Clearly, the West, like most of the rest of the nation, has become a Republican stronghold since the 1972 elections. Actually, the West has been supporting the GOP presidential candidates during the entire postwar period, as Tables 6.4 and 6.5 indicate.

The Democrats have won less than 30% of the states and less than 20% of the electoral votes cast in the West since 1948 (see Tables 6.4 and 6.5). When one examines the alternative indicator of the Democratic percentage of the popular vote for president, as opposed to electoral votes cast, the results reveal a similar Republican dominance. In this regard the percentages of the 1970s and 1980s are merely continuations of a long-term pattern. The West in presidential elections is GOP territory!

Table 6.4   Western States' Presidential Election Votes, 1948–84, by States

Region	Times Voted for Dem.	Times Voted for Rep.	Dem. Percent
Mountain	23	65	26.1
Pacific	15	32	31.9
West	38	97	28.1
U.S.A.	4	7	36.4

Note: This table indicates how often states in the two western subregions, the West and the nation voted for the Democratic or Republican candidate in presidential elections. For example, states in the Mountain region have voted 23 times for Democratic presidential candidates and 65 times for Republican candidates.

Source: Compiled by the authors from federal election reports.

Table 6.5   Western States' Presidential Election Votes, 1948–84, by Electoral Votes

Region	Dem. Electoral Votes	Rep. Electoral Votes	Dem. Percentage of Electoral Votes
Mountain	67	272	19.8
Pacific	119	462	20.5
West	186	734	20.2
U.S.A.	1,821	3,434	53.0

Source: Compiled by the authors from federal election reports.

CONGRESSIONAL COMPETITION

On the U.S. Senate and congressional levels, however, it is a quite different story. Table 6.6 presents data on the Democratic party percentage of House of Representatives seats in the West since 1978. Table 6.7 presents Democratic party congressional election vote percentages in the West's subregions during the 1982, 1984 and 1986 elections.

In each of these elections the West elected a majority of Democratic party candidates to the House, despite the fact that the Mountain states have returned only about one-third of their House delegations as Democrats. The overall western index for House races in the 1970s is 58.1, with the Pacific regional index at 70.8 (the highest index number in this chapter), and the Mountain states' index at 50.3. In sharp contrast, during the early 1980s all the indexes drop: Pacific, 53; Mountain, 31; and West, 39. Obviously, during the 1980s, the Republicans have become the majority party in western U.S. House elections.

Table 6.6   House of Representatives Elections in the West, 1980–84, by Democratic Percentage of Vote

Region	1980	1982	1984
Mountain	46.5	45.0	37.6
Pacific	49.4	53.4	51.5
U.S.A.	51.3	56.2	52.8

Source: Compiled by the authors from federal election reports.

Table 6.7   House of Representatives Elections, 1978–86, by Democratic Party Percentage of Seats

Region	1978	1980	1982	1984	1986
Mountain	47.3	36.8	34.8	29.2	37.5
Pacific	66.1	56.1	62.3	60.7	59.0
West	61.3	51.3	54.8	51.8	52.9
U.S.A.	63.4	55.9	61.8	58.2	59.3

Source: Compiled by the authors from federal election reports.

A similar pattern has occurred in U.S. Senate elections in the West. Of the 185 western Senate races since 1946, the Democrats have won 96 or 51.9%. During the 1970s, the index was 51.4 for the West, 55.4 for the Pacific, and 48.9 in the Mountain states. Again, the indexes have declined in the 1980s to 47 (West), 51 (Pacific) and 44 (Mountain).

FEDERAL-LEVEL PARTY COMPETITION: A SUMMARY

Overall, the federal-level competition index during the 1970s supported the two-region concept. The Pacific region index scores were 56.7 (1970s) and 54.4 (1980s). The Mountain states' index scores went down from 45.1 to 35.7 from the 1970s to the 1980s. The West's index scores reflected this increased Mountain states' support for the Republicans: 49.6 in the 1970s to 40.6 in the 1980s.

REDEFINING PARTY COMPETITION

It was noted early in this section that previous assessments of party competition in the West were based on a broad definition of what constituted two-party competition. Here we suggest a new set of classifications that are more useful in understanding the degree of competition found in the thirteen western states. The classification of *one-party control* is based on a party controlling more than 65% of that subcategory of seats or offices. A party is described as *two-party* (*Democratic/Republican*) *dominant* if it controls from 55% to 65% of the seats or offices in a particular subcategory; and the designation *two-party* (*Democratic/Republican*) *leaning* when a small majority (50.1% to 55%) of seats or offices in that subcategory favors one party.

PARTY COMPETITION IN THE WEST, ITS SUBREGIONS
AND ITS STATES: A SUMMARY

By applying this new classification of party competition to the indexes set out in the tables, we can present a picture of party competition in the West, its subregions and its states since 1970. Table 6.8 sets this out for the West as a whole and for the subregions. This table provides both a breakdown of competition for various offices, and overall ratings for these offices by subregion and for the West as a whole. Then in Table 6.9 the overall index scores and competitive classification for each state are listed for the two periods covered by the analysis.

It is very important to view party competition as a dynamic variable. It is constantly changing from election to election. It is also important, as we have stressed throughout this section, to view it not as a composite, as set out in Table 6.9, but through the various levels and types of offices. This is because, from the perspective of practical politics, the degree of competition at the various levels and in the various types of offices is likely to shape both the effectiveness of political participation and the policy process. As the indexes in Table 6.8 indicate, from the 1970s to the 1980s changes in party competition occurred in twenty-one of the twenty-seven index categories.

What then have we learned about changes in party competition in the West since 1970? Of the twenty-seven indexes, only three reflect one-party control situations: Pacific statewide offices (Democratic), Mountain presidential (Republican) and Mountain House (Republican). Overall, the West moved from "two-party Democratic leaning" to the equivalent Republican category. This represents a relatively minor shift. The West in general is Democratic territory on the state level, with a few major exceptions such as Utah and Wyoming, and it is Republican on the federal level, with the major exceptions of Pacific states such as California and Hawaii. The Pacific states are Democratic on the state and federal levels, while the Mountain states tend to be mixed on the state level and strongly Republican on the federal level. (See Tables 6.1 and 6.2 for further amplification.)

Table 6.8   Party Competition in the Subregions and the West, by Office Levels

	1970s	*1980s*
Subregion: Pacific States		
State-Level		
Governor	Two-party Democratic leaning	no change (n.c.)
Statewide	Two-party Democratic dominant	One-party Democratic control
State Leg.	Two-party Democratic dominant	n.c.
Overall State	Two-party Democratic dominant	n.c.
Federal-Level		
President	Two-party Republican dominant	n.c.
Senate	Two-party Democratic dominant	Two-party Democratic leaning
House	One-party Democratic control	Two-party Democratic leaning
Overall Fed.	Two-party Democratic dominant	Two-party Democratic leaning
Overall IPC[a]	Two-party Democratic dominant	Two-party Democratic leaning
Subregion: Mountain States		
State-Level		
Governor	Two-party Democratic leaning	Two-party Democratic dominant
Statewide	Two-party Democratic dominant	Two-party Republican leaning
State Leg.	Two-party Republican leaning	Two-party Republican dominant
Overall State	Two-party Democratic leaning	Two-party balanced
Federal-Level		
President	Two-party Republican dominant	One-party Republican control
Senate	Two-party Republican leaning	Two-party Republican dominant
House	Two-party Democratic leaning	One-party Republican control
Overall Fed.	Two-party Republican leaning	Two-party Republican dominant
Overall IPC[a]	Two-party Republican leaning	Two-party Republican dominant
Region: West		
State-Level		
Governor	Two-party Democratic leaning	Two-party Democratic dominant
Statewide	Two-party Democratic dominant	n.c.
State Leg.	Two-party Democratic leaning	Two-party Republican leaning
Overall State	Two-party Democratic dominant	Two-party Democratic leaning
Federal-Level		
President	Two-party Republican dominant	n.c.
Senate	Two-party Democratic leaning	Two-party Republican leaning
House	Two-party Democratic dominant	Two-party Republican dominant
Overall Fed.	Two-party Republican leaning	Two-party Republican dominant
Overall IPC[a]	Two-party Democratic leaning	Two-party Republican leaning

[a]IPC = Index of Party Competition.

Source: Compiled by the authors.

Table 6.9   Overall Party Competition in the Thirteen Western States: A Comparison of the 1970s and 1980s

Classification of Party Competition	1970s		1980s	
	State	Index	State	Index
One-party Democratic	Hawaii	74.6	Hawaii	73.7
Two-party Democratic dominant	Nevada	61.3	Montana	57.4
	New Mexico	58.4	California	56.4
	Washington	57.5		
	Montana	56.2		
	California	55.1		
Two-party Democratic leaning	Oregon	50.4	Washington	51.8
Two-party Republican leaning	Colorado	48.0	New Mexico	49.0
	Alaska	46.8	Nevada	48.2
	Utah	46.4	Colorado	47.5
			Alaska	45.4
Two-party Republican dominant	Arizona	44.2	Oregon	44.5
	Wyoming	41.9	Arizona	39.3
	Idaho	39.5	Idaho	36.7
One-party Republican	None		Wyoming	34.3
			Utah	28.5

Source: Compiled by the authors.

Party Realignment and Western Politics

WHAT IS REALIGNMENT?

Understanding something about the elements of party competition and recent voting patterns in the West can help us in tackling another question about electoral and partisan trends in western politics. This question relates to the issue of party realignment in the region.

The question of party realignment has so dominated the profession of political science during the 1980s that it is often referred to as the *R* word. Party realignment refers to the study of patterns of party success and failure in elections over a long period of time and the determination of shifts in the voting patterns. If significant and durable changes occur in the form of *voters changing their partisan loyalties from one party to the other,* it is called "realignment." If mixed patterns occur as a result of *reduced voter loyalties to parties in general—*

that is to say, reduced partisanship and an increase in the number of "independent" voters—then this situation is called "dealignment."

The concept of party realignment comes from V. O. Key's 1955 seminal article on the theory of critical elections.[29] Key's "critical elections" were characterized by a "short, sharp dramatic movement of voters away from one party." Such elections were also characterized by high turnouts, a rise in split-ticket voting, and sharp swings from one party to the other from election to election. A realigning election results from large-scale switches in voter support of the major parties, the development of a new set of issue cleavages that separate the parties, and the realization that there is a new majority party at all levels of government.

In 1959, Key added the idea of "secular realignment," in which the realignment may take place at different levels of politics on a gradual basis.[30] In 1983, James Sundquist suggested that realignment may take place first on the national level and then on the lower levels of politics at a later time.[31] It was Burnham who developed the notion that "dealignment" may be a more appropriate description of changing political loyalties than "realignment."[32]

HAS THE WEST REALIGNED INTO A REGION
OF REPUBLICAN DOMINANCE?

While most political scientists now argue that realignment has probably not occurred on the national level of American politics, some suggest that regional realignments may have occurred.[33] The two regions that have attracted the most scrutiny have been the South and the West.[34] Among the indications of possible realignment in the West have been high voter turnouts. Of the thirteen western states, five Mountains states (Colorado, Idaho, Montana, Utah and Wyoming) and three Pacific states (Alaska, Hawaii and Oregon) have turnout rates that are usually above the national average. But since most of these states have long traditions of high turnouts, it is difficult to argue that this is significant evidence to support the idea of realignment in the region.

Next to the examination of election results, the best data we have to examine the question of realignment come from public opinion poll questions focusing on party self-identification and issue positions. Nationally, a strong plurality of public self-identification with the Democratic party continued from the 1930s until the early 1980s when the Reagan victories sharply eroded the Democratic edge. By 1984, it appeared that the Republicans might have caught up and perhaps even surpassed their Democratic rivals. By the late 1980s, however, it appeared that the GOP tide was ebbing.

In the Mountain states subregion, the Republicans have become the dominant party in terms of voter self-identification. Stone has shown that this region has shifted from being one of the most Democratic regions in the nation to the most Republican region. He documents a 16-percentage-point change from 48% Democratic identification to 32% over the period since the 1950s.[35] Conversely, the GOP identifiers went from 18% to 33%—the highest regional support level for Republicans in the nation. The increase in Republican identifiers came from a variety of sources, including in-migration and the conversion of long-term residents.

While Democratic party losses in terms of voter identification were greater in the South than in the Mountain states, the outcomes by the late 1980s were very different. The difference is striking that while the Democratic party lost strength in the South, the Republicans gained relatively little there. The Democratic party still retains its position as the South's premier party, but the party has lost its edge as the Mountain West's leading party to the Republicans. The Pacific states, on the other hand, tend to follow the national patterns quite closely. There, Democratic party identification dropped from 47% in the 1950s to 43% in the 1980s, while the Republican party support declined from 31% to 24% in the 1980s.[36] Thus, an examination of public opinion data on party self-identification in the two subregions supports the conclusion that the Mountain states may have realigned from the Democratic party to the Republicans, but that the Pacific states have a pattern of only minor dealignment.

The second set of public opinion evidence that is pertinent to an understanding of realignment deals with the public's attitudes and positions on the key political issues of the period. Residents of the Mountain states have long exhibited a high level of hostility toward the federal government. Miller, Ritt and Stone discovered that as the national Democratic party moved from emphasizing development of economic infrastructure such as highways and dams to the development of social infrastructure programs such as education and health care, the reaction of the Mountain states to heightened government intervention was increasingly negative.[37] When the Republican party began to nationalize the issues developed in its congressional campaigns, these conservative issues found a receptive audience in the Mountain West.[38] In terms of ideological identification, the Mountain West has replaced the South as the most conservative region of the nation, especially in its opposition to federal government programs in social policy areas.

This conservative philosophy is duplicated in the voting ratings of the region's congressional delegation. Senators such as Orrin Hatch (R-Utah), Jake Garn (R-Utah), Jim McClure (R-Idaho) and Malcolm Wallop (R-Wyoming) have replaced senators like John Stennis (D-Mississippi) and Jeremiah Denton (R-Alabama) as the most conservative members in the U.S. Senate.[39] As the national Democratic party has moved sharply to the left on social issues since the late 1960s, the traditionally conservative Mountain West has found itself more and more comfortable with the conservative positions of the Republican party. As was the case with party self-identification, the Pacific states followed the national trends and became even more liberal than in previous decades.

Data from the 1988 elections confirm that these ideological trends continue. The *New York Times*/CBS Election Day exit polls discovered that next to the South, the West has the largest proportion of self-described conservative voters (35% as compared with 38% of southern voters). But the West also has the second highest proportion of liberal voters (18% compared to 23% in the Northeast). In terms of party self-identificaton of 1988 voters, the West was the only region in the nation with a Republican plurality (38% to 37% for the Democrats).[40]

The indexes of party competition presented earlier in this chapter support the argument that two quite different phenomena are occurring in the West. First, like the rest of the nation, westerners are increasingly reluctant to vote for Democratic presidential candidates. Consequently, one realignment conclusion that may be argued is that a presidential-level realignment may have occurred in the West. However, realignments are difficult to declare because historical perspective is a necessity. No one could be sure that the two Roosevelt victories of 1932 and 1936 were the beginning of a realignment, until the late 1940s or early 1950s. The rest of the data from federal election results are much less supportive of the realignment argument. Can one suggest that the Mountain states have realigned on the presidential and congressional levels without mentioning that the Democrats are still very competitive in U.S. Senate races in that subregion and in the West as a whole?

Arguing that realignment has taken place becomes even more difficult when the state-level offices are examined. As we noted earlier, the Democrats during the 1970s had gubernatorial and statewide office indexes (Democratic percentage of total seats during the period) of

55 and 58 in the Mountain states and 59 and 49 in the 1980s. The western state-level combined indexes for the 1970s and 1980s were 55.8 and 53.6 respectively. Only by arguing that a "rolling realignment" (one office at a time over an extended period) is the appropriate model for analyzing what is happening in the West can one defend the idea of realignment. What would seem to better describe the western situation is a pattern of individual state realignments and dealignments rather than a regional realignment.

Take, for example, the interesting cases of Alaska, Idaho and New Mexico. Alaska has a Democratic party that is quite strong on the state level, but unable to compete effectively on the federal level. Idaho and New Mexico have the same pattern. This may be evidence of dealignment or, alternatively, of very sophisticated voters who can establish long-term patterns of party loyalties that are office- and political-level specific. It could also reflect the power of incumbency or of various other factors. Other states such as Utah, Wyoming and Arizona have shifted sharply toward the Republican party in the last decade. Are such shifts enduring over time and thus evidence of state-level realignment, or are they just short-term reactions to specific issues and candidates being presented by the two major parties? Clearly, changes are occurring; change is a constant in partisan politics. But it is not yet clear whether these changes will be durable or just for the short term.[41]

Although the results from the 1988 elections have not been included in the indexes, the overall patterns changed only slightly. In the West, the Democrats gained one house seat and lost one governorship. The house seat was gained in the Pacific subregion and the governorship lost in the Mountain states. Despite this loss, the Democrats still hold a majority of Mountain state governorships, and overall in the West the Democrats hold nine of the thirteen governorships. The Democrats also improved their position in the state legislatures by holding slightly over half of all the state legislative seats in the West (50.7%). The large Democratic majorities in the Pacific states (63%) balance the almost comparable large Republican majorities in the Mountain states (56%). Still, the Democrats managed to increase their share of legislative seats in the Mountain states from their 1986 totals.

THE PROSPECT OF FUTURE REALIGNMENTS IN THE WEST

Projections about future realignment trends in the West must take into account the region's central political challenge: maintaining the flow of national government funds (a tacit acknowledgment of economic and political dependence) while appearing to be independent through support of less government regulation. Since the mid-1970s Republican candidates have successfully emphasized the latter half of this equation, particularly in the Mountain states. In the future the ability of both parties to meet the challenge depends on several economic and political factors.

A central economic element is whether the West experiences uniform growth or is further split into "haves" and "have-nots." In the 1970s economic growth patterns favored the Sunbelt, which included most of the region. Voters expected a booming economy and could afford ideological opposition to government. Economists now speak of a "bi-coastal economy" in which Atlantic and Pacific Coast states experience economic growth, but the country's midsection (based heavily upon agriculture, manufacturing, and natural resource extraction) lags behind. Continuation of bi-coastal growth patterns could threaten Republican electoral hegemony in the Mountain states. If voters face trade-offs between ideological preferences and acquiring economic subsidies to regain growth, rhetoric may give way to the needs of the pocketbook.

A political challenge also faces Democrats in the Pacific states. Here the trend toward the Republican party has been skillfully deflected by redistricting in California, and by the ability of regional Democrats to "denationalize" campaigns by relying on local or state issues. Whether this political deflection can continue into the 1990s is questionable.

Conclusions

The two central mechanisms linking citizens and government in the policymaking process that have been evaluated in this chapter are *direct legislation* and *political parties*. Despite falling short of the original populist and progressive expectations, the direct legislative process in the West does allow the "issue public" greater participation in policymaking, gives the political process a vitality not found in other regions, and will doubtless remain a distinctive aspect of the region's politics.

The role of western parties as vehicles of political participation reflects western political culture and western traditions. Parties offer a form of representation that in both the major parties and in most minor parties tends to support the individualistic, nonideological and small-government themes found throughout the West. Western parties and their elected representatives offer a pragmatic mix of relatively frugal government combined with an emphasis on major policy areas of interest to western voters, such as environmental protection and educational enhancement. The political realignments and dealignments that have affected the West in recent years have occurred within these party traditions.

Western parties foreshadowed the rise of conservative political values and with the West's "favorite son," former California governor Ronald Reagan, brought those values to the highest office in the nation. Today, the party and ideological divisions of the West, more than of any other region in the nation, mirror national-level patterns. Thus, in terms of reflecting the attitudes of the western electorate, western parties appear to be doing an efficient job.

Compared to parties in other regions, however, western parties are relatively weak in organization and leadership, and they are not very significant influences on the policymaking process. Parties in all thirteen western states have developed within a political system that over the years has produced and been dominated by powerful interest groups. The parties have learned to coexist with these groups, and increasingly interest groups have come to realize that they must use parties to achieve their policy goals. The great significance of interest groups in the policymaking process as well as being vehicles of political participation in the West will be examined in the following chapter.

Notes

1. Eugene C. Lee, "The American Experience, 1778–1978," in *The Referendum Device*, ed. Austin Ranney (Washington: American Enterprise Institute, 1981), 58.

2. Citizens' League, *Initiative and Referendum . . . "NO" for Minnesota* (Minneapolis: Citizens' League, 1979), 21–22.

3. David Magleby, *Direct Legislation: Voting on Ballot Propositions in the United States* (Baltimore: Johns Hopkins University Press, 1984), 96.

4. David H. Everson, "The Effects of Initiatives on Voter Turnout: A Comparative State Analysis," *Western Political Quarterly* 34 (September 1981), 415–25.

5. California's most controversial proposition, the 1978 Jarvis-Gann Proposition 13, was scheduled in the June primary election, and therefore is not counted in this calculation.

6. Magleby, *Direct Legislation*, 86.

7. *Ibid.*, 90.

8. Proposition 65 in California proposed greater restrictions on hazardous waste, Washington State's Referendum 40 concerned whether a high-level nuclear waste repository should be located in the state, and three Oregon propositions (14–16) dealt with nuclear waste and nuclear weapons.

9. Jack Broom, "What Give Adams the Edge?" *Seattle Times*, November 5, 1986.

10. George Skelton, "Experience Aided Governor, Cranston," *Los Angeles Times*, November 5, 1986.

11. John S. Shockley, *The Initiative Process in Colorado Politics: An Assessment* (Boulder: Bureau of Governmental Research and Service, University of Colorado, 1980), 9.

12. Douglas Shuit and Kenneth Reich, "130 Million Spent on Ballot Issue Campaigns," *Los Angeles Times*, November 4, 1988.

13. Edward G. Carmines and James A. Stimson, "The Two Faces of Issue Voting," *American Political Science Review* 74 (March 1980), 78.

14. Lee, "The American Experience," 56.

15. Alexander J. Groth and Howard G. Schultz, *Voter Attitudes on the 1976 California Nuclear Initiative*, Institute of Governmental Affairs Environmental Quality Series, 25 (Davis: University of California, 1976); Deborah R. Hensler and Carl Hensler, *Evaluating Nuclear Power: Voter Choice on the California Nuclear Initiative* (Santa Monica, Calif.: Rand Corporation, 1979); Robert C. Benedict *et al.*, "The Voters and Attitudes Toward Nuclear Moratorium Initiatives," *Western Political Quarterly* 33 (March 1980), 7–23.

16. Clive S. Thomas, "The Alaska Public Offices Commission: The Development and Evaluation of a Watchdog Agency," paper presented at the 1984 annual meeting of the Pacific Northwest Political Science Association, 2–3.

17. Ruth K. Scott and Ronald J. Hrebenar, *Parties in Crisis: Party Politics in America* (New York: John Wiley and Sons, 1984), 336.

18. Thomas R. Dye, *Politics in States and Communities*, 6th ed. (Englewood Cliffs, N.J.: Prentice Hall, 1988), 129–31.

19. *Ibid.*, 131.

20. Wayne L. Francis, "Leadership, Party Caucuses and Committees in the U.S. State Legislatures," *Legislative Studies Quarterly* 10 (1985), 243–57.

21. Hugh LeBlanc, "Voting in State Senates: Party and Constituency Influences," *Midwest Journal of Political Science* 13 (February 1969), 36.

22. Austin Ranney, "Parties in State Politics," in Herbert Jacob and Kenneth Vines, eds., *Politics in the American States*, 3rd ed. (Boston: Little, Brown, 1976).

23. *Ibid.*; and John F. Bibby, Cornelius P. Cotter, James L. Gibson, and Robert Huckshorn, "Parties in State Politics," in Virginia Gray, Herbert Jacob

and Kenneth N. Vines, eds., *Politics in the American States: A Comparative Analysis*, 4th ed. (Boston: Little, Brown, 1983), 66.

24. See, for example, Ronald J. Hrebenar and Clive S. Thomas, *Interest Group Politics in the American West* (Salt Lake City: University of Utah Press, 1987), chap. 1.

25. Six office indexes are generated for each of the thirteen states, for a total of seventy-eight indexes. Additionally, for each state, a state and a federal combined index is produced. Finally, indexes are calculated for each of the two subregions, and an overall western competition index is prepared. The office-specific indexes are calculated by averaging the mean Democratic party vote for the single seat offices (president, U.S. senator and governor) and the mean Democratic percentages of seats won in the multiseat offices (House of Representatives, statewide, state-level offices and the state legislatures). The means for the five Pacific states, the eight Mountain states, and the thirteen western states form the three regional indexes.

26. The number of these state-level offices varies a great deal from state to state. Some states elect only two or three such officials (governor, secretary of state, attorney general); while other states elect up to eight officials. Only those who run as partisan candidates are counted in this index.

27. Malcolm E. Jewell and David M. Olson, *Political Parties and Elections in American States*, 3rd ed. (Chicago, Ill.: Dorsey Press, 1988), 282.

28. Walter Dean Burnham, "American Politics in the 1970s," in William N. Chambers and Walter Dean Burnham, eds., *The American Party Systems*, 2nd ed. (New York: Oxford University Press, 1975); and Walter Dean Burnham, *Critical Elections and the Mainspring of American Politics* (New York: W. W. Norton, 1970).

29. V. O. Key, Jr., "A Theory of Critical Elections," *Journal of Politics* 17 (February 1955), 3–18.

30. V. O. Key, Jr., "Secular Realignment and the Party System," *Journal of Politics* 21 (1959), 198–210.

31. James L. Sundquist, *Dynamics of the Party System* (Washington, D.C.: The Brookings Institution, 1981 and 1983).

32. Burham, *Critical Elections*, 193.

33. For the perspective of those who strongly argue that realignment has occurred in the Mountain West, see Peter F. Galderisi *et al.*, eds., *The Politics of Realignment: Party Change in the Mountain West* (Boulder, Colo.: Westview Press, 1987); and Raymond Wolfinger and Michael Hagen, "Republican Prospects: Southern Comfort," *Public Opinion* (October/November 1985), 8–13.

34. See Paul A. Beck, "A Socialization Theory of Partisan Realignment," in *Controversies in American Voting Behavior*, Richard G. Niemi and Herbert F. Weisberg, eds. (San Francisco: Freeman, 1976); Bruce A. Campbell, "Patterns of Change in the Partisan Loyalties of Native Southerners," *Journal of Politics* 39 (1977), 730–61; Bruce A. Campbell and Richard J. Trilling, eds., *Realignment in American Politics* (Austin: University of Texas Press, 1980); Philip E. Con-

verse, "On the Possibility of Major Political Realignment in the South," in *Elections and the Political Order*, Angus Campbell *et al.*, eds. (New York: John Wiley and Sons, 1966); Ronald Brownstein, "The West Is Regan Country, Giving Democrats Little Hope in 1984," *National Journal* (May 12, 1984), 929–34; Cal Clark and B. Oliver Walter, "Symposium on Politics in the West: The 1980 Election," *Social Science Journal* 18 (October 1981); and Robert C. Benedict, "Alignment and Realignment in the 1986 Western Elections: A Preliminary Analysis," paper presented at the 1987 annual meeting of the Western Political Science Association. Also see Benedict's chapter, "Policy Change and Regional Alignment" in Galderisi *et al.*, *The Politics of Realignment*, 129–44.

35. Walter J. Stone, "Regional Variation in Partisan Change: Realignment in the Mountain West," in Galderisi *et al.*, *The Politics of Realignment*.

36. *Ibid.*

37. Arthur Miller, "Public Opinion and Regional Political Alignment," and Stone, "Regional Variation in Partisan Change," both in Galderisi *et al.*, *The Politics of Realignment*.

38. Miller, "Public Opinion and Regional Realignment," 100.

39. See Michael Barone and Grant Ujifusa, *Almanac of American Politics, 1988* (Washington, D.C.: National Journal, 1987); or the annual ideological ratings of each representative and senator in the *National Journal*.

40. *The New York Times*, November 10, 1988.

41. Two recent publications also have addressed the question of the changing nature of the western states' party systems. These are Gerald R. Webster, "Presidential Voting in the West," *Social Science Journal* 25, 2 (1988), 211–32; and Paul Kleppner, "Politics Without Parrties: The Western States, 1900–1984" in Gerald D. Nash and Richard W. Etulain, eds., *The Twentieth-Century West: Historical Interpretations* (Albuquerque: University of New Mexico Press, 1989), 295–338.

7

INTEREST GROUPS
AND LOBBYING

Clive S. Thomas

A HUNDRED YEARS AGO, HENRY M. YERINGTON AND
Charles "Black" Wallace doled out thousands of dollars a year in cash
and kind to Nevada state legislators and other public officials to keep
them favorably disposed to their business. Their business, and thus
their political interest, was railroads—the Virginia and Truckee Railroad and the Central Pacific Railroad respectively.[1] Nevada, like most
states in the Union and especially the West, experienced a period
around the turn of the century when railroad interests were *the dominant force* in state politics. The state of Wyoming was literally the
creation of the Union Pacific Railroad.[2] Consequently, the railroad
company was the major interest in state politics for years afterward.[3]

Both the Northern Pacific and the Great Northern Railroads exerted considerable influence in the states of Montana, Idaho and Washington; as did the Atchison, Topeka and Santa Fe Railroad in New Mexico and Arizona. And the Southern Pacific Railroad dominated California politics until the reforms of the progressive era.

In all but a few western states the political clout of the railroads has long since waned. Yet the influence and importance of interest groups—from oil and gas companies to state employees to senior citizens—live on. In many western states, interest groups are the major determinants of how politics are structured, what issues and problems are dealt with by government, and which ones are ignored. This contrasts with several states in the Northeast and the upper Midwest where political parties and other components of the political system play the major role in structuring politics and setting the policy agenda.

Therefore, because of their prominence, interest groups are especially important as vehicles of political participation in the West. In this chapter we explore and evaluate the role of these interest groups in state politics in the West. This will involve a consideration of the types of groups active in the West both past and present; the regulation of group activity; the influence of groups on public policy-making; and the strategies and tactics they use to achieve their goals (including the role of lobbyists). All this is built around the theme of comparing interest group activity in the West with its counterparts in the other three regions of the nation.

Interest Groups, Interests and Lobbies

Exactly what is an *interest group?* Those who study these groups in politics have never fully agreed on a definition. For our purpose, however, we may define an *interest group* as *any association of individuals, whether formally organized or not, that attempts to influence public policy.* This is the definition used in the Hrebenar–Thomas study, the most recent and extensive examination of interest groups in the states.[4] As a broad definition, its major advantage is that it includes not only groups like bankers, environmentalists and labor unions but also the so-called "hidden groups and lobbies"—that is, those not required to register under state law. The most important of these hidden lobbies is government itself, particularly state agencies. As these and other governments are a particularly important "lobbying force" in western states, to ignore them would be to provide an incomplete and rather distorted perspective on the role of interest groups in the West.[5]

We also need to distinguish an *interest group* from an *interest* and a *lobby*. An interest group is a specific organization like the Wyoming Truckers Association, which is an association of trucking companies. The members of this organization are also part of the broader *interest* category of transportation. This includes bus companies, air carriers, railroads, and petroleum suppliers. Truckers are also part of the even broader category of the Wyoming business *lobby*, which includes all those groups and organizations—such as oil and gas companies, bankers, retailers, liquor dealers, and a host of others—that are interested in promoting conditions favorable to business operations. On occasion, however, members of an *interest* or *lobby* find themselves on opposite sides of a political issue. This could be the case if the truckers were to seek higher weight limits for trucks on state roads, a move which the railroads might oppose, fearing it would cut their business.

Political Parties and Interest Groups as Vehicles of Political Participation

At several points in this book we have alluded to the strength of interest groups and the weakness of political parties in the West. We now begin our consideration of interest groups by explaining why this situation exists and what it means for political participation and for public policymaking in the western states.

The major means of political participation in the West, as in the rest of the nation, is by voting in elections. Yet state elections take place only every two or four years, and because of the oversimplified nature of the choices available (voting either for or against a candidate, yes or no on a ballot proposition), the messages they send are usually vague and often contradictory. Therefore, elections need to be supplemented with more specific, direct and regular links between the public and elected officials. Political parties and interest groups provide these major day-to-day links. In some aspects of their role as vehicles of political participation, parties and groups complement each other, while in other ways they compete.

The purposes of parties differ from those of interest groups in three major ways. First, political parties seek to win elections for the purpose of formally operating the machinery of government. In contrast, interest groups attempt only to influence public policy in their particular area of concern, and do not seek to run the government. Second, at least in the United States, parties have much broader support and a more wide-ranging set of policy goals than do interest groups. Groups generally represent a very narrow constituency, such as ranchers, lawyers, public utilities or environmentalists, and usually focus only on those issues which affect their members. Third, whereas political parties exist almost solely for political purposes—*i.e.*, winning elections and operating government—in most cases interest groups do not.

Usually political representation before government is only one of the purposes of most interest groups. For example, the primary purpose of the various groups that make up the education lobby is to deliver educational services, and the priority of most professional groups, such as pharmacists, lawyers and doctors, is to enhance professional knowledge and standards. The importance of political activity and lobbying among the member services provided by an interest group will be mainly a function of the purpose of the group and the extent to which public policy affects the achievement of that group's goals.

The political role of an interest group is a consequence of its need to influence public policy for the benefit of its members. Achieving influence involves a two-stage strategy. First, the group must gain access to government decision-makers—legislators, the governor and bureaucrats—and second, it must influence their actions. The pursuit of this access and influence among interest groups complements and competes with similar pursuits by political parties. The three major functions that groups and parties share are: (1) securing political benefits in the form of policies, as discussed above; (2) providing political representation; and (3) facilitating the election process.

In their representational role, interest groups, like political parties, act as a means for aggregating the needs and policy preferences of their members and articulating these to government. A particularly important role of groups, but much less significant for parties, is the provision of information to policymakers. The informational role of interest groups is essential to the governmental process, because both political and technical information is essential to public policymaking. Organizations as diverse as those representing utilities, insurance companies, trailer court owners, and gambling interests are often the most knowledgeable in their particular fields. Groups often lend their expertise in drafting bills and amendments. Control over technical information is an important component of group power. This is one reason why government agencies are significant lobbying forces.

As vehicles of representation, however, interest groups are far from ideal. The major problem is that not all segments of the population are represented equally in interest groups. The bias is toward the better educated, higher income, white, and male segments of the population. Nonwhites, minorities (including women), the less well educated and lower income segments are underrepresented by interest groups in the political process.[6] As umbrella organizations embracing a host of groups and interests, parties are far more representative political organizations.

Besides endorsing certain candidates and perhaps openly opposing others, interest groups can participate in elections in three major ways: by recruiting candidates, by providing campaign support in the form of workers and other services, and by contributing money. While all three have increased in recent years, the proliferation of political action committees (PACs), which have the primary and often sole purpose of channeling money to candidates, has been phenomenal.

While the complementary role of interest groups and parties has provided essential elements of political participation, the competition between them in this regard has had the most impact on the operation of state politics and policymaking. In fact, while it is far from a simple relationship, a characteristic of state politics is that the stronger the parties are, the less influential interest groups will be; and the weaker the parties, the greater will be the impact of interest groups.[7] In this competitive situation, interest groups have come out on top in most states through the years and have continued to consolidate their position. This has been the case particularly in the West.[8]

In the West, as elsewhere, a major reason for the political power of interest groups is that their relatively homogeneous constituency and narrowly defined goals make them more effective agents of representation for specific interests than parties. Parties have been less effective because they are essentially broad coalitions of interests and tend to pursue broad issues and policies, as opposed to the concerns of small and very narrow interest groups. Consequently, those seeking specific policy goals in the states, and particularly in the western states, have been more likely to use an interest group than a political party. Also, over the years the narrower constituency and policy focus of interest groups have made them very adaptable to their political environment. On the other hand, political parties, with their much

broader base of representation, their cumbersome organizational machinery, and their more general, long-term, and nebulous goals, have
far less ability to adapt. In addition, interest groups have often filled
the void in state political systems by taking over essential political
functions, such as candidate recruitment and the financing of election
campaigns that parties would not or could not perform. In fact, the
increased role of groups in the financing of elections has been primarily responsible for their increased prominence and power in recent
years.

Their adaptabilty, performance of essential political functions, and
unparalleled success in securing benefits have made interest groups
a consistent and prominent feature of state politics. Add to this the
fact that political parties were weak from the start in the West, and
that they were prevented from developing strong organizations as a
result of populist and progressive reforms: then it is easy to understand why in most western states interest groups have been and
remain the major influence on public policymaking.

Similarities and Differences in Interest Group Systems

While interest groups continue to be very influential in the politics
of all western states, there is variation, and in some instances considerable variation, among the thirteen states in the make-up and
operation of their group systems. The group system in California, for
instance, is far more diverse and developed than those operating in
states like Montana, Idaho and Alaska. In Table 7.1 we set out eight
factors that help account for such similarities and differences. Specifically, this information will shed light on three key aspects of group
activity as it relates to political participation and state public policymaking in the West: (1) the types of interest groups that are active;
(2) the methods they use in pursuing their goals; and (3) the power
that they exert.

These eight factors and their components are interrelated. A change
in one may reflect or lead to a change in one or more of the other
factors. Any change at all is likely to affect the nature of group activity,
and major changes will have a significant impact on the interest group
and lobbying scene in a particular state, or even on the states as a

Table 7.1   Eight Major Factors Influencing the Make-up, Operating Techniques and Impact on Public Policy of Interest Group Systems in the States

Factor	Influence
1. *State Policy Domain*	Constitutional/legal authority of a state affects which groups will be politically active. Policies actually exercised by a state affect which groups will be most active. The policy priorities of a state will affect which groups are most influential.
2. *Centralization/Decentralization of Spending*	This refers to the amount of money spent by state governments versus that spent by local governments. The higher the percentage of state spending on individual programs and overall on services, the more intense will be lobbying in the state capital.
3. *Political Attitudes*	Especially relevant are political culture, and political ideology viewed in terms of conservative/liberal attitudes. Affects the type and extent of policies adopted; the level of integration/fragmentation and professionalization of the policymaking process; acceptable lobbying techniques; and the comprehensiveness and stringency of enforcement of public disclosure laws, including lobby laws.
4. *Level of Integration/ Fragmentation of the Policy Process*	Included are strength of political parties; power of the governor; number of directly elected cabinet members; number of independent boards and commissions; initiative, referendum and recall. These influence the number of options available to groups: greater integration decreases them, while more fragmentation increases the options.
5. *Level of Professionalization of State Government*	Includes state legislators, support services, and bureaucracy, including the governor's staff. Impacts the extent to which public officials need group resources and information. Also affects the level of professionalization of the lobbying system.
6. *Level of Socioeconomic Development*	Increased socioeconomic diversity will tend to produce: a more diverse and competitive group system; a decline in the dominance of one or an oligarchy of groups; new and more sophisticated techniques of lobbying, such as an increase in contract lobbyists, lawyer-lobbyists, multiclient/multiservice lobbying firms, grassroots campaigns and public relations techniques, and a general rise in the professionalization of lobbyists and lobbying.
7. *Extensiveness and Enforcement of Public Disclosure Laws*	Includes lobby laws, campaign finance laws, PAC regulations, and conflict of interest provisions. These provisions increase public information about lobbying activities. Such information has impacted the methods and techniques of lobbying, in turn this has affected the power of certain groups and lobbyists.
8. *Level of Campaign Costs and Sources of Support*	As the proportion of group funding increases, especially that from PACs, group access and power increases.

Sources: Adapted by the author for the West from fig. 4.1 in Clive S. Thomas and Ronald J. Hrebenar, "Interest Groups in the States," chap. 4 in Virginia Gray, Herbert Jacob and Robert Albritton, eds., *Politics in the American States: A Comparative Analysis*, 5th ed. (Glenview, Ill.: Scott Foresman/Little, Brown, 1990).

whole. We can now use this information to understand the development, role and effectiveness of groups as vehicles of political participation in the West.

THE DEVELOPMENT OF INTEREST GROUP SYSTEMS IN THE WEST

From territorial days until the 1960s the interest group systems in the West, like those in most states, were very narrowly based. A narrow range of interests was represented in state capitals and a handful of powerful interests dominated the group system and often the state politics as well. This becomes easier to understand after considering the factors that influence interest group activity in the states as set out in Table 7.1. In this period all the western state economies were almost entirely dependent on three forms of livelihood—agriculture, natural resource extraction, and railroads. Alaska, with one federally owned railroad, and Hawaii, with no railroads, were equally dependent upon shipping companies. Furthermore, the way that economic development occurred in the early West meant that most states were dependent on one or a very few business enterprises.

The railroads were important as employers and because for several years they held a transportation monopoly. Even after the advent of the truck and the airplane, the railroads were for many years (and in many instances remain) the only feasible means of moving freight in the vast region of the West. In most states one or two mining or other primary product companies were the other dominant economic interests. In Arizona it was Phelps Dodge and other copper and mining concerns; in Montana it was the Anaconda Company, also a copper concern; in Oregon and Alaska it was the lumber and pulp companies; and also in Alaska, the salmon canneries. In Hawaii it was the pineapple and sugar interests.

The dominant philosophy of *laissez faire* meant that the role of the states was far less extensive than it is today. As a consequence, state bureaucracies were small and the level of professionalism of the state civil service was low. Professionalism was also minimal among elected state officials, especially legislators. Because of the small range of policy areas in which the states were involved, most legislatures met only once every two years. Public disclosure provisions were also minimal; and where they existed they were loosely enforced. With all this, plus the traditional weakness of parties and political institutions, it is easy to see why all western states were dominated by a few powerful economic interests until the 1960s.

As in other regions of the nation, business interests were dominant in the West. Besides the organizations we have already mentioned, banks were also important political forces. Beginning around the turn of the century, agricultural groups such as state farm bureaus and stockgrowers and commodity associations also began to develop a political voice in western state capitals. From the late 1930s on, these were joined by local government groups, labor unions and education interests, especially schoolteachers. Together these five interests—business, agriculture, labor, local government and education—formed the major interests operating in the state capitals of the West, and in the states in general, in the early 1960s.

One long-lasting aspect of the state lobbying scene that resulted from these loose environmental constraints both in the West and elsewhere was that most famous, or perhaps notorious, of stereotyped lobbying styles—the wheeler-dealer. This style is easier to recognize than to define. Generally, it refers to a powerful lobbyist who operates in an aggressive and flamboyant manner and is willing to use a variety of methods—some of which may be suspect—to achieve his or her goals. As with many other aspects of the pre-1960s lobbying community, it is impossible to determine how widespread the wheeler-dealers were in the states. The nature of politics at the time and the lack of public disclosure and professionalism, however, lead to the conclusion that this was the dominant lobbying style.

It is hard to determine when the changes began that were to transform state interest groups' activity. By the late 1960s, however, they were well under way. At the root of these changes was a confluence of factors transforming almost all aspects of American life since World War II. Among these was the increasing importance of the service sector of the economy. Changes in the attitude about the role of government in society brought about by modern American liberalism have also been important; as have increases in urbanization, the standard of living, and the level of education. There has been an increase in political efficacy on the part of many sectors of society, particularly in minority groups; and, a related point, a general increase in political awareness was brought about by the civil rights movement, the Vietnam War and Watergate. These developments have transformed interest group activity in state capitals in the West, as elsewhere, in several significant ways.

Public Disclosure of Lobbying Activities: Registered and Nonregistered Groups

To appreciate fully the consequences of these developments on interest group activity in the western states, we need to realize that actual lobbying activity is much more extensive than public disclosure information about interest groups reveals. This is because in the West several types of groups and interests are not required to register. Consequently, there are many nonregistered or "hidden groups and lobbies" at work in the western state capitals.

As Table 7.1 (Factor 7) sets out, there are four types of provisions helping to provide some public monitoring of interest group activity: lobby laws; conflict of interest provisions; campaign finance disclosure; and rules regulating the activities of PACs. As previously noted, while the first three types of laws existed in most western states before the 1970s, they were usually weak and casually enforced. It took the Watergate affair of 1973–74 to generate a reform movement across the nation against political corruption, and more extensive and stringently enforced public disclosure laws resulted. This movement also included the regulation of PACs. These were burgeoning largely as a result of declining political parties, rising campaign costs, and, in many states, the imposition of limits on campaign contributions.

Throughout the West in the 1970s, new agencies like California's Fair Political Practices Commission and Washington's Public Disclosure Commission were created to administer these public disclosure provisions. An indication of the fervent activity attempting to regulate western PACs can be gleaned from Table 7.2. This lists the agency in each state primarily responsible for the regulation and monitoring of PAC activity. It also lists the year the major provisions were enacted and the years that major revisions to those laws were made. Utah (1988) and Nevada (1989) were the last two states in the West, and indeed in the nation, to enact statutes specifically regulating PACs.

It is, however, state lobby laws that provide the most specific and comprehensive information about interest group activity. The thrust of these laws is to provide public information and throw light on group activities rather than to restrict or attempt to control them. In fact, because of the provisions relating to the right to "petition government" in the First Amendment to the U.S. Constitution and similar provisions in many state constitutions, attempts to restrict lobbying would run into serious constitutional problems. These laws, however, vary in their inclusiveness, their reporting requirements, and the stringency with which they are enforced. The variations for the western states can be seen in Table 7.3.

In particular, the differences in *who is* and *who is not* required to register as a lobbyist under the various state laws produce a wide variation in the number of persons registering as lobbyists, as well

Table 7.2   Agencies Responsible for PAC Registration in the Western States

State	Agency	Year of Major Law/Revisions
Alaska	Alaska Public Offices Commission	1974,[a] 1975, 1980, 1985
Arizona	State Elections Officer (Sec. of State)	1974, 1978, 1979,[a] 1980, 1984, 1985
California	California Fair Political Practices Commission	1974,[a] amended yearly since
Colorado	Elections Officer (Sec. of State)	1974,[a] 1975, 1976, 1978, 1979, 1980, 1983, 1984, 1985, 1986, 1987
Hawaii	Campaign Spending Commission, State Ethics Commission	1974,[a] 1976, 1978, 1980
Idaho	Elections Division (Sec. of State)	1974,[a] 1976, 1977, 1983
Montana	Commissioner of Political Practices	1975,[a] 1979, 1987
Nevada	Elections Division (Sec. of State)	1989
New Mexico	Director of Elections (Sec. of State)	1978,[a] 1981, 1985
Oregon	Government Ethics Commission	1971, 1973, 1975, 1977, 1979, 1983, 1985, 1987[a]
Utah	Lieutenant Governor	1988
Washington	Public Disclosure Commission	1972[a] (Ballot initiative), 1975, 1977, 1979, 1982, 1984, 1985, 1986, 1987
Wyoming	Elections Assistant (Sec. of State)	1973,[a] 1985

[a]Year major provisions enacted.

Source: Michael R. Young, "Political Action Committees in the American West" (unpublished manuscript, University of Alaska, Juneau, 1988). Updated by Clive S. Thomas.

as those registering as lobbying organizations (that is, the employers or clients of lobbyists). These variations are set out in Table 7.4. A glance at Tables 7.3 and 7.4 leads to questions about the value of registration information as an indication of both the types of interests that lobby and the actual amount of lobbying that takes place. For example, common sense would lead us to assume that there would be more lobbyists and lobbying activity in California with its 28 million inhabitants and with one of the most diverse interest group systems in the nation than in Montana with less than 1 million people and a narrower range of groups. According to Table 7.4, however, Montana has more lobbyists. In fact, Arizona, New Mexico, Utah and Wyoming also have more lobbyists than California, according to the public disclosure records. This is not the practical reality: there are probably more people lobbying in Sacramento than in any state capital in the country and certainly many more than in any other western state.

Table 7.3 Legal Definition of Lobbyists, Their Reporting Requirements, and Prohibited Lobbying Activities in the 13 Western States

	AK	AZ	CA	CO	HI	ID	MT	NV	NM	OR	UT	WA	WY
DEFINITION INCLUDES:													
Legislative/parliamentary lobbying	*	*	*	*	*	*	*	*	*	*	*	*	*
Administrative agency lobbying	*	*	*	—	*	—	—	—	—	—	*	*	—
Elective officials as lobbyists	—	—	—	*	—	—	—	—	—	*	—	*	—
Public employees as lobbyists	—	—	—	—	—	—	*	—	—	*	*	*	—
Specified level of compensation received by lobbyist	—	—	*	*	*	*	—	—	—	—	*	*	*
Specified amount spent on lobbying	—	—	—	*	*	—	—	—	—	*	*	*	—
Specified amount of time spent lobbying	*	—	*(c)	—	*	—	—	—	—	*	*	*	—
REQUIRED TO REGISTER:													
Those having contact with state officials	*	*(b)	*	*	*	*	*	*	*	*	—	(ag)	—
Those employing individuals having contact (employers/clients)	*	*(b)	*	—	*	—	*	—	—	*	*	*	—
Public officials lobbying in their official capacity	—	—	—	—	—	—	—	—	(s)	—	—	*	—
Other	(a)	—	—	—	—	—	—	—	—	(ad)	—	—	(ag)
PROHIBITED ACTIVITIES													
Lobbyists making campaign contributions at any time	—	—	—	—	—	—	—	—	—	*	—	—	—

Lobbyists making campaign contributions during legislative sessions	—	—	—	—	—	—	—	—	—	—
Lobbyists making expenditures in excess of ($) per official per year	—	—	—	—	—	100	—	—	—	—
Solicitation of lobbyists by officials or employees for contributions or gifts	—	—	(d)	—	(f)	—	—	—	—	—
Other					(f,h m, aa)		(f)	(f, m)		*

KEY:

* Application exists.

— Application does not exist.

(a) Those compensated to have contact and the clients of the lobbyist.

(b) Principal must register and identify the lobbyist(s).

(c) Number of contacts.

(d) Lobbyists making gifts in excess of $10 per month per official.

(f) Contingency basis lobbying.

(h) Instigating legislative and/or administrative action for the purpose of obtaining employment in support or defeat thereof.

(m) Making false statements or misrepresentation to legislators.

(s) Those compensated for attempting to influence the outcome of legislative matters.

(aa) Using information from lobbyists reports in soliciting contributions.

(ad) Anyone exceeding 16 hours or $50 in a calendar quarter, influencing or attempting to influence legislative action (not limited to direct communication).

(ag) Any person paid to represent interest of another in affecting legislation.

Source: Adapted by the author from COGEL [Council on Governmental Ethics Laws], Campaign Finance, Ethics & Lobby Law Blue Book 1988–89: Special Report (Lexington, Ky.: COGEL through the Council of State Governments, 1988), table 21, pp. 157–59. Reprinted with permission.

Table 7.4   Number of Registered Lobbyists and Their Employers/Clients in the 13 Western States in a Typical Year During the 1980s

	Lobbyists	Lobbyists' Employers/Clients
Alaska	225	225
Arizona	4,500	600
California	700	n.a.[a]
Colorado	475–500	250
Hawaii	150	100
Idaho	270	n.r.[b]
Montana	750	300
Nevada	500	n.r.[b]
New Mexico	750	n.r.[b]
Oregon	700	900
Utah	800–900	n.a.[a]
Washington	800	700
Wyoming	800	430

[a]n.a.: information not available.

[b]n.r.: not required to register.

Source: Adapted by the author from COGEL [Council on Governmental Ethics Laws], *Campaign Finance, Ethics & Lobby Law Blue Book 1988–89: Special Report* (Lexington, Ky.: COGEL through the Council of State Governments, 1988), table 21, pp. 157–59. Reprinted with permission.

The comparisons in Table 7.4 are distorted because of the differences in the definition of a *lobbyist* and who is required to register as set out in Table 7.3. States like Utah and Oregon require public employees to register as lobbyists, thus they tend to have higher numbers. California and Hawaii exempt public employees from registering. Differences in other provisions lead to further distortions.

As we mentioned in considering our definition of an *interest group*, the largest nonregistered or hidden lobby in the states is state government—particularly state agencies, boards and commission—and local governments. Because of the particular reliance of the West on government, these are very significant lobbying forces in western states, even in California. The Hrebenar–Thomas study revealed that as many as one-third of those "lobbyists" working the halls of government in the West on any one day represented government. Therefore, to obtain an accurate picture of interest group activity in the West, we cannot ignore government, even though studying its lobbying role presents problems that are due to the absence of information.

Interests Active in the Western States Today

Since the 1960s there has been a great expansion in group activity along three dimensions. First, there has been an expansion in the number of groups seeking to influence state government. Second, the range of interests has also expanded as new interests—such as groups organized around social issues, public interests, and single issues—have entered the political arena, and as traditional interests have fragmented. Fragmentation has been particularly evident within the business and local-government lobbies. Individual corporations and businesses along with cities and special districts (especially school districts) have increasingly lobbied on their own. They have done so because, although they may remain part of an umbrella organization—chamber of commerce, trade association, municipal league— they see their specific interests as not being fully served by the umbrella group. The third dimension of this expansion is that groups are lobbying harder than they did twenty or even ten years ago: they have more regular contact with public officials, and they use more sophisticated techniques.

Given the shortcomings of lobby registration records, we use the definition stated at the beginning of this chapter in order to obtain as accurate a picture as possible of the range of groups and interests operating in western state capitals today. This range is shown in Table 7.5. Interests are listed on the basis of two criteria. The first criterion is the extent of their presence in the thirteen states, which is indicated by the two columns. The second criterion is whether an interest is continually active in the states where it is present, or intermittently active in some or all of the states where it exists. Both continually and intermittently active interests are listed in order of the estimated intensity of their lobbying efforts across the region.

The bulk of the interests appear in the first column indicating they are present in all thirteen states. Although not all are continually active, this means that a very broad range of interests, both public and private, operate in the West today. In terms of time and money, however, probably as much as 75% of the lobbying effort is attributable to the twenty interests in the "continually active" category.

The increasing prominence of several interests is worth noting. We have already metioned individual cities, special local government districts, and state agencies. The most prominent agencies in terms of lobbying effort in all states are the departments of education or public instruction, transportation and welfare in addition to state

Table 7.5   Interests Active in the Western States

Type	Present in All 13 States[a]	Present in 1 to 12 States
Continually Active	Individual business corporations[a]	Railroads
	Local government units (cities, districts, etc.)	Health care corporations
	State departments, boards and commissions	Agribusiness corporations
	Business trade associations[b]	Latino groups
	Utility companies and associations (public and private)	Gambling/race tracks/lotteries
	Banks and financial institutions/associations	Commercial fishers
	Insurance companies/associations	
	Public employee unions/associations (state and local)	
	Universities and colleges (public and private)	
	Schoolteachers unions/associations	
	Local government associations	
	Farmers' organizations/commodity associations	
	Traditional labor unions	
	Labor associations (mainly AFL-CIO)	
	Environmentalists	
	Oil and gas companies/associations	
	Hospital associations	
	Tourism groups	
	Mining companies	
	Sportsmen's groups (esp. hunting and fishing)	
Intermittently Active	Doctors	Taxpayers groups
	Trial lawyers/state bar associations	Native American groups
	Retailers' associations	Animal rights groups
	Contractors/real estate	Welfare rights groups
	Liquor interests	Foreign businesses (esp. from Japan)
	Communication interests (telecommunication, cable TV, etc.)	Children's rights groups
	Truckers	Media associations

Women's groups
Groups for the arts
Pro and anti abortion groups
Religious groups
Senior citizens groups
Social service groups and coalitions
Good government groups (League of Women Voters, Common Cause)
American Civil Liberties Union
Federal agencies
Black American groups
Groups for the physically and mentally handicapped
Student groups
Nurses
Chiropractors
Parent teacher associations
Consumer groups
Veterans' groups
Moral Majority
Community groups
Pro and anti gun control groups

Pro and anti smoking interests

[a]An unavoidably broad category. It includes manufacturing and service corporations with the exception of those listed separately, *e.g.*, private utilities and oil and gas companies. These and other business corporations were listed separately because of their frequency of presence across the western states.
[b]Another unavoidably broad category. It includes chambers of commerce as well as specific trade associations, *e.g.*, truckers, air carriers, manufacturers' associations, etc.

Sources: Adapted by the author for the West from table 4.1 in Clive S. Thomas and Ronald J. Hrebenar, "Interest Groups in the States," chap. 4 in Virginia Gray, Herbert Jacob and Robert Albritton, eds., *Politics in the American States: A Comparative Analysis,* 5th ed. (Glenview, Ill.: Scott Foresman/Little, Brown, 1990); and from the thirteen state chapters in Ronald J. Hrebenar and Clive S. Thomas, eds., *Interest Group Politics in the American West* (Salt Lake City: University of Utah Press, 1987).

universities and colleges. Associated with this rise of government lobbying has been the increased prominence of public sector unions, particularly state and local employees' and teachers' unions. Ideological groups, which are also often single-issue groups such as anti-abortionists, have also become active in recent years. Public interest organizations, particularly good government, senior citizen, and—most of all—environmentalist groups are other forces that now have a significant presence in all western state capitals.

Interests listed in the other column tend to be newly formed groups, such as consumer and animal rights groups, or those representing an interest concentrated in certain states, such as gambling and commercial fishing.

By any definition or categorization, this range of interests is no longer narrow, though it is important to note that the diversity of the group system will vary from state to state. It is also important not to equate *presence* with *power*. The active presence of a group or interest does not by itself assure success in achieving its goals. As we shall see in the following sections, some of the interests listed in Table 7.5 are very effective most of the time, while others have very little influence at all.

Interest Group Influence on Public Policy

In the study of interest groups, the concept of group power is used in two distinct but interrelated ways. It may refer either to the power of individual groups, interests and lobbies or to the power or impact of interest groups as a whole on the political system of a particular state.

The Hrebenar–Thomas study defined the *power* of an individual group, interest or lobby as *its ability to achieve its goals as it defines them.* Many problems face those who attempt to measure the power of individual groups. These problems arise from the fact that there are numerous variables or influences involved, several of which are extremely volatile or dynamic in nature. Among them are political climate and public opinion as well as power relationships between public officials. For our assessment of the West, we rely on the Hrebenar–Thomas study, which used a combination of quantitative and qualitative techniques to measure power of individual groups.[9] The results are set out in Tables 7.6 and 7.7.

Table 7.6 lists the interest groups in each state that are the most effective and those that are of the second level of effectiveness. Table

7.7 ranks interests in terms of their effectiveness across the West as a region and compares these rankings with those for the fifty states as a whole. By examining these two tables and by comparing them with Sarah McCally Morehouse's assessment of group power in the states a decade ago,[10] we can detect several trends and offer some observations.

One observation is that the days of states being run by one or two dominant interests—the Union Pacific Railroad in Wyoming, the "Big Five Companies" in Hawaii, the salmon canneries in Alaska—are virtually gone. In other words, there are no longer any "company states." To be sure, many states still have a single prominent interest, such as Boeing in Washington State, gambling in Nevada and oil in Wyoming, Alaska and New Mexico. But these interests must share power with other groups. Thus, as the result of expanding political pluralism, the days when one interest could dictate policy on a wide range of issues appears to be gone. We should be careful, however, not to assume that the decline of the dominance of individual interests has also meant the decline of interest group systems as a whole. This has certainly not been the case, as we will explain.

As to the power status of the so-called traditional interests in the West—business, agriculture, labor, education, and local government—three of these have maintained or enhanced their power while two have lost ground. Education interests (especially schoolteachers), local governments, and business remain very influential. Contrary to some predictions, increased political pluralism and fragmentation within the business community do not appear to have significantly affected its power. To be sure, some businesses have experienced an erosion of their political power in certain states. These include the railroads and some natural resource enterprises such as mining. However, these have been replaced by service and other businesses among the ranks of the most powerful groups. On the other hand, agriculture and traditional labor have suffered some loss of power, even though they still rank among the most influential interests.

In the case of labor, political power has passed from the traditional unions to public employees such as teachers and state and local public employees. The rise of state employees associations is one of the most noteworthy phenomena in the changing configuration of interest group power in western state capitals. It appears to be linked to the increased role of government since the 1960s. This rise in the importance of government has also enhanced the power of many state agencies,

Table 7.6   The Most Influential Interest Groups in the 13 Western States

State	Interest Groups
Alaska	*Most effective:* AK Municipal League (and individual municipalities); state and local govt employees (esp AK State Employees Assn, AK Public Employees Assn); NEA-Alaska (and the education lobby in general); environmentalists; oil industry
	Second level: AK Native groups; Alascom (telecommunications); contractors; AFL-CIO and traditional labor unions; trial lawyers; insurance lobby (esp medical underwriters); Chamber of Commerce
Arizona	*Most effective:* AZ Manufacturers Assn; AZ Chamber of Commerce; AZ Farm Bureau; AZ Business Council; AZ Mining Assn; League of AZ Cities and Towns; AZ Ed Assn[a]; utilities (esp AZ Public Service Company, the Salt River Project)
	Second level: AZ Fed of Labor; Assn of Retired Employees; Firemen's Assn; farm groups (other than the Farm Bureau); The Liquor Assn; AZ Assn of Counties; realtors; banks; health and medical groups; senior citizens; individual manufacturers (esp Motorola and others involved in electronics and computers)
California	*Most effective:* CA Manufacturers Assn; Standard Oil of CA; CA Farm Bureau; The Wine Institute (wine makers); CA Medical Assn[b]; Bank of America; Pacific Bell; CA Assn of Realtors; CA Bar Assn; CA State Employees Assn; Western Growers Assn (formerly CA Growers Assn)
	Second level: CA Teachers Assn; Uni of California; AFL-CIO; CA Bankers Assn
Colorado	*Most effective:* CO Assn of Commerce and Industry; CO Assn of Realtors; financial institutions (esp independent bankers, savings & loans); education (esp CO Ed Assn, universities and colleges); local govts (esp CO Municipal League, CO Counties, Inc.)
	Second level: Transportation interests (esp CO Motor Carriers); cattle ranchers and agricultural groups; water interests (conservation and irrigation); construction industry; oil; corrections (police, sheriffs, community corrections); trial lawyers; district attorneys; occupational groups (esp doctors)
Hawaii	*Most effective:* Big business (esp banks, developers, agribusiness, Business Roundtable); HI School Teachers Assn; public employees (esp the HI Government Employees Assn); traditional labor unions (esp the International Longshoremen and Warehousemen's Union); tourist industry
	Second level: Mainland and foreign investment interests (esp from Japan) and their local representatives (law firms, realtors, etc.); small business; Native Hawaiian groups; immigrant groups (esp Filipinos); education interests; environmentalists; insurance industry; lawyers; health care groups; public interest groups
Idaho	*Most effective:* ID Power Company; ID Ed Assn; ID Farm Bureau; ID Cattlemen's Assn; Assn of Commerce and Industry; Assn of ID Cities; mining and forest industries; Mormon Church
	Second level: AFL-CIO; Associated Taxpayers of ID
Montana	*Most effective:* MT Power Company (utility); MT Ed Assn; MT State AFL-CIO; MT Chamber of Commerce; MT Stockgrowers Assn
	Second level: MT Bankers Assn; Burlington Northern Railroad; Women's Lobby Fund; Local Government Coalition (League of Cities and Towns, MT Assn of Counties); Environmental Coalition (Environmental Information Center, Northern Plains Resource Council, Audubon Soc.); MT Coal Council
Nevada	*Most effective:* NV Resorts Assn (Las Vegas casinos); Associated General Contractors; Clark County (Las Vegas area); interstate banks (esp Citibank, Security Pacific Corp., First Interstate, Valley, American Express); utilities (esp NV Power Company, Sierra Pacific Resources, Southern California Edison, Los Angeles Dept of Water and Power); NV Gaming Assn (casinos from outside Las Vegas); corporate mining (esp Freeport McMoran, Newmont Gold, FMC Gold); NV Sheriffs and Police Chiefs Assn
	Second level: NV Assn of Counties; City of Las Vegas; NV Trial Lawyers Assn; NV Mining Assn (small mine owners); NV State Ed Assn; NV League of Cities; State of NV Employees Assn; NV Women's Lobby

State	Interest Groups
New Mexico	*Most effective:* Utilities (esp Public Service Company of NM, Southwestern Public Service Company, El Paso Electric, El Paso Natural Gas Company); schoolteachers (NM Ed Assn, NM Fed of Teachers); oil and gas (NM Oil and Gas Assn, Independent Petroleum Assn, and individual producers); local govts (esp NM Municipal League, NM Assn of Counties, City of Albuquerque)
	Second level: AFL-CIO; insurance industry; NM Trial Lawyers Assn; NM Bankers Assn; telecommunications industry; liquor lobby (esp NM Beverage Alcohol Wholesalers, NM Liquor Dealers Assn); NM Hospital Assn
Oregon	*Most effective:* Associated OR Industries; K-12 education lobby (esp OR Ed Assn, OR Council of School Administrators, OR School Boards Assn); AFL-CIO; public employees unions (esp the OR Public Employees Union, American Federation of State County and Municipal Employees); OR Med Assn; women's group coalition (OR chapter of the National Organization of Women, Women's Political Caucus, Women's Rights Coalition); higher education (institutions and faculty)
	Second level: American Electrical Assn (high-tech companies); utilities (Pacific Power and Light, Portland General Gas and Electric, Northwest Natural Gas); banks and savings and loans; forest product companies (esp Crown-Zellerbach, Weyerhaeuser); insurance lobby (esp auto and health); local govts (esp League of OR Cities, City of Portland, and Eugene); agriculture; State Bar Assn; port authorities
Utah	*Most effective:* Mormon Church; oil and gas (esp the UT Petroleum Assn, the Western Petroleum Marketers Assn); UT Public Employees Assn; UT Ed Assn; utilities (esp Mountain Fuel, UT Power and Light); banking (esp the UT Bankers Assn); business groups; local govts (esp Salt Lake City, Salt Lake County); AFL-CIO
	Second level: Mining groups; agricultural groups; industrial groups; UT Taxpayers Assn; higher ed (esp the State Board of Regents, the University of Utah)
Washington	*Most effective:* WA Ed Assn; WA State Labor Council (and labor in general); Assn of WA Business; WA Fed of State Employees; Boeing; finance and banking; senior citizens; United for WA (business PAC only); utilities; forest products
	Second level: Wine and beer; agriculture; environmentalists; contractors and developers; commercial fishing
Wyoming	*Most effective:* WY Mining Assn; WY Ed Assn; banks and financial institutions; farm groups (esp Stock Growers Assn, Farm Bureau); insurance (esp medical liability underwriters); WY Med Soc; Trial Lawyers; WY Truckers Assn; WY Liquor Dealers Assn
	Second level: WY Assn of Municipalities; Union Pacific Railroad; WY Public Employees Assn; Uni of Wyoming; oil and gas; WY Outfitters (tourism group); WY Heritage Soc. (business development group, funds the WY Heritage Foundation, a public policy think tank)

Note: Abbreviations used in this table are:
  AFL-CIO = American Federation of Labor–Congress of Industrial Organizations
  Assn = Association
  Ed = Education
  esp = especially
  Fed = Federation
  govt = government
  Med = Medical
  NEA = National Education Association
  Uni = University
[a]The designation *Education Association* in the formal name of a group indicates a schoolteachers' organization, *e.g.*, the Washington Education Association.
[b]The designation *Medical Association* in the formal name of a group indicates a general practitioners' organization, *e.g.*, the Oregon Medical Association.

Source: Adapted for the West by the author from Appendix A "The Most Influential Interests in the Fifty States" in Virginia Gray, Herbert Jacob and Robert Albritton, eds., *Politics in the American States: A Comparative Analysis*, 5th ed. (Glenview, Ill.: Scott Foresman/Little, Brown, 1990). This Appendix was compiled by Clive S. Thomas and Ronald J. Hrebenar from the Hrebenar-Thomas study of interest groups in the fifty states.

Table 7.7   Ranking of the 20 Most Effective Interests in the 13 Western States Compared with the 50 States as a Whole

Interest and Rank in West	Overall Rank in the 50 States	Number of States in the West in Which Interest Ranked among:		
		Most Effective	Second Level of Effectiveness	Less Effective
1. Schoolteachers' organizations (predominantly NEA)	1	11	2	0
2. Utility companies and associations (electric, gas, telephone, water)	6	8	3	2
3. General business organizations (chambers of commerce, etc.)	2	7	3	3
4. General local government organizations (municipal leagues, county organizations, etc.)	10	6	5	2
5. State and local government employees (other than teachers)	12	6	4	3
6. Individual banks and financial institutions	7	6	3	4
7. Bankers' associations (includes savings and loan associations)	3	5	5	3
8. Manufacturers[a] (companies and associations)	4	5	4	4
8. Traditional labor associations[a] (predominantly the AFL-CIO)	5	5	4	4

8. Agricultural commodity organizations[a] (stockgrowers, grain growers, etc.)	18	5	4	4
11. General farm organizations (mainly state farm bureaus)	10	4	5	4
12. Mining companies and associations	26	4	3	6
13. Oil and gas[a] (companies and associations)	13	4	2	7
13. Individual cities and towns[a]	24	4	2	7
15. Lawyers (predominantly state bar associations and trial lawyers)	8	2	6	5
16. Doctors/general practitioners (state medical associations)	11	3	3	7
17. Insurance (companies and associations)	13	3	2	8
18. Universities and colleges (institutions and personnel)	19	2	4	7
19. K-12 education interests (other than teachers)	16	3	1	9
20. Contractors/builders/developers	22	2	3	8

[a]Tied ranking

Source: Rankings for the West are based on Table 7.6. They were calculated by allocating 2 points for each "most effective" placement and 1 point for each "second level of effectiveness" placement and adding the totals. Where a tie in total points occurs, where possible, interests are ranked according to the number of "most effective" placements. Overall rankings for the fifty states are taken from table 4.2, "Ranking of the Forty Most Effective Interests in the Fifty States," in Clive S. Thomas and Ronald J. Hrebenar, "Interest Groups in the States," chap. 4 in Virginia Gray, Herbert Jacob and Robert Albritton, eds., *Politics in the American States: A Comparative Analysis*, 5th ed. (Glenview, Ill.: Scott Foresman/Little, Brown, 1990). Rankings in that table were calculated similarly to those for the West in this chapter.

particularly the departments of education and the state university systems.

Less significant but steady gains have been made by environmentalists, minority groups (including women's groups), senior citizens, and the various components of the health care industry other than doctors. None of these rank in Table 7.7. They place twenty-first, twenty-fifth, twenty-seventh and thirty-first in the West respectively. Recently, single-issue groups have also achieved some successes: for example, taxpayers' groups in California and Idaho; ABATE, a Wyoming group opposing mandatory crash helmets for motorcyclists; and Mothers Against Drunk Driving (MADD) in several western states. However, many of these groups are now inactive or declining in influence. The issue of tort reform, particularly the attempt to place a cap on awards in damage suits, brought three of the best-financed and best-organized interests—doctors, lawyers and insurance companies—into the ranks of the most effective interests in the West during the latter 1980s.

The relatively high ranking in Table 7.7 of some interests in the West when compared with the fifty states as a whole indicates the importance of government and certain types of economic activity to the region's economy and thus to its political life. We have already mentioned state and local employees associations, ranked twelfth overall but sixth in the West. Other examples are utility companies and associations, general local government organizations, individual towns and cities, agricultural commodity associations, and the oil and gas industry. Mining companies and associations provide the greatest contrast of all. These rank twenty-sixth in the fifty states as a whole but twelfth in the West.

The successes of other interests, such as social issue groups, do not appear to have been significant enough across the western states to emerge as a trend. Indeed, the changes in the configuration of interest group power across the West, as in the other states, has been far less dramatic over the last twenty-five years than the major expansion in interest group activity might lead us to assume. This is not surprising when we consider the factors that constitute individual groups' power. The players in the game may have changed by the addition of new groups, but the rules of success, particularly command of resources and building up long-term relationships with public officials, remain virtually unchanged.

Turning to *overall interest group power*, Hrebenar–Thomas defined this as *the extent to which interest groups as a whole influence public policy when compared to other components of the political system, such as political parties, the legislature, the governor, etc.* Attempting to assess this is fraught with problems similar to those of assessing individual interest group power. However, drawing on research from the Hrebenar–Thomas study, we have classified the fifty states according to interest group impact on state policymaking systems. This classification is presented in Table 7.8.

States listed in the *dominant* column are those in which interest groups as a whole have an overwhelming and consistent influence on policymaking. The *complementary* column includes those states where groups have to work in conjunction with, or are constrained by, other aspects of the political system. More often than not this is the party system, but it could also be a strong executive branch, competition among groups, the political culture or a combination of all these. The *subordinate* column represents a situation where the group system is consistently dominated by other influences in the policymaking process. The absence of any states in this column indicates that interest groups are not consistently subordinate in any state. The *dominant/complementary* column includes those states whose group systems alternate between the two situations or are in the process of moving from one to the other. Likewise, the *complementary/subordinate* column includes those states where the group systems alternate between being complementary and subordinate. Except for Colorado, all the western states fall in either the dominant or the dominant/complementary column. As a region, the West has interest group systems that are surpassed in their overall impact only by the South.

Interest Group Tactics and Lobbyists

In the West, as elsewhere, the use and misuse of political power by railroad interests during the late nineteenth century helped leave a legacy of distrust and suspicion among the public toward interest groups, and particularly the lobbyists who represent them. Over the years this attitude was reinforced by the fact that many interest groups have been willing to use almost any means, sometimes illegal ones, to influence government decisions. While these negative images live on, however, the passage of public disclosure laws and an increase in public awareness over the last twenty years has changed the way that groups and lobbyists do business.

The four direct avenues of access and influence that groups use are: election campaigns, the legislature, the executive branch (in-

Table 7.8   Classification of the 13 Western States by Overall Impact of Interest Groups and Comparison with States in Other Regions

		States Where the Overall Impact of Interest Groups Is:			
Region	Dominant	Dominant/ Complementary	Complementary	Complementary/ Subordinate	Subordinate
West	Alaska New Mexico	Arizona California Hawaii Idaho Montana Nevada Oregon Utah Washington Wyoming	Colorado		
Midwest		Nebraska Ohio Oklahoma	Illinois Indiana Iowa Kansas Michigan	Minnesota	

Region				
South	Alabama, Florida, Louisiana, Mississippi, South Carolina, Tennessee, West Virginia	Arkansas, Georgia, Kentucky, Texas, Virginia	North Carolina	Missouri, North Dakota, South Dakota, Wisconsin
Northeast	Maine, Maryland, Massachusetts, New Hampshire, New Jersey, New York, Pennsylvania			Connecticut, Delaware, Rhode Island, Vermont

Source: Adapted by the author from table 4.3 in Clive S. Thomas and Ronald J. Hrebenar, "Interest Groups in the States," chap. 4 in Virginia Gray, Herbert Jacob and Robert Albritton, eds., *Politics in the American States: A Comparative Analysis,* 5th ed. (Glenview, Ill.: Scott Foresman/Little, Brown, 1990).

cluding the bureaucracy), and the courts. Public relations and media campaigns, and to a lesser extent activities such as demonstrations and sit-ins, form the major indirect tactics. By far the most common and still the most effective of group tactics is the use of lobbyists. In fact, until very recently it was the only tactical device used by the vast majority of groups, and it remains the sole approach used by many of them today.

We define a *lobbyist* as *a person designated by an interest group to represent it to government for the purpose of influencing public policy in that group's favor.* The popular press and even some academics refer to lobbyists as if they were all the same in terms of their roles and background. This generalization could not be further from the truth. There are, in fact, five different categories of lobbyists. These, with their major attributes, are set out in Table 7.9. It is important to distinguish among these five categories because the various types of lobbyists have different assets and liabilities, including their backgrounds and experience, and thus they are perceived differently by public officials. Such perceptions will determine the nature and extent of the most crucial factor in a lobbyist's business—his or her power base. In turn the nature and extent of this power base will affect the way lobbyists approach their job of influencing public officials.

Overall, the state capital lobbying community has become much more pluralistic and has advanced greatly in its level of professionalism during the last twenty years. Contract lobbying appears to have made the greatest strides in professionalism, but in-house lobbyists, particularly those representing associations, have also made such advances. While the level of professionalism varies from state to state, its general increase among contract lobbyists is evidenced by several developments. These include an increase in the number of those working at the job full-time; the emergence of lobbying firms, which often provide a variety of services and represent as many as twenty-five clients; and an increased specialization on the part of many contract lobbyists in response to the increasing complexity of government. George Soares, for example, specializes in representing several California agricultural commodity and agribusiness groups, such as the California Avocado Commission and the Agricultural Chemicals Association.[11]

Do these developments mean that the wheeler-dealer has passed from the lobbying scene in western state capitals? In the raw form in which they used to exist, the answer is probably yes. However, the most successful lobbyists today are wheeler-dealers under a more sophisticated guise. Like the old wheeler-dealers, they realize the need for establishing and maintaining good relations with public officials. This includes everything from participating in election campaigns to helping officials with their personal needs. In addition this modern-day wheeler-dealer is very aware of the increased importance of technical information, the increased professionalism and changing needs of public officials, and the increased public visibility of lobbying. The result is a low-key, highly skilled and effective professional who is a far cry from the old popular image of a lobbyist.

Since the 1960s, several factors have led to other tactical devices to supplement the work of the lobbyist. These factors include increased competition between interest groups as their numbers expanded, the changing needs of public officials, and an increased public awareness of both the activities and potential of interest groups. The new tactical devices that have been developed include mobilizing grass-roots support through networking (sophisticated member contact systems); public relations and media campaigns; building coalitions with other groups; and contributing workers and especially money to election campaigns, particularly by establishing a PAC.

It is important to note, however, that such tactics are not viewed as a substitute for a lobbyist. Rather they are employed as a means of enhancing the ability of lobbyists to gain access to and to influence public officials. Shrewd and experienced group leaders and lobbyists choose the most cost-efficient and politically effective method they can to achieve their goals. In most cases this means establishing a legislator-lobbyist contact that involves a minimum of other group members. They employ the newer techniques only if absolutely necessary. This is partly because creating public relations campaigns, setting up networks and contributing to election campaigns are all very costly. Equally important is the axiom that the more people involved in a campaign and the more complex the strategy, the harder it is to orchestrate. Nevertheless, for the reasons related above, these new techniques are being widely and increasingly used.

Finally, it is important to note that interest group activities at the state level do not usually take place in isolation. Either directly or indirectly, their activities and tactics are often connected with, and affected by, group activities at the federal and local level. Many state groups have national affiliates. The National Education Association, for example, has an extensive and sophisticated national organization providing aid and advice to its local state affiliates. State affiliates also sometimes participate in lobbying in Washington, D.C. At the same

Table 7.9   Five Categories of Lobbyists, Their Recruitment, Gender, and Approximate Percentage of the State Capital Lobbying Community in the West

Category	Definition	Recruitment	Gender	Percentage
1. Contract Lobbyists	Those hired on contract for a fee specifically to lobby. They often represent more than one client. Approximately 20% represent five or more clients.	Many, especially the most successful, are former elected or appointed state officials, usually legislators or political appointees, and sometimes former legislative staffers. An increasing number are attorneys from capital law firms and public relations and media specialists. Some are former in-house lobbyists. Few are former career bureaucrats.	Predominantly male, ranges from approximately 80% in California to about 90% in Idaho; higher in less professionalized lobby states.	Make up from 15%–25% of the state capital lobbying community; higher in more professionalized lobby states.
2. In-House Lobbyists	Employees of an association, organization or business, who as part or all of their job act as a lobbyist. These represent only one client—their employer.	Most have experience in the profession, business or trade which they represent, e.g., education, medicine, oil and gas, retailing, labor union activities. Much less likely than contract lobbyists to have been public officials (though more likely to have been so in less professionalized lobby states).	Approximately 75% male, 25% female.	Constitute from 40%–50% of the lobbying community—the largest category in most western state capitals.
3. Government Lobbyists and Legislative Liaisons	Employees of state, local, and federal agencies, who as part or all of their job represent their agency to the legislative and executive branches of state government. Thus, these also represent only one interest. They include state	Legislative liaisons are often career bureaucrats with broad experience in the agency or government unit that they represent. Some are political appointees and an increasing number are recruited from the ranks of legislative	Approximately 25%–35% of legislative liaisons are female; higher in more economically and socially diverse states, such as California and Washington.	Difficult to estimate as several western states do not require government personnel to register as lobbyists. A rough estimate for all government lobbyists in the West is between 25% and 40%. Tends to be higher in western

	government agency heads and senior staff, both elected and appointed officials of local governments, and some federal officials. To specifically monitor their relations with the legislature, most state agencies and some local governments and federal agencies appoint a person designated as a legislative liaison.	staffers. No common recruitment pattern exists for government lobbyists as a whole.	states where state and local government employment is highest.
4. Citizen or Volunteer Lobbyists	Persons who, usually on an *ad hoc* and unpaid basis, represent citizen and community organizations or informal groups. They rarely represent more than one interest at a time.	Too varied for meaningful categorization; but most are very committed to their cause.	Difficult to estimate as many are not required to register as lobbyists. However, it appears that the majority, and in some western states as high as 80%, are female.	An estimate is from 10%–20% of the state capital lobbying community.
5. Private Individual, "Hobbyist" or Self-styled Lobbyists	Those acting on their own behalf and not designated by any organization as an official representative. They usually lobby for pet projects, direct personal benefits, or against some policy or proposal that they find objectionable.	Other than self-recruitment, no common pattern.	Difficult to estimate as many are not required to or do not register as lobbyists. Most are probably male.	Difficult to estimate, but probably less than 5%.

Source: Adapted for the West by the author from fig. 4.2 in Clive S. Thomas and Ronald J. Hrebenar, "Interest Groups in the States," chap. 4 in Virginia Gray, Herbert Jacob and Robert Albritton, eds., *Politics in the American States: A Comparative Analysis*, 5th ed. (Glenview, Ill.: Scott Foresman/Little, Brown, 1990); and from the thirteen state chapters in Ronald J. Hrebenar and Clive S. Thomas, eds., *Interest Group Politics in the American West* (Salt Lake City: University of Utah Press, 1987).

time, local chapters of state schoolteachers' associations often lobby their local school boards. Large corporations like IBM and some oil companies set general policies on political involvement, which are followed by the state offices of these organizations. According to Zeigler, there is also an increase in interstate cooperation and funding of groups.[12] This is particularly the case with ballot propositions involving social issues such as abortion funding, gun control, and attempts to restrict smoking. During the 1988 elections in Oregon, for example, a ballot measure to restrict smoking in public places was defeated with the aid of some skillful polling and public relations largely financed by out-of-state tobacco interests.

Conclusion: How Different Are Interest Group Systems in the Western States?

As with most aspects of western politics and government, the interest group systems and interest group politics in the western states exhibit both similarities and differences when compared with the other thirty-seven states. If we ask whether there are any features of interest group activity that are uniquely western, the answer is probably no. This is because, while there are certainly variations in group systems and activity between regions, these are essentially circumstantial rather than indigenous or uniquely regional. This is illustrated by the fact that California's interest group system is far more akin to the populous and economically and socially diverse states of the Northeast and Midwest than to those of most of its western neighbors. Furthermore, developments in the past twenty-five years have tended to reduce differences in group systems and group politics across the states as these become more and more like their counterparts in Washington, D.C.

Nevertheless, despite variations among the thirteen states, the West continues to exhbit some common characteristics in its interest group systems. Some of these set it apart from the rest of the nation. These circumstantial differences can be traced to a combination of the following factors, all of which are recurring influences on western poltics: (1) the nature of the western economy, based on resource extraction, recreation and government; (2) the region's relatively weak political institutions; (3) the populist-progressive tradition; and (4) in many western states, conservatism and a relatively low level of government professionalism. Consequently, natural resource interests have been more prominent in the West than in other regions, and in some states in recent years environmentalists have risen to prominence. Government has been a particularly important lobbying force, especially in the last two decades, as have government-related organizations, particularly those of teachers as well as of state and local employees. The group systems as a whole have been very powerful, and in this regard are surpassed only by those in the South. Outside of California, which remains in the forefront of interest group and lobbying developments, western systems are generally among the least developed in terms of professionalism.

For a long time only a very narrow range of groups was represented in western state capitals. For much of the region's history, therefore, interest groups were a select preserve, rather exclusive and sometimes exclusionary in their role as vehicles of political participation. While there have been major developments over the last two decades in the range of groups operating in western state capitals, resulting in increased political participation for causes and individuals not previously represented, the old entrenched economic and institutional interests still exert the most consistent influence on public policy. These are primarily business, labor and professional groups, as well as state and local government agencies. It is their command of extensive resources that has enabled them to maintain, and in some cases enhance, their influence. Therefore, while the days of blatant corruption associated with some early lobbyists may be long gone, and there are more westerners represented by interest groups, in the West as elsewhere interest groups are still far from an ideal means of political participation.

Notes

1. Don W. Driggs, "Nevada: Powerful Lobbyists and Conservative Politics," in Ronald J. Hrebenar and Clive S. Thomas, eds., *Interest Group Politics in the American West* (Salt Lake City: University of Utah Press, 1987), 86–87; Russell R. Elliott, *History of Nevada*, 2nd ed. rev. (Lincoln: University of Nebraska Press, 1987), 158–61.

2. Maury Klein, *Union Pacific: Birth of a Railroad: 1862–1893* (Garden City, N.Y.: Doubleday, 1987), 369.

3. Tim R. Miller, *State Government: Politics in Wyoming* (Dubuque, Iowa: Kendall/Hunt, 1981), 66–67.

4. The Hrebenar–Thomas study is the first fifty-state study of interest

groups. It involved seventy-eight political scientists and took over six years to complete—1983–89. This chapter draws on material from that study. In particular, the material on the West is drawn in part from Hrebenar and Thomas, *Interest Group Politics in the American West;* and the comparisons between the West and the other states are drawn mainly from Clive S. Thomas and Ronald J. Hrebenar, "Interest Groups in the States," chap. 4 in Virginia Gray, Herbert Jacob and Robert Albritton, eds., *Politics in the American States: A Comparative Analysis,* 5th ed. (Glenview, Ill.: Scott, Foresman/Little, Brown, 1990).

5. Interest groups are often referred to as *special interests, political interest groups* or as *pressure groups.* In this chapter we use only the term *interest group.*

6. E. E. Schattschneider, *The Semisovereign People: A Realist's View of Democracy in America* (New York: Holt, Rinehart and Winston, 1960), 20–46; Kay Lehman Schlozman and John T. Tierney, *Organized Interests and American Democracy* (New York: Harper & Row, 1986), 58–87; L. Harmon Zeigler, "Interest Groups in the States," in Virginia Gray, Herbert Jacob and Kenneth N. Vines, eds., *Politics in the American States: A Comparative Analysis,* 4th ed. (Boston: Little, Brown, 1983), 99, 104–6; and L. Harmon Zeigler and Hendrik van Dalen, "Interest Groups in State Politics," in Herbert Jacob and Kenneth N. Vines, eds., *Politics in the American States: A Comparative Analysis,* 3rd ed. (Boston: Little, Brown, 1976), 110–12.

7. Zeigler and van Dalen, "Interest Groups in State Politics," 94–95; Zeigler, "Interest Groups in the States," 111–17; Sarah McCally Morehouse, *State Politics, Parties and Policy* (New York: Holt, Rinehart and Winston, 1981), 116–18, 127; Belle Zeller, *American State Legislatures,* 2nd ed. (New York: Thomas Y. Crowell, 1954), 190–93.

8. Hrebenar and Thomas, *Interest Group Politics in the American West,* 149–52.

9. The Hrebenar–Thomas methodology involved a combination of survey research, interviews with public officials, and examination of what little existing literature was available. Each of the seventy-eight contributors was given a set of guidelines to follow in this and other aspects of the investigation of group activity in their state. Because of variations and unique circumstances in certain states absolute consistency in methodology was not possible to achieve.

10. Morehouse, *State Politics, Parties and Policy,* table 3.2 "Listing of the Significant Pressure Groups by State," 108–12.

11. John C. Syer, "California: Political Giants in a Megastate," in Hrebenar and Thomas, *Interest Group Politics in the American West,* 42.

12. Zeigler, "Interest Groups in the States," 117–18.

8

THE POLITICS
OF WOMEN
AND ETHNIC
MINORITIES

F. Chris Garcia,
Christine Marie Sierra and
Margaret Maier Murdock

*T*HE POLITICAL ADVANCES MADE BY WOMEN AND
ethnic minorities, especially in recent years, as well as their increasing
potential for power in politics at both the national and regional levels,
are now well recognized by political observers. As a result, the study
of contemporary American politics is marked by an ever-broadening
interest in the politics of these groups. This chapter will examine the
politics of women and ethnic minorities in the western region of the
United States.[1] Our purpose is to shed light on these groups' political
status, their political attitudes and patterns of participation, and the
policy issues that concern them in this specific region of the country.

Such a broad topic requires the imposition of certain limits on our discussion. While we present demographic data for each of the western states, we develop our discussion of women and ethnic minorities largely in light of their general group experiences in the region (or in some cases the nation) as a whole. We address specific states in this region selectively to illustrate certain points. It should be noted that we incorporate Texas into our analysis, thus focusing our study on fourteen rather than thirteen states as most authors have done in this book. Texas is often considered a southern state in scholarly analysis. However, it is also intrinsically a part of the history, politics and culture of the American Southwest. Thus we include it here as part of a special subregion within the West.

Likewise, it would be impossible to discuss in detail all the ethnic minorities residing in the western states. Consequently, we focus on the major racial/ethnic minority groups whose importance in regional politics is most apparent. Central to our analysis are the politics of Mexican Americans[2] and American Indians—the "territorial minorities" of the Southwest and Northwest. Material on other significant minorities—blacks, Asians, and other Hispanic groups—is included, but to a lesser extent.

Women and Ethnic Minorities: Diversity and Commonality

At first glance it would appear that the rich and varied histories and political experiences of women, Mexican Americans, American Indians, and the other groups examined here would defy generalization and common treatment. Not only are there major differences *across* these groups, but there are differences *within* each group as well. Numerous factors such as age, social class and political ideology, to name only a few, create distinctions among individuals within the same group. For example, national surveys indicate that women differ more among themselves in their attitudes on certain political issues than they do as a group from men.[3] Persons of Mexican origin prefer various ethnic self-labels, such as Hispano, Chicano, or Mexican American, depending in part on the region or state in which they reside.[4] For American Indians, clan and tribal distinctions are central features in their personal lives as well as in their social organization.[5]

As this chapter will point out, such internal group distinctions are important to consider when examining and evaluating the political behavior of these various groups. Women and ethnic minorities, however, also share certain characteristics of overriding importance. The common features of their various experiences become clear when we look at their political, economic and social status in the United States, both historically and in the contemporary period.

Of fundamental importance to the major racial/ethnic groups discussed here is the nature of their incorporation into American society and their group experiences within the political system.[6] In short, the incorporation of these groups into U.S. society is marked by a history of conquest, violence, and the exercise of coercive force by the state. As distinct racial and ethnic populations, they have been subject to discrimination, cultural repression, and political exclusion and powerlessness.

American Indians were incorporated into the U.S. political system as a result of conquest. Western subjugation of Indian people began in the fifteenth century with the arrival of European settlers on the North American continent. European domination of indigenous communities came as the result of war, violence, disease and cultural conquest.

Anglo-American domination of Indian people has been similarly marked by conflict and violence. Official U.S. government policy toward Indians has vacillated over time from genocidal extinction to tribal termination and cultural assimilation. The coercive power of the state is plainly seen in the government's confiscation of Indian lands and the forceful relocation of Indian populations onto reservations.[7]

The population of Mexican origin in the United States can also be considered as "people of conquest."[8] Like American Indians, this population of mixed Spanish and Indian heritage had established settlements in what is now the American Southwest as early as the sixteenth and seventeenth centuries. Major contact with Anglo-Americans from the East did not occur until the nineteenth century. This contact likewise was marked by violent confrontation.

As a result of the war with Mexico from 1846 to 1848, the United States acquired a vast territory, which included the present states of New Mexico, Nevada, California, and parts of Colorado, Arizona and Utah. Texas had declared its independence from Mexico in 1836 and was admitted to the Union in 1845. Those Mexican inhabitants who chose to remain in the ceded territory (most of the native Mexican population) thereafter became U.S. citizens. However, they were incorporated into U.S. society as an economically and politically subordinated group. Their treatment by the dominant society as second-class citizens has extended well into the twentieth century.

The U.S. government's coercive power over Mexican communities has been exercised particularly through immigration policies carried out by the Immigration and Naturalization Service and the Border Patrol. Deportations of people of Mexican origin, including U.S. citizens, numbered in the hundreds of thousands during the 1930s and 1950s.[9]

The incorporation of black Americans into U.S. society began with the institution of slavery. Brought to this country as property, blacks were subjected to numerous forms of white domination, violence and cultural repression for over two centuries under the slave system. Not until the adoption of the Civil War amendments to the U.S. Constitution were blacks accorded the legal and political rights of other citizens. Notwithstanding such constitutional guarantees, racial subordination of blacks continued in the nineteenth and twentieth centuries.

Chinese and Japanese populations, while originally welcomed for their labor, were officially barred from entering the United States during the nativist periods of the late nineteenth and early twentieth centuries. Governmental control over the Asian population was clearly exercised in the policy of Japanese relocation during World War II.[10]

Each of these racial and ethnic groups also shares in a history of discrimination. They have been segregated and confined to certain occupations through discriminatory and racist employment practices.[11] They have also been denied access to quality education and other social goods and benefits. Most importantly, they have been excluded in the past from participating in the political process.

After the Civil War, black disenfranchisement in the South resulted from both informal and formal methods of exclusion. The adoption of the white primary and grandfather clauses, and the requirements of literacy tests and poll taxes for voting, worked to deny black people their right to vote. Another historical method that continues to be used to dilute the impact of racial bloc voting is the gerrymandering of districts.

American Indians and Mexican Americans in the Southwest have also encountered numerous obstacles in exercising the franchise. Both groups have had to pursue litigation to challenge unfair election requirements and procedures, such as those mentioned above. For Indians, the denial of their basic right to vote has had a particularly long history. Indians were not granted citizenship until Congress passed the Indian Citizenship Act in 1924. Notwithstanding this federal law, state legislatures continued to exclude Indians from voting. Arizona and New Mexico did not grant Indians the right to vote until 1948. Utah became the last state in the Union to grant Indians the franchise in 1956.[12] Adoption of the Voting Rights Act in 1965, and its extension to language minorities in 1975, finally put a halt to most of these methods of disenfranchisement.

The historical experiences of women—those of the majority culture—in the American political system departs in significant ways from the histories of these racial and ethnic minorities. Women's incorporation into U.S. society, for example, is not marked by overt and systematic conquest, violence or cultural oppression. At the same time, however, these women as a group have experienced discrimination, inequality and political exclusion. Women, in fact, did not win the right to vote in federal elections until 1920, with the passage of the 19th Amendment. They, too, have been occupationally segregated into "women's work," and denied certain social, economic and educational advantages that were available to men.

To be sure, there have been vast improvements over the years in the political and social status of all these groups. However, the legacy of discrimination, inequality, and political powerlessness has a continuing impact on each of these groups. As will be noted below, the socioeconomic status of none of these groups in general equals that of white men, though Asians do present some exceptions to this general pattern. Moreover, each of these groups continues to be underrepresented in decision-making positions and in the political processes of this country.

In short, women and racial/ethnic groups examined here continue to occupy a *subordinate status* in American politics and society at both the national and regional levels. As such, they constitute "minority" groups in contemporary American politics. It is important to note that women are not a numerical minority, since they constitute slightly over half of the population. As used in this chapter, "minority" status for women refers to their unequal sociopolitical standing as a group in relation to men in U.S. society.

The following section provides an overview of demographic and socioeconomic characteristics of major ethnic groups and women in the western states. The subsequent sections of our chapter provide overviews of critical dimensions of the politics of women and ethnic minorities in the American West. Our discussion includes a focus on political culture and attitudes, patterns of political participation and representation, and policies and issues of major significance to these groups.

Demographic Profile of Minorities in the West

Because of variations in their geographic concentration, ethnic and racial minority groups have varying influences in different regions of the United States. Especially important in the West are Asians, Hispanics and Indians, who tend to be concentrated more heavily in the western United States than in other areas of the nation. Blacks, on the other hand, are more heavily concentrated in regions outside the West. Consequently, black political influence tends to be more pronounced in the South and in the major urban areas of the Northeast and Midwest than in the West.

Additionally, each of these racial and ethnic groups is concentrated in specific western states, and their influence varies accordingly. Asians have more influence in California and Hawaii than in most of the other western states. Hispanic influence is prominent in Texas, California and New Mexico. American Indians significantly affect state and local politics in Alaska, Arizona and New Mexico. Thus, for each of these groups (except for blacks), their concentration in the West implies more political power, potential and real, there than in other parts of the country.

For obvious reasons, women are more evenly spread throughout the general population of the United States. Thus, as a group, their political status and influence are not primarily linked to a geographic distribution of their numbers. While women outnumber men in the United States 51.4% to 48.6% (a difference of 6,450,779 persons), this margin is slightly smaller in the West, where women constitute only a 50.6% majority. Table 8.1 shows the numbers of women relative to men for each minority group, by state, for the western United States. In Alaska, Hawaii, Nevada and Wyoming, women are a numerical minority.

Table 8.1 also shows the size, absolute numbers and percentage of the state population of each minority group by sex and by state, as well as for the whole United States according to the 1980 census. It is clear from this table that, except in Hawaii, whites outnumber all minority groups in each of the western states. In Hawaii, whites constitute less than one-third of the population. More than half of the population is made up of Asians and Pacific Islanders; Japanese alone constitute 24.9% of the population in Hawaii. While this proportion of minority groups is indicative of the unique character of Hawaii's cultural heritage, such a distribution is not typical in the western states. With the exceptions of California, Hawaii, New Mexico and Texas, whites constitute more than 70% of the population in each of the western states. In six states—Idaho, Montana, Oregon, Utah, Washington and Wyoming—whites make up more than 90% of the population.

Except for the case of the Asian and Pacific Islander population in Hawaii, Hispanics make up the single most numerous minority group in the western states. In the U.S. as a whole, Hispanics constitute almost 7% of the population. However, in Arizona, California, Colorado, Hawaii, Nevada, New Mexico and Texas—half of the western states—they constitute a much larger sector of the population. Hispanics are especially concentrated in Arizona, California, New Mexico and Texas, where they constitute between 16% and 37% of the state populations.

While blacks nationwide make up slightly less than 12% of the national population, their concentration in the western states is much smaller; only in Texas is there a similar proportion.

American Indians make up only a tiny portion of the nation's population, about one percent. However, many of the western states show significantly larger concentrations of American Indians. Alaska, in particular, has the largest proportion (16.1%). Arizona, Montana and New Mexico also have American Indian populations considerably above the percentage in the national population. In the West, only Hawaii and Texas have smaller proportions of American Indians than exist in the national population.

CHARACTERISTICS OF MINORITY GROUPS

While numbers may give some indication of the kind of economic, political, and social power a group can wield, numbers alone cannot tell the entire story. Table 8.2 gives the percentage of persons who graduated from high school, the median family income, percentage of families below the poverty level, and levels of unemployment among minority groups in the fourteen western states. This table shows clearly where the educational and economic advantages lie: whites tend to have higher percentages of persons who have graduated from

Table 8.1 Minority Population by State

	Total		White		Black		Hispanic		Native		Asian and Pacific Islanders	
	Number	Percent	Number	Percent	Number	Percent	Number	Percent	Number	Percent	Number	Percent
U.S.	226,545,805		180,602,838	79.72	26,091,857	11.52	14,603,683	6.45	1,432,807	0.63	3,550,605	1.57
Female	116,498,292	51.42	92,707,560	51.33	13,770,602	52.78	7,329,350	50.19	725,889	50.66	1,835,937	51.71
Male	110,047,513	48.58	87,895,278	48.67	12,321,255	47.22	7,274,333	49.81	706,918	49.34	1,714,668	48.29
Alaska	401,851		306,899	76.37	13,533	3.37	9,057	2.25	64,776	16.12	7,695	1.92
Female	188,906	47.01	142,658	46.48	7,582	56.03	4,195	46.32	32,234	49.76	4,065	52.82
Male	212,945	52.99	164,241	53.52	5,951	43.97	4,862	53.68	32,542	50.24	3,631	47.18
Arizona	2,718,215		2,028,725	74.63	72,410	2.66	444,102	16.34	146,461	5.39	22,888	0.84
Female	1,379,472	50.75	1,033,012	50.92	34,741	47.98	222,252	50.05	74,924	51.16	12,617	55.12
Male	1,338,743	49.25	995,713	49.08	37,669	52.02	221,850	49.95	71,537	48.84	10,271	44.88
California	23,667,902		15,850,775	66.97	1,784,086	7.54	4,541,300	19.19	189,700	0.80	1,242,157	5.25
Female	12,001,798	50.71	8,086,286	51.02	911,542	51.09	2,243,613	49.40	97,055	51.16	633,951	51.04
Male	11,666,104	49.29	7,764,489	48.98	872,544	48.91	2,297,687	50.60	92,645	48.84	608,206	48.96
Colorado	2,889,964		2,394,430	82.85	99,752	3.45	341,435	11.81	17,394	0.60	32,747	1.13
Female	1,456,323	50.39	1,209,280	50.50	48,436	48.56	170,707	50.00	8,597	49.43	17,314	52.87
Male	1,433,641	49.61	1,185,150	49.50	51,316	51.44	170,728	50.00	8,797	50.57	15,433	47.13
Hawaii	964,691		311,068	32.25	16,966	1.76	71,399	7.40	2,605	0.27	555,845	57.62
Female	469,719	48.69	143,992	46.29	5,520	32.54	34,464	48.27	1,066	40.92	281,406	50.63
Male	494,972	51.31	167,076	53.71	11,446	67.46	36,935	51.73	1,539	59.08	274,439	49.37
Idaho	943,935		887,691	94.04	2,670	0.28	36,560	3.87	9,926	1.05	6,403	0.68
Female	472,970	50.11	446,666	50.32	1,008	37.75	16,432	44.95	4,958	49.95	3,602	56.25
Male	470,965	49.89	441,025	49.68	1,662	62.25	20,128	55.05	4,968	50.05	2,801	43.75

Montana	786,690		734,490	93.36	1,699	0.22	10,103	1.28	37,022	4.71	2,937	0.37
Female	394,104	50.10	367,664	50.06	614	36.14	4,995	49.44	19,041	51.43	1,581	53.83
Male	392,586	49.90	366,826	49.94	1,085	63.86	5,108	50.56	17,981	48.57	1,356	46.17
Nevada	800,493		666,807	83.30	50,565	6.32	54,130	6.76	13,373	1.67	14,561	1.82
Female	395,321	49.38	329,017	49.34	25,030	49.50	25,946	47.93	6,660	49.80	8,162	56.05
Male	405,172	50.62	337,790	50.66	25,535	50.50	28,184	52.07	6,713	50.20	6,399	43.95
New Mexico	1,302,894		690,236	52.98	22,298	1.71	477,051	36.61	103,102	7.91	7,118	0.55
Female	660,696	50.71	349,434	50.63	10,612	47.59	241,204	50.56	53,742	52.13	4,130	58.02
Male	642,198	49.29	340,802	49.37	11,686	52.41	235,847	49.44	49,360	47.87	2,988	41.98
Oregon	2,633,105		2,459,399	93.40	36,798	1.40	66,164	2.51	28,672	1.09	39,303	1.49
Female	1,337,155	50.78	1,252,210	50.92	17,429	47.36	31,032	46.90	14,331	49.98	20,780	52.87
Male	1,295,950	49.22	1,207,189	49.08	19,369	52.64	35,132	53.10	14,341	50.02	18,523	47.13
Texas	14,229,191		9,370,023	65.85	1,688,947	11.87	2,982,583	20.96	43,632	0.31	128,109	0.90
Female	7,231,263	50.82	4,760,970	50.81	876,751	51.91	1,498,227	50.23	21,072	48.29	66,660	52.03
Male	6,997,928	49.18	4,609,053	49.19	812,196	48.09	1,484,356	49.77	22,560	51.71	61,449	47.97
Utah	1,461,037		1,351,222	92.48	9,425	0.65	60,045	4.11	19,045	1.30	19,602	1.34
Female	736,327	50.40	682,955	50.54	3,891	41.28	29,010	48.31	9,774	51.32	9,893	50.47
Male	724,710	49.60	668,267	49.46	5,534	58.72	31,035	51.69	9,271	48.68	9,709	49.53
Washington	4,132,156		3,734,289	90.37	104,085	2.52	121,286	2.94	61,153	1.48	105,438	2.55
Female	2,080,163	50.34	1,885,031	50.48	47,962	46.08	57,320	47.26	31,007	50.70	56,024	53.13
Male	2,051,993	49.66	1,849,258	49.52	56,123	53.92	63,966	52.74	30,146	49.30	49,414	46.87
Wyoming	469,557		431,503	91.90	3,186	0.68	24,535	5.23	7,892	1.68	1,953	0.42
Female	229,023	48.77	210,631	48.81	1,399	43.91	11,640	47.44	4,016	50.89	1,113	56.99
Male	240,534	51.23	220,872	51.19	1,787	56.09	12,895	52.56	3,876	49.11	840	43.01

Source: Department of Commerce, Bureau of the Census, 1980.

Table 8.2   Minority Group Economic Status by State

State/Status	White	Hispanic	Black	Native	Asian and Pacific Islunders
Alaska					
% High School Graduates	83.2	80.9	85.0	59.4	76.8
Median Family Income	27,294	18,774	18,674	15,921	25,201
% Below Poverty Level	6.0	11.7	9.2	25.3	6.6
% Unemployed	8.2	12.4	14.4	20.3	6.5
Arizona					
% High School Graduates	76.1	44.4	60.6	42.4	73.9
Median Family Income	19,947	15,468	13,724	10,371	19,618
% Below Poverty Level	6.9	18.2	22.6	40.1	14.3
% Unemployed	5.5	8.8	11.2	14.4	4.5
California					
% High School Graduates	76.6	43.6	68.5	65.7	76.3
Median Family Income	22,748	16,081	14,887	16,548	23,449
% Below Poverty Level	6.5	16.8	20.6	15.2	9.7
% Unemployed	5.8	9.6	11.1	11.8	4.6
Colorado					
% High School Graduates	80.2	48.6	74.4	68.1	77.2
Median Family Income	21,822	15,412	15,732	15,339	20,933
% Below Poverty Level	6.2	18.4	18.7	19.1	12.6
% Unemployed	4.6	9.4	8.7	10.7	4.9
Hawaii					
% High School Graduates	85.7	64.4	91.5	83.5	67.3
Median Family Income	20,792	16,479	12,764	13,114	24,680
% Below Poverty Level	7.4	15.4	11.5	15.4	7.5
% Unemployed	5.8	7.5	12.9	10.0	4.0
Idaho					
% High School Graduates	74.6	38.7	74.4	55.4	77.8
Median Family Income	17,669	12,294	12,961	11,897	16,975
% Below Poverty Level	9.1	34.8	13.3	29.7	14.1
% Unemployed	7.8	11.8	11.0	17.8	6.3
Montana					
% High School Graduates	75.2	58.1	80.3	56.0	63.6
Median Family Income	18,691	16,463	14,226	11,767	13,345
% Below Poverty Level	12.3	20.2	25.8	39.7	32.7
% Unemployed	7.8	11.5	11.3	20.3	10.3

State/Status	White	Hispanic	Black	Native	Asian and Pacific Islanders
Nevada					
% High School Graduates	76.9	56.8	61.4	59.5	76.5
Median Family Income	21,879	18,332	15,424	15,728	18,434
% Below Poverty Level	7.9	10.5	25.1	22.9	15.3
% Unemployed	5.7	6.8	9.1	10.7	4.7
New Mexico					
% High School Graduates	73.4	50.6	62.8	47.4	74.7
Median Family Income	18,429	13,512	12,063	10,826	17,090
% Below Poverty Level	15.3	29.3	33.8	45.7	29.0
% Unemployed	5.9	9.3	13.1	14.6	5.7
Oregon					
% High School Graduates	76.1	57.4	68.0	62.6	74.7
Median Family Income	20,210	15,917	13,409	14,809	18,536
% Below Poverty Level	10.4	21.4	31.6	26.5	22.4
% Unemployed	8.1	12.0	14.2	17.3	7.1
Texas					
% High School Graduates	65.7	35.5	53.0	63.2	77.5
Median Family Income	20,955	13,293	13,042	17,302	21,005
% Below Poverty Level	12.1	33.3	31.8	18.6	19.0
% Unemployed	3.4	6.4	6.9	5.8	4.0
Utah					
% High School Graduates	80.9	52.1	69.7	52.8	75.5
Median Family Income	20,205	16,499	15,041	11,853	17,500
% Below Poverty Level	10.6	22.8	27.2	40.8	24.8
% Unemployed	5.3	9.3	9.9	12.8	5.6
Washington					
% High School Graduates	78.3	55.5	72.6	63.2	75.3
Median Family Income	21,989	14,993	15,833	14,778	21,520
% Below Poverty Level	9.2	19.4	24.0	29.2	16.1
% Unemployed	7.1	11.1	11.4	16.2	6.6
Wyoming					
% High School Graduates	78.8	49.4	75.4	63.4	74.3
Median Family Income	22,666	19,047	14,073	15,805	18,359
% Below Poverty Level	5.5	11.3	14.1	19.8	16.4
% Unemployed	4.0	6.9	6.9	8.2	2.5

Source: U.S. Department of Commerce, Bureau of the Census, 1980.

high school, just as they tend to have higher incomes, lower levels of unemployment, and fewer families below the poverty level.

On the whole, Asians and Pacific Islanders constitute the ethnic group whose socioeconomic indicators are closest to those of whites. This group is comparable to whites in terms of education, income, and employment levels. In fact, on a few measures their socioeconomic characteristics are higher than those of whites. At the same time, blacks in western states tend to have slightly higher educational and income levels than American Indians and Hispanics. But that is not an entirely consistent pattern. Indeed, in a few states—primarily in California and Texas—American Indians are slightly more advanced in economic and educational terms than are Hispanics and blacks.

Scholars offer many explanations for variations in the socioeconomic status among majority and minority groups. Social and economic features peculiar to each state and to the region as a whole at least partially explain variations in the quality of life across groups. For example, areas with a booming economy and expanding employment opportunities allow more opportunities for socioeconomic advancement. At the same time, educational systems that remain unresponsive to multicultural education, or areas with persistent patterns of discrimination in housing and employment retard group chances for socioeconomic advancement. Additionally, cultural traditions that stress education and financial stability, such as the Asian cultures, may be a factor in producing higher income and educational levels.[13]

Overall, Table 8.2 shows ample evidence that minority groups are definitely disadvantaged in terms of economic and educational status. These groups therefore lack some of the essential bases for political achievements, which can, in turn, have continuing and negative effects on their economic and educational status.

DEMOGRAPHIC CHANGES AND THEIR POLITICAL RAMIFICATIONS

Since World War II there has been continuous population growth in the West, especially growth created by migration from other parts of the nation and immigration from other countries. This postwar growth, especially that caused by immigration, has resulted in both larger numbers and larger concentrations of minorities throughout the West. These concentrations have allowed for more interaction with the dominant political system and have provided the basis for increased political, economic, and social power for minority groups.

However, as discussed above, minorities are a long way from having even a proportionate share of the resources in the West.

Such a situation produces a number of significant questions concerning the long-term consequences of demographic change. How will the politics of the West be changed with the increasing numerical strength of minority groups? As the relative size and power of groups change, how will majority–minority relations be affected? Will minority groups compete or coalesce with one another to produce a common agenda for western politics? And, finally, what will be the consequences should the political system attempt to curtail the growth and impact of these racial and ethnic groups? Such questions will prove significant well into the twenty-first century.

Patterns of Political Participation: Political Cultures, Attitudes and Organization

POLITICAL CULTURES

A distinguishing feature of minority political participation in the West is that in general it tends to be distinct from that of the majority culture in both its nature and degree. Hispanics, Indians, blacks, and Asians tend to participate in politics to a lesser degree than do their white or Anglo[14] counterparts. Since they all have experienced discrimination, a significant portion of members of these groups have a less than positive attitude toward politics. In some cases, this includes negative attitudes toward electoral participation, the political system, and its institutions and officials. In other cases, it is manifested as a feeling of neutrality toward and separation from politics and government at any level.

As discussed in Chapter 2, the interplay between a group's own cultural values and the group's interactions with the dominant society produces a set of orientations toward politics that can be termed "political culture." Each of these western ethnic minority groups has its own distinctive political culture. But because of their common experience of discrimination and generally lower economic status, some aspects of their political cultures are common to them all.

The oldest of the western ethnic minority cultures is that of the American Indians. Given their unique history as indigenous settlers of the western hemisphere, Indians have the most distinctive political culture among the groups. To some degree, the reservation system has permitted Indians to keep intact their own life-styles, traditions, and languages. Furthermore, their ownership of large amounts of territory, as well as membership in semisovereign political systems, make Indian patterns of political culture and political participation unique. As the most officially separate of the ethnic groups in the United States, they have a relationship to governmental institutions and processes that is marked by some distance, autonomy and independence.

There are several dozen distinct tribal groupings of American Indians in the western United States. Consequently, their political culture may more accurately be considered as a multitude of political cultures. Each retains some degree of separation from the local, state and national governments of the United States, and each varies in its degree of assimilation into the dominant society. Approximately half the Indian people do not live on their tribal lands, but instead are "urban Indians" who have chosen to live in urban communities.[15]

Many American Indian political cultures are marked by an integration with the religion and politics of their own tribes. Most Indian tribal political systems are a combination of their own ancient sociopolitical systems and some forms of modern American constitutional government. Generally, American Indians are very supportive of their own systems and participate quite naturally in them, while being somewhat less enthusiastic in their participation in the politics of the outside system.[16]

The other "territorial" minority in the West is the Mexican American, or Hispanic.[17] As is the case with American Indians, Hispanic political culture reflects this group's historical origins in the Southwest and its experiences as a racially oppressed group in this region of the United States. In turn, the southwestern United States continues to be distinctive in that it retains a substantial Hispanic flavor throughout its culture. A significant amount of the political culture in the Southwest also reflects the historical and geographical closeness of Mexico and contiguity with the rest of Latin America.

Substantially more research has been done on the political culture of Mexican Americans than on that of American Indians, though the existing research is still minimal. Mexican Americans of the West tend to participate less in politics and government than do Anglos, although that difference has been decreasing.[18] Moreover, there have been some exceptions to this generality, such as the high level of participation of Hispanics in northern New Mexico.[19] In the past, these lower levels of involvement have been attributed to values alledgedly innate in Hispanic culture, such as fatalism, personalistic politics and envy of leaders. However, much of the more recent research, especially that done by Hispanic scholars, has indicated that nonparticipatory attitudes and behavior are more likely the result of feelings of exclusion and powerlessness caused by discrimination by the majority culture rather than simply the reflection of any innate values.[20] In fact, the differences among many aspects of the political culture of Hispanics and Anglos seem to be minimal, particularly in cases where Hispanics have been involved in social accommodation for at least a few generations, such as in northern New Mexico and the lower Rio Grande Valley of Texas.

Like American Indians and Hispanics, Asian Americans are also a culturally heterogeneous group. Much of their culture has been retained as a result of their separation, both voluntary and involuntary, in ethnic enclaves in certain areas of the West. The cultural values of Americans of Japanese ancestry, perhaps combined with their historic experience with relocation during World War II, appear to have subsequently promoted their accommodation into mainstream American society. For example, education for lucrative, professional jobs has been stressed among Japanese Americans because these are "secure" positions.[21]

The early legal prohibitions against Chinese involvement in political processes of any kind, including testifying in court against whites, laid the foundations for low political participation among the Chinese immigrants. This discrimination also forced on them a social and political isolation that has been difficult to overcome, though that is changing in states like California.[22]

Peoples from many other Asian cultures have settled throughout the West, usually in quite separate and distinct communities. During the late 1970s, large numbers of people from the Southeast Asian countries of Vietnam, Laos, and Cambodia immigrated to the United States. They have established small but numerous communities throughout the inland West as well as in the coastal areas.[23] As others have done, these immigrants bring with them their own cultural traditions and history. As new immigrants, their concerns focus on fundamentals: earning a living; obtaining housing, education, and health care; and learning to live in a different culture and political system. As a result, these new immigrants have had little involvement in the mainstream of the political system.

While Americans of African ancestry have been scattered throughout the West since the 1800s, it is doubtful that an African American culture distinctive to the West has emerged. Most areas in the western states have only very small percentages of blacks in their populations. However, there are large black populations in the large urban areas of California and Texas. In these areas, it is likely that black Americans share the political culture of the majority of their co-ethnics throughout the United States: a political culture marked by the after-effects of oppression and discrimination.

Women have been one of the relatively powerless groups in the United States. Despite the fact that equal political rights for women were first granted by a western state (Wyoming), political equality for women in the West is far from a reality.[24] Because women occupy a subordinate status in the political system, one perhaps would expect to find a political culture resembling that of a previously disenfranchised group. It is, however, almost impossible to generalize about a political culture for women because women are such a large and heterogeneous grouping. Nevertheless, some important observations can be offered.

Women have made great strides since the 1960s and 1970s in the area of political participation. Indeed, women's rate of participation in the 1980s, at least in terms of voting, is comparable to that of males.[25] Similarly, there is evidence that some aspects of women's political culture now resemble those of men, including attitudes supportive of participation in politics.[26] On the whole, there seems to be a great deal of optimism among women about their rapidly expanding opportunities in the social, economic, and political spheres, despite their realization that they do not yet share fully in the resources of the system.

MINORITY POLITICAL ATTITUDES

Systematic inquiry into the political attitudes of most ethnic minorities has been sorely lacking. Only a few tentative generalizations can be drawn at this point. In general, the political attitudes of minorities are, as one would expect, somewhat more critical of government than those of white Americans.[27] Blacks, Hispanics, American Indians and Asians often are more critical of public authorities in government and the policies they have produced.

This is not to say that these groups are any less supportive of the fundamental values of American democrary, such as freedom, liberty, justice and equality. Opinion research into the attitudes of black, Hispanic and Indian children, for example, has shown that they believe at least as strongly in these concepts in their ideal sense as do white Americans.[28] Interestingly, in light of the irrational fear of some, these studies also show that blacks and Hispanics are as patriotic as Americans of the majority culture. That is, they evidence an equally high level of positive emotion toward the American political community, while at the same time evidencing some special feeling toward their homelands, e.g., Africa and Mexico.

Traditional measures of attitudes that underlie political participation, such as civic duty, political efficacy and political trust, are usually at lower levels for these ethnic minorities than for core-culture Americans.[29] That these ethnic attitudes are slightly less positive is not surprising. What is surprising is the degree of similarity between the political attitudes of minorities and those of the majority culture, given these groups' history of political discrimination and differential treatment.

Further investigation is necessary to elaborate upon the political attitudes of these groups and, more specifically, their attitudes in individual states. Some public opinion polls in the states have begun to include larger samples of ethnic minorities in order to learn more about the political opinions of these groups, who are becoming increasingly important participants in the American political system.

GENERAL PATTERNS OF POLITICAL PARTICIPATION AND ORGANIZATION

Racial and ethnic minorities have pursued multiple strategies to advance their groups' political rights and interests. Since electoral politics in all its manifestations was prohibited to them both by law and by tradition, these groups have often been forced to go outside the system and engage in the politics of direct action. That is, they have employed unconventional and sometimes "radical" political tactics to make their interests heard. In the past, political resistance to the dominant society has included the use of force. Particularly during the nineteenth century, Indians and Hispanics resorted to armed struggle to resist encroaching Anglo-American influence on their lands. In Mexican communities in Texas, California and New Mexico, "social bandits" engaged in fence-cutting, robbery, and skirmishes with Anglos to protect their rights and property.[30]

The direct-action political strategies of the activist decades of the 1960s and 1970s provide additional examples of unconventional politics. The United Farm Workers of America (UFW), under the leadership of Cesar Chavez, acquired political and economic leverage through the use of the consumer boycott. Numerous Chicano organizations participated in rallies, marches, demonstrations, and sit-ins to voice their opposition to police brutality, unequal educational opportunity, the Vietnam War, and other issues. American Indian activists participated in "fish-ins" in the Pacific Northwest to demand protection of their traditional land and fishing rights. In addition, their territorial occupations of California's Alcatraz Island and Wounded Knee, South Dakota, brought American Indian grievances to national attention.[31]

Minority groups have achieved both positive and negative results from engaging in alternative forms of political participation. Perhaps the most significant success of direct action during the 1960s and 1970s lies in the increased political awareness that minority group movements generated within their own communities, as well as among the general population.

Substantive gains for minority groups have most clearly been made, however, through the use of the courts. Organizations such as the Mexican American Legal Defense and Educational Fund (MALDEF) and other civil rights groups have sought to remedy unfavorable political arrangements through the courts. It was in the courts that, on a national level, blacks were successful in safeguarding their rights when other agents of government remained discriminatory. They won favorable court interpretations based on post–Civil War constitutional amendments. Foremost among these decisions was the 1954 Supreme Court case of *Brown v. Board of Education*, which struck down the doctrine of separate-but-equal—the foundation of racial segregation in the South.

In the 1970s and 1980s, Hispanics and Indians won court battles which helped to correct the political inequalities fostered by the malapportionment of local and state legislative bodies. Key decisions also struck down several instances of at-large, multi-member districts, which worked against the probabilities of a numerical minority wielding electoral power.[32]

Litigation has been a key element in American Indian efforts to protect their rights for several reasons. Indians bear a special legal relationship to the federal government and enjoy a special political status under the U.S. Constitution.[33] Thus, their grievances often involve legal and constitutional questions. Furthermore, their opportunities for conventional political success are seriously limited by their small numbers. During the 1980s, they have increasingly turned to the courts for redress of grievances and protection of their land, mineral and water resources, especially from infringement by state and local government.

Another political strategy involves the organized use of interest groups. The late 1970s and 1980s witnessed concerted efforts on the part of women and minorities to form interest groups or pressure groups to engage in lobbying at the national level. Numerous women's groups and minority organizations established headquarters or located branch offices in Washington, D.C. Examples of such Washington-based groups are the National Council of La Raza and the National Association of Latino Elected and Appointed Officials (NALEO), the American Indian Congress, and the National Organization for Women. These organizations have been working to secure favorable policy decisions from federal officials, such as legislation guaranteeing equal opportunities, including the Equal Rights Amendment. They have been useful resource centers as well for local and state minority groups.

PATTERNS OF POLITICAL REPRESENTATION
FOR WOMEN AND ETHNIC MINORITIES

The activist decades of the 1960s and 1970s, in conjunction with political organizing during the 1980s, have produced notable increases in formal political representation for women and ethnic minorities. Gains in representation have been most clearly made at the local level, with some improvement at the state and national level as well.

The farm workers' movement and related Chicano political activities during the mid-1960s produced significant changes in the rural areas of the western states. Most notably in California and Texas, communities with majority Chicano populations wrested control of local governments from the Anglo minorities which formerly held power. City councils, school boards, county commissions, local judgeships and even elected executive positions such as mayorships, were filled by newly activated Chicano majorities supporting their own co-ethnics at the local level.[34] Overall, Hispanic official representation in government has increased from just a few hundred in the 1950s to over three thousand elected officials in the mid-1980s.[35]

American Indian activism of the 1960s and 1970s appears to have had a similar impact on Indian communities. American Indian voting in the elections of the core culture has been on the increase. In largely Indian areas, such as northern and western New Mexico and the state of Alaska, Indian people have elected their co-ethnics to local government bodies such as school boards and county commissions. In Alaska, several hundred Eskimos and Aleuts hold local offices, surpassing the total number of Indian officials found throughout the rest of the forty-nine states.[36]

Blacks in the western region of the United States have been part of the larger national black civil rights movement that has helped them gain more social, educational and economic resources within the system. Some degree of increased political participation, including office-holding, has resulted. However, the West has given blacks no special advantages politically beyond those earned by the national black civil rights movement.

Asian Americans, especially Chinese and Japanese Americans, have increased their participation and political influence, particularly in local elections in California. In 1971, Norman Y. Mineta was elected mayor of San Jose, California, thus becoming the first Japanese-American mayor of a big city on the U.S. mainland. Three years later, Mineta won election to the U.S. Congress.[37] In 1985, Michael Woo became the first Asian to be elected to the Los Angeles city council. His "near landslide" victory pointed out that despite their small numbers, Asians can still be elected to public office.[38] Japanese Americans continue to play a significant role in Hawaiian politics, as evidenced by their high levels of political participation and the numerous political offices they hold throughout the state.[39]

Increased participation and representation has been reflected at the state level as well, although not with the same rate of success. Illustrative of the difference between political successes at the local and the state levels is the history of La Raza Unida Party (LRUP) in Texas. Although successful in winning majority control of many small south Texas cities, when LRUP went statewide in its attempts to elect a governor, it mustered only 6% of the statewide vote. It is difficult for a group that has only 5% to 35% of the population to elect one of its members to a statewide post. Thus, the politics of numbers tend to provide minority groups with better opportunities for representation on the local than the state level.

Nevertheless, some important statewide positions have been won by Mexican American candidates. At one point during the 1970s, two of the five southwestern states had Hispanic governors, Jerry Apodaca in New Mexico and Raoul Castro in Arizona. On the other hand, no black, Indian, or Asian governors have yet been elected in modern history in the western states, outside of Hawaii.[40] Likewise, only a handful of women have served as governors across the country. The early decades of the twentieth century witnessed the election of two women governors in the West, Miriam "Ma" Ferguson in Texas and

Nellie D. Tayloe Ross in Wyoming. In recent history, however, only one woman has been elected governor in a western state: Dixie Lee Ray was elected governor of Washington in 1977.[41]

Beyond gubernatorial positions, other notable examples of minority candidates elected to statewide posts are Wilson Riles as superintendent of public schools, Mervyn Dymally as lieutenant governor and March Fong Eu as secretary of state, all in California. As noted previously, Hawaii has a history of Asian Americans serving in elective office; they have attained positions at the highest levels of state government, including the office of governor, lieutenant governor and attorney general, as well as party leadership positions in both houses of the state legislature.[42] As many successful minority candidates have shown, the traditional political art of coalition-building is a necessity for gains in electoral politics beyond the local level.

Since state legislators are not elected in statewide elections, but instead are chosen from smaller legislative districts throughout the state, the most noticeable increases in ethnic representation have been made in the legislatures of the western states. Table 8.3 shows the percentage of state legislative seats held by blacks, Hispanics, and women in the fourteen states of the West in 1985.

Although these percentages point to persistent patterns of underrepresentation for all of these groups, they also reflect the gains made over the past several decades. Hispanic representation is reflected in only those areas with high concentrations of Hispanics—that is, the five southwestern states. While New Mexico Hispanics retain their significant influence from the past, major increases in the ranks of Hispanic legislators have occurred in Arizona, Colorado, California and Texas. Some legislative leadership positions have also been won by Hispanics in Colorado, Arizona and New Mexico.

As Table 8.3 indicates, blacks are found in several state legislatures in the West, but their presence is limited. Among the fourteen western states, California and Texas have the largest percentage of blacks in their legislatures. However, some black legislators have assumed important legislative roles, such as Willie L. Brown, Jr., who served as speaker of the assembly in the California state legislature.

Asians and American Indians hold state legislative seats in those states where their numbers are greatest. Asian representation is greatest (approximately a majority) in Hawaii's state legislature. In 1986, there was only a handful of American Indians in the state legislatures of Alaska (6), Arizona (3), Colorado (1), Idaho (2), Montana (3), New Mexico (5) and Wyoming (1).[43]

Table 8.3   Percent of State Legislative Seats Held by Blacks, Hispanics, and Women in 1985

State Legislature	% Black	% Hispanic	% Women
Alaska	1.7	0.0	18.3
Arizona	2.2	13.3	20.0
California	6.7	5.8	12.5
Colorado	3.0	9.0	24.0
Hawaii	0.0	1.3	18.4
Idaho	0.0	0.0	19.0
Montana	0.0	1.3	14.7
Nevada	4.8	0.0	15.9
New Mexico	0.0	30.4	11.6
Oregon	3.3	0.0	20.0
Texas	7.7	12.7	8.8
Utah	1.0	0.0	6.7
Washington	2.0	0.0	23.8
Wyoming	1.1	0.0	25.5

Sources: Black Elected Officials: A National Roster 1986, 15th ed. (Washington, D.C.: Joint Center for Political Studies, 1986); *National Directory of Women Elected Officials 1985* (Washington, D.C.: National Women's Political Caucus, 1985); and U.S. Department of Commerce, Bureau of the Census, *Statistical Abstract of the United States 1987,* 107th ed., 241, table 415.

Compared to minority groups, women hold higher percentages of state legislative seats. However, women also make up approximately 50% of the populations in these various states (the major exceptions being Alaska, Hawaii, Nevada, and Wyoming). Consequently, they still are far from achieving the level of representation that their numbers warrant. While more women have been elected to state office across the country since the 1950s and 1960s, surprisingly little change in the number of women representatives in state legislatures has occurred from 1975 to 1985. Moreover, as one study concludes, over this same decade women's level of proportional representation dropped in many states for one or more years.[44]

Clearly, while gains in political representation for all groups have occurred, there is much room for improvement, in the West as well as throughout the country.

MINORITIES AND POLITICAL PARTIES

Throughout U.S. history, the major political parties have sought the participation of minorities only when it was to their advantage to do so. That is, these previously excluded elements typically were brought into the party system when a party badly needed to increase its potential electoral strength and had nowhere else to turn. When these groups have participated in party affairs, it has usually been under conditions stipulated by the party. Most often this has meant exchanging electoral support for various forms of partronage for individuals, especially in public sector employment. This has always produced the danger of cooption of potential leaders of these minorities into the system without any gains for the rank and file or the general communities of the ethnic groups.

Minorities have generally not occupied influential positions in the party hierarchy itself, although a few "token" ethnics have been used as window dressing to claim that one party or another was most supportive of a particular group's political agenda. Yet, outside of New Mexico, ethnic minorities are not significantly represented among the ranks of the party hierarchies.

In general, it has been the Democratic party that has been most open to the ethnic minorities in the West. The Republican party's social exclusivity and conservative policy positions have not made a comfortable home for most socioeconomically disadvantaged minorities. The partisan affiliation of distinctive ethnic minority groups, however, is best reflected in their psychological membership—that is, the identification that each group may feel with the major parties. In all states of the West, Hispanics, American Indians and blacks identify in large majorities with the Democratic party. The largest proportion of Democratic party identifiers occurs among the blacks, who identify at about 80–90%. Overall, Mexican Americans in the West identify as Democrats at about 65–70% rates. Partisan loyalties appear to be more divided in the Asian community. Voter registration in 1984 in California indicated that Asians affiliated equally with the Democratic and Republican parties (42% registered Democratic; 41% Republican; 16% declined to state).[45]

Women, being by far the largest and most socioeconomically diverse group, have divided loyalties with regard to political parties. In the past they have been slightly more Democratic than their male counterparts, but not by large proportions.[46] Since the party reforms of the 1960s and 1970s, at least in the Democratic party, party rules now call for quota representation of ethnic minorities. Both parties have also reserved places for both males and females in their state delegations to the national party organization and the national conventions.

In sum, ethnic minorities and women in the West have made significant gains in the area of political representation and organization, especially over the past three decades. In response to these, some favorable public policies have been secured. Yet these groups have not achieved the level of social, economic, and political equity that the American way of life and, more specifically, the frontier opportunities of the West have made available to others.

Public Policies and Issues of Concern to Women and Ethnic Minorities

The issues that have been of particular concern to minority groups in the West are important to assess, for in a sense they form the "guts" or substance of minority group politics—they provide the basis for group demands on the political system. To the extent that they capture the attention of the general public and the political decision-makers, minority group issues also shape public policy. Thus, minority group issues impact the larger society as well as the minority populations themselves.

It is important to point out that issues that generate minority group mobilization are not necessarily issues that the groups themselves have chosen to address. Minority group action often is a response to policies and issues that originate outside the group, from sectors of the dominant society. In many cases, minority groups perceive such issues or policies as threatening to their rights. Thus, they seek to defend their communities against issues and policies that are not of their choosing. In the end, because these issues must be dealt with, they become "minority issues."

ISSUE IMPORTANCE AT THE MASS LEVEL

Although few in number, opinion surveys have been conducted among certain minority populations in the West to determine what minority respondents think are the most important (i.e., serious) problems facing their community and the country. The results, while far from definitive, do suggest some underlying patterns in issue importance among minority groups.

Overall, four major types of issues appear to be at the forefront of minority group concerns. They can be broadly described as (1) economic issues, (2) socially disruptive issues, (3) public service issues and (4) discrimination/race relations issues. Surveys conducted in San

Antonio, Texas, and East Los Angeles, California, show that in the early 1980s Mexican Americans considered unemployment and crime to be the most serious problems in their local communities. The respondents indicated lack of education, inadequate public services, and discrimination as also being significant issues of concern.[47]

A 1984 cross-cultural survey of minorities in California found that unemployment was an important issue for Latinos, Asians and, most especially, for blacks. In addition, discrimination, race relations, and education emerged as important problems specifically facing these racial/ethnic groups.[48] Surveys of American Indians in New Mexico and Arizona clearly indicate that unemployment or the lack of jobs has also been of major concern to Indian communities. Unlike other minority groups, however, American Indians specifically list alcoholism and drug abuse among their most serious community problems. Additional issues of importance include housing, education, public services, and poverty.[49]

The evidence indicates that minority group populations tend to be mostly concerned with issues that relate directly to their quality of life and the immediate material circumstances in which they live. Political scientists have referred to these concerns, taken as a whole, as *welfare issues*. They can be distinguished, for example, from *status issues*, which concern a group's overall status or political and social position in society.[50] Demands for equal rights and increased minority representation in government, for example, could be considered status issues.

Are ethnic minorities more concerned with welfare issues than Anglos/whites? Are there gender differences on the question of issue importance? Unfortunately, both of these questions remain largely unexplored. A study of Anglos and Mexican Americans in San Antonio, Texas, indicates that generally both groups identify similar types of issues as important to them, but they rank them differently in terms of significance.[51] There is some evidence that men and women perceive the importance of many national and international issues differently, as do ethnic minorities in relation to whites, but gender differences on the community level remain largely unexplored.[52]

MINORITY LEADERSHIP CONCERNS AND
PRIORITY ISSUES

Those who represent minority concerns to the dominant society include a wide array of individuals, groups and organizations. Individuals who hold elected or appointed positions in government (including tribal governments), the directors and members of minority and women's organizations, and community leaders and activists are considered important group representatives.

In examining the nature of minority group and women's activism, it is apparent that their group representatives and leaders recognize welfare issues as major concerns facing their respective constituencies. Numerous minority and women's groups have organized around such issues, demanding better jobs, education, housing and public services for themselves and their children. But it is also clear that other types of issues have served as important bases for minority group mobilization.

Generally speaking, the issues upon which minority group activism has focused also involve the larger questions of *group status* and *empowerment*. That is, those who organize and advocate for the interests of minority populations and women largely attempt to do three things: (1) protect the civil rights of their group, (2) elevate their group's status within the larger society, and (3) enhance and extend the group's power and influence throughout society.

These larger concerns have involved ethnic minorities and women in conflict and controversy with sectors of the dominant society over questions such as constitutional rights and protections, territorial rights, language and culture, political power and self-determination. When concerns with welfare issues are included, one can appreciate the complexity and full range of the policy and issue agenda that minority groups encounter.

The minority political agenda described above is not peculiar to the western states. Rather, it is a national agenda that assumes particular characteristics in different regions of the country. Examples of how this complex agenda has taken form in the West will be highlighted through a few examples.

Strengthening the constitutional and legal protections for minority and women's rights has met with both successes and failures. Particularly successful have been the legal challenges to state and local electoral arrangements that have proven discriminatory to minority populations. For example, Mexican American groups have been at the forefront of the legal battles in California, Colorado, New Mexico and Texas to replace at-large electoral systems with single-member district elections and to ensure that minority voting rights are protected through the reapportionment and redistricting process.[53]

In the area of employment discrimination, affirmative action plans for women and minorities in hiring and promotion continue to be upheld in the courts. Women's rights advocates were especially pleased with the outcome of a California employment case, *Johnson v. Transportation Agency, Santa Clara, California*. On March 25, 1987, in a 6-to-3 decision, the U.S. Supreme Court upheld the affirmative action plan of the City of Santa Clara, which marked "the first time the Supreme Court upheld the use of affirmative action plans for women."[54] Other efforts to enhance the constitutional and legal rights of minorities and women have met with less favorable results. The women's movement suffered a disappointment when the Equal Rights Amendment (ERA) was not incorporated into the U.S. Constitution. By the deadline for ratification, June 30, 1982, only thirty-five of the necessary thirty-eight states had ratified the amendment. Arizona, Nevada and Utah were among the fifteen states that did not ratify the ERA; Idaho ratified the amendment but subsequently sought to rescind that action.[55] In many state legislatures across the West, state funding for abortions continues to be challenged. And some issues, such as pay equity for women and minorities and comprehensive child care legislation, appear to be far from resolved.

Of special significance in the West and Southwest is public policy concerning land, water and other natural resources. For American Indians, other native peoples and Mexican Americans, policies in this area often threaten their "territorial rights" as indigenous inhabitants or original settlers of the area. From their perspective, controversies over land claims and water use, grazing and fishing rights and natural resource development have posed vital threats to their material livelihood as well as to their group status and influence in their homelands—areas in which they have historically resided.

In recent years, American Indian interest groups have had significant success through litigation challenging state governments over land rights. Strong and unified leadership and a significant presence in the state secured for Indian people a land claims settlement in Alaska in 1971 that was heralded as a "phenomenal accomplishment."[56] Treaty fishing rights for American Indians in western Washington State have also been subject to intense litigation and community struggle.

Similarly, for Hispanos in northern New Mexico and southwest Colorado, land rights have historically served as the basis for group mobilization. Groups such as the Chama Land Rights Council continue to advocate Hispano access and control over "la tierra." However, Hispano grievances have not met with the same success as have Indian claims.

Intrinsically tied to issues of territorial rights are questions of language and cultural preservation. For American Indians, their homelands are more than simply geographic locations of residence. They are imbued with religious, cultural and symbolic meaning as well. The American Southwest, once Mexican territory, evokes similarly strong feelings of cultural identity among many Mexican Americans.

Given their sense of place in this region, these groups have at times resisted (or at least resented) the increasing presence and influence of Anglo-Americans among them. For many, Anglo-American dominance translates into encroachment on their cultural rights to language, religion and self-determination. Consequently, policies that seek to protect and preserve such rights, such as bilingual education and the use of bilingual ballots, find significant support within these populations.[57]

During the 1980s, efforts to declare English the official language of the country, through the adoption of an amendment to the U.S. Constitution, have stirred much controversy in the West. Hispanic leaders and interest groups are at the forefront of the opposition to such efforts. They contend that the "English-only movement" represents a nativist and racist attack on multiculturalism in the United States. They point out that the proposed amendment appears to be a symbolic gesture, recognizing the importance of the English language in this country's heritage. However, its intent is to permit legislation that will eradicate the culture and language protections that non–English-speaking minorities currently enjoy.[58]

U.S. English, a national organization promoting the constitutional amendment, has declared publicly its intention to overhaul bilingual education programs and to eliminate provisions for bilingual ballots when the Voting Rights Act is under congressional review in 1992. U.S. English and its allies have taken their language policy initiative to the state level. In 1986, voters in California overwhelmingly approved an initiative declaring English the official language of the state. However, in New Mexico, similar efforts failed. By the end of 1987, a total of thirteen states had declared English as their official language. Numerous other states will consider similar proposals in the years to come. In Colorado and Arizona, English-language measures appeared on the November 1988 ballot and passed in both states.[59]

Conclusion

The search for political power is clearly a concern around which all the groups discussed here have mobilized. The 1980s were marked by renewed group interest in pursuing electoral strategies aimed at increasing levels of formal political representation. Consequently, voter registration and education campaigns have been launched among all of these ethnic communities to increase their political interest and expand their electoral strength. Women's organizations have increasingly sponsored training workshops to enhance the political skills of women to foster their growing participation in politics. Electoral contests involving minority and women candidates have spurred grassroots organization as these elections assume symbolic importance for group power. The quest for political power has registered some significant victories in the West. In the end, however, it remains an ongoing campaign across the country for all groups.

Fundamentally embedded in many of these issues concerning group status and empowerment is the nature of these groups' control over their own affairs and destinies. At different times, in different ways, each has asserted its rights to some form of self-determination. For Indians, tribal sovereignty is the critical issue. Black and Chicano demands in the past have ranged from community control of local institutions to the creation of separatist states. The feminist agenda has sought to expand women's control over their own lives, beginning with the most personal (i.e., reproductive rights).

Self-determination in the 1980s perhaps can best be characterized as the quest for cultural pluralism. That is, minority groups and women seek to change the dominant-subordinate relationships that characterize their social and political lives. They seek more equitable relationships—a sharing of power across all social groups and a fundamental recognition of the value of cultural diversity in the collective experience of all Americans. As women and ethnic minorities continue to assert their political agendas in western politics, the viability of cultural pluralism will be increasingly tested.

Notes

1. For purposes of this chapter, the West is composed of fourteen states: Alaska, Arizona, California, Colorado, Hawaii, Idaho, Montana, Nevada, New Mexico, Oregon, Texas, Utah, Washington and Wyoming. Unlike the authors of other chapters in this book, we have included Texas in our analysis. See discussion in text.

2. The terms *Mexican American* and *Chicano* are used interchangeably to refer to the Mexican-origin population in the United States. The term *Hispanic*

refers to the Spanish-origin population in the United States, of which Mexican Americans make up the majority. According to the U.S. census, in 1987 the Hispanic population in the United States divided into the following groups: Mexican Americans 63%, Puerto Ricans 12%, Cubans 5%, and Central and South Americans, along with "Other Hispanics," compose 19% of the total Hispanic population.

3. Keith T. Poole and L. Harmon Zeigler, *Women, Public Opinion, and Politics: The Changing Political Attitudes of American Women* (New York: Longman, 1985).

4. John A. Garcia, "Yo Soy Mexicano . . . : Self-Identity and Sociodemographic Correlates," *Social Science Quarterly* 62 (March 1981), 88–98.

5. Murray Wax, *Indian Americans: Unity and Diversity* (Englewood Cliffs, N.J.: Prentice Hall, 1971).

6. The literature on specific racial and ethnic groups is extensive. Important overviews include: Hanes Walton, Jr., *Invisible Politics: Black Political Behavior* (Albany, N.Y.: State University of New York Press, 1985) and *Black Politics: A Theoretical and Structural Analysis* (Philadelphia, Pa.: Lippincott, 1972); Rodolfo Acuna, *Occupied America: A History of Chicanos*, 3rd ed. (New York: Harper & Row, 1988); F. Chris Garcia and Rodolfo O. de la Garza, *The Chicano Political Experience: Three Perspectives* (North Scituate, Mass.: Duxbury Press, 1977); Joan Moore and Harry Pachon, *Hispanics in the United States* (Englewood Cliffs, N.J.: Prentice Hall, 1985); Vine Deloria, Jr., and Clifford M. Lytle, *The Nations Within: The Past and Future of American Indian Sovereignty* (New York: Pantheon, 1984) and *American Indians, American Justice* (Austin: University of Texas Press, 1983); and Vine Deloria, Jr., ed., *American Indian Policy in the Twentieth Century* (Norman: University of Oklahoma Press, 1985).

Bibliographies include Hanes Walton, Jr., "The Recent Literature on Black Politics," *PS* 18 (Fall 1985), 769–80; Albert Camarillo, ed., *Latinos in the United States: A Historical Bibliography* (Santa Barbara, Calif.: ABC-CLIO, 1986); Francis Paul Prucha, *A Bibliographical Guide to the History of Indian-White Relations in the U.S.* (Chicago: University of Chicago Press, 1977) and *U.S. Indian Policy: A Critical Bibliography* (Bloomington: Published for the Newberry Library by Indiana University Press, 1977).

7. Deloria and Lytle, *The Nations Within*, and Deloria, ed., *American Indian Policy in the Twentieth Century.*

8. Christine M. Sierra, "Chicano Political Development: Historical Considerations," in *Chicano Studies: A Multidisciplinary Approach*, ed. Eugene Garcia, Francisco Lomeli, and Isidro Ortiz (New York: Teachers College Press, Columbia University, 1984), 79–98.

9. Juan R. Garcia, *Operation Wetback: The Mass Deportation of Mexican Undocumented Workers in 1954* (Westport, Conn.: Greenwood Press, 1980), and Abraham Hoffman, *Unwanted Mexican Americans in the Great Depression: Repatriation Pressures, 1929–1939* (Tucson: University of Arizona Press, 1974).

10. Peter Irons, *Justice at War: The Story of the Japanese American Internment Cases* (New York: Oxford University Press, 1983).

11. For a specific focus on the American Southwest, see Mario Barrera, *Race and Class in the Southwest: A Theory of Racial Inequality* (Notre Dame, Ind.: University of Notre Dame Press, 1979).

12. Daniel McCool, "Indian Voting," in Deloria, *American Indian Policy in the Twentieth Century*, 105–16.

13. Judy Tachibana, "California's Asians," *California Journal* (November 1986), 535; and Robert W. Gardner, Bryant Robey, and Peter C. Smith, *Asian Americans: Growth, Change, and Diversity, Population Bulletin* 40 (October 1985), 24–27.

14. Used extensively in the American Southwest, the term *Anglo* refers to non-Hispanic whites.

15. Lynn Simross, "The Plight of Native Americans on the 'Urban Reservation,'" *Los Angeles Times*, April 16, 1986, sec. V, p. 2, and Michael A. Dorris, "The Grass Still Grows, the Rivers Still Flow: Contemporary Native Americans," *Daedalus: Journal of the American Academy of Arts and Sciences* 110 (Spring 1981), 59–60.

16. Deloria and Lytle, *The Nations Within*; Fred R. Harris and LaDonna Harris, "Native Americans and Tribal Governments in New Mexico," chap. 8 in *New Mexico Government*, ed. F. Chris Garcia and Paul L. Hain, rev. ed. (Albuquerque: University of New Mexico Press, 1981), 182; and McCool, "Indian Voting."

17. Rodolfo O. de la Garza, Anthony Kruszewski, and Tomas A. Arciniega, eds., *Chicanos and Native Americans: The Territorial Minorities* (Englewood Cliffs, N.J.: Prentice Hall, 1973).

18. John A. Garcia and Carlos H. Arce, "Political Orientations and Behaviors of Chicanos: Trying to Make Sense Out of Attitudes and Participation," in *Latinos and the Political System*, ed. F. Chris Garcia (Notre Dame, Ind.: University of Notre Dame Press, 1988), 125–51.

19. F. Chris Garcia, "Manitos and Chicanos in New Mexico Politics," in *La Causa Politica: A Chicano Politics Reader*, ed. F. Chris Garcia (Notre Dame, Ind.: University of Notre Dame Press, 1974), 271–80.

20. See, for example, the historical studies of Albert Camarillo, *Chicanos in a Changing Society: From Mexican Pueblos to American Barrios in Santa Barbara and Southern California, 1848–1930* (Cambridge, Mass.: Harvard University Press, 1979); Arnoldo De Leon, *The Tejano Community, 1836–1900* (Albuquerque: University of New Mexico Press, 1982); and Mario T. Garcia, *Desert Immigrants: The Mexicans of El Paso, 1880–1920* (New Haven: Yale University Press, 1981).

21. Tachibana, "California's Asians," 540.

22. *Ibid.*, 537.

23. Gardner *et al.*, *Asian Americans*, esp. 5–12.

24. T. A. Larson, *History of Wyoming* (Lincoln: University of Nebraska Press, 1965), 78–82.

25. Adjusting for differences in age, employment status, education, and other characteristics, men and women show comparable rates of voter registration and turnout. Indeed, among the more highly educated, women have slightly higher rates of voter turnout than their male counterparts. James MacGregor Burns, J. W. Peltason, and Thomas E. Cronin, *Government by the People*, Bicentennial Edition 1987–89 (Englewood Cliffs, N.J.: Prentice Hall, 1987), 226; and Poole and Zeigler, *Women, Public Opinion, and Politics*, 121–27.

26. Poole and Zeigler, *Women, Public Opinion, and Politics*, 129–40.

27. Paul Abramson, *The Political Socialization of Black Americans: A Critical Evaluation of Research on Efficacy and Trust* (New York: Free Press, 1977); Robert R. Brischetto and Rodolfo O. de la Garza, *The Mexican American Electorate: Political Participation and Ideology* and *The Mexican American Electorate: Political Opinions and Behavior Across Cultures in San Antonio*, Occasional Papers Nos. 3 and 5 (Austin: Joint Publications of the Southwest Voter Registration Education Project, San Antonio Texas, and the Hispanic Population Studies Program of the Center for Mexican American Studies, University of Texas at Austin, 1983 and 1985); Rodolfo O. de la Garza, ed., *Ignored Voices: Public Opinion Polls and the Latino Community* (Austin: Center for Mexican American Studies, University of Texas at Austin, 1987); Garcia and Arce, "Political Orientations and Behaviors of Chicanos"; and Louis Harris, *The Anguish of Change* (New York: W. W. Norton, 1973).

28. Charles S. Bullock and Harrel R. Rodgers, Jr., eds., *Black Political Attitudes: Implications for Political Support* (Chicago: Markham, 1972); F. Chris Garcia, *Political Socialization of Chicano Children: A Comparative Study with Anglos in California Schools* (New York: Praeger, 1973); Edward S. Greenberg, "Black Children and the Political System," *Public Opinion Quarterly* 34 (Fall 1970), 333–45; and Margaret Maier Murdock, "Political Attachment Among Native Americans: Arapahoe and Shoshoni Children and the National Political System," *Social Science Journal* 20 (April 1983), 41–58.

29. Brischetto and de la Garza, *The Mexican American Electorate: Political Opinions and Behavior*, and *Political Participation and Ideology*; Bruce E. Cain and D. Roderick Kiewiet, *Minorities in California* (Pasadena: California Institute of Technology, 1986); Garcia and Arce, "Political Orientations and Behaviors of Chicanos"; and Dale C. Nelson, "Ethnicity and Socioeconomic Status as Sources of Participation: The Case for Ethnic Political Culture," *American Political Science Review* 73 (December 1979), 1024–38.

30. See, for example, Robert J. Rosenbaum, *Mexicano Resistance in the Southwest: "The Sacred Right of Self-Preservation"* (Austin: University of Texas Press, 1981).

31. Rex Weyler, *Blood of the Land: The Government and Corporate War Against the American Indian Movement* (New York: Vintage Books, 1982).

32. Richard Santillan, "The Latino Community in State and Congressional

Redistricting: 1961–1985," *Journal of Hispanic Politics* 1 (1985), 52–66, and *The Hispanic Community and Redistricting, Volume II* (Claremont, Calif.: Rose Institute of State and Local Government, Claremont McKenna College, 1984).

33. Harris and Harris, "Native Americans and Tribal Governments in New Mexico."

34. John Staples Shockley, *Chicano Revolt in a Texas Town* (Notre Dame, Ind.: University of Notre Dame Press, 1974).

35. National Association of Latino Elected and Appointed Officials (NALEO), *National Roster of Hispanic Elected Officials* (Washington, D.C.: NALEO Education Fund, Inc., 1984).

36. Systematic information on American Indian elected officials is scarce. The only directory available for this study was Teresa Brito-Asenap, *National Indian Elected Officials Directory* (Albuquerque, N.M.: National Indian Youth Council, 1986). This directory listed eighty-eight Indian local officials in Alaska. However, scholars familiar with Alaska politics indicate that Native American officials number well into the hundreds in that state.

37. John H. Culver and John C. Syer, *Power and Politics in California*, 3rd ed. (New York: Macmillan, 1988).

38. Frank Clifford, "Woo's Victory—Asians Come of Political Age," *Los Angeles Times*, June 6, 1985, sec. I, p. 1.

39. Neal R. Peirce and Jerry Hagstrom, *The Book of America: Inside 50 States Today* (New York: W. W. Norton, 1983), 870; *State Elective Officials and the Legislatures 1987–88* (Lexington, Ky.: The Council of State Governments, 1987), 28–29; and Michael Barone and Grant Ujifusa, *The Almanac of American Politics, 1988* (Washington, D.C.: National Journal, 1987).

40. Most recently, George Ariyoshi served as governor of Hawaii from 1974 to 1986. John D. Waihee, a native Hawaiian, was elected as governor in 1986. His term expires in 1990. See Peirce and Hagstrom, *The Book of America*, 870; and Barone and Ujifusa, *Almanac of American Politics*, 314.

41. In 1988, Arizona's governor Evan Mecham was impeached and convicted of official misconduct while in office. During Mecham's impeachment trial, Rose Mofford, the secretary of state, became acting governor. Upon Mecham's conviction and removal from office, Ms. Mofford was sworn in as governor on April 5, 1988. She will serve out Mecham's term through 1990, whereupon she may seek reelection to office in her own right. *Facts on File,* April 8, 1988, 236, and April 15, 1988, 253; Roy R. Glashan, comp., *American Governors and Gubernatorial Elections, 1775–1978* (Westport, Conn.: Meckler Books, 1979).

42. Peirce and Hagstrom, *The Book of America*, 870; and *State Elective Officials and the Legislatures 1987–1988*, 28–29.

43. Brito-Asenap, *National Indian Elected Officials Directory*, and information supplied by the authors.

44. R. Darcy, Susan Welch, and Janet Clark, *Women, Elections and Representation* (New York: Longman, 1987), 48.

45. Brischetto and de la Garza, *The Mexican American Electorate: Political Participation and Ideology,* 4–6; Cain and Kiewiet, *Minorities in California,* 18–20.

46. Poole and Zeigler, *Women, Public Opinion, and Politics.*

47. Rodolfo O. de la Garza and Robert R. Brischetto, *The Mexican American Electorate: Information Sources and Policy Orientations,* Occasional Paper No. 2 (Austin: Southwest Voter Registration Education Project, San Antonio, Texas, and the Hispanic Population Studies Program of the Center for Mexican American Studies, University of Texas at Austin, 1983), 6–7.

48. Cain and Kiewiet, *Minorities in California,* vol. 1, 25.

49. National Indian Youth Council, *American Indian Political Attitudes and Behavior Survey: Data Report* (Albuquerque, N.M.: National Indian Youth Council, 1983); *Navajo Indian Political Attitudes and Behavior Poll* (Albuquerque, N.M.: National Indian Youth Council, 1984); and *National American Indian Political Attitudes and Issues Poll* (Albuquerque, N.M.: National Indian Youth Council, 1986).

50. Rodolfo O. de la Garza and Adela I. Flores, "The Impact of Mexican Immigrants on the Political Behavior of Chicanos: A Clarification of Issues and Some Hypotheses for Future Research," in *Mexican Immigrants and Mexican Americans: An Evolving Relation,* ed. Harley L. Browning and Rodolfo O. de la Garza (Austin: Center for Mexican American Studies, University of Texas at Austin, 1986), 211; S. J. Makielski, Jr., *Beleaguered Minorities: Cultural Politics in America* (San Francisco: W. H. Freeman, 1973), 157–59.

51. Brischetto and de la Garza, *The Mexican American Electorate: Political Opinions and Behavior Across Cultures,* 17.

52. Poole and Zeigler, *Women, Public Opinion, and Politics,* 57–58.

53. Santillan, "The Latino Community in State and Congressional Redistricting."

54. National Women's Political Caucus, "U.S. Court Endorses Affirmative Action," *Women's Political Times* (Spring 1987), 3; and Mexican American Women's National Association, "Supreme Court Rulings Victory for Women and Minorities," *MANA* (Spring 1987), 2.

55. Nadine Cohodas, "ERA Dies as Deadline Passes; Amendment Is Reintroduced," *Congressional Quarterly Weekly Report,* July 3, 1982, 1585.

56. Theodore W. Taylor, *American Indian Policy* (Mt. Airy, Md.: Lomond Publications, 1983), 22.

57. Cain and Kiewiet, *Minorities in California;* de la Garza and Brischetto, *The Mexican American Electorate: Information Sources and Policy Orientations;* and National Indian Youth Council, *National American Indian Political Attitudes and Issues Poll.*

58. Raul Yzaguirre, "The Perils of Pandora: An Examination of the English-Only Movement," *Journal of Hispanic Policy* 2 (1986–87), 5–8.

59. Antonia Hernandez, "English-Only Busca Destruir Nuestra Existencia, Cultura y Tradicion," *Replica* (September 1988), 22–23; and David Rapp, "Providing Bilingual Education: An Issue Laden with Meaning," *Congressional Quarterly Weekly Report,* April 18, 1987, 733–35.

III

State and Local Government Institutions and Public Policy in the West

9

WESTERN STATE
LEGISLATURES

Paul L. Hain

TO GAIN A SENSE OF WHO HAS POWER IN A STATE, one should devote a few weeks to immersing oneself in the activities of the state legislature, observing both legislators and lobbyists. One will discover that although each legislator has an equal vote on the floor, some legislators have much greater power than others. An astute observer will also discover that certain lobbyists are unusually influential. In this and most other features, the thirteen western state legislatures are similar to the thirty-seven other American state legislatures. All these thirteen are bicameral, all have specific powers granted by their respective state constitutions, and all perform similar functions within the state political system. But in some ways the western state legislatures *are* different from most of the other thirty-seven state legislatures. This chapter will focus on some of those similarities and differences and what effect they have.

Names, Terms of Office, and Size of Legislatures

The upper chamber of every American state legislature is called the senate. The western states grant their senators four-year terms of office much more regularly than do the other states of the Union. In the West only Arizona and Idaho have the two-year senate term found in ten of the thirty-seven other states.

Western senates are smaller than average—a feature that makes service especially attractive, since small legislative chambers are more personal than large ones and in a small chamber each legislator's vote is more important than in a large chamber. Seventeen of the fifty state senates have more than forty-five members; only two of them (Montana and Washington) are in the West. In contrast, seven of the ten smallest senates (thirty or fewer members) are in the West: Alaska has the smallest of all, with twenty members, followed by Arizona, Hawaii, Nevada, Oregon, Utah and Wyoming. This is not too surprising, given the relatively small populations of most western states.

All thirteen western states have two-year terms of office for the members of the lower (larger) legislative chamber. (Five nonwestern states have four-year terms.) Eleven of the western states call this larger chamber the house of representatives, the title used in forty-one states. California and Nevada, however, call the larger chamber the assembly.

As with state senates, the western lower chambers also are relatively small. Thirty-two of the forty-nine lower chambers in the U.S. have 100 or more members. Only one of the western lower chambers (Montana) is that large, while nine of the nation's eleven lower chambers with seventy-five or fewer members are in the West.

When referring to the entire state legislature, eleven of the thirteen western states use the term *legislature,* as do sixteen nonwestern states. Eighteen of the thirty-seven nonwestern states join Colorado in preferring the term *general assembly.* In Oregon the house and senate constitute the Oregon legislative assembly.[1]

Legislative Functions

Legislatures perform several different functions in the American system of the separation of powers in government. The differences in various states' constitutional grants of legislative power, of course, affect whether and how the different legislatures perform various functions. But one should remain aware of the theoretical distinction between the constitutional grant of power and the political function.

Lawmaking is the central function of American state legislatures. Judges, elected executives, and bureaucrats also make binding policy decisions, but to be legitimate those decisions must be consistent with constitutional and statutory provisions. If the legislature disapproves of decisions implementing the law, it can change the law underlying the disliked executive or judicial decision. It is through enactment and/or repeal of statutes (or, as appropriate, successfully proposing amendments to the state constitution) that the legislature changes the criminal code or laws governing divorce, creates or dismantles state agencies or enacts a state budget.[2]

Representation of one's constituents and of one's section of the state is also an important legislative function.[3] Equality of representation (summed up by the phrase "one person, one vote") has been at the heart of the battles over legislative apportionment since the 1960s. As will be discussed below, the western states were among those with the most malapportioned legislatures in the early 1960s.[4]

Largely because of western states' small populations (except in California) most western state legislators represent fewer constituents than do nonwestern legislators. They thus tend to be more accessible to their constituents than is the case with their nonwestern counterparts. They are often elected (or sometimes challenged) with a campaign that relies on going from door to door in their district. This is especially the case in Alaska, Hawaii, Idaho, Montana, Nevada, New Mexico, Utah and Wyoming, where a member of the lower chamber usually represents fewer than twenty thousand people.

Women and nonwhite Americans often point to the importanct of what is known as "descriptive representation." They argue that ordinary citizens would have more faith in the government if the legislature more closely approached to being a mirror of the personal characteristics of the population. As was discussed in Chapter 8, increasing the number of women and minority legislators probably would lead to different policy outcomes in a number of important policy areas.

Representation includes not only attempting to ensure that any new statute (including the state budget) is consistent with the values and needs of one's community back home but also helping one's constitutents find their way through the governmental maze and occasionally interceding with a state agency on a constituent's behalf. These constituent requests for help in coping with the bureaucracy, coupled with the electoral benefits to legislators of responding, have led many state legislatures to provide their members with a personal staff on a year-round basis to help the members in their constituent service chores and to assist them in other ways. A decade ago a year-round personal staff was much more frequent among eastern and midwestern legislatures than in the West, but in recent years the West has almost caught up.[5]

Legislative oversight, which consists of checking executive agencies of state government to ensure compliance with the law and the legislature's policy preferences, is the third major function of state legislatures. The oversight function—a part of the checks and balances between the branches of government—is usually carried out quietly, through informal dialogues between the legislators and the executive agency personnel. But an agency occasionally gets so out of step with the preferences of the legislators that the legislative leaders feel compelled to hold formal "oversight hearings." Continued legislative dissatisfaction can result in (*a*) budget cuts for the offending agency, (*b*) changes in the agency's statutory authority or mission, (*c*) legislatively mandated changes in agency procedures, and/or (*d*) in damaged bureaucratic careers.[6]

In addition to the major functions discussed above, state legislatures also have a *judicial function* and a *leadership selection function.* The judicial function includes the possibility of impeaching judicial and executive officials as well as disciplining errant legislators. Only Oregon, among the fifty states, does not provide for impeachment. The power of impeachment (the power to bring formal charges) lies with the lower chamber of the legislature in forty-seven states and with the single legislative chamber in Nebraska. Forty-five states, including eleven in the West, try the impeached official in the state senate. If convicted, the official is removed from office and can be prohibited from subsequently holding public office. (Criminal punishment for the same offences can also occur.)

Alaska's constitution reverses the normal procedure and gives the power of impeachment to the state senate, with the house conducting the trial. In 1985 Alaska held the first impeachment hearings concerning an incumbent governor since those in Tennessee in 1931. The Alaska senate, where the hearings were held, settled for a resolution reprimanding the governor.[7]

The other recent use of the impeachment power against a governor was also in the West. On February 5, 1988, the Arizona house voted to impeach Governor Evan Mecham, who was also the subject of a recall petition and an indictment. On April 4, after dropping the issue of his concealing a $350,000 campaign loan, the Arizona senate found the governor guilty of obstruction of justice and of illegally lending $80,000 in state money to his auto dealership. Mr. Mecham was removed from office but the vote to prohibit him from subsequently holding public office failed. He later was found not guilty of the criminal charges brought in state court.[8]

The legislature's leadership selection function includes not only the selection of legislative leaders but also involvement in the selection of various executive and judicial officers. The thirteen western senates, as in the other states, have the power to approve or reject gubernatorial appointments to various boards, commissions and high administrative posts.[9] But western state legislatures are much less involved in judicial selection than are some eastern legislatures. The legislatures of three eastern seaboard states elect all of their states' judges, and a fourth elects appellate judges. In contrast, twelve of the thirteen western legislatures have no formal role in the selection of their states' judges. Insofar as judicial selection systems are concerned, it seems that the western progressive tradition has been translated into direct elections of judges or a version of the "Missouri plan." Neither involves the legislature in judicial selection. The western exception is Hawaii, where some judges are appointed by the governor subject to senate confirmation.[10]

Legislative Powers and Constraints

With the exceptions noted above, the powers of the western state legislatures are all similar. Although the state legislatures are granted sweeping powers, they are restricted by various provisions of the state and national constitutions. Constitutional provisions protect individual liberties (e.g., freedom of religion) from governmental abuse and also prohibit such actions as passing bills of attainder or ex post facto legislation. State constitutions often require certain legislative procedures, such as requiring that the title of each bill clearly state what the bill does and that a journal be kept. State constitutions also restrict the legislature's power to tax. Analysis of constitutional restrictions on taxation can give the student of politics a good idea of the power of various interests in the state. The California Constitution (Article XIII, Sec. 3i), for instance, exempts grapevines from property taxation for three years after the season in which they were planted in vineyard form. Most scholars believe such provisions belong in the taxation statutes rather than the constitution, but the protected interests want them in the constitution where they are more difficult to eliminate.

A comparison of the powers of state legislatures requires awareness that the reality of power sometimes differs from what the constitution suggests. For example, New Mexico's constitution seems to grant full control over preparing the state budget to the governor and his or her subordinates. And they do indeed prepare the executive budget. But by statute the interim Legislative Finance Committee also holds budget hearings and produces a recommended budget. That legislative budget is more influential with most legislators than is the executive budget.

Most western states also provide for direct popular participation in the legislative process. Such provisions limit the legislature's power. As has been noted in earlier chapters, the initiative originated in the West as part of the progressive program of the early 1900s and is found much more frequently among the western states than elsewhere.

THE VETO

A major limitation on the powers of most state legislatures is the governor's veto, found in every state but North Carolina. The votes required to override a veto vary from a majority to two-thirds of the members in each legislative chamber. All western states require a two-thirds vote, either of those present (Montana, New Mexico, Oregon and Washington) or of the elected membership. Forty-three states grant the governor an *item veto* over appropriations bills, meaning that the governor can reduce or eliminate individual items in the appropriations bill without having to veto the entire bill. Such authority adds greatly to the power of a conservative governor facing an activist legislature, but is of less use to an activist governor facing a conservative legislature. Only Nevada in the West denies its governor the item veto.[11]

LEGISLATIVE SESSIONS

Western states, overall, limit their legislative sessions a bit more than do the states in the rest of the nation. As recently as 1962 only nineteen state legislatures scheduled regular annual sessions. Today the unusual states are the seven (including Montana, Nevada, and Oregon in the West) whose legislatures still meet only every other year. Only California and Idaho, in the West, place no limit on the number of days the legislature may meet each year, and Oregon does not limit the number of days its biennial session can run. Ten non-western states have annual legislative sessions of unlimited length.[12]

LEGISLATIVE LEADERS

The lower chambers of the state legislatures are all required to elect a speaker (presiding officer) by majority vote on the floor. State constitutions either designate the lieutenant governor as *ex officio* president of the senate or require the senate to elect a president by majority vote on the floor. Organization of each chamber is usually along party lines, although control of a chamber by a cross-party coalition has recently become less of a rarity, especially in the West. Democrat Willie Brown of California, for instance, was initially elected speaker of the assembly with crucial Republican support. The Democratic speaker of the Alaska house of representatives, Jim Duncan, was removed in 1981 by a coalition of Republicans and dissident Democrats. And during the past decade both chambers of the New Mexico legislature have been formally controlled during some sessions by a coalition of Republicans and conservative Democrats.

The speaker of the lower chamber of the state legislature generally is the most powerful member of that chamber and is a state official of substantial independent power. Indeed, the national and state media attention directed at both the late Jesse Unruh and present California assembly speaker Willie Brown suggest an office of great power—power that is enhanced by the uncertainty of just how long the incumbent will retain the post. Speakers occasionally serve for a decade or more, but this seldom happens in the West. Although there are no legal restrictions on how long one person may serve as speaker of the lower chamber, the western states have a greater turnover in that office than do the other states. For example, California, Hawaii and New Mexico are the only western states in which two or more speakers served three or more terms between 1947 and 1980, while that is the case in thirteen of the other thirty-seven states.[13]

Thirty state senates have the lieutenant governor as *ex officio* president by constitutional mandate. The other twenty senates elect a presiding officer from among the membership. Western states prefer the latter approach, but tend to deny their senate presidents any extensive powers. In the West, only California, Idaho, Nevada, New

Mexico and Washington assign the lieutenant governor to be the senate presiding officer. Lieutenant governors seldom make a career in that office, but Washington's John A. Cherberg served thirty-two years in that capacity, through January 1989, setting a record.[14]

Where the lieutenant governor is *ex officio* president of the senate, the powers of the senate president are seldom great. After all, the lieutenant governor might not be a member of the senate majority party and might not have any prior legislative experience. Power in such a senate is more diffuse than in a chamber where the members elect one of their own to preside.

Thirteen of the twenty senates that elect their own presiding officer give him or her powers similar to those of the speaker of the lower chamber, but that occurs less frequently in the West. Of the eight western senates that elect their own president, only Arizona, Oregon and Utah given him or her authority to appoint members and chairs of standing committees. Ten of the twelve nonwestern senates with elected presidents do so.[15]

The authority of other senate leaders is affected by whether the lieutenant governor is *ex officio* senate president. Where that is the case, the president pro tem or majority leader, or both, tend to have more formal power than in a senate that elects a president from among its members. Under either kind of senate organization, of course, one ignores the president pro tem and the party floor leaders at one's peril.

Among the twenty state senates that elect their own president, the western senates have a higher than average turnover in the top spot. Half of the eight western senates in this category had no president who presided more than four years between 1947 and 1980. That was the case for only one-fourth of the nonwestern senates in this set. The pattern of leadership stability is just the opposite where the lieutenant governor is senate president. All five western states in this category had above-average tenure in the president pro tem position from 1947 through 1980.[16]

Professional vs. Amateur Legislatures

State legislatures can be fairly well classified into three categories by the degree to which they are professional legislatures. Some clearly are professional legislatures; some clearly are "citizen" (or amateur) legislatures. The others (semiprofessional) fall in between. In most cases the western state legislatures lie near the "citizen" end of that distribution.

The three types of legislatures are analogous to three types of football teams. At one end of the spectrum are the professional football teams, whose members see themselves as professional football players. At the other end of the spectrum are the members of football teams at small colleges which retain the ideal of the student-athlete and do not provide athletic scholarships. The small college football players are likely to consider themselves college students who enjoy football. In the middle are the major college football powers, whose team members may be unsure whether they are primarily college students or primarily football players.

The National Football League of state legislatures includes nine states, only one of which (California) is in the West. Seven of those states paid each of their legislators $33,000 or more annual salary as of October 1987, plus various expenses. These professional legislatures, which require year-round activity from their members, pay them enough to enable them to live on their legislative salary even if they have no other occupation. These legislatures also provide substantial staff and information services to the members. California legislators, for example, receive annual salaries of $40,816 (in 1989) and $82 per day unvouchered expense allowance while in session. They also have a generous pension plan, reimbursement for 90% of the cost of a leased automobile up to $400 per month, a telephone credit card, a comprehensive insurance package, and up to $244,900 per year per member for office and staff expenses.[17]

The small college equivalent among the state legislatures are those that are clearly "citizen" (*i.e.*, amateur) legislatures made up of people for whom legislative sessions consume sixty days or less per year, whose legislative compensation (if any) is far too little to live on, and who earn their livings from activities outside the legislature. They primarily identify themselves as attorneys, businesspeople, ranchers, and the like, who are temporarily serving as legislators. New Mexico, Utah and Wyoming provide clear examples of citizen legislatures. New Mexico pays no salary, but its legislators receive $75 per day for expenses while the legislature is in session or while at interim committee meetings, as well as mileage for one round trip to the capital each session and to each interim committee meeting. Legislative sessions in New Mexico last sixty days in odd-numbered years and thirty days in even-numbered years. Utah pays legislators $65 per day salary plus mileage, and up to $55 per day of expenses for members who reside away from the capital. The legislature can meet for forty-five days each year, but met for only twenty days in 1984. The Wyoming legislature meets for forty days in odd-numbered years and twenty days in even-numbered years. Members receive 35 cents per mile for one round trip to the capital plus $75 per day salary and $60 per day for expenses. Only limited centralized nonpartisan staff assistance is available to the legislators of these three states. Idaho and Montana are also close to the "citizen" end of the spectrum.

Most members of citizen legislatures lose money while serving— a fact that causes the membership of citizen legislatures to be skewed, even more than elsewhere, toward prosperous citizens. That skewing is evident from Table 9.1, which presents the salaries, gender and occupations of western state legislators. One gets a sense of the differences among the legislatures from such a table, but as with many political phenomena it is difficult to convey the full reality in tabular form. The table shows the occupation listed first by legislators in response to a questionnaire. But what occupation should be listed for a small-town representative who divides her time between her house in town and her ranch, actively participates in the management of the ranch and of a small bank in which she is the largest shareholder and devotes several days per week to the practice of law as the senior member of a three-member firm? Similarly, it is difficult to distinguish between legislators in the "business owner" category like the senator who, with his wife, worked sixty-hour weeks for years to develop a profitable dry-cleaning business, and other ones who have substantial inherited wealth. And of course the "full-time legislator" category includes some wealthy people who can afford to devote themselves to legislative business; some whose spouses earn enough to permit the family to get by with only the legislative salary in addition; and some—primarily in California, among the western states—who were public sector employees (*i.e.*, teachers, social workers, or legislative aides) who realized they could earn as much money and have more job satisfaction by serving in the legislature.

Despite the limits of Table 9.1, it is clear that substantial differences exist in the backgrounds and perspectives of California legislators versus Wyoming legislators, or those in Utah versus those in Washington State. Similar differences exist between the membership of the twelve nonprofessional western state legislatures and that of the eight professional nonwestern legislatures mentioned above. Such differences among legislators reflect not only the structure of the legislatures but also the economic, social, and cultural differences among

Table 9.1   State Legislators: Gender and Occupations (Percent of Legislators in Each Category, 1986)

State	Number of Legislators	Women %	Attorney %	Real Estate %	Insurance %	Education %	Full-time Legislator %	Agriculture %	Business Owner %	Business Executive %	Non Mgmt. Business Employee	Salary (as of Oct. 87)
Alaska	60	18	12	3	0	5	0	2	40	8	7	$22,140/yr
Arizona	90	20	3	7	2	10	13	7	14	9	4	$15,000/yr
California	120	13	18	3	4	6	36	9	13	1	0	$37,105/yr
Colorado	100	24	18	5	3	14	9	11	11	9	2	$17,500/yr
Hawaii	76	17	18	7	3	10	14	3	17	8	0	$15,600/yr
Idaho	105	21	8	2	2	7	0	30	13	6	2	$30/day
Montana	150	15	9	3	3	8	0	32	12	5	9	$52/day
Nevada	60	17	10	3	2	3	0	6	11	11	16	$130/day
New Mexico	112	12	18	6	1	2	0	9	23	11	12	—0—
Oregon	90	20	12	2	3	13	7	14	17	4	8	$11,028/yr
Utah	104	7	13	9	1	12	0	12	25	1	3	$65/day
Washington	147	24	8	3	1	5	0	7	14	10	3	$15,500/yr
Wyoming	92	26	10	2	1	13	0	27	17	10	3	$75/day
Western States Total	1,305	18	12	4	2	8	6	15	17	7	5	—
United States Total	7,461	17	16	4	3	8	11	10	14	6	5	—

Source: Adapted from Beth Bazar, "State Legislators' Occupations: A Decade of Change" (Denver: National Conference of State Legislatures, 1987). The first occupation listed by each legislator is reported. Salary data are from "Summary: Legislators' Compensation and Benefits," October 31, 1987 (Denver: National Conference of State Legislatures, mimeo, 1987).

the various states. Those differences are reflected in the way legislative decisions are made and in the policies that are enacted into law. To a large extent the difference between professional legislatures and citizen legislatures can be summed up by noting that professional legislatures are more oriented toward change and governmental activism, while the citizen legislatures tend to favor the status quo.

As the federal system grows increasingly complex, as state populations increase, and as state officials find less consensus concerning "how things should be done," greater state activity seems to become necessary even in states with a strong ideological commitment to minimal government. If the citizen legislature is to be an effective branch of a more active government (presumably restraining government's growth and activity), the legislature must have increasing numbers of committees that meet during the interim between legislative sessions. Such interim committees permit the exploration of various problems in depth. But the increased demands on legislators make it ever more difficult for the ordinary citizen legislator to earn a living and they also create pressure for more staff support and additional compensation to the legislators, even in states (including most of those in the West) where the ideal of the citizen legislature remains part of the political belief system. An Alaska legislator, discussing such considerations, quite accurately complained on the floor of the house that "all of this is discouraging normal people from running for the legislature."[18]

In between those legislatures which are clearly citizen legislatures and those which are clearly professional are the thirty or so legislatures whose members devote so much time to legislative service that serving in the legislature interferes with their principal occupations, but whose total legislative income is not enough to live on comfortably. These legislatures also tend to provide an intermediate level of staff support. Many such legislatures have a variety of compensation components, making it difficult to estimate the members' total income from legislative service. It is below that provided to members of the professional state legislatures, so that, not unlike Big Ten football players, these legislators can be considered "semiprofessional." Members of these legislatures feel they need long enough sessions to address their states' problems, but many strongly prefer the ideal of a citizen legislature to a professional legislature. As the demands of these semiprofessional legislatures take increasing amounts of time and effort, however, their members find it increasingly difficult to maintain a private occupation. Still, many members resist the shift to a professional legislature. The ideal of the citizen legislature or, if needed, the semiprofessional legislature, seems to harmonize better with the dominant cultural values of most western states than does the model of the professional legislature. In the West only heavily urbanized California has accepted the professional legislature.

As can be seen in Table 9.1, seven of the thirteen western states (54%) pay their legislators $10,000 per year or more, plus expenses. Twenty-four of the thirty-seven nonwestern states (65%) do so. In all, 46% of the legislatures in the West are citizen legislatures, or are close to it, as compared to 35% of the legislatures in the other states.[19]

Whether a state has a professional or a citizen legislature does seem to matter. Citizen legislatures tend to be found in less populated and less industrialized states. In citizen legislatures the members are mostly people who can afford to serve. Sessions are short, staff is scarce, and even legislators who have served numerous terms have limited legislative experience because the sessions are so short. Such legislators often are dependent on others (including lobbyists) for information. Committees have little time to analyze collectively the problems that need solving. When interim committees are utilized to explore these problems in depth, the legislators discover that their time commitments begin to seem open ended.

Professional state legislatures tend to be found in the more industrialized, urbanized states. The professional state legislature tends to have fewer wealthy members and more members who have made careers in the public sector, including those whose career is elective office. There is greater staff assistance and more time to evaluate problems collectively. Legislative norms develop more firmly and loom larger in the individual legislator's perspective. States with professional state legislatures tend to enact public policies that are more protective of tenants, welfare clients and workers, more acceptable to consumer groups, and generally less unfavorable to people in lower economic levels than do states with citizen legislatures. Those differences in policy choices seem to result partly from the differences between the two types of legislatures and partly from differences in the political cultures and socioeconomic environments of the states with the different types of legislatures.[20]

MEMBERSHIP TURNOVER

Legislative observers pay great attention to the turnover rate of state legislators. Low turnover rates, of course, mean that the existing structure of power in the legislature is unlikely to change dramatically.

Nor are major state policies likely to change. Furthermore, legislatures with low turnover rates have experienced members whose knowledge base permits them, when they perceive the need, to act contrary to the preferences of bureaucrats and lobbyists and to hold their own in the continual struggle for power against the constitutional officers of the other branches of government. Over the past few decades there has been a national trend toward lower turnover rates in state legislatures. Western senates have turnover rates similar to the rest of the nation, while the lower chambers in the West are somewhat above the national average in turnover rates.[21]

Reapportionment in the West

The "reapportionment revolution" of the 1960s began with the Tennessee case of *Baker v. Carr* in 1962. In that case the U.S. Supreme Court ruled for the first time that state legislative apportionment cases were justiciable, meaning that federal courts could take jurisdiction of such cases and hear them on their merits. The court also held that when deciding apportionment cases the courts should apply the equal protection clause of the Fourteenth Amendment to the U.S. Constitution. The federal district court subsequently ruled that the great population disparities in Tennessee house districts violated the equal protection clause and ordered Tennessee to reapportion its house so that all districts contained approximately the same number of people. Such a standard for apportionment is normally referred to as "one person, one vote." A similar decision concerning state senates was issued in 1964. Thus, by 1964, the U.S. Supreme Court had ruled that the "one person, one vote" standard applied to districting of both legislative chambers.[22]

In 1970 an astute observer of western state politics noted that in the West only Oregon had a fair population-based legislative apportionment before the series of federal court orders. Eleanore Bushnell further observed that the West "was particularly stubborn in its preference for the status quo—area representation—and, consequently, unusually slow in accommodating to the apportionment rulings."[23] In every state the rural sparsely populated counties were overrepresented.

The median percentage of the state's citizens theoretically able to elect a majority of the upper house in the West was 18.1% before compliance with orders to reapportion; in the other thirty-seven states the median was 36.9%. The median percentage theoretically able to elect a majority of the lower house in the West was essentially the same as in the nation: 38.4% for the West, 38.6% for the rest of the country.[24]

The Nevada, New Mexico and Utah lower chambers were even more badly skewed in favor of rural areas than the others. The percentage of a state's voters theoretically able to elect a majority of the members of those chambers ranged from 27.0% in New Mexico to 29.1% in Nevada. Only Alaska, Arizona, California and Oregon had districting plans under which at least 45% of the voters were required to elect a majority of the lower chamber membership.[25]

The most malapportioned state senates in the early 1960s, and the percentage of the state's voters theoretically able to elect a majority of the state's senators, were Nevada (8.0%), California (10.7%), Arizona (12.8%), New Mexico (14.0%), Montana (16.1%), and Idaho (16.7%). Those states basically used counties as the basis for senate apportionment. Before the court decisions, Los Angeles County (with a 1960 population of 6.5 million people) had one California state senator, as did a three-county district with a total population of 15,000 people. Similar differences in senate district populations were common throughout the western states.[26] Because the senates had been more seriously malapportioned, the impact of the "reapportionment revolution" was greater in western senates than in western lower chambers. Still, the percentage of members from rural areas declined dramatically in both chambers, and the legislatures became much less captive to rural interests and to the Western Myth, except to the extent that urban residents and their elected representatives chose to perpetuate that myth.

The population variance of legislative districts in every state was greatly reduced in the late 1960s and early 1970s. Although precise guidelines were not promulgated by the Supreme Court, and different cases saw different methods of determining the fairness of the various state reapportionments, many observers believed that the courts would continue to move toward minimal variation in the populations of electoral districts. But in 1973 (*Mahan v. Howell*) the U.S. Supreme Court (with some new justices) approved a Virginia state legislative reapportionment that had substantial population variation between districts. The reasoning was that the variation was a consequence of using political subdivision boundaries in the districting, and that doing so was important to helping citizens know who their legislator was.

An even greater deviation was permitted Wyoming in its reapportionment that followed the 1980 census. The ideal district based on that census and a sixty-two-member house would have contained some 7,500 people. But Niobrara County (the state's smallest, with a population of 2,924) wanted its own representative in the Wyoming house and persuaded the legislature to add one more house seat and award it to Niobrara County. The Wyoming League of Women Voters challenged the reapportionment (*Brown v. Thomson*), but the U.S. Supreme Court upheld the Wyoming apportionment on a 5-to-4 vote, even though the largest house district in Wyoming contained 9,496 people and the smallest had only 2,924.[27] Whether a new guideline has been set is not yet clear, but it is possible that the rule of equality among legislative districts may be modified, as the Supreme Court's membership changes, to permit greater variation in the populations of legislative districts in order to take into account county and municipal boundaries in the apportionment process. If so, rural and small-town areas could once more become systematically overrepresented in state legislatures.

Other western states have also struggled with legislative reapportionment. California went through an extensive political turmoil before accomplishing its reapportionment following both the 1970 and the 1980 censuses. Those conflicts were not just between the two major political parties or various regions of the state, but also included extensive participation by Hispanic and black organizations.[28]

Arizona's 1960 and 1970 reapportionments achieved approximately equal populations per district only with extensive judicial involvement and, as in California, resulted in increased minority representation in the state legislature. Republican reapportionment plans passed a special session of the legislature in 1981 over Democratic governor Babbitt's veto. The Democratic party filed suit against the new law and the U.S. Department of Justice expressed specific concerns. An out-of-court settlement was reached, which met those concerns and left most incumbent Hispanic legislators fairly secure. In some ways the goals of Hispanic legislators and activists (mostly Democrats) were compatible with the goals of Anglo Republicans, who created some safe Hispanic-dominated Democratic districts in their effort to create an optimal number of fairly safe Republican state legislative districts.[29]

New Mexico's history of post-*Baker* reapportionment activity has been characterized by reluctant obedience to the federal courts. That was the case in 1982 as well. The Democratic senate majority was fragile; the house was governed by a coalition of conservative Democrats and Republicans. The apportionment enacted in January of 1982 was based on a "votes cast" formula for estimating the populations of various precincts. Under this plan each precinct was assumed to have the same proportion of the county's population as its proportion of the county's votes cast in the gubernatorial election. The resulting precinct population estimates systematically underestimated populations in minority and working class precincts and systematically overestimated populations in middle class precincts. That, of course, meant more legislators from middle class neighborhoods and fewer from poor and minority neighborhoods. A three-judge federal panel said the plan was unconstitutional and ordered the legislature to devise an apportionment using census-based estimates of precinct population. The legislature did so in an acrimonious special session. But even that apportionment plan was subsequently modified by court order because it discriminated against Hispanics in some counties.

The western states have been more willing than other states to take the reapportioning function away from the legislature. As of 1980 four western states (Alaska, Colorado, Hawaii and Montana) had reapportionment commissions as compared to eight of the other thirty-seven states. Washington State followed suit in 1984.[30]

Reapportionment commissions do not take the politics out of reapportionment, but they do remove the decision from the legislature, whose members have an intense personal interest in the details of the plan but who are also the best informed on the consequences of any particular change in district boundaries. The Colorado commission was created following the unseemly Colorado general assembly battles after the 1970s census. In 1981 the commission, consisting of four legislative leaders, three gubernatorial appointees, and four members appointed by the chief justice of the state supreme court, seems to have developed an reapportionment plan in a less partisan manner than the apportionment a decade earlier.[31]

The Montana commission must submit its reapportionment plan to the legislature for review and criticism. The commission then considers legislative comments, may or may not make subsequent revisions, and sends its plan to the secretary of state, at which point the plan goes into effect.[32] After the Washington State commission submits its plan to the legislature the legislature has thirty days to alter the plan, but changes must pass by a two-thirds vote in each chamber.[33]

One might ask why all the western states but Oregon required court orders in the decade following *Baker v. Carr* before accepting a fair apportionment of their legislatures, and why some required further prodding by the federal courts after the 1980 census. The dominant values of the West, after all, include egalitarianism. But, as earlier chapters have discussed, westerners are ambivalent about federal government authority. Furthermore, the resistance to court-ordered reapportionment came from incumbent legislators, especially those from rural or semirural districts who feared (often correctly) that reapportionment would end their legislative service. Further, many rural and small-town legislators, like their constituents, apparently truly believed in the Western Myth of rugged individualism and felt that rural citizens were the repository of such values. There is also some scattered evidence that many legislators thought the urban newcomers did not have a sufficient stake in the state to be entitled to an equal voice in state affairs. For instance, in 1949 New Mexico amended its constitution to grant every county one (and only one) state senator, regardless of population. But newly created Los Alamos County was, for purposes of senate representation, considered part of the county from which it had been severed. Los Alamos County, after all, was populated almost entirely by newcomers who worked at the Los Alamos National Laboratory.

Rural and small-town dwellers may fret about being outnumbered in the state legislature by representatives of urban areas, but the legislators from those rural areas are disproportionately experienced. A study of recruitment to the Oregon legislative assembly, for instance, concluded that in rural and small-town constituencies the social cost of challenging an incumbent state legislator is much greater than in metropolitan areas, while the benefits are less.[34] Rural incumbents occasionally are challenged, but less frequently than urban incumbents. The result is greater average seniority among rural/small-town legislators and, in all probability, disproportionate influence in the legislature. Such is the case in Alaska, for instance, where Anchorage legislators hold nineteen of forty seats in the house and eight of twenty in the senate. But:

> Rural legislators have tended to be disproportionately influential. . . . Non-Anchorage legislators on the whole have longer tenure in office . . . [and] in the mid-1980s averged twice as long in office as did Anchorage area members. . . . This long tenure in office translates into power. . . . During the fourteenth legislature (1984–86), for example, one senator from a non-Anchorage

region got an appropriation for his district reinserted by threatening future action. He reportedly said that while he was in the minority now, he would be in the majority in the future and would not forget those who had voted against him on an issue so vital. . . . During the fourteenth legislature a significant indicator of the influence of rural Alaska was the fact that both the senate and house finance committees were chaired by Natives from rural Alaska.[35]

Summary

For the most part, western state legislatures are much like the legislatures of the other states, but some regional skewing is obvious. For instance, the West leans more toward citizen legislatures than does the rest of the nation. In part because of the progressive heritage of the West, western legislatures are much more likely than others to share legislative authority with the voters. Three-fourths of the western states provide for the initiative whereas barely one-fourth of the other states do so. Prior to judicial intervention in the *Baker v. Carr* era, the West contained some of the most malapportioned legislative chambers in the nation, and some western states have been among the most stubborn in resisting the "one person, one vote" rule. Perhaps as a result, western states have been more willing than the others to remove the reapportionment function from the state legislature.

While the rural and small-town legislators probably will continue to have less competition and thus greater average tenure and influence than their urban colleagues, the members of the western state legislatures will become increasingly urban over the next few decades and presumably will gradually grow less responsive to the values of the Western Myth of rugged individualism and self-reliance. The states that now have citizen legislatures are under pressure to provide more staff assistance to members and greater compensation to offset lost income as the legislature takes up increasing amounts of the members' time. A slow movement to more semiprofessional legislatures is almost certain, and in the more populous states the gap between semiprofessional and professional may narrow. Still, as long as the West has states with small populations, small numbers of people per legislator, and large open spaces, its legislatures are likely to retain many of the characteristics—and policy orientations—of the citizen legislature.

Notes

1. Council of State Governments, *The Book of the States, 1986–87* (Lexington, Ky.: Council of State Governments, 1986), table 3.1.

2. For in-depth discussions of legislative authority and the importance of legislative action to legitimize governmental decisions, see John C. Wahlke, Heinz Eulau, William Buchanan, and LeRoy C. Ferguson, *The Legislative System* (New York: John Wiley and Sons, 1962), especially chap. 1; and Fred R. Harris and Paul L. Hain, *America's Legislative Processes: Congress and the States* (Glenview, Ill.: Scott Foresman, 1983), chap. 2. Parts of this chapter draw on research done for the Harris and Hain book and its revision.

3. For an extensive theoretical discussion of representation, see Hanna Pitkin, *The Concept of Representation* (Berkeley: University of California Press, 1972). For a more extensive and somewhat different discussion of the functions of the American legislature, see William J. Keefe and Morris S. Ogul, *The American Legislative Process: Congress and the States,* 6th ed. (Englewood Cliffs, N.J.: Prentice Hall, 1985), chap. 1.

4. Eleanore Bushnell, "Introduction," and "The Court Steps In," in Eleanore Bushnell, ed., *Impact of Reapportionment on the Thirteen Western States* (Salt Lake City: University of Utah Press, 1970).

5. *The Book of the States, 1986–87*, table 3.17, "Staff for Individual Legislators"; and *The Book of the States, 1980–81*, table 30, "Staff for Individual Legislators." Brian Weberg and Beth Bazar, *Legislative Staff Services: 50 State Profiles* (Denver: National Conference of State Legislatures, 1988).

6. For an insightful discussion of state legislative oversight activities, see Richard E. Brown, ed., *The Effectiveness of Legislative Program Review* (New Brunswick, N.J.: Transaction Books, 1979). Chaps. 3 and 6 discuss the 1973 oversight of the State Public Utilities Commission in Hawaii and the 1974 analysis of the Montana Workman's Compensation Division.

7. Clive S. Thomas, "'The Thing' that Shook Alaska: The Events, the Fallout, and the Lessons of Alaska's Gubernatorial Impeachment Proceedings," *State Legislatures* 13, 2 (February 1987), 22–25; *The Book of the States, 1986–87*, table 2.8, "Impeachment Provisions in the States."

8. *The New York Times*, April 6, 1988.

9. This "advise and consent" power sometimes enables key senators to obtain policy concessions from the executive which they probably could not otherwise obtain. In 1979, for instance, "the chairman for the [Hawaii] Senate's Energy Committee held up the reappointment of Hideo Kono as the director for the Department of Planning and Economic Development in order to obtain a concession from that department to allocate more funds to the university for alternative energy studies." James C. F. Wang, *Hawaii State & Local Politics* (Hilo: Wang Associates, 1982), 256–57.

10. *The Book of the States, 1980–81*, 156–57.

11. *The Book of the States, 1986–87*, table 3.14. Alaska has a unique provision

that requires a three-quarters vote of the membership of the legislature to override vetoes of appropriations bills and bills to raise revenue.

12. *The Book of the States, 1986–87*, table 3.2.

13. Malcolm E. Jewell, "Survey on Selection of State Legislative Leaders," *Comparative State Politics Newsletter* (May 1980), 8.

14. Hugh A. Bone, "Record Setting Incumbent Retires in Washington State," *Comparative State Politics Newsletter* (December 1988), 2.

15. *American State Legislatures: Their Structures and Procedures*, rev. ed. (Lexington, Ky.: Council of State Governments, 1977), tables 2.6 and 4.6.

16. Malcolm E. Jewell, "Survey on Selection of State Legislative Leaders," 11.

17. "Summary: Legislators' Compensation and Benefits," October 31, 1987 (Denver: National Conference of State Legislatures, mimeo, 1987). Pennsylvania legislators' annual salaries rose to $47,000 and California legislators' salaries to $40,816 effective December 1, 1988, while New York legislators' salaries rose to $57,500 as of January 1989. The other states paying legislators $33,000 or more per annum, plus expenses, are Illinois, Massachusetts, Michigan, and Ohio. Wisconsin legislators receive $29,992, while New Jersey legislators get $25,000. Also, see John H. Culver and John C. Syer, *Power and Politics in California*, 2nd ed. (New York: John Wiley and Sons, 1984), chap. 6.

18. Stephen F. Johnson, "The Alaska Legislature," in Gerald A. McBeath and Thomas A. Morehouse, eds., *Alaska State Government and Politics* (Fairbanks: University of Alaska Press, 1987), 236.

19. "Summary: Legislators' Compensation and Benefits," October 31, 1987.

20. Lance T. LeLoup, "Reassessing the Mediating Impact of Legislative Capability," *American Political Science Review* (June 1978), 616. For an insightful philosophical examination of how a professional state legislature functions, see William K. Muir, Jr., *Legislature: California's School for Politics* (Chicago: University of Chicago Press, 1982).

21. Richard G. Niemi and Laura R. Winsky, "Membership Turnover in U.S. State Legislatures: Trends and Effects of Districting," *Legislative Studies Quarterly* (February 1987), table 1.

22. Robert G. Dixon, Jr., *Democratic Representation: Reapportionment in Law and Politics* (New York: Oxford University Press, 1968), 263.

23. Eleanore Bushnell, "Introduction," in Bushnell, *Impact of Reapportionment*.

24. *Ibid.*, 2.

25. *Ibid.*, 23.

26. *Ibid.*, 23 and 80.

27. Tim R. Miller, *State Government: Politics in Wyoming* (Dubuque, Iowa: Kendall/Hunt, 1985), 73; Janet Clark and B. Oliver Walter, "Wyoming's Reapportionment: Does It Make a Difference?" paper presented to the 1983 annual meeting of the Western Political Science Association.

28. James D. Driscoll, *California's Legislature* (Sacramento: Center for California Studies, California State University, 1986), 74–77; Carlos Navarro and Richard Santillan, "The Latino Community and California Redistricting in the 1980s: Californios for Fair Representation," in Richard Santillan, ed., *The Hispanic Community and Redistricting* (Claremont, Calif.: The Rose Institute, 1984).

29. John A. Garcia, "Reapportionment in the Eighties: The Case of Arizona and Chicanos," in Richard Santillan, ed., *The Hispanic Community and Redistricting*.

30. *The Book of the States, 1980–81*, 86–87. Thor Swanson, William F. Mullen, John C. Pierce, and Charles H. Sheldon, eds., *Political Life in Washington* (Pullman, Wash.: Washington State University Press, 1985), 111. In Alaska the governor and the commission together reapportion the legislature.

31. Robert S. Lorch, *Colorado's Government* (Boulder: Colorado Associated University Press, 1983), 155–61.

32. James J. Lopach, *We the People of Montana* (Missoula, Mont.: Mountain Press, 1983), 64–66.

33. Thor Swanson *et al.*, eds., *Political Life in Washington*, 111.

34. Lester G. Seligman, Michael R. King, Chong Lim Kim, and Roland E. Smith, *Patterns of Recruitment: A State Chooses Its Lawmakers* (Chicago: Rand McNally, 1974), 69.

35. Stephen F. Johnson, "The Alaska Legislature," 235.

10

GUBERNATORIAL POLITICS

Raymond W. Cox III

CATEGORIZING THE ROLE AND INFLUENCE OF WEST-
ern governors is a time-sensitive exercise. While the framework for
authority set forth in constitution and statute provides relatively stable reference points, the reality of gubernatorial power is largely determined by the changing political culture of the state and region,
and the personality and ability of the individual governor. The prominence of an individual governor in a particular state is most influenced by the policies, politics and programs of the time. The legacy
of a particular governor is in the changed expectations by the public
of how future governors should act. Clearly, the governorship represents for most politicians the culmination of a political career and

the best opportunity to shape a state's future in a way that is deeply personal.

Any examination of gubernatorial politics is necessarily a study of history—primarily the political and cultural history of the state and region. Constitutions, no less than statutes, are historic documents that reflect the political, social and economic concerns of the leaders of a particular time.[1] The commonalities that exist in the West largely reflect the fact that most of the constitutions of the region are the products of the 1880s and 1890s. The governments of that era reflect both a need for leadership and a distrust of the exercise of leadership. Thus the governor is granted strong veto authority (particularly in the use of the item veto), yet the executive authority is fragmented through the election of several "executive" officials. The shift away from progressive-era sentiments in some states accounts for much of the variation in gubernatorial authority that now exists in the region. The relatively uniform political culture that produced similar constitutional frameworks has not held. As was suggested in Chapter 2, from the perspective of political culture the region known as the West is a cluster of subregions, not a monolith. Despite the variation that now exists, the appropriate starting point for this examination is the constitutional powers granted to (or withheld from) the governors of the West. Once this background has been established, the variations that are the product of political, cultural, statutory and individual change since the "founding" of each state can then be examined.

Progressives, Populists and Constitution Writers

The political values and ideals of the progressive era dominate the constitutions of the western states. Virtually all the states have governments that reflect the business-regulatory, antipolitics, pro-education and direct democracy ideals of the period. The progressives felt that some aspects of policymaking were too important to be left to politics and politicians. Policy was not to be made by corrupt legislatures, but by independent boards and commissions. The administration of policy was made more democratic, on the one hand by separately electing (sometimes in nonpartisan elections) executive officials and making use of initiative and referendum, and on the other hand by permitting the recall of those officials. Distrust of government was high and any mechanism for fragmenting government authority was considered desirable.

This perspective was not conducive to the creation of a strong executive authority. The primary concern of the progressives was not governors but rather legislatures, which was the reason for "sheltering" policy areas such as education, civil service, mine safety and railroad regulation behind independent boards and commissions. Further, management activities such as financial management, the administration of the justice system, and record-keeping were protected through the ballot box. The end result was that the executive branch was as severely constrained as the legislative branch in the progressives' quest to rid government of corruption and "politics." The ability of a governor to coordinate and administer a coherent set of policy initiatives was all but completely circumscribed. The new governors found themselves the nominal leaders of governments that were quite capable of pursuing multiple and conflicting policies simultaneously; but except under extraordinary circumstances (the election of Hiram Johnson in California is the best example) these governments were incapable of concerted action to address a broad range of problems. While not as weak, institutionally, as the governors of Arkansas, Texas and Florida, the new governors of the West were not in a position to be vigorous policy advocates.

In contrast, the influence of the governor in legislative matters was relatively strong. Either by constitution or statute the authority to prepare the budget was vested in the governor (though in some states, such as Colorado, a powerful legislative budget committee had reasserted a strong legislative prerogative). Further, the ability to veto items in bills and/or the appropriations act is shared by all except the governor of Nevada. (See Table 10.1.) Finally each governor has the authority to call the legislature into special session, which was a particularly powerful tool at a time when most legislatures met biennially.

In general the expectation was that neither governors nor legislators would be activists in the policy arena. Rather, other officials with narrow functional responsibility would see to the administration of those activities for which a consensus already existed, such as promotion of primary and secondary education, regulation of railroads, honest accounting procedures, safe mines, and fair administration of justice. (See Table 10.2.)

Larry Sabato has best summarized the perspective on the governorship as it existed at the turn of the century:

Table 10.1   Gubernatorial Veto Power in the West

State	Veto	Item Veto	Legislative Override
Alaska	yes	yes	$2/3$ & $3/4$[a]
Arizona	yes	yes	$2/3$
California	yes	yes	$2/3$
Colorado	yes	yes[b]	$2/3$
Hawaii	yes	yes	$2/3$
Idaho	yes	yes	$2/3$
Montana	yes	yes	majority
Nevada	yes	no	majority
New Mexico	yes	yes	majority
Oregon	yes	yes	majority
Utah	yes	yes	$2/3$
Washington	yes	yes	majority
Wyoming	yes	yes	$2/3$

[a]Revenue and appropriation bills require a three-fourths vote by the legislature to override a veto. All other bills require a two-thirds vote.
[b]Appropriations bill only.

Source: Adapted from *The Book of the States, 1984–85* (Lexington, Ky.: Council of State Governments, 1985).

> The seeds of executive disaster were sown in this period with the adoption of the "long ballot." More and more public offices were filled by popular election. . . . This loss of administrative control caused a corresponding loss of coordinated action. Governors were frequently hamstrung by the executive departments they were supposed to rule. . . .
> . . . the governorship was not empowered to break the heavy chains that bound it to a minor role in government. Governors had neither the basic constitutional and statutory authority, nor the control over their branch of government that would be necessary for them to loom larger.[2]

The contrast between the progressive-era governments and the two established in the 1950s is striking. With the exception of a lieutenant governor, who runs jointly with the governor, there are no other elected executives in Alaska and Hawaii. Speaking about the governorship of Hawaii, James C. F. Wang notes, "Comparatively speaking, the State of Hawaii, through its constitution and historical tradition, concentrates an enormous amount of political power in the governor."[3] In contrast, the numbers of separately elected officials,

Table 10.2   The Fragmented Executive: Separately Elected Constitutional Offices

State	Lt. Gov.	Sec. of State	Attorney General	Treasurer	Superintendent of Public Instruction	Other
Alaska	(1)	(7)	—	—	—	—
Arizona	—	yes	yes	yes	yes	(2, 10)
California	yes	yes	yes	yes	—	(3)
Colorado	(1)	yes	yes	yes	—	(3)
Hawaii	(1)	(6)	—	—	—	—
Idaho	yes	yes	yes	yes	yes	—
Montana	yes	yes	yes	—	yes	(4)
Nevada	(1)	yes	yes	yes	—	(3)
New Mexico	(1)	yes	yes	yes	—	(5)
Oregon	—	yes	(6)	yes	yes	—
Utah	yes	(7)	yes	yes	—	(5)
Washington	(1)	yes	yes	yes	yes	(5, 8, 9)
Wyoming	—	yes	—	yes	yes	—

(1) Gov.–lt. gov. run as team
(2) Corporation commissioners (public utilities)
(3) Comptroller
(4) Public utilities, by statute not constitution
(5) Post audit
(6) Attorney general, by statute not constitution
(7) Lt. gov. serves as sec. of state
(8) Insurance commissioner, by statute
(9) Commissioner of natural resources, by constitution
(10) State mine inspector, by constitution
Source: Adapted from *The Book of the States*, 1984–1985.

compounded by the use of independent boards, widely disperse executive power in most western states.

In a commentary specifically about Arizona, but which would fit all but the Pacific Rim states, Mason and Hink summarize the weaknesses of the governorship as follows:

1. Dispersion of authority and responsibility.
2. Illogical groupings of functions within agencies.
3. Complexity and inconsistency in forms of agencies.
4. Inappropriate functions and excessive numbers of boards and commissions.
5. *Ex officio* membership on boards and commissions.[4]

The antigovernment attitude at the turn of the century has given way to one that is more tolerant of executive authority. The high visibility of the states' governors, through the National Governors' Association (NGA), in the effort to redirect and reform social welfare policy[5] is a clear indication of the prominence of the governors and the centrality of state government to most U.S. domestic policy. Further, specific steps have been taken to change the constitutional and statutory basis of gubernatorial authority in many states.[6]

Nonetheless, not all efforts to strengthen the governorship have succeeded. In 1970, the State of Nevada put a two-term limit on future governors.[7] In that same year New Mexico voters rejected a constitution that, among other provisions, would have made several constitutional offices subject to gubernatorial appointments and granted reorganization authority to the governor.[8] A decade later in 1980 New Mexico voters rejected a proposal to permit the governor to seek a second term.[9] Thad Beyle ends his 1983 study of the governorship on this pessimistic note:

> The governors . . . make the decisions, set the priorities, and see that the programs are implemented. Yet the milieu in which they must carry out these responsibilities is difficult at best. . . . they face resurgent legislatures seeking at a minimum a sense of parity with the governor . . . and they often find key parts of the executive branch in the control of separately elected officials, or policy boards which they have varying abilities to influence. They are part of a federal system in which the partner at the top is cutting back not only in programs and grant-in-aid funds, but also reducing its responsibilities to answer to the needs of our state and local communities. And now finding themselves faced with a tighter revenue situation than at any time in the recent past, governors must decide whether to raise taxes or cut back on programs and activities in their state governments. Neither choice is attractive to governors or the people they serve.[10]

Pessimistic or not, these comments firmly place the governor at the center of the state policymaking process. The ability of a governor to succeed is founded on three essential elements: legal authority; the expectations of the public; and his or her desire and willingness to pursue change. With few exceptions, legal authority to act has been given to the governors of the West. More important, public expectation is that the governors ought to be more activist in the policy arena. While the political attitudes of at least the Rocky Mountain West remain highly skeptical of government (particularly Wyoming, Idaho, Nevada, Utah and New Mexico), governors throughout the region seem to enjoy more latitude but are conversely burdened with higher expectations than were their predecessors. How the governorships have changed in the last three decades from a position of relative weakness to one of being able to control their own political destinies is the subject of the next section.

Changing Gubernatorial Authority

THE GOVERNOR AS MANAGER

The last three decades represent a period of considerable upheaval in state government. Academic interest in state politics and government, which had been on the wane since the Great Depression, was somewhat revived in the late 1950s. Coincidentally, many within government were trying to come to grips with a growing set of problems. The result was that the period since the late 1950s has been one of the most significant periods of state government reform in U.S. history.[11]

The question of managing government was to move to the forefront of gubernatorial concerns in the 1960s. The problems inherent in such management are significant. Not the least of these was the fact that the financial and institutional capacities to handle problems that were regional or national in scope were still lacking in many states. Former governor Tom McCall of Oregon in a 1970 interview for a symposium of the American Society for Public Administration (ASPA) characterized the problem in this way:

> The gradual displacement of governing control from the statehouse to Washington, D.C., has come about for a number of reasons, not the least of which has been the demonstrated inability and in certain cases a blatant unwillingness on the part of states to grapple with many of our pressing problems. Also, one cannot overlook the fact that the federal government has the capability of raising and collecting revenues on a much more massive scale than is true of the states. Thus, the federal government has assumed control of many program areas by default simply because it and only it has had the financial resources to undertake these responsibilities.
>
> I believe those of us in positions of authority in state government must make every effort to stem the tide of ever-increasing control which is flooding Washington. If we do not, I fear that not only will government in general become even less responsive to the will of the people, but also, that we may well place in jeopardy our democratic way of life.[12]

Major changes have been made in the structure of state governments throughout the country. The reorganizations of the 1960s had two purposes: (1) the rationalization of the formal state government structure; and (2) control of state agencies, which were managed at the state capital, but were increasingly controlled by funding from Washington. The need to put the organizational as well as the structural house of government in order was becoming paramount. Governor Welsh of Indiana commented at the ASPA symposium:

> Just to enumerate these areas, and then consider them in light of the turmoil in our society today, is to emphasize the awesome responsibility with which state government is charged. It also demonstrates the importance, to me at any rate, of seeing to it that our state governments are strengthened and supported, for I do not believe it is possible for these problems to be dealt with or resolved by any other level of government.[13]

The governors of the period were adamant in their belief that the future lay in the construction of a partnership between the federal government and the states. Governor John Dempsey (Connecticut) had this to say on the necessity of the partnership:

> Most of the issues that government faces in the 1970s cannot be contained, nor can they be solved, within particular political boundaries.
>
> The governors must continue and intensify their efforts toward further federal-state cooperation in developing and implementing programs in such areas as welfare, control of air and water pollution, transportation, and others where individual states can exercise only limited control.
>
> The problems of the cities, including poor housing, high unemployment and underemployment, crime, and inadequate education and health facilities, will remain problems indefinitely if they are regarded as strictly local problems.
>
> Their scope is such that they are beyond the capacity of individual municipal governments, or of state governments.
>
> The state can, however, and must, be the agent for bringing together the resources of all levels of government, as well as the private sector, for the purpose of developing and carrying out an effective urban program.[14]

The period of reorganization as a reform movement extended over two decades. During that period a subtle shift in emphasis began to appear. The heavy reliance on restructuring weakened during the early 1970s. In 1967 the Committee for Economic Development was still pushing for cabinet-style governments with limited span of control to provide the governor with authority similar to that of a corporate chief executive officer. The constitutional changes in California reinforcing the control of reorganization by the governor and the massive statutory reorganizations in Colorado are two examples of these changes.[15] Increasingly, however, those inside state government became aware of the limits to a single-minded focus on structure. The goal of an improved government process could not be achieved simply through structural reform. Although better machinery and processes could make better governments more likely, they do not in themselves guarantee progress. The period 1969–74 is particularly significant in the evolution of state government organization. This period was marked by a rapid shift in the number and kinds of issues that were being brought before state government for solution: the environment, energy conservation, nuclear power, crime in the streets, waste disposal and management, water quality, mass transit, and more. The disillusionment with government that seemingly dominates the political scene today had not yet taken hold. Quite the contrary, the level of government effort continued to rise. The level of dollars and the type and variety of state and federal programs designed to "solve" society's problems grew.[16]

"Managing government" was no longer thought of in terms of limiting the number of persons reporting to the governor, or of specialization of work tasks. The management of government requires a pro-active planning and control system, which not only can attempt to resolve current problems but also is capable of reacting to new issues and new problems, and of defining, understanding, and controlling such issues and problems. The governors were acquiring the tools for becoming the central figures in state policymaking. Reputations were to be made in the policy issues that governors confronted. Policy issues quickly became linked to certain governors—water issues with Babbitt (Arizona); environmental issues with McCall (Oregon) and Evans (Washington); nuclear power with Ray (Washington); and the death penalty with Anaya (New Mexico).

The important point is that management as a generic issue was for the first time of more than academic interest. The earlier focus on structural realignment had laid the foundation for this new examination of government organization. The nature and direction of this examination, however, was quite different from the earlier review. Rather than discussing the number of departments that should report to a governor or the efficacy of placing a planning office within the governor's office rather than within budgeting, the discussion focused on coordinating and managing the information and resources available to the state in developing policy or improving services. A further aspect of the shift to management focus was the growth of efforts to establish formal linkages to resources and groups outside the government. As is illustrated by the comment of former governor Dempsey (Connecticut), the idea of public/private initiatives in the cities is at least two decades old. For the purposes of this discussion, a more important development was the enhancement of the research and planning capacity of state government through the use of university faculties. Like many other suggestions the link between the universities and the governor's office is at least as old as the "Wisconsin Idea" of Robert LaFollette.[17] Unfortunately, few states followed the lead of Wisconsin. In the early 1970s several conferences were held with the specific purpose of examining means to strengthen university-gubernatorial relations. New or expanded efforts in California, Illinois, New York, Alabama and elsewhere were a by-product of these meetings.[18]

The survival handbooks for governors were made part of the literature on complex organizations because that is certainly what even the smallest of states had become. In *Governing the American States*, the Center for Policy Research of the National Governors' Association found that of the eleven most difficult and demanding aspects of the job of being governor, six related to the management or control of state government.[19] "The traditional management and administration activities, once estimated to take less than 15 percent of any Governor's time, seem now to be the most important part of the job. Some look back on previous generations and wonder how the chief executive could function without using a sophisticated system of budget and planning analysis."[20] (See Table 10.3.)

While state government and the office of governor have changed considerably for those working within them, it is less clear that the general public perceives these shifts to be as dramatic or, for that matter, even for the better. Changes occur at different times and at different rates because of all the factors noted above. The structure, personnel, leadership style, political circumstances, and financial position of a state all influence *when, if* or *how* change is to occur. Further, there is the very real problem of perception of change. Somehow, people find massive structural reorganizations reassuring—an indication that something is being done. Changes in the less public aspects of government, such as increased professionalism among line and

Table 10.3   Most Difficult and Demanding Aspects of Being Governor

- Working with the legislature
- Interference with family life
- Ceremonial demands on time
- Invasion of privacy
- Long hours
- Tough decisions
- Working with the federal government
- Intramural governmental squabbles
- Day-to-day management of state government
- Working with the press
- Building and keeping staff

Source: Center for Policy Research, *Governing the American States* (Washington, D.C.: National Governors' Association, 1978), 4.

staff personnel, or a shift to a management focus of the state planning and policy office, may have far greater long-term impact on state government than any major reorganization. Yet the general public is much less likely to be aware of what is going on and much less able to perceive a positive change. In reflecting on the question of managing the bureaucracy, former Illinois governor Daniel Walker made these comments:

> Nobody cares. The media doesn't care whether you're actually managing state government or not. There's not glamour to it. Very few people care about it. Actually, the only satisfaction you get is what you see in terms of results. It's the satisfaction of the job. It's not a political plus—no question about it. In terms of getting votes or a better image or a better reputation, you'd better spend your time somewhere else. I don't think that it's going to hurt you that much. I just don't think that politically or image-wise you're going to get very much out of the fact that it's damn hard work. That makes most governors just walk away from it and leave it to the apparat [*sic*]. I think that is very unfortunate.[21]

Those governors who took the time and effort to try to manage were not always successful. Nevertheless, management is recognized as a critical and complex problem for any governor. What is significant is that despite the limited political pay-off increasing numbers of governors and senior gubernatorial staff have seized these ideas and tried to apply them in their states.[22]

MANAGING THE WESTERN STATES

The changes in structure and management described above have had considerable influence in the West. Major constitutional and statutory changes were made in California in the 1960s, placing responsibility for the organization of government in the hands of the governor. By statute Colorado radically reorganized the executive departments, giving the governor far more management and administrative control.[23] The chief beneficiary of these 1968 and 1971 changes was Governor Richard Lamm, who served from 1973 to 1987 and came to dominate the Colorado political scene despite facing a hostile Republican legislature throughout his tenure.[24] While progress has been somewhat slower in New Mexico, the reorganizations initiated by Governor Jerry Apodaca (1975–79) have been described as "a major political achievement" that has made the "executive branch of government . . . demonstrably more responsive to gubernatorial direction than in the past."[25] These changes have meant that the role of manager of government has effectively fallen upon the shoulders of the governor. In fact, today in the West the ability of the governor to control, direct and lead the state bureaucracy is a major factor in judging the success of the governor.[26]

Following the lead of the National Governors' Association and the Council of State Planning Agencies, states such as Arizona, Utah, Washington, Oregon and Idaho sought to strengthen the governorship by augmenting staff policy and planning capabilities. While these changes are more difficult to institutionalize, considerable interest was expressed by governors in enhancing the policy management capacity of their states. Such policy management efforts were typically focused in the governors' offices.[27] The size and character of the gubernatorial staff has changed radically from the days when a staff meant a secretary and possibly a receptionist.

The staff changes, and obviously the statutory and constitutional changes, helped reshape the governor's office along with the opportunity to direct state policy, in some instances for the first time. Larry Sabato aptly summarized the new gubernatorial organization and authority: "In the executive sphere, governors have done well, not only in successfully orchestrating constitutional revisions and reorganizations, but also in consolidating and fortifying their control of administration."[28]

A few states, such as Idaho, Nevada and Wyoming, were relatively untouched by the constitutional and statutory reforms of the 1960s and 1970s. Nonetheless, the changes in staffing patterns and in the general expectations of the role of the governor as leader have touched virtually every state. Mullen and Swanson's comment on the authority of Washington State's governor applies almost universally: "The citizen tends to assume the governor possesses more authority than the constitution and statutes in reality allow. An energetic and able chief executive, nevertheless, is able to have significant impact on state policy."[29]

The first piece in the puzzle of the changing impact of the governor is establishing a firmer constitutional and statutory basis of authority. The second aspect of gubernatorial influence is the role of the governor as political leader before the legislature and within the political parties.

The Governor as Political Leader

Unlike the reforms of the 1960s and 1970s, which were essentially national in scope, an understanding of western governors as political leaders requires a regional or even a state-by-state focus. However, at least two generalizations are possible about western governors. First, the plural executive typically has not limited the political influence of the governor as much as might be expected. Second, constitutional restrictions were more often focused on the legislatures than on the governor. The opportunity to dominate the political arena exists for most governors. Even the recent resurgence of state legislatures, which has increased the willingness of the legislatures to challenge the governor, has not appreciably altered the relatively strong position of western governors.

In general the governors of the West have the upper hand in dealing with their legislatures. With the exception of activist legislatures in California, Hawaii and Oregon, none of the legislatures of the West are regarded as particularly innovative or powerful.[30] Conversely, the governors of the region have the constitutional and statutory tools to be effective. While legal and partisan political authority gives the governor the advantage, it may not be fully or effectively exercised. As Coleman Ransome, Jr. observed over thirty years ago, "These powers and techniques place the governor in a position to wield considerable influence in the legislative process. Whether he in fact assumes the role of legislative leader is another matter and depends on such factors as his party leadership, the customs and traditions of the state, and the governor's own view of the proper gubernatorial role."[31]

The bases of that power rest in the constitutional responsibilities of the governor in legislative affairs. The ability to call the legislature into special session and the existence of the line-item veto (except in Nevada) give the governor two powerful tools for confronting the legislature. Also, the constitutional mandate of "one-man, one-vote," which in the West affected primarily the Rocky Mountain states, has given the governor more control over the legislature because the "governor and legislature now represent the same constituency."[32]

The relative impact of the governor in legislative affairs is somewhat blunted by a strong legislative role in the appropriations process. Despite the ability to item-veto appropriation lines in all but Nevada, where no item veto exists, the tradition has remained that the legislature has played a prominent and even dominant budgetary role in Colorado, New Mexico, Washington, Wyoming and elsewhere.[33] Also, in states such as California[34] strong gubernatorial budget authority is challenged by an equally strong legislative involvement in budgetmaking.

Relatively few states have granted the governor sufficient authority so that the legislature has not retained some influence in the budget process. Obviously, the "new" states of Alaska and Hawaii, with constitutions that attempt to centralize control in the executive, have granted their governors such influence, at least in theory. Also, the states of Utah and Washington, which mandate through their state constitutions an executive budget and permit considerable control over the allocation of funds, have done the same.[35]

Legislative-gubernatorial relationships are greatly influenced by partisan politics. This is played out in two areas. First, the frequency with which the governor and legislative majority are of different parties in many of the western states greatly colors the gubernatorial-legislative relationship. Second, the expectation in some states that the governor will also be party leader alters that relationship.

As mentioned above, the situation where the legislative majority and the governor are of different parties is common in the West. (See Table 10.4.) For example, in twelve of the last twenty years in California a Republican has been governor, but the Democratic party has held majority control of both houses the entire time, and recently the lieutenant governor has also been a Democrat. In Arizona, Colorado, Idaho and Wyoming, Democrats held the governorship from 1975 to 1987, yet the majority party in at least one house of the legislature has been Republican during that entire period. A similar split existed from 1977 to 1985 in Utah. In contrast, only Hawaii and New Mexico have been consistently controlled by one party—the Democrats in both cases—for the last two decades. With the election of Republican Garrey Carruthers in New Mexico in 1986, only Hawaii continues to display that consistency.

Other states have been "competitive" in that neither party has been able to dominate the governor's office or the legislature. The result has typically produced splits, but at one point in time the split may be a Democratic governor and a Republican legislature (Washington State in 1979–80), at another time it may be a Republican governor and a Democratic legislature (Washington State in 1974–75).

A party split in the state capital seemingly would heighten partisanship and legislative-gubernatorial tensions. Conversely, single party dominance should reduce partisanship and related tensions. Those expectations are not always met, however. For example, Bruce Babbitt, a Democrat, was relatively successful during his second full term in his relationship with the Arizona legislature.[36] Also, Governor Herschler of Wyoming maintained a good working relationship with the legislature for most of his twelve years in office.[37] Governor Dan Evans of Washington State was a highly respected Republican governor in a state with predominantly Democratic legislatures during his tenure. On the other hand, Democratic governor Jerry Brown was not more successful in his legislative relations than his successor, Republican governor Deukmejian, despite Democratic majorities in both houses of the California legislature during the entire period. Also, the legislative problems of New Mexico governor Toney Anaya were considerable from the very first[38] as were those of Evan Mecham in Arizona.[39]

The role of the governor as a party leader is critical in evaluating the political leadership of the governor. Several factors must be considered in evaluating the party role of the governor. First, when a strong party leader becomes governor, his or her influence may extend beyond the term of office. For example, Thomas Burns built the Democratic party in Hawaii and dominated it before he was elected governor in 1962 and afterwards into the 1970s.[40] Also, the California Republican party is still dominated by Reagan supporters, who took over when he became governor in 1966.[41] On the other hand states such as Washington, Idaho and Alaska have never had a tradition of gubernatorial-dominated parties. This is partly to be attributed to the greater independence of the voters of these states, who do not identify as closely with the political parties.[42] Speaking of Washington State politics, Mullen and Swanson comment that "unlike the governors

Table 10.4　A Legacy of Conflict: Partisan Differences Between the Western Governors and the Legislatures

	AK			AZ			CA			CO			HI			ID			MT			NM			NV			OR			UT			WA			WY		
	G	H	S	G	H	S	G	H	S	G	H	S	G	H	S	G	H	S	G	H	S	G	H	S	G	H	S	G	H	S	G	H	S	G	H	S	G	H	S
1943-44	#	#	#	#	#	#	X	X	X	X	X	X	#	#	#	X	X	X	X	X	X	#	#	#	#	#	X	X	X	X	#	#	#	#	#	#	#	X	X
1945-46	#	#	#	#	#	#	X	X	X	X	X	X	#	#	#	X	X	X	X	X	X	#	#	#	#	#	X	X	X	X	#	#	#	#	#	#	#	X	X
1947-48	#	#	#	#	#	#	X	X	X	X	X	X	#	X	X	#	X	X	X	X	X	#	#	#	#	#	X	X	X	X	X	X	X	X	X	X	X	X	X
1949-50	#	/	#	X	#	#	X	X	X	X	X	#	X	X	X	X	X	X	X	X	X	#	#	#	#	#	X	X	X	X	/	X	X	X	X	X	X	/	X
1951-52	#	/	X	X	#	#	X	X	X	X	X	X	X	X	X	X	X	X	X	X	X	X	X	X	#	#	X	X	X	X	X	X	X	X	X	X	X	X	X
1953-54	X	X	#	X	#	#	X	X	/	X	X	X	X	X	X	X	X	X	X	X	X	X	X	X	#	#	X	X	X	X	X	X	X	#	X	X	X	X	X
1955-56	X	#	#	#	#	#	#	#	#	#	#	#	X	X	#	X	X	X	X	X	X	#	#	#	#	#	X	/	#	#	X	X	X	#	X	X	#	X	X
1957-58	X	#	#	#	#	#	#	#	#	#	#	#	X	X	#	X	X	X	X	X	X	#	#	#	#	#	X	#	#	#	X	X	X	#	X	X	#	X	X
1959-60	#	#	#	X	#	#	#	#	#	X	X	X	X	X	#	X	X	X	X	X	X	#	#	#	X	#	X	#	#	#	#	#	#	#	X	X	#	X	X
1961-62	X	#	#	X	#	#	#	#	#	#	#	#	X	#	#	X	X	X	X	X	X	#	#	#	X	#	X	#	#	#	X	#	X	X	X	X	X	X	X
1963-64	#	/	#	X	#	#	#	#	#	#	#	#	X	#	#	X	X	X	X	X	X	#	#	#	X	#	X	#	#	#	#	#	#	X	X	X	#	X	X
1965-66	X	X	X	X	#	#	X	#	#	X	X	X	#	#	#	X	X	X	X	X	X	#	#	#	X	#	X	#	#	#	#	#	#	X	X	X	#	X	X
1967-68	X	#	X	X	#	#	#	#	#	X	X	X	#	#	#	X	X	X	X	X	X	#	#	#	X	#	X	X	X	X	#	#	#	X	X	X	#	X	X
1969-70	X	#	#	X	#	#	#	#	#	X	X	X	#	#	#	X	X	X	X	X	X	#	#	#	X	#	X	X	X	X	#	#	#	X	X	X	#	X	X
1971-72	#	#	/	X	#	#	X	#	#	X	X	X	#	#	#	X	X	X	X	X	X	#	#	#	X	#	/	#	#	#	#	#	#	X	X	X	X	X	X
1973-74	#	#	X	X	#	#	X	#	#	X	X	X	#	#	#	X	X	X	X	X	X	#	#	#	X	#	X	#	#	#	#	#	#	X	X	X	X	X	X
1975-76	X	#	#	#	#	#	#	#	#	X	X	X	#	#	#	X	X	X	X	X	#	#	#	#	#	#	X	#	#	#	#	#	#	/	#	#	#	X	X
1977-78	X	#	#	#	#	#	#	#	#	X	X	X	#	#	#	X	X	X	/	X	X	#	#	#	#	#	X	#	#	#	#	#	#	/	#	#	#	X	X
1979-80	X	#	#	X	#	#	#	#	#	X	X	X	#	#	#	X	X	X	X	X	X	#	#	#	X	#	X	#	#	#	#	#	#	X	#	#	#	X	X
1981-82	X	#	#	X	#	#	#	#	#	X	X	X	#	#	#	X	X	X	X	X	X	#	#	#	X	#	X	#	#	#	#	#	#	X	#	#	#	X	X
1983-84	X	#	#	X	X	X	X	#	#	X	X	X	#	#	#	X	X	X	X	X	X	#	#	#	X	#	X	#	#	#	#	#	#	X	#	X	#	X	X
1985-86	#	X	X	X	X	X	X	#	#	X	X	X	#	#	#	X	X	X	X	X	X	#	#	#	X	#	X	#	#	#	X	X	X	#	#	#	#	X	X
1987-88	#	#	#	#	X	X	X	#	#	X	X	X	#	#	#	X	X	X	X	X	/	/	#	#	X	#	X	#	#	#	#	#	#	X	#	#	#	X	X
1989-90	#	#	X	X	X	X	X	X	X	X	X	X	#	#	#	X	X	X	X	X	X	X	#	X	X	#	X	#	#	#	X	X	X	#	#	X	#	X	X

Note:　G = Governor　　# = Demo
　　　　H = House　　　　X = GOP
　　　　S = Senate　　　 / = Split

of some states, Washington's chief executive draws relatively little strength from the role of party chief . . . each major party is factionalized, with the governor heading but one faction. . . . Neither party commands the adherence of a majority in the electorate."[43]

In much of the West the power base of the governor is, at least at the time of first election, outside the party.[44] Only through successful reelection and longevity in office do such governors assume the mantle of party leadership. However, that leadership is not likely to transcend leaving office. Governors such as Bruce Babbitt in Arizona, Richard Lamm in Colorado, John Evans in Idaho and Scott Matheson in Utah could dominate for a time, but their control of the party apparatus was linked to their position, and was quickly dissipated. For example, Evans lost a U.S. Senate bid after leaving office, and a Republican replaced Matheson at the governor's mansion in Utah. Babbitt, who was briefly a candidate for the Democratic nomination for president in 1988, remains quite influential in Arizona Democratic circles, but the individual he endorsed as his successor lost in the Democratic primary, and because of later splits in the Democratic party the Republican nominee Evan Mecham won with 40% of the vote in a three-way race.[45] Of these four governors only Richard Lamm was succeeded by a governor from his own party. This is ironic because Lamm never actively sought to dominate Democratic politics in Colorado.

Frequently the party leader is someone other than the governor. For example, with their restriction to a single term most New Mexico governors have more influence before they reach that office. The Arizona Republican party has been dominated for thirty years by former U.S. Senator Barry Goldwater, and not by the numerous Republican governors of the 1950s, 1960s and early 1970s. State Representative Ted Strickland has been the head of the Colorado Republican party since the 1970s, yet he has lost elections for governor twice, in 1978 and 1986.

This relative lack of gubernatorial influence can be attributed to two factors, which can be seen as specific to particular regions and states. In the northern Rocky Mountain area (Montana, Colorado, Idaho) the basic independence of the voters has kept party identity relatively low. Thus, a person has not had to be a party insider in order to secure the nomination for governor. Along the Pacific Rim (Alaska, Washington, Oregon, Nevada, California) the competitiveness of office has rarely left any governor in power long enough to take effective control of the party apparatus. In both areas personalities have been the key to party control. Individuals who may or may not ever be governor dominate the party apparatus. Also, by direct personal appeal to the public, a gubernatorial candidate may succeed to that office without party support.

The Governor as Political Personality

The twentieth century has produced a number of powerful personalities who have dominated state and regional politics for long periods. Robert LaFollette in Wisconsin, Nelson Rockefeller in New York, Huey Long in Louisiana, William Borah in Idaho and Ronald Reagan in California came to national prominence after serving as governors of their respective states. The West has had a significant array of individuals who by force of personality carried a political party for many years. Given the competitiveness of many states and the heightened "independence" of western voters it should not be surprising that personalities can dominate for a period. The list is, therefore, quite long. John Burns in Hawaii virtually created the Democratic party on those islands in the late 1940s. Since he was elected governor in 1962 virtually all state offices have been controlled by that party, which never held a statewide office until 1958.[46] In Arizona, Governor George Hunt served seven terms over the first twenty years of statehood and ushered in a period of Democratic domination of state politics. On the other hand Barry Goldwater in Arizona resurrected what in the 1940s was a moribund Republican party and by the late 1960s had made it the majority party in the state's politics.[47] Dan Evans served as governor of Washington State for twelve years, and was elected to the U.S. Senate in 1983, despite a bias in state politics favoring the Democratic party. Ronald Reagan's 1966 election as governor of California was the starting point of a resurrection of that state's Republican party that continues today. Paul Laxalt was able to increase the influence of the Nevada Republican party, first as governor and then as U.S. senator, in a state dominated by Democratic Clark County (Las Vegas). For lasting impact, Hiram Johnson of California may have been the most important western governor. His election in 1910 set a pattern of election of progressive governors that would last into the 1960s. Also, the shape of California politics, with its emphasis on the initiative process, nonpartisan elections for some state offices, and the emergence of the governor as the central figure in policymaking and administration can be traced to Johnson's tenure.[48]

Table 10.5   Where Did They Come From?

State	Governor	Year Elected	Previous Occupation
Alaska	Cowper	1986	Legislator/lawyer
Arizona	Mofford[a]	1987	Secretary of state
California	Deukmejian	1986	Incumbent
Colorado	Romer	1986	State treasurer
Hawaii	Waihee	1986	Lt. governor
Idaho	Andrus	1986	Former federal cabinet official/governor
Montana	Stephens	1988	Radio commentator/state senator
Nevada	Miller[b]	1988	Lt. governor
New Mexico	Carruthers	1986	Federal agency official/college professor
Oregon	Goldschmidt	1986	Former cabinet official/mayor
Utah	Bangerter	1984	Speaker Utah house
Washington	Gardner	1984	County executive
Wyoming	Sullivan	1986	Lawyer

[a]Gov. Mecham was impeached and Secretary of State Rose Mofford became governor.
[b]Gov. Bryan resigned upon his election to the U.S. Senate and Lt. Gov. Miller became acting governor.

In this region that can boast of numerous significant twentieth-century political personalities, many were never governor. Henry "Scoop" Jackson of Washington State, Gale McGee of Wyoming, Mike Mansfield of Montana, Barry Goldwater of Arizona, all made their reputations in the U.S. Senate, but each had a major influence on the politics of his state. There is, nonetheless, an expectation that the governor will dominate the political spotlight, if only during his tenure in office.

The seeming importance of personalities has meant that in a number of states strong individuals have emerged as candidates for governor or other office who were not closely tied to either political party. While most of them have had some elected political experience, not all were strong party activists, though few would be characterized as complete outsiders. (See Table 10.5.) As noted earlier, George Deukmejian was not the party choice in the 1982 California Republican primary, but he succeeded there, and in the general election that November. Evan Mecham was a decided outsider in Republican circles who had sought the Republican gubernatorial nomination five times,

Table 10.6   Where Did They Go?

State	Governor	Year	Sought Re-election	Won/ Lost	Other Office	Present Occupation
Alaska	Sheffield	1986	yes	L		Business
Arizona	Babbitt	1986	no		Lost in bid for nomination for president, 1988	
California	Deukmejian	1986	yes	W		
Colorado	Lamm	1986	no			Teaching/ attorney
Hawaii	Ariyoshi	1986	no			Attorney
Idaho	Evans	1986	no		Lost bid for U.S. Senate	
Montana	Swinden	1980	no			Farming
Nevada	Bryan	1986	*a*		U.S. Senate	
New Mexico	Anaya	1986	no			Attorney
Oregon	Atiyeh	1986	yes	L		Attorney
Utah	Matheson	1984	no			Attorney
Washington	Spellman	1984	yes	L		
Wyoming	Herschler	1986	no			Ranching

*a*Resigned in the middle of his term.

won the nomination twice and finally, in 1986, became a plurality governor after a Democratic party split produced two candidates (Bill Schulze ran as an independent). In 1982 in Alaska, Bill Sheffield was nominated and elected governor despite strong primary opposition from persons more closely tied to the Democratic party than he.[49] It has been said that virtually every race for governor in Alaska since 1970 has revolved around personality issues and has been won with the aid of personal political organizations and not the parties.[50] In New Mexico Governor Carruthers succeeded in the Republican primary by distancing himself from party politics and particularly from the gubernatorial-legislative squabbles that had characterized the preceding Anaya administration.[51] Even Toney Anaya, a Democrat, had run an anti-*patrón*, antipolitical establishment campaign in his 1982 run for governor.[52] Former governor Victor Atiyeh of Oregon was regarded as a maverick within the Republican party when he served as a state legislator and was not that party's first choice. The same could be said of Democrat Dixie Lee Ray who served as a one-term governor in Washington State. Finally, as noted earlier, former gov-

Table 10.7   Gubernatorial Authority and Cultural Expectations of Government Activism

Cultural Expectations of Government Activism	Gubernatorial Authority		
	Low	Medium	High
Low	Nevada New Mexico Wyoming Utah Idaho		
Medium	Arizona	Montana Washington Colorado	Alaska
High			Hawaii California Oregon

ernor Richard Lamm of Colorado was never a party insider before his nomination in 1974, the prelude to twelve years in office. It should not be surprising that given their lack of a strong tie to the party, few governors go on to other elective office once their terms as governor are over. (See Table 10.6.)

The Governor as Policymaker

The ultimate role of the governor is that of shaper of public policy. In this convergence of legal authority, political skill, and popular and personal expectation the opportunity for policymaking emerges. As was suggested above, the popular expectations of a prominent gubernatorial role in policymaking have grown in the last three decades. Also, in most western states the legal barriers have been lowered. The factor of political skill is more difficult to evaluate, in part because the other factors may blunt the efforts of a skillful politician and, conversely, a governor of relatively modest skill may succeed because of a strong legal foundation for action.

The first level of analysis is to examine the relationship between institutional or legal authority and cultural expectations of government.[53] The easiest way to visualize this is to contrast strength of gubernatorial authority with strength of government as permitted by the political culture. This analysis gives a sense of the opportunity to impact policy. (See Table 10.7.)

Table 10.7 suggests that on balance governors in the West are not capable of significant long-term political change, and certainly not without the active participation of the state legislatures. Those in the best position would seem to be the governors of California, Hawaii, Alaska and Oregon. However, this judgment must be tempered by the realization that the legislatures of these states are quite active and would not readily cede a dominant policymaking role to the governor. The threat of "competition" in policymaking is less in Montana, Washington and Colorado. From this perspective a vigorous issue-oriented governor could easily dominate state politics (as Evans of Washington and Lamm of Colorado in fact did). This opportunity is enhanced by the party competitiveness of these states, which places a premium on personality to attract voters. The placement of Arizona presents some problems. The raised expectations (relative to authority) are primarily the result of nine years of activism from Bruce Babbitt. He set a pattern of expectation much higher than previous governors. Further, the continued in-migration to that state brings more persons into the area who have higher expectations of government service provision because of the higher levels of service they probably received in other states.

The placement of New Mexico as a state with low expectations is based on the decline in the Hispanic (the most Democratic) segment of the population. As the state becomes more Anglo and conservative the expectations of government are likely to decline.

What of the governors of the other states ranked low on both scales? These are predominantly states where a governor can be relatively passive yet be regarded as a success. It would also seem likely that a vigorous or activist governor would be successful for a short time. But over the long haul that activism would be counterproductive as voters are not likely to accept the activist gubernatorial style. The example of Bruce Babbitt in Arizona runs counter to this thesis. However, the growth of the last two decades has changed the dominant political cultural outlook of that state. It remains very conservative, but is more amenable to certain government intervention, particularly in the areas of environmental policy and education. An analysis of the Arizona governorship by Everett, which applies equally to governors from any state with low authority and low expectations, notes:

> Though in weak position, he has more influence than any other official in the state, and most people hold him accountable for

the effective and efficient administration of state government. How effective a governor is depends, to a large degree, on his personality and how he uses his "good offices." Some governors have taken a creative role in all matters, while others have restricted their operations to constitutional and statutory duties.[54]

The other aspect of the role of the governor as policymaker involves gubernatorial relations with the bureaucracy. The structural changes made in state government were aimed at giving the governor more control over the bureaucracy. This issue is somewhat broader than the question of who appoints the agency heads, though that in itself is an important question. Two aspects of this issue are the ability to fire as well as appoint agency personnel, and the breadth of coverage of the merit system, which determines the kind of patronage the governor can utilize.

Because western states emerged during the progressive era, it is not surprising that a strong commitment to civil service and nonpatronage hiring is common in the West. As Sabato remarks, "In the late nineteenth century the institution of paronage became the focus of attack for the burgeoning Progressive Movement."[55] He goes on to note that over 95% of all positions in Utah state government are covered by civil service, and in the state of Washington the governor appoints only about three hundred of the thirty thousand state employees.[56] But the issue of control includes not only appointment but also extends to removal from office. Often it is not so much a question of patronage hiring, as of removing people who are perceived to be incompetent or simply unwilling to pursue aggressively the programs and policies of the new governors. In Utah, Arizona and Wyoming, the power of removal has been constrained by the courts and statute so that removals, except for malfeasance, are virtually impossible.[57] In other western states the governor is given considerably more latitude. Notable for this broad grant of power are Colorado, New Mexico, Hawaii and Alaska.[58]

The most complex situation is that of California. In addition to a very large cadre of senior civil service officials, California created in 1963 the Career Executive Service, which is a group of some fifteen hundred senior personnel who fill policymaking roles, but retain some civil service rights. (This program was the model for the federal Senior Executive Service created by the Civil Service Reform Act of 1978.) The governor of California controls policy with the aid of a rather large staff (over five hundred), and then through the Career Executives. It is in "managing" the Career Executives that the governor manages and directs policy.[59]

In general, the management aspect of the gubernatorial role is a much more prominent part of the work-day of a modern governor than it was twenty or thirty years ago.[60] In only a few states are the powers of the governor sufficiently restricted so that being a manager is made problematic. The authority is in place, the public expects a responsive bureaucracy, and to the extent that they have the opportunity and willingness to manage, governors can gain a considerable degree of control over the direction of routine state policy.

CONCLUSION

In 1956 Coleman Ransome stated that governors function in "three broad areas of operations—policy formation, public relations, and management." This statement is no less true today. If anything, the last three decades have produced considerable change to increase the policy formation and management capacity of the governors. These changes are most apparent in the West because constitutional and political tradition originally left most western governors decidedly weak in both the policy and management areas.

The modern western governor has, with few exceptions, the staff, the authority, and the popular support to implement his or her chosen political agenda. This does not mean that the governor has carte blanche. The legislatures of the West have been similarly vigorous in increasing their policymaking and decision-making capacity. Governors still have to convince a sometimes reluctant and always skeptical legislature in order to implement new policies. In addition, all but the governors of Alaska and Hawaii must contend with political rivals in the form of the other elected executives. And of course no governor can ever stray too far from the accepted political norms of his or her state electorate no matter how efficacious that governor may believe the policy, or how broad he or she perceives the "mandate" to be. Whether in an earlier time when restrictions were many or today when authority and expectations are much higher, the crucial factor is the personality and vigor of the person who is elected governor. This will determine the success of a governor's tenure in office.

Where do governors go after being governor? Their one political chance seems to be only as a governor, since they are unlikely to move on to another office after four or eight years as the state's chief executive. Even in that effort they must compete with an often hostile legislature and "colleague" executives who have their own political agendas. Does this make western governors different from their counterparts in the other thirty-seven states? In general the answer would seem to be no, though the West is more likely to experience a partisan split between the governor and the legislature than are the other states. On the other hand there are fewer activist legislatures in the West. This does not, however, automatically yield more power to the governor, because the popular expectations for a vigorous, pro-active government are low.

What do the governors think of their experience? When the National Governors' Association asked that question the response was overwhelming: the governorship was the single greatest experience of those who have held the office.[61] They have a sense that they are "in charge." The immediacy of the impact of policy decisions at the state level contributes greatly to this feeling of being at the top despite the institutional and organizational barriers to rapid, concerted action. It would seem to be inconceivable that a governor, given the opportunity to do it over again, would decline the chance to be governor.

Notes

1. Coleman B. Ransome, Jr., *The Office of the Governor in the United States* (University: University of Alabama Press, 1956); Larry Sabato, *Goodbye to Good-Time Charlie*, 2nd ed. (Washington, D.C.: Congressional Quarterly Press, 1983).

2. Sabato, *Goodbye to Good-Time Charlie*, 6–7.

3. James Wang, *Hawaiian State and Local Politics* (Hilo, Hawaii: Wang Associates, 1982), 366.

4. Bruce Mason and Heinz Hink, *Constitutional Government in Arizona*, 4th ed. (Tempe: Arizona State University, 1972), 169–70.

5. "To Form a More Perfect Union" (National Conference on Social Welfare, Washington, D.C., 1985).

6. Lynn Muchmore, "The Governor as Manager," in Thad Beyle and Lynn Muchmore, *Being Governor* (Durham, N.C.: Duke University Press, 1983), notes that between 1965 and 1980 some twenty-two states undertook reorganizations and government restructuring to aid the governor.

7. Albert C. Johns, *Nevada Government and Politics* (Dubuque, Iowa: Kendall/Hunt, 1971), 63.

8. Elmer E. Cornwell, Jr., Jay Goodman, and Wayne Swanson, *State Constitutional Conventions* (New York: Praeger, 1975), 144.

9. Alan Reed, "The Plural Executive," in F. Chris Garcia and Paul L. Hain,

New Mexico Government, rev. ed. (Albuquerque: University of New Mexico Press, 1981), 89.

10. Thad Beyle, Lynn Muchmore, and Robert Dalton, "Conclusion" in Beyle and Muchmore, *Being Governor*, 206.

11. For an extended discussion of state government reform in this period, see "State Government: The Evolution of the Laboratories of Democracy" in Raymond W. Cox III, *Intergovernmental Relations as an Instrument of Political Change*, a report to the National Science Foundation #82-SP-0840, November 1984, 16–37.

12. "Symposium on the American Governor in the 1970s," *Public Administration Review* 30(1) (January/February 1970), 37.

13. "Symposium on the Governor," 25.

14. *Ibid.*, 27.

15. John Culver and John Syer, *Power and Politics in California*, 2nd ed. (New York: John Wiley and Sons, 1984), 50; Robert S. Lorch, *Colorado's Government* (Boulder: Colorado Associated University Press, 1979), 207–8.

16. According to a 1986 study by the Advisory Commission on Intergovernmental Relations, the number of categorical programs declined in the 1960s then rose sharply through the 1970s. Such programs have been in decline again since 1981.

17. The Wisconsin Idea was that the universities had a responsibility to aid governmental decision-making by preparing policy analyses and conducting research on behalf of government. The university was to provide the same services that the Municipal Research Bureau at Columbia University was providing to New York City.

18. Abdo I. Baaklini, ed., *Linking Science and Technology to Public Policy* (Albany: State University of New York, 1979).

19. *Governing the American States* (Washington, D.C.: National Governors' Association, 1978).

20. *Reflections on Being Governor* (Washington, D.C.: National Governors' Association, 1981), 5.

21. *Ibid.*, 281. In questionnaires sent to the thirteen western governors, most of them agree that Walker's views remain correct, though Governor Carruthers of New Mexico disagreed quite vigorously.

22. *Ibid.*, 5. In the questionnaires sent to the current governors in the West, most disagree with the lack of public interest and awareness expressed by Walker. The linkage between policy and management that has become recognized by governors throughout the nation is, I believe, responsible for the changed emphasis. Walker's definition of management is much narrower than that used today. See Raymond Cox, "The Expanding Role of the Western Governor as a Manager," *The Western Governmental Researcher* 4, 3 (Winter 1989).

23. Lorch, *Colorado Government* (1979), 207–8.

24. Neal Peirce, "Prophet," *The Arizona Republic*, January 21, 1987.

25. Harold Rhodes, "The Cabinet and Other Appointive Agencies," in Garcia and Hain, eds., *New Mexico Government*, rev. ed., 89, 106.

26. Gary Hamilton and Nicole Biggart, *Governor Reagan, Governor Brown* (New York: Columbia University Press, 1984). Also, it has been argued that the easy reelection of Governor Deukmejian of California in 1986 was due to his perceived ability to control state government with a minimum of difficulty, *i.e.*, to be a "good manager." See *Congressional Quarterly Weekly Report* 44(45) (November 8, 1986), 2858.

27. Cox, *Intergovernmental Relations as an Instrument of Political Change*, 1–15.

28. Sabato, *Goodbye to Good-Time Charlie*, 88.

29. William Mullen and Thor Swanson, "The Executives and Administration," in Thor Swanson, William Mullen, John Pierce and Charles Sheldon, eds., *Political Life in Washington* (Pullman: Washington State University Press, 1985), 93.

30. *Arizona Republic*, January 7, 1987, A10. The best study of the innovation in the state legislatures remains Jack Walker's classic 1969 study, "The Diffusion of Innovations Among American States," *American Political Science Review* 63(3) (1969), 880–99.

31. Ransome, *The Office of Governor in the United States*, 148.

32. Sabato, *Goodbye to Good-Time Charlie*, 88.

33. Robert Lorch, *Colorado's Government*, rev. ed. (Boulder: Colorado Associated University Press, 1983), 191–93; Alan Reed, "The Plural Executive," 20; Herman H. Trachsel and Ralph Wade, *The Government and Administration of Wyoming* (New York: Thomas Y. Crowell, 1953), 75; Tim R. Miller, *State Government: Politics in Wyoming* (Dubuque, Iowa: Kendall/Hunt, 1981), 147–50; and John B. Richard, *Governmental Politics of Wyoming* (Dubuque, Iowa: William C. Brown, 1966), 68.

34. See Culver and Syer, *Power and Politics in California*, and Michael J. Ross, *California: Its Government and Politics*, 2nd ed. (Monterey, Calif.: Brooks/ Cole, 1984).

35. Homer Durkham, *State and Local Government in Utah* (Salt Lake City: Utah Foundation, 1954), 39. While this dominance was noted over thirty years ago, discussions with scholars on state politics suggest that such gubernatorial control remains. Mary Avery, *Government of Washington State*, rev. ed. (Seattle: University of Washington Press, 1973), 31.

36. Joel Nilsson, "Water Code a Monument to Babbitt's Political Arts," *Arizona Republic*, January 7, 1987, A10.

37. In a state that is strongly Republican, and despite a growing recession in the state, Herschler had a 60% approval rating when he left office. Cal Clark, Janet Clark and B. Oliver Walter, "From Boom to Bust: The Implications of a Declining Economy for the 1986 Wyoming Elections," a paper presented at the Annual Meeting of the Western Political Science Association, Anaheim,

Calif., March 26–28, 1987. See also Tim R. Miller, *State Government: Politics in Wyoming*, 140.

38. Jose Garcia, "The 1982 Gubernatorial Transition in New Mexico: A Farewell to Patron Politics," in Thad L. Beyle, ed., *Gubernatorial Transitions: The 1982 Election* (Durham, N.C.: Duke University Press, 1985), 337–40.

39. Mecham was in trouble with both the electorate and the legislature from the day he took office. On April 4, 1988, the Arizona senate convicted him under articles of impeachment drawn by the Arizona house of representatives. He was removed from office and the secretary of state, who was acting governor during the impeachment trial, became governor.

40. See Tom Coffman, *Catch a Wave*, 2nd ed. (Honolulu: University of Hawaii Press, 1973) and Wang, *Hawaiian State and Local Politics*.

41. See Culver and Syer, *Power and Politics in California*, Ross, *California: Its Government and Politics*, and Hamilton and Biggart, *Governor Reagan, Governor Brown*, for discussion of the control of the Republican party by Reagan supporters. Such party control is relatively recent. Through the 1950s, cross-nomination in the primary meant that statewide candidates such as Knight and Warren sought the nomination of both parties. Control was much more personal while in office.

42. Robert H. Blank, *Regional Diversity of Political Values: Idaho Political Culture* (Washington, D.C.: University Press of America, 1978); Boyd A. Martin, *Idaho Voting Trends* (Moscow, Idaho: Idaho Research Foundation, Inc., 1975).

43. Mullen and Swanson, "The Executives and Administration," 80.

44. George Deukmejian, despite many years of legislative and state office experience, was not the choice of Reaganites, who supported Lt. Gov. Mike Curb in the Republican primary in 1982.

45. *Congressional Quarterly Weekly Report* 44(45) (November 8, 1986), 2859, 2864.

46. A very good history of the emergence of the Democratic party in Hawaii is found in Coffman's *Catch a Wave*, 2nd ed.

47. Ray Everett, *Arizona History and Government* (Phoenix: Arizona Board of Regents, 1977).

48. Hamilton and Biggart, *Governor Reagan, Governor Brown*, 55–62.

49. Gerald McBeath, "Alaska's Governor" in Gerald A. McBeath and Thomas A. Morehouse, eds., *Alaska State Government and Politics* (Fairbanks: University of Alaska Press, 1987), 268–69.

50. *Ibid.*, 262, 269.

51. *Congressional Quarterly Weekly Report* 44 (23) (June 7, 1986), 1293.

52. Garcia, "The 1982 Gubernatorial Transition in New Mexico," 338.

53. As suggested earlier, most of the West by tradition has sought relatively weak or passive governments. So the characterization of a state as permitting a strong government must be taken with a grain of salt. All judgments about strength are obviously subjective.

54. Everett, *Arizona History and Government*, 159–60.

55. Sabato, *Goodbye to Good-Time Charlie*, 67.

56. *Ibid.*, 68.

57. Durham, *State and Local Government in Utah*, 48; Mason and Hink, *Constitutional Government in Arizona*, 161; Everett, *Arizona History and Government*, 162; and Trachsel and Wade, *The Government and Administration of Wyoming*, 71.

58. Lorch, *Colorado's Government* (1983), 192; Reed, "The Plural Executive," 20; Wang, *Hawaiian State and Local Politics*, 368; and Victor Fischer, "Alaska's Constitution" in McBeath and Morehouse, *Alaska State Government and Politics*, 28–29, 41.

59. Hamilton and Biggart, *Governor Reagan, Governor Brown*, 10.

60. Cox, "The Expanding Role of the Western Governor as Manager."

61. *Reflections on Being Governor*, 81.

11

JUDICIAL SYSTEMS AND PUBLIC POLICY

John H. Culver

*I*N HIS BOOK ABOUT THE FIRST YEAR OF LAW SCHOOL, Scott Turow says, "I had always thought that the legislatures made all the rules and that judges merely interpret what has been said." He adds, "I'm not sure where I got that idea, either in high-school civics or, more likely, from TV."[1] Turow thus identified a perception of the judiciary held by many, that judges are nonpolitical interpreters of laws with no policymaking role. This impression is incorrect, as Turow notes, and as demonstrated by the numerous examples in the federal and state courts. When the U.S. Supreme Court rules that the right of privacy means that a woman can elect to have an abortion during the first trimester of her pregnancy (*Roe v. Wade*, 1973) or the

California supreme court holds that the state's capital punishment law is unconstitutional (*People v. Anderson*, 1972), public policies are being made.

Neither high-school civics texts nor television shows do a credible job of explaining the nation's judicial system. The basics may be covered—there are two judicial systems, one federal and one in the states, and the function of the courts is to resolve legal disputes—but confusion is frequently the result. Most civics texts ignore or understate the policymaking role of the courts as well as the linkage between the judiciaries and the political cultures of the states. Unlike the single chief executive and legislative body within the individual states, the fifty state judicial systems are composed of a variety of courts at various levels. It is left to the states to decide what courts should be established, how judges should be selected, and the types of disputes that are to be resolved in these courts. These legal systems mirror state politics in much the same fashion as do state executives and state legislatures.

For too many years, the study of state courts was neglected on the assumption that the major legal issues and the policy implications that emanated from those decisions were the province of the federal courts in general, and the U.S. Supreme Court in particular. Obviously, the federal courts are important, but in terms of the volume of legal business transacted in the courts, it is in the state courts where most cases begin and end. In 1985, for example, more cases were appealed to the California supreme court (4,370) than to the U.S. Supreme Court (4,289); and the Hawaii supreme court had only 900 fewer cases appealed to it than did the federal high court. There are almost twice as many judges in the thirteen western states as in the entire federal judiciary. Fortunately, the last twenty years have witnessed a dramatic increase in scholarly attention to the importance of the state judiciary.

This chapter examines the judicial systems in the western states. Special attention is directed to their policymaking role, the contrasts between the state judiciaries and the federal judicial system and the question of whether there is a regional uniqueness to the courts in the West as compared to those in other regions of the country. This assessment thus begins with a discussion of judicial policymaking, then moves on to the organization of western state courts, and finishes with an examination of how judges are selected.

Two interwoven themes ease the task of understanding the judicial systems in the western states. First, state courts are a reflection of the social, economic and political history of each state.[2] Second, judicial institutions and processes in these states are quite similar; the key element that gives the state judiciaries their distinctiveness lies with the judges who staff the courts at the various levels. A trial judge in Los Angeles is part of the local legal culture of that area just as the judge in rural Utah or Nevada is identified with the prominent norms of those areas.

The Western Judiciaries and Public Policy

Turow's remarks point to the fact that the role state judiciaries play in the formulation of public policies is, in contrast to the legislative and executive branches of government, the least understood by the public. However, the courts can, and do, play an important role, whether in defining the rights of those suspected or criminal behavior, dismantling the legal barriers that perpetuate discriminatory housing patterns, or promoting environmental protection. Moreover, the tolerance of the public in response to judicial policymaking is part of a state's political culture as defined by Elazar (see Chapter 2). States such as California, where the progressive spirit is well entrenched, tend to have activist supreme courts. Similarly, the populist-progressive tradition in Oregon and Washington is reflected in the decisions of the high courts in those states. The Alaska supreme court has been praised for its decisions that mirror "the cherished individualism of the nation's last frontier."[3] By contrast, the political culture in a state such as Utah, with its strong Mormon influence, is not very supportive of activist policymaking.

Beginning in the early 1970s, state supreme courts have looked to their own constitutions for support of decisions that have expanded the scope of personal rights beyond what the federal Supreme Court has established. The view of John C. Sheehy, a justice on the Montana supreme court, characterizes this new independent spirit. In complaining about the rigidness of the federal Supreme Court in defining individual rights, Sheehy said,

> Instead of knuckling under to this unjustified expansion of Federal judicial power into the perimeters of our state power, we should show our judicial displeasure by insisting that in Montana, this sovereign state can interpret its Constitution to guarantee rights to its citizens greater than those guaranteed by the Federal Constitution.[4]

Justice Sheehy's opinion has been transformed into judicial policies in a number of state high-court decisions. Thus the Alaska supreme court in 1975 held that the personal use and possession of marijuana by adults in their own homes fell within the meaning of Alaska's constitutional guarantee of privacy (*Ravin v. State*). The California supreme court, widely regarded as a politically progressive and independent tribunal, established landmark rulings in the areas of consumer protection, public school financing, capital punishment, and the rights of the accused. The Oregon and Hawaii supreme courts have been less tolerant (*e.g.*, pro-suspect) than the U.S. Supreme Court on questions concerning the admissibility of evidence in criminal cases. The Oregon supreme court has also extended free speech protection to adult-bookstore owners beyond that held to be protected under the First Amendment by the federal high court in obscenity cases. Similarly, the Colorado supreme court in the mid-1980s expanded the privacy rights of citizens beyond the limits established by the federal courts. The Nevada supreme court has established numerous precedents in the area of legalized gambling that will affect how casinos operate in other states (when and if they decide to turn to this source of taxation to augment state revenues).

State supreme courts can make public policies by aggressively seizing the opportunity to act or by declining to do so and thus maintaining the status quo. For example, the California supreme court ruled in 1971 that public schools must be funded on an equitable basis (*Serrano v. Priest*). When a similar case was appealed from Texas to the U.S. Supreme Court two years later, the federal high court found that disparities in school financing did not violate the equal protection clause of the U.S. Constitution (*San Antonio Independent School District v. Rodriguez*, 411 U.S. 1, 1973). Despite that ruling, the California legislature changed its funding formula to conform to the California high court decision. Soon after the *Serrano* decision, the state supreme courts in Arizona, Oregon, Colorado and Idaho heard challenges to inequitable financing in their own states. They decided not to follow California's lead, although this precedent was subsequently adopted by the Washington State supreme court (1977) and the Wyoming supreme court (1983). As Ken Wong discusses in Chapter 14, the federal and state judiciaries have been actively involved in educational policymaking in the states, not just in regard to school financing, but also in the provision of educational programs for the needy and equal opportunity regulations.

The ability of the justices to create public policies rests upon several conditions. Most important, there has to be a majority of like-minded justices on the state high court. The composition of the court justices rests in turn on who appointed them to the bench. A governor with a conservative political orientation will not knowingly appoint a judge to the bench who has a liberal view of creative judicial policymaking. Thus, since states such as Utah, Nevada and Idaho are unlikely to elect liberal governors, it is doubtful that governors from those states would appoint liberal judges to the high court. Second, since all state supreme court justices in the western states must face the voters at one time or another, the justices are mindful of the prevailing public attitudes, the influence of the media in the state, the powerful interest groups in the state, and the likelihood of organized opposition to their decisions. All of these factors are important at election time.

One generally associates judicial policymaking with rulings concerning civil liberties and the environment. However, courts can also affect public policy in cases concerning economic activity. This is illustrated in the area of tort law, which involves civil wrongs of a noncontract nature. An example of a tort action would be the question of who is responsible for damage resulting from a defective product— the manufacturer, the seller or the buyer? Cases in tort law can shift the economic burden from manufacturers to consumers or from governmental units to insurance companies. In one analysis of tort law reform in the states since World War II, the supreme courts in New Jersey, Michigan, Kentucky, California and Washington, among others, were characterized as having taken activist policy positions. By contrast, the supreme courts in Alaska, Hawaii, Idaho, Montana and New Mexico were regarded as having pursued a policy of judicial self-restraint—that is, they had not seized the opportunity to be innovative in tort law reform.[5] As noted in this analysis, these latter states are largely rural and have small populations. A state supreme court such as Montana's may not have had an opportunity to be particularly creative in this area.

While state judiciaries can be powerful and creative in policymaking, they are restrained in two major ways. First, unlike state legislatures or state executives, which can enact laws that change public policies when the political climate supports such actions, the judiciary is confined to dealing with the cases that come to it. State judiciaries cannot simply decide, for example, that the time is ripe to pronounce sweeping environmental reforms without the specific environmental case at hand. Equally important, the state judicial systems cannot enforce their own decisions. They depend upon state legislatures, governors, state attorney generals and mayors, among other public officials, to ensure compliance with judicial decisions. When legislatures enact new policies, funds are appropriated for enforcement. The courts lack the appropriations power of legislatures and governors.

Perhaps the most basic question concerning judicial policymaking is whether the courts are the appropriate institutions to engage in this activity. Advocates of a policy of judicial self-restraint emphasize that legislatures are the accepted vehicles to formulate public policies. Proponents of judicial activism counter that the courts can properly engage in policymaking when the legislatures are not responsive to social-legal problems. The most obvious example of this can be seen in the situation of blacks in the South until the 1950s when the U.S. Supreme Court began invalidating racial discrimination laws. Without such federal judicial action, black citizens would have had to wait until the all-white state legislatures decided it was time to grant black residents the rights they presumably were guaranteed by the U.S. Constitution.

State supreme courts cannot be classified as wholly activist or nonactivist. Some courts may be prone to policymaking in some areas, but not in others. Once again, Elazar's concept of political culture, as discussed in Chapter 2, may help us to understand those issues where the courts feel most and least comfortable in making public policies. In 1977, the Washington State supreme court held that the dismissal of a homosexual male high-school teacher was valid as his "fitness" had been impaired. By contrast, the California supreme court arrived at the opposite conclusion in a similar case that same year.[6] As examples in this chapter illustrate, the policymaking aspects of state high courts are a function of the composition of the courts, the political culture of the state, public opinion, the judicial tradition in the state, and the economic foundations of the state. Changing public attitudes may sweep out liberal or conservative governors and shift the ideological balance in the legislatures. They may also affect the state supreme courts, which are the locus of judicial policymaking. Courts that were regarded as progressive and innovative a decade ago may now acquiesce to other political bodies in terms of policymaking. The opposite also holds true. Jacob's statement on the policymaking role of the judiciary is put well: "Courts are intruders in the policy arena and bring to it a degree of unpredictability."[7]

The Organization of Western State Courts

There is no regional distinctiveness to the organization or structure of the western state courts, nor is there a unique method of judicial selection that sets the West apart from the rest of the country. Rather, as one scholar has noted, the "structure and operation of American courts have been shaped by *strong traditions of local control of justice and judicial independence.*"[8]

There is a common hierarchy in the structure of the courts in all the states, although the names of the courts may vary from state to state as discussed below. Basically, there are four levels of state courts: (1) the state court of last resort (the supreme court); (2) the intermediate appellate courts, although not all states have them; (3) the general trial courts; and (4) courts of limited jurisdiction. Figure 11.1 illustrates two different judicial systems. Note that the Alaska court organization is a unified court model wherein there are no county or city courts and funding comes entirely from the state. However, there is a proliferation of courts of limited jurisdiction in New Mexico and funding comes from both the state and local units of government.

SUPREME COURT

Each of the thirteen western states has a supreme court, staffed by between five and nine justices who serve for terms ranging from six to twelve years (see Table 11.1 for data on each state supreme court). These courts have the final say on questions of interpretation of state constitutions and state laws. While a decision made by a state supreme court may be appealed to the U.S. Supreme Court, the nine members of the federal high court usually leave matters of state law to their brethren on the state supreme courts. The supreme courts have discretionary appellate jurisdiction—that is, the majority of their business consists of hearing appeals from decisions reached in the trial courts. With the exception of cases involving capital punishment, the state high courts decide which cases they will hear. In those cases involving a death sentence, most states provide for automatic appeal to the state supreme court.

The majority of cases that come on appeal to the state supreme courts are civil matters involving disputes between private parties. Typical civil suits involve personal injury, property damage, contracts, and disputes between individuals. Appeals on criminal matters involve individuals who have been convicted of violating a state law.

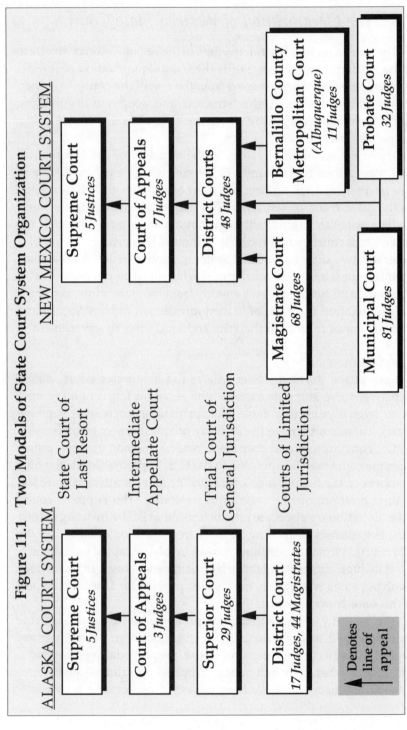

Figure 11.1   **Two Models of State Court System Organization**

Sources: Alaska Court System, 1988 Annual Report; Judicial Department, State of New Mexico, Annual Report, 1988.

Table 11.1   Characteristics of Western State Supreme Courts

State	Number of Justices	Length of Term (yrs.)	Method of Selection
Alaska	5	10	merit plan
Arizona	5	6	merit plan
California	7	12	merit plan (modified)
Colorado	7	10	merit plan
Hawaii	5	10	merit plan/senate confirms
Idaho	5	6	nonpartisan election
Montana	7	8	nonpartisan election
Nevada	5	6	merit plan
New Mexico	5	8	merit plan (modified)
Oregon	7	6	nonpartisan election
Utah	5	10	merit plan
Washington	9	6	nonpartisan election
Wyoming	7	8	merit plan

Sources: Compiled from most recent annual reports for the courts in individual states.

For example, the Alaska supreme court handled 338 civil appeals in contrast to 98 criminal appeals in 1987–88. When a state supreme court reverses the decision of a lower court, the case then goes back to the trial court for a new trial consistent with the decision of the state high court.

INTERMEDIATE APPELLATE COURTS

This level of the judicial hierarchy refers to those courts, commonly known as courts of appeal, which fall between the supreme court and the main trial courts. The appeal courts do not hear cases in the manner of the trial courts, but instead serve as the first line of appeal for litigants who are dissatisfied with the decision of the trial court. The purpose of the intermediate appellate courts is to determine whether or not the original trial was conducted in a satisfactory and proper manner. In most cases, judges on the courts of appeal read the transcripts of the case at hand and uphold the lower court's decision. The often monotonous processing of these cases prompted this candid response from one California appellate jurist:

> Once in a while I cheat a little bit to get an interesting case out of there, but generally I try to give the more interesting cases to other judges who have more time to devote to them. My job is

to get rid of the garbage, because I get rid of the garbage faster
than anyone else.[9]

If the lower court's decision is upheld by the appellate court, it
may then be appealed to the state supreme court. Because the intermediate appellate courts are created to lessen the caseload demand
on the state supreme courts, they usually are not present in states
where the population is relatively small. However, Alaska—one of
the two smallest states in the country in population—is an exception.
Also, as a result of the increasing number of appeals brought to the
Idaho supreme court in the early 1980s, which caused delays of two
to three years before the cases could be heard, the Idaho legislature
created an intermediate appellate court. Of the thirteen western states,
there are no intermediate appellate courts in Montana, Nevada, Utah
and Wyoming.

Everyone has the right to appeal a lower court decision, except
the state if it loses in a criminal prosecution. However, most defend-
ants in criminal cases give up the right to appeal because the vast
majority (approaching 90% in some states such as California) of such
cases are resolved by plea bargaining. *Plea bargaining* is the common
term used to describe the process whereby some criminal charges
against a defendant will be dismissed if the defendant pleads guilty
to one or several others. This procedure works to the advantage of
both sides—the state saves the taxpayers' time and money by avoiding
a trial and the defendant customarily avoids being prosecuted on the
most serious offense. On the civil side of the law, out-of-court settlements work the same way and resolve the majority of civil suits that
are filed in court. The plaintiff (the person bringing the court action)
receives some compensation, though not as much as demanded initially, from the respondent (the person or company being sued). In
the vast majority of the cases that are appealed, the decision of the
trial court is upheld. Unlike the case filings for the state supreme
courts mentioned above, there is more of a balance between civil and
criminal appeals in the intermediate appellate courts.

THE TRIAL COURTS

Whatever their name (usually "superior court" or "district court"),
the main trial court of general jurisdiction disposes of the bulk of
nontraffic cases that constitute the business of the judiciary. Put another way, the trial courts handle the serious criminal and major civil
cases for the states. Felony criminal cases and civil suits, usually

involving more than ten thousand dollars, are heard by the trial courts. Felony cases are those in which a sentence of one year or more in state prison can result if a verdict of guilty is returned. Murder, assault and battery, rape, possession of narcotics with intent to sell, robbery, and the like are examples of felony cases. A common civil suit handled by the trial courts is divorce. The various trial courts of general jurisdiction and the courts of limited jurisdiction in the western states are identified in Table 11.2.

COURTS OF LIMITED JURISDICTION

The municipal courts (sometimes called "magistrate," or "circuit" courts) deal with traffic infractions, minor civil suits, and misdemeanor criminal cases, such as shoplifting and public intoxication. Juvenile cases are often heard by these courts, as are small claims actions involving minor noncriminal disputes between individuals. Sometimes nonattorney judges, or magistrates, are used in some of these lower courts. States may also establish courts designed to handle only certain types of cases. For example, the water court in Montana adjudicates water rights in that state's eighty-five water basins. Hawaii maintains a special land court, which handles registration of land, petitions for subdivisions and easements; it also has a tax appeal court in Honolulu to adjudicate tax disputes.

A number of the states also maintain justice courts (sometimes called "justice of the peace courts"). Generally these courts are involved only in minor civil cases, misdemeanor infractions, and violations of county ordinances. Today, justice courts in Arizona, California, Nevada, Oregon and Wyoming are confined to small towns and rural counties that lack a municipal court. In the effort to professionalize the judiciary, some states have abolished the justice courts. For example, New Mexico abandoned its justice courts in the early 1960s after a series of hearings revealed that the judges' legal qualifications and training were so paltry and embarrassing as to make them expendable. As one report concluded, "Most JP courts in New Mexico are operated ineptly, imcompetently, and inefficiently. On more than a few occasions, they are operated contrary to law."[10]

Judicial Selection

Just as there are a variety of state courts, so, too, there are a number of different methods for selecting judges to serve on them. The debate over the best method of judicial selection has been waged for decades

Table 11.2   Courts of General and Limited Jurisdiction in the Western States

State	General Jurisdiction	Limited Jurisdiction
Alaska	superior courts (29)	district courts (17 judges, 44 magistrates)[a]
Arizona	superior courts (101)	municipal courts (112 plus 58 part-time judges); justice of the peace courts (84)
California	superior courts (777)	municipal courts (642); justice courts (83)
Colorado	district courts (104)[b]	county courts (111)
Hawaii	circuit courts (17)	district courts (22); land court and tax appeal court (1)
Idaho	district courts (33)	magistrates court (73)
Montana	district courts (36)	city courts (50); municipal (1); justice of the peace courts (84)
Nevada	district courts (35)	municipal courts (25); justice of the peace courts (55)
New Mexico	district courts (56)	Bernalillo metropolitan court (Albuquerque) (11)[c]; magistrate court (68); municipal court (81); probate court (32)
Oregon	circuit courts (85)	district courts (58); municipal courts (124); justice courts (38)
Utah	district courts (29)	circuit courts (37); justice of the peace courts (144)
Washington	superior courts (131)	district courts (109); municipal courts (85)
Wyoming	district courts (17)	county courts (19); municipal courts (77); justice of the peace courts (14)

Note: Number of judges for each court in parentheses.

[a]Magistrates are nonattorney judges designated to hear limited cases.

[b]This figure includes the 25 district judges in Denver who sit on the Denver district court, juvenile court and probate court. Denver is both a city and county and has the only county court that is not part of the state court system.

[c]The Bernalillo metropolitan court is found only in Bernalillo County and handles minor civil cases and limited felony and misdemeanor cases. The majority of these cases arise from the largest city in the state, Albuquerque.

Sources: Compiled by the author from the most recent annual reports for the county from the individual states and from *The Book of the States 1986–87* (Lexington, Ky.: The Council of State Governments, 1986).

and there is no indication that a consensus is near at hand. At the federal level, judicial selection is fairly straightforward. The president nominates an individual to a court vacancy and the U.S. Senate acts as the confirmation body. Once the nominee has been confirmed, that individual serves for life, assuming good behavior. This system is not without defects. Critics correctly point out that a nominee's professional qualifications often become secondary to his or her political and legal philosophy. The prominence of a judge's judicial views in the appointment process was demonstrated in 1986 when President Reagan sought to nominate a conservative replacement for Justice Lewis Powell, who had earlier announced his retirement from the Supreme Court. Reagan's first nominee, Judge Robert Bork, was rejected by the Senate on the grounds that his narrow judicial philosophy was contrary to the open-mindedness expected from a Supreme Court justice. The president's second nominee, Judge Douglas Ginsburg, also a judicial conservative, withdrew his nomination after he admitted having smoked marijuana while he was a professor at Harvard Law School. In early 1987, Reagan's third nominee to the vacancy, Judge Anthony Kennedy, was confirmed. While Kennedy's past decisions suggested that he would be more like Justice Powell, a moderate conservative, his record on the high court suggests he votes with the conservative bloc.

A second criticism often leveled is that this procedure is not particularly democratic because federal judges have no accountability to the public. Since judges in both the state and federal judiciaries often make public policies as a reslut of their decisions, the argument goes, should not the public have some decision as to who serves on the courts? This line of reasoning is only accepted at the state level, however. In the thirteen western states, the governors may initially appoint some judges to judicial vacancies, but citizens can turn those jurists out of office if enough of them so desire. Thus, in direct contrast to the federal system whereby no judge is voted on by the public, all judges must face the voters at some time or another in the states.

METHODS OF SELECTION

The western states have experimented with several different methods of judicial selection in an effort to achieve both judicial independence and public accountability. This is no easy task, for there exists a basic philosophical debate over how much independence judges should enjoy and how much accountability the public should demand. On the one hand, judges must be capable of rendering decisions without fear of reprisals from governors, legislators or other public officials, as well as the citizenry. Without this freedom and insulation from political pressures, judges would be either little more than surrogates for elected officials or would have to render decisions according to popular opinion. On the other hand, because judges can make public policies as a result of their decisions in specific cases, citizens should have some voice on the appropriateness of those policies.

The merit plan is used to staff bench vacancies at the supreme court and intermediate appellate court level in the majority of the thirteen western states. However, elections are utilized in four states, and California employs its own modified merit plan procedure. These mechanisms, along with other features of the state high courts, are illustrated in Table 11.1. Under the merit plan (also known as the Missouri Plan), a nominating panel usually composed of judges, lawyers and laypersons recommends three qualified individuals to the governor, who then selects one of the three to fill the vacancy. Within a few years after assuming the bench, the new judge appears on a retention ballot for a public vote. The retention ballot lists only the new justice(s) with perhaps other justices whose terms have expired and who now seek reconfirmation for a new term. Voters are asked to mark the ballot in confirmation of or opposition to the justice(s). In most circumstances, the justices are routinely confirmed without controversy. However, as well be discussed below in a case study from California, confirmation is not always assured. According to merit plan advocates, this system de-emphasizes politics in judicial selection since the governor can only select from the pool of nominees drawn up by the nominating panel. At the same time, justices do need public confirmation, thereby addressing the accountability issue. When the term of office expires, those justices seeking an additional term must run against their record rather than against a challenger.

While the Missouri Plan has been characterized as a nonpolitical judicial selection mechanism, it is quite political nonetheless. Bar politics play a role in determining which lawyers' names make the nomination list, and most governors look for nominees with judicial views compatible with their own. For example, when Governor Evan Mecham of Arizona had an opportunity to fill a vacancy on his state's supreme court, he initially rejected all three nominees submitted by the Commission on Appellate Court Appointments on the grounds that none represented the political philosophy he desired. However, he eventually recanted and appointed Judge James Moeller to the vacancy. As the governor said at the time, "I thought Judge Moeller would make decisions based on the Constitution and on precedent. It's important to get judges who don't legislate from the bench. We see eye to eye on that."[11]

Idaho, Montana, Oregon and Washington State have opted for nonpartisan elections for the selection of supreme court justices. These elections are contested affairs, although the candidates' partisan affiliation is not indicated on the ballot. Until recently, New Mexico was the only western state to have partisan elections for the supreme court. But in 1988 New Mexico voters ratified a constitutional amendment in favor of a modified merit selection plan. Under the new procedure, which appears to give the party controlling the statehouse an advantage, judicial vacancies will be filled by merit selection. However, unlike the procedure in other states, jurists in New Mexico must initially stand for reelection on a partisan ballot; subsequent elections are by a nonpartisan retention ballot.

Critics of election methods charge that elections require judges to campaign for voter support, that they have to worry about raising sufficient funds to win contested elections, and that the public really is largely ignorant about what judges are supposed to do. The governor still plays an important role in staffing vacancies on the high courts in these election-system states. For example, some three-fourths of the justices who served on the Washington State supreme court between 1948 and 1974 were initially appointed to the bench by the governor.[12]

The method employed in the selection of appellate court judges is usually also used for the selection of trial court judges in the western states, although there are exceptions. In California, for instance, appellate court justices are nominated by the governor, confirmed (or rejected in rare cases) by a three-member Commission on Judicial Appointments, and then subjected to a popular vote at the next gubernatorial election. However, the state constitution specifies that superior court and municipal court judges must run on a competitive nonpartisan ballot for their six-year terms. In reality, most of these lower court judges reach the bench by gubernatorial appointment. Once on the bench, they can be challenged by others, but at least their brief tenure on the bench provides them with the right to list themselves as "incumbents," a label that generally ensures continued service on the court. In Arizona, appellate court judges and trial court judges in counties of over 150,000 population are selected by the merit plan. However, trial court judges in the less populated counties are elected on a nonpartisan ballot.

The careful reader will probably have realized by now that the only western state in which the legislature plays a role in judicial selection is Hawaii. Even there, that role is limited to the confirmation of trial and appellate court judges. In only three East Coast states—Rhode Island, South Carolina and Virginia—does the legislature appoint judges at the appellate court level. In two of these states—South Carolina and Virginia—the legislature also appoints judges to lower court positions. Judicial reformers, who have long been advocates of *decreasing* the role of politics in judicial selection, see this legislative role as *increasing* the politicization of judicial selection.

Once on the bench, judges usually are secure for as long as they want to serve regardless of the method by which they obtained their seat on the bench. For example, of the thirty-two trial court judges who appeared on retention ballots in Alaska, Arizona and Colorado between 1964 and 1984, only seven were defeated.[13] Similarly, in California only 19 superior court judges were rejected by the voters between 1958 and 1980 in 125 contested elections.[14] In Idaho, Montana and Utah, an unchallenged trial court judge appears on a retention ballot; if there is a challenge, then the incumbent and challenger appear on a nonpartisan ballot. This arrangement favors the incumbent, particularly if that individual has the resources to raise an impressive war chest to discourage would-be challengers.

RACIAL AND GENDER REPRESENTATIVENESS

There are two main points to note about judicial selection. First, judges are selected by a variety of methods. Second, regardless of which system a state employs, each system works to the advantage of some groups over the others. Thus, for example, women and minority candidates fare better today when governors make the final selection (or the initial one as in California). Judicial elections generally favor male attorneys because of the preponderance of male lawyers in the states, the fact that they are in a better position to raise campaign funds, and the public's image of judges as men.

The issue of gender and race bias in voting for judges is a difficult one to measure for two reasons. First, it has been only recently that the elevation of a woman (or black or Hispanic) to the bench has come to be expected rather than treated as an unusual event. Second, few voters willingly admit to public opinion pollsters that they voted for or against a judicial candidate because of that person's race, ethnicity or sex.

Nevertheless, the names of judicial candidates often provide voters with "cues" as to the individual's sex, race and ethnicity. One recent study on gender and ethnic factors in Oregon's nonpartisan judicial elections indicated that black judicial candidates received a substantially higher number of votes in black voting precincts than in predominantly white precincts and that women were more disposed to favor female judicial candidates than were male voters.[15]

As was noted in an earlier chapter, Hawaii stands out as the only state in the Union where Anglos are in a minority. The dominant Asian population is reflected in the non-Anglo composition of the Hawaiian judiciary. Four of the five members of the Hawaii supreme court (as of 1988) are of Asian ancestry (the other is an Anglo). Similarly, two of the three members of Hawaii's intermediate court of appeals are Asian. However, one has to drop down to the circuit courts, the state's main trial courts, to encounter any women jurists. Not surprisingly, the large Hispanic population of New Mexico is represented throughout the state's judiciary.

TENURE IN THEORY AND PRACTICE

Regardless of the method by which judges reach the bench, and whether they sit at the trial or appellate level, the position is usually their own for as long as they want it. If an incumbent judge is rejected by the voters, it is likely due to his or her decisions in one or more controversial cases. When superior court judge Alfred Gitelson ruled in 1970 that the County of Los Angeles had to institute busing to achieve racial integration in area schools he was defeated at the polls the following November. Gitelson's unsuccessful reelection bit became a referendum on school busing, even though an appeal stayed his order soon after it was issued.

Similarly, the unpopular sentences handed down by District Judge Paul Liamos, Jr., a trial court judge in Wyoming, in several criminal cases were sufficient to arouse public opinion and lead to his defeat in 1984. In one case, Judge Liamos suspended all but sixty-one days of a one-to-five-year prison sentence for a convicted child molester. In another case, Liamos sentenced a seventeen-year-old boy to a five-to-fifteen-year prison sentence upon his being convicted of killing his father.[16] This second case received national attention as the lad had claimed self-defense to prevent his father from continuing to physically abuse the family.

Most but not all judicial elections lack controversy. In 1984, several "law and order" groups spearheaded a drive to defeat Justice Hans Linde, who was serving on the Oregon supreme court. While that effort was unsuccessful, a similar move to oust Rose Bird and several of her colleagues from the California supreme court was successful. The campaign against Bird demonstates the clash between judicial independence and judicial accountability.

CASE STUDY: THE 1986 CALIFORNIA SUPREME COURT ELECTIONS

When Democrat Jerry Brown was governor of California from 1975 to 1982, his appointees to the state supreme court included the first woman, first black person, and first Hispanic to be appointed to the court. Brown's appointment of Rose Bird to be chief justice in 1977 marked the first time that a woman had been chosen to lead a supreme court in the western states. Brown also broke ranks with his predecessors by appointing a number of women, blacks and Hispanics to the courts of appeal and to the lower courts.

Controversy surrounded Bird during her nine tumultuous years on the California supreme court. For one thing, her personal style caused friction among longtime staff employees. In addition, she voted with the majority in a decision that reduced the amount of prison time a convicted rapist had to serve, and she was accused of withholding several decisions in controversial cases until after the November 1978 elections (when she would appear on a retention ballot) to ensure her confirmation. Bird won confirmation by a narrow two-percentage-point majority. Later that month Bird requested that the state Commission on Judicial Performance investigate the allegation that she deliberately withheld several decisions for political reasons. The ensuing probe of the court neither confirmed nor refuted the charge, but the sometimes public and sometimes secret hearings did reveal a court torn by personal bickering and petty jealousies.[17]

Although it is not unusual for one or two California appellate court justices to be on the ballot at the same time striving for public confirmation, in November of 1986 six of the seven state supreme court justices were scheduled to be confirmed either for the first time or for additional terms in office. Bird and two other of Jerry Brown's appointees—Cruz Reynoso and Joseph Grodin—were among those subject to the public vote and who had been targeted for defeat by opposition groups. The campaign against Bird, Reynoso and Grodin was waged by several organizations with impressive financial backing, supported by Governor George Deukmejian, a Republican, and virtually all other state Republican politicians, a number of prominent attorneys and law school professors. The opposition campaign was also endorsed by several influential newspapers. While many of the past issues surfaced, the thrust of the anti–Bird/Reynoso/Grodin effort was directed at their handling of death penalty cases. In the sixty-one capital cases that had come before Bird, she had voted to reverse the convictions and/or sentences in all of them. Reynoso had voted in support of a death penalty conviction only once in the forty-five capital cases in which he participated, and Grodin upheld only five out of the forty in which he had participated.

Ultimately, over nine million dollars was spent by the various sides in the contest. Even by California standards, such an amount of money expended on a nonpartisan judicial election fueled the arguments of the many experts who lamented that judicial elections are becoming more like elections for other political positions. Another disquieting aspect of the campaign involved the use of brief television ads. The anti-Bird side effectively used television spots to portray Bird, Reynoso, and Grodin as soft on crime, unsympathetic to the victims, and antagonistic to the wishes of the citizens of the state. In contrast, Bird's organization—the Committee to Conserve the Courts—countered with its own television ads which featured the chief justice, who defended the independence of the judiciary with the non-too-subtle suggestion that without individuals like her, American courts would be no more tolerant of individual rights than those in the Soviet Union and South Africa.[18] The response of the voters was clear. Bird was rejected by 66% of the electorate, Reynoso by 60%, and Grodin by 57%. The other three justices were confirmed by large margins.

The defeat of Justices Bird, Reynoso and Grodin enabled Governor Deukmejian to appoint three of his nominees to the high court at the beginning of his second term in office. The three new justices quickly joined two other Deukmejian appointees from his first term as governor (1983–86). When George Deukmejian took office in 1983, five of the seven justices had been appointed by his predecessor, Jerry Brown. In 1990, only one Jerry Brown–appointed justice, Allen Broussard, remains. The Deukmejian appointees are experienced and respected jurists who adhere to the governor's philosophy of judicial self-restraint. As a result of these staffing changes, there is a conservative majority on the court for the first time in almost three decades. This dramatic change in the composition of the court will undoubtedly result in decisions that will be less protective of the rights of criminal suspects than was the Bird court. One can anticipate that California's twenty-year moratorium on the implementation of the death penalty will soon end. In the first three years of the new court, the justices have voted to affirm the death sentence in fifty-eight of the eighty-three capital cases they have reviewed. By contrast, the "Bird Court" upheld only four death sentences from the sixty-eight capital cases that it reviewed in the period from 1977 to 1986.

The unanswered question, of course, is whether the 1986 California supreme court elections were an aberration or whether future judicial retention elections, including those outside the state, will be equally politicized. According to most observers, California's rejection of Bird, Reynoso and Grodin was an isolated event brought on by a number of unusual factors that are unlikely to be repeated. At the same time, the decision of the voters may well cause jurists to think twice about potential public reaction before they render a formal decision on cases involving controversial issues.

Conclusion

The state judiciaries in the western states—indeed in all of the states—are quite similar from an institutional perspective. That is, there is a judicial hierarchy that includes the lower courts and the appellate courts; the selection of judges is by one or more of five different methods; and the processing of cases through the courts follows a well-worn path. It is the political tradition within a state that gives the state courts their individual quality by establishing informal rules to cover such questions as: Are women at a disadvantage in trying to reach the bench? Does the supreme court appear to favor the accused over the victim? Does the governor have a major role in staffing the courts? Do judges have unfettered freedom to pronounce significant conservative or liberal public policies from the bench? In some states the answer to all these questions is yes, while in others it is no.

This assessment of the western states' judiciaries leaves other questions unanswered as well. For example, what are the boundaries of policymaking—*i.e.*, to what extent can the courts establish policies that run counter to the opinions held by a majority of the state's residents? Is there a way by which judges can be selected solely for their legal qualifications and open-mindedness; or are all methods of judicial selection ultimately politically biased? Is the judiciary culpable in assuming policymaking powers that constitutionally belong to the other branches of government, as some charge, or have the executive and legislative branches abrogated their obligation to resolve controversial issues and simply left them to the judiciary?

If the answers to these questions do not come easily, be assured that they have eluded knowledgeable legal scholars for years.[19]

Notes

1. Scott Turow, *One L* (New York: Penguin, 1981), 31.

2. Charles H. Sheldon, "The Uniqueness of State Legal Systems: Nevada, Utah, and Vermont," *Judicature* 52 (March 1970), 333–37.

3. Mary Cornelia Porter and G. Alan Tarr, "State Supreme Courts: Some Old Inquiries for a New Situation," in Porter and Tarr, eds., *State Supreme Courts* (Westport, Conn.: Greenwood Press, 1982), 4–5.

4. Quoted in Robert Pear, "State Courts Surpass U.S. Bench in Cases on Rights of Individuals," *New York Times*, May 4, 1986, I:1.

5. See Lawrence Baum and Bradley C. Canon, "State Supreme Courts as Activists: New Doctrines in the Law of Torts," in Porter and Tarr, eds., *State Supreme Courts*, 83–108.

6. See Stanley H. Friedelbaum, "Independent State Grounds: Contemporary Invitations to Judicial Activism," in Porter and Tarr, eds., *State Supreme Courts*, 23–53.

7. Herbert Jacob, "Courts," in Virginia Gray, Herbert Jacob and Kenneth N. Vines, eds., *Politics in the American States: A Comparative Analysis*, 4th ed. (Boston: Little, Brown, 1983), 241.

8. Henry R. Glick, *Courts, Politics and Justice* (New York: McGraw-Hill, 1983), 19.

9. John T. Wold and Gregory Caldeira, "Perceptions of 'Routine' Decision-Making in Five California Courts of Appeal," *Polity* 13 (Winter 1980), 339.

10. State Judicial System Study Committee, "The Courts in New Mexico," report to the Twenty-fifth Legislature, Santa Fe, New Mexico, 1961, 43.

11. Sam Stanton and Brent Whiting, "Non-Activist Judge Appointed to Supreme Court," *Arizona Republic* (Phoenix), February 14, 1987.

12. Philip L. Dubois, *From Ballot to Bench* (Austin: University of Texas Press, 1980), 206.

13. William K. Hall and Larry T. Aspin, "What Twenty Years of Judicial Retention Elections Have Told Us," *Judicature* 70 (April–May 1987), 343.

14. Charles G. Bell and Charles M. Price, "Running for Judge in California: Superior Court Elections, 1978–1980," *California Data Brief* 6 (June 1982).

15. Nicholas P. Lovrich, Jr., Charles H. Sheldon, and Erik Wassman, "Gender and Ethnic Factors in Nonpartisan Judicial Elections: The Oregon Experience," paper presented at the 1987 Western Political Science Association Annual Meeting, Anaheim, Calif.

16. Kenyon N. Griffin and Michael J. Horan, "Ousting the Judge: Campaign Politics in Judicial Elections," paper presented at the 1986 Western Political Science Association Annual Meeting, Eugene, Ore.

17. See Preble Stolz, *Judging Judges* (New York: The Free Press, 1981). For a different analysis, see Betty Medsger, *Framed: The New Right Attack on Chief Justice Rose Bird and the Courts* (New York: Pilgrim Press, 1983).

18. See John T. Wold and John H. Culver, "The Defeat of the California Justices: The Campaign, the Electorate, and the Issue of Judicial Accountability," *Judicature* 70 (April–May 1987), 348–55.

19. See Harry P. Stumpf, *American Judicial Politics* (San Diego: Harcourt, Brace Jovanovich, 1988), esp. chap. 2, "Law and the Judicial Function."

12

FINANCING STATE
AND LOCAL
GOVERNMENT

David R. Berman

THE IDEAL CALIFORNIA LEGISLATOR WAS ONCE DE-
fined as a person "who votes for all appropriations, and against all
taxes."[1] Indeed, legislators in California and other western states *are*
under pressure to increase spending *and* to reduce taxes and, from a
political point of view, would gladly do both if they had the opportunity. Unfortunately, on both the state and local levels a choice has
to be made between cutting taxes and increasing spending.

This chapter explores these and the various other dilemmas of
finanical policymaking in western states. More broadly, we are concerned with the general context in which decisions regarding taxing
and spending are made and with how decision-makers go about their

tasks. We are also concerned with the nature of the outputs or decisions that have been made. In particular, we look at the way funds have been distributed among particular programs and how the burden of paying for the costs of government has been allocated. In short, we ask: Who benefits? And who pays?

A number of themes emerge in exploring financial policymaking and financial policies in the West. One is that historical influences, traditions, values, geography and economic conditions have, in a number of respects, made the politics of finance in western states somewhat distinct and different from that in other regions of the country. A similar set of factors accounts for additional variation within the western region. It is not unusual, for example, to find differences between the Mountain West and the Pacific West.

Much of the following discussion provides information comparing the West with other regions or comparing states and localities within the western region. A broader aim of this chapter, however, is to indicate not so much what is unique about the West or any particular group of states within this region, but what factors have been and currently are generally important in influencing the financial problems and policies of state and local governments in the western part of the country. In this respect it is important to note that as in other parts of the nation, financial decision-making in the West is greatly influenced by general nationwide economic conditions and by policies pursued by the federal government.

This chapter begins with an overview of broad constraints and limitations on financial policymaking. This is followed by a discussion of financial policymaking, spending and revenue patterns, and, in the last section, long-term trends and problems relating to financial responsibility in western states.

General Constraints and Limitations

The ability of state and local officials in the West to raise and spend revenues is conditioned by a host of intergovernmental, legal, economic and political conditions. In this section we look into some of the most important of them.

INTERGOVERNMENTAL CONDITIONS

Public finance in the United States has been influenced greatly by a complex set of relationships among the governments. Some problems have to do with relationships between states or between localities. State policymakers, for example, are aware that a high tax or a low level of services can prompt both industry and people to "vote with their feet" by moving to another state. This problem is even more severe for localities because moving from one locality to another is easier than moving from one state to another. Thus, the task for decision-makers is to arrive at a set of tax and spending policies which they hope will both satisfy existing demands and, assuming that further growth is desired, be attractive to industry and people in other jurisdictions.

On a fundamental level, each sector of government—federal, state, local—also is in competition for the taxpayer's dollar. Through a system of grants and shared revenues, however, revenues raised by one level of government are distributed to another level with various restrictions on how the monies may be spent. Much of what state and local governments in the West spend comes from the national government, and much of what local governments spend comes from the state. Some current trends and problems in intergovernmental aid, including important developments in state-local relations, are discussed below.

Although the federal government has played an important role in the finances of state and local governments in all regions of the country, it has played a particularly strong role in the West. As mentioned before, the West has long been the home of politicians who condemn federal spending with the same intensity that they condemn the exploitative "Eastern Establishment." At the same time they have been eager to funnel as much of that federal spending as possible into their own states. Most favored has been federal support for water projects, highways, and other improvements that promote development of the economy such as farming or mining.

While seeking more developmental aid, western politicians also have attempted to place the burden of financing federal projects for their states on taxpayers in other parts of the country. Indeed, adoption of the major revenue producer of the national government, the U.S. income tax, was strongly supported in the West as a means by which the relatively low-income residents of this area could shift the burden of financing western developmental programs to the relatively wealthy residents of the Midwest and East. Largely for this reason, in 1912–13 the Income Tax Amendment was quickly and almost unanimously ratified in nearly all western state legislatures.[2] The subsequent growth of federal revenues and programs soon meant, in the words of western historian Gerald D. Nash, "a change of masters for the West, from Wall Street to Pennsylvania Avenue, from foreign and eastern financiers to the White House, Congress, and the administrative agencies in Washington."[3]

Westerners came to resent their dependency on the federal government, however. In the 1960s, western politicians, particularly those in the Mountain region, became extremely critical of some federal programs providing funds for states and localities. The major battles took place over the propriety of accepting federal aid for social programs, such as welfare and education. In this period a large number of new programs were instituted as part of the New Frontier and Great Society programs of national administrations. Campaigning in Goldwater's Arizona in the 1960s, gubernatorial candidate Samuel P. Goddard, a Democrat, contended: "It is immoral to refuse federal aid for education and accept it for sugar beets. It is immoral to refuse federal aid for the crippled and accept it for reclamation."[4] Goddard, who was elected governor two years later, was instrumental in bringing more federal aid for social programs into the state.

While the battle over the propriety of accepting federal aid for social programs is less intense today than in the 1960s, doubts still linger. Many western politicians appear to have an unusually dim view of anything that looks like a welfare program, regardless of whether it is paid for by the federal government or by state or local funds. Many politicians also view federal programs in areas like education as a threat to state authority that will lead sooner or later to increased demands for large amounts of additional state and local spending from their own revenues.

Perhaps more important to western politicians than the question of whether they should accept federal aid is the fact that federal aid has not been an altogether reliable source of revenue: the amounts and conditions of aid have varied with the philosophies of national administrations and national economic conditions. In the late 1980s federal aid was on a downswing, forcing states and localities to become more dependent on their own revenue sources.

In considering the broad influence of the federal government on state and local finances in the West as elsewhere, one should note the importance of changes in federal taxes as well as spending policies. Thus, in recent years, several states have had to reshape their tax systems because of the Tax Reform Act of 1986, which ended the practice of allowing taxpayers to deduct state and local sales taxes from their federal income tax payments. This change made sales taxes less acceptable to taxpayers, particularly in comparison to state and local income taxes, which continued to be deductible on federal returns. Consequently, states and localities were encouraged to abandon the sales tax in favor of the other sources of revenue.

LEGAL CONDITIONS

State and local policymakers must live with a wide variety of legal limitations on their ability to raise and spend revenues. Some limitations are imposed by federal law while others are self-imposed, such as those found in state constitutions and statutes. Among the federally imposed limits, the fact that federally owned lands cannot be made subject to state taxation has been troublesome in western states. This is particularly irksome because over half of the land area of the thirteen western states is under control of the federal government. State laws often impose bans on certain types of taxes and limits on tax rates. The ability of state and local governments to borrow is limited by the state constitutions and laws that impose limits on the amount of debt and require voter approval of bonds.[5] Under state laws, as noted below, state legislatures are also required to have balanced budgets.

Many of the more general existing limitations on spending and taxing were imposed as the result of the "taxpayers' rebellion" of the late 1970s and early 1980s. This rebellion reflected the public distrust of government and, more directly, the perception that government spending and taxes were too high.[6] In many states, public pressure produced laws limiting spending increases to a fixed percentage or to changes in personal income. The rebellion was first manifested in June 1978 when California voters adopted Proposition 13 (the Jarvis-Gann initiative) to limit increases in property taxation. In California, property taxes are now below the national average whereas, before Proposition 13, they were 50% higher than the national average.[7]

Another characteristic of state laws in the West is the earmarking or dedication of revenues for various purposes or programs. It is common, for example, to earmark revenues derived from state gasoline taxes for highway programs—and only for highway programs. States have also determined that certain percentages of the general sales tax or the receipts derived from the sale of lottery tickets should be automatically allocated to various programs, such as school aid.[8]

Western states, particularly those in the Mountain West, are considerably above average in the extent to which they earmark taxes.[9] On a nationwide basis, about 21% of all state tax revenues are earmarked for certain functions. Comparable percentages are 29% in

Arizona, 25% in Colorado, 32% in Idaho, 60% in Montana, 44% in New Mexico, 52% in Nevada, 48% in Utah, 26% in Washington State and 69% in Wyoming. Many of these states have earmarked unusually large amounts of funds for highway building. The remaining western states, all in the Pacific category, are below the national average in the proportion of earmarked revenues.[10]

Earmarking of funds is commonly used as a means of selling a new revenue system to the voters or to the state legislators. A lottery, for example, may be easier to support if it is known in advance that the funds will be put to some good purpose, such as education or parks and recreation. In some instances, however, the earmarking of funds is less of a constraint than it might appear. Earmarked revenues, for example, may be used to replace general fund revenues spent on a particular function. The freed-up revenues, in turn, may be spent on any program the legislature chooses. Thus, though the law may require that lottery proceeds go to support education, revenues from this source may simply replace revenues derived from the property tax, which, in turn, could be used to finance a wide range of general government activities.

Legislative flexibility may be most seriously impaired by earmarking in the area of highway financing. By putting gasoline taxes in the highway fund, one can guarantee a certain level of support for road building and maintenance. At the same time the earmarking severely limits the ability of the lawmakers to respond to pressing conditions. Thus, even though lawmakers might feel that revenues in the highway fund could be better used for other purposes they will be prevented by law from making such a diversion.

Overall, in looking at the broad pattern of self-imposed legal limitations in western states, we find a relatively strong concern with fiscal responsibility. This keeps spending in check and, in the case of earmarking, shows an unusually strong distrust of legislative discretion. The distrust may well reflect lessons learned from an earlier era when few restrictions were placed on the ability of western legislators to raise and spend revenues. Not to exclude any particular branch of government, one can also find a considerable distrust of elected officials other than legislators and of administrators in state law. A 1912 law still on the books in Arizona, for example, forbids the state treasurer from leaving the state without special permission from the governor or the legislature.

GENERAL ECONOMIC AND POLITICAL CONDITIONS

Besides the law, it is commonly recognized that a factor of central importance to those who would raise governmental revenues is the

Table 12.1   Personal Income by State—1984

State	Per Capita Income	Rank in West	Rank in U.S.
Alaska	$17,487	1	1
California	$14,487	2	5
Colorado	$13,847	3	8
Nevada	$13,320	4	12
Hawaii	$13,042	5	17
Washington	$12,792	6	19
U.S. Average	$12,778		
Wyoming	$12,224	7	27
Arizona	$11,841	8	30
Oregon	$11,611	9	33
Montana	$10,546	10	40
New Mexico	$10,262	11	43
Idaho	$10,092	12	45
Utah	$9,733	13	48

Source: *Book of the States: 1987–88* (Lexington, Ky.: Council of State Governments, 1987), 439.

amount of wealth within their jurisdiction which can be drawn upon for taxation. This depends, in turn, on the level of economic development and the ability to attract industry and high-income taxpayers.

For much of the nation's history, western states have had relatively underdeveloped economies. The scarcity of local wealth in much of the West and the desire to keep taxes at a level that would encourage investment have functioned over the years to place severe limits on the level of public spending and have made balanced budgets and frugality the standards by whcih public officials have been judged.

Currently, there is considerable variation in the wealth in individual western states. As Table 12.1 indicates, on a per capita basis, personal income in western states in 1984 ranged from $9,733 in Utah to $17,487 in oil-rich Alaska. Altogether, seven of the thirteen western states were below the national average in per capita income and six were above the national average. With the one exception of Oregon, those below the national average—and thus in a relatively uncomfortable position when it comes to raising revenues—are in the Mountain West.

Much of the West remains not only relatively poor but also highly unstable in regard to economic conditions. Nearly every western state has a long history of the here today, gone tomorrow boomtowns built around some extractive industry. While many towns have diversified their economies, some still remain dependent on a few economic activities. States and communities lacking economic diversity are subject to the most extreme feast or famine conditions. An example is the state of Alaska, which with an essentially "one crop" (oil) economy has found its revenues largely dependent on the price of energy. After the fall in world energy prices in 1986, the state revenues declined by almost 40%. With this there came a drastic cutback in state programs.

Ultimately, decisions concerning spending levels and who pays and who benefits are highly political in nature. These battles in the West, like others in state politics, are likely to invoke divisions along party, ideological, regional and/or interest group lines. On the local level we see similar lines of division, though there is less overt partisan conflict because of the widespread employment of nonpartisan elections. As indicated in the discussion of Proposition 13, the ready availability of initiative and referendum procedures in the West has made governments in this region particularly susceptible to popular opinion regarding financial matters. Taxpayers have frequently used these devices to reject large spending programs[11] and to impose overall limits on the abilty of state and local officials to raise and spend revenues. Taxpayer resistance to attempts to raise revenues has commonly manifested itself in times of economic stress. Given taxpayer opposition, governors and a good many mayors have often faced the following dilemma: "They cannot operate their governmental programs without increased revenues, and they cannot increase their revenues and be reelected to office."[12]

Financial Decision-Making

Much of what state and local officials in the West do in regard to raising and spending revenues is influenced by conditions, legal and otherwise, over which they have little direct control. Within these boundaries, however, state and local officials do have considerable discretion along with a number of choices to make in arriving at a budget that balances revenues and expenditures. Equally important choices involve allocating the benefits and costs of government. In this section we will look at the participants in policymaking, focusing for the most part on the state level and the general processes that are followed there.

THE PLAYERS

The state government officials most directly involved in financial decision-making are legislative leaders (especially those sitting on appropriations, taxation, and budget committees), governors and their staffs, and the heads of various departments. These legislative leaders appear to have a greater direct influence over taxing and spending decisions in the smaller western states. In the larger states, influence has shifted over the years to governors, who, with the help of professional staffs, are better able than legislative committees to grapple with a large bureaucracy and complicated financial problems.

The governor of California, perhaps a harbinger of the future in other western states, is in an unusually strong position to influence financial decisions. Working through the department of finance, California governors as disparate in style as Ronald Reagan (1967–75) and Jerry Brown (1975–83) were able to exert a strong central control over the spending and legislative proposals of the various state departments. Department heads have been careful to make their demands in terms compatible with the policy positions of the governors.[13] The California governor not only has access to considerable expertise, but also has a line item-veto that allows him or her to reduce or eliminate items in appropriations acts.[14] This gives the governor a relatively strong bargaining position with the legislature because appropriation bills have to be passed by at least two-thirds of the members.[15]

BUDGETING

The functions of coupling anticipated revenues with spending needs and allocating funds among programs are accomplished both at the state and at the local levels through a budgeting system. Budgets are considered each year in seven states (Alaska, Arizona, California, Colorado, Idaho, New Mexico and Utah) and biennially in six states (Hawaii, Montana, Nevada, Oregon and Washington in odd years and Wyoming in even years). The actual significance of these different systems has not been studied. There are those who favor a two-year cycle on the grounds that it offers a greater opportunity for planning and more in-depth program analysis. Those in favor of annual budgeting argue that it provides greater immediate control over spending. On the political level, annual budgeting has been seen by legislators as most conducive to maximizing their ability to control the budget. Biennial budgeting, on the other hand, has been equated with an increased role for the governor and his or her staff at the expense of the legislature.[16]

All the western states have executive budgeting systems, which make the governor the principal budgetmaking authority. The process begins when department heads propose expenditures for the next year (or next two years in the biennial systems) to budgeting officials in the governor's office. These proposals are examined and revised in the light of anticipated revenues and in accordance with the governor's policy preferences. The revised proposals are then submitted to the legislature as the governor's budget. Legislatures in all the states have unlimited power to change, increase or decrease the items. Essentially the same process is followed by local governments, though it is far less formal in the smaller units. Many western localities have a council-manager form of government. In these communities budgetmaking is instigated by a city manager rather than a mayor.

During the budgeting process most attention is focused on non-committed revenues (that is, those not earmarked by law for a specific purpose), which flow into what in most jurisdictions is called the *general fund*. The budgetary strategy employed by administrative agencies that derive all or most of their revenues from this fund depends in large part on the level of anticipated general fund revenues. When revenues are increasing, agencies are likely to seek gubernatorial and legislative support for new or expanded programs. When general revenues appear to be on the decline, agencies are likely to see their central mission to be one of protecting what they have—that is, preventing cuts in the existing programs.[17]

When times are generally good, as they were in much of the West from the 1940s through the late 1970s, budgets are likely to increase by small increments from year to year, thus providing benefits to numerous groups. Cutting back in times of stress, on the other hand, has entailed the politically more difficult task of taking away benefits or transferring them from one group to another.

BALANCING EXPENDITURES AND REVENUES

State laws in all western states require the adoption of balanced budgets. Though there is really no penalty for lawmakers who fail to comply with these laws, the laws appear to be taken seriously. In Montana, for example, a constitutional provision that appropriations "shall not exceed anticipated revenues" has encouraged legislators to be so conservative in estimating revenues that the state frequently comes up with a budget surplus.[18]

In attempting to balance expenditure demands with revenues, one might either begin with an examination of what needs to be spent and the willingness at least to consider an increase in taxes if it turns out that there is not enough revenue to cover the expenses or one could begin by assuming that total spending should be limited to the revenue that is raised through the existing system, even if this means eliminating worthy programs. Budgetmakers in western states—again more so in the Mountain than Pacific regions—in recent years appear generally to have favored the second of these approaches.[19]

On those occasions when western legislatures have taken advantage of unusual circumstances to increase their revenues—for example, to tax oil and gas companies—their actions have been followed by a somewhat frantic scramble over what to do with the new revenues. In Montana, for example, adoption of the severance tax in 1973 provoked conflict over whether the funds should be used to increase aid to affected boomtowns, be put in a trust fund for future use, or be used as a substitute for other taxes. Generally, there was "a tendency for every underfunded cause to view the severance tax as the source of new revenue."[20] Ultimately, the new revenue was distributed among a number of funds.

Spending and Revenue Patterns

Despite the need in recent years to make cutbacks (see Chapter 13), the expenditures of state and local governments in the West have steadily increased since the 1940s. As Table 12.2 indicates, moreover, since 1976 the combined total of state and local government spending in most western states has been above the national per capita average. The only consistent exceptions have been in the Mountain West states of Arizona, Idaho, and Utah. The remainder of this section will focus on the allocation of funds among various programs; patterns and issues involving intergovernmental transfers; state and local revenue sources; and some questions concerning equity or fairness in raising revenues.

ALLOCATION PATTERNS

The largest category of combined state and local expenditures in western states has been education (see Table 12.3). Education is also the largest category of expenditure for the state governments and for the local governments when considered separately. Among local units much of the responsibility for education is assumed by independent

Table 12.2   Combined Direct General Expenditures of State and Local Governments, Total (in Millions of Dollars) and Per Capita (in Dollars)

State	1976 Total	1976 Per Capita	1980 Total	1980 Per Capita	1984 Total	1984 Per Capita
Alaska	1,178	3,079	2,503	6,257	4,553	9,106
Arizona	2,611	1,150	4,205	1,547	6,350	2,080
California	30,734	1,428	43,413	1,834	60,390	2,357
Colorado	3,266	1,264	4,558	1,578	7,006	2,204
Hawaii	1,567	1,767	1,877	1,945	2,524	2,429
Idaho	913	1,099	1,289	1,366	1,711	1,709
Montana	949	1,260	1,392	1,769	1,958	2,376
Nevada	868	1,423	1,492	1,867	2,181	2,394
New Mexico	1,304	1,116	2,156	1,658	3,510	2,465
Oregon	3,155	1,355	5,001	1,899	6,372	2,383
Utah	1,379	1,118	2,359	1,615	3,383	2,048
Washington	4,379	1,212	7,359	1,440	9,889	2,274
Wyoming	632	1,612	1,100	2,335	1,995	3,904
United States		1,191		1,622		2,132

Source: Statistical Abstract (Washington, D.C.: Government Printing Office, 1978, 1982–83, and 1987).

school districts. Total educational expenditures covering elementary and secondary schools and public universities constitute better than a third of the total state and local spending in Arizona, Colorado, Idaho, Montana, New Mexico, Oregon, Utah, Washington, and Wyoming. For Alaska, Arizona, Colorado, Idaho, Montana, New Mexico, Utah, and Wyoming, the second largest category of expenditures is highways. Welfare is ranked second in California, Hawaii and Washington, and virtually tied for second with highways in Oregon. Health and hospitals are ranked second in Nevada.

Compared to the rest of the nation, state and local governments in the West are about average in the extent to which they give priority to local education (seven of the states are above the national average, six below), and considerably above average when it comes to the percentage of the budget spent on higher education (Alaska and Nevada being the major exceptions) and on highways (California, Hawaii, and Oregon being the exceptions). Perhaps the distinguishing characteristic of western states, however, is the relatively low priority given by all of them, except for California, to public welfare.

On one level, explanations for the various spending patterns are

Table 12.3   Percentage Distribution of Combined State and Local Expenditures by Function, 1984 (Compared with U.S.)

	Education	Highways	Welfare	Health and Hospital	Other
Alaska	26.5	10.6	5.2	3.2	54.5
Arizona	38.6	9.3	7.8	5.8	38.5
California	32.2	4.7	15.3	8.9	38.9
Colorado	38.2	9.6	9.2	8.4	34.6
Hawaii	28.1	7.0	11.6	7.2	46.1
Idaho	37.2	12.6	7.9	10.2	32.1
Montana	38.6	13.6	9.5	5.5	32.8
Nevada	25.5	10.1	5.5	11.1	47.8
New Mexico	38.1	12.3	6.9	8.6	34.1
Oregon	37.8	7.6	7.6	6.4	40.6
Utah	42.2	10.9	8.4	6.0	32.5
Washington	36.8	9.1	10.3	7.8	36.0
Wyoming	39.1	14.8	4.1	9.6	32.4
United States	35.0	7.9	12.9	9.2	35.0

Source: Advisory Commission on Intergovernmental Relations, Significant Features of Fiscal Federalism (Washington, D.C.: Government Printing Office, 1986).

to be found in the budgetary procedures and political infighting discussed earlier. Underlying these activities, however, are other factors which help explain what appear to be distinct and recurring allocation patterns in much of the West. For example, the relatively large amount spent on highways is due in part to the relatively large land areas, diffused populations, and difficult terrains found in western states. In regard to education, because of historically sparse populations and limited wealth, the West has had fewer private colleges than the East, and thus has had to rely far more on public funds to develop higher education systems. The low priority generally given to welfare is commonly attributed to an attachment among westerners to the frontier values of rugged individualism and self-reliance. While helping one's neighbor was part of life on the western frontier, emphasis was placed on reciprocal aid rather than handouts or charity. Just how or why these values have survived in the West, if indeed they have, is not altogether clear. One might also contend that to some extent, the goal of economic development has minimized concern for problems of poverty. Whatever the underlying reasons, contemporary public opinion in western states, particularly in the Mountain West, does indeed appear to be the most conservative in the nation on welfare issues.[21] Given this, it is not surprising to find welfare given low priority in these states.

Table 12.4   State Aid to Local Governments, 1984

State	Amount (in thousands of dollars)	Per Capita (in dollars)
Alaska	1,183,094	2,366
Arizona	1,547,438	507
California	19,125,775	747
Colorado	1,522,105	479
Hawaii	25,231	24
Idaho	408,686	408
Montana	293,193	356
Nevada	487,427	535
New Mexico	967,744	680
Oregon	993,012	390
Utah	610,987	370
Washington	2,290,339	515
Wyoming	529,687	1,037

Source: Book of the States: 1987–88 (Lexington, Ky.: Council of State Governments, 1987), 442.

INTERGOVERNMENTAL PATTERNS

As noted earlier, the flow of taxpayer contributions to state and local governments is complicated somewhat by the fact that money raised by one level of government is frequently shifted to another. Intergovernmental transfer within western states come mostly in the form of various types of state aid programs for local governments. Much of this aid goes to support elementary and secondary education.

Compared to other regions, state governments in most western states have assumed a strong role in aiding local governments. Currently, the top three states in the country in terms of per capita state aid to local governments are Alaska, Wyoming, and California. Also among the top thirteen states in terms of such aid are New Mexico, Nevada, Washington, Arizona and Colorado.[22] As Table 12.4 indicates, only Hawaii departs radically from the pattern of strong state support. State aid per capita in Hawaii is the lowest not only in the West but also in the nation as a whole because the state government directly administers programs in education and other areas which, in other states, are local responsibilities.

In most jurisdictions, increased state aid has been welcomed by local officials, who have been hard hit by increased costs and by the cutbacks in federal aid to numerous localities. Making this aid less welcome, however, is the fact that increases in state aid have been accompanied by greater state control in such areas as education. The problem appears to have surfaced early in California where the approval of Proposition 13 was followed by large increases in state aid—up from 10 billion dollars to 15 billion dollars from 1978 to 1980—and to some 19 billion dollars in 1984 as the state moved to offset local government losses in property tax revenues. Although this aid was well received by local officials, the shift was also viewed with some alarm because it tended to increase state control and—in the opinion of some—to contribute to an erosion of local self-government.[23]

The dependence of both state and local governments, in the West as elsewhere, on federal aid has been on the decline in recent years. Still, even in the mid-1980s, state and local governments in three western states—Idaho, Montana and Utah—received better than 20% of their total revenues from this source. Compared with the rest of the nation, however, governments in the West as a whole are not currently distinctive in their reliance on federal funds: seven western states are above the national average in reliance on federal aid while six are below (see Table 12.5).

TAXES AND OTHER REVENUE SOURCES

The shifting of funds from one level of government to another should not obscure the fact that state and local governments themselves raise most of the money they spend. The major source of tax revenue for most of the state governments has been the general sales tax though some, such as California, Colorado and Oregon, have also looked to income taxes for substantial portions of their revenues. The major source of tax revenue for local governments in the West as in the rest of the nation has been the property tax.

In addition to the "big three" tax sources—income, sales, and property—a number of states and localities have special sources. Nevada, for example, derives nearly half of its general fund revenues from taxes and license fees on the gambling industry. Severance taxes on the removal of natural resources such as oil, gas, coal, minerals, and lumber have been imposed by several western states. In some cases, these taxes represent a long uphill struggle against corporate interests headquartered in the East that invested the large amounts of capital needed to develop the energy resources or minerals.

During the 1970s, severance taxes became particularly important

Table 12.5   Percentage Distribution of Combined State and Local Revenues by Source, 1984 (Compared with U.S.)

	Federal Aid	Property Tax	Sales Tax	Income Tax	Other Sources
Alaska	8.2	7.3	1.0	0.0	83.5
Arizona	13.4	16.7	21.5	8.3	40.1
California	18.7	15.2	16.8	14.2	43.1
Colorado	15.6	19.0	18.0	10.3	37.1
Hawaii	19.4	11.0	24.3	15.3	30.0
Idaho	20.6	14.5	13.7	12.9	38.3
Montana	20.9	22.7	0.0	8.0	48.4
Nevada	13.8	12.6	19.1	0.0	54.5
New Mexico	15.1	4.8	15.2	1.7	63.2
Oregon	19.2	23.1	0.0	18.4	39.3
Utah	20.6	14.2	17.1	10.5	37.6
Washington	15.7	16.7	29.4	0.0	38.2
Wyoming	18.6	22.2	8.2	0.0	51.0
United States	17.9	17.8	13.9	11.9	38.5

Source: Advisory Commission on Intergovernmental Relations, *Significant Features of Fiscal Federalism* (Washington, D.C.: Government Printing Office, 1986).

in Alaska, Montana, New Mexico and Wyoming because of soaring energy prices. In Alaska, revenues from the oil and gas industry enabled the state to abolish its income tax in 1980 and launch a "share the wealth" program. The latter consists of a state savings account— the Alaska Permanent Fund—created by public referendum in 1976, into which certain oil revenues are deposited. Earnings on its investments are then distributed to each Alaskan resident on a yearly basis.

In recent years, western state and local governments have gone into new revenue areas, especially lotteries—which are popular and, from the lawmaker's point of view, far preferable to levying new taxes or increasing the existing ones. The current trend toward lotteries first caught on in the East and Midwest, although several western states, when they became financially strapped, have joined the movement.[24] Lotteries, however, provide only a small percentage of the revenue (around 3%) for the states that have adopted them.

State lotteries were common in western states during the nineteenth century. They were abandoned because of scandals and unethical practices. Many people continue to question if the state should be in the business of operating a gambling enterprise or be actively engaged in encouraging people to gamble. Lotteries also can be considered regressive in that, in theory, low income people spend a greater percentage of their income on lottery tickets than do rich people (the tickets are the same price for rich and poor alike). At the same time, while the evidence is skimpy, it appears that, in fact, people in the very lowest category of income participate less in lotteries than do other income groups.[25]

While lotteries have been politically popular and thus easy to adopt, other tax changes have been difficult to make. Numerous attempts, for example, have been made in the State of Washington to provide a better balanced tax system by adopting personal and corporate net income taxes. Such proposals have failed in the legislature, at the polls, and/or in the courts. Washington State, as a consequence, has relied heavily on general and selective sales taxes. To further complicate matters, because Oregon voters have repeatedly rejected a sales tax, Washingtonians living along the Oregon border have an opportunity to evade their state's sales tax by shopping in another state.[26]

SOME QUESTIONS OF EQUITY

A number of criteria may be used to evaluate the equity or fairness of revenue policies. By one common standard a tax is fair if it is imposed on those who benefit directly from the manner in which the tax receipts are spent. Thus a tax on gasoline is equitable because it is levied for the most part on people who use the highways and it is used to build or maintain roads. Similarly, lawmakers have also commonly concluded that the costs of various services, such as sewer extensions, should be borne in large part by those who beneift from them or, as in the case of a municipal golf course, those who use them.

Another criterion is that taxes and other revenue measures should be based on the ability to pay. They are considered *progressive* if they take a larger percentage of a rich person's income than of a poor person's income and *regressive* if they have the opposite effect. Over most of this century, progressive taxes have generally been viewed as the most desirable; though this goal has been difficult to achieve in practice. In recent years, however, the concept that taxes should be proportional to income—that is, that everyone should pay the same percentage regardless of how much they make—has become more popular. This notion was reflected in the federal Tax Reform

Table 12.6   Direct Tax Burdens for a Married Couple with Two Dependents Living in the Largest City in Each State (Selected State and Local Taxes, 1982, as a Percentage of Income)

City	Income Level			
	$17,500	$25,000	$50,000	$100,000
Anchorage, AK	1.8%	1.5%	1.2%	0.9%
Phoenix, AZ	4.1	4.7	5.3	4.9
Los Angeles, CA	4.1	4.5	5.9	8.0
Denver, CO	4.1	4.3	4.6	4.7
Honolulu, HI	5.2	6.4	7.5	8.1
Boise, ID	5.6	6.5	7.3	7.3
Billings, MT	4.3	4.5	5.1	5.2
Las Vegas, NV	2.4	2.2	1.7	1.2
Albuquerque, NM	3.1	3.4	3.9	4.4
Portland, OR	7.8	8.6	9.0	9.7
Salt Lake City, UT	6.4	6.9	6.7	5.8
Seattle, WA	4.3	3.8	2.9	2.1
Casper, WY	2.4	2.1	1.6	1.1

Note: State and local taxes include income, general sales, and property.

Source: Advisory Commission on Intergovernmental Relations, *Significant Features of Fiscal Federalism*, Special Insert (Washington, D.C.: Government Printing Office, 1984).

Act of 1986 and will undoubtedly be reflected in tax policies at the state and local levels.

Some idea of the actual impact of state and local taxes in western states in regard to the older "ability to pay" criterion is shown in Table 12.6. This table presents the impact of state and local taxes (income, general, sales, property) on families with different levels of income living in the largest city in each of the thirteen western states. The table contains considerable variety. In Los Angeles, Portland, and Honolulu there are relatively high rates which increase with income (that is, progressive taxation). On the other hand, there are relatively low rates and a regressive system in Anchorage and Casper. Historically, state and local taxes in the West as in the nation as a whole have had a somewhat regressive impact.

State and local decision-makers faced with the task of raising revenues have to worry about the overall effects of their tax policies. For example, they have to be concerned with whether high tax rates will cause working people and businesses to leave the area, or, for those businesses unable to leave, to lay off workers—and overall, the possibility of a taxpayers' rebellion at the next election. Given these concerns, states and local officials have felt it prudent to get as much revenue as possible from outside their jurisdictions. One way of doing this is through the adoption of a general sales tax, which is imposed on out-of-state tourists as well as local residents. This is one reason why such taxes have been popular and lucrative in states like Arizona, Hawaii, and Nevada.

Shifting some—if not much—of the tax burden to residents of other states can also be accomplished through severance taxes. Thus in the late 1970s, as western states increased their severance taxes on oil, gas and coal, eastern states dependent on these energy sources complained that the taxes were being unfairly passed along to their citizens. Westerners, however, defend such taxes on the grounds that they are necessary to avoid and partially make up for abuses the West has suffered in the past.[27] Speaking for many in the West, Montana's U.S. senator Max Baucus declared:

> Montanans are willing to contribute to the resolution of this Nation's energy predicament. . . . At the same time, it must be emphasized that Montana will not serve as a resource colony. The state has a history well remembered by my generation of Montanans. The natural resource bounty of Montana was plundered again and again with little concern for the stability and future of the area.
>
> Too often, the result was impoverished families, disintegrated neighborhoods, busted towns. We have pledged that this past will not be mirrored in our future—and we deserve to be taken seriously in this quest.
>
> We are setting aside coal tax revenues to pay the costs of coal development and to provide a balanced framework for stable, diverse economic development in the future. A state like Montana has that right. It has that power. And it has that duty to future generations.[28]

In a more indirect manner westerners have historically shifted much of the burden of taxation to citizens of other regions by securing the adoption of favorable federal taxation and spending policies. Yet questions about the equity of such tax shifting have been the subject of continued debate.

Fiscal Responsibility, Development, and Stress

Over the years, financial policymakers in the West have generally demonstrated a commitment to the doctrine of fiscal responsibility.

This doctrine, as Frederick C. Mosher and Orville F. Poland noted several years ago, "urges frugality in public spending, a balanced budget, the liquidation of the public debt, and government as small and as close to the people as possible."[29]

Along with this, however, westerners have long placed emphasis on the desirability of economic growth. The goal of economic development has had three main implications. First, it has helped foster dependency on outsiders, particularly eastern corporate investors and the federal government. Second, it has led to recurring resentment in the West over being treated as an economic and political colony of the United States. Third, it has encouraged state and local governments to assume the task of encouraging investment as their principal task. Creation of a climate for investment has been taken to require making transportation improvements, protecting property rights, keeping taxes low, imposing only minimal regulations on business, and doing what can be done to keep labor costs down. Social welfare has not been viewed as a major long-term responsibility of government because economic development is expected to bring general prosperity.[30]

The growth thesis and its corollary assumptions about the role of government have been dominant sentiments in the West. Yet pursuit of the goal has had a further implication: as actual growth has taken place, the accompanying dislocations and changes have created pressures leading to an expanded role for government and indeed to an open conflict with the doctrine of fiscal responsibility. Growth appears to have created pressures toward centralization at the state level, increased reliance on executive leadership, more regulation, larger budgets, and increased stress on state and local revenue systems.

Notes

1. John Gunther, *Inside U.S.A.* (New York: Harper and Brothers, 1947), 31.

2. See the account by Bob Gleason, "When the States Gave the Income Tax to the Federal Government," *Intergovernmental Perspective* (Fall 1985), 10–12.

3. Gerald D. Nash, *The American West in the Twentieth Century* (Albuquerque: University of New Mexico Press, 1977), 192.

4. Quoted in David R. Berman, "Political Culture: Change and Conti-

nuity," in *Culture and Values in Arizona Life* (Phoenix: Arizona Academy, 1987), 115–30.

5. For details on deficit limitations, see annual editions of *The Book of the States* published by the Council of State Governments.

6. David B. Magelby, "The Movement to Limit Government Spending in American States and Localities, 1970–1979," *National Civic Review* (May 1981), 271–76, 282.

7. James S. Fay, Anne G. Lipow, and Stephanie W. Fay, eds., *California Almanac, 1986–87* (Los Angeles: Presidio Press, 1985).

8. Lottery revenues are either channeled into general revenue funds, which can be spent for any purpose, or into special funds earmarked for particular purposes. In Arizona, funds are split between the local transportation and the general funds. In Colorado lottery revenues go for capital construction, conservation, parks, and recreation. California earmarks lottery proceeds for education. Funds are distributed to public school districts on a per capita basis. The Oregon lottery, which began in 1985, was prompted by losses from a declining timber industry. Its revenues were earmarked for projects and programs selected by the state legislature and designed to improve the state's economy.

9. Steven D. Gold, "The Pros and Cons of Earmarking," *State Legislatures* (July 1987), 28–31.

10. The percentages of these states are: Alaska, 2%; California, 13%; Hawaii, 5%; and Oregon, 19%. The figures are for 1984. See Gold, "The Pros and Cons of Earmarking."

11. See Charles M. Price, "The Initiative: A Comparative State Analysis and Reassessment of a Western Phenomenon," *Western Political Quarterly* 28 (June 1975), 243–62; and Hugh A. Bone and Robert C. Benedict, "Perspectives on Direct Legislation: Washington State's Experience, 1914–1973," *Western Political Quarterly* 28 (June 1975), 330–51.

12. Frederick C. Mosher and Orville F. Poland, *The Costs of American Governments* (New York: Dodd, Mead, 1964), 1.

13. See Gary C. Hamilton and Nicole Woolsey Biggart, *Governor Reagan, Governor Brown: A Sociology of Executive Power* (New York: Columbia University Press, 1984), 97.

14. In most of the other western states, governors have the power to veto or eliminate specific budget items in appropriation bills, but cannot simply reduce the amounts.

15. See Sydney Duncombe and Richard Kinney, "The Politics of State Appropriation Increases," *State Government* (September/October 1986), 113–23.

16. See *Annual or Biennial Budgets?* (Lexington, Ky.: Council of State Governments, 1972).

17. Duncombe and Kinney, "The Politics of State Appropriation Increases."

18. James J. Lopach, ed., *We the People of Montana: The Workings of a Popular Government* (Missoula, Mont.: Mountain Press, 1983), 203.

19. Duncombe and Kinney, "The Politics of State Appropriation Increases."

20. Lopach, *We the People*, 267.

21. Arthur H. Miller, "Public Opinion and Regional Political Realignment," in Peter F. Galderisi *et al.*, eds., *The Politics of Realignment: Party and Change in the Mountain West* (Boulder, Colo.: Westview Press, 1987), 94–97.

22. See Vance Kane, "State Aid to Local Governments," *Book of the States 1987–88* (Lexington, Ky.: Council of State Governments, 1987), 438.

23. See James Ring Adams, *Secrets of the Tax Revolt* (New York: Harcourt Brace Jovanovich, 1984), 172.

24. Currently half of the states and the District of Columbia operate lotteries. In the West, lotteries are found in Arizona, California, Colorado, Idaho, Montana (as part of a regional lottery with South Dakota), Oregon and Washington. Thus far, Alaska, Hawaii, New Mexico, Nevada, Utah and Wyoming have resisted the urge to adopt a lottery system. In Nevada such proposals have historically encountered the opposition of gambling interests, which, as might be expected, are anxious to avoid governmental competition. On this latter point, see Gilman M. Ostrander, *Nevada: The Great Rotten Borough, 1859–1964* (New York: Alfred A. Knopf, 1966), 203.

25. This may, of course, be due to not having resources beyond a subsistence level to participate. See David R. Berman and Bruce D. Merrill, "The Arizona Lottery," *Comparative State Politics Newsletter* (April 1982), 22–23.

26. See Donald R. Burrows and Don C. Taylor, "Public Financing in Washington: The Role of Taxation," in Thor Swanson *et al.*, *Political Life in Washington* (Pullman: Washington State University Press, 1985), 179–95.

27. See Richard Lamm and Michael McCarthy, *The Angry West: A Vulnerable Land and Its Future* (Boston: Houghton Mifflin, 1982).

28. *Congressional Record* (July 8, 1981), S7220.

29. Mosher and Poland, *The Costs of American Governments*, 2.

30. See Berman, "Political Culture."

13

WESTERN LOCAL GOVERNMENTS AND PUBLIC POLICY

Cal Clark and Janet Clark

*L*OCAL GOVERNMENTS ARE THE ONES CLOSEST TO the people, and they perform many, if not most, of the basic public services for Americans—refuse collection and police protection, keeping potholes filled and utility users billed and administering tax rolls and election polls. Thus, they should be more accessible and more adaptable to political change than the more distant state and federal institutions. Yet there is far less public awareness about local government and politicians than about the leaders and bodies at higher levels; and, at least most of the time, local political issues draw far less interest than does the drama of national or even state politics.

This mixture of closeness and invisibility especially applies to the

West. The "individualistic culture" that Daniel Elazar sees as marking most of the West[1] should make small-scale local government and "friends and neighbors" politics attractive. Yet the region's vast and sparsely settled spaces exacerbate the problems of knowing who local officials are and what is involved in local public policies. Furthermore, as will be seen, these characteristics of western communities have contributed to a financial crisis that threatens to undermine the vitality and perhaps even the viability of many of the region's local governments.

This chapter examines three of the most important characteristics of local governments in the West. The first section discusses the overall structure of western local government systems; the second considers their public policies and basic activities; and the third argues that the fiscal crisis in American local governments is especially pronounced in the West. Finally, a concluding section summarizes the problems and prospects of local governments in the West.

The Structure of Local Governments

The U.S. Constitution leaves the creation and regulation of local governments solely to state constitutions and statutes in the belief that systems of local government should be designed to fit local conditions. Thus the nature and structure of local government might well be expected to vary radically among states in response to different socioeconomic settings and political philosophies. Yet almost all the states have basically the same structure of local government. While there are fifty separate state systems of local government in the United States, their make-up is very similar. The area of almost every state is divided into counties (Alaska has boroughs and Louisiana has parishes) within which are cities and municipalities. In general, most of the county services are directed at areas outside municipal borders. For example, the county sheriff's department generally patrols the rural regions of a county and leaves the mean streets of the cities and towns to the city police except when emergencies arise; the city and county have their own street and road departments with separate responsibilities for different stretches of pavement; and so on. In addition to the general services provided by counties and municipalities, public education is administered by separate school districts in most of the states, and a plethora of "special districts" have been created for such diverse activities as sewage removal, irrigation, public housing and health care.

The inertia that limits local government structures is perhaps best illustrated by the case of Montana, whose 1972 constitution contained provisions explicitly seeking to promote major reforms in local government. It was hoped that these reforms would follow a Jeffersonian tradition of bringing government closer to the people by increasing the powers of local government, allowing more flexibility and diversity in the organization of local governments and promoting participatory democracy at the local level. The centerpiece was the provision for mandatory "voter review of local government" every ten years. Under this system, local government study commissions would be elected in every county and municipality which would review the current structure of government and suggest an alternative to it for a voter referendum between the existing and proposed systems. Thus, it was hoped, reform would be promoted through grass-roots initiatives. In the first round of voter review in the mid-1970s, about one-sixth of the proposed changes in form of government were adopted, but there did not seem to be much popular enthusiasm about the process. Thus, whether this experiment in reform and populism was successful or not depended upon one's predilection for declaring a glass half full or half empty. In contrast, the second round of voter review in the mid-1980s drew little interest and resulted in almost no change.[2]

Tables 13.1 and 13.2 summarize the local government systems in the thirteen western states in the 1980s. Table 13.1 presents the numbers of the four different types of local governments by state in 1987; and Table 13.2 indicates their relative importance in total local government spending for 1981–82. There are several noteworthy items in these tables. First, the counties have much more spending power compared with the cities in the West than elsewhere in the nation. There are five times as many municipalities as counties in the West, which is only slightly less than the six to one ratio for all the U.S. Yet total county and city spending is almost equal in the West, while cities spend 75% more than counties nationwide. This is not simply the result of an absence of urban centers, since the West now resembles the rest of the nation in its proportion of urbanized population.[3] Among the western states, there is some tendency for the most pastoral, like Montana and Wyoming, to have the highest relative county spending, and for some of the most urbanized, like Alaska, Arizona and Colorado, to have the highest relative city spending. However, this relationship is far from perfect. Counties slightly outspend cities in California; and city budgets exceed county budgets almost fourfold

Table 13.1   Types of Local Governments, 1987

State	Total Number	Number per 1000 Pop.	Counties	Municipalities	School Districts	Special Districts
Alaska	233	.32	14[a]	149	56	14
Arizona	576	.18	15	81	227	253
California	4,331	.16	57	442	1,098	2,734
Colorado	1,593	.49	62	266	180	1,085
Hawaii	18	.02	3	1	0	14
Idaho	1,065	1.06	44	198	118	705
Montana	1,243	1.52	54	128	547	514
Nevada	272	.20	16	33	77	146
New Mexico	331	.22	33	98	88	112
Oregon	1,502	.56	36	240	350	876
Utah	530	.32	29	225	40	236
Washington	1,779	.40	39	266	297	1,177
Wyoming	424	.84	23	95	56	250
West	13,897	.28	425	2,222	3,134	8,116
U.S.	86,242[b]	.36	3,042	19,200	14,777	29,532

[a]Number of boroughs.
[b]Includes townships in nonwestern states.

Sources: 1987 Census of Governments: Volume 1, Government Organizations (Washington, D.C.: Bureau of Census, U.S. Department of Commerce, 1988), 3, 5; *County and City Data Book, 1988* (Washington, D.C.: Bureau of Census, U.S. Department of Commerce, 1988), 2.

in New Mexico. Perhaps western states have yet to react to the growing importance of metropolitan centers because of the recentness of urbanization.

Second, while most people think of local government in terms of "general purpose" units like cities and counties, in sheer numbers school districts and single-purpose "special districts" make up most of the total. Sheer numbers, however, should not be confused with political importance. For example, special districts account for 15% or more of total local government spending in only three western states, indicating that they have only a marginal role in the provision of public services. In contrast, school districts are important in overall local government finance, spending almost a third of public local funds both in the West and nationwide. Interestingly enough, school districts control a disproportionately high level of local government resources in most of the Mountain states (Montana, Wyoming, Idaho and Utah), as well as in Oregon. Rather than belying the normally conservative image of the Mountains states by implying a special focus on education, this probably reflects an absence of large cities and a

Table 13.2   Local Government Expenditures, 1981–82 (in Millions of Dollars)

State	Total Expenditures	County	Municipality	Township	School District	Special District
			Percent by Unit			
Alaska	$1,656	36%	63%	0%	0%	2%
Arizona	$4,370	18	29	0	35	19
California	$42,088	30	28	0	30	13
Colorado	$4,733	16	36	0	36	13
Hawaii	$578	25	75	0	0	1
Idaho	$881	22	23	0	45	11
Montana	$1,029	31	18	0	46	5
Nevada	$1,210	44	19	0	33	5
New Mexico	$1,631	11	41	0	48	1
Oregon	$3,812	17	25	0	46	13
Utah	$2,009	15	21	0	41	24
Washington	$8,463	11	20	0	26	44
Wyoming	$1,164	30	21	0	42	6
West	$73,624	25	28	0	31	16
U.S.	$313,365	21	36	3	30	11

Note: Rows may not sum to 100% because of rounding off.

Source: 1982 Census of Governments, Volume 4, Government Finances, No. 5 Compendium of Government Finances (Washington, D.C.: Bureau of Census, U.S. Department of Commerce, 1982), 166, 168, 169, 171, 172, 178, 179, 193, 195, 198, 204, 211, 214, 217.

conservative attitude toward municipal and county spending levels, which depresses their budgets. Thus, the high percentage of school spending reflects less an emphasis on education than a lack of emphasis upon other local government functions.

Third, while the West's "individualistic" culture might be expected to promote a proliferation of local governments, this evidently is not the case. For example, the number of local governments per thousand people is significantly lower for the West than for the entire nation, although many of the Mountain states (Colorado, Idaho, Montana and Wyoming) are well above the national average, probably reflecting both their individualist cultures and their rural expanses. In addition, no western state now has townships located within counties, as do twenty of the thirty-seven states outside the West. Alone among the western states, the Washington State constitution permits counties to form townships, but only two have done so in the past, and all townships in that state were abolished by the mid-1970s.[4] Evidently, the sparse populations outside municipal boundaries render the formation of subcounty governments impractical. Consequently, many western counties are huge in size, larger in fact than Rhode Island or even Connecticut. Finally, while the West's individualistic culture might also suggest a hankering for special districts this is not the case either, since special districts spend significantly more than the national norm in only three western states.

While the local government system of almost every western state can be comfortably described in terms of these basic units, many idiosyncratic variations exist in how they are combined. A striking contrast results when comparing Alaska and Hawaii which, at least on the surface, have several common characteristics: separation from the U.S. mainland; a common late admission to the Union; clearly defined state-local divisions of responsibility; school districts that are largely integrated with general purpose local government units; the lowest number of special districts in the nation, next to Delaware; and smallness (in population for the former and size for the latter). Yet they differ drastically in their systems of local government. Hawaii may well have the simplest in the U.S. and Alaska the most complex.

In Hawaii, there are four counties in all, including the combined city-county of Honolulu, as well as what may be the only "noncounty" county in the nation—Kalawoo County on Molokai Island, which is conterminous with Hansen's Disease Settlement and is administered by the state's department of health. Alaska, with the largest land mass and the next-to-the-smallest population in the nation, divided about 45% of the state into fourteen "supercounties" called *boroughs*, including three consolidated city-boroughs (Anchorage, Juneau and Sitka). The largest, the North Slope Borough, which includes the Prudhoe Bay oil field, is approximately the size of Idaho, yet its population is only 12,000. The rest of the state, comprising the rural or bush areas, constitutes what is called the *unorganized borough*, which includes many small municipalities and Native villages. In theory and law, the state legislature acts as the governing council of the unorganized borough. Furthermore, the rural local government system in Alaska is supplemented by for-profit and nonprofit Native Corporations, which were founded by the federal Alaska Native Claims Settlement Act of 1971 and have been estimated to provide about half of the social and public services to Native Alaskans. In addition, there are various other Native governments in the state.[5]

Compared with the exotic frontiers of Alaska and Hawaii and the populism of Montana, county and muncipal government systems in the rest of the West appear rather mundane and can be described straightforwardly and succinctly.[6] States divide their territories into counties, usually encompassing the whole state. Municipalities or cities, however, are founded on specific sites whenever the population, economic, and political conditions warrant "incorporation" in the eyes of the residents and, in many western states, when they meet a minimum-size requirement. Incorporation is almost obligatory for even medium-sized towns with, say, several thousand population. For smaller communities, the choice of whether or not to declare themselves a municipality may be more controversial. Sometimes the question hinges on financial considerations, such as whether gaining federal revenue-sharing funds will outweigh losing services provided by the county. At other times, the issues can be idiosyncratic and even ironic. For example, the "South Valley" near Albuquerque, New Mexico, threatened to incorporate as a separate municipality in the late 1980s in order to preserve its traditional rural life-style from the encroaching metropolitan center.[7]

Municipal forms of government are the most variegated, with three basic types of systems being used in the West: (1) *the mayor-council system*, in which an elected mayor is the chief executive with a legislative council; (2) *the council-manager system*, in which an appointive city manager serves as chief executive responsible to an elected council; and (3) *the commission system*, in which there is no manager and the elected commissioners act as department heads in the municipal administration. Counties, in contrast, have fewer differences in their organizational structure. They are generally governed by elected councils, usually made up of three to five members. In most of the West, these are called county commissioners, although they go by other titles in a few places—board of supervisors in Arizona and California, borough assemblies in Alaska, and, to make names especially confusing, county courts in thirteen of Oregon's thirty-six counties. School districts and special districts are usually administered by boards. School boards are almost always elected by the population in a school district. Board members for special districts can be either elected directly or appointed by other local governments, with the latter method being more popular.[8]

Given that county and municipal populations can vary from the thousands (or even hundreds) to the millions, it is not surprising that many states divide their local governments into different types based upon total population and assessed valuation of property within a jurisdiction, thus giving somewhat different powers and organizations to different classes of cities and counties. For example, Alaska,

Nevada, and Utah each have three categories of cities; and in Washington State, with its four classes of cities, voter approval is necessary in order to change status. Sometimes these divisions get a little out of hand, though. New Mexico's thirty-three counties are divided into nine classes, several of which have only one county. Many of the western states also have "home rule" provisions, which allow the local governments taking this option to have greater flexibility in their organizational structures and fiscal affairs. In California, for instance, most of the largest cities have adopted such "charters," but in Washington State only five of the thirty-nine counties have adopted home rule because state law has attached enough strings to make such independence of questionable value.[9]

Local Government Public Policies and Activities

Governments are constituted, of course, to do things for their people, despite the adage that "that government is best which governs least"—a view widely shared in the individualistic and conservative West, especially in regard to the federal government.[10] This section on public policy in the West will look at three characteristics of the activities or public policies of western local governments: (1) the form of government adopted, especially by minicipalities, since this has important implications for their policy performance; (2) the distribution of budgetary expenditures by local governments since this directly measures what they are doing; and (3) the functional responsibilities of special districts, since this provides an indirect measure of citizens' demands for public services not provided by their counties and municipalities.

While popular images view the West in terms of desolate deserts and majestic mountains, the region is now quite urbanized in terms of where people live and differs little from the nation as a whole in extent of urbanization, although the region's urban transformation dates only from World War II. In fact, as illustrated by the date in Table 13.3, which details the proportion of state populations living in cities of over fifty thousand, almost half of all westerners live in urban centers. More than half the residents of Arizona, California, and Colorado live in large cities. Almost half of Alaskans can be found in Anchorage, and the same proportions of Nevadans in Las Vegas–North Las Vegas and Reno–Sparks. A quarter to a third of the citizens

Table 13.3   Urban Characteristics of the West

State	Percent of Population in Cities of over 50,000*	Government for Cities over 25,000*		
		Mayor	Manager	Commission
Alaska	43%	1	0	0
Arizona	60	0	9	0
California	57	3	157	0
Colorado	52	2	16	0
Hawaii	35	2	0	0
Idaho	11	3	3	0
Montana	17	2	2	0
Nevada	42	1	4	0
New Mexico	32	1	7	0
Oregon	22	1	8	1
Utah	26	3	4	2
Washington	22	6	10	1
Wyoming	11	1	1	0
West	47	26	221	4

*Cities of different sizes used because of manner in which data reported.
Source: *County and City Data Book, 1988* (Washington, D.C.: Bureau of Census, U.S. Department of Commerce, 1988), 602–728.

of the other western states (excepting Idaho, Montana and Wyoming) are much more city slickers than rural rubes.

Consequently, some western historians now view the urbanization of the West as the most important change over the last half-century, in that it has allowed the region greatly to decrease its economic dependence upon other parts of the nation. In particular, a series of growth spurts triggered by the siting of defense bases, the growth of the high-tech defense industry, the energy boom, America's trade reorientation toward the Pacific and tourism have stimulated urban growth and created population centers large enough to become regional centers for economic distribution and production. Politically, western urban government in general shifted from domination by development-oriented businessmen during the mid-1940s to the mid-1960s, to polities more responsive to the professional middle class and minority groups in the 1970s.[11]

Thus urban politics and government are certainly of central importance in the West. In fact, the West has played a leading role in the national movement for urban reform and government reorganization. In the United States as a whole, the twentieth century has seen a major change in municipal and urban government from elected mayors to city managers as part of reform efforts to decrease political corruption and patronage and increase administrative professionalism and skills. The West, with its individualistic political culture and distrust of "bosses," took a leading role in these reform efforts of the progressive movement; and California in particular became a model of good government reform, the legendary prewar corruption of the "City of Angels" notwithstanding.[12]

Table 13.3 also includes the number of cities over 25,000 population in each western state having each of the three different forms of municipal government. These data show that reform has been quite popular in the West, since the two types of reformed governments— the council-manager and commission systems, especially the former— are dominant, more so than in the nation as a whole. Many of the cities that retain elected mayors, however, rank among the largest and most economically powerful in their state or region (Albuquerque, Anchorage, Boise, Denver, Honolulu, Los Angeles, San Francisco and Seattle), suggesting that politicians are especially loath to give up power where there are enough local resources at stake to make power worth having. Furthermore, these large metropolitan centers have quite heterogeneous populations in terms of ethnic and class composition, implying a need for political conciliation and leadership rather than professional administration.

Another structural reform that is popular in theory, but not in practice, is to create consolidated city-county governments to produce greater administrative coherence, lessen political rivalries, and save scarce local funding. Some of the largest cities in the West, such as Denver, Honolulu and San Francisco, have adopted this form of government, as have a couple of cities facing very special circumstances. For example, there is a consolidated city-county government in Los Alamos, New Mexico, which essentially consists of national laboratories. Montana's experiments in local government include two city-county consolidations (Butte/Silver Bow and Deer Lodge/Anaconda) that were created as part of the reforms occurring from the "voter review of local government" in the mid-1970s—although they were far from uncontroversial, as is suggested by the following quotation from an irate letter to the editor:

> Won't these consolidationists and do-gooders ever learn? If they

want to live in a decent, clean, and progressive town, why don't
they go somewhere else?[13]

Thus, while the West was a leader in municipal reform because it was
consistent with the western political culture, these same values of
individualism, conservatism and suspicion of big government militate
against local government consolidation, whatever its alleged payoffs
in terms of efficiency and administrative rationality.

The structure of local government is considered a public policy
issue because it is assumed to affect the operations or actual policy
implementation of these bodies. Table 13.4 provides an overview of
the public policies of local governments in the West by presenting the
proportions of local government spending in each western state devoted to the variety of purposes that compose about 80% of local
government budgets. School districts are excluded from this analysis
because they are treated in detail in the next chapter. Thus, the figures
in Table 13.4 represent the combined spending of counties, municipalities, and special districts.

It is clear that local governments provide many basic services, but
most of these are quite mundane and not the subject of much political
interest except of course when scandals erupt. Public safety, transportation, sanitation, general administration, public utilities, and interest payments form well over half the local government budgets
nationwide and in every western state. The fact that local public policy
is not connected with high political drama should not be taken to
mean that these issues are necessarily considered inconsequential by
the citizenry, though. Whether it means being protected from drug
dealers on urban streets or having the snow plowed off rural roads,
a public service can have a tremendous impact on people's daily
lives—perhaps only becoming fully apparent by its absence. For example, some county commissioners in rural counties in states like
Montana and Wyoming divide control over road systems into personal
areas. Their ability to determine where road repairs are made and
cattle guards placed then becomes an important patronage source,
akin to giving out city jobs in "urban machines."

The relative priorities that local governments in the West place
upon the individual policy categories also reflect the generally conservative nature of western politics.[14] Local governments in the West
generally spend less of their total budgets than the national average
on welfare (except for California), health (except for California and
three Mountain states where local governments have a heavy re-

Table 13.4 Percent Distribution of Local Government Budgets, 1981–82

State	General Admin.	Public Safety	Transportation	Sewers and Sanitation	Public Utilities	Welfare	Health	Housing and Urban Dev.	Environment	Interest
Alaska	8%	10%	10%	9%	16%	1%	4%	6%	4%	15%
Arizona	8	13	9	8	34	2	7	2	7	6
California	7	14	7	5	19	14	12	3	5	2
Colorado	8	11	10	7	13	9	8	2	5	4
Hawaii	10	19	9	13	21	1	1	2	8	3
Idaho	11	14	16	10	9	1	20	2	6	2
Montana	11	12	17	8	5	4	6	5	6	6
Nevada	13	20	15	5	7	2	18	3	7	4
New Mexico	8	15	11	9	23	1	8	2	5	10
Oregon	11	16	17	6	20	1	7	4	5	4
Utah	8	11	9	5	48	1	5	1	4	4
Washington	4	8	8	4	56	1	5	2	3	2
Wyoming	10	11	14	9	10	1	19	1	8	10
West	7	13	8	6	25	9	9	3	5	3
U.S.	6	11	8	7	29	7	10	4	3	4

Note: Combined spending of counties, municipalities, and special districts (and townships for total U.S. figures). Rows may not sum to 100% because of rounding errors.

Source: 1982 *Census of Governments, Volume 4, Government Finances, No. 5 Compendium of Government Finances* (Washington, D.C.: Bureau of Census, U.S. Department of Commerce, 1982), 166, 168, 169, 171, 172, 178, 179, 193, 195, 198, 204, 211, 214, 217.

sponsibility for hospitals), and housing and urban development. In contrast to this lower-than-average concern with these liberal policy areas, local governments in the West give higher budgetary priority than the nation as a whole to the public safety and transportation areas that conservatives look on with more favor. The regional percentages for the West, incidentally, are fairly close to the national average for several of these items because California, which is not very typical of the West, accounts for 59% of the region's local government spending.

In terms of the other policy areas, all thirteen western states have above-average spending on the environment, but this reflects less liberal environmental protectionism than the development of natural resources through such means as water projects. All the western states except Washington spend more of their budgets on general administration than the average elsewhere in the nation. Thus, despite the proclaimed western aversion to the evils of bureaucracy, these are high-cost governments, presumably because many of them are small units that cannot take advantage of the economies of scale (see the following section). Three western states (Washington, Utah and Arizona) devote very sizable amounts of their local government resources to "public utilities"—a category that happens to include liquor stores. However, many of these utilities more than pay for themselves since they provide a very significant proportion of local revenues. Finally, three energy states (Alaska, Wyoming and New Mexico) have high interest payments because of the need to raise money for new infrastructure and projects in rapidly growing areas. Many of these communities, however, rapidly declined after the bust in energy products in the mid-1980s, leaving many local government facilities underutilized.

Special districts represent the most "local" of local governments and hence might be expected to be especially attractive in the West. Most are smaller than counties; and almost all perform a single function (administering a hospital or irrigation district, providing utilities or sanitation services, and so on). Their advantages include the ability to deliver services and allocate costs to the groups or areas directly involved, to serve as a mechanism to get around debt and spending limits on other local governments, and to bring government "close to the people." They also possess several disadvantages—such as the higher costs of small government, contributing to the fragmentation of government within an area, and their invisibility to the general population.[15]

The invisibility of these governments in the West is well attested to by a New Mexico case from the mid-1970s. According to state law, the state provided matching funds for qualifying special districts. An enterprising state official, who was in charge of this program, certified that a fictitious special district in the southern part of the state had been formed, thus qualifying it for state aid. He then deposited the state monies, several hundred thousand dollars, in a local bank where the special district allegedly was and made payments to a dummy corporation for "services rendered." Unfortunately for himself, he stayed in his state job for several more years until the scam unraveled. He was apprehended at the Albuquerque airport when he belatedly tried to take it on the lam. Certainly this is quite a reminder that governments "close to the people" are not necessarily known to the people.

Table 13.5 describes some of the characteristics of special districts in the West. Special districts might seem especially appropriate for the region's wide-open spaces and individualistic political culture. In addition to the fact, noted earlier, that special districts have an above-average share of local government finance in only three western states, the growth in the number of special districts during the 1970s and 1980s was higher than average in only three states (Arizona, Montana and Nevada). The growth of western special districts, moreover, evidently was not stimulated as elsewhere in the nation by attempts to get around limits on other local governments since they grew at exactly the national rate in California, the home of the "taxpayers' revolt." In contrast, there was a tremendous expansion of special districts in Montana as part of that state's populist movement in local government, but their financial role remains minuscule (see Table 13.2) suggesting a rather limited policy impact from their proliferation.

The types of special districts emphasized in the West deviate from national norms in several interesting ways. First, western conservatism is reflected in a comparative dearth of special districts in the areas of education, health, housing, and sanitation. Second, the West as a whole is well above average in the proportion of fire districts and those falling into the residual "other" category. The reason for the latter is that western states are far more likely than others to have cemetery districts, perhaps harking back to the days when vigilantes created their own special districts by bringing business to the "boot hills" around the West. Finally, while only a few of the western states have a disproportionate number of natural resource districts, water and irrigation districts are extremely important in the parched West

Table 13.5   Characteristics of Special Districts

State	Total Number, 1987	Growth Rate, 1972–87	Percent by Function[a]						
			Education/ Health	Transportation	Fire	Nat. Resources/ Parks	Housing/ Sanitation	Public Utilities	Other
Alaska	14	All new	0%	0%	0%	0%	93%	7%	0%
Arizona	253	181%	5	1	46	33	7	6	1
California	2,734	23	7	3	14	25	13	15	23
Colorado	1,085	34	3	1	20	21	29	12	14
Hawaii	14	–7	0	0	0	100	0	0	0
Idaho	705	30	9	9	17	27	10	3	26
Montana	514	99	4	1	25	23	18	5	23
Nevada	146	93	9	7	10	23	19	7	23
New Mexico	112	13	3	0	0	65	11	8	13
Oregon	876	6	3	4	31	28	8	17	10
Utah	236	34	5	2	5	34	17	14	22
Washington	1,177	15	7	4	35	18	10	15	11
Wyoming	250	23	4	1	18	47	11	2	18
West	8,116	27	6	3	21	26	14	12	18
U.S.	29,532	24	10	4	17	25	22	12	10

[a]Rows may not sum to 100% because of rounding errors.

Source: 1987 Census of Governments: Volume 1, Government Organizations (Washington, D.C.: Bureau of Census, U.S. Department of Commerce, 1988), 5, 20–21.

and account for the relatively high degree of spending by special districts in Arizona and Utah.

Washington State stands out as having by far the most fiscally important special districts, which control almost half of local government spending in the state as compared to a quarter in Utah, the western state with the next greatest special district spending (see Table 13.2). In Washington, this is the result of state statutes, which are quite permissive regarding the formation of special districts. Consequently, the state has a variety of special districts for public utilities, port administration, fire protection, conservation and water management, many of which have huge budgets. Moreover, special districts in Washington are independent of other local governments since their managing boards are directly elected; and many have become highly effective in lobbying the state legislature. Consequently, by the late 1980s other units of local government had become jealous of their powers and unsuccessfully petitioned the legislature to clip their wings. Thus, we see that special districts are not always invisible and can become a public policy issue in and of themselves.[16]

Local Governments and Fiscal Stress

The 1970s and 1980s witnessed a growing financial crisis for many local governments in the United States as the nation's economy reeled from "stagflation" and as higher levels of government reduced intergovernmental aid to localities because of their own severe fiscal problems.[17] In addition to the general financial crisis of local governments everywhere, the West's local governments face other specific disadvantages. First, the normal financial problems of local governments are exacerbated by the boom-bust cycles that operate in much of the western economy. Second, the West is characterized by small rural local governments, which have high costs of administration and operation. Third, recent urban development in the West has created some special fiscal problems. Finally, these economic problems make western cities and counties more financially dependent upon the federal government and more vulnerable to changes in federal priorities than are their counterparts elsewhere in the United States. The West, then, faces fiscal stress from a variety of sources.

The boom-bust cycle creates severe problems for state and particularly local governments. Tremendous capital outlays are needed for expanding road networks, sanitation systems, health care and schools; law enforcement expenditures escalate because of the social strains accompanying rapid growth, and so on and on. Moreover, the prospect of a down or bust cycle raises serious questions regarding the long-term feasibility of financing major increases in capital projects when population declines in the near future will (or might) lead to the underutilization of expensive public infrastructure projects.[18]

The problems of responding to this boom-bust cycle are exacerbated by the dependent nature of local governments, which can thwart their ameliorative actions. Examples of this are easy to find in the West. In both Idaho and Montana—two of the states in the region hardest hit by the 1980s recession—the state legislature refused to act on a number of proposals that would have provided "local options" for raising much-needed new revenues. This refusal created a good deal of bitterness among the local government officials. The courts have also stifled local governments' attempts to raise new monies. For example, Pocatello's attempt to charge utility fees for street maintenance was voided by the U.S. Supreme Court in 1989. Even more broadly, a crisis arose in local finance in Washington State in the late 1980s when the state's business and occupational tax was declared unconstitutional; the state legislature then refused to support any major new tax initiative for several years.[19]

All this implies that local governments in the West have been especially subject to fiscal stress; and this suspicion is confirmed by the data in Table 13.6 on two indicators of fiscal stress: (1) the growth, or more accurately nongrowth, of "real" (that is, adjusted for inflation) state and local spending during 1978–81, and (2) the number of tax increases in each state. For the nation as a whole, state and local spending grew minutely at the rate of 0.5% a year in real terms, reflecting the economic crisis and the taxpayers' revolt of that era. Spending in the West did not even match this low standard because nine of the thirteen western states had lower growth rates. Moreover, the West contained seven of the fifteen states whose budgets declined in real terms over this period, including the two with the greatest declines—Hawaii and Idaho. Interestingly, though, while the cutbacks of Proposition 13 in California dominated national publicity, several other western states facing economic recessions actually had more severe cutbacks; namely Hawaii, Idaho, Montana and Nevada. The economic picture would have been even bleaker had not the oil price explosion of 1979 greatly enriched the coffers of the energy-rich states of Alaska, Wyoming, and New Mexico.

These spending cutbacks occurred despite the fact that the West was increasing taxes at a slightly greater rate than the nation as a

Table 13.6   Indicators of Fiscal Stress for State-Local Governments

State	Annual Percentage Change in Real per capita State-Local Expenditures, 1978–81	Number of Tax Increases, 1981–82
Alaska	14.54%	0
Arizona	–0.01	2
California	–0.73	1
Colorado	–0.42	1
Hawaii	–3.76	0
Idaho	–1.93	2
Montana	–1.34	0
Nevada	–0.99	3
New Mexico	3.59	2
Oregon	0.23	4
Utah	0.36	4
Washington	1.84	5
Wyoming	6.41	0
West	0.28	1.85
U.S.	0.54	1.62

Source: John Shannon and Susannah E. Calkins, "Federal and State-Local Spenders Go Their Separate Ways," *Intergovernmental Perspective* 8 (Winter 1983), 26–27.

whole. The western states averaged 1.85 tax increases in 1980–81 compared to 1.62 for the rest of the nation. Only four states in the West (including energy-rich Alaska and Wyoming) did not implement tax increases. Such statistics are surprising given the fact that only two or three years earlier the West had been the spawning ground for the taxpayers' revolt. The statistics are also a strong indication of the severity of the budgetary crisis that faced most of the region. However, some influence of the taxpayers' revolt can be seen in the fact that the western states were much more reluctant to increase general sales or income taxes, relying instead on fuel, alcoholic beverages, and cigarette tax hikes.[20] While these taxes have much narrower bases, they do have the advantage of taxing "luxuries" and "sins." It is also noteworthy that the greatest taxing activity occurred in the Pacific Northwest states of Oregon and Washington where tax hikes were used to support modest spending increases, implying that the relatively liberal image of these states within the region is justified.[21] In any event, these data on budgetary stress certainly demonstrate that local governments in the West had special problems in the early 1980s.

A second problem for the West comes from the fact that despite the growing urban concentration of its total population, many of its local governments are small and rural in nature. The costs are substantially greater on a per capita basis to provide public services to the small and dispersed populations of rural areas simply because they cannot take advantage of economies of scale. Consequently, per capita state-local spending in the West is considerably higher than in the nation as a whole (see Chapter 12). In addition to being more expensive to operate, most rural governments are not large enough to hire skilled technical and planning personnel who could help them operate more effectively. Many rural areas also suffer from stagnating economic bases. Thus, they have exceedingly high costs coupled with comparatively low abilities to pay.[22]

The harsh fiscal conditions in smaller communities are strongly implied by the data in Table 13.7, which compares the economic conditions in counties with fifty thousand population or more with those of less than fifty thousand population. Counties were considered economically distressed if they met either of two conditions: (1) if they had a 1983 money income per capita of less than $7,500, which of itself was about 25% below the U.S. average; (2) if they had an income per capita growth rate of less than 20% between 1979 and 1983, which of itself was only half the rate of inflation.

This table demonstrates that economic conditions in rural areas were considerably worse than in larger communities. About one-quarter of the larger counties show significant stress on each indicator, while slightly over half of the smaller counties do. This relationship also holds for all the western states except California, Hawaii and Washington, where the economic conditions in large and small counties are relatively equal. The type of economic stress differs greatly between states, however. On the one hand, Arizona, Idaho, New Mexico, Utah and rural Colorado are fairly poor but growing in relative affluence. On the other hand, Nevada, Oregon, Wyoming, rural Alaska and California, and urban Washington are more prosperous but suffering from declining growth. The collapse of the oil market in the mid-1980s further added greatly to the economic distress of such oil patch and coal states as Alaska, Montana, New Mexico and Wyoming. Thus, these data on general economic conditions again demonstrate that almost every state in the West is subjected to significant economic stress of one kind or another.

Since urbanization in the West has been a relatively recent development, it might be expected that city budgets in the West would

Table 13.7 County Size and Economic Stress

	Counties over 50,000			Counties under 50,000		
State	Number	Percent with 1983 Money Income per capita under $7,500[a]	Percent with 1979–83 per capita Income Growth under 20%	Number	Percent with 1983 Money Income per capita under $7,500[a]	Percent with 1979–83 per capita Income Growth under 20%
Alaska	2	0%	0%	19	21%	36%
Arizona	10	60	20	5	100	60
California	41	20	22	17	18	59
Colorado	10	0	0	53	42	23
Hawaii	3	0	0	1	0	0
Idaho	6	17	0	38	84	55
Montana	4	0	25	52	64	67
Nevada	2	0	50	15	20	73
New Mexico	7	57	14	26	85	23
Oregon	15	20	93	21	38	90
Utah	5	40	20	24	88	67
Washington	16	0	38	23	22	22
Wyoming	2	0	50	19	32	100
West	123	19	29	313	53	52

[a]Money income averages 80% of personal income for the western states. Thus, this is equivalent to personal income per capita of approximately $9,375.

Source: Local Population Estimates: West (Washington, D.C.: Bureau of Census, U.S. Department of Commerce, 1986), *passim.*

have some new and distinctive characteristics. The implications of this for city fiscal health are mixed, at least in theory. On the one hand, rapidly growing cities must make massive investments in infrastructure and service start-ups, and the previous findings about the relatively low levels of city spending compared with counties suggest that their revenue bases are restricted. On the other hand, they do not have the long history of patronage politics of many of the older cities, which pushes up the cost of government considerably.[23]

On balance, the negative factors outweigh the positive ones by a substantial extent, as illustrated in the sophisticated analysis of the fiscal health of a national sample of cities by Helen Ladd and John Yinger. Ladd and Yinger developed an index of "fiscal health" for seventy-one cities (twenty from the West) based on the ratio between standardized measures of "expenditure needs" and "revenue raising capacities." The summary index of fiscal health is the difference between capacity and need taken as a percentage of capacity. Table 13.8 reports this index for 1972 and 1982 for the western cities included in the analysis.

In the early 1970s, the fiscal health of western cities looked good, both in absolute terms and in comparison with American urban centers as a whole. Twelve of the twenty cities from the West had capacities at least 3% greater than their needs, which suggests a minimum degree of fiscal health and was better than the national average of 0%. Over the next decade the fiscal health of all American cities fell by 5%, indicating that the average metropolitan center was beginning to experience significant fiscal strain. The fiscal condition of cities in the West, however, virtually collapsed during this decade. By 1982, twelve were below the national average, and another three had negative ratios. Los Angeles had the worst fiscal health in the nation; and Oakland, Sacramento, and Salt Lake City also were in the "bottom ten." Honolulu, Sacramento, Salt Lake City and Santa Ana suffered a particularly sharp drop in their fiscal health, while significant improvement occurred only in Phoenix and San Francisco among the twenty western cities included in the study.[24] Clearly, cities in the West face an abnormally high fiscal crisis.

The major reason for the poor fiscal health of these western cities turns out to be the result of their low revenue-raising capabilities. For example, western cities are much less able to "export" taxes to non-residents than are cities elsewhere in the nation.[25] City revenue systems are generally determined by state law. This low capacity of western cities probably stems from regional conservatism against granting

Table 13.8   Indices of City Fiscal Health in West, 1972 and 1982

	1972		1982	
	Index Value (%)	*Rank out of 71*	*Index Value (%)*	*Rank out of 71*
Anaheim, Calif.	19.1%	12	–2.0%	34
Denver, Colo.	–1.3	44	–4.9	39
Garden Grove, Calif.	38.1	3	15.1	16
Honolulu, Haw.	16.3	13	–7.8	45
Long Beach, Calif.	3.3	37	–7.1	43
Los Angeles, Calif.	–28.0	63	–79.7	71
Oakland, Calif.	–12.9	55	–33.2	62
Ogden, Utah	6.8	31	–5.6	40
Ontario, Calif.	8.3	27	–2.1	35
Phoenix, Ariz.	–4.5	48	11.4	19
Portland, Ore.	–10.6	54	–10.2	47
Riverside, Calif.	13.6	16	10.4	21
Sacramento, Calif.	3.1	38	–43.0	65
Salt Lake City, Utah	0.6	42	–34.3	63
San Bernadino, Calif.	13.1	18	–3.3	36
San Diego, Calif.	–6.0	52	–16.0	53
San Francisco, Calif.	–7.3	53	8.0	25
San Jose, Calif.	15.7	14	16.7	14
Santa Ana, Calif.	8.1	29	–17.2	54
Tucson, Ariz.	30.9	5	19.8	11
West	5.3	33	–9.2	40
U.S.	0.0	35	–4.9	35

Note: Index is calculated by taking the difference between standardized measures of a city's revenue capabilities and service responsibilities (*i.e.*, assuming that each city takes equal advantage of its resource base and provides basic public services of equal value) divided by revenue capability. Thus, the index measures the percentage by which resources exceed or fall short of needs.

Source: Helen F. Ladd and John Yinger, *America's Ailing Cities: Fiscal Health and the Design of Urban Policy* (Baltimore: Johns Hopkins University Press, 1989), 210–11.

taxing powers, as well as the fact that most of the West did not have to grapple with urban fiscal problems until quite recently.

Given these fiscal problems, local governments in the region would seem to merit special aid from higher levels of government. Indeed, small rural governments—such as those in the West—clearly benefited from the Nixon administration's New Federalism, which sought to reduce the emphasis on urban-targeted programs through such initiatives as the Revenue Sharing program. The sweeping presidential

Table 13.9   Federal Aid to Local Governments

State	Total General Revenue per capita		Federal Aid per capita	
	1977–78	1984–85	1977–78	1984–85
U.S. Average	$987	$1,484	$99	$91
	State Index of U.S. Average[a]			
Alaska	219	279	186	263
Arizona	129	106	131	85
California	149	124	119	96
Colorado	123	112	105	71
Hawaii	54	39	152	100
Idaho	84	69	77	71
Montana	99	97	88	135
Nevada	160	113	139	81
New Mexico	88	95	131	121
Oregon	121	103	176	163
Utah	90	97	81	86
Washington	107	101	102	116
Wyoming	147	189	95	102
West	139	121	122	105

[a]This index is derived by dividing the state figure by the national average. Thus, the index is 100 when the state and national averages are the same, 115 when local revenues in or federal aid to a state are 15% greater than the national average, and so forth.

Sources: Advisory Commission on Intergovernmental Relations, *Significant Features of Fiscal Federalism, 1987 Edition* (Washington, D.C.: U.S. Government Printing Office, 1987), 48; Advisory Commission on Intergovernmental Relations, *Significant Features of Fiscal Federalism, 1979–80 Edition* (Washington, D.C.: U.S. Government Printing Office, 1980), 78.

victory of Ronald Reagan in 1980 and the ensuing "Reagan revolution" in domestic taxing and spending policies had a major impact on fiscal federalism, but one that worked to the disadvantage of the West. The Reagan administration proved successful at cutting federal aid, which hurt local governments throughout the nation. Moreover, despite Reagan's frontal attack on social programs, political pressures protected individual transfer payments much more than they did direct grants to local governments, such as the Revenue Sharing program that benefited the West.[26]

In fact, the West did lose out in the "Reagan revolution" in intergovernmental relations, as illustrated by the data in Table 13.9, which confirm several of the previous arguments about fiscal stress in the

West. First, local governments in the West are clearly high cost in the sense that they spend more on a per capita basis than do their counterparts in other regions—although this difference narrowed over the 1980s due to budgetary constraints in the West. An obvious exception to this is Hawaii, whose local governments have very low spending because of the concentration of fiscal power at the state level. Second, federal aid as a proportion of local government general revenues fell sharply from 10% to 6% between 1977–78 and 1984–85 for the nation as a whole, indicating that all local communities were forced to rely more upon their own resources—which are usually confined to the narrowest and least progressive tax bases, such as a heavy reliance on the property tax (see Chapter 12). Third, most western states were advantaged by the system of federal transfers in the late 1970s since they received higher-than-average amounts of aid. This advantage was largely lost, however, during President Reagan's first term. Most of the western states experienced significant decreases in their aid flows relative to the national average, and by 1985 the advantage of the West as a whole was a minuscule 5%.[27]

Implications

Local governments in the West, in sum, come in all shapes and sizes. In California, San Bernardino County contains over twenty thousand square miles and Los Angeles County over 7 million people. Yet there also are many municipalities with less than two hundred residents and "paper" special districts with almost no budgets or staff. Thus it is hard to generalize about them. Yet several features appear particularly salient. First, while the local governments are close to the people and perform many basic public services, they are generally far removed from the drama provided by issues of national politics. Thus, they tend to be "invisible" to the public. Second, the conservative and individualistic political culture of the West has resulted in a narrower focus on basic services in their public policy mixes than occurs elsewhere in the nation. Yet these same cultural traits helped stimulate the West's leading role in the progressive movement for municipal reform. Finally, local governments are quite dependent upon higher levels of government in terms of structural and policy limitations and intergovernmental aid.

These characteristics, moreover, serve to exacerbate the fiscal stress on western local governments created by the factors discussed in the last section—boom-bust economic cycles, new cities with restricted revenue powers, high-cost rural governments, and declining inter-governmental aid. The fact that local governments primarily are limited to basic services means that budget cuts visibly affect much of the population. For example, proliferating potholes, uninvestigated burglaries, and long lines for getting license plates quickly draw public ire. However, the "invisible" nature of local government means that it is hard to mobilize the public; and the dependent status of these bodies constrains their actions even more.

Unfortunately, the financial problems facing local governments in the region appear to be a permanent part of the western scene. During the late 1970s, rapid economic growth in much of the West, especially the Sunbelt and the mineral-producing states, and growing federal aid programs produced a prosperity that many thought would become permanent. The economic bust and declining federal support of the 1980s brought rapid disillusionment on that score, however. Thus, in the foreseeable future of the West, local government finances will almost assuredly remain the victim of periodic cyclical crises; and fiscal austerity and cutback management will probably remain dominant themes in the public policies of many local governments.

Notes

1. Daniel J. Elazar, *American Federalism: A View from the States* (New York: Thomas Y. Crowell, 1966), chap. 4. None of the western states, except Nevada, is conceived as having a totally individualistic culture, but the individualistic culture is clearly stronger in the West than in any other part of the nation (see Elazar's classification of states, 97).

2. James J. Lopach, ed., *We the People of Montana . . . The Workings of a Popular Government* (Missoula, Mont.: Mountain Press, 1983), 214–17, 241–53.

3. Carl Abbott, "The Metropolitan Region: Western Cities in the New Urban Era," in Gerald D. Nash and Richard W. Etulain, eds., *The Twentieth-Century West: Historical Interpretations* (Albuquerque: University of New Mexico Press, 1989), 71–73.

4. Thor Swanson, William F. Mullen, John C. Pierce, and Charles H. Seldon, eds., *Political Life in Washington* (Pullman: Washington State University Press, 1985), 168.

5. David C. Maas, "Federalism in Alaska," in Gerald A. McBeath and Thomas A. Morehouse, eds., *Alaska: State Government and Politics* (Fairbanks: University of Alaska Press, 1987), 83–110; Clive S. Thomas and Anne F. Lee, "Alaska and Hawaii in the Federal System: A Comparison of Problems, Per-

ceptions and Perspectives," paper presented at the Annual Meeting of the Western Political Science Association, Eugene, Oregon, March 20–22, 1986; and personal communication, Clive S. Thomas, University of Alaska, Juneau.

6. Case studies of local government in individual states can be found in Mary W. Avery, *Government of Washington State*, rev. ed. (Seattle: University of Washington Press, 1973), chaps. 7 & 8; Bernard L. Hyink, Seymon Brown, and Ernest W. Thacker, *Politics and Government in California*, 11th ed. (New York: Harper & Row, 1985), chap. 9; Lopach, *We the People of Montana*, chap. 7; Robert S. Lorch, *Colorado's Government* (Boulder: Colorado Associated Universities Press, 1983), chaps. 3–6; Maas, "Federalism in Alaska"; and Maurilio E. Vigil, "Local Government in New Mexico," in F. Chris Garcia and Paul L. Hain, eds., *New Mexico Government*, rev. ed. (Albuquerque: University of New Mexico Press, 1981).

7. Personal communication, Paul Hain, University of New Mexico.

8. Robert S. Lorch, *State and Local Politics: The Great Entanglement*, 3rd ed. (Englewood Cliffs, N.J.: Prentice Hall, 1989), chaps. 9 & 10.

9. Swanson *et al.*, *Political Life in Washington*, 163.

10. Arthur H. Miller, "Public Opinion and Regional Political Realignment," in Peter F. Galderisi, Michael S. Lyons, Randy T. Simmons, and John G. Francis, eds., *The Politics of Realignment: Party Change in the Mountain West* (Boulder, Colo.: Westview Press, 1987), 86–90.

11. Carl Abbott, "Western Cities," 71–98.

12. John D. Buenker, *Urban Liberalism and Progressive Reform* (New York: Charles Scribner's Sons, 1978); Richard Hofstadter, *The Age of Reform* (New York: Random House, 1955); George L. Mowry, *The California Progressives* (Berkeley: University of California Press, 1951); and Walter D. Rowley, "The West as Laboratory and Mirror of Reform," in Gerald D. Nash and Richard W. Etulain, eds., *The Twentieth-Century West*, 339–57.

13. Quoted in Lauren S. McKinsey, "Montana Voter Review: City–County Consolidations," paper presented at the Annual Meeting of the Western Social Science Association, Tempe, April 29–May 1, 1976.

14. For discussions of various manifestations of political conservatism in the West, see Galderisi *et al.*, *Politics of Realignment: Party Change in the Mountain West*.

15. Lorch, *State and Local Politics*, 243–47.

16. Personal communication, Nicholas Lovrich, Washington State University.

17. Roy Bahl, *Financing State and Local Governments in the 1980s* (New York: Oxford University Press, 1984).

18. Don D. Detomasi, "Public Service Fiscal Impacts," in Gene F. Summers and Arne Selvik, eds., *Energy Resource Communities* (Madison, Wis.: MJM, 1982), 169–88.

19. Personal communications by Hugh Bone of the University of Washington, Richard Foster of Idaho State University, Nicholas Lovrich of Wash-

ington State University, and Dave Sharpe and Keneth Weaver of Montana State University.

20. For example, the West (which contains 26% of the American states) accounted for 39% of the fuel tax increases, 30% of the alcoholic beverage and cigarette tax increases, but only 13% of the general sales and income tax increases. See John Shannon and Susannah E. Calkins, "Federal and State-Local Spenders Go Their Separate Ways," *Intergovernmental Perspective* 8 (Winter 1983), 27.

21. Paul Hagner and William F. Mullen, "Washington: More Republican, Yes; More Conservative, No," *Social Science Journal* 18 (October 1981), 115–29; and James Klonoski and Ann Aiken, "Oregon: Still Liberal but Slipping," *Social Science Journal* 18 (October 1981), 87–101.

22. Garrey E. Carruthers, Eugene C. Erickson, and Kathryn N. Renner, *Delivery of Rural Community Services: Some Implications and Problems* (Las Cruces, N.M.: New Mexico State University Agricultural Experiment Station, 1975); Paul Eberts and Marwan Khawaja, "Causal Factors Affecting Local Fiscal Stress in U.S. Northeast Counties," *Cornell Rural Sociology Bulletin Series*, 149 (June 1987); William F. Fox, *Size Economies in Local Government Services: A Review* (Washington, D.C.: U.S. Department of Agriculture, 1980); The Report of the President's Task Force on Rural Development, *A New Life for the Country* (Washington, D.C.: U.S. Government Printing Office, 1970); and Jim Seroka, ed., *Rural Public Administration: Problems and Prospects* (Westport, Conn.: Greenwood Press, 1986).

23. Terry Nichols Clark, "The Irish Ethic and the Spirit of Patronage," *Ethnicity* 2 (December 1975), 305–59; and Terry Nichols Clark and Lorna Crowley Ferguson, *City Money: Political Processes, Fiscal Strain, and Retrenchment* (New York: Columbia University Press, 1983), chaps. 5 & 6.

24. Helen F. Ladd and John Yinger, *America's Ailing Cities: Fiscal Health and the Design of Urban Policies* (Baltimore: Johns Hopkins University Press, 1989), chap. 9.

25. *Ibid.*, chaps. 3 & 6.

26. Paul R. Dommel, "Trends in Intergovernmental Relations: Getting Less, but Enjoying It More (Maybe)," in Norman Walzer and David L. Chicoine, eds., *Financing State and Local Governments in the 1980s: Issues and Trends* (Cambridge: Oelgeschlager, Gunn & Hain, 1981), 91–108; and George E. Peterson, "Federalism and the States: An Experiment in Decentralization," in John L. Palmer and Isabel Sawhill, eds., *The Reagan Record: An Assessment of America's Changing Priorities* (Cambridge: Ballinger, 1984), 217–59.

27. These themes are developed in much more detail in Cal Clark and Janet Clark, "Federal Aid to Local Governments in the West: An Irony of the Reagan Revolution," *Policy Studies Review* forthcoming, 1990.

14

STATE AND LOCAL GOVERNMENT INSTITUTIONS AND EDUCATION POLICY

Kenneth K. Wong

*P*UBLIC EDUCATION CONSTITUTES AN IMPORTANT POL-icy domain in the American states. State and local spending on elementary and secondary schools often amounts to one-third of all government expenditures. School districts across the states are hiring thousands of teachers to educate the future generations of this nation. Effective schooling is often seen as the best way to combat such major and pervasive social problems as poverty and use of drugs. As a major federal report recently pointed out, "Our Nation's schools . . . are routinely called on to provide solutions to personal, social, and political problems that the home and other institutions either will not or cannot resolve."[1]

This chapter examines educational policy in the western states. We will focus exclusively on public elementary and secondary education and will not consider post-secondary policy. The analysis begins with a discussion of the socioeconomic trends and the political-administrative context within which the western public schools operate. Differences and similarities between the West and the nation will be discussed. It should be noted that most of the socioeconomic trends in public education in the West are substantially affected by the presence of one state—namely, California. The approach here is first to compare the national trend to that of the entire western region so as not to differentiate variations within this group of thirteen states. This aggregate comparison will be followed by a discussion of inter-state differences.

The second part of this chapter will pay particular attention to the politics of three major school-policy areas, namely, school finance reform, programs that promote educational equity and the current back-to-basics movement. In each of these areas, governmental institutions and political processes have played a major role. While state court rulings have guided the restructuring of school finance, the federal government has played an active role in expanding services for special-needs children. More recently, state legislatures have had to cope with fiscal pressure generated from the taxpayer movement.

The Socioeconomic Context

ENROLLMENT TRENDS

Public school enrollment in the western states continues to decline in the mid-1980s. However, this enrollment reduction in the West is much slower than in the nation as a whole. While the U.S. as a whole has lost 11% of its public school population since 1977, the thirteen western states have experienced a modest 3% loss as indicated in Table 14.1. As a result, enrollment in the West as a proportion of the entire nation has jumped from 18.4% to 20.2%. In the mid-1980s, one out of five students was attending school in the West. While seven western states suffered losses, six states gained in school population. These enrollment changes range from a 28% increase in Utah to a 9% decline in Montana. The absence of a sharp enrollment decline in the West is due to the fact that none of the seven declining states have experienced a loss of over 10% of their enrollment, while, of the six states that have gained enrollment, Alaska, Utah, and Wyoming have experienced significant jumps.

Table 14.1   Trends in Public School Enrollment in Western States, 1977–86

	1977–76 (in nearest 000s)			1985–86 (in nearest 000s)			Percentage Change, 1977–86		
	Total	Elementary	Secondary	Total	Elementary	Secondary	Total	Elementary	Secondary
Alaska	91	65	26	106	77	29	16.5%	18.5%	11.5%
Arizona	503	354	149	508	351	157	1.0	-0.8	5.4
California	4,380	2,940	1,440	4,144	2,836	1,307	-5.4	-3.5	-9.2
Colorado	570	385	185	549	377	173	-3.7	-2.1	-6.5
Hawaii	175	118	57	164	111	52	-6.3	-5.9	-8.8
Idaho	200	136	64	210	151	59	5.0	11.0	-7.8
Montana	171	113	58	155	109	46	-9.4	-3.5	-20.7
Nevada	142	96	46	152	103	50	7.0	7.3	8.7
New Mexico	285	192	93	272	195	77	-4.6	1.6	-17.2
Oregon	475	317	158	445	304	141	-6.3	-4.1	-10.8
Utah	314	216	98	403	299	104	28.3	38.4	6.1
Washington	781	524	257	739	500	239	-5.4	-4.6	-7.0
Wyoming	91	62	28	104	76	28	14.3	22.6	0.0
Western States	8,178	5,518	2,659	7,951	5,489	2,462	-2.8	-0.5	-7.4
(as percent of U.S. Total)	(18.4%)	(18.4%)	(18.6%)	(20.2%)	(20.4%)	(19.8%)			
U.S. Total	44,335	30,012	14,323	39,350	26,920	12,430	-11.2	-10.3	-13.2

Sources: 1976–77 data from National Center for Education Statistics, *Digest of Education Statistics, 1977–78*, table 29, "Enrollment in Public Elementary and Secondary Day Schools by Level and by State: Fall 1976 and Fall 1977" (Washington, D.C.). 1985–86 estimated figures from NCES, *Digest of Education Statistics, 1985–86*, table 25, "Enrollment in Public Elementary and Secondary Schools, by Level and by State: Fall 1981 to Fall 1985" (Washington, D.C.). Percentage calculations are the author's.

For the West as well as the nation as a whole, much of the decline in student population occurs at the secondary level. Over the past ten years, the thirteen western states have lost 7% of their secondary student enrollment—only about half as much as that of the U.S. as a whole. Altogether, eight states have experienced significant decline in their secondary population. As shown in Table 14.1, Montana lost the most—about one out of five of its high school group. This was followed by New Mexico (17%), Oregon (11%), California and Hawaii (both 9%), Idaho (8%) and Washington and Colorado (both 7%). Conversely, among the four states that have gained in secondary enrollment, only in Alaska has the growth rate exceeded 10%.

The trend in elementary enrollment is somewhat different. The West, unlike the nation, has experienced only a modest 0.5% decline. Though seven states are losing some of their elementary population, only Hawaii exceeds a 5% decline. In contrast, four states have enjoyed sharp increases as shown in Table 14.1. Utah has had a 38% growth, followed by Wyoming's 23%, Alaska's 19% and Idaho's 11%. As a result, the western share of the nation's elementary enrollment has increased from 18.4% to 20.4%. In short, the West has had a much slower rate of enrollment decline than the nation as a whole.

Public schools in the West, like those of the nation as a whole, have a visible minority population. In the 1980s, minorities constituted one-fourth of the student body in the western states. There are, of course, variations among the thirteen states, as indicated in Table 14.2. Nonwhites in Hawaii, New Mexico and California exceed 40% of public school enrollments. Of course, the Asian/Pacific Islander group is the majority in Hawaii. In contrast, Utah, Wyoming, Idaho and Oregon have a very modest minority presence. While California seems to maintain a multiracial school community, most western states have an uneven share in the size of various racial/ethnic groups.

The states also differ in the size of their minority groups. The West has a much smaller black population: 3% as compared to the nation's 16% in 1981. Both California and Nevada have a sizable black student population; while in Idaho, Montana, Utah and Wyoming, blacks are virtually absent. The Hispanic enrollment suggests a different pattern. This group, which constitutes 11% of the student population in the West, exceeds the 8% national average. Hispanics are particularly concentrated in New Mexico, where they constitute almost half of the entire student body. California, Arizona and Colorado also have a substantial Hispanic enrollment. Very few Hispanic students are found in Alaska, Hawaii and Montana.

Table 14.2   Enrollment by Racial and Ethnic Groups in Western States, 1981

	% White	% Black	% Hispanic	% Asian/ Pacific Islander	% American Indian/ Alaska Native	% Total Minority
Alaska	71.6	3.9	1.6	2.3	20.6	28.4
Arizona	66.3	4.2	24.2	1.1	4.1	33.7
California	57.1	10.1	25.3	6.6	0.8	42.9
Colorado	77.9	4.6	15.3	1.7	0.5	22.1
Hawaii	24.8	1.4	2.0	71.4	0.2	75.2
Idaho	91.8	0.5	4.6	1.0	2.1	8.2
Montana	87.9	0.3	1.2	0.8	9.8	12.1
Nevada	81.1	9.5	5.2	2.2	2.0	18.9
New Mexico	43.0	2.2	46.5	0.6	7.8	57.0
Oregon	91.5	2.1	2.6	2.2	1.7	8.5
Utah	92.7	0.5	3.5	1.5	1.8	7.3
Washington	85.9	3.4	4.0	3.7	3.0	14.1
Wyoming	92.5	0.7	5.3	0.4	1.0	7.5
Western States	74.2	3.3	10.9	7.3	4.3	25.8
U.S. Total	73.3	16.1	8.0	1.9	0.8	26.7

Source: National Center for Education Statistics, *Digest of Education Statistics, 1985–86* (Washington, D.C.), table 33, p. 39.

The sharpest difference between the West and the nation as a whole exists in the Asian and the Native American groups (see Chapter 8). The western school population consists of over 7% Asian and 4% Native Americans. Hawaii's Asian/Pacific Islander students constitute over 70% of its public school enrollment. Except for California, the Asian enrollment remains quite modest in the other western states. At the same time, Native Americans are highly concentrated in Alaska, and have a visible presence in both Montana and New Mexico.

THE INSTRUCTIONAL STAFF

Consistent with enrollment decline, the number of teachers has been reduced from 382,000 to 365,000 in the western states since 1977. Much of the decrease can be attributed to California alone. This 4.4% reduction in the teaching force has exceeded the national average, despite the fact that the country as a whole has suffered a greater decline in enrollment.

To be sure, changes in the teaching staff have varied among the thirteen states, as illustrated in Table 14.3. As could be expected, much of the increase in the number of teachers has occurred in the states that have gained enrollment. For example, Wyoming has increased its teaching staff by 41% in response to a 14% rise in enrollment. Expansion in the instructional staff has also occurred in Alaska (28%), Nevada (23%), Utah (21%), Arizona (12%) and Idaho (6%). Despite their declining enrollment, New Mexico, Washington and Oregon continued to hire additional teachers. The remaining four states generally responded to student reduction by cutting their instructional staff. For example, teacher reduction exceeded 10% in California and Hawaii between 1977 and 1984.

Partly due to enrollment decline and partly because of teacher retention, the pupil-to-teacher ratio has declined. The pupil-per-teacher count in the western states decreased from 21.2 to 19.7 between 1977 and 1984. This trend is quite similar to that of the nation as a whole as suggested in Table 14.3. Of the thirteen western states, only California and Hawaii, both of which have undertaken substantial teacher reduction, have experienced an increase in the pupil-to-teacher ratio.

On the whole, teachers' salaries in the West have been slightly ahead of the nation. In 1985, the average teacher salary in the West was $24,850, which is about 6% higher than the national average. To be sure, variations exist among the western states. Alaska offers by far the highest salary, and while most western states cluster around the mid-twenties, Idaho was the only western state that had an av-

Table 14.3 Number of Teachers and Enrollment per Teacher in Public Schools

	Total Number of FTE[a] Teachers			Number of Pupils per Teacher		1985 Average Teacher Salary	1985 Teacher Salaries as % of Total School Spending
	1976–77	1983–84	% Change	1976–77	1983–84		
Alaska	4,475	5,747	28.4%	20.4	16.2	$39,751	25.1%
Arizona	23,482	26,268	11.9	21.4	19.2	23,380	40.7
California	204,000	174,290	-14.6	21.5	23.5	26,300	31.1
Colorado	28,452	28,421	-0.1	20.0	19.1	24,456	37.6
Hawaii	7,914	7,007	-11.5	22.1	23.2	24,628	34.7
Idaho	9,277	9,847	6.1	21.6	21.0	19,700	40.1
Montana	9,580	9,479	-1.1	17.8	16.2	21,705	33.9
Nevada	5,995	7,366	22.9	23.7	20.4	22,520	36.3
New Mexico	12,887	14,532	12.8	22.1	18.6	22,064	30.1
Oregon	23,942	24,409	1.9	19.8	18.3	24,889	35.5
Utah	12,952	15,650	20.8	24.3	24.2	21,307	33.8
Washington	33,690	34,757	3.2	23.2	21.2	25,610	32.2
Wyoming	4,991	7,010	40.5	18.2	14.4	26,709	30.6
Western States (as percent of U.S. Total)	381,637 (17.4%)	364,783 (17.2%)	-4.4	21.2	19.7	24,848	34.7
U.S. Total	2,193,000	2,125,756	-3.1	20.2	18.5	23,546	36.6

[a]FTE = Full-time equivalent.

Sources: National Center for Education Statistics, *Digest of Education Statistics, 1977–78,* table 66, p. 66; National Center for Education Statistics, *Digest of Education Statistics, 1985–86,* table 39, p. 45; C. Emily Feistritzer, *The Condition of Teaching: A State by State Analysis, 1985* (Princeton, N.J.: Carnegie Foundation, 1985).

erage teacher salary below $20,000 in 1985. Despite interstate differ-
ences in pay scale, only Arizona and Idaho spent over 40% of their
school funds on teachers' salaries. In most western states, teachers
salaries amount to about one-third of the total school expenditure.

SCHOOL SPENDING

School spending on a per pupil basis has continued to increase
into the mid-1980s. As Table 14.4 shows, even when inflation is taken
into account, western states increased their per pupil current expenditure by 27% between 1976 and 1983. This rate of increase was more
than the national average. Alaska and Wyoming, two states that have
gained enrollment, show the biggest increase—an almost 50% jump.
More limited gains occurred in Utah, Arizona, Idaho and California.
Of these, only California has seen a decline in its pupil population.

Nevertheless, these persistent gains in per pupil spending have
not exceeded the growth in the states' earning capacity. Total school
expenditure as a portion of personal income actually fell from 6.2%
to 5.7% in the western states between 1977 and 1983. Similar declines
also occurred in the nation as a whole. Only three western states
(Alaska, Oregon and Wyoming) increased their school spending when
measured against the state's personal income. Moreover, in 1983,
public school expenditures constituted about one-fourth of all state
and local governmental spending in the western states as a group.
In Alaska, Hawaii and Nevada, school spending amounted to less
than one-fifth of all governmental expenditures. On the other hand,
in Montana public education expenses amounted to almost 30% of
all governmental spending.

INCREASE IN STATE SUPPORT

Over the past twenty years, state governments have begun to
assume a primary fiscal responsibility in public education. Equally
significant is the fact that local governments have substantially reduced their contribution to public schools. At the same time, the
federal role remains limited. The emergence of the state role has
occurred quite rapidly in the West.

By 1983, state governments in the West contributed 58% of school
expense as compared to only 48% in the nation as a whole (see Table
14.5). In contrast, while local governments at the national aggregate
level assumed 45% of the educational costs, that figure was only 34%
in the western region. In other words, the fiscal responsibility in
school policy has been restructured since the mid-1960s when local

Table 14.4 School Expenditure Trends in the Western States

| | Current Expenditure Per Average Daily Attendance | | | | | Total School Expenditure as % of Personal Income | | Elementary/Secondary School Spending as % of All State/Local Functions |
| | 1975–76 | | 1982–83 | | Percentage Change 1976–83 | 1976–66 | 1982–83 | |
	Current $	Constant $ᵃ	Current $	Constant $ᵃ				
Alaska	$3,009	$1,658	$7,325	$2,469	49%	7.8%	8.0%	17.1%
Arizona	1,420	782	2,524	851	9	6.0	4.6	25.5
California	1,510	832	2,733	921	11	5.3	3.9	21.2
Colorado	1,456	802	3,171	1,069	33	5.8	4.4	27.7
Hawaii	1,616	890	3,239	1,092	23	5.0	4.7	17.1
Idaho	1,125	620	2,052	692	12	6.2	5.1	24.8
Montana	1,586	874	3,289	1,108	27	7.0	6.9	29.7
Nevada	1,354	746	2,613	881	18	4.9	3.9	19.2
New Mexico	1,284	707	2,901	978	38	7.2	6.9	26.9
Oregon	1,786	984	3,504	1,181	20	5.4	5.9	26.3
Utah	1,172	646	2,013	678	5	7.4	6.3	28.2
Washington	1,546	852	3,211	1,082	27	5.4	4.9	24.2
Wyoming	1,670	920	4,045	1,363	48	7.3	8.1	27.4
Western States	1,580	871	3,278	1,105	27	6.2	5.7	24.3
U.S. Total	1,509	831	2,948	993	19	5.4	4.6	24.3

ᵃ1967 = 1.00.

Sources: National Center for Education Statistics, *Digest of Education Statistics 1977–1978,* table 73, p. 73, and table 72, p. 72; National Center for Education Statistics, *Digest of Education Statistics 1985–1986,* table 75, p. 86, table 74, p. 85, and table 15, p. 17.

Table 14.5   School Revenue by Sources and by State in Percentages, 1964, 1976, 1983

	1964				1976				1983			
	Total in million $	Federal %	State %	Local %	Total in million $	Federal %	State %	Local %	Total in million $	Federal %	State %	Local %
Alaska	40.4	26.5	50.7	22.8	254.5	21.4	61.9	16.6	607.1	7.7	78.0	14.3
Arizona	180.7	7.2	31.0	59.9	774.7	10.3	45.7	44.0	1,257.2	9.6	58.4	32.0
California	2,592.0	3.5	37.0	58.9	7,993.3	8.3	42.4	49.3	11,210.6	8.8	68.1	23.1
Colorado	250.0	6.4	23.4	71.1	923.8	7.4	40.7	51.9	1,900.2	4.5	40.3	55.2
Hawaii	72.0	12.0	67.6	20.4	268.8	12.8	87.2	—	497.8	11.9	87.9	0.1
Idaho	68.8	8.1	30.7	61.2	239.5	9.1	48.2	42.7	413.5	9.1	59.1	31.7
Montana	85.1	6.5	25.4	68.1	276.2	9.4	50.9	39.7	536.2	7.8	48.8	43.3
Nevada	51.2	7.4	49.8	42.7	198.9	8.3	37.5	54.2	375.3	5.4	49.6	45.0
New Mexico	132.5	10.5	68.5	20.9	371.0	23.0	59.4	17.5	834.1	12.4	74.8	12.8
Oregon	261.7	2.5	30.4	67.1	843.7	7.8	26.1	66.2	1,505.6	5.9	31.0	63.1
Utah	133.8	6.0	49.6	44.2	385.4	9.1	54.6	36.3	884.3	6.0	54.0	40.1
Washington	413.5	5.0	61.2	33.8	1,232.0	9.2	61.1	29.7	2,524.9	6.2	74.8	19.0
Wyoming	45.3	5.2	41.3	53.4	160.3	7.1	30.9	61.9	566.7	3.1	28.8	68.1
Western States	4,327	8.2	43.6	48.2	13,922.1	11.0	49.7	39.3	23,113.5	7.6	58.0	34.4
U.S. Total	20,544.2	4.4	39.3	56.3	70,802.8	8.8	43.9	47.4	116,912.0	7.1	48.3	44.6

Sources: National Center for Education Statistics, *Digest of Education Statistics 1967*, table 66, p. 55; National Center for Education Statistics, *Digest of Education Statistics 1977–78*, table 66, p. 66; National Center for Education Statistics, *Digest of Education Statistics 1985–86*, table 70, p. 81.

communities exceeded their state governments in financial support for public schools. In the 1960s, only four western state governments provided over 50% of the school revenue. This figure increased to six during the 1970s, and further jumped to eight by 1983.

These dramatic shifts are uneven among the thirteen western states, however. Schools in Wyoming, Oregon and Colorado continue to rely heavily on local property tax revenue. Wyoming experienced the sharpest drop in state support, from 41% to 29% between 1964 and 1983. Another dramatic example is Oregon, where the property tax constitutes eighty-seven cents of every dollar of locally raised revenue on a per pupil basis.[2] In contrast, state governments have played a primary fiscal role in Hawaii, Alaska, New Mexico and Washington State since the 1960s. The highly centralized pattern in Hawaii is partly due to the state's imperial tradition. In six states, there is a gradual shift toward a larger state role. These include Arizona, California, Idaho, Montana, Utah and (during the 1970s and the 1980s) Nevada.

Unlike that of local and state governments, the federal role in education finance remains limited. During the 1950s and the early 1960s, much of the federal funding was channeled through the impact aid program, in which local districts were compensated for the presence of property-tax-exempted military bases and federally owned properties. For example, Alaska gained a sharp increase in federal support in the early 1960s, shortly after the state legislature voted to accept federal impact aid.[3] States also received supplementary support for vocational training projects. During this period, the western states as a group received 8% of their school revenues from federal grants.

Since the mid-1960s, federal grants have been significantly expanded into a variety of programs for special-needs children. Among the major federal programs were compensatory aid (Title I, now Chapter I, of the Elementary and Secondary Education Act), bilingual projects, Native American education, school desegregation grants and special education.[4] But even in the period of federal activism in the 1970s, federal assistance accounted for only one-tenth of educational cost in the western states. However, both Alaska and New Mexico received substantial federal support. For example, the Los Alamos district in New Mexico received 50% of its funds from two federal sources: the Atomic Energy Commission and the Impact Aid Programs. Nonetheless, by the early 1980s federal funds had diminished to less than 8% in the western states overall. These federal dollars exceeded 10% in only two states—namely, Hawaii and New Mexico—and remained very limited in Wyoming and Colorado. Wyoming has a tradition of viewing federal school grants with caution. Two years after the National Defense Education Act (NDEA, 1958) was enacted, the Wyoming legislature reversed its earlier decision and pulled the state out of this program. It was not until 1965 that a majority of the legislature permitted the state to receive federal NDEA funds and subsequent federal grants. Wyoming thus became the last state in the union to participate in the NDEA.[5] Similarly, Colorado has maintained a strong sense of localism, drawing on the state's culture of "rugged individualism and self-reliance."[6] In short, the most significant fiscal trend in public education is the persistent rise in the state role and the concomitant decline in both local and federal involvement.

The Administrative and Political Context

Centralization is the dominant trend in the organization of public education. At the local level, just as hundreds of small districts are being consolidated into fewer large districts, school policies are increasingly formulated by the school superintendent and a few top professional administrators.[7] At the same time, fewer and fewer school issues are left in the hands of local school-board members. Instead, expanding state educational agencies and increasingly professionalized state legislatures are exerting more extensive control over school policymaking.

TENDENCIES TOWARD CENTRALIZATION

Looking for a more economical way of providing uniform educational services, states have moved toward the consolidation of school districts. Smaller districts were said to have difficulties in retaining high-quality teachers, upgrading school facilities and maintaining an enriched curriculum. At the same time, these districts often required a much higher per pupil cost, thereby imposing a heavier burden on the local property taxpayers.[8] Consequently, the number of school districts was reduced from 128,000 in 1930 to 71,000 in 1951 for the nation as a whole. The states' efforts to contain school costs by consolidating smaller districts continued in the postwar decades. In the 1950s and 1960s, most state legislatures enacted laws to reduce the number of school districts, thereby providing better service coordination and cutting administrative costs. As a result, the number of school districts has continued to be substantially reduced.

Over the past three decades, 4,700 districts have been eliminated in the western states, as indicated in Table 14.6. By 1984, the West

Table 14.6   District Consolidation in Western States

	Number of School Districts			Percent of Change	
	1952	1967	1984	1952–67	1967–84
Alaska	108	27	53	–75.0%	96.3%
Arizona	329	298	221	–9.4	–25.8
California	2,044	1,187	1,030	–41.9	–13.2
Colorado	1,333	183	181	–86.3	–1.1
Hawaii	1	1	1	0.0	0.0
Idaho	281	117	115	–58.4	–1.7
Montana	1,386	873	561	–37.0	–35.7
Nevada	177	17	17	–90.4	0.0
New Mexico	107	90	89	–15.9	–1.1
Oregon	995	390	309	–60.8	–20.8
Utah	40	40	40	0.0	0.0
Washington	560	360	299	–35.7	–16.9
Wyoming	313	173	49	–44.7	–71.7
Western States	7,674	3,756	2,965	–51.1	–21.1
U.S. Total	71,117	23,464	15,747	–67.0	–32.9

Sources: 1951–52 data from Council of State Governments, *The Book of the States, 1982–83*, vol. 24, table 7; 1966–67 data from National Center for Education Statistics, *Digest of Education Statistics 1967*, table 57, p. 44; 1983–84 data from National Center for Education Statistics, *Digest of Education Statistics 1985–86*, table 53, p. 59.

had fewer than three thousand school districts, each of which holds an average of twenty-seven hundred students. These districts range from the half-million enrollment in the Los Angeles Unified School District down to hundreds of districts with fewer than a hundred pupils. As noted above, district consolidation continued rapidly during the 1950s and 60s, but has since slowed down. The rate of district reduction in the West is slower now than the national trend. Between 1951 and 1967, while the nation reduced its 71,100 districts by two-thirds, the western region trimmed its 7,700 districts by only one-half. During this period, the sharpest decline occurred in Nevada, Colorado, Alaska, Oregon and Idaho. Following the passage of the School District Organization Act of 1959, Colorado consolidated 950 districts into 180 districts in an eight-year period. The Oregon 1957 School District Reorganization Act succeeded in bringing down its 700 districts by almost half in a ten-year period.[9] In recent years, district reduction has slowed down in most of the western states. Between 1967 and 1984, only 21% of the region's school districts were eliminated. While Wyoming and Montana continued to undertake major cuts, Alaska has actually increased its number of districts by almost 100% since the late 1960s, after having cut them by 75% in the 1950s.

Both district consolidation and the diminishing local fiscal role in public education are evidence of a more assertive state role in school matters. In his examination of thirty-six school-policy areas in the early 1970s, Wirt proposed the concept of a centralization score in assessing the state government's role in all fifty states.[10] The scale ranges from the lowest level of centralization (high local autonomy) with a score of zero (0.0) to the highest level of state policy control with a score of six (6.0). The average score for all fifty states was 3.56, which suggests that the state government generally exercises more control than local districts over school affairs. This pattern comes as no surprise. From a constitutional perspective, local districts are seen as agencies of the state educational system. The states enjoy almost complete control over personnel, compulsory attendance, accreditation, curriculum, graduation standards, and such housekeeping matters as calendar, records, and accounting procedures. Localities generally maintain more discretion over district organization, guidance and counseling, pupil-teacher ratios, and extracurricular activities.[11]

Despite its populist political culture, the West on the average has a slightly higher centralization score (3.62) than the national average. Interestingly, the West includes both the most centralized state (*i.e.,* the one-district state of Hawaii, with a score of 6.0) and the state that allows for the greatest local autonomy (*i.e.,* Wyoming, with a score of 1.86). Washington, Oregon, Colorado, New Mexico and California also had higher centralization indices than the national average. In contrast, a greater degree of local autonomy was found in Alaska, Arizona, Idaho, Montana, Nevada and Utah.

Growth in administrative activities of public schools has not brought about as sharp an increase in spending on administrative purposes in the West as in other regions of the nation (see Table 14.7). While all states increased their administrative spending in public education by 73%, the western states' spending increased by only 21% in real dollars between 1964 and 1980, a period generally recognized as one of major growth in the educational bureaucracy. As a result, the western portion of the nation's school administrative expenses dropped from 23% to 16% during this period. Of the thirteen western states, Alaska experienced by far the greatest increase, a 580% rise in administrative spending, while California actually reduced its admin-

Table 14.7   Public School Spending for Administrative Purposes in Constant Dollars

	1963–64 (in $ 000s)	1979–80 (in $ 000s)	1964–80 % Change
Alaska	3,030	20,638	580%
Arizona	6,135	14,507	136
California	120,511	81,531	–32
Colorado	8,905	24,395	174
Hawaii	3,321	9,516	187
Idaho	2,629	4,061	54
Montana	4,281	5,038	18
Nevada	1,404	2,730	94
New Mexico	4,409	6,194	41
Oregon	10,250	19,470	90
Utah	3,127	3,714	19
Washington	12,908	23,783	71
Wyoming	2,377	8,186	220
Western States	171,421	184,449	21
U.S. Total	744,770	801,374	73

Note: 1967 = 1.00.

Sources: National Center for Education Statistics, Digest of Education Statistics 1967, p. 59; National Center for Education Statistics, Revenue and Expenditure for Elementary and Secondary Education, Fiscal Year 1980, p. 20.

istrative expense by one-third, in large part due to the 1978 passage of a tax limitation measure, Proposition 13. Arizona, Colorado, Hawaii, Nevada, Oregon, Washington, New Mexico and Wyoming all showed significant increases. At the same time, from 1964 to 1980 administrative activities remained fairly stable in Idaho, Montana and Utah.

SOURCES OF ACCOUNTABILITY AND RESPONSIVENESS

These centralizing tendencies notwithstanding, policymaking in education is subject to numerous sources of accountability which allow for citizen participation, interest group input, and political response.

The selection of state school boards and the state chief school officers (e.g., commissioner of education, superintendent of public instruction) is largely determined by the electorate in most western states. The methods of selection of chief school officers and the state school board in the western states have undergone changes in the postwar decades. In comparing the methods of selection between the late 1940s and the early 1980s, several trends emerge. First, a greater number of state school boards is elected by the people, although several states continue to allow the governor to appoint the board members. Second, more chief school officers are now appointed by the state school board, fewer are directly elected by the people, and none are appointed by the governor.

As a result, by 1981 two sets of selection systems were prevalent in the western states. The first system has a popularly elected board that in turn appoints the chief school officer. This system is found in five states: Colorado, Hawaii, Nevada, New Mexico and Utah. The second consists of a governor-appointed board, whose members have to work with a popularly elected chief school officer. This system is found in another five states: Arizona, California, Montana, Oregon and Wyoming. Only in Alaska are both the board and the chief school officer appointed—the board by the governor and, at least in theory, the commissioner of education by the board. In practice, the board rarely chooses anyone the governor does not want. Idaho is the only western state where both the board and the officer are popularly elected; while in Washington State voters elect the school officer, and local school boards from congressional districts choose the members of the state board. These current selection practices indicate major changes over the past several decades. In 1947, for example, only Alaska and Hawaii (both were territories at that time) had an appointed chief school officer, and the remaining eleven states elected the top school official. Since then, voters in five states have delegated to the state board the selection of the top administrator. Under this arrangement, the professional administrator is expected to develop a better working relationship with the board. While the public increasingly prefers a competent professional as the chief school officer, voters continue to view the board as a representative body.

The educational policy process provides numerous access points for interest group participation. In this regard, it is important to note that the pressure group system in public education has gone through various phases of development in the American states. During the 1950s and 1960s, state educational affairs were largely dominated by coalitions of major professional and occupational groups with a broad range of policy concerns from wages to curriculum. Among the most prominent were the two sets of teacher unions: the state teachers' associations (affiliates of the National Education Association, or NEA) and state teachers' federations (affiliates of the American Federation of Teachers, or AFT). Other organized interests included state school board associations, state school administrators' associations, and classified school employees' groups.[12] To the extent that these different groups formed a broad alliance, state legislatures had to deal with a "monolithic" set of educational interests, as Laurence Iannaccone once observed.[13]

Since the mid-1960s, interests among these groups have become more diverse. As an increasing number of states legalized collective bargaining for teachers, rivalry intensified between the NEA affiliates and the AFT affiliates, which were fighting for representational rights. The AFT and its affiliates continued to maintain a stronghold in big-city districts, enjoying a half-million membership, and retaining sole collective bargaining rights in major eastern cities such as New York, Chicago, Detroit, Cleveland, Philadelphia and Washington, D.C.[14] Since the 1960s, the NEA and its affiliates have gained their membership in mid- and small-sized districts. By the late 1970s, NEA represented about 87% of the public school teachers. NEA's decisions to move into contract negotiation and to adopt sanctions as a means to resolve administration-teacher disputes during the early 1960s contributed to its growth in subsequent years. For example, sanctions were applied to Utah in the mid-1960s that led to the beginning of NEA-sponsored work stoppages.[15] The organization thus became more involved in state and local policy, and by the late 1960s its membership was responsible for one-third of all teachers' work stoppages. In the early 1970s, NEA and its state and local chapters began contributing to political campaigns. The California teachers' unions combined ranked second only to the state's powerful oil industries in campaign contributions in the 1974 election.[16] In Oregon, teachers' unions topped the list of PAC contributions to statewide elections during the 1980s. Where taxpayers organized campaigns to place limits on spending and taxing, teacher groups and other public employee unions have often formed the core of a counter-coalition.[17]

Of the 1.7 million NEA members, over 356,000 (or 21%) come from the thirteen western states.[18] In Hawaii, Oregon, Utah and Washington, at least 70% of the professional, instructional, and administrative staff belong to the NEA. In contrast, less than 30% of the school staff in New Mexico joined the NEA–New Mexico in the mid-1980s. Among the thirteen western states, the California Teachers Association has the largest membership, over 164,000, whereas NEA–Alaska has only 5,700 members.

During the late 1960s and the early 1970s, more vigorous lobbying activities came from special-needs groups. Advocacy organizations for the handicapped, migrant children, and minorities primarily focused on school policy that affected particular disadvantaged groups and targeted their efforts to bring about reform through new legislation or court action.[19] As Murphy described these interest group activities, "they have helped to raise the consciousness of various groups about their needs; they have helped to change common perceptions about the scope of governmental responsibility for solving social problems; they have helped to spur the growth of special interest groups in the states."[20] As will be discussed below, state court decisions initiated by the disadvantaged have brought about more equitable distribution of state school funds, new categorical services for the needy, and an expansion of equal opportunity regulations. By the 1980s, however, spending for special-needs programs had slowed down, in part due to taxpayer pressure for fiscal retrenchment.

Equity in School Finance

To a certain extent, the increase in state fiscal support for public education has been facilitated by events beyond the control of the state legislative and executive branches. Throughout the 1970s, state courts put pressure on state legislatures to bring about a more equitable school finance system. In the late 1970s and the early 1980s, taxpayer opposition to increases in local property taxes and to an overall rise in governmental spending imposed a new set of fiscal constraints on local districts. The shift from local to state funding was designed to relieve the property tax burden. Finally, the proliferation of federally funded school programs for the needy had a stimulative effect in encouraging both matching and supplemental state contributions. During the early 1980s, however, a greater state role in special programs was needed to replace diminishing federal funds.

The movement toward reforming the statewide school finance system started in 1967 in California when John Serrano and other parents, concerned about poor school services for their children in the Los Angeles area, brought a class action suit against the state of California.[21] In the landmark ruling of *Serrano v. Priest* (1971), often referred to as *Serrano I,* the California supreme court handed down a 6-to-1 decision in favor of the parents. According to this ruling, significant interdistrict disparities in school spending due to uneven distribution of taxable wealth violated the equal protection provisions of the state constitution. In this case, a sharp disparity in school spending existed between the wealthy Beverly Hills district and the nearby Baldwin Park district. While the former had a tax rate that was less than half as much as the latter, it was able to come up with twice as many school dollars on a per student basis during 1968–69. As the court opinion stated, "affluent districts can have their cake and eat it too; they can provide a high quality education for their children while paying lower taxes. Poor districts, by contrast, have no cake at all."[22] Shortly after the court decision, the California legislature adopted what became the first of several school finance reform plans enacted throughout the 1970s.[23] At the same time, similar charges were filed by parent plaintiffs in several other states.

Within two years, however, *Serrano I* was questioned by a U.S. Supreme Court ruling on a case in Texas. In *Rodriguez v. San Antonio* (1973), the U.S. high court in a 5-to-4 decision reversed a federal district court ruling. It concluded that since education does not constitute a fundamental interest under the U.S. Constitution, the state can choose to preserve local control by not interfering in interdistrict fiscal inequities. In line with *Rodriguez*, the state supreme courts in Arizona (1973), Washington (1974), Oregon (1976), Colorado (1976) and Idaho (1975) ruled that the statewide system did not violate the state constitution despite interdistrict funding inequity.

Despite *Rodriguez*, the pressure for a more equitable allocation of state school funds continued. Among the most significant state rulings that rejected the local control notion in *Rodriguez* was *Serrano II* (1976). Following *Serrano I*, all factual evidence went through a vigorous examination process. It took five years for the California high court to reach its final ruling. In *Serrano II*, the California supreme court upheld its earlier decision in favor of the parents. In the post–*Serrano II* period, the state high courts in Washington and Wyoming also ruled as unconstitutional the state school financing system. Costly services for special-needs students were brought to the states' attention by big-city districts in several legal suits, including *Seattle v. Washington*.

By 1978, over twenty states had adopted reforms in their school finance system nationwide. In the West, seven states enacted funding reform during the peak of the reform years of the mid-1970s. Both California (1973) and Washington State (1977) implemented reforms in response to the state high court ruling of unconstitutionality. Though found to have operated a state school system within the bound of the state constitutional provisions, Arizona moved toward a series of reforms that began in 1974. By 1980 the legislature had consolidated all school finance programs into a block grant and assumed primary obligation for local capital projects. Shortly after a trial court found the system at fault in 1973, the Colorado legislature reduced the tax burden of property owners by placing limits on school revenue growth.[24] Although no suits against their statewide systems were filed, Montana, New Mexico and Utah carried out major changes in state school funding policy in 1973. After some delays following the unconstitutionality ruling, Wyoming instituted a new plan in 1983 in which all districts have to levy the same tax rate and are required to achieve a minimum spending level for each student.[25]

Through a revised set of general aid allocation formulas, these reformed states have gradually reduced the gap between local wealth and school spending by distributing a greater amount of state funds to poor districts.[26] Several arrangements for this are found in the western states. Utah, Washington and California have "foundation programs," laying a base-line revenue for students in poor districts. Districts are required to levy a local property tax up to a state-designated maximum. State dollars are channeled to make up the difference between local tax revenue and the minimum level of school spending. In addition to these foundation programs, Utah and other states have adopted a more complicated "multitiered" subsidy approach. Under this system, districts are rewarded with additional state dollars for any tax efforts that go beyond the required tax rate. Since 1973, Colorado has provided for an equal amount of school funds to all districts that levied the same tax rate. Parts of the Wyoming finance plan have been controversial: In the "recapture" provisions, districts in Wyoming that are able to raise more money than the basic spending level are required to return to the state portions of their excess tax dollars.[27] In Colorado, Arizona and several other western states, school finance reforms have relieved local property tax burdens.[28]

Encouraged by the proliferation of federal grants since the late 1960s, states have looked for new ways to finance special-needs programs. Most western states have set up categorical programs, separate from the general aid allocation, for compensatory instruction, bilingual projects, and special education. Other western states, such as Utah, New Mexico and Wyoming, assign additional points, often referred to as a "weighted formula," to the handicapped and other special-needs students. The weighted formula takes into account the extra cost in providing services to the disadvantaged.

TAXPAYER PRESSURE

Finance reform slowed down during the late 1970s and early 1980s not only because of the economic recession but, perhaps more important, because of citizen-based campaigns against state and local taxation and spending. If parents in poor districts resorted primarily to litigation for funding redistribution, property taxpayers largely used methods of direct democracy to halt increases in local taxation and spending. These citizen-initiated movements had mixed success. Nonetheless, fairly widespread organized discontent has succeeded in sending a strong political message to governors and legislators, who have modified their perspectives on fiscal policy. As Citrin assessed the long-term impact of Proposition 13 in California: "Austerity and self-reliance have become new symbols of legitimacy. Politicians increasingly speak the language of trade-offs and constraint, rather than progress and social reform."[29] How to cope with new spending limitations will remain a major challenge to state policymakers for quite a while.

Indeed, signs of taxpayer opposition to school levies had begun to emerge before the passage of Proposition 13 in California in 1978. As early as 1970, a majority of school bond requests had failed to be approved by the voters at the nationwide level.[30] In California, local taxpayers were so dissatisfied with a sharp increase in local school contributions during Ronald Reagan's governorship that between 1966 and 1971 they rejected 50% of all local tax increases for school operation and 60% of the school bond levies for capital purposes.[31] According to a 1969 poll, 56% of Californians preferred to see a greater state role in financing public education.[32] Nevertheless, elsewhere in the western region a majority of the public continued to support school bonding well into the mid-1970s. In 1974, 1975 and 1976, voters in the western region approved school bond elections by 85%, 55% and 54% respectively.[33] In Colorado, voters repeatedly rejected measures to limit governmental spending throughout the 1970s.

Discontent among taxpayers in the western region became more widespread, however, during the time of the much-publicized campaign of Proposition 13 in California in 1978. In this regard, the West seemed consistent with the national sentiment. According to a 1978 national Gallup Poll, when asked to identify their dissatisfaction with various taxing sources for public schools, 52% of the respondents mentioned property tax, as compared to only 21% for federal sources and 20% for state funding.[34] In that year alone, nine of the thirteen western states saw organized citizen efforts to curb property tax increases and/or spending increases.[35] In California, Colorado, Idaho, Montana, Nevada, Oregon and Utah, voters pushed for limitation of property tax increases. Taxpayers in Arizona focused on spending limitation, while Washington State residents attempted to institute a ceiling on both taxing and spending. Taxpayer discontent was virtually absent, however, in Alaska, Hawaii, New Mexico and Wyoming. In Alaska, the state has assumed the primary fiscal responsibility for school expense largely through corporate and severance taxes on oil and gas companies.[36]

Of all the measures on the ballot during the peak of the taxpayer revolt in the western states, only California's Proposition 13 and Idaho's Proposition 1 gained approval. Passage of these measures was often attributed to strong citizen demand for tax equity following failure of the legislatures to take action. In Idaho, largely because of dissatisfaction with the lack of legislative action to reduce property taxes, 58% of the voters approved Proposition 1. The passage of this measure, however, did not mean that the voters were critical of local schools. According to an Education Commission of the States (ECS) survey during the election, 75% of Idaho residents did not want to see schools suffer as a result of Proposition 1.[37] Moreover, voters in the states that rejected these measures often enjoyed substantial state support in school finance. Without exception, teacher associations and other public employee groups formed the core in the coalition against the tax relief drive. According to an ECS study, the Colorado spending limitation referendum would have been rejected even if its proponents had had enough money to launch a statewide campaign. This is because a majority of Coloradans were found to be more satisfied with both governmental and educational spending than were people elsewhere. In 1978, in Oregon Measure 6 (similar to Proposition 13) was rejected by a narrow margin of 52% to 48%, a sharp reversal of an earlier 66%–22% support margin based on a pre-election poll. This tax limitation drive was seriously contested by a broad-based coalition consisting of the governor, education interests, and other public employee groups, and by widespread media opposition to Measure 6.[38]

Equal Educational Opportunity in the West

The prominent state role in school spending has been further encouraged by the adoption of legislation that promotes equal educational opportunity. In this regard, federal school policy during the

Great Society era of the mid-1960s and the 1970s has played a crucial role.[39] Even in 1983, at a time when the Reagan administration was cutting back on educational spending, the thirteen western states received $500 million in federal compensatory aid for disadvantaged children, $160 million in handicapped education grants (P.L. 94-142) and $110 million in vocational training funds.[40] These funds for the western states amounted to 18% of all federal allocations for the three programs. California received by far the largest amount of federal assistance, which included $290 million in compensatory education funds, $84 million in special education, and almost $60 million in vocational grants. Arizona, Colorado, Oregon and Washington received substantial vocational education subsidies. Wyoming and Nevada received the smallest amount of compensatory school assistance, while Alaska received only $1.8 million in special education.

SCHOOL DESEGREGATION

Fiscal assistance notwithstanding, the federal government's regulatory impact in public education has been even more far-reaching in promoting educational equity. In no area of school policy is the exercise of federal judicial power more important than in the racial desegregation of school districts. Although racial segregation in schools was most visible in the deep South, it existed in other regions as well, including the West. Judicial activism coupled with vigorous federal enforcement had significantly reduced racial segregation in southern public schools by the late 1970s.[41] In the western states, however, although progress has continued to be made since the 1960s, racial school integration seemed to remain at a moderate level even in the mid-1980s. According to Orfield, in 1984 in the western region (which includes all the states in our study except Alaska and Hawaii), 35.1% of white students attended black neighborhood schools. This level of integration was lower than the South's 41% as well as the nation's 35.8%. A similar pattern is found when one looks at the Hispanic enrollment figures. In 1984, 36.6% of white students went to Hispanic neighborhood schools in the western states. This figure is only slightly higher than the national average of 33.7%.[42]

To be sure, the level of racial integration varies among western states, each of which has a different socio-demographic character. At the same time, much of the variation in integration is affected by the implementation of court-ordered school desegregation plans in such major metropolitan areas as Seattle, Denver, Las Vegas, San Diego and Los Angeles.[43] In the early 1980s, substantial integration between black and white students was found in Denver, Riverside, Seattle, Colorado Springs, Las Vegas and Tacoma. School segregation of Hispanics was higher in Los Angeles, Albuquerque, Tucson, Fresno and San Diego.[44]

COMPENSATORY EDUCATION

While desegregation policy often affects major metropolitan areas, where minority groups are more heavily concentrated, other federal programs for equal educational opportunity have a statewide impact. In compensatory instruction, Native Indian programs and bilingual education, state legislation is by and large modeled after federal policy. Proliferation of federal mandates has encouraged states to expand their own services for special-needs groups.[45] When a uniform set of national standards is applied to all states, state decision-makers do not have to worry about whether their services for the disadvantaged are likely to generate costly consequences, such as in-migration of the special-needs population and the out-migration of taxpayers. Having overcome this policy dilemma, in which state decision-makers are caught between moral justification and fiscal constraint, federal programs can in fact generate "stimulative" effects, encouraging states to allot additional spending for special-needs groups.

By the late 1970s and early 1980s, a majority of the western states had enacted their own remedial instruction programs, providing supplemental funding in support of federal policy. In California, Arizona, Washington and Hawaii, state dollars are channeled through a grant based on the count of eligible students. Utah gives additional weight to the disadvantaged in its general funding formula, while Oregon and Hawaii award project grants to communities with special needs.[46] State funds for remedial services, however, are largely modest and have fallen behind inflation. While most western states spend no more than a few million dollars, California continues to maintain the largest state compensatory education program in the West: in 1981, for example, California allocated over $160 million to 756,000 disadvantaged pupils. Other states serve a much smaller clientele, such as Washington's 22,500, Utah's 5,000 and Hawaii's 2,000. States also differ in their program scope. While California allows local districts to assign priority to early grades, the Hawaii program focuses on grades nine through twelve. Washington State gives equal attention to the participants' low-income backgrounds as well as their achievement level, while Utah provides local districts with considerable flexibility by allowing state dollars to be used at both elementary and secondary levels. California, Montana, Alaska and Washington also have well-established statutes in the area of Native/Indian education.[47]

BILINGUAL EDUCATION

State programs for students with limited English proficiency have been encouraged by several federal initiatives. These include the 1970 Department of Health, Education and Welfare guidelines against native-origin discrimination; Title VII assistance to the language minority under the Elementary and Secondary Education Act; and the 1974 *Lau v. Nichols* U.S. Supreme Court decision. In *Lau*, the court ruled that school districts are responsible for providing instructional programs to students with minimal English proficiency. By the early 1980s, twenty states in the nation provided funding for their bilingual programs. In the West, mandatory bilingual rules (for example, services must be provided as long as the district has eight or more students with limited English proficiency) were adopted in Alaska (1975), California (1972), Colorado (1975) and Washington (1979). More permissive legislation has been passed in Arizona (1969), Hawaii (1979), New Mexico (1974), Oregon (1979) and Utah. In Montana, Idaho, Nevada and Wyoming, no statute on bilingual programs exists. In the West, as in other parts of the country, state dollars are channeled in at least five different ways. New Mexico allots "weights" to its students with limited English proficiency, while Utah, Arizona and Washington State generally adopt a basic amount on a per student basis. California, which operates the largest bilingual program, reimburses districts for their excess costs. Oregon provides project grants, while Hawaii and Alaska channel state aid to classroom units. California leads the West in the scope of its bilingual education program. It serves over 325,000 students through a $15 million state program. Both Arizona and New Mexico operate a sizable bilingual program, providing services for 20,000 and 27,000 pupils respectively. In Arizona, California, Colorado, Hawaii, Utah and Washington, students with limited English proficiency in K–12 grades are eligible. Programs in Alaska, New Mexico and Oregon have focused on the elementary level. These interstate differences in bilingual education policy are related to the varying political strength of minority groups in each state, as Chapter 8 suggested.

SERVICES FOR HANDICAPPED STUDENTS

Finally, unlike bilingual and compensatory education, all fifty states now mandate instructional programs for the handicapped between the ages of five and seventeen. Very often, state provisions on special programs are promoted by special interest groups in the state capital.[48] In the early 1980s, New Mexico became the last state in the nation to participate in the federal program for the education of handicapped students (P.L. 94-142). All states now provide funding for these services, although their allocation mechanisms differ. In Arizona, New Mexico, Utah and Washington, special education students are given additional points in the state aid formula. Nevada, Alaska and Wyoming channel funding to classroom/instructional units. The school districts' "excess" costs are reimbursed by the state in Montana, Idaho, Colorado, California and Oregon. Unlike compensatory education and bilingual projects, a substantial portion of K–12 students are enrolled in special education because of the well-defined federal mandates. In the West, over 8% of all public school pupils are enrolled in state-subsidized special programs. Utah has the largest enrollment, with over 11% of public school pupils attending special education classes; while Hawaii's 6% is the smallest in the West. Although it did not receive federal funding under P.L. 94-142 until 1984, New Mexico provides special services to 7% of its pupils. Indeed, practically every state has increased its support for special services quite sharply in a relatively short period of time since the 1975 passage of the federal P.L. 94-142 program. Between 1976 and 1981, every western state doubled its spending on special education. California, for example, increased its spending from $210 million to $420 million, while Idaho's program budget jumped from $9 million to $22 million.[49] Though it was not participating in the federal program during this period, New Mexico expanded its own program from $13 to $30 million.

IMPACT OF THE NEW FEDERALISM

As the federal government shifted toward devolution of program responsibility beginning in the early 1980s,[50] states have responded accordingly by allowing for greater local discretion on educational equity issues. The West is no exception. In Utah and Washington, the legislature has adopted the block grant approach, allowing local discretion in setting priorities on special programs. In 1980, Arizona consolidated its major categorical programs into its general aid allocation, in which local districts are given more flexibility in the use of funds.[51] This prompt legislative action in Arizona was perhaps triggered by the extensive influence on school spending enjoyed by special-needs groups. Under vigorous lobbying from special education groups, state legislators committed the state to write off 90% of the excess costs in programs for the handicapped. Taking advantage of the state largesse, local districts were reportedly shifting students from other remedial programs to special education projects.[52] As federal policy changed, some state legislatures were quick to delegate to districts the decisions over the use of special education funds, thereby ridding themselves of intense lobbying from special interests.[53]

But if special interests are pre-empted by decategorization, policy generalists seem to have gained new political influence. These generalists include elected officials, such as school-board members, governors, legislators, and chief state school officers, as well as top appointees in education agencies. The most obvious example is the role of the legislatures. In 1981, more than twenty legislatures adopted laws that allowed legislative oversight over federal education funds, such as the newly created block grant, known as Chapter II of the Education Consolidation and Improvement Act.[54] At the same time, legislators became more dependent upon administrative generalists in the education agencies for information and technical advice. In the end, it seems that the political vacuum created by the decline of special interests will be filled by the rise of generalists. The generalists, often backed by citizen concerns for accountability and efficiency, have played the leading role in the current movement toward curricular reforms.

The Back-to-Basics Movement

The current back-to-basics movement has been going on for more than a decade. During the mid-1970s, citizen concerns for minimal competency in students' reading, writing, and calculating skills prompted dozens of state legislatures to adopt new school policy. On the one hand, these public concerns reflected declining public confidence in the performance of public schools. According to a 1976 Gallup Poll, only 41% of the respondents gave their local schools either an *A* or a *B* grade.[55] At that time, a majority of the public identified basic skills and school discipline as the two most important ways to improve education quality. Conversely, only 27% suggested raising teachers' standards, and even fewer (14%) mentioned improvement in teachers' salaries. On the other hand, concerns about the students' basic skills seem to have reflected an awareness of cost-effectiveness issues during a period of shrinking tax dollars, declining enrollment, and a stagnant economy. By 1978, over half of all states had undertaken steps, through either legislation or state school board rulings, toward adopting stricter graduation standards in basic skill areas and establishing testing programs to be administered early at the secondary level.[56] Although minimal competency legislation failed in Arizona, the Oregon state department of education mandated that local districts set higher graduation standards. Utah implemented "Outcome Based Education" programs. California legislation enacted in 1976 required proficiency testing from grade seven and up. The Washington legislature tied state funds to the local implementation of basic achievement plans.[57] By 1977, over 40% of the public were aware of the back-to-basics movement.[58]

With the publicity resulting from the 1983 federal report, *A Nation at Risk*, the reform movement has gathered new momentum and taken on a broader agenda. Citing disturbing trends in the decline of student achievement and the shortage of teachers in basic-skill areas, the federal report sought "to generate reform of our educational system in fundamental ways . . . and to renew the Nation's commitment to schools."[59] As a keen observer pointed out, "in the seventies . . . the seeds of the reform movement were sown. Its green shoots broke ground in 1983 when a plethora of proposals made the need for reform visible to the American public."[60] The policy debate of the mid-1980s has gone beyond the basic skills of graduating seniors, and has moved into areas of teaching competency and teacher training as well as comprehensive curricular reform. Much of the recent policy debate, known as "the second wave" of reform, is related to three broad areas of school performance: personnel development (for example, teacher quality), graduation standards and disciplinary matters, and curriculum.

Different strategies to facilitate personnel development have been adopted in the West.[61] This seems consistent with the western states' long reform history. In the early 1900s, California and Utah were the first two states in the nation to require a four-year college degree for secondary schoolteachers. Twenty years later, California again became the first state to require a college degree for teachers in elementary schools.[62] In the current reform, California, Idaho, Montana, Oregon and Utah have strengthened their standards on teacher preparation and certification. Policies that deal with teacher shortages and programs that facilitate professional development for both teachers and administrators are popular in Alaska, Arizona, Hawaii, Washington and Wyoming. California, Hawaii and Idaho paid particular attention to the salary issue; again, Idaho, California and Utah adopted the master teachers program. This latter identifies and rewards teachers who have demonstrated effective teaching in the classroom. Utah has set aside 50% of all school appropriations for the "Career Ladder System." The 1987 Oregon legislature funded a $3 million "Teacher Support Project" and a $400,000 Teacher Corps program.

The West has also made efforts to strengthen graduation requirements and school discipline. A majority of the western states introduced stricter graduation requirements, while Alaska, through its School Activities Association, tied academic standards to student participation in extracurricular activities. Anchorage, a district that represents 40% of the Alaskan enrollment, adopted an even stricter set of guidelines. Less than half of the western states enacted new college admissions requirements or introduced new student testing. Similarly, few states seemed interested in policy on school discipline and grade promotion. Only Alaska, California and Washington demonstrated a general interest in these issues that are designed to govern student behavior.

Finally, on the restructuring of the curriculum, California is clearly ahead of all the other western states in adopting wide-ranging major reform measures. General curriculum reform was also adopted by Alaska, Arizona, Montana, New Mexico and Washington. The latter four states, together with California and Wyoming, also strengthened their academic enrichment programs. Much less popular in the West are textbook policy, academic recognition programs, an extended school day and specialized schools. Most of these proposals were not seriously considered in Wyoming, Utah, Nevada, Montana, Alaska and Idaho.

Western states are uneven in their pace of school reform. The slower process in some states may be explained by fiscal constraints in a sluggish economy; constitutional limitations on legislative interference in school matters; tenure laws that govern teacher-administration relations; and the political clout of educational interest groups. To be sure, each of these factors affected each state in different ways. For example, New Mexico was adversely affected by the decline in its oil-based economy during the early 1980s, while the constitution in Colorado prohibits statewide selection of textbooks. Oregon and California have powerful teachers' unions, while Colorado and Wyoming enjoy a strong tradition of local autonomy. The Colorado Association of School Executives has often succeeded in circumscribing legislative actions on curricular matters.[63] States that achieved reform often were led by strong political coalitions (including the governor and key legislators) toward reform. California's state senator Gary Hart (not to be confused with the former presidential candidate with the same name) and the state school chief officer, Bill Honig, for example, are strong reform advocates.

Even more important, legislative success on reform proposals seems to be largely dominated by state legislatures and the state school board. Proposals that come from both the legislature and the state school board have the greatest chance of success. According to the author's preliminary analysis of a 1985 survey, out of the 174 major reform proposals being considered in the western region, 53 (30.5%) were initiated from legislatures and 63 (36.2%) came from state school boards.[64] Governors submitted 9%, while various task forces and commissions were responsible for 13.8%. State education agencies and chief school officers proposed 9.8% of all policy innovations. Of these 174 submitted proposals, however, only 89 were finally adopted. Of them, 83, or 93.3% of the total, were traced to either the legislature or the state school board. Policy initiations from other reform sources, including the governor, have largely failed in the legitimation process. The prominence of state legislators in the current reform is largely consistent with the literature on education policymaking in the American states. According to a recent six-state study, state lawmakers who specialize in education policy are most capable of influencing their colleagues in voting on school matters. These influential legislators are labeled "the insiders."[65]

Conclusion

School policy in the West is made in a social and political context that is somewhat different from that of the nation as a whole. For one thing, the West has not experienced as steep an enrollment decline as has the nation. Again, schools in the West have a higher proportion of Hispanics, Asians, and Native Americans, but fewer blacks. In recent years, the states have played a greater role in financing public education. Tendencies toward policy and administrative centralization notwithstanding, educational spending for administrative purposes has not risen rapidly.

The politics of educational policy in the West, however, are not unlike the national pattern. In this regard, governmental institutions and political processes have played an important role in the making of school policy. While school finance reform in the 1970s was brought about by court rulings, programs that promote equity were often the result of intensive lobbying from the disadvantaged groups at both the national and the state levels. Tendencies toward greater educational equality, however, have been slowed down since the early 1980s. While federal cutbacks on special-needs services and policy devolution allow for greater state and local discretion in setting program priorities, localities have been subject to pressure from organized taxpayer groups toward property tax relief. In recent years, public concern for effective schools has further directed governmental attention to the basics. In short, educational policy in the West, as in the nation, seems to have shifted from special-needs concerns to the issue of improving general school quality for all. Yet, given the new spending limits in many western states in the post–Proposition 13 era, whether policymakers can effectively cope with competing goals (*i.e.*, excellence versus equity) will remain a central policy challenge for some time to come.

Notes

The author acknowledges Doug Mitchell for his comments on an earlier draft of this chapter.

1. National Commission on Excellence in Education, *A Nation at Risk* (Washington, D.C.: U.S. Government Printing Office, 1983), 6.

2. National Center for Education Statistics, *Revenues and Expenditures for Public Elementary and Secondary Education Fiscal Year 1980* (Washington, D.C.: U.S. Government Printing Office, 1982), table 4, p. 17. A more extensive examination of the state role in public school financing is presented in Kenneth Wong, "State Fiscal Support for Education: The 'Parity to Dominance' View Examined," *American Journal of Education* 97 (4) (August 1989).

3. Jim B. Pearson and Edgar Fuller, eds., *Education in the States: Historical Development and Outlook* (Washington, D.C.: National Education Association, 1969), 40–41, 57.

4. Paul E. Peterson, Barry Rabe, and Kenneth Wong, *When Federalism Works* (Washington, D.C.: Brookings Institution, 1986).

5. Pearson and Fuller, eds., *Education in the States*, 1410–11.

6. *Ibid.*, chap. entitled "Colorado."

7. Harvey Tucker and Harmon Zeigler, *Professionals Versus the Public: Attitudes, Communication, and Response in School Districts* (New York: Longman, 1980).

8. Edgar Fuller and Jim B. Pearson, eds., *Education in the States* (Washington, D.C.: National Education Association, 1969), 139.

9. *Ibid.*, 12.

10. Frederick M. Wirt, "School Policy Culture and State Decentralization,"

chap. 6 in Jay D. Scribner, ed., *The Politics of Education* (Chicago: University of Chicago Press, 1977), 164–87.

11. *Ibid.* Also see Frederick Wirt and Michael Kirst, *Schools in Conflict* (Berkeley: McCutchan, 1983), 232–33.

12. Wirt and Kirst, *Schools in Conflict*, chap. 8. Also see J. Alan Aufderheide, "Educational Interest Groups and the State Legislature," in Roald Campbell and Tim Mazzoni, Jr., eds., *State Policy Making for the Public Schools: A Comparative Analysis* (Berkeley: McCutchan, 1976).

13. Laurence Iannaccone, *Politics in Education* (New York: Center for Applied Research in Education, 1967), chap. 3.

14. Lorraine McDonnell and Anthony Pascal, *Organized Teachers in American Schools* (Rand Corporation, 1979).

15. Fuller and Pearson, *Education in the States*, 673.

16. McDonnell and Pascal, *Organized Teachers*, 67.

17. Efrem Sigel, Dantia Quirk, and Patricia Whitestone, *Crisis! The Taxpayer Revolt and Your Kids' Schools* (White Plains, N.Y.: Knowledge Industry Publications, 1978).

18. Calculations are based on *NEA Handbook 1985–86* (Washington, D.C.: National Education Association, 1985).

19. Alan Rosenthal and Susan Fuhrman, *Legislative Education Leadership in the States* (Washington, D.C.: Institute for Educational Leadership, 1981); Susan Fuhrman and Alan Rosenthal, eds., *Shaping Education Policy in the States* (Washington, D.C.: Institute for Educational Leadership, 1981).

20. Jerome T. Murphy, "Progress and Problems: The Paradox of State Reform," chap. 8 in Ann Lieberman and Milbrey W. McLaughlin, eds., *Policy Making in Education* (Chicago: University of Chicago Press, 1982), 204.

21. David Long, "Rodriguez: The State Courts Respond," *Phi Delta Kappan* (March 1983); Walter Garms, James Guthrie, and Lawrence Pierce, *School Finance* (Englewood Cliffs, N.J.: Prentice Hall, 1978), 36–43 and 75–95; Nelda Cambron-McCabe and Allan Odden, eds., *The Changing Politics of School Finance* (Cambridge, Mass.: Ballinger, 1982); Allan Odden and L. Dean Webb, eds., *School Finance and School Improvement* (Cambridge, Mass.: Ballinger, 1983).

22. As cited in Garms, Guthrie, and Pierce, *School Finance*, 38.

23. Michael Kirst and Stephen Somers, "California Educational Interest Groups: Collective Action as a Logical Response to Proposition 13," *Education and Urban Society* 13 (2) (1981), 235–56; Betsy Levin, Michael Cohen, Thomas Muller, and William Scanlon, *Paying for Public Schools: Issues of School Finance in California* (Washington, D.C.: Urban Institute, 1972).

24. Robert Palaich, James Kloss, and Mary Williams, *Tax and Expenditure Limitation Referenda* (Denver: Education Commission of the States, 1980), 38.

25. John Augenblick, "The Current Status of School Financing Reform in the States," chap. 1 in Van Mueller and Mary McKeown, eds., *The Fiscal, Legal, and Political Aspects of State Reform of Elementary and Secondary Education* (Cambridge, Mass.: Ballinger, 1986); Tyll Van Geel, "The Courts and School

Finance Reform: An Expected Utility Model," chap. 4 in Cambron-McCabe and Odden, eds., *The Changing Politics of School Finance*.

26. Stephen Carroll, *The Search for Equity in School Finance* (Santa Monica, Calif.: Rand Corporation, 1979); Allan Odden, Robert Berne, and Leanna Stiefel, *Equity in School Finance* (Denver: Education Commission of the States, 1979).

27. Augenblick, "The Current Status of School Financing Reform in the States."

28. *The Book of the States 1978–79* (Lexington, Ky.: Council of State Governments, 1978), 329–59.

29. Jack Citrin, "Introduction: The Legacy of Proposition 13," in T. Schwadron, ed., *California and the American Tax Revolt* (Berkeley: University of California Press, 1984), 58.

30. Philip Piele and John Stuart Hall, *Budgets, Bonds, and Ballots* (Lexington, Mass.: Lexington Books, 1973).

31. Levin *et al.*, *Paying for Public Schools*.

32. *Ibid.*, 59.

33. National Center for Education Statistics, *Bond Sales for Public School Purposes 1973–74, 1974–75, and 1975–76* (Washington, D.C.: U.S. Government Printing Office).

34. Phi Delta Kappan, *Gallup Polls of Attitudes Toward Education 1969–1984: A Topical Summary* (Bloomington, Ind.: Phi Delta Kappan, 1984), 23.

35. Sigel *et al.*, *Crisis!*

36. Susan Hansen, "Extraction: The Politics of State Taxation," chap. 12 in Virginia Gray, Herbert Jacob, and Kenneth N. Vines, eds., *Politics in the American States: A Comparative Analysis*, 4th ed. (Boston: Little, Brown, 1983).

37. Palaich *et al.*, *Tax and Expenditure Limitation Referenda*, 53.

38. *Ibid.*

39. Peterson *et al.*, *When Federalism Works*. Also see Paul E. Peterson, *Making the Grade* (New York: Twentieth Century Fund, 1983).

40. E. Kathleen Adams, *A Changing Federalism: The Condition of the States* (Denver: Education Commission of the States, 1982), 54–55.

41. Gary Orfield, *Public School Desegregation in the United States, 1968–1980* (Washington, D.C.: Joint Center for Political Studies, 1983).

42. Gary Orfield and Franklin Monfort, "Are American Schools Resegregating in the Reagan Era?" Working Paper No. 14, National School Desegregation Project, University of Chicago, 1986.

43. Gary Orfield, *Must We Bus?* (Washington, D.C.: Brookings Institution, 1978); David Kirp, *Just Schools* (Berkeley: University of California Press, 1982). On the San Diego case, see Peterson *et al.*, *When Federalism Works*, 201–8.

44. Orfield, *Public School Desegregation in the United States, 1968–1980*, 43–47.

45. Peterson *et al.*, *When Federalism Works*, chap. 1.

46. Adams, *A Changing Federalism*.

47. Education Commission of the States, *Indian Education: An Overview of State Laws and Policies* (Denver: Education Commission of the States, 1980).

48. Murphy, "Progress and Problems," in *Policy Making in Education.*

49. Adams, *A Changing Federalism.*

50. Michael Knapp and R. A. Cooperstein, "Early Research on the Federal Education Block Grant: Themes and Unanswered Questions," *Educational Evaluation and Policy Analysis* 8 (2) (Summer 1986), 121–37.

51. Susan Fuhrman, "State-Level Politics and School Financing," chap. 3 in Cambron-McCabe and Odden, eds., *The Changing Politics of School Finance.*

52. *Ibid.*

53. *Ibid.*

54. Knapp and Cooperstein, "Early Research on the Federal Education Block Grant," *Educational Evaluation and Policy Analysis.* Also see "A Special Issue: Rethinking the Federal Role in Education," *Harvard Educational Review* 52 (4) (November 1982).

55. Phi Delta Kappan, *Gallup Polls*, 18.

56. *The Book of the States, 1978–79.*

57. Ben Brodinsky, "Back to the Basics: The Movement and Its Meaning," *Phi Delta Kappan* (March 1977), 526.

58. Phi Delta Kappan, *Gallup Polls*, 32.

59. National Commission on Excellence in Education, *A Nation at Risk*, 6. Also see Congressional Budget Office, "Educational Achievement: Explanations and Implications of Recent Trends" (Washington, D.C.: CBO, 1986). The CBO study suggests that achievement trends cannot be directly linked to school performance declines.

60. Chris Pipho, "States Move Reform Closer to Reality," *Phi Delta Kappan* 68 (4) (December 1986), K2.

61. U.S. Department of Education, *The Nation Responds* (Washington, D.C.: U.S. Government Printing Office, 1984).

62. Fuller and Pearson, eds., *Education in the States*, 21.

63. Keith Hamm, "The Role of 'Subgovernments' in U.S. State Policy Making: An Exploratory Analysis," *Legislative Studies Quarterly* 11 (3) (August 1986).

64. "Changing Course: A 50-State Survey of Reform Measures," *Education Week* (February 6, 1985), 11–30.

65. Catherine Marshall, Douglas Mitchell, and Frederick Wirt, "The Context of State-Local Policy Formation," *Educational Evaluation and Policy Analysis* 8 (4) (Winter 1986), 347–78. Also see E. H. Wahlke, W. Buchanon, and L. C. Ferguson, *The Legislative System: Explorations in Legislative Behavior* (New York: John Wiley and Sons, 1962); and Kenneth Wong, "Policymaking in the American States: Typology, Process and Institutions," *Policy Studies Review* (Spring 1989).

IV

Intergovernmental Relations and Public Policy in the West

15

UNDERSTANDING INTERGOVERNMENTAL RELATIONS IN THE WEST

Robert J. Waste and Clive S. Thomas

*A*T 5:04 P.M. ON TUESDAY, OCTOBER 17, 1989, AT THE PEAK of the rush hour, northern California was rocked by the second strongest earthquake in U.S. history. Measuring 7.1 on the Richter Scale, it killed over two hundred people, left thousands homeless for weeks, and caused billions of dollars' worth of property damage. It also dislocated and damaged the infrastructure including water and sewer systems, telephone service and roads and bridges. The task, and the cost, of dealing with the immediate concerns of rescuing people and providing medical and other services, as well as the long-term effort of rebuilding were far too big for any one organization or government to undertake alone. Besides help from private agencies like the Red

Cross, the emergency required a concerted effort of local, state and federal agencies to provide both funds and expertise for the enormous tasks of recovery.

What is true in emergency situations like this is also true in the formulation and implementation of the majority of public policies. While it is important to understand the structure and operation and the role of the various governments in the West, it is equally important to bear in mind that rarely does one level of government—be it federal, state or local—have exclusive domain in the formulation and implementation of any given policy area. Most policies involve the interaction of two and often three levels of government. This is the case, for example, for highways, education, health, public safety and even alcohol and drug abuse prevention programs.

Therefore to see a complete picture of the policymaking and implementation process in these and other areas, we need to understand something about how and why the various levels of government interrelate. For this reason, the final chapters of this book will focus on the various facets of intergovernmental relations as they affect the West.

Robert Jay Dilger has captured the essence of intergovernmental relations in the following passage:

> Intergovernmental relations encompass all the relationships that exist between and among all the various governmental units in the given polity. In the United States, intergovernmental relations refers to the relationships between and among the 82,341 governmental units currently in existence. There are fifty state governments and one national government. There are also 3,041 county governments, 19,076 municipal governments, 16,734 townships, 14,851 school districts, and 28,588 special districts (created for flood control, fire protection, library systems, etc.). . . . Intergovernmental relations also encompasses the relationships between and among the representatives of these 82,341 governmental units.[1]

Thus, *intergovernmental relations* (IGR) in the West refers to the interaction among federal, state, regional, county, city and special district governments, their employees and elected officeholders. This complex web of intergovernmental relations is the result of the American belief in federalism, and the creation of the federal system in the United States.

American federalism, properly speaking, refers to a system of divided authority or responsibility (technically referred to as *legal sovereignty*) between the federal and state governments. How this authority is to be divided is set out in the U.S. Constitution and in numerous federal court decisions. Legally, local governments, local government compacts and interstate organizations do not acquire their authority from the U.S. Constitution or federal laws, but from their states or member governments. Thus they are excluded from the strictly constitutional-legalistic definition of federalism. In practice, however, these local governments and government compacts play a very important role in the day-to-day operation of the federal system by administering state and federal programs, and by developing and implementing policies and programs of their own. For this reason, understanding IGR—viewed in the broad sense as a web of state, local, national and regional government interaction—is crucial to comprehending the American tradition of federalism. So while federalism and IGR are not, strictly speaking, synonymous, for the purposes of this chapter we will use them interchangeably.

Students of western politics need to be familiar with the IGR system in the West in order to understand much that is crucial to politics, power, government, administration and policymaking in the thirteen western states. There are thirteen state governments, 425 county governments, more than 2,200 municipal governments, over 3,000 school districts, and approximately 8,200 special districts in the West.[2] In fact, intergovernmental relations in the West are so vast that the various western governments are part of five interlocking IGR systems. These are:

1. A federal-state IGR system comprising the federal government and thirteen state governments.
2. A state-local government IGR system comprising each state government and its counties, cities and special districts.
3. Interstate relations and compacts between western states.
4. Federal-local relations involving direct dealings between federal agencies and local governments in the West.
5. Local-local relations and sometimes formal agreements between local governments both within the same state and sometimes across state boundaries.

This "five IGR" schema is a heuristic device—an oversimplification for purposes of explaining the extremely complex IGR system in the West. In reality, the five systems make up one vast confusing and shifting network of governmental units, employees, officeholders and alliances. But without the artificial device of dividing the IGR system into five more or less comprehensible channels or facets, IGR in the West would almost be impossible to visualize or explain. Figure 15.1 sets out the various facets of the IGR system in the West.

A key theme of this chapter is the argument that the senior partner in the first two facets of the intergovernmental system in the West—the federal government in federal-state IGR, and the states in state-local IGR—set the agenda and exert the primary influence on politics and policies in the West. States are greatly influenced by policy decisions made in Washington, D.C., just as local governments are greatly influenced by decisions made in their respective state capitals. The power that the federal and state governments can exert as senior partners in the IGR system is based upon three interrelated factors: (1) the granting of constitutional authority and the accumulation of court decisions reinforcing that authority; (2) their broad and flexible budgetary authority and the size of their revenues; and (3) their power to regulate many activities performed by the governments within their jurisdictions.

In this chapter we also explore the five-part IGR schema set out above and explain how the parts interact to develop policies and thus affect the lives of westerners. All this will set the scene for understanding the similarities and differences in the western IGR system and provide a basis for a fuller appreciation of the chapters on land, water and environmental policy that follow.

Changing Views of Federalism

Evolution in the western states' relations to each other and to the federal government is related to evolution in the national pattern of federalism. Therefore it will be useful to begin our consideration of IGR by tracing how IGR has evolved from a period in which federalism was discussed in terms of "dual federalism" to the much more recent use of the term "bamboo-fence federalism."

DUAL FEDERALISM

In the early years of the nation the U.S. Supreme Court often favored the interests of the national government over those of the states. The major force behind this was Chief Justice John Marshall who served from 1801 to 1835. He broadly defined the "necessary and proper" clause of the U.S. Constitution in order to protect the national government from experiencing the same weaknesses vis-à-vis the state governments that beset the earlier Articles of Confed-

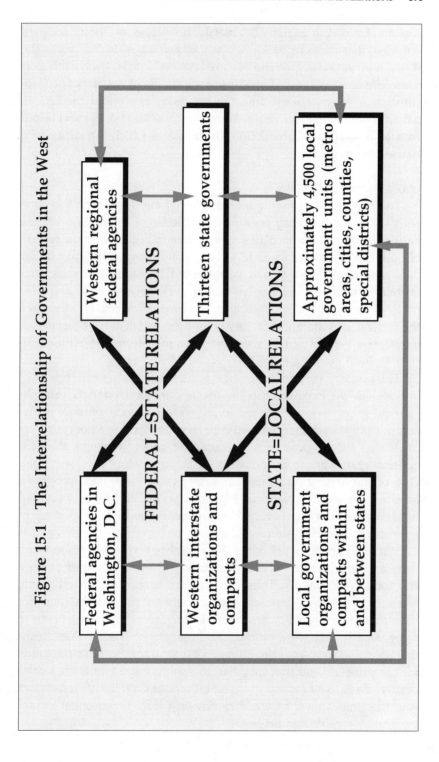

Figure 15.1   The Interrelationship of Governments in the West

eration. Following Marshall, Chief Justice Roger B. Taney adopted the view that came to be known as *dual federalism*. In this view, the states and national government are seen as equals, each with permanently fixed powers. The supremacy clause of the national Constitution is seen as protecting the necessary powers of the federal government, while the Tenth Amendment is viewed as carving out an area of exclusive jurisdiction for the states which the supremacy clause cannot touch.[3]

COOPERATIVE FEDERALISM

The New Deal of Franklin D. Roosevelt and his attempt to cope with the dire emergency presented by the Great Depression led the national government to play a greater role in regulation and control of both the private and public sectors than had been the case under dual federalism. This period was marked by the rise of *cooperative federalism*, which, as Henig has noted, was: "a new style and new philosophy of federalism distinguished by *joint undertakings* between the federal and state governments and the expansion of the use of *federal grants-in-aid* (direct transfers of money from the national to state or local governments)."[4]

The primary vehicle for the new federal role during the New Deal period was the expansion in the use of *categorical grants*. These categorical grants were designed to aid state and local officials in the administrative and financial hardships of implementing a host of newly mandated federal programs. It should be noted, however, that categorical grants began in the early 1900s, well before the New Deal. One of the earliest and most important categorical grant programs for the West was the National Highway Act of 1916, which provided funds for the then largely rural West to develop the basis of the present interstate highway system.

What is important about the New Deal period is that these years were a time of major expansion of earlier categorical grants to state and local governments. These grants were narrowly targeted grants to assist in specific purposes, such as help for the elderly, highway construction, public housing and aid for the poor. Many of these categorical grants were *matching* and *competitive* grants. This meant that state and local governments needed to supply some of the funds for the projects, and that they had to apply for the grants on a competitive basis. The federal government under cooperative federalism was the final arbiter of whether or not a local government would eventually receive a grant-in-aid.

CREATIVE FEDERALISM

In addition to the financial-budgetary relationship providing financial assistance to state and local governments, since the 1930s the federal government has increasingly developed an important role in regulation. This increasing propensity of the federal government to regulate state and local conditions in such areas as worker safety, civil rights, transportation and the environment, was a key element of the *creative federalism* associated with the presidency of Lyndon Johnson (1963–69).

It was President Johnson's declaration of a "War on Poverty" that set the nation on a course leading to creative federalism. As Jeffrey Henig has also noted, this new course involved "a shift in the nature of cooperative federalism toward a more adversarial relationship."[5] During this period, federal officials began to use the considerable resources of the federal government to compel states and localities to participate in programs and assume responsibilities—especially in such areas as civil rights and aid to the poor—that many would have preferred not to undertake. Eventually this resulted in a backlash against centralized federal authority, and a loosening of the federal grip under the *new federalism* of the Nixon administration.

NEW FEDERALISM (NIXON)

In his *new federalism* President Nixon (1969–74) attempted to bring the federal government closer to state and local governments, and to loosen some of the strings involved in the categorical grant process. He did this by dividing the country into several regions, and mandating that a federal headquarters for each major federal agency be located in a key city within each region.

Nixon succeeded in supplementing the old categorical grant system with a newer *block grant* system in which funds were granted to localities for broad purposes with little or no supervision by federal officials. In the most dramatic example of new federalism in action, Nixon lobbied Congress successfully for the passage of *general revenue sharing*, a program that provided funds to all states and local governments on a formula based on population. The population-based formula contained few restrictions on the uses of the monies by state and local governments. Two less sweeping block grant programs were included in the 1973 Comprehensive Employment and Training Act (CETA) and the 1974 Community Development Block Grant Act (CDBG). Collectively, while they did not replace the earlier categorical grants, these three programs did make available a great deal of federal money to a large number of jurisdictions without the heavy hand of supervision that had characterized the earlier cooperative federalism and creative federalism periods.

THE NEW PARTNERSHIP

During his presidency (1977–81) Jimmy Carter stressed three themes that were important to what he labeled a *new partnership* approach. These were: "(1) the need for a more precise targeting of federal aid to the most hard-pressed communities, (2) greater use of public funds as levers in stimulating private investment, and (3) his intent to mount a full-fledged attack on red tape and the paperwork morass hindering efficient government on all levels."[6] Despite his short tenure, Carter was able to advance his program on two fronts. He created an Urban Development Action Grant program (UDAG), which targeted money for competitive urban and rural development projects. He also launched a major study of red tape and paperwork involved with the various federal categorical and block grant programs.

NEW FEDERALISM (REAGAN)

Since we will discuss the Reagan administration's variant of *new federalism* in more detail below, it is only necessary here to mention that the early Reagan years and the focus on budget reductions at the federal level resulted in the demise of several key programs. Many of the categorical programs, such as UDAG and CETA, were eliminated, the remaining programs were consolidated or "blocked" together into broad programs having less federal "strings" and funds. Finally, the centerpiece of Nixon's new federalism—general revenue sharing—was eliminated in favor of reducing the overall size of the federal budget, and reducing the size and scale of government assistance to state and local governments to build low-cost housing, decreased dramatically during the Reagan administration. For example, the overall budget for programs administered by the Department of Housing and Urban Development decreased from a high of $24 billion in 1980 to a low of $8 billion in 1988.

Understanding Federalism and the
Overall Intergovernmental Relationship

Before turning to a discussion of IGR in the West, we will explain two further views of federalism: *picket-fence federalism,* and a more recent variant, *bamboo-fence federalism*. Explaining them will help bring some systematic understanding to the complex and often confusing pattern of the overall IGR system operating in the American West.

PICKET-FENCE FEDERALISM

The former governor (now U.S. senator) of North Carolina, Terry Sanford, once described federalism as a picket fence in which government is composed of a series of vertical pickets. In this "fence," government has several specific functions, such as public health and welfare, education, civil defense, aid to agriculture, regulation of mining and so on. Administrators in these specific functional areas talk frequently and easily with their counterparts at the other levels of government. Thus, a county agricultural agent may speak with state agricultural officials in the state capital, or just as frequently with federal agricultural officials in the federal regional office, or with the federal headquarters in Washington, D.C. The key to this view is the fact that a county agricultural agent will communicate frequently with his or her functional counterparts in the IGR system, but will rarely, if ever, have the need to communicate on a professional basis with other officials of the same governmental level—a county welfare or county health official, for example.

Writing in the late 1960s, Sanford described *picket-fence federalism* in the following manner:

> Government is not, in these major programs at least, like a rail fence, with three rails one above the other, one for the national, one for the state, and one for the cities and local governments. It is more like a picket fence. The lines of authority, the concerns and interests, the flow of money, and the direction of programs run straight down like a number of pickets stuck into the ground. There is, as in a picket fence, a connecting cross slat, but that does little to support anything. In this metaphor it stands for the governments. It holds the pickets in line; it does not bring them together. The picket-like programs are not connected at the bottom. Maybe we need to find some way to connect them, some close-to-the-ground exchange for all that our agencies do.[7]

BAMBOO-FENCE FEDERALISM

As David Walker has noted, by the mid-1970s, local, state and federal administrators tended to describe Sanford's picket fence in more flexible terms. In this revised view:

> A fence would still appear to be the proper metaphor, but not

the sturdy, solid wood variety. One of bamboo would be more apt—given its somewhat softer materials, its elaborate horizontal wiring system, and its greater capacity to bend to prevailing winds.[8]

Walker developed the metaphor of *bamboo-fence federalism* to capture the fact that vertical functionalism and isolation of government officials have continued after 1970, but that the IGR system as a whole has grown somewhat more flexible. This increased flexibility is due to increased professionalism on the part of state, local and federal officials, plus realization by all the IGR players that a need exists for greater realism and greater flexibility if the IGR system is to function successfully.

IGR in the West: The Differences and the Similarities

Intergovernmental relations in the thirteen western states are both similar and distinct from IGR in the rest of the United States.

THE DIFFERENCES

These differences are less numerous than the similaries yet perhaps more important. The West differs from the prevailing patterns of IGR in the rest of the nation in two key aspects, which are recurring themes throughout this book. First, as the Sagebrush Rebellion and the Proposition 13 taxpayer revolt of the 1970s illustrate, westerners are deeply distrustful of governmental authority, both at the federal and state level. However, the animosity of westerners toward the federal government has run much longer and probably runs a good deal deeper than do such feelings toward their state and local governments in the region.[9] Second, the federal government is the single largest landholder in the West, with holdings that include national forests, parks, recreation areas, Forest Service lands, hydro-electric projects, grazing lands and waterways, managed by the Department of the Interior, the Bureau of Land Management and the Forest Service, among other agencies. These two factors provide a special context for western federalism.[10] We shall have occasion below to return to this theme in our discussion of the administrative role of the federal government in the West.

THE SIMILARITIES

Like the other states in the Union, western states are players in a system of federalism or IGR characterized by what Michael Reagan and John Sanzone have described as federally dominated "permissive federalism" in which, although "there is a sharing of power and authority between the national and state governments, the state's share rests upon the permission and permissiveness of the national government."[11]

Local governments in the West—including counties, cities and special districts such as school districts—have much the same relation to their respective state governments as the state governments have to the federal government. That is to say, the IGR system within each of the western states mirrors on a smaller scale the federal-state IGR system. Local governments—particularly cities and special districts— are legal corporations created by the legislatures of their respective states. In fact, following a decision by Judge John F. Dillon of the Iowa supreme court in 1868, and now widely referred to as "Dillon's Rule," a state legislature has the power to create, legally control and even disband its local governments.[12]

State-federal intergovernmental relations and state-local intergovernmental relations share the other characteristics noted earlier in Chapter 4. Western state constitutions provide many examples of overlap between state and local government functions. Education, public health and public safety are the major, but by no means the only examples. Despite this, there are also certain spheres of authority of local governments that cannot be touched by the states, and vice versa. Additionally, local governments are able to tax and raise revenue, but they are often dependent on the state for financial assistance.

Because these lines of authority, independence and dependence are confusing and subject to change over time, Martin Grodzins has urged scholars to depict this relationship as a "marble cake" rather than as a "layer cake."[13] The marble cake analogy is meant to illustrate that even though the federal or state government has the upper hand in legal authority, resources and policy initiative, the lines of authority are often blurred. Who, for example, has the authority to protect the environment and reduce air pollution in western states and cities? Or who is the final arbiter of the water quality or sewage treatment provided by local governments in the West? The answer, untidy as it is, is that many partners—including the federal government, the states, counties, special districts, and cities (all members of the basic western IGR system) join together to regulate and protect the environment of the western states. Actual federal-state or state-local government relationships in the West thus often take on more the shape of a confused swirl than a neatly divided co-equal set of layers.

The Five Facets of IGR in the West

1. FEDERAL-STATE RELATIONS: THE PERVASIVE INFLUENCE OF THE NATIONAL GOVERNMENT

Because it is the senior partner in the federal-state IGR system, the federal government has long exercised an administrative role in the western states. Indeed, the issue of which "layer" in the federal-state intergovernmental relations system "owns" or is best situated to regulate the use of natural resources such as land, water and/or minerals is one of the most contentious political issues in the West. The debate about who does or should regulate these resources in the West is one of the key elements of the dissatisfaction with the federal government in the West, one manifestation of which was the Sagebrush Rebellion.

Largely because of its all-pervasive importance, the administrative role of the federal government and the character of "permissive federalism" are different in the West than in other states and regions. True, like the rest of the country, the federal "partner" is the dominant partner and, also as in other regions, this dominance extends to an administrative role for the federal government in such apparently "local" issues as the quality of the drinking water, speed limits on the state freeways, or the operation and condition of state prisons. The difference in the West, however, is that the federal government is not simply the "senior partner" in the western federal-state IGR system, but it is also the largest single land holder in the region. Thus, the character of the federal presence in the West is unique. For westerners, the federal government is not only constitutionally, politically and financially the dominant partner, it is also, in many cases, quite literally the landlord.

As Richard Foster noted in Chapter 4, this all-pervasive presence of the federal government, manifested in its supervisory and regulatory role, its financial aid, and its land ownership, underlies what he describes as the unique "political schizophrenia" in the West. The omnipresence of the federal government is both a necessity to the functioning of the sometimes shaky western economies and at the same time a constant irritant to western plans and sensibilities.[14] We can argue that these resentments have led directly to efforts by the westerners who have been elected president to restructure the federal-state IGR system to decrease the influence of the federal government in state and local matters. The new federalism of both Richard Nixon and Ronald Reagan, while national in its scope, may be viewed as efforts by presidents from the West to redress grievances long simmering in the region which have led to such movements as the Sagebrush Rebellion and the Proposition 13 taxpayer revolt of the late 1970s.

Thus, President Nixon addressed both national and western concerns when he divided the country into ten administrative regions.

> By the end of Nixon's administration, nine domestic departments or agencies were covered by this structure. In addition, their key field representatives served as members of the federal regional councils (FRC's) which were assigned both an interdepartmental coordinative and an intergovernmental liaison role. Attempts to delegate "sign-off" discretion in managing grants from Washington, D.C., to the field produced the claim, in 1972, that at least 190 grant programs had been decentralized administratively.[15]

By the late 1980s most government departments and agencies had a branch office available to state and local government officials, and citizens. Thus, western officials and citizens interested in the federal fisheries policy could get an answer in Seattle; California cities could contact a grant administrator for a federal program run by the Department of Housing and Urban Development in San Francisco; and state and local officials in the Southwest could deal directly with representatives of the Department of Energy in Albuquerque instead of in Washington, D.C.

2. STATE-LOCAL RELATIONS

We explained earlier that the state-local IGR system in the West mirrors that of the federal-state IGR system. There is a dominant senior partner (the state government) which—as in the "permissive federalism" that characterizes federal-state relations—shares a small measure of its powers with local governments. The cities, as we also noted earlier, are corporations legally chartered by the legislature of each state. The county governments are even more directly under state control since they are technically subdivisions of the state government, legally designated as "quasi-municipal corporations" created by the state for its administrative convenience.[16] In recent years, several western states, as Blair has noted,

> have turned to the use of administrative controls to regulate the incorporation of new governmental units [including cities, townships, and special districts]. State commissions to review incorporation or annexation proposals exist in several states and countywide review agencies have been established in other states. Both types of review agencies are empowered to make decisions as to the appropriateness of the proposals before them and to approve or disapprove them with or without amendment.[17]

Thus, state governments not only share power with local governments, but in many cases the state government regulates county, city or special district governments directly.

Western states have also formed commissions to oversee and administer various other aspects of life within their state boundaries and which directly impact the operation of local government. These include: mental health care and the licensing of physicians, the regulation of coastal areas, agricultural labor relations, the arts, air pollution and civil rights. In addition, in California a commission was formed in the late 1980s to investigate the role of "self-esteem" in the state and local workforce. Other administrative roles played by state government in the West include key roles played by state judicial systems and water agencies.

3. WESTERN INTERSTATE ORGANIZATIONS AND COMPACTS

Interstate organizations (ISOs) and compacts, sometimes referred to as multistate organizations, are another example of the interaction that occurs between government units in the West. ISOs are developed to promote the common interests of two or more states. Some are formed by a compact between the member states that outlines the duties and responsibilities of each member. These compacts are enforceable contracts that must receive consent from the U.S. Congress, as mandated by Article I, Section 10, of the U.S. Constitution, which states: "No State shall, without the consent of Congress . . . enter into any Agreement or Compact, with another State." Along with giving its consent, the federal government sometimes becomes a member of these ISOs, sharing the duties and responsibilities of the other members. Most ISOs, however, need no congressional approval.

Although ISOs have been in existence since the founding of the nation, primarily as compacts defining common state boundaries, it was not until the early twentieth century that they began to expand their scope of interest and increase their membership. This growth can be traced to the greater complexity of modern society and the need for innovative governmental techniques to deal with this.[18]

In the western states, two examples of early ISOs were the Four Corners Regional Commission and the Old West Regional Commission. These were established to promote economic development. The former, established in 1966, included Arizona, Colorado, New Mexico, Utah and Nevada, together with the U.S. Department of Commerce. The Old West Regional Commission, established in 1972, was similar to Four Corners in scope, and had a membership of Montana, Wyoming, North Dakota, South Dakota and Nebraska. Like Four Corners, the Old West also included a partnership with the federal government.[19]

In 1975, concern over energy resources led to the formation of the Western Governors' Regional Energy Policy Office. Richard Lamm, governor of Colorado, along with governors of the other Mountain states, felt that a unified organization was necessary to deal with energy resource development. In 1979, the regional energy policy office went through some refinement and a new organization, the Western Governors' Policy Office was formed. This office, like its predecessor, was concerned with energy resources. Its bargaining position was increased through added financial support and new members, particularly Alaska. It also increased its scope, adding natural resources like water and agriculture to its agenda. In 1984, this organization was reorganized as the Western Governors' Association (WGA). Comprising eighteen western states, two territories and one commonwealth, its main purposes are to facilitate the exchange of ideas on regional issues, to promote its members' interests both nationally and internationally, and to compile and analyze business, governmental and educational data of its member governments.[20] WGA holds an annual meeting at which members discuss policy issues and set an agenda for the coming year. Along with its main office in Denver, WGA has an office in Washington, D.C., for the major purpose of monitoring federal actions that may affect its members.

Not all ISOs have such a broad focus as WGA and its predecessor. The Western Interstate Commission for Higher Education, for example, is concerned only with interstate cooperation in post-secondary education. Some western states, such as Alaska, lack the educational resources for specialized schools for medicine and law; the commission provides the students of these states with the opportunity to attend specialized schools in other western states without having to pay nonresident tuition, and thus enables these states to deal with their shortage of doctors and other professionals.

Visit U.S.A. West, with the five Pacific and three of the Mountain states as members, is an ISO that promotes tourism in this eight-state region. The Western States Association of Tax Administrators is an ISO that facilitates information exchange between tax administrators throughout the western states. These types of ISOs are designed to pool resources in an area of mutual concern to the member states.

Table 15.1 shows ten examples of ISOs in operation in the West today. It provides an indication of the scope and membership of ISOs in the region. This, however, is far from an exhaustive list: the Western Governors' Task Force in 1976 found over one hundred such organizations in the western states, focusing on energy, water, the environment, education, and a host of other areas.[21] ISOs, like other areas of intergovernmental cooperation, are constantly changing to meet the needs of an increasingly complex society and thus the changing needs of state governments.

4. FEDERAL-LOCAL RELATIONS

Federal-local relations in the West have been crucial to the development of the region. Projects like the interstate highways and schemes such as the Central Valley Project in California, the Salt River Project in Arizona, and the Bonneville Dam project in the Pacific Northwest produced roads, dams, electric power and recreation facilities, and made water available for irrigation, commercial and domestic use. Neither the states nor the local governments could have afforded to finance such massive and expensive projects by themselves. And the federal government could not have undertaken them without the active participation and support of local as well as state governments.

The federal-local IGR connection became increasingly important with the advent of creative federalism in the mid-1960s, with its focus on trying to ameliorate the major problems of America's decaying metropolitan areas and large cities. With their malapportioned legislatures favoring rural interests, the states had not given these urban problems the attention that they warranted. So the federal government increased direct aid to cities—including Seattle, Los Angeles, Denver, Portland and others in the West—for urban renewal of de-

Table 15.1   Ten Western Interstate Organizations with Their Member States

Organization	Member States												
	Alaska	Arizona	California	Colorado	Hawaii	Idaho	Montana	Nevada	New Mexico	Oregon	Utah	Washington	Wyoming
Council of State Governments–Western Office (CSG)	X	X	X	X	X	X	X	X	X	X	X	X	X
Western Governors' Association (WGA)	X	X	X	X	X	X	X	X	X	X	X	X	X
Western Interstate Commission for Higher Education (WICHE)	X	X	X	X	X	X	X	X	X	X	X	X	X
Western States Foundation/Senate Western Coalition (WSF/SWC)	X	X	X	X	X	X	X	X	X	X	X	X	X
Western Association of Fish and Wildlife Agencies (WAFWA)	X	X	X	X	X	X	X	X	X	X	X	X	X
Western Council of State Foresters (WCSF)	X	X	X	X	X	X	X	X	X	X	X	X	X
Western Interstate Energy Board (WIEB)	X	X	X	X	X	X	X	X	X	X	X	X	X
Western U.S. Agricultural Trade Association (WUSATA)	X	—	X	X	X	X	—	—	X	X	X	X	X
Western States Association of Tax Administrators (WSATA)	X	X	X	X	X	X	X	X	X	X	X	X	X
Visit U.S.A. West (Tourism Organization)	X	X	—	—	X	X	—	X	—	X	—	X	—

Note: CSG, WGA, WSF/SWC, WCSF, WIEB, WSATA contain more members than the 13 western states.

Source: Western Governors' Association, *Western Multi-State Organization Directory,* 1987.

caying downtown areas, public transport facilities, pollution control, and improvement of law enforcement, among other functions.

The 1980s, as we have seen, saw a cutback in federal aid, including that to the local governments. Nevertheless, the federal-local IGR relationship, particularly the financial connection, is still vitally important. This was particularly evident in the estimated $4 billion of federal disaster relief that northern California communities received to deal with the devastation of the October 1989 earthquake.

Earlier in 1989 the importance of the federal-local financial connection was made particularly evident when the Bush administration stepped up the war on drugs. Part of the complex strategy for combating the problem was drug education programs in the schools, local rehabilitiation programs and increased law enforcement. The war could not be won without the cooperation of local governments, especially those of large cities such as Los Angeles, where the drug problem had reached enormous proportions. And the cities could not step up their effort unless they received increased financial and other assistance from the federal government.

5. THE RELATIONSHIP BETWEEN LOCAL GOVERNMENTS

There is often a need for relations between various local governments in the West. Typically, a regionwide need for a service such as mass transit, water, or utilities, or the need to tackle a problem such as crime or air pollution, will result in several local governments cooperating to pool their talents and take advantage of lower costs of the service or amenity provided. Often local governments will establish an intergovernmental compact or organization to deal with the service or issue. One example is BART, the Bay Area Rapid Transit District, which provides public transport for San Francisco and many other communities in the surrounding metropolitan area. Another is SCAG, the Southern California Association of Governments. This association attempts to cope with such common regional problems as smog and congested freeways.

While most local government compacts are formed within state boundaries, when the need arises such organizations are developed across state borders. California and Nevada, for example, have a regional government compact—The California-Nevada Tahoe Regional Planning Agency—to clean up pollution in Lake Tahoe and to plan for managed growth in the Lake Tahoe basin, which straddles the border between the two states. Similarly, local water districts in California cooperate with local water districts in Arizona to exchange water in times of drought, and to plan for managing the scarce water resources of the rivers used by water districts in both states.

Another important way in which local officials from varying jurisdictions interact within and across state lines is through local government associations. Some of these, such as the League of Arizona Cities and Towns, the Wyoming Association of Municipalities, and Colorado Counties Incorporated, are general organizations that bring together elected and appointed officials of all types. Others, such as the New Mexico Association of School Administrators, the Alaska Association of Chiefs of Police, and the Oregon Chapter of the American Planning Association, are organizations representing specific local government professionals.

Whether general or specific, such local government organizations pursue the major objectives of enhancing their abilities to perform their service by lobbying state and federal officials for increased funding and an improved operating environment, and by disseminating information and advancing professionalism among their members. Annual meetings, conventions and conferences, such as that of the League of California Cities, bring together local officials to exchange ideas and plan common strategies. Regional and subregional interaction is facilitated by such organizations as the Western Interstate Regional meeting of the National Association of Counties and the Pacific Northwest City Managers Association.

Finally, it is important to emphasize once again that the division we have made here between the five facets of the IGR relationship is for the purpose of explaining the complexities of the overall intergovernmental relations system. Rarely, for example, will local governments interact, either through a compact or otherwise, without some involvement, whether direct or indirect, of the state or federal governments. The five aspects of IGR are inextricably connected: the decisions and actions of one facet of interaction will almost always impact one, and often all four, of the other facets of activity.

Relations Between Western Governments and Foreign Governments

Because the relations between western governments and foreign governments are transnational and do not take place entirely within the American federal system, we have not included them in the representation of IGR set out in Figure 15.1 or in the facets of IGR explained in the last section. In practice, however, these relations are a sixth facet of IGR in the West as well as in other regions of the nation.

It is, of course, primarily the federal government that engages in relations with foreign governments. This is because of the role in foreign relations accorded the national government by the U.S. Constitution and also because the states are prohibited in that document (Article I, Section 10) from entering into any "Agreement or Compact . . . with a foreign Power." Nevertheless, state and local governments have always interacted with foreign governments for a variety of reasons. Such interactions have increased markedly over the last twenty-five years; and some western governments have been at the forefront of this development. Several factors have prompted these increased interactions with foreign governments and their various cities and localities. As far as the West is concerned, these have been primarily the result of: (1) the expansion and increasing interdependence of the world economy; (2) increased immigration, especially from Mexico and the Far East; (3) a rising demand for educational and cultural exchanges; and (4) the need to deal with problems of resource use and the environment.

Not all western state and local governments are affected equally by the actions of foreign nations; and the desire among western governments to promote foreign contacts also varies. Location is an important factor here. Obviously, states bordering on Canada and Mexico will likely have more concern with the actions of these countries than will Colorado, Nevada, Oregon, Utah and Wyoming which have no international borders. Similarly, the Pacific states of Alaska, California, Hawaii, Oregon and Washington will be affected more by issues relating to trade with the Far East and the Pacific Rim nations than will the Mountain states.

Alaska provides some interesting examples of policy conflict and cooperation arising between a western state government and foreign governments as the result of location. In its relations with Canada, Alaska has cooperated on such issues as the management of caribou and other game that wander between the two nations, and on the delivery of services to remote areas, including education and public safety. But Alaska and Canada have engaged in bitter conflict over the rights to the salmon catch. Similarly, Alaska has cooperated with South Korea, Japan and Taiwan on many trade issues, including the shipment of coal and lumber. But again it has been locked in a bitter struggle with these nations over the interception by their fishing fleets of salmon on the high seas. This not only prevents the fish from returning to spawn in Alaskan streams but also in time will reduce the catch of Alaska fishermen. As noted above, constitutionally these problems can only be resolved through the tortuous process of international diplomacy and by treaties between the federal government and the countries concerned. The fact that Alaska has no part in this process and that these problems go unresolved for years adds to the feeling of helplessness to manage their own affairs on the part of some Alaskans. This further intensifies their antipathy toward the federal government.

Probably the major and certainly the fastest-growing area of relations between state and local governments in the West and foreign governments and localities relates to trade and the promotion of economic ties, especially with the Pacific Rim nations. Many western states have established trade offices in Japan, Taiwan and other Asian countries. As might be expected, California leads the way. In fact, not only the State of California but also several of its larger cities— Los Angeles, San Francisco and San Diego—have established such foreign trade offices. Besides being good for business this is also good for politics, as many California cities have substantial populations of Asian descent.

IGR in the West and Changes in Federal and State Administrations

Intergovernmental relations in the West change along with changes in personnel and in philosophy at both the federal and state levels. Changes in the IGR system in the West can also take place via the use of local or statewide initiative, recall and referendum campaigns. A new administration in Washington, D.C., will likely affect foreign policy and thus to some degree will impact the relations of western state governments with foreign governments and localities. In terms of the domestic operation of IGR, two examples will illustrate that a new administration at either the state or federal level or changes mandated by the electorate of a western state through the direct legislation process can cause significant changes in the IGR system.

In California dramatic changes in the relationship between county and state government and the suddenly tax-poor counties, cities and special districts was a direct effect of the successful 1978 campaign for Proposition 13 led by Howard Jarvis and Paul Gann.[22] The property tax limitations enacted in California and in several other western states dramatically changed the relationship of the local governments to their state governments. They greatly limited the amount of property taxes that local governments can levy against property owners, and exacerbated the financial dependence of local governments on the state legislatures for subventions or financial "bail out" legislation.

At the federal level, with the election in 1980 of Ronald Reagan, westerners widely believed that Reagan's policy of new federalism would decrease red tape and federal "strings" attached to matching funds and grants to state and local governments. And certainly the Reagan administration brought some benefits to state and local governments in the West. It created some new state and local programs and encouraged certain policy initiatives. Most notable were the Job Training and Partnership Act (JTPA), and the administration's support of unsuccessful efforts in Congress to enact legislation calling for the creation of urban enterprise zones in low-income city neighborhoods to try to attract business and industry by a combination of tax breaks and other incentives. This was coupled with a call for increased privatization of functions and services formerly provided by federal, state and local governments. This latter aspect of the administration's attempt to change the IGR system met with a mixed reaction from local officials in the West.

According to a 1986 survey of municipal officials in all thirteen western states, while some reductions of red tape and strings did take place in the Reagan administration, those responding to the survey were disappointed with the amount that remained.[23] While 60% reported satisfaction with Reagan's new federalism in 1981, only 43% of the same group of municipal officials were "satisfied" or "very satisfied" with it in 1986.[24]

The survey revealed that the widespread negative attitude prevalent among these officials by 1986 was based on their negative reaction to the effects of three major changes in IGR implemented by the Reagan administration. These were: (1) a largely successful attempt to lower expenditures targeted for municipal areas and state programs; (2) a short-lived federal-local "swap" in which the federal government would assume responsibility for Medicaid in exchange for the states assuming responsibility for AFDC (Aid to Families with Dependent Children); and (3) the "blocking" or consolidation of several federal-local programs and the elimination of several state and local grant programs, including the Comprehensive Employment Training Act (CETA), General Revenue Sharing (GRS), and Community Development Block Grants (CDBG).[25]

Conclusion: Past, Present and Future IGR in the West

As we have shown, intergovernmental relations in the West can be broken down into five distinct (but very much interconnected) sets of relationships between the governments of the region: (1) the federal government and western state government; (2) the state governments and the thousands of city, county, regional and special district governments in the West; (3) the thirteen western states; (4) federal and local governments; and (5) local governments both within the same state and sometimes across state lines. The history of politics, government and public policymaking in the West is basically a history of the workings of this vast intergovernmental network and, over time, the gradual erosion of local autonomy and political power in favor of increased power in the hands of the federal and state governments.

The national and state governments have grown in power and influence because: (1) they are the "senior" partners in their respective IGR systems from a constitutional perspective; (2) they have superior financial resources; (3) many of the tasks of "local" governments require the resources or expertise of the centralized federal or state government; and (4) in the case of the federal government, the dominant IGR "partner" is the largest land holder in the West. For all these reasons political power and policymaking initiative have tended to drift away from local government in the West, and toward the state capitals and Washington, D.C.

Yet, despite increased centralization and the dominance of the federal and state governments in the IGR relationship, local governments and intergovernmental compacts, both interstate and intrastate, are essential partners in the western IGR system, and in fact are now more important than ever before. Over the years, cooperation, especially in financial relations, between the five facets of IGR in the West, and to some extent transnational governmental relations, have made it possible to solve problems that would not otherwise have been resolved. Whatever the political complexion of the governments in Washington, D.C., the state capitals, city halls and county seats, this interdependence is likely to increase and IGR become even more significant in the West, as elsewhere, as society grows even more complex and citizens demand increased services and solutions to chronic problems such as drugs, crime and pollution.

An overview of the basic principles of IGR in the West is an aid to understanding some of the specific policy areas that these inter-governmental relations impact. The following chapters will amply illustrate the intricacies and importance of the IGR system in the region.

Notes

1. Robert Jay Dilger, ed., *American Intergovernmental Relations Today: Perspectives and Controversies* (Englewood Cliffs, N.J.: Prentice Hall, 1986), xv.

2. *Census of Governments* (Washington, D.C.: U.S. Bureau of the Census, 1982); see also Chapter 13, Table 13.1.

3. Michael Reagan and John Sanzone, *The New Federalism*, 2nd ed. (New York: Oxford University Press, 1981), 20–21.

4. Jeffrey R. Henig, *Public Policy and Federalism: Issues in State and Local Politics* (New York: St. Martin's Press, 1985), 15.

5. *Ibid.*, 15–16.

6. David Walker, *Toward a Functioning Federalism* (Cambridge, Mass.: Winthrop, 1981), 112.

7. Terry Sanford, *Storm over the States* (New York: McGraw-Hill, 1967), 80.

8. Walker, *Toward a Functioning Federalism*, 128. See also Walker, "Federal Aid Administrators and the Federal System," in *Intergovernmental Perspective* 3, 4 (Fall 1977), 10–17.

9. See Thomas G. Alexander, *A Clash of Interests: Interior Department and Mountain West, 1863–96* (Provo, Utah: Brigham Young University Press, 1977); Gene M. Gressley, "Regionalism and the Twentieth Century West," in Jerome O. Steffen, ed., *The American West: New Perspectives* (Norman: University of Oklahoma Press, 1979); Richard D. Lamm and Michael McCarthy, *The Angry West: A Vulnerable Land and Its Future* (Boston: Houghton Mifflin, 1982); Arthur Miller, "Public Opinion and Regional Political Alignment," in Peter Galderisi et al., eds., *The Politics of Realignment: Party Change in the Mountain States* (Boulder, Colo.: Westview Press, 1986); Ken Robison, *The Sagebrush Rebellion: A Bid for Control* (Blackfoot, Idaho: Save Our Public Lands, 1981); and Ira Sharkansky, *Regionalism in American Politics* (Indianapolis: Bobbs-Merrill, 1970).

10. Neal R. Peirce, *The Mountain States of America: People, Politics and Power in the Eight Rocky Mountain States* (New York: W. W. Norton, 1971).

11. Reagan and Sanzone, *The New Federalism*, 175.

12. *City of Clinton v. Cedar Rapids and Missouri Railroad Company*, 924 Iowa 455, 1868. See also George S. Blair, *Government at the Grass-Roots*, 4th ed. (Pacific Palisades, Calif.: Palisades Publishers, 1986), 21.

13. See Martin Grodzins, "Centralization and Decentralization in the American Federal System," in Robert A. Goldwin, ed., *A Nation of States: Essays on the American Federal System* (Chicago: Rand McNally, 1965), 1–23.

14. See John G. Francis and Richard Ganzel, eds., *Western Public Lands: The Management of Natural Resources in a Time of Declining Federalism* (Totowa, N.J.: Rowman and Allanheld, 1984); Richard Ganzel, ed., *Resource Conflicts in the West* (Reno: Nevada Public Affairs Institute, 1983); and Frank J. Popper, "The Timely End of the Sagebrush Rebellion," *The Public Interest* 76 (Summer 1984), 61–73.

15. Walker, *Toward a Functioning Federalism*, 104.

16. George S. Blair, *Government at the Grass-Roots*, 3rd ed. (Pacific Palisades, Calif.: Palisades Press, 1981), 24.

17. *Ibid.*

18. The Council of State Governments, *Interstate Compacts and Agencies* (Lexington, Ky.: Council of State Governments, 1983), vi.

19. Lynton R. Hayes, *Energy, Economic Growth, and Regionalism in the West* (Albuquerque: University of New Mexico Press, 1980), 59.

20. *Western Multistate Organization Directory* (Denver: Western Governors' Association, 1987), 11.

21. Hayes, *Energy, Economic Growth, and Regionalism in the West*, 58.

22. John O. Sears and Jack Citrin, *Tax Revolt: Something for Nothing in California* (Cambridge, Mass.: Harvard University Press, 1982).

23. Robert J. Waste and Roger W. Caves, "New Federalism, Reaganomics and Western Cities: The View of Municipal Officials," paper presented at the Annual Meeting of the Western Political Science Association, 1986.

24. *Ibid.*

25. See also Dale Rogers Marshall and Robert J. Waste, *Large Cities and the Community Development Act* (Davis: University of California at Davis, Institute of Governmental Affairs, 1977); and Waste and Caves, "New Federalism, Reaganomics and American Cities: A Research Note," paper presented at the Annual Meeting of the Western Political Science Association, 1987.

16

LAND AND NATURAL RESOURCE POLICY, I: DEVELOPMENT AND CURRENT STATUS

R. McGreggor Cawley and Sally K. Fairfax

*A*S EARLIER CHAPTERS HAVE MADE ABUNDANTLY clear, the presence of the federal public lands affects virtually all aspects of western politics. In this chapter and the next we will investigate the evolving character of public land policy to discover why it occupies this central role in western affairs. While the sheer magnitude of the federal estate is a key component of the situation, size alone does not explain the intensity of conflicts like the Sagebrush Rebellion that have periodically erupted in the West. It seems plausible, therefore, that other factors must be at work here.

One such factor is situated in understanding the history of the public lands. From the time the original thirteen colonies first contemplated forming a union to the present day, public land policy has provided an important arena for structuring the relations among governments in this country. In consequence, discussions about land use have always carried on an implicit dialogue regarding the distribution of power among the various governmental units. In developing this theme, we will argue that the modern image of active federal management and control being at loggerheads with state interests is a relatively recent phenomenon. Throughout most of this country's history, public land policy has been the result of negotiations in Congress to resolve a maturing set of disputes among the states.

The purpose of the present chapter is to establish a historical context for public land policy, and then to examine the three themes that have structured the modern dialogue between the federal government and the western states. These themes are: (1) the changing national agenda; (2) multiple user conflict; and (3) bureaucratic fragmentation. In the following chapter we will use two case studies in an attempt to demonstrate that despite federal dominance, state and local governments have always had an important part in the making of public land policy.

From Public Domain to Federal Lands

In the heat of the Sagebrush Rebellion, a disgruntled Select Committee on Public Lands of the Nevada legislature declared that "federal policies affecting the West . . . are made in ignorance of conditions and concerns in the West, . . . those policies are made for a so-called national constituency without regard for western problems."[1] Two hundred years earlier, an equally chagrined inhabitant of the western territories had proclaimed: "I do certify that all mankind, agreebale to every constitution formed in America, have an undoubted right to pass into every vacant country, and form their constitution. . . . Congress is not empowered to forbid them, neither is Congress empowered . . . to make any sale of the uninhabited lands to pay the public debts."[2] It would seem, then, that western complaints about national policies are not a recent phenomenon.

The apparent parallel between these statements, however, should not be interpreted as an indicator that little has changed. To the contrary, the structure of land policy has undergone significant shifts over the last two centuries. Our goal in this section is to outline briefly the contours of these changes, using as our theme a little-noticed modification in nomenclature that has taken place over the last fifty years. Whereas it was once standard procedure to refer to the public lands as the *public domain*, they are now generally called the *federal lands*. The story behind this transformation, we believe, provides an important context for understanding both modern land policy and modern intergovernmental relations.

Our story begins in 1776 with the recognition that successful prosecution of the Revolution required a central government capable of coordinating the efforts of the thirteen colonies. Immediately after adopting the Declaration of Independence, the Continental Congress began consideration of such a central government in the form of the Articles of Confederation. Although several issues became points of contention, the question of the "western reserves" represented the single roadblock to a unanimous adoption of the Articles.

Seven of the original states claimed exclusive jurisdiction over the "western reserves." These land claims were not inconsequential: Virginia claimed 164 million acres, Georgia 94 million and North Carolina 58 million—all lying westward of what are now the boundaries of those states. Two problems emerged in this situation. First, the claims among these states overlapped; and second, several small states that did not border on the western reserves—most notably Maryland—argued they should have equal access to those lands. Under the Articles, the central government had no control over western lands claimed by the states and "could not interfere in the matter of state boundaries except through an elaborate system of arbitration."[3] As a result, ratification of the Articles remained in jeopardy.

After extended negotiations, the claimant states agreed to cede the western reserves to Congress. This action settled the immediate crisis, but it also raised a new problem—what to do with the ceded lands? This was an especially troublesome question in light of the fact that the Articles provided no authority for Congress on the matter. Nevertheless, the Congress enacted a resolution defining how it would handle the ceded lands. The General Land Ordinance of 1785, unprecedented for its brevity and durability, established three basic principles that determined congressional land policy for over 120 years:

(1) that the lands were to "be disposed of for the common benefit of the United States";

(2) that the lands "shall be granted and settled at such times and under such regulations as shall hereafter be agreed on by the United States in Congress assembled"; and

(3) that the lands shall become new states, which shall "become members of the Federal Union, and shall have the same rights of sovereignty, freedom and independence as the other states."[4]

In short, the 1785 Ordinance created the "public domain."

Rapid westward expansion, though it was the goal of Congress, precipitated growing confrontations between European settlers and Native Americans. On one occasion, in fact, Congress dispatched troops to force settlers off land they had occupied in violation of a treaty between the United States and the "Indian Nations." Such incidents as these led Congress to adopt the General Land Ordinance of 1787 which provided "for the establishment of States, and permanent government therein, and for their admission to a share in the Federal councils, on an equal footing with the original states." The purpose of the 1787 ordinance was to combine the basic principles from the 1785 ordinance with a clear statement of Congress's authority to regulate matters in the western territories. This latter theme was reinforced several months later when the Constitutional Convention delegates adopted language that became Article IV, Section 3 of the Constitution: "The Congress shall have power to dispose of and make all needful rules and regulations respecting the territory or other property belonging to the United States."

There is a sense in which this early history seems to fit the modern image of a confrontation between the federal government and the states (or territories). And yet the actual record points in another direction. The key reference point here is Congress. Under both the Articles and the initial version of the Constitution, Congress served as a forum in which states worked out their disputes through bargaining and negotiation. In consequence, these early acts were not "federal policies" in a modern sense but rather agreements among the states about joint goals for the public domain.

The period from the 1790s to the 1880s was a time of national expansion. In consequence, land policy sought to accomplish two major goals: first, acquisition of the continent; and second, development of the nation through the sale and/or grant of those lands to states, organizations, and individuals. The first major expansion of the public domain came in 1803 when President Thomas Jefferson negotiated the Louisiana Purchase with France, adding over 500 million acres to the federal estate. The last major acquisition occurred in 1867 with the purchase of Alaska from Russia. Thus, in sixty-five years the public domain grew from 200 million acres (the amount ceded by the original states) to roughly 1.8 billion acres.

The disposal of the public domain was equally ambitious. Policies during this period provided for the sale and grant of public lands:

—to generate revenue for the national treasury;
—to stimulate settlement of the frontier regions;
—to reward military service;
—to encourage internal improvements (schools, roads, canals, railroads, etc.);
—to encourage exploitation of raw materials.

One measure of the effectiveness of these policies is that by the early 1900s, most of the public domain west of the original states and east of the 102nd meridian (roughly parallel to the eastern boundary of Colorado) had been converted into state and/or private property.

Although the disposal era appeared to be a period of general agreement regarding the purpose of the public domain, it was actually punctuated with a myriad of conflicts. What is important for our purposes, however, is that the form of these conflicts followed the general pattern established in the late 1700s. Once again, Congress served as the focal point for a series of disputes that pitted the "old states" of the east against the "new states" in the west.

The new states pushed for cession of all the federal lands within their boundaries. They claimed these lands as a prerequisite to the equality promised in the General Ordinance of 1787 and in previous cession agreements. Failing to achieve that, they bargained for grants of land and money, for speedy land surveys and sales, and for concessions to "squatters" on the public domain.[5] The old states took the position that the public domain existed only because of the "common blood, sword and purse" of the original thirteen colonies and challenged the constitutionality of statutes under which federal lands were granted to benefit economic development in western territories.[6]

At first, the expanding number of new states in Congress led to policies of increasingly generous land grants. As the nineteenth century drew to a close, however, the distinction between new states and old states was more problematic. Many of the early new states (primarily those east of the Mississippi River) joined with the old states in efforts to assure that the remaining public lands would serve the common benefits of all the states through permanent federal land reservations. This was not an inconsequential development, since most of the remaining public domain existed in the West as it is defined in this book, and most of the western states were still in territorial status. But other forces were also at work in the last decades of the nineteenth century.

Speaking of the period from the 1870s to the 1920s, historian Robert Wiebe suggests: "An age never lent itself more readily to sweeping, uniform description: nationalization, industrialization, mechanization, urbanization:"[7] In a society preoccupied with these values, the importance of land is increasingly measured in terms of the resources base it provides. What occurred during this time, in other words, was that broad policy discussions about the public domain became narrow dialogues about specific resources needed for an industrial society. Moreover, these resource dialogues were given a sense of urgency by the growing predictions regarding the potential for a serious resource crisis looming in the nation's future. As President Theodore Roosevelt explained to the first conference of the nation's governors:

> We began with an unapproached heritage of forests; more than half the timber is gone. We began with coal fields more extensive than those of any other nation and with iron ores regarded as inexhaustible, and many experts now declare that the end of both iron and coal is in sight. . . . The enormous stores of mineral oil and gas are largely gone. . . . Finally, we began with soils of unexampled fertility, and we have so impoverished them by injudicious use and by failing to check erosion that their crop-producing power is diminishing instead of increasing.[8]

The intersection of these concerns and the changing congressional attitude, then, was the basis for a new direction in land policy—a basis for converting the *public domain* into the *federal lands*.

A brief summary of some major land acts during this time will help to demonstrate our argument. Yellowstone National Park was reserved in 1872, marking the beginning of the national park system. The General Land Law Reform Act of 1891 established federal forest reserves, which subsequently became the national forest system. A significant portion of the mineral estate was reserved in federal ownership by the Mineral Leasing Act of 1920. And finally, the Taylor Grazing Act of 1934 brought the remaining public lands under federal control, leading to what Louise Peffer characterized as "the closing of the public domain."[9]

The shift from disposal of the public domain to retention of the federal lands carried significant implications regarding the structure of intergovernmental relations. On the one hand, the federal lands were placed under the administration of a bureaucracy staffed by professionally trained managers. This move set the stage for an ongoing series of confrontations between the western states and the federal land management agencies. On the other hand, the role of the states, which is often downplayed in contemporary analyses of federal land policy, actually assumed growing importance.

Although they are interrelated, we will separate these factors into two discussions. The remainder of this chapter will consider how the changing national agenda, interest group conflict, and bureaucratic fragmentation have structured confrontations between the western states and the federal managers. In the next chapter, we will return to the evolving role of states in the policy process.

The National Agenda

The rise of the progressive movement in the first decades of the twentieth century ushered in a new era of intergovernmental relations. One facet of progressivism—the conservation movement—crafted the initial agenda for federal land management. While the political implications behind the conservation movement have been the subject of considerable debate,[10] for our purposes the key feature of this era was the introduction of scientific management principles for the efficient use of federal land resources. Although the conservation movement did embody a recreation and preservation impulse, as demonstrated by the creation of the national park system, its main thrust remained "development." As Gifford Pinchot, a chief spokesman for the conservation movement, consistently argued: "The first principle of conservation is development, the use of natural resources now existing on this continent for the benefit of the people who live here now."[11]

Despite such reassurances, westerners expressed both skepticism and open hostility toward conservation. On the one hand, the specter of increasing portions of land being retained in federal ownership led to charges that the federal government was purposely retarding the natural growth of the West. On the other hand, the prospect of federal managers (frequently portrayed as "snobbish Eastern bureaucrats"[12]) controlling the exploitation of western resources, and thus the major economic activity in the region, was even more objectionable.

The early conservationists, however, proved extremely adept at pacifying the public outcry throughout the West.[13] Their primary theme was that federal management did not mean the end of exploitation activities but rather a new era of more orderly and less wasteful development. In the long run, the argument went, these new practices would brighten the western economic horizon by freeing that region from the "rape, ruin and run" mentality that had dominated earlier exploitation activities. Moreover, negotiations in Congress during this time helped sweeten the pot by earmarking revenues generated from the public lands for return to the western states. (We will explore this point more fully in the next chapter.)

Although these efforts did not completely pacify the western opposition, a truer measure of their success lies in the fact that conservation has become the reference point for determining the legitimacy of public land policy initiatives. Despite the often heated character of public land disputes, there remains a basic agreement that policies should serve the goal of "wise use." During the first half of the twentieth century, "wise use" defined in terms of managed development dominated the agenda. However, in the years following World War II the meaning of conservation began to change, signaling an important shift in the national agenda.[14]

Expanding prosperity, leisure time, and mobility for the population in the United States gave rise to renewed demands for policies more attentive to recreational pursuits and the preservation of the public lands in their natural state.[15] By the 1960s, these demands had captured the land use agenda, as demonstrated by two key events. First, in 1964, after nearly a decade of controversy, Congress enacted the Wilderness Act. In so doing, it created a new category of public lands which were to be managed so as to protect their "primeval character and influence." Though not a complete victory for preservation advocates, in that limited development activity, including mineral exploration, was permitted in the wilderness system, the Wilderness Act clearly identified "preservation" as the primary management mandate.

The second event occurred in 1965 when President Lyndon Johnson delivered a "Special Message to Congress on Conservation and Restoration of Natural Beauty." In this message, Johnson pointed to booming population growth, urbanization, and the poisonous byproducts of technology as forces that called for a "new conservation." This new conservation, Johnson explained,

> must be not just the classic conservation of protection and development, but a creative conservation of restoration and innovation. Its concern is not with nature alone, but with the total

relationship between man and the world around him. . . . In this conservation the protection and enhancement of man's opportunity to be in contact with beauty must play a major role.[16]

By the end of the decade, the new conservation had become "environmentalism" and in signing the National Environmental Policy Act into law on January 1, 1970, President Richard Nixon declared that the 1970s were to be the "Environmental Decade." Four months later, the environmental movement was officially christened by "Earth Day" celebrations throughout the country.

Despite this early enthusiasm, the "Environmental Decade" contained ambiguous elements. On the one hand, policies enacted during the late 1960s and early 1970s demonstrate a concerted effort to place preservation and restoration of the natural environment above economic development in the use of the federal lands. But, on the other hand, the advent of the energy crisis directed national attention to the rich energy resources in the West as a way to free the country from its foreign dependence. The primary consequence of these countervailing forces was a series of conflicts that intersected on the plane of intergovernmental relations.

Perhaps the best example of these conflicts was the confrontation over controlling growth associated with energy development in the West. A consistent focus of federal environmental policy was the need for planning efforts directed at controlling growth and development. These efforts were not always welcomed in the West, but the region's changing political climate, in combination with federal enforcement, gave clear indication that environmental protection was firmly established in the national agenda. At the same time, federal reaction to the energy crisis—"Project Independence"—suggested that the West was on the verge of a massive growth era.

While striking a balance between environment and energy is a thorny problem, the West found itself in a special bind. Efforts to secure federal impact assistance for the communities located near federal energy development projects were answered with the argument that expansions in local and state tax bases brought about by the growth in combination with increases in federal royalty payments to the states would provide sufficient revenues to mitigate impact. Additional federal aid, therefore, would amount to a "windfall" profit for the West. And yet when Montana and Wyoming increased severance taxes in an attempt to develop state revenues for impact mitigation, they were accused of trying to "hold up" the rest of the nation.[17] The Montana tax subsequently became the subject of a U.S. Supreme Court case, and though Montana won the challenge, the controversy raised troublesome signals about the role of the states in the federal system.[18]

The "changing national agenda," though a convenient shorthand expression, is somewhat misleading. Rather than *the federal government* changing its policies, the evolving federal lands agenda has been largely the product of interest group interaction. It is to this issue that we now turn.

Multiple User Conflict

While interest groups of one sort or another have always been involved in land policy,[19] retention of the federal lands under active management created a political climate in which group activity has flourished. The groups involved in modern land management can be divided into three general categories:

1. *Commodity interests*, which refers to groups involved in the development and/or extraction of public land resources like timber, fuel and nonfuel minerals, and domestic livestock forage.
2. *Recreational interests*, which refers to those groups seeking to use the public lands for activites like hiking, camping, hunting, and off-road vehicles.
3. *Environmental interests*, which refers to those groups seeking to preserve and/or restore the natural environments of the public lands.

These categories provide a basis for multiple sets of conflicts.

For example, commodity users frequently charge that environmental and recreational policies "lock up" federal land resources, thereby precluding development activity. Conversely, environmental/recreational interests charge that development activity reduces recreational opportunities and leads to irreversible damage of the natural environment. Moreover, off-road vehicles have done serious damage to the public lands, leading to conflict between environmental and recreational interests. Finally, conflict can also emerge among groups within these interest categories. Mining, timbering and grazing are not always compatible; nor is off-road vehicle use always compatible with hiking and camping.

The early conservationists were well aware of the potential for conflict, but buoyed by a faith in scientific management, they believed that interest group activity could be controlled through a careful calculation of the "greatest good for the greatest number for the longest time."[20] When put to practice, this adage became "multiple use management." The Multiple Use Sustained Yield Act of 1960, for instance, directed that the national forests be "administered for outdoor recreation, range, timber, watershed, and fish and wildlife purposes." A similar mandate was given to the Bureau of Land Management by the Federal Land Policy and Management Act of 1976.

Implementation of multiple use management has seldom gone smoothly. Commodity users continued to charge that federal agencies pursue misdirected and unresponsive policies, while conservation/ environmental groups complain that their interests are ignored because federal agencies have been "captured" by commodity users. However, as former chief forester Richard McArdle explained, user dissatisfaction is a routine component of the manager's job:

> Let me make it completely clear that I think being in the middle is exactly where we ought to be. I believe that our inability to satisfy completely each and every group of national forest users is a definite sign of success in doing the job assigned to us. When each group is somewhat dissatisfied, it is a sign that no group is getting more than its fair share.[21]

Conflict may be an inevitable consequence of multiple use management, but the missing variable in this equation is the western states.

Indeed, despite the fact that most of the major land conflicts of this century have been posed in the language of intergovernmental disputes, the exact role of the western states has remained ambiguous. Since the advent of the conservation movement, the western states have been portrayed as agents for commodity production. Such an image has been reinforced by the ongoing importance of resource extraction in the region's economy and by commodity users who consistently phrase their claims in the rhetoric of states' rights. In consequence, the ability of the western states to act as responsible managers has remained problematic.

Commodity users have enjoyed considerable influence in the West, but the same is true of all the states carved from the public domain. What makes the West different, then, is that it joined the Union after the conservation movement had transformed national development from a decentralized, state-oriented process into a centralized, federal activity. In an arena thus structured, there is little room for discussion of states as independent actors. Multiple use management anticipates only two categories of players: resource users and land managers.

Suspicions about the western states' capability and/or willingness as managers has led, in turn, to their classification as users. It may be, therefore, that the western states' claim of unequal status in the federal system is more accurate than commonly recognized.

Bureaucratic Fragmentation

One of the most frequently cited passages regarding the meaning of *conservation* comes from Gifford Pinchot's autobiography, *Breaking New Ground*. Therein Pinchot explains:

> Suddenly the idea flashed through my head that there was a unity in the complication—that the relation of one resource to another was not the end of the story. Here were no longer a lot of different, independent, and often antagonistic questions, each on its own separate little island, as we had been in the habit of thinking. In place of them, here was one single question with many parts. Seen in this new light, all these questions fitted into and made up the one great central problem of the use of the earth for the good of man.[22]

At first glance, this statement seems appropriate to the modern concept of ecological management—a concept of holistic management predicated on the view that natural resources exist in an interrelated system. However, the actual context of this quotation is bureaucratic politics.

Describing the political landscape in the early 1900s, Pinchot points to the existence of "twenty-odd Government organizations in Washington which had to do with natural resources."[23] The mere existence of multiple agencies was not the problem. Instead it was this:

> Every Bureau chief was for himself and his own work, and the devil take all the others. Everyone operated inside his own fence, and few were big enough to see over it. They were all fighting each other for place and credit and funds and jurisdiction. What little co-operation there was between them was an accidental, voluntary, and personal matter between men who happened to be friends.[24]

Thus, Pinchot's statement of holistic management has less to do with natural resources than with bureaucratic unity—a unity he likened to the formation of the United States from thirteen separate colonies.

Although conservation as a resource management philosophy has

Table 16.1   Federal Agencies Responsible for Federal Lands, and Percentage of Land Each Controls

Federal Agencies	% of Land Under Their Control
Bureau of Land Management	46
Forest Service	26
Fish & Wildlife Service	12
National Park Service	10
Department of Defense	3
Other[a]	2
Total	99[b]

[a]Primarily lands administered by the Bureau of Indian Affairs, Bureau of Reclamation, and the Army Corps of Engineers.

[b]There are other agencies that regulate land use even though they possess minimal land holdings; these include the Soil Conservation Service (SCS) and the Agricultural Conservation Program (ACP) in the Department of Agriculture, and the Office of Surface Mining (OSM) in the Department of Interior.

Source: U.S. Department of Interior, Bureau of Land Management, *Public Land Statistic 1984* (Washington, D.C.: Government Printing Office, 1984).

become deeply embedded in natural resource policy, it has not provided either unity or harmony among natural resource management agencies. Table 16.1 lists the principal federal agencies with direct administrative responsibility for the federal lands and the percentage of land under their control.

Nearly every facet of natural resource policy, moreover, has a story of bureaucratic competition. Despite his call for unity, Pinchot exploited the growing antagonisms between western stock raisers and the Department of Interior in order to expand the Forest Service's control of the national forests. He also carried out an unsuccessful campaign to transfer the national parks from the Department of Interior to the Forest Service. Part of the controversy surrounding the creation of the national wilderness system, in turn, centered on the continuing competition between the Forest Service and the Park Service.[25]

Marc Reisner summarized the impact of competition between the Army Corps of Engineers and the Bureau of Reclamation in the following manner: "the Corps of Engineers and the Bureau squandered their political capital and billions in taxpayers' money on vainglorious rivalry, with the result that much of what they really wanted to build does not now exist and probably never will."[26] Browne and Meier suggest that in addition to the Soil Conservation Service (SCS) and the Agricultural Conservation Program (ACP), "seven other USDA agencies . . . both independently and cooperatively sponsor 34 programs with soil and water projects related to SCS and ACP efforts."[27] And these examples only scratch the surface of the interagency competition web that has developed in the natural resource policy arena.

Bureaucratic fragmentation results from a variety of factors. Scientific management, with its emphasis on resource categories and expertise, creates a climate in which specialized problems are viewed as requiring specialized agencies. Hence, the national forests require management by professionally trained foresters.[28] Interest groups understand that agencies with narrow missions are easier to influence than ones with broader missions. Western stock raisers dominated the Bureau of Land Management for thirty years because its primary mission was regulating grazing.[29] Bureaucrats understand that narrowly defined missions with specialized clienteles lead to greater autonomy. Former secretary of the interior Harold Ickes referred to the Army Corps of Engineers as an "insubordinate and self-seeking clique."[30] Moreover, bureaucratic fragmentation seems to be a natural extension of the political fragmentation upon which the Constitution of 1787 was founded.

As might be expected, assessing the actual impact of this fragmentation is largely a matter of interpretation. Throughout the post–World War II era, concerns about efficient resource use and greater control over the bureaucratic structure have generated calls for reorganization and consolidation, including a recurring proposal for the creaton of a federal department of natural resources.[31] On the other hand, Nienaber and McCool assessed the situation in *Staking Out the Terrain*, and concluded that bureaucratic competition may have actually produced better policies than would have resulted from a monolithic structure.[32]

As with increased group activity, bureaucratic fragmentation creates confusion in the intergovernmental dialogue. Although western complaints are typically lodged against the "federal government," such an expression actually represents a convenient shorthand for frustration with the diverse, often contradictory, policies pursued by federal agencies. A brief survey of the 1970s policy landscape will help demonstrate this point.

In 1977, President Jimmy Carter announced the deauthorization of several federal reclamation projects. In doing so he brought an end to the era of large-scale federally funded dams in the West. While this action was troublesome in its own right (see Chapter 18), it came at a time when federal plans for massive developments of coal and oil shale, as well as strict federal surface mine reclamation standards, pointed to a future of intensified competition over scarce western water resources. Despite the perceived need for energy development, the Carter administration pushed for expansion of the wilderness system and withdrew 110 million acres of Alaskan lands from development activity. Finally, in the fall of 1979, the Defense Department announced plans to locate the infamous "race track" MX missile system in the Great Basin area of Nevada and Utah. Touted as the largest construction program in history, the MX system ignited a heated political debate.[33]

Although the racetrack proposal was eventually defeated, and energy development never reached the scale anticipated, the 1970s did seem to provide an endless barrage of federal policies made with little regard for the "conditions and concerns" of the West. It is not surprising, therefore, that the 1970s should end in a major conflict linking public lands policy with intergovernmental relations. As Philip Burgess, then executive director of the Western Governors' Policy Office, explained at a national Sagebrush Rebellion conference in 1980:

> Amid our different approaches to the appropriate course of action is an underlying agreement among us—an agreement on the general attitude of the sagebrush rebellion. This attitude insists on the need to strengthen the role of the states and local governments at all levels of decisionmaking in the American federal system— and especially decisions about the management and regulation of our lands. . . . And it is an attitude that demands that the various interests that constitute our West stand together in order that our common fears and concerns—and our aspirations as well—are heard by the nation.[34]

Summary

If our story ended here, we would have a rather dismal conclusion. The shift from disposal of the public domain to active management of the federal lands has exacted a heavy toll on the western states. Unable to stake out an independent posture, the western states have been relegated to a sideline position in the ongoing struggle among interest groups and federal agencies. But fortunately our story does not end here.

Although post–World War II discussions have generally ignored the role of states and localities in public land policy, more recent trends suggest that subnatioinal governments may be emerging as central players. Indeed, despite suspicions about state management capabilities, environmental policy has actually expanded the role of subnational governments. Moreover, the western states have responded by expanding their institutional capabilities. It is to these developments that we will turn in the next chapter.

Notes

1. Nevada State Legislature, Select Committee on Public Lands, press release issued November 26, 1979.

2. Quoted in Merrill Jensen, *The New Nation* (New York: Alfred A. Knopf, 1963), 357.

3. Thomas Abernathy, *Western Lands and the American Revolution* (New York: D. Appleton–Century, 1937), 365. Abernathy also concludes, in what is regarded as the classic study of the subject, that the large vs. small states (or landless states vs. states with land claims) sobriquet is a bogus characterization of the conflict. Chronicling the role of land speculators in foreign relations, the war effort, and subsequent efforts to establish a union, Abernathy concludes that the conflict was among land speculators, not between coalitions of states of different sizes. He casts the speculators as manipulators of different levels of government: speculators that were claiming the land through control of state government vs. those seeking control by challenging the alleged state claims and asserting primacy of the federal government (see p. 172). For the purposes of this discussion, the goals and motives of the advocates at the state and federal levels are less significant than the patterns by which they negotiated their differences.

4. Henry Steele Commager, *Documents in American History, Volume 1* (Englewood Cliffs, N.J.: Prentice Hall, 1973), 119–20.

5. *Squatters* were those who settled illegally on land in advance of the mandatory land survey and then came into conflict with bona fide purchasers of the land over title. "Squatter's Rights" issues were ultimately resolved to the benefit of the squatter—that is, the person who had actually lived on and settled the land.

6. Thomas C. Donaldson, *The Public Domain: Its History with Statistics*, U.S. Congress, House of Representatives, Document 47, part 4 (Report of the Public Land Commission), 46th Cong., 3d Sess. July 1881, at 256 for references concerning the constitutionality of such grants.

7. Robert H. Wiebe, *The Search for Order, 1877–1920* (New York: Hill and Wang, 1967), 12.

8. Theodore Roosevelt, "Opening Address by the President." *Proceedings of a Conference of Governors in the White House*, ed. Newton C. Blanchard (Washington, D.C.: Government Printing Office, 1909), 7–8.

9. E. Louise Peffér, *The Closing of the Public Domain* (Stanford: Stanford University Press, 1951).

10. See, for example, the debate summarized by excerpts in Roderick Nash, *The American Environment: Readings in the History of Conservation*, 2nd ed. (Reading, Mass.: Addison–Wesley Publishing Company, 1976), 79–93.

11. Gifford Pinchot, *The Fight for Conservation* (Seattle: University of Washington Press, 1967), 43.

12. Nash, *The American Environment*, 64.

13. Elmo R. Richardson provides an excellent account of these efforts in *The Politics of Conservation: Crusades and Controversies, 1879–1913* (Berkeley: University of California Press, 1962).

14. Grant McConnell, "The Conservation Movement—Past and Present," *Western Political Quarterly* 7 (1954), 463–78.

15. Samuel Hays, *Beauty, Health, and Permanence: Environmental Politics in the United States, 1955–1985* (New York: Cambridge University Press, 1987).

16. Lyndon B. Johnson, "Special Message to Congress on Conservation and Restoration of Natural Beauty," in *Public Papers of the Presidents: Lyndon B. Johnson* (Washington, D.C.: U.S. Government Printing Office, 1965), 156.

17. R. McGreggor Cawley and Kenyon Griffin, "Regional Equity: The Politics of Severance Taxation," in *Resource Conflicts in the West*, Richard Ganzel, ed. (Reno: Nevada Public Affairs Institute, 1983), 80–93.

18. James J. Lopach, "The Supreme Court and Resource Federalism: *Commonwealth Edison Co. v. Montana*" in John G. Francis and Richard Ganzel, eds., *Western Public Lands: The Management of Natural Resources in a Time of Declining Federalism* (Totowa, N.J.: Rowman and Allanheld, 1985), 282–302.

19. Two of the more famous (or infamous) examples from earlier times were land speculators and the railroads.

20. Pinchot, *The Fight for Conservation*, 48.

21. McArdle quoted in Phillip O. Foss, ed., *Recreation* (New York: Van Nostrand, 1971), 401.

22. Pinchot, *The Fight for Conservation*, 322.

23. *Ibid.*, 319.

24. *Ibid.*, 321.

25. Craig W. Allen, "Wilderness Preservation as a Bureaucratic Tool," in Phillip O. Foss, ed., *Federal Lands Policy* (Westport, Conn.: Greenwood Press, 1987), 127–38.

26. Marc Reisner, *Cadillac Desert: The American West and Its Disappearing Water* (New York: Viking-Penguin, 1986), 221.

27. William P. Browne and Kenneth J. Meier, "Choosing Depletion? Soil Conservation and Agricultural Lobbying," in Susan Welch and Robert Mei-

wald, eds., *Scarce Natural Resources: The Challenge to Public Policy Making* (Beverly Hills: Sage Publications, 1983), 257–58.

28. Herbert Kaufman, *The Forest Ranger* (Baltimore: Johns Hopkins University Press, 1960).

29. Phillip O. Foss, *Politics and Grass: The Administration of Grazing on the Public Domain* (Seattle: University of Washington Press, 1960).

30. Arthur Maass, *Muddy Waters: The Army's Engineers and the Nation's Rivers* (Cambridge: Harvard University Press, 1951), xiv.

31. Mister Z, "The Case for a Department of Natural Resources," in Dennis L. Thompson, ed., *Politics, Policy and Natural Resources* (New York: The Free Press, 1972), 146–55.

32. Jeanne Nienaber and Daniel McCool, *Staking Out the Terrain: Power Differentials Among Natural Resource Management Agencies* (Albany: State University of New York Press, 1985).

33. Lauren Holland and Robert C. Benedict, "The Great Basin States and the MX," in Ganzel, *Resource Conflicts in the West*, 60–79; Paul J. Culhane, "Heading 'Em Off at the Pass: MX and the Public Lands Subgovernment," in Foss, *Federal Lands Policy*, 91–110.

34. Philip M. Burgess, "Rebels with a Cause: The Sagebrush Movement and the Future of Federalism," in *Agenda for the '80s: A New Federal Land Policy* (Salt Lake City: League for the Advancement of States' Equal Rights, 1981), 13.

17

LAND AND
NATURAL RESOURCE
POLICY, II:
KEY CONTEMPORARY
ISSUES

Sally K. Fairfax and
R. McGreggor Cawley

*T*HIS CHAPTER USES TWO CASE STUDIES TO SUPPORT
our thesis, stated in the previous chapter, that subnational governments are assuming a more important role in natural resource policy.
The first case concerns the evolution of programs that share receipts
from development of federally owned resources with the states and
localities in which the resources are located. The second case puts
recent litigation over the role of state law in federal land management
into its historic context. States and localities receive up to 90% of the
gross receipts from the sale and lease of federally owned timber, coal,
oil, gas, forage and a host of other resources.[1] The conventional wis-
dom that these payments to states and counties are required in order

to compensate for the financial burdens created by federal land ownership and the tax exempt status[2] of the federal lands is ubiquitous, and also incorrect on at least two counts. First, generally speaking, federal land ownership does not create any identifiable financial losses.[3] Second, receipt-sharing programs are as old as federal land ownership itself, and do not depend on recent theories about burdens. Broadly speaking, they originated in the General Land Ordinance of 1785 and the subsequent accession statutes at a time when the federal holdings were presumed to be temporary and there were, moreover, precious few surrounding governments to be burdened.

A more accurate view of the receipt-sharing case is as a continuation of the shifting regional coalitions of states and their supporters bargaining in Congress, which characterized nineteenth-century land policy. Confronted with the congressional policy shift from land disposition to land retention, the western states became sophisticated in insisting that they should be compensated with a share of the revenues produced by development of the retained resources. Eastern states, in turn, understood that increasing assertions of national authority over public lands would meet less resistance in the western states received a generous share of the revenues. Thus public land receipt sharing looks very much like an attempt to "buy" western states' compliance with the permanent retention of federal lands within their boundaries.

The second case concerns the Granite Rock litigation, in which the U.S. Supreme Court addressed the question of whether federal or state law is controlling on federal lands. The specific issue involved a private mining claim located in a national forest in California's coastal zone. The Court's decision employs pre-emption analysis, which involves the resolution of apparent conflicts between federal and state law in any policy area, from personal liability to regulation of nuclear power plants.[4] The question of whether or not federal law, which under the U.S. Constitution is the supreme law of the land, supersedes or pre-empts conflicting state law has been commonplace for most of U.S. history in other policy fields.[5] It has only recently, however, become a factor in public land litigation.

Pre-emption is an important question because in major environmental legislation of the 1970s Congress directed that states play the lead role in regulation of air pollution and water pollution, coastal zone protection and toxic substances control. Moreover, the days are gone when western state legislatures held the range livestock industry in an uncritical embrace[6] or sought federal subsidies for water development without regard to efficient resource allocation or environmental consequences.[7] For the first time in their history the western states are inclined to regulate more stringently than the federal government. Thus increasingly capable western state governments are urged by an equally diverse array of interest groups to pursue distinctive agendas on the federal lands.

When taken together, these cases suggest a pattern of enhanced state and local participation in the management of the federal holdings, and a declining motivation in eastern states to spend tax dollars to purchase western compliance. In addition, the once sharp distinction between eastern and western priorities has become less pronounced as urbanization has spread throughout the West. We will conclude this chapter by suggesting that a reduction in the authority the federal government exercises over the western public lands is a plausible future scenario. This may not produce a change in management priorities—if we agree that westerners are not all that different in their values from the nation as a whole. Westerners may indeed become even more sensitive to environmental degradation of their region—for aesthetic, spiritual or tourism reasons—than the environmental/conservation movement, which has been typically regarded as stronger in the East. Whatever one's response to that suggestion may be, looking at the near and distant past better prepares us to see patterns and to speculate on how they might evolve in the future.

Receipt Sharing

Budgetary pressures at all levels of government have focused attention on revenue aspects of federal resource management, which were generally ignored until recently. The Reagan administration's efforts to rescind programs granting states and localities a share of such revenues[8]—or at least to shift the basis for calculating the share to a percentage of net rather than gross receipts[9]—have raised questions about the history and the original context of the sharing. The western states' traditional posture on this issue has been that because federal lands are exempt from state and local taxation they are financial burdens on states and localities. This position is seriously undermined by this historical inquiry, in which receipt sharing emerges as an equalizer in two centuries of efforts to facilitate radical changes in expectations regarding federal land ownership.

As noted in the previous chapter, the overriding goal of nine-

teenth-century land policy was disposal of the public domain in order
to form and settle new states. Receipt sharing played an essential role
in that process. In the accession statutes, new states were required
to waive interest in and taxing authority over the federal lands within
their jurisdiction. Moreover, they were obliged to agree to hold newly
patented[10] federal lands exempt from state and local taxation for five
years. The Congress insisted on this in order to allow settlers time to
become established before having to pay state and local taxes. As a
quid pro quo, new states were given a percentage of land sales receipts, and they bargained for land grants. The new state of Ohio,
joining in 1803, received one section in each township to support
development of public schools, and 5% of the proceeds from sale of
federal lands.

As the new states became more numerous and powerful in Congress, they received more generous portions. The California accession
statute, passed in 1850, indicates the broadening scope of the negotiations and the increasing generosity of Congress to the new states.
However, hostility to the admission of California as a free state and
the belief that her rich mineral deposits made "liberality toward it less
necessary" resulted in Congress being less generous.

> True, it was the first state to be given two sections for public
> schools [later the ante was raised to four sections] . . . and Cal-
> ifornia was given 6,400 acres for public buildings and 46,080 acres
> for a seminary (less than Florida). [But,] California did not receive
> salt springs, 5 per cent of the net proceeds from lands sales, direct
> grants for railroads or wagon roads as Minnesota, Kansas, and
> Oregon had, or the double allotment of land for internal im-
> provements, or the four sections in each township that it had
> asked for.[11]

As the nineteenth century closed, eastern states spearheaded a
growing congressional commitment to reserving western lands from
disposition. By retaining areas in perpetual federal ownership, Congress seemed to be reasserting the "common benefits" theory advocated by the original states in the 1780s.[12] That is, the public land
resources were to serve to the benefit of the entire nation. This new
policy was to be most thoroughly implemented in the evolving concept of forest reserves.

In the General Land Law Reform Act of 1891, Congress took major
steps to retain in federal ownership large amounts of public domain
land.[13] A provision of the 1891 act established general authority for

the president to reserve from private entry large areas of the public domain in order to protect the forest cover, hence the watersheds.[14] Although this authority was redefined nearly out of existence in 1907,[15] most western national forest lands were reserved by that time, and the idea of permanent federal land ownership was beginning to take hold.

NATIONAL FOREST REVENUES

Part of the bargaining accompanying the shift noted above led Congress to adopt the national forest receipt-sharing program in 1908. Confusion about the purpose of the receipt-sharing program is evident in the fact that it took three years and three separate riders on annual appropriations bills to establish it. At the heart of the confusion was a muddled understanding as to the nature and purpose of the land reservations.

One congressional conversation on the sharing proposal suggests that the funds were viewed as money owed to the states because the Forest Service had leased or sold resources within national forest boundaries without regard to the fact that lands previously granted to the states were included within those boundaries.[16] The payments were also justified as compensation for the loss of the states' normal 5% share of the receipts from land sales on areas that would never be sold.[17] One major proponent of the proposal described the share simply as "a gift" to the new states.[18]

The issue was further clouded by the fact that Congress was divided on the specific management mission for the forest reserves. Proposals for reserve management ranged from preserves allowing sales of only small amounts of timber to "tree farms" that would either turn a profit for the federal government or at least raise enough money to pay for the costs of administration. In 1908, however, Congress made the receipt-sharing program permanent and set the state's fraction at 25% of net receipts. It also provided that the money was to be spent for road and school purposes in the county or counties where national forests are located.[19] This provision continued the pattern obvious in nineteenth-century grants to states: the shared receipts were to be used in support of internal development.

MINERAL LEASING ACT OF 1920

When Congress passed the Mineral Leasing Act more than a decade later, many of the ambiguities apparent in the early discussion of national forests were clarified. Under the original formula for receipt sharing the state was to receive 37.5% of the mineral-leasing revenues directly and without any "earmark" (regarding support for schools or transportation) as to how the money would be spent. An additional 52.5% was to be deposited in the Reclamation Fund, which had been established to provide monies for dam construction in seventeen western states. This became necessary after the original pay-as-you-go scheme, which relied on receipts from early reclamation projects to fund subsequent ones, failed to produce enough money.[20]

Receipt sharing appears to have had two purposes under the 1920 act. First, it was justified by the fact that the lands were permanently reserved, as payment to states and counties in lieu of the property taxes that taxing jurisdictions would have been able to levy on land values had the land passed into private hands.[21] Second, states anticipated substantial economic activity and population growth once leasing was established. With that growth would come need for public services—particularly roads and schools—normally financed through taxes. Since the reserved lands were not taxable, the payments were ostensibly necessary.

Not surprisingly the mineral leasing system was ardently sought by conservation groups. It solidified the federal commitment to land retention and in contrast to the 1872 General Mining Act, it gave the federal government control over the timing, location and intensity of development of fuel and sedimentary deposits. It would be an error, however, to assume that the states were not also beneficiaries of the leasing system. Much of the federally owned coal to which western development interests sought access lay under private land as a result of the Stockraising Homestead Act of 1916.

In that act, Congress belatedly recognized arid conditions in the intermountain West by allowing homesteaders to patent 640 rather than 160 acres per homestead. Although 640 acres was generally still not adequate for a ranch, eastern representatives in Congress were so impressed by their generosity that they retained in federal ownership all the minerals underlying lands patented under the 1916 act.[22] The result was that the developers could not obtain access to the minerals, as they had in the past, by patenting the "surface estate." Thus, there *had to be* a leasing system, or the "severed minerals estate" would be lost to development forever.

In the process of devising a leasing program, the western states argued that they were giving up enormous authority to regulate minerals development within their jurisdiction—plus, the fact that they were also acquiescing in permanent land retention—and hence they ought to be compensated for the burdens created. Because western development interests saw enormous economic advantage in developing the federal minerals, the logic of the burdens argument is not entirely clear. There was inequity in the western states' inability to tax and regulate the development of federal lands within their boundaries. However, western states *could* regulate the development of privately held resources, but were not inclined to do so during the early decades of this century. Hence, it is not clear why development of federally owned resources, and the attendant need for roads and other concomitants of population growth, would be especially burdensome.

The fact is that the states welcomed the development of both federally and privately held resources—but claimed in Congress that federal developments were burdensome and therefore required compensation. The eastern states in effect paid the western states for acquiescing in an expanded assertion of the "common benefits" argument from earlier days. Combining the states' direct share of the receipts with the percentage allocated to the Reclamation Fund, also benefiting western states, 90% of the revenues from development of western leased minerals was returned to the states.[23]

PAYMENT IN LIEU OF TAXES ACT (PILT)

This pattern of the eastern states compensating western states when extending land reservations or their management may have ended in 1976 with the passage of the long-sought Payments in Lieu of Taxes Act. This act provided payments to counties, ostensibly in lieu of state and local taxes (to which federal land holdings are not subject). The PILT Act promises ten cents to seventy-five cents per acre to the counties in which federal "entitlement land" is located. Two things about this act are significant in the context of the East/West bargains that have characterized all the programs previously discussed. First, the theory justifying the payments is that *any* federal land holding is a financial burden to the jurisdiction in which it is located. Second, the payments are dependent upon annual appropriations by Congress. Unlike receipt sharing, payments are not automatically disbursed by the responsible agency.

Although the congressional debate on the act is filled with pitiful assertions of burdens created by the federal presence,[24] there is no connection in the statute between the payments and the alleged burdens. It is the mere presence of federal holdigns that justified the payments. Significantly, national parks are "entitlement lands" justifying PILT payments.

The irony is unmistakable—for establishment of national parks is typically sought by localities and justified by Congress in part because the designation generally provides a fiscal boon to the localities.[25] However, in the PILT Act parks lands are treated as a burden and compensated. This made sense only because it had the effect of extending the payments program to eastern states without whose support the program would not have passed. The statute may be understood as evidence of pork-barrel politics in Congress—federal monies were being handed out, and everybody stood in line. Regardless of the justification, everybody "got theirs." However, there appears to be more to it than just that: including the eastern states is a significant new wrinkle in the old pattern of bargains.

In 1976, the eastern states were willing to pay for western acquiescence in a broad array of programs expanding federal authority over federal lands.[26] The PILT program was something new—although long sought by western interests—and there was no corresponding expansion of federal authority. It is reasonable to assume that the eastern states were unwilling to go along without there being something in it for them too. Hence, the inclusion of parks—an inclusion that annually sends about one-third of the PILT payments to eastern states.[27] This whole deal can be viewed as a reassertion of the old "common benefits" posture of eastern states. Interestingly enough, however, it has been clarified and intensified in recent years.

PATTERNS FOR THE FUTURE?

During the federal budget crisis there were significant cutbacks in congressional investments in management of western lands.[28] There have also been continuing efforts to reduce or curtail the resource receipt sharing—to calculate state payments as a percentage of net rather than gross receipts, for example, or to eliminate them altogether.[29] This suggests two things. First, the "federal-ness" of federal lands may be so well established that eastern states are no longer willing to compensate western states for acquiescing in a well-established fact. Second, when federal dollars are scarce, "common benefits" have a reduced value to eastern states. This further suggests the possibility that eastern states, in an effort to reclaim some of the revenues previously used to purchase western acquiescence, may be willing to cede some control back to the western states.

Evidence to support that speculation is found, in part, in the growing role western states and localities are playing in the management of federal lands. The environmental decade of the 1970s ushered in a period of rapidly expanding state capabilities. Federal air and water quality legislation required states to develop programs or submit to federal standards and regulation. The same programs provided federal grants to support state efforts. In the process of responding to the combination of mandate and opportunity, and benefiting from a generally expanding national economy, states enhanced their management abilities, modernized their legislative and executive branches, and upgraded their capacity to govern.[30]

By 1975, for example, all the western states had consolidated their environmental pollution control programs in either a reorganized health department or a specialized environmental agency.[31] In addition, all of the western states except Colorado had some mechanism for coordinating statewide land use by the mid-1970s.[32] Whether or not these institutional arrangements are effective is debatable, of course, but the effectiveness of federal agencies is no less problematic. The more important point is that the western states do have the capability for shared management responsibility.

The whole pattern of shared management authority is, however, at risk in the jurisprudence of federal-state relations known as pre-emption. Can these trends continue if the courts find that the states have no authority to share management responsibilities? That issue will be addressed in the second case study.

Granite Rock Litigation

The Granite Rock litigation has many earmarks of federalism studies of a bygone era—it is at one level a juridical inquiry into the constitutional and statutory allocation of power between state and national governments. However, the Granite Rock case is one of relatively few Supreme Court decisions pertaining to the federal lands, and one of even fewer in which federal and state authority over the federal lands comes into direct conflict. Not surprisingly, therefore, it is also one of the few in which the Supreme Court has applied standard concepts of pre-emption analysis of public lands issues.

THE FACTS OF THE CASE

The facts of the case are fairly simple. The Granite Rock Company mines chemical-grade white limestone on an unpatented mining claim located in the Big Sur area of the California coast.[33] The claim is in the Los Padres National Forest, near a congressionally designated wilderness area, a state park, the drainage of the Little Sur River and scenic resources of undisputed international stature. In February 1981, following the preparation of an environmental assessment as required by NEPA (National Environmental Policy Act), the U.S. Forest Service approved the Granite Rock Company's proposed plan of mining operations.

Subsequently, the California Coastal Commission (CCC) informed Granite Rock that its mine was located in California's coastal zone, and that the company was required to secure a permit from the CCC before commencing operations. The Granite Rock Company refused to apply for a permit and sued to enjoin the CCC from requiring a permit. The company argued that the federal government's grant of rights to miners and its regulation of the miners' activities on federal lands constitute such a comprehensive regulatory scheme that it preempts any state effort to regulate or otherwise interfere with the federal patent holder's exercise of rights.[34]

TESTS FOR PRE-EMPTION

To reiterate the familiar tests for pre-emption, the Supreme Court's decision in Granite Rock relied upon a recent case:

> [S]tate law can be pre-empted in either of two general ways. If Congress evidences *an intent to occupy a given field*, any state law falling within that field is pre-empted. If Congress has not entirely displaced state regulation over the matter in question, state law is still pre-empted to the extent it *actually conflicts* with federal law, that is, when it is impossible to comply with both state and federal law, or where the state law stands as an obstacle to the accomplishment of the full purposes and objectives of Congress.[35]

Although these criteria may appear straightforward, they are actually quite slippery in application. As we shall see, apparently contradictory precedents make it difficult to predict outcomes.

Express Pre-emption and "Occupying the Field." In an important precedent supportive of state regulation (*Rice v. Santa Fe Elevator Corp.*), the Supreme Court concluded that occupation of the field will not be presumed unless it is the "clear and manifest purpose of Congress."[36] That is, pre-emption can be justified if Congress specifically indicates that federal law supersedes state law in a given area. Yet, in a similar case from the same period, the Supreme Court took the opposite tack. In *First Iowa Hydro-Electric Cooperative v. Federal Power Commission* the

Supreme Court held that the Federal Power Act (FPA) pre-empted an Iowa law requiring a state permit for water before construction of a hydroelectric facility. The ruling not only ignored the fact that the FPA contained no clearly stated and manifest purpose of Congress to pre-empt the field; it also ignored a specific provision [Section 9(b)] that required each license application to be accompanied by "satisfactory evidence of compliance with state laws as to bed and banks and the appropriation diversion and use of water for power purposes." The Court concluded that Congress intended the Federal Power Act to be a "complete scheme of national regulation which would promote the comprehensive development of the water resources of the Nation," and that it left "no room or need for conflicting state regulation."[37]

"Actual Conflict"—Regulation versus Prohibition.   Case law is similarly inconclusive regarding the second standard, sometimes called the "actual conflict" standard. Cases considering this issue assume that states have concurrent jurisdiction over federally regulated private activities unless state regulation is clearly prohibited by federal law. The issue, then, is frequently discussed in terms of state *regulations*, which would not be pre-empted because they are an extension of concurrent powers, and state *prohibitions*, which would be disallowed because they preclude activities which Congress intends to permit. Hence, the Court looks for actual conflict between the federal and state regulatory schemes.

The Ninth Circuit Court of Appeals recently invalidated the efforts of Ventura County, California, to establish an open space in an area including national forest land that had been leased for oil exploration. Without either inquiring into what effect the county permit requirement would have on the lessee's operations or considering the importance of congressional programs and purposes identified since passage of the 1920 Mineral Leasing Act, the court determined that mineral leasing was the overriding purpose of the forest land. It concluded that the "federal government has authorized a specific use of federal lands, and Ventura cannot prohibit that use . . . in an attempt to substitute its judgment for that of Congress."[38]

Thus, Ventura County's permit represented a *prohibition* and could be pre-empted by federal law. Yet, another decision, this time from a state supreme court, concluded that the exercise of state concurrent authority would not necessarily be prohibited because the regulation frustrated one of the purposes of a federal program.[39] What we discover, then, is that neither of the tests for pre-emption is grounded in firm precedents regarding the federal lands.

PRE-EMPTION AND THE GRANITE ROCK DECISION

Although the courts tend to style these pre-emption cases as a conflict between sovereigns, the disputes are not normally between the federal and the state governments. Typically a third party sues, arguing that one sovereign, rather than the other, has authority to regulate, because the plaintiff wishes to avoid whichever regulatory scheme is more onerous. This pattern is clear in the Granite Rock litigation.

Faced with a state permit requirement, the company alleged that the state had no authority to require a permit and refused to apply for one. Its position relied on the *Ventura County* and *First Iowa* decisions, and ignored the fact that the responsible federal agency (the Forest Service) made no effort to deny state authority. On the contrary, the Forest Service's plan approval, not unlike Section 9(b) of the Federal Power Act, explicitly stated that compliance with all relevant state law was a prerequisite to operating under the permit. The agency's environmental assessment stated that a permit from the Monterey Air Pollution Control District was needed in order to *understand* state and federal air quality standards.

The Supreme Court very narrowly upheld the California Coastal Commission's position. On the "occupation of the field" standard, it simply stated that it would not presume pre-emption. It found no intent to pre-empt in the federal government's regulation of unpatented mining claims; it further stated that administrative regulations, to be pre-emptive, must "declare any intention to pre-empt state law with some specificity."[40] Returning to the *Rice Elevator* standard the Court looked for a clearly stated congressional intent to pre-empt. Finding none, it refused to presume it.

In regard to the "actual conflict" standard, the decision creates a *possibility* of state regulation that did not appear to exist in *Ventura County* and *First Iowa*. The Court reiterated the need to find *actual conflict* between federal and state schemes before making a finding of pre-emption. Thus, in the absence of actual permit conditions, the Supreme Court refused to assume that there would be conflict. From the state perspective, therefore, *Granite Rock* is an improvement over *Ventura County* and *First Iowa*. But the Court was clear that it was concluding

> only that the barren record of this facial challenge has not demonstrated any conflict. We do not, of course, approve any future

> application of the Coastal Commission permit requirement that
> in fact conflicts with federal law.[41]

That is, the Court's ruling applied only to the specific situation in dispute and should not, therefore, be interpreted as a broader precedent.

This narrowness is troubling to state officials because the Court continues to view the activities of third parties on the federal lands as embodying federal government purpose. When coupled with language scattered elsewhere in the decision, it suggests that the Court is likely to look with disfavor on state regulation that impedes in *any* way the claimholder's exercise of its rights. The dissenters in the decision (the vote was 5–4 so the dissent is especially important) were even clearer, arguing that state land-use planning is automatically pre-empted on federal lands.[42]

CONSEQUENCES OF GRANITE ROCK
FOR WESTERN RESOURCE MANAGEMENT

The narrowness is also troubling because it bodes ill for the future of environmental and resource management in the western states. The decision ignores numerous realities about the western federal lands: (1) the diversity of congressional purposes for federal land management; (2) the important role that Congress has directed that states play in achieving those purposes; (3) the legitimacy of state interests in federal resource management; and (4) the complex matrix of federal-state interactions that has long been a part of western resource management. Finally, it ignores the erosion of federal management capabilities during the last decade.[43]

Comparing the *Granite Rock* decision to *First Iowa* illustrates the importance of diversity of congressional purposes for federal land management. *First Iowa* involved one federal agency (the Federal Power Commission), one federal statute (the Federal Power Act), and one over-arching federal purpose (generation of hydroelectric power). Minerals management on national forest lands typically involved a minimum of seven federal agencies in four federal departments operating under no fewer than fifteen major land management statues (not including any of the major 1970s environmental legislation).[44] The goals of the federal programs are not compatible—and picking any one of them as *the* overriding federal goal is absurd on its face.

This becomes even more absurd when the state's role in major environmental statutes of the 1970s is acknowledged. At issue in the

Granite Rock case was the Coastal Zone Management Act, in which Congress directed the states to undertake programs to protect the coast and provided planning and other grants to support the effort. Congress has also decided to address air and water quality and toxic substance control by encouraging and/or requiring state action. Preempting the state programs of federal lands creates management vacuums where federal land managers are not authorized, required, or equipped to fill in the gaps.[45]

Less familiar, perhaps, but equally important is the state's role in managing federal lands. The federal land retention program evolved slowly, long after state regulation of many western resources was well established. In many cases, Congress has not seen fit to dislocate the state scheme, but relies on and has included state regulatory programs in federal management schemes. Wildlife programs are the most familiar—state game regulations have long applied on federal lands and hunters for game on federal lands procure state licenses.[46] Similarly, state oil and gas regulation was well developed before the passage of the Mineral Leasing Act in 1920. Federal oil lessees are subject to the full range of state requirements regarding well spacing, production quotas, field unitization, and the like.[47]

If these state regulations are disallowed, the federal land management agencies will simply have to replicate the programs. The threat of pre-emption also undercuts states' efforts to protect their own legitimate interests. Federal land management agencies do not, for example, consider off-site impacts of energy development on federal lands when they conduct social and environmental analyses for environmental impact statements required by NEPA. If state efforts to protect proximate environments and communities are disallowed, a major component of reasonable planning for resource use and development will be truncated.

A mindless judicial embrace of federal supremacy over federal lands puts all these facets of the federal-state management partnership at risk. It is unlikely that the federal land management agencies will be able to take up the slack if the courts hand them exclusive authority for all or even some of the potentially pre-empted state programs. Federal management capacities are declining and are not likely to expand during the near future. In 1988 the Forest Service had, for example, 15% fewer professional employees than it had in 1980.[48]

Conclusions

What are the lessons to be learned from this and the preceding chapter? We suggest the following. First, federal supremacy over the public lands is far more problematic than commonly assumed. A close reading of history demonstrates that changing attitudes and coalitions among states in Congress was a key factor in the transformation of the public domain into the federal lands. Second, conflict over the management of the federal lands has been orchestrated by competition among interest groups and federal agencies. In the process, the western states have been unable to establish in independent role, and therefore are at a disadvantageous position in the traditional inter-governmental arena. This situation is clearly apparent in the case studies. Eastern support for management of the federal lands appears to be declining just at the time when the courts appear inclined to restrict burgeoning state and local efforts to participate in planning and management of those lands.

Although there are no easy answers, there are some general directions that could be pursued. One possible approach is that the courts could be pursuaded, in future cases, that it is folly to disrupt longstanding and increasing successful cooperative management in order to exalt some historically inaccurate notion of federal supremacy. Congress could perhaps take a hand in convincing the courts to encourage, rather than discourage, the evolving pattern of intergovernmental relations. Finally, there needs to be greater awareness that, in the words of John Francis, "the western states themselves have grown in sophistication in statutes, personnel, and their respective abilities to contribute to public lands decision-making."[49]

Notes

1. Sally K. Fairfax and Carolyn E. Yale, *The Federal Lands: A Guide to Planning, Management, and State Revenues* (Covelo, Calif.: Island Press, 1987), discuss a variety of revenue-producing programs on the federal lands.

2. Discussed generally in Sally K. Fairfax, "Interstate Bargaining over Revenue Sharing and Payments in Lieu of Taxes: Federalism as if States Mattered," in Phillip O. Foss, ed., *Federal Lands Policy* (Westport, Conn.: Greenwood Press, 1987).

3. *Tax exempt* is not the same thing as *tax immune*. See, for a lucid discussion, *Van Brocklyn v. Tennessee*, 117 U.S. 151 (1886).

4. See, for example, two recent important cases: *Silkwood v. Kerr-McGee*, 464 U.S. 238 (1984); and *Pacific Gas and Electric Corp. v. State Energy Resources Conservation and Development Commission*, 461 U.S. 190 (1983).

5. See, for an early example, *Gibbons v. Ogden*, 22 U.S. (9 Wheat.) 1 (1824).

6. For complaints about livestock operators' political power, see E. Louise Peffer, *The Closing of the Public Domain* (Stanford: Stanford University Press, 1951), and William Voigt, Jr., *Public Grazing Lands* (New Brunswick, N.J.: Rutgers University Press, 1976).

7. Marc Reisner, *Cadillac Desert: The American West and Its Disappearing Water* (New York: Viking-Penguin, 1986), is a recent entry into the long list of volumes on that subject.

8. Fairfax and Yale, *The Federal Lands*, 74–78, note 1.

9. The Reagan administration repeatedly attempted, in its yearly budget proposals, to deduct administrative costs before distributing the state and local share of these revenues. By various estimates, the change would have cost western states and local governments from $300 million to $400 million per year.

Each year, however, the proposal ran into stiff resistance from the beneficiaries, and the proposal was never made into law. In its report on the 1987 Budget Bill, the Senate Appropriations Subcommittee on the Interior complained: "For the fourth year in a row, the Committee fails to see why states should be forced to bear the burden of the Federal Government costs and has deleted the proposed bill language" (99th Congress, 2d Session, Senate Report 99-397, Dept. of the Interior and Related Agencies Appropriation Bill, 1987, August 13, 1986, 35).

10. *Patented* is a legal term which, in this context, means to take title to or obtain a final deed for public domain land. A homesteader, for example, would enter an area, stake a claim, engage in the required activities—such as building a house of specified dimensions and living there for a specified number of years—and having demonstrated that the requirements had been met—that is, having "proved up" the homestead—the settler could "patent" the land.

11. Paul W. Gates, *History of Public Land Law Development* (Washington, D.C.: U.S. Government Printing Office, 1968), 303–4.

12. See the discussion in the previous chapter.

13. Samuel T. Dana and Sally K. Fairfax, *Forest and Range Policy*, 2nd ed. (New York: McGraw-Hill, 1980), chap. 2.

14. See A. Dan Tarlock and Sally K. Fairfax, "No Water for the Woods: A Critical Analysis of *United States v. New Mexico*," *Idaho Law Review* 15, (1979) 509–54, for a discussion of the ramifications of the meaning of those apparently self-evident terms.

15. Peffer, *The Closing of the Public Domain*, chap. 5, note 6.

16. Fairfax, "Interstate Bargaining," 106, note 2.

17. *Ibid.*

18. *Ibid.*

19. *Ibid.*

20. *Ibid.*

21. Fairfax and Yale, *The Federal Lands*, 151–52, note 1.

22. Dana and Fairfax, *Forest and Range Policy*, 103–4, note 13.

23. Fairfax and Yale, *The Federal Lands*, 59, note 1.

24. Fairfax, "Interstate Bargaining," 85, note 2.

25. *Ibid.*

26. *Ibid.*

27. *Ibid.*

28. Sally K. Fairfax and Richard Cowart, "Judicial Nationalism vs. Dual Regulation in Public Lands Federalism: Granite Rock's Uneasy Compromises," *Environmental Law Reporter* 17 (July 1987), 10276–87; 10286, note 118.

29. *Ibid.*, note 9.

30. Richard Cowart and Sally K. Fairfax, "Public Lands Federalism: Judicial Theory and Administrative Reality," *Ecology Law Quarterly* 15 (3) (1988), 375–476.

31. Jon Grand, "Environmental Management: Emerging Issues," *The Book of the States, 1984–85* (Lexington, Ky.: Council of State Governments, 1985), 454.

32. Council of State Governments, "Natural Resource and Environmental Management," in *The Book of the States, 1976–1977* (Lexington, Ky.: Council of State Governments, 1977), 478.

33. Cowart and Fairfax, "Public Lands Federalism," 10277–78, note 28.

34. *Ibid.*

35. *Silkwood v. Kerr–McGee Corp.*, cited in *California Coastal Commission v. Granite Rock Co.*, 107 S. Ct. 1419 (1987), 17 ELR 20565, citations omitted.

36. *Rice v. Santa Fe Elevator Corp.*, 331 U.S. 218 (1987), 230.

37. *First Iowa Hydro-Electric Cooperative v. Federal Power Commission*, 328 U.S. 152 (1946) at 182.

38. *Ventura County v. Gulf Oil Corp.*, 601 F2d 1080 (1976) at 1084.

39. *State ex. rel. Andrus v. Click*, 97 Idaho 791, 554 P. 2d 969 (1976).

40. *California Coastal Commission v. Granite Rock Corp.*, 17 ELR 20566.

41. *Ibid.*, 20569.

42. *Ibid.*, 20572 (Scalia dissenting).

43. Cowart and Fairfax, "Public Lands Federalism," 10286, note 28.

44. *Ibid.*, 10281, note 65.

45. *Ibid.*, 10281. See also, Susan Bartlett Foote, "Regulatory Vacuums: Federalism, Deregulation, and Judicial Review," *University of California Davis Law Review* 19 (1985), 113–52; 113.

46. See generally George C. Coggins and Michael E. Ward, "The Law of

Wildlife Management on Federal Public Lands," *Oregon Law Review* 60 (1981), 59–155.

47. Cowart and Fairfax, "Public Lands Federalism," note 28, note 113 and text accompanying. See also, *U.S. v. California* 483, U.S. 645 (1978).

48. Cowart and Fairfax, "Public Lands Federalism," note 28, note 118.

49. John G. Francis, "Public Lands Institutions and Their Discontents," in Foss, ed., *Federal Lands Policy*, 74, note 2.

18

INTERGOVERNMENTAL RELATIONS AND WESTERN WATER POLICY

Tim De Young

CROSSING THE GREAT PLAINS, ONE NOT ONLY SEES BUT feels the beginning of the West. Near the 100th meridian, humidity drops precipitously, trees steadily give way to shrubs and grasslands, then eventually to a stark landscape of cactus and sage. Rivers and streams only occasionally break the brown monotony but when they do, startling oases of lush vegetation and shade emerge. Entering the West's cities and towns, one soon forgets the harsh realities of the region's dry climate as lawns, golf courses and parks enhance life-styles just as they do anywhere in middle America. On the outskirts, irrigated fields look—at least to the casual observer—much like fields back east. Crops and orchards flourish in long, neat rows, and in nearby mountains, forests and cascading streams contribute to the perception that water is ample enough to supply the needs of society and the natural environment.

Despite the green facade, water is not plentiful in the West. Rainfall averages less than twenty inches per year in most of the region. The Pacific coastal regions of California, Oregon, Washington, Alaska and Hawaii are notable exceptions but even in these states, semiarid regions are to be found inland. Hidden from view is a complex life support system that includes the "hardware" of dams, wells, pipelines and treatment facilities and the "software" of federal, state and local water policies and programs. It is a multibillion-dollar enterprise built through cooperation, compromise and controversy, a system that lets westerners forget their region's aridity.

Constructed in large part by federal agencies such as the Bureau of Reclamation and the U.S. Army Corps of Engineers, financed by federal tax dollars and administered by a combination of state and local water agencies, most of the technically and economically feasible supply projects—and not a few questionable ones—have already been built. Now, with the system largely completed, increasing demand for relatively finite and fully allocated supplies has become the key policy challenge. As in many policy areas, a declining federal role has characterized water policy in recent years. In consequence, the western states have begun to assume greater responsibility for water management.

How well do the western states manage water? What are the key water policy issues confronting state government? What will be the role of the federal government in future water policy decisions? To answer these questions, this chapter first presents a basic model of policy change. Next, the traditional dominance of the federal government in water policy is traced followed by an examination of the relatively recent shift of authority to state governments and to a lesser extent, the private sector. State responses to management demands then are highlighted drawing upon recent developments in selected western states. The chapter concludes with a summary and discussion of emerging water policy issues.

A Model of Policy Change

Years ago, Mark Twain observed that in the West whiskey is for drinking and water is for fighting about. Another wag concluded that you can flirt with a westerner's lover, but don't mess with his water.

Both aphorisms reflect the high saliency of western water issues. Wherever water is scarce, local inhabitants develop a special interest in water policy based on the largely accurate view that water is an essential ingredient of their area's economic well-being. In her study of western water development politics, Ingram notes that strong local sentiments about the importance of water development create an environment of risks and rewards especially attractive to locally based political interests.[1] Any model of water policy change thus should be sensitive to the role of local individuals and groups.

The West's political culture further reinforces the notion that local interests should heavily influence water policy. Fierce individualism characterizes the most arid regions of the West from Montana to Arizona.[2] The West's faith in private enterprise has helped create an environment generally opposed to heavy governmental involvement. As we shall see, even when government programs are implemented, steps are taken to assure local, if not private, control.

More generally, water policy evolution can be characterized by the relative importance over time of private versus public sectors and, within the public sector, by the relative importance of federal versus state initiatives. James Q. Wilson's observations about the evolution of public policy are helpful in this regard.[3] According to Wilson, new policies, that is, assumptions of authority by government, are adopted only after there has been a change in opinion or a new perception of old arrangements sufficient to remove control from private hands and place it on the public agenda. For example, the failure of private attempts to develop water supplies may lead to government-financed water development projects.

Revisions to existing public policies follow a similar pattern. Public policies are revised when implementation fails to resolve issues about the propriety of the policy, "the ideological and normative issues" related to whether a governmental role is appropriate, or when the distribution of costs and benefits is unacceptable to a sufficient proportion of the public.[4] For example, federal subsidies to irrigators may be revised when significant opposition occurs. A public program may be abandoned, significantly modified, or responsibility may shift to a different level of government. As will be discussed later, dissatisfaction with public water policies has led to a call for the privatization of certain water decisions.

Wilson's approach acknowledges and builds upon Theodore Lowi's seminal classification of public policies by three "arenas of power," distributive, regulatory, and redistributive.[5] A *distributive* policy is one that provides specific benefits to specific groups without regard to limited resources or impacts upon others. Opposition to distributive policies is limited and debate over policy tends to be pragmatic, not ideological. Irrigation projects, for example, can be seen as distributive because they promote the economic development of water-short regions. Regions may compete against one another for government assistance, but regional representatives such as members of Congress can resolve differences by supporting each other's projects. As we will see, this "you scratch my back, and I'll scratch yours" approach to policymaking was especially popular during the water development era.

A second characteristic of the distributive policy arena is the presence of fairly autonomous political coalitions which some have called "iron triangles."[6] An iron triangle typically is composed of legislators, administrators and special interest groups. The pork-barrel era of water policy involved relatively stable coalitions between key western congressmen, the Bureau of Reclamation, and farming or local development interests. The demise of these coalitions reflects an end to this era and the advance of the current policy regime, one that is largely regulatory.

Regulatory policies involve rules that govern the behavior of a defined group. In the American political system, the power to regulate domestic affairs generally is reserved to the states. A shift from distributive to regulatory policies thus suggests a shift from federal to state policy arenas. Like distributive policies, regulatory decisions provide benefits to specific groups but regulatory benefits are somewhat different because they result from distinctions that protect established interests. For example, privately owned water rights, legal rights to use water from a given supply, are regulated by each of the western state governments. In all but one of the western states, Hawaii is the exception, a prior appropriation system has been used that follows a simple "first in time, first in right" formula for determining priority of use. Owning a "senior" or older water right provides significant benefits because in times of shortage water first must go to those with the oldest rights even if such allocations harm others. That is, even if they do not get any water! Regulatory distinctions thus result in benefits to certain rights owners and costs to others. Conflict in the regulatory arena is essentially political, a struggle over who gets what, when, and how. As Lowi and others have noted, opposing groups often form along ideological lines with liberals versus conservatives, pro-development groups versus environmentalists, and so on.

A *redistributive* policy also engenders political conflict because resources are reallocated from one group to another. Interbasin transfers of water, for example, can be seen as redistributive because water supplies and attendant benefits are redistributed from areas of origin to areas of destination. The classic and much publicized case is Los Angeles's "destruction" of the Owens Valley. As fictionalized in the movie *Chinatown*, the Los Angeles Aqueduct provided the growing metropolis with an assured supply of water. But as the movie and other accounts suggest, water came at the expense of the agricultural economies in the Owens and San Fernando valleys. The primary beneficiaries were a select group of particularly greedy, if not corrupt, individuals. When the policy debate about the aqueduct actually occurred near the turn of the century, the redistributive potential was largely ignored, especially by Angelenos. They were largely concerned about the costs of building the system and distributing the water.[7] In other words, they looked at the policy proposal in practical distributive terms. At the same time, farmers saw the proposal as redistributive, a ruthless scam to rob them of precious water. Can a policy be both distributive and redistributive?

Both Lowi and Wilson emphasize that perceptions of policy, rather than any actual distinctions, determine whether a policy will be characterized as distributive, regulatory or redistributive. For example, a water project may be considered distributive at a particular point in time but later—as calculations of costs and benefits change—the same project may be considered essentially redistributive. As policy perceptions change, levels of support also will vary. Some policy theorists contend that perceptions change as a function of learning over time. Others note that when new groups become active in policy arenas, the infusion of new perceptions also may affect levels of support for established practices.[8]

Before moving on, the water policy model's two key assumptions can be summarized: First, the role of local groups and individuals in the formation and implementation of water policy is particularly important. Due to the West's political culture and semiarid environment, strong support for water policies that tend to reward private and local initiatives should be expected. Second, shifts in the respective roles of private and public groups and within the public sector, changes in responsibilities between federal, state and local levels of government will be found. Such changes will be caused by variations in perceptions over time about the propriety of certain policies and by the range of participants involved in water policy processes. With these assumptions in mind, the evolution of western water policy can now be considered.

Building the System

More than any other resource, the development and control of water has characterized the history of the West. Like any human enterprise, water development has produced a wide array of social and environmental costs and benefits. Fortunes have been made by bringing water to the desert, and abortive attempts have caused heartbreak and financial ruin. Natural environments have been decimated to satisfy growing populations, and barren tracts of desert have been transformed into the world's most productive farmlands. Traditional Hispanic and Indian communities have seen their water rights and way of life threatened or destroyed by an onslaught of water-dependent development, while large water storage projects have produced excellent recreational sites and relatively inexpensive supplies of hydroelectric power.

Even some of the staunchest critics of the region's water policy history acknowledge the positive impacts of the western water development. In his excellent study, *Cadillac Desert*, Marc Reisner concedes:

> Millions of people and green acres took over a region that, from appearances, is unforgivingly hostile to life. It was a spectacular achievement, and its worst critics have to acknowledge its positive side. The economy was, no doubt, enriched. Population dispersion was achieved. Land that had been dry-farmed and overgrazed and horribly abused was stabilized and saved from the drought winds [sic]. "Wasting" resources—the rivers and aquifers—were put to productive use.[9]

At the same time, Reisner and others conclude that the costs have been great. Wild and scenic rivers and groundwater reserves have been lost. A national irrigation program designed to subsidize small farmers has benefited large agribusiness corporations whose excess production depresses national crop prices. Environmental degradation due to excessive or improper irrigation is a largely unpaid bill that will burden future generations.

These sacrifices have been made for a system that is not particularly efficient. A significant portion of developed water supplies—as much as 90% in some western states—is used by irrigated agriculture at heavily subsidized rates, even in situations where buyers are willing to pay as much as ten times more for the same water.[10] The system is fraught with disincentives to water conservation as well as obstacles to the reallocation of water to higher economically valuable uses. In short, the mirage of water prosperity conceals a system under stress.

THE EARLY YEARS

Securing safe and sufficient supplies of water has been a fundamental problem in the West for centuries. Water development initially occurred through local initiatives rather than as a result of state or federal programs. With perfect hindsight, we can see that local efforts even though quite popular were inhibited by a shortage of capital for building all but the simplest systems. Private systems were at a special disadvantage because the need for significant start-up capital often was coupled with no means to compel prospective beneficiaries to share the costs. The early history of private water supply ventures was thus littered with failures.[11] In many cases, responsibility was assumed by public agencies.

In the case of drinking water, municipalities often consolidated a number of small private companies. Los Angeles, for example, replaced several private water companies with its own Department of Water and Power (DWP) at the turn of the century. Private developers tended to support the transition as a means to ensure adequate supplies of water without which their investments would become worthless.[12] These early capitalists found that by insulating public agencies from popular control—the DWP was controlled by an appointive board dominated by wealthy and powerful individuals—they could have the advantages of the public coffers with few of the disadvantages. Similar assumptions of responsibility were made in most states, as communities formed water boards, mutual domestic companies or analogous institutions. The extent of popular control varied, but regardless of region, local developers and bankers have dominated municipal water policy.

Building irrigation systems was accomplished in a somewhat different manner. To overcome the twin problems of capital formation and compulsory cost sharing, proponents of local irrigation projects turned first to mutual domestic associations, not for profit organizations that allowed the pooling of resources. The mutual domestic approach worked exceptionally well in Utah where the collective spirit of the Mormons along with the church's hierarchical authority structure are important factors. In their first fifty years, the Mormons had about 6 million acres under full or partial irrigation in several states.[13] Though successful for smaller projects, the mutual domestics rarely could afford to build larger systems. Impressed by the success of a collective approach, however, local interest groups in many regions turned to their state legislatures for help.

In 1865, Utah became the first western state to pass legislation enabling the formation of "irrigation districts," state political subdivisions possessing some but not all of the powers given to counties and municipalities.[14] In 1877, California followed with the Wright Act, a statute that became the standard for similar legislation subsequently passed in seventeen western states, all except Alaska and Hawaii.[15] Irrigation district formation offered considerable incentives to local irrigators, including the power to levy compulsory assessments on benefited lands within the district, the authority to issue bonds, and exemption from state and local taxes for district property.

Throughout the West, hundreds of irrigation districts were formed, but not without controversy. The collective approach that was so successful for the Mormons was anathema to many individualists. Landowners with sufficient water supplies or those with unirrigated yet taxable urban tracts within districts protested the compulsory taxation feature. The debate was couched in terms of the propriety of governmental involvement, with detractors claiming that districts amounted to "communism and confiscation." Eventually, the constitutionality of the Wright Act was considered by the U.S. Supreme Court in *Fallbrook Irrigation District v. Bradley,* 164 U.S. 112 (1896). Holding the act to be constitutional, the Court pointed out that in light of the aridity of most western states and the public importance of promoting irrigation, state legislatures were justified in taking unprecedented measures. This decision symbolizes the first of many compromises that individualists would need to make in their conquest of the arid West.

Despite legislative and judicial support, the early record of irrigation districts is not impressive. In California, for example, only nine of the fifty-two irrigation districts formed in 1887 were still operating in 1915.[16] Defaults on loans depressed bond markets in some states, which soon led to state regulatory restrictions on district formation and closer supervision of fiscal management.[17] The states' public irrigation districts thus suffered the same fate encountered by earlier private efforts. Further development was stymied unless a different approach could be developed. In looking for help, local interests found a willing benefactor in the federal government.

THE FEDERAL CONSTRUCTION ERA

Federal dominance first in navigation and then in irrigation was made possible by significant national support for governmental assistance in the settlement of the West. Federal programs had distinct advantages including superior technical skill, deep pockets for financing construction and the jurisdictional ability to build projects by hydrologic, rather than political boundaries. The emerging importance of the U.S. Army Corps of Engineers after the Civil War provided an excellent example of federal competence. Despite significant private construction during the canal era of 1817–38, the nation's inland navigation system was both incomplete and inefficient.[18] After the Civil War, the Corps of Engineers planned, financed and maintained a vast system of canals, rivers and harbors throughout the East thus providing a basic infrastructure for a growing industrial economy. The Corps of Engineers expanded its operations to the West by building numerous bridge, flood control and shore maintenance projects. An even larger assumption of responsibility occurred through the passage of the Reclamation Act of 1902. Because the act remains the centerpiece of western irrigation development, its implementation deserves special consideration.

The 1902 Reclamation Act was an adaptation of the 1862 Homestead Act, a program designed to spread Thomas Jefferson's moralistic vision of a nation of citizen farmers. Like the Homestead Act, eligibility to receive water from federal projects was to be based on a 160-acreage limitation, residency requirements, and antispeculation provisions. Farmers were to repay project costs at no interest, a considerable subsidy but by no means a free ride.[19] Predictably, most western senators and congressional representatives at first opposed enactment, characterizing the heavy governmental role as unnecessary, socialistic and paternalistic.[20] But against a backdrop of largely unsuccessful private and state irrigation attempts and nearly two decades of abnormal drought and cold, the protestations were largely symbolic.

More than any other program, projects by the Bureau of Reclamation epitomize distributive public policy. As explained above, the distributive policy arena is characterized by a politics of mutual non-interference where elected politicians obtain benefits for their home

region by "logrolling," a vote-trading procedure, and pork-barrel legislation, omnibus authorization bills that contain a collection of individual project authorizations. Another technique used to "bring
home the bacon" was to attach a project authorization as an amendment to unrelated but important legislation.[21]

Typically, a member of Congress and local economic interests formed
an iron triangle with bureau officials to gain approval for pet projects.
State governors, legislators and top officials often acted as brokers,
adding their support to create an even more potent plea for federal
assistance. Not only did westerners support one another's reclamation projects, they often supported eastern water projects in trade for
eastern states' support. Throughout the West, congressional leaders
enhanced their careers by delivering reclamation projects. The list of
names is impressive including Texas's Lyndon Johnson, Utah's Frank
Moss, Idaho's Frank Church, Washington's Henry Jackson, Colorado's Wayne Aspinall, California's Bernie Sisk and New Mexico's
Clinton Anderson. Due to the influence of these individuals, federal
agencies dominated Western Water Facilities construction from the
late 1940s until the early 1960s. Unfortunately, the main virtue of
many of these projects was political feasibility. Several projects could
not be justified in terms of their economic efficiency or environmental
impact. The reclamation program thus was reflective of the distributive myth that resources are unlimited and the costs to others are
minimal.

Had reclamation benefits gone to small farmers willing to live on
or near 160-acre parcels, the program would have conformed to legislative intent and more generally to the moralistic ideal of settling
the West with a society of self-sufficient individual farmers. But implementation subverted these goals in two important ways. First, the
federal subsidy went to speculators and other owners of large parcels
in certain cases. Primarily in California and Arizona, speculators had
bought out struggling farmers, amassing tracts well in excess of the
160-acre limit. In other areas, notably California's San Joaquin Valley,
large land holdings were typical before federal involvement. To make
sure these individuals did not receive benefits, Congress passed the
Omnibus Adjustment Act of 1926.[22] Owners of "excess lands" (parcels
greater than 160 acres) who were to receive federally subsidized water
were ordered to sign recordable contracts that would force them to
sell such lands by project completion at pre-project prices. Contracts
were to be signed and enforced by local irrigation districts under the
supervision of the bureau. But the Bureau of Reclamation and local

districts had little incentive to enforce the contracts because large landowners generally could repay project costs more easily than small farmers and because agency personnel were more oriented to water management than to land reform.[23] In consequence, big farms were subsidized. According to the bureau's own estimates, about 10% of the land benefited by reclamation water (1,117,029 of 10,554,567 total irrigable acres) was owned by excess landowners as late as 1980.[24] Moreover, 90% of the excess landowners reside in California, where about 40% of bureau-benefited land is located.

Despite the implementation problems or perhaps because of them, the reclamation program remains a cornerstone of western development. Bureau of Reclamation dams and ancillary facilities are found in every western state providing vast quantities of water and the hydroelectric power to pump more water to thirsty lands and people. Table 18.1 lists major projects in each of the thirteen western states. Not only has the bureau helped to irrigate the West, bureau policies have encouraged the formation of thousands of irrigation districts. Irrigation and conservancy districts, the progeny of the federal era, distribute about one-half of all water used in the West, even though they include less than a third of the irrigated acreage.[25] Although special districts technically are political subdivisions of the states, in actual practice they are relatively independent governments whose influence is considerable.[26] Before looking at special districts and other state water management institutions, it is important to discuss briefly the declining importance of the federal government in water policy.

THE DECLINE OF THE FEDERAL ROLE

Successful policy implementation, more than any other factor, ended federal dominance in western water policy. Most of the technically feasible sites have been developed and most of the region's major rivers have been dammed and diverted. Remaining development opportunities will be extremely costly.

The end of the construction era has had inestimable political consequences. With the federal subsidy pie largely distributed, the basis for political coalitions has been undermined. Throughout the West, congressional leaders who had based, or at least enhanced, their careers on delivering federal water projects have been replaced, usually by representatives of an emerging urban majority. Congressional construction authorizations to the Bureau of Reclamation began to plummet in the mid-1970s and a search for new roles for the bureau has begun.[27]

Table 18.1   Major Bureau of Reclamation Projects in 13 Western States

State	Project	Year Completed	Irrigated Acres
Alaska	Eklutna[a]	1955	N/A
	Crater–Long Lakes–Snettisham[a]	1969	N/A
Arizona	Salt River	1971	53,046
	Gila	1957	91,527
	Central Arizona	under construction	
California	Boulder Canyon	1954	517,936
	Klamath	1921	68,942
	Central Valley	1944	75,574
Colorado	Colorado–Big Thompson	1959	628,588
	Fryingpan–Arkansas	1975	269,600
Hawaii	Molokai	under construction	4,415
Idaho	Boise	1912	173,971
	Minidoka	1942	188,908
Montana	Milk River	1946	100,403
	Sun River	1908	82,199
	Pick–Sloan Missouri Basin, e.g., Helena Valley	1958	13,867
Nevada	Humboldt	1939	33,900
	Newlands	1906	62,932
New Mexico	Rio Grande	1916	77,606
	Middle Rio Grande	1961	58,081
	San Juan–Chama	1976	2,118
Oregon	Owyhee	1939	63,796
	Deschutes	1957	42,117
	Vale	1938	33,118
Utah	Central Utah	1980	16,893
	Moon Lake	1938	78,337
	Weber River	1931	93,580
Washington	Columbia River	1978	515,457
	Yakima	1975	218,068
	Chief Joseph Dam	1964	23,607
Wyoming	North Platte	1925	52,827
	Kendrick	1955	20,132
	Shoshone	1910	82,985

[a]Indicates power plants.

Source: From Bureau of Reclamation, "Summary Statistics Index," 1986.

It would be inaccurate to conclude that the decline was only due to a largely completed construction agenda or even the replacement of reclamation proponents. Changing perceptions about the costs and benefits of distributive programs are an underlying factor. In the late 1950s, natural resources economists began to argue that the marginal costs of large-scale projects were increasing rapidly while the number of productive project sites decreased.[28] Economic analyses of large, interbasin water transfer projects also indicated that the benefits of western irrigation entailed significant costs to agriculture elsewhere. More groups began to see the reclamation program as essentially redistributive. Agricultural profits had been shifted from the Midwest where massive irrigation projects were unnecessary, to the West at considerable and continuing expense to the federal taxpayer.[29] As such views gained in popularity, national support for western irrigation began to erode.

At the same time, analyses of the benefits of reservoirs for flood control indicated that nonstructural measures, such as flood insurance, zoning and warning systems, were more cost-effective in many situations. Most of these measures required state and local implementation.[30] Against a backdrop of an increasing national debt coupled with the rising tide of fiscal conservatism, these critiques gained a growing national audience.

Opposition also came from the environmental movement that emerged in the 1960s. The passage of the Wilderness Act (1964), the Water Resources Planning Act of 1965, the Wild and Scenic Rivers Act (1968) and the National Environmental Policy Act of 1969 are testimonials to their growing political power. Many proposed water projects were derailed, and a significant number of potential sites was protected from future development by "wild and scenic" or "wilderness area" designations. President Carter's infamous "hit list" of proposed federal projects symbolized the growing opposition, as the focus of water policy shifted from distributive, construction-oriented technical programs of the federal government to nonstructural, regulatory policies and programs of the states.

Managing the System

Reduced federal policy leadership and financial support have created a vacuum that the states are struggling to fill. Although federal assistance to both water resource development and pollution control has declined, federally mandated requirements, such as the cleanup deadlines of the Clean Water Act, remain in force. Similarly, court-ordered compliance deadlines in water quality protection typically cannot be modified. Finally, federal agencies are asserting increasing demands for water both to secure instream flows in national parks and forests and to fulfill substantial water rights claims for Indian reservations. In addition to federal concerns, the states must deal with a wide range of water-related problems including infrastructure decay, increasing demands for relatively finite supplies, and emerging water quality problems. The complexity of contemporary water resource problems represents a formidable challenge. To determine state capabilities to meet these challenges, we consider first the states' legal authority.

LEGAL CONTROL OF WATER

Most of the western states developed their water laws solely under the prior appropriation doctrine, a "first in time, first in right" system invented in the West.[31] California, Oregon and Washington, like most eastern states, also recognize the riparian doctrine, where the right to use water is a function of owning land along a stream, lake, or river. However, most rights and all new uses are governed by prior appropriation systems in these states. Hawaii has a unique blend of ancient and modern rights but, as discussed below, this state has begun to develop laws, policies and programs that are similar to those of the other western states. In prior appropriation states, the right to divert water for use is established as a private property right subject to review by a state agency, board or tribunal, which determines if the private use of water meets the criteria of "beneficial use." Defining the water right in this way allows the state to act on behalf of other users when the right to use must be shared or when other rights are affected by transfers or misuse.

State regulation of an individual's right to use water is based upon state constitutional definitions of water as a public good, owned by the state, people or public.[32] At roughly the same time that state legislatures were enabling the creation of irrigation districts, the public ownership provisions became the basis for the creation of state water agencies. Beginning with Wyoming in 1890, each of the western states, except Colorado, enacted legislation that created an administrative system to enforce the right to divert water and to resolve disputes over water allocation.[33] Over time, public ownership has encouraged the development of elaborate regulatory systems within prior appropriation states. These systems include sophisticated water supply monitoring, permits, and detailed adjudication procedures for quantification of claims.

In 1982, the U.S. Supreme Court dealt a nearly lethal blow to the public ownership principle. In *Sporhase v. Nebraska*, 485 U.S. 941, the Court held that state ownership of groundwater was a legal fiction. Traditionally, groundwater was assumed to be the subject of exclusive state control, much like land use. Accordingly, interstate compacts to apportion shared surface waters made little or no mention of groundwater. Moreover, several western state constitutions prohibited the exportation of groundwater. In *Sporhase*, the Court held that groundwater exportation bans were unconstitutional restrictions on interstate commerce. States could not allow their own residents to buy and sell groundwater rights while denying the same rights to out-of-state residents. In addition, the Court rejected Nebraska's contention that the public trust doctrine, that allowed the state to act as trustee of natural resources for the public, created a proprietary interest in a state's water resources. The Court recognized, however, that a state has a heightened police power, or regulatory interest, in water resources by virtue of the public trust doctrine. A state thus can allocate scarce resources to meet current and future in-state demands if the allocation is not arbitrary, that is, if it is the result of a comprehensive water management system.

In response to *Sporhase*, perceptions about the propriety of state involvement in water management have changed. Even those western states that traditionally avoided water policymaking by deferring to private, municipal, or federal entities have become much more active. Colorado, a state that relies heavily on state water courts for water use regulation and management, has asserted a state proprietary interest in groundwater located under state-owned lands. Montana is actively appropriating unappropriated water as part of a regional planning process, and New Mexico has begun a similar process.[34] Other states in the region have been relatively more active in the development of affirmative state management policies and programs. In the following paragraphs, state efforts in these areas are compared.

STATE WATER PLANNING AND MANAGEMENT

Because the traditional federal role has been to bestow benefits on local constituencies, primarily irrigation districts and municipalities, the states have received relatively small amounts of federal monies to develop water resources management capabilities. The most significant type of federal aid to the states was planning assistance grants administered by the now defunct U.S. Water Resources Council. Through this assistance, states were encouraged to initiate comprehensive and integrated water planning and management. By federal definition, a comprehensive plan would incorporate water quality and quantity as well as land-use planning elements into a single coordinated process. Planners and implementers were not to be separated. Integration would be achieved by assigning responsibility via a unified legislative mandate to a single natural resource agency. The federal ideal was to achieve a total management program for water and related land resources planning and management.[35]

Of course the federal prescriptions are based on normative criteria which assume that states should be comprehensive, should integrate, should plan and so on. Conceivably, a state's lack of progress toward these objectives may indicate a deliberate decision not to follow the federally recommended path to water management success. Nevertheless, describing the structures and functions of state water management organizations provides a starting point for interstate comparisons.

In each state, two types of water agency are generally found. Cabinet-level executive departments typically include an agency responsible for water rights, use permits and other quantity concerns, and an agency responsible for pollution control, safe drinking water standards and other quality concerns. In some states, a single agency is responsible for both quantity and quality. In contrast to administrative departments, boards or commissions (hereafter boards) typically are policymaking or advisory bodies whose members are appointed, usually by the governor, with advice and consent by the legislature. Hawaii is an interesting exception. Appointment to this state's Board of Land and Natural Resources is a shared responsibility of the governor and the legislature.[36]

In most states, boards include state agency representatives either as regular members or as nonvoting *ex officio* members. As with departments, boards usually are responsible only for water quality or water quantity. In some states, however, water quality boards have water quality experts as members and vice versa. Theoretically, having representatives of various agencies on a board will enhance communication and, hence, the coordination of state policy efforts. Integration of water management thus may be achieved through formal organizational linkages rather than by consolidation of functions within a single agency.

Table 18.2 compares state water management in the thirteen west-

Table 18.2 Water Management Agencies in 13 Western States

State	Boards/Commissions		Executive Departments	
	With Interagency Members	Without Interagency Members	Quality	Quantity
Alaska	Water Resources Board		Environmental Conservation	Natural Resources
Arizona	Water Commission Water Quality Control Commission			Water Resources
California		Water Quality Control Board Water Commission	Health Services Water Resources	Water Resources
Colorado		Water Quality Control Commission	Health	State Engineer Natural Resources
Hawaii	Land & Natural Resources Board	Water Resources Commission	Land & Natural Resources	Land & Natural Resources
Idaho		Water Resources Board Board of Health	Health & Welfare	Water Resources
Montana	Water Pollution Control Advisory Council	Natural Resources & Conservation Board Health & Environmental Sciences Board	Health & Environmental Sciences	Natural Resources & Conservation
Nevada		Environment Commission Board of Health	Conservation & Natural Resources Human Services	Conservation & Natural Resources
New Mexico	Water Quality Commission	Interstate Stream Commission	Health & Human Services	State Engineer
Oregon	Strategic Water Management Group	Water Resources Commission Environmental Quality Commission	Environmental Quality	Water Resources
Utah		Water Resources Board Water Pollution Control Commission	Health	Natural Resources
Washington			Ecology	Ecology
Wyoming	Water Development Commission	Board of Control Environmental Quality Council	Environmental Quality	State Engineer

Source: Compiled from relevant state statutes.

ern states. Listed first are boards according to type of membership. Alaska, Arizona, Hawaii, Montana, New Mexico, Oregon and Wyoming are states that require such interagency members on some or all of their boards or commissions. In New Mexico, for example, the state engineer who is responsible for water supply regulation, also is a member of the Water Quality Commission, the agency responsible for establishing water quality policy. In addition, the state engineer serves as a member of the Interstate Stream Commission, an agency that represents the state in interstate and international water matters. In Arizona, the Water Commission includes two *ex officio* members, the commissioner of state lands and the chair of the Arizona Power Authority. Interagency representation is even more extensive on Arizona's Water Quality Control Commission, an advisory body that includes directors of five executive agencies including the Department of Water Resources. Interagency representation is required in Montana and Oregon, too, but in these states, the interagency board does not make policy, it only serves an advisory function.

A brief look at the evolution of water management agencies in Wyoming suggests some limitations in the snapshot of boards provided by Table 18.2. The Wyoming Water Development Commission (WWDC) qualifies as a board with interagency members because the state engineer and the administrator of the water division of the Department of Economic Planning and Development serve as *ex officio* members. However, the nine voting members are appointed at-large by the governor upon recommendations from the state's regional water superintendents. In 1979, the WWDC replaced the Governor's Interdepartmental Water Conference, a board largely composed of agency personnel from all of the state's major departments. Some observers conclude that the WWDC was designed to exclude environmental interests and produce a pro-development bias.[37] In any event, Wyoming, unlike many other states, decided to reduce interagency representation on a key water policy board.

Boards without interagency representatives can be found in California, Colorado, Idaho, Montana, Nevada, Oregon and Utah. Usually, representation is regional with one member from each hydrologic region. In contrast, some states list public and private sectors that must be represented. For example, Utah's Water Pollution Control Committee requires one member each from a list of interest groups: mineral industries, food processing industries, municipalities, fish and wildlife and so forth. In a classic example of the West's disdain for bureaucrats, the Utah statutes explicitly bar any state employee from service on this committee.

Though interagency representatives are not allowed to serve on certain boards in several states, coordination of board and agency efforts may result from institutional location. For example, Colorado's Water Quality Control Commission is formally part of the Department of Health. Similarly, Idaho's Water Resources Board is located within the Department of Water Resources. In contrast, Alaska's Water Resources Board reports directly to the governor. However, Alaska's Commissioner of Environmental Conservation is an *ex officio* member of the board and the Commissioner of the Natural Resources Department is the executive secretary.

Washington appears to be the only western state that has abandoned state water boards and commissions altogether. State legislation allocates significant planning and management authority for water and related land resources to the Department of Ecology. The state thus conforms to the federally recommended omnibus management approach to natural resources. Only two other states in the Union, Florida and Delaware, have enacted programs as comprehensive as that of Washington State.[38]

California is the only other state in the West that has consolidated water quality and quantity concerns within a single state agency. However, authority for water quantity permits and water quality planning and management is assigned to the Water Resources Control Board, a quasi-judicial state agency that oversees the Department of Water Resources (DWR). In addition to water quantity and quality management, the DWR is the state's major water planning agency. Despite the apparent power of California's state water agencies, the golden state is also distinguished by the relative autonomy of its local water districts. Nevertheless, Washington State and California appear to be leaders in the development of comprehensive state water management.

Idaho is an interesting example of some of the difficulties that a western state can encounter when it seeks to change established policies and programs. In 1978, the Idaho legislature passed a water policy and planning act that directed the relevant state agencies to develop a comprehensive plan that included consolidation of state water quantity and quality planning and administration. In 1983, the Idaho Supreme Court ruled that the act was unconstitutional because the legislature could not require legislative approval of a water plan or supplant the Water Resources Board's power to set official state water policy.[39] The Idaho case suggests that changing water policies and structures will be a long and arduous task.

Other states have been able to implement significant changes, but not without years of effort. After several years of federal prodding, Arizona finally enacted a groundwater reform act in 1980. Unlike earlier attempts, the act provides a statewide regulatory structure for the reduction of agricultural consumption as well as incentives for reallocation of water from agriculture to municipal and industrial users.[40] In 1987, Hawaii enacted a state water code—after several years in which proposed legislation had died—and created its Commission on Water Resources. In addition, the Board of Land and Natural Resources was directed to begin comprehensive land and water planning. In both states, the declining dominance of agriculture in water policy decisions was a key factor that allowed reform.

The organizational structure of state water management is a useful point of departure, but such information does not directly tell us how effectively water is managed, nor does it identify who actually makes water policy decisions within each state. Nevertheless, only two western states, Washington and California, have made water policy the primary responsibility of a single state agency. More often, western states fragment the responsibility for water management among various state agencies. Overlap of functions may exist or, even worse, some management functions may not be the responsibility of *any* state-level agency. On the other hand, interagency boards may enhance both coordination and efficiency. Another way to compare state water policy is to look within each state to local water agencies.

THE RELATIVE INFLUENCE OF LOCAL WATER AGENCIES

In contrast to eastern states, the western states are distinguished by the important role that local interests play in the determination of water policy. In the West, local discretionary authority varies considerably. California, home of the nation's most powerful special water districts, provides an interesting example. Underlying California's state level agencies is a complex local water industry. In addition to municipal and county governments, approximately one thousand special purpose district agencies have been granted the power to levy taxes, exercise eminent domain, issue bonds, enter into contracts, construct works, and charge for services.[41] In consequence, state and local organizations manage water resources in two separate spheres of influence. The state is responsible for the regulation of water quality, custodial management of surface and groundwater rights, and large-scale water projects, while local organizations are free to develop, allocate and manage water supplies. The two spheres of influence may make it difficult to coordinate water quality, and surface and groundwater management.

Similar patterns exist throughout the West because in each of the states, except Alaska and Hawaii, special districts have significant discretionary authority over water management. The trend toward integration of state water management appears to be moving at a faster rate in states that do not possess an infrastructure of local water management organizations. States with strong, independent local organizations generally have not been able to develop a unified statewide approach.[42] Some states, including Washington, Oregon and California, have attempted to control the proliferation of special districts by creating local agency formation commissions. Others, notably Nebraska and Florida, have reorganized existing water districts into larger regional "super districts."[43] The important role of local water districts is the second dimension of state water policy.

PRIVATE WATER MARKET TRANSACTIONS

Throughout the region, population growth and continued urbanization coupled with stable or declining agricultural water demands has created pressures to reallocate water. In most cases, water is moving from agriculture to municipal, industrial and recreational uses. Reallocation of water to more highly valued uses such as recreation and industry could bring revitalization of local economies without government subsidies or other forms of public assistance, but a number of "institutional impediments" inhibit or prevent reallocation. These include jurisdictional boundaries and state administrative and statutory restrictions.

A persistent and increasingly popular reallocation approach is offered by a group of "new resource economists" who advocate the removal of impediments and the establishment of private markets.[44] To function efficiently, markets require private ownership of water rights, voluntary exchange by numerous buyers and sellers, and a government role limited to specification of water rights and enforcement of contracts. Allowing water to "flow uphill to money" via unfettered private transactions has special appeal to western individualists and those who tend to oppose governmental solutions. Because the prior appropriation doctrine generally allows voluntary transfers by private rights owners, the West seems to be especially well suited to private reallocation. In fact, Saliba has documented the existence of rudimentary private water markets in California, Arizona, Colorado, Nevada, New Mexico and Utah.[45] Private transactions appear to be particularly popular in Colorado and New Mexico—states that have not developed extensive administrative controls over water use.

Despite these examples, water rights often are not in private hands but instead are owned in large blocks by public agencies. Once again, special water districts play a pivotal role because districts tend to oppose market transfers between willing participants if water will move outside the district's jurisdiction.[46] State governments also may inhibit markets to cushion the impact of reallocation upon agriculture.[47] For example, Arizona, California and Montana have passed area-of-origin protection statutes primarily to restrict interbasin reallocations of water.[48]

Throughout the region, however, state legislatures have begun to pass laws that promote private market transactions. For example, Oregon recently enacted a law that allows irrigators to sell water "saved" by the use of improved conservation techniques. Washington and Hawaii are also among the growing list of states that have established rules for short- and long-term transfers of water.[49]

Whereas private sales rarely occur across water agency jurisdictional boundaries in any state, agencies increasingly negotiate contracts with other agencies to share, sell or lease water. For example, since 1987 the Idaho Water Bank has redistributed surplus water from federal Snake River basin projects to willing buyers. The most provocative example of intergovernmental cooperation is a proposed agreement between two water districts in California: the Imperial Irrigation District (IID) and the Metropolitan Water District (MWD). If it proves successful, MWD will receive 10,000 acre-feet of IID's Colorado River entitlement in exchange for financing water conservation facilities in IID's service area. An interesting aspect of this deal is that IID contemplates no net loss of water; the water sold to MWD will come from improvements in operating efficiencies that will result from ditch lining.[50] Another example comes from Utah where the Bureau of Reclamation is considering purchasing water rights from private individuals and water companies on behalf of the Central Utah Water Conservancy District.[51]

The emergence of water markets, then, is the third dimension by which western states can be compared and contrasted. Significant transaction costs suggest that major reallocations will be the result of intergovernmental agreements, and not private market transactions.

Conclusion

For most of the twentieth century, federal water agencies have responded to demands for assistance by the West's local interests. Old habits are hard to break. Local activists will continue to try to bring some of the pork home even if costs far exceed benefits. A continued federal presence is also likely because of federal water claims and water quality regulations.

Until recently, the western states had played an instrumental role for dominant federal, private, and local water developers. State policies generally were designed to resolve disputes and record claims, with little attention paid to active stewardship of a scarce natural resource. But as the distributive policy era ends, the states face increasing demands for relatively finite supplies, demands that are particularly fierce and are likely to increase.[52] To their credit, the states have responded with a diverse array of regulatory policies and programs.

Perhaps the diversity is due to insularity. In each of the widely separated state capitals, westerners have developed whatever mix of private, public, or quasi-public institutions that seemed appropriate. To the extent that the region's parochialism and vestiges of strong individualism persist, state leaders will continue to fashion distinctive approaches to water management. Yet within this diversity, identifiable patterns have emerged. The spread of irrigation districts is an early example, and the widespread adoption of marketlike reallocations of water is a more recent one. Even though homegrown solutions and local autonomy will continue to characterize the region's water management, a trend toward uniform statewide controls and incentives is evident, if not inevitable.

Whether it is from the sugar plantations of Hawaii or the beanfields of New Mexico, thirsty, growing cities demand water for homes, industry and recreation. Even though most supplies have been developed, significant amounts of water can be "produced" by using water more efficiently. Agriculture, the king of uses, will continue to be the primary target. States and their political subdivisions have been reluctant to impose the heavy hand of government in limiting water use, but this reluctance will surely fade. Sooner or later, state governments increasingly will be called on to reallocate water. In some states, reallocation of water will rend the social fabric of rural communities, especially communities that rely on irrigated agriculture. In other states, the effects will be less severe.

In a sense, water allocation problems are a mirage. The often intense political struggles over who gets what water, when, and how seem to be the real issues. From a larger perspective, the western states may face even tougher challenges in the form of environmental protection. The water pollution problems evident in many western states are the result of generations of neglect in the use of the region's most precious resource. As water is used and reused by more people for more purposes, the West's limited waters increasingly will be threatened. In light of the region's dependence on these supplies, water quality problems should become the focal point for the future.

Notes

1. Helen M. Ingram, *Patterns of Politics in Water Resources Development: A Case Study of New Mexico's Role in the Colorado River Basin Bill* (Albuquerque: University of New Mexico, Division of Government Research, 1969; reprinted as *Water Politics: Continuity and Change*, University of New Mexico Press, 1990).

2. See chapters 1 and 2 above.

3. James Q. Wilson, *Political Organizations* (New York: Basic Books, 1973), chap. 16.

4. *Ibid.*, 330–34.

5. Theodore J. Lowi, "American Business, Public Policy, Case Studies, and Political Theory," *World Politics* 16, 4 (1964).

6. See, for example, Daniel McCool, *Command of the Waters* (Berkeley: University of California Press, 1987).

7. William Kahrl, *The Water and the Power* (Berkeley: University of California Press, 1982); Vincent Ostrom, *Water and Politics* (Los Angeles: Haynes Foundation Press, 1953).

8. See, for example, Paul Sabatier, "Knowledge, Policy Oriented Learning, and Policy Change: An Advocacy Coalition Framework," *Knowledge* 8 (June 1987), 649–92; Hugh Heclo, "Issue Networks in the Executive Establishment," in Anthony King, ed., *The New American Political System* (Washington, D.C.: American Enterprise Institute, 1978).

9. Marc Reisner, *Cadillac Desert: The American West and Its Disappearing Water* (New York: Viking-Penguin, 1986), 503.

10. Delworth Gardner, "Institutional Impediments to Efficient Water Allocation," *Policy Studies Review* 5, 2 (1985), 353–636.

11. Lenni Beth Benson, "Desert Survival: The Evolving Western Irrigation District," *Arizona State Law Journal* 2 (1982), 377–417.

12. Kahrl, *Water and Power.*

13. Reisner, *Cadillac Desert*, 2.

14. Benson, "Desert Survival," 385.

15. 1887 California Statute 29, chap. 34.

16. Erwin Cooper, *Aqueduct Empire* (Glendale, Calif.: Arthur H. Clarke, 1968).

17. Benson, "Desert Survival," 399.

18. Henry P. Caulfield, Jr., "U.S. Water Resources Development Policy and Intergovernmental Relations," in John G. Francis and M. Richard Ganzel, eds., *Western Public Lands* (Totowa, N.J.: Rowman and Allanheld, 1984), 232–47.

19. Mark Wilson, "Reclamation Subsidies and Their Present-Day Impact," *Arizona State Law Journal* 2 (1982), 497–527.

20. Reisner, *Cadillac Desert*, 114–15.

21. Ingram, *Patterns of Politics*, chap. 1.

22. P. L. 69-287, 44 Stat. 636 (codified in various sections of 43 U.S.C.).

23. Reisner, *Cadillac Desert*, 121.

24. U.S. Department of the Interior, Water and Power Resources Service (Bureau of Reclamation), "Acreage Limitation: Draft Environment Report" (Washington, D.C.: U.S. Government Printing Office, 1981).

25. John Leshy, "Irrigation Districts in a Changing West: An Overview," *Arizona State Law Journal* 2 (1982), 345–76.

26. Tim De Young, *Discretion Versus Accountability: The Case of Special Water Districts: Challenge for the Future* (Boulder: University of Colorado, School of Law, Natural Resources Center, 1983); Merrill R. Goodall and John D. Sullivan, "Water District Organization: Political Decision Systems," in Ernest A. Englebert, ed., *California Water: Planning and Policy* (Davis: California Water Resources Center, 1979), 207–28.

27. John Leshy, "After the Concrete Sets: The Future Role of the Bureau of Reclamation in Western Water Management," in *Workshop Proceedings, Western Water: Expanding Demand/Finite Supplies* (Boulder: University of Colorado, School of Law, Natural Resources Center, June 1986).

28. Charles W. Howe, "The Coming Conflicts over Water," in *Western Water Resources: Coming Problems and the Policy Alternatives*, symposium sponsored by the Federal Reserve Bank of Kansas City, September 27–28, 1980 (Boulder, Colo.: Westview Press, 1980).

29. Charles W. Howe and William Easter, *Interbasin Transfers of Water* (Baltimore, Md.: Resources for the Future, 1962).

30. Caulfield, *U.S. Water Resources Development Policy*, 221.

31. Frank J. Trelease and George A. Gould, *Cases and Materials on Water Law*, 4th ed. (St. Paul, Minn.: West Publishing, 1986), 12–15.

32. George E. Radosevich, "Better Use of Water Management Tools," in *Western Water Resources: Coming Problems and the Policy Alternatives*, 262–63.

33. George A. Gould, "Water Use and the Appropriation Doctrine," in *Workshop Proceedings, Western Water: Expanding Demand/Finite Supplies*.

34. 49th Montana State Legislature, *Final Report of the Select Committee on*

Water Marketing (January 1985); New Mexico Water Resources Research Institute and University of New Mexico Law School, *State Appropriation of Unappropriated Groundwater: A Strategy for Insuring New Mexico a Water Future* (January 1986).

35. For a good summary of federal objectives, see National Water Commission, *Water Policies for the Future* (Washington, D.C.: U.S. Government Printing Office, 1973).

36. Except where noted this section is based on relevant state statutes.

37. R. McGreggor Cawley and Charles Davis, "Changing State-Federal Relations in Water Resource Policy: The Case of Wyoming," paper delivered at the 1983 Annual Meeting of the Western Political Science Association, Seattle, March 25.

38. U.S. Water Resources Council, *State of States: Water Resources Planning and Management* (Washington, D.C.: U.S. Government Printing Office, 1981).

39. *Idaho Power Company v. State*, 104 Id. 570, 661 P.2d 736 (1983).

40. Dale Pontius, "Groundwater Management in Arizona: A New Set of Rules," *Arizona Bar Journal* (October 1980), 28–52; Arizona Revised Statutes, vol. 15, chap 45 (1980).

41. Goodall and Sullivan, "Water District Organization," 208.

42. Terry Edgmon and Tim De Young, "Categorizing State Models of Water Management," in John G. Francis and M. Richard Ganzel, eds., *Western Public Lands*, 232–47.

43. *Ibid.*

44. See, for example, Terry Anderson, *Water Crisis: Ending the Policy Drought* (Baltimore, Md.: Johns Hopkins University Press, 1983).

45. Bonnie C. Saliba, "Do Water Markets Work? Market Transfers and Trade-Offs in the Southwestern States," *Water Resources Research* 23, 7 (July 1987), 1113–22.

46. Tim De Young and Hank C. Jenkins-Smith, "Privatizing Water Management: The Hollow Promise of Free Markets," in Zachary T. Smith, ed., *Water and the Future of the Southwest* (Albuquerque: University of New Mexico Press, 1989).

47. Gary Weatherford and Helen Ingram, "Legal Institutional Limitations on Water Use," in Ernest A. Englebert, ed., *Water Scarcity: Impact on Western Agriculture* (Berkeley: University of California Press, 1984), 69.

48. Lawrence J. MacDonnell and Charles W. Howe, "Area-of-Origin Protection in Transbasin Water Diversions: An Evaluation of Alternative Approaches," *University of Colorado Law Review* 57 (1986), 527–48.

50. Dennis B. Underwood, "A Case Study: Imperial Valley, CA," in *Workshop Proceedings, Western Water: Expanding Demand/Finite Supplies*.

51. *Water Market Update Newsletter.*

52. John A. Folk-Williams, *What Indian Water Means to the West* (Santa Fe, N.M.: Western Network, 1982); F. Lee Brown, "Conflicting Claims to the Southwestern Water: The Equity and Management Issues," *Southwestern Review of Management and Economics* 1, 1 (Spring 1981), 35–60.

19

WESTERN
GOVERNMENTS
AND
ENVIRONMENTAL
POLICY

Sheldon Kamieniecki,
Matthew A. Cahn, and
Eugene R. Goss

*T*HE MINING AND PROCESSING OF URANIUM ORE, AN
operation primarily confined to the West, has led to serious health
and environmental problems. For example, from the early 1900s until
the middle of the 1920s high-grade uranium ore was shipped from
the Colorado Plateau in western Colorado to Denver, where it was
refined into pure radium. At that time many people believed that
radium had special healing properties, and many regularly drank
water that had sat for days in urns containing radium. In addition,
tailings from the refinement process were often mixed with cement
in the construction of buildings. Builders, unaware of the potential
health hazards of continuous exposure to low levels of radiation (*e.g.,*

cancer), added the tailings because they provided a cheap filler and improved the consistency of wet cement. Once the dangers of exposure to radiation became known, these practices ceased. The milling sites were shut down and buried, and buildings and roads were built on top of them. Unfortunately, the sites continued to release radiation, exposing thousands of unaware workers and citizens for decades.

The Denver radium sites are just one example of the many serious environmental problems faced by the thirteen western states. Due to the nature and complexity of these problems, various agencies and levels of government in the West have had to work together to solve them. This chapter examines the role of such intergovernmental relations in the development of environmental policy in this region. The first section discusses how the ethos of the West has shaped intergovernmental relations and environmental policymaking over time. The following sections analyze government reaction to several environmental problems, including the Denver radium sites, the Exxon tanker oil spill near Valdez, Alaska, the removal of old-growth timber in the Northwest and air and water pollution in California. This is followed by an examination of intergovernmental relations involving the federal government, the western states and Mexico. Possible future trends in intergovernmental relations and environmental policymaking in the West are reviewed at the conclusion of the chapter.

Ethos of the West

To a large extent, the sight of the natural scenic beauty combined with an understanding of the ethos of the West help one to grasp the nature of intergovernmental relations and environmental policy in the region's thirteen states. John Muir discovered an aspect of the West a hundred years ago that is increasingly being rediscovered by Americans today—that the West is graced with great natural beauty. Among the natural wonders in the West are Mauna Kea in Hawaii, the tallest mountain in the world from base to top; the ecologically rich Prince William Sound in Alaska; the ruggedly spectacular forests and coastlines of Washington, Oregon and California; Yosemite and Sequoia national parks in California; the Grand Canyon in Arizona; Yellowstone National Park in Montana and Wyoming; the Sawtooth Mountains of Idaho; and the alpine vistas of the Colorado Rocky Mountains. Americans and especially westerners deeply cherish these places, and they consider them to be irreplaceable treasures.

Many of these natural wonders might appear quite different today were it not for the strong environmental protectionist values most westerners share. John Muir was one of the first to translate his deep concern for preserving the environment into action.[1] His early messianic crusade to save the Hetch Hetchy Valley in Yosemite sounded the call for environmental activism in the West. For Muir, nature was to be valued above human aspirations and should be worshiped rather than manipulated to fulfill material desires. In this respect, he differed from those in the conservation movement who were responsible for establishing national parks and forests and encouraging armies of tourists to visit them annually. Muir sought the unequivocal preservation of nature, primarily for nature's sake and secondarily for providing a spiritual resource for humankind.[2]

The conservation movement was a well-intentioned offshoot of the progressive movement of the early 1900s. Teddy Roosevelt was among the leaders of the movement who regarded the western lands as a national resource to be carefully managed by prudent federal stewardship. This did not preclude the exploitation of the public lands and national forests for tourism, hunting, lumber, minerals and energy resources. As a reflection of this perspective, a balance among competing demands for natural resources was established and maintained.

The Sierra Club, founded by John Muir in 1892, is regarded today as the leading environmental organization in the United States. The Sierra Club, with its headquarters in San Francisco, enjoys considerable grass-roots support and is especially influential in the West. Muir is a legendary figure there and continues to influence western attitudes from the grave.[3]

The environmental movement in the West has faced a political challenge unlike that faced in other parts of the country. Many of its initiatives have needed the force of federal law to have any impact on state policy. Leaders of the movement have therefore turned to Congress, the federal courts, and various federal agencies in order to gain leverage in public policymaking in the western states. Particularly in the West, the Environmental Protection Agency (EPA), established by Congress in 1970, has been stringently enforcing the Clean Air Act. In addition, the Office of Surface Mining (in the Department of the Interior), established in 1977, has been overseeing the implementation of the Surface Mining Control and Reclamation Act. Many westerners, however, have traditionally resented the interference of the federal government in what are perceived as local matters.

Herein lies the dilemma faced by public-spirited westerners over the past century, a dilemma that frequently has been resolved to the detriment of the natural environment. Westerners love the great natural beauty that surrounds them, but this beauty also attracts tourists and encompasses enormous amounts of timber, mineral and energy resources. Tourism, logging and mining have historically been the foundation of local economies throughout the region.[4] When workers in the lumber industry are faced with a choice between saving old forests and feeding their families, their otherwise strong respect for and love of nature will usually take second place. This is a predicament that westerners have faced for years. The conflict is often framed as one between developers and environmentalists, and to a large degree that is accurate. But it is also a conflict within the hearts and minds of people who reside near or within the West's great scenic beauty. This inner conflict is one in which contradictory values fight for control of rational thought. In some states, such as Oregon and California, environmental values often prevail. In other states, such as Utah and Wyoming, economic values more often win out. This deep historical conflict among competing values sets the West apart from other regions of the country and provides the backdrop for studying intergovernmental relations and environmental policy in these western states.

The Denver Radium Sites

A major environmental policy problem faced by all the state governments in the West is how to manage the transportation and disposal of hazardous and toxic wastes. Due to the West's rich uranium reserves and the central role the region has played in the development of the atomic bomb and nuclear energy, this issue also has encompassed the disposal of radioactive materials. In fact, the federal government will probably designate one of the western states, possibly Nevada, as a national site for the long-term storage of highly radioactive wastes. As the introduction to this chapter implies, the city of Denver is one of several places that has been touched by the issue.

The first clue that a serious problem might exist in the city of Denver was uncovered in late January 1979.[5] Don Hendricks was the chief of the Office of Radiation Programs at the EPA's Las Vegas, Nevada, facility at the time. While working in an EPA research library, he discovered a reference in an old document to a "large radium mill" that had operated close to downtown Denver from 1914 to 1917. He became concerned about the final disposition of the mill and immediately contacted the regional EPA office in Denver which, in turn, contacted the Colorado State Department of Health. The exact location of the site was ascertained with the help of the Denver Public Library's city directories from that era. The site, owned and operated by the Robinson Brick and Tile Company, was visited and surveyed on February 8, 1979. The walls of two buildings on the site were found to be emitting radiation above federal standards.

News of this finding spread rapidly, and investigative reporters and private citizens were asked to help in locating other abandoned sites. The Interagency Regulatory Liaison Group (IRLG)—consisting of the U.S. Consumer Product Safety Commission, the EPA, the federal Food and Drug Administration, the federal Food Safety and Quality Service and the U.S. Occupational Safety and Health Administration—was contacted and its aid requested. The U.S. Department of Energy (DOE) provided a specially equipped helicopter and the EPA a scanning van, which were used to locate additional radium sites in and around Denver. After two months of searching and investigation, about forty sites had been discovered. Approximately two-thirds of the sites were found to be emitting "low levels" of radiation in excess of federal standards. The Colorado State Department of Health later conducted epidemiological studies of workers who had been employed on several of the sites for long periods of time and found no evidence of widespread health problems such as cancer.

The investigation into the scope and seriousness of the Denver radium problem received unprecedented cooperation both within and between all levels of government. At the local level, support services were provided by the city and county of Denver, the Office of Civil Defense and the health departments of El Paso, Boulder and Jefferson counties. Albert J. Hazle, the director of the Radiation and Hazardous Wastes Control Division in the Colorado State Department of Health, took the lead in coordinating the intergovernmental efforts at the request of the governor of Colorado. The Colorado Department of Natural Resources, the Colorado Department of Highways and the Colorado Department of Law all played a central role at the state level in addressing the issue. In addition to the IRLG, the DOE and the EPA Region VIII office, other federal agencies lent their expertise and services to the operation (*e.g.*, the U.S. Geological Survey and the

U.S. Nuclear Regulatory Commission). Finally, Denver's congressional representative, Patricia Schroeder, who believed the sites should be immediately abated and removed where possible, attempted to tie the radium sites' cleanup to the passage of the Superfund bill in the U.S. House of Representatives. She stated in a speech on the House floor that it was the House's intent to place Colorado radium sites under the jurisdiction of the measure. The EPA later agreed to this after the Superfund bill became law in 1980.

Because Albert Hazle, the Colorado State Department of Health and the regional EPA office were willing to take the initiative to examine the problem closely, they managed to avoid any significant political turmoil. No doubt, the extensive media coverage this issue received, as well as the many telephone calls and letters from concerned citizens, initially accounted for the overall high level of cooperation among the various agencies involved. This cooperation continued, however, long after the excitement had died down, though in less dramatic fashion. Perhaps a steel linked fence, with its many connections at different angles, best describes the nature of intergovernmental relations on this policy issue. As a consequence, many of the Denver radium sites, particularly those that posed a potential danger to human health, were eventually abated.

The Exxon Valdez Oil Tanker Spill

The coastal areas of Alaska, Washington, Oregon and California contain many scenic vistas as well as a large number of fragile ecological reserves. Consequently, environmentalists have long feared a catastrophic oil spill along the Pacific Coast tanker route from Alaska to southern California. On March 24, 1989, their worst fears were realized as a super oil tanker, owned and operated by the Exxon Oil Company, ran aground on Bligh Reef in Prince William Sound in Alaska. About 10.8 million gallons of North Slope crude oil spilled from the tanker and was spread by rough weather and high seas along 1,244 miles of the shoreline.[6] By November 1989, the known casualty toll numbered 980 sea otters, 138 bald eagles, and 33,126 sea birds.[7] The local fishing economy suffered greatly. Despite an intensive cleanup effort by Exxon and the U.S. Coast Guard, the local ecosystem and the once pristine coastline may never return to their original state.

The political conflict resulting from the handling of the spill received national attention as environmentalists and Exxon executives used television to demonstrate graphically to the public their divergent perspectives on the incident. One news report showed the pathetic oil-soaked sea otters lying dead on a black oil-stained shore. Environmentalists, in the report, argued that Exxon and government officials acted too slowly in trying to contain the spill and the ensuing oil slick. Another report showed a "clean beach" and shots of wildlife that had seemingly escaped the effects of the spill. The message in this latter report, of course, was that Exxon was doing its job. Regardless of who scored well in the battle over public support, the ecologically catastrophic oil spill and the controversy surrounding its cleanup are likely to have a significant effect on how local, state and federal officials jointly prepare for and clean up future oil spills along the Pacific Coast and in other parts of the country.

Initially, amid threats of legal action by various agencies and levels of government, Exxon agreed to clean up the oil spill. The Coast Guard provided a portion of the labor, equipment and supplies for the cleanup. Environmentalists speculate that Exxon took the initiative as a public relations move to pre-empt litigation. Perhaps the company also wished to soften the overall negative impact of the spill on its upcoming efforts to obtain permission from Congress to begin exploration and drilling in the Arctic National Wildlife Refuge located on Alaska's North Slope. By late August 1989, the cleanup had involved nearly twelve thousand workers, twelve hundred boats, and one hundred aircraft.[8]

After spending in excess of one billion dollars trying to clean up the worst oil spill in America's history, Exxon suspended its massive operation in September 1989, leaving Alaska's sullied shoreline to a winter of uncertainty. The giant oil company argued that impending winter storms in the area would pose a serious danger to its workers and equipment. While the oil company publicly congratulated itself and began a final public relations campaign to reverse the negative image it had acquired, state and local officials complained about the work left undone in Prince William Sound and the Gulf of Alaska. The state maintained that 57% of the original spill remained unrecovered.[9] As a result, the state sued in state superior court in Anchorage for punitive and compensatory damages, in addition to requesting a substantial negligence fine.[10] Presumably, the state's decision to file in state rather than in federal court reflected its desire for a more sympathetic hearing.

William Reilly, the administrator of EPA, publicly urged Exxon to continue and even expand its cleanup efforts well into 1990, and his assessment concerning Exxon's cleanup was cautiously positive.[11] Bowing to political pressure from various sources, the oil company agreed to return in spring 1990 to resume the cleanup. To the chagrin of many state and local officials, however, the federal government refrained from funding and implementing its own comprehensive cleanup plan. In the opinion of some state and local officials, Exxon's campaign contributions during the 1988 presidential election had not been forgotten by the Bush administration.

One lesson for policymakers seems clear as a result of this disastrous accident. Clearly, the complacency of Exxon, the Alyeska oil consortium, the State of Alaska, the EPA and the Coast Guard before the incident caused them to be caught by surprise. This is probably because for many years oil shipping through these sensitive ecological areas had been free of significant mishaps. Most experts agree that the equipment necessary to contain a spill of this size effectively was not in place and that this seriously hindered early attempts to keep the oil from spreading. Moreover, during the critical twenty-four-hour period immediately following the accident, officials from the State of Alaska, the Coast Guard, EPA and Exxon could not agree on a basic plan of action. This breakdown of decision-making and lack of prior planning delayed action and probably exacerbated the ultimate spread of oil across the sea and shoreline. In sharp contrast to the handling of the Denver radium sites, cooperation within and between agencies and levels of government was almost nonexistent at the outset of the crisis. Plans are currently being made to improve intergovernmental relations in the event of another oil spill along the Pacific Coast.

The Exxon oil spill underscores the schizophrenia westerners feel about protecting their environment on the one hand, and furthering rapid economic growth on the other hand. While Alaskans are dismayed at the death of fish and wildlife and the harm caused to the scenic beauty of the area, they know very well that over 80% of their state's revenues come from oil.[12] Clearly, Alaskans want the oil industry in their state. However, if this episode is an indication of future trends, the state of Alaska will probably exercise more regulatory control over the industry in the future.

Cutting of Old-Growth Timber in the Northwest

The raging controversy over old-growth timber in Oregon, Washington and northern California is another example of how competing values concerning environmental protection and economic growth have influenced intergovernmental relations and public policy. Thus far, due to the conditions underlying the controversy, intergovernmental relations have primarily involved units of government at only the federal level. At issue is the future of the last remaining public-owned stands of old-growth Douglas fir, Western hemlock, and California redwood. Most of these forests are managed by either the U.S. Forest Service (Department of Agriculture) or by the Bureau of Land Management (BLM, Department of Interior).

The economic stakes are extremely high. The timber industry in Oregon alone directly employs 67,400 workers and provides one-third of the state's manufacturing jobs.[13] Public policy decisions concerning federal forest management affect private timber companies because they depend upon public forests as a source of timber. Privately owned forests simply cannot fill the need for lumber under current economic conditions and management practices.

Environmentalists, of course, view these forests differently. In their opinion, old-growth forests support unique ecological systems. Stands of majestic trees with trunks four to five feet in diameter and many centuries old form the structural canopy for the complex system of microorganisms, insects, plants, and animals below. Among these inhabitants is the Northern spotted owl, which is now considered to be an indicator species of old-growth forests. As a canary in a coal mine was once used to signal dangerous conditions for miners, so is the Northern spotted owl monitored to learn the health of other species in old-growth forests. As the old-growth forests have diminished, so has the number of Northern spotted owls. As a consequence, environmental groups filed separate suits against the Forest Service and the Bureau of Land Management seeking to protect the owl from extinction by challenging pending timber sales that would potentially affect the owl's habitat. Judges in both cases at the federal district trial court level ordered temporary injunctions on the proposed timber sales until data about the spotted owl could be obtained. The effect of these rulings was to halt the harvest and processing of hundreds of millions of board feet of lumber.

In late 1988 and early 1989, as lumber mills began threatening layoffs, the political climate changed. Senator Mark Hatfield, a Republican from Oregon, organized support for a bill in Congress to limit the injunctive power of courts over federal timber sales (a position strongly backed by the timber industry). Meanwhile, environmental organizations, including the Oregon Natural Resources Council and the Sierra Club Legal Defense Fund, successfully persuaded the U.S. Fish and Wildlife Service to consider officially designating the Northern spotted owl an endangered species, thereby guaranteeing federal protection for it. On September 6, 1989, an injunction restricting the BLM from selling timber that potentially contained the spotted owl habitat was overturned by the U.S. Ninth Circuit Court of Appeals in San Francisco.[14] This ruling came on the heels of a highly publicized hearing concerning the spotted owl held by the Fish and Wildlife Service in Redding, California. At this hearing, dominated by loggers and lumber mill workers, evidence was produced from a timber industry–financed study that appeared to show a prolific presence of spotted owls in the area's national forests.[15]

Although the injunction against the BLM had been overturned, that against Forest Service sales still stood. The timber industry grew steadily more agitated. On the other side, public opinion about the spotted owl was mixed at best, and probably highly antagonistic at worst. On September 29, 1989, a House–Senate conference committee approved a compromise that limited court-imposed injunctions on timber sales, allowed 9.6 billion board feet of timber to be cut in 1989 and 1990, permanently withdrew 700 million board feet from harvest, and minimized "fragmentation of significant old-growth forest stands" to mitigate damage to the spotted owl's habitat.[16]

The conflict intensified when a panel of government scientists issued a report in spring 1990 concluding that continued logging of old-growth forests was threatening the spotted owl with extinction. The scientists, some of whom were from the U.S. Forest Service, called for a ban on up to 40% of the available timberland in the Pacific Northwest in order to protect the bird. Finally, after much deliberation, the U.S. Fish and Wildlife Service officially declared the spotted owl a "threatened" species in summer 1990. The Bush administration has proposed to limit the cutting of old-growth forests, but not near the level recommended by scientific experts.

This episode underscores the pervasive influence of the federal government in the West. Environmental groups and the timber industry both attempted to use the federal courts, Congress, and the federal bureaucracy to realize their particular goals pertaining to the disposition of lands in their states. Historically, this has been a bittersweet process. For the average Oregonian on either side of the issue there is trepidation about having such important decisions made so far from home. As for the combatants in the controversy, neither side received everything it wanted. However, environmentalists are optimistic. In the view of Jim Bloomquist of the Sierra Club, "Congress clearly is on record as saying for the first time that old-growth [forest] is an important national resource and is worthy of significant federal protection."[17]

Water Quality Policy in Southern California

Many areas of the West have experienced rapid population growth since the 1960s. The comfortable climate and outstanding economic and employment opportunities, especially in the Sunbelt cities, are mainly responsible for attracting people to the West. The population explosion has successfully fueled local businesses, dramatically increased land and housing sales, and added considerably to the tax coffers of some states. On the negative side, having more people has led to urban and suburban sprawl, extensive freeway systems and less green space, traffic congestion and noise, air and water pollution problems and a general decline in the quality of life.

Southern California, most notably, has experienced the benefits and costs of a burgeoning population. In February 1989 the Los Angeles *Times* conducted a comprehensive survey of Los Angeles County residents about the overall quality of life in the area. Surprisingly, 48% of those interviewed said that they had considered moving away in the past year.[18] Among the negative aspects of living in Los Angeles, air and water pollution ranked third, closely following crime and traffic congestion.

Clean water is also an essential component of a high quality of life. Robert Gottlieb, a professor of urban planning, recently challenged the southern California Metropolitan Water District (MWD), which is a regional government agency responsible for the distribution of water to arid southern California, to help address the deteriorating quality of life by focusing more on water quality and less on developing new sources of water solely for the purpose of growth.[19] Gottlieb's thesis is that in the dry Southwest, urban growth can be indirectly managed by changing the mission of water agencies from acting as purveyors to serving as stewards and managers. If water quality rather than water quantity becomes the focal point, perhaps other policy spheres directly bearing on the quality of life in southern California can also be improved.

Plenty of work needs to be done to satisfy current water needs, and the increasing pollution of water only hurts this effort. Californians are already alarmed by the taste and possible health problems of their water, and they now consume more privately marketed bottled water than do residents of any other state.[20] While there is some question about the quality of some bottled water, this behavior is certainly indicative of people's distrust of the quality of the water entering their homes.

In 1988, as part of a comprehensive weeklong series on water in California, the *Los Angeles Herald Examiner* undertook a spot check of six water sources around Los Angeles. Using a state-certified laboratory, they found "that most contaminants in the sampled water were byproducts of chlorination."[21] Obviously, this threatens the continued reliance on chlorination as the principal means to disinfect the water supply.

Following prodding by the federal government, both the Los Angeles Department of Water and Power (DWP) and the MWD are attempting to improve the quality of the water they supply to southern California. In a pamphlet distributed by the DWP, the agency showcases its Los Angeles Aqueduct Filtration Plant.[22] In the discussion of the operation of the facility, DWP touts the use of ozone gas to replace chlorine as the primary disinfectant. This will allow the DWP to comply with new, tougher EPA standards for drinking water. The MWD, however, only recently converted its treatment plants to chloramine, which reduces contaminants better than chlorine but not as well as ozone gas. As a result, the MWD may have to spend as much as 200 million dollars more in order to convert its plants to ozone and meet EPA standards. Assuring the supply of safe drinking water is technologically possible but very expensive.

As the preceding chapter indicated, competition for water between agriculture and the growing urban areas of the West is increasing. This competition is bound to raise the price of water. As the price increases, public attitudes will probably change. If water prices become high enough, consumers might begin to recognize their own importance in the formation of quality standards. For now, tap water is cheap enough in Los Angeles that dissatisfied customers can afford to purchase bottled water and other beverages, and use tap water mainly for cleaning and for watering the garden. How long this situation will last is unknown. The problem is compounded by a general shortage of water supplies in the Southwest. Water pricing involves a complex set of agreements between water districts and the federal government, between municipalities and water districts, and between state governments. Water is highly political, and therefore water prices may remain artificially low, reflecting cross-subsidies and inequitable arrangements.

Furthermore, since the passage of the ambitious 1972 Federal Clean Water Act and its subsequent amendments, a struggle over meeting water quality guidelines has ensued among EPA, state agencies, and local communities in the West. Generally, progress has been slow, and many water sources, including those used for recreation, remain polluted. This is partly because of the speculative nature of many of EPA's early quality standards, which often were impossible to meet under existing technology. However, most of the water pollution is attributed to inadequate waste treatment facilities, the discharge of toxic wastes by industrial and manufacturing firms, and the release of chemicals used in mining, ranching and agriculture. The powerful interest groups that represent these activities, especially in California, have been able to forestall effective state implementation of mandated federal standards.[23] The patience of EPA is running low, and the California State Water Resources Board has been under increasing pressure to move quickly to meet federal water quality standards. While there has been some cooperation among federal, state and local government officials on this issue, for the most part intergovernmental relations concerning water quality in California have been marked by conflict. Greater cooperation within and between levels of government is required before significant improvements in water quality can be achieved.

Air Quality Policy in Southern California

Air pollution may be the most serious environmental problem the West faces today. A combination of burning fossil fuels in power plants, heavy reliance on automobiles and other motorized vehicles for transportation, and natural mountain barriers is primarily responsible for the air pollution in different parts of the region. In southern California, where air quality has suffered most, automobiles are responsible for about 60% of the pollution. Lead, sulfur dioxide, carbon monoxide, nitrogen oxides, and ozone are "cooked" by the sun to form a dangerous mixture of photochemical smog. The smog hurts the development of children's lungs; causes severe eye irritation, headaches, and respiratory problems in adults; kills plants and trees; and damages property. Long-term health effects, such as emphysema, are also thought to be associated with constant exposure to smog. While California has enacted strict automobile emission requirements since 1970, initial gains have been offset by continuous population growth. Recognizing this trend, the EPA has threatened to cut off all federal funds for California highway construction and transportation if southern California does not come into compliance with federal clean air standards in the near future.

As a consequence, the South Coast Air Quality Management District (AQMD) and the Southern California Association of Governments (SCAG) recently drafted and approved a bold and comprehensive plan to bring southern California into compliance with National Ambient Air Quality Standards by 2007.[24] State, regional and local officials, business interests, and environmental and community groups were all involved in the formulation of the program. The plan was developed through five years of negotiations between state and local officials in particular, and therefore enjoys a statewide consensus. The plan has been approved by the California Air Resources Board and now awaits final approval by EPA. The entire project could not have been completed without close intergovernmental cooperation. The proposed air pollution program may become a model for air policy nationally, and it has also attracted international attention.

The backbone of the plan is the recommended use of clean fuel alternatives such as methanol for motorized vehicles. The plan calls for over 120 specific controls that would result in, among other things, 40% of all new private automobiles and 70% of all new commercial trucks and buses running on methanol by 1999. Chemicals, solvents, paints, household cleaners and similar materials will be reformulated to reduce the release of fluorocarbons (which cause smog). Finally, the new policy requires higher emission and mileage standards for highway vehicles, improved mass transit and increased housing on transit hubs to ease commuting.

While the plan's language is strong, it may be more symbolic than practical. Policy implementation depends upon the participation of local communities, whose primary motivation to comply is the improved traffic flow that would result. Moreover, the state must adopt the specific recommendations of the plan as law. Even before that can happen, the federal government will determine the final shape of the plan.

Nonetheless, the plan may be a preview of environmental policies to come. If state and federal agencies adopt the plan's recommendations and suggested regulations, the program will drastically reduce air pollution in southern California. An effective plan will also demonstrate the need for close intergovernmental relations in the formulation of environmental policies. In many ways California is implementing an experimental program. If it is successful, other states, the nation, and perhaps other countries will follow suit.

Transnational Intergovernmental Relations and Environmental Policy

As explained in Chapter 15, sometimes federal, state and local governments cooperate with foreign governments in order to solve common policy problems. As has often been said, pollution knows no boundaries. The governments of Mexico and Canada have in the past participated in the abatement of such problems as acid rain and water pollution. In the area of environmental policy, therefore, intergovernmental relations have often taken on an international flavor.

Acid rain has been a major problem in the West. The increased acidity of rainfall in certain areas of the West has had a detrimental effect on plants, forests, waterfowl, fish and other living organisms in lakes and streams. Sulfur dioxide, once in the atmosphere, can be transformed into an acid that falls back to earth in precipitation. During the 1980s copper smelters—a majority of them in Arizona and New Mexico—accounted for most of the sulfur dioxide released into the atmosphere between the Sierras in California and the Rocky Mountains. Downwind monitoring stations, some as far away as Wyoming and Idaho, have detected changes in sulfate concentrations in rain and snow in direct proportion to variations in smelter emissions.[25] These smelters will have to install advanced pollution control equipment in order to decrease sulfur dioxide emissions and the resulting acid rain.

There is concern in western states, however, that a new large Mexican smelter in operation at Nacozari across the border from Arizona will drastically increase acid rain in the region. Environmental scientists believe that sulfur dioxide emissions in the West could eventually increase by over 50%, primarily because the prevailing winds around Nacozari blow toward the north. As a result, the United States and Mexican governments, with input from EPA and several western states, negotiated an agreement under which Mexico will add pollution controls to the plant and the United States will act to reduce pollution from American smelters. American copper producers, however, have requested extensions of their deadlines for installing expensive pollution control equipment. If American companies are granted extensions, Mexico might refuse to follow through on the agreement. The natural environment in the West will suffer if this occurs.

In terms of improving water quality, efforts to treat sewage on the United States–Mexico border have recently benefited from the cooperation of local San Diego and Tijuana officials as well as leaders in the capitals of both countries. Many residents of the Mexican border town remain without regular plumbing, allowing wastes to enter rough channels that drain to the north. Also, Tijuana's sewage pipes frequently break down, thus augmenting the flow. As a result, much of the city's sewage—about 10 million gallons a day—ends up in the fetid Tijuana River, which drains on the U.S. side.[26] At the mouth of the river on the American side are a slough and a national estuarine sanctuary, one of the few on the West Coast, which attract many types of wildlife, including endangered species. Environmentalists feel that the sewage seriously threatens the delicate ecosystem as well as human health. In fact, a 2½-mile stretch of beach just north of the border has been quarantined for more than six years because of the sewage.

Brian Bilbray, a San Diego county supervisor, and other state and local officials helped bring pressure on both national governments to relieve the problem. Following the elections of President George Bush and President Carlos Salinas de Gortari in 1988, both of whom had emphasized environmental concerns in their campaigns, the United States agreed to fund the project and the Mexican government agreed to the building of a binational facility to treat its wastes. A historic United States–Mexico environmental pact signed in Washington in October 1989 could end the decades-long spillage of Tijuana sewage. The agreement commits both nations to the construction of a San Diego–based facility, costing about 200 million dollars, that would treat wastes from Mexico.[27] The facility is scheduled to be in operation by 1993.

Prospects for the Future

The rapid growth of the West has placed tremendous stress on the natural environment. Population growth, tourism, lumbering, mining, and the heavy burning of fossil fuels to fulfill energy and transportation needs have all adversely affected the quality of life in the region. The schizophrenia westerners feel about achieving economic prosperity and protecting their environment helps to explain current public policy. While there have been significant improvements in environmental quality on some fronts, many areas of the West are still experiencing severe pollution problems and shortages of natural resources. Unless something is done, many other areas will soon encounter similar problems.

First and foremost, westerners must decide to what extent they are willing to enjoy economic growth at the expense of the environment. Slow-growth movements have emerged in a number of local communities in the region, and many cities have proposed slow-growth legislation. In addition, many communities have already adopted pollution control, recycling and conservation measures.

Emerging as the nation's trend-setter in pollution control, California has initiated steps to curtail substantially the burning of fossil fuels by the year 1999. Taking California's lead, Congress has amended President Bush's Clean Air Act provisions to extend California's already tough emission standards to the rest of the nation by 1994.[28] This will lower by 39% the amount of hydrocarbons automobiles can emit and reduce nitrogen oxide emissions by 60%.[29]

Federal officials are also likely to learn from California's plan to manage solid waste. In 1989, the state enacted an extremely comprehensive solid waste bill—the Integrated Waste Management Act. This bill requires cities and counties to reduce and recycle 25% of their waste by 1995 and 50% by the year 2000. Citizens and businesses will be asked to reduce the amount of their garbage, and to separate newspaper, aluminum, glass and certain plastics for recycling. While critics have argued that it is unrealistic to expect households to separate trash before pickup, in those areas where recycling has been implemented results have been encouraging. In fact, in some areas the existing plants are unable to keep up with the supply of recyclable material. Such local experiments suggest that site separation is workable and that building additional plants will allow more garbage to be recycled.

Intergovernmental relations in the area of environmental policy are likely to be strained as the West moves into the next century. Although a recent comparative fifty-state study ranked California, Oregon and Washington among the best managers of the environment (numbers one, two, and ten, respectively), nearly all the remaining western states were ranked in the bottom half of the nation.[30] In order to maintain and improve the region's environment and quality of life, westerners will have to make significant changes in their life-styles. Many of these changes will infringe upon the traditional freedoms westerners have enjoyed. Interest groups in the individual states and localities are likely to contest restrictive legislation at every juncture, thus increasing political tensions and leading to immense friction within and between levels of government. Such political turmoil can be avoided if westerners and others realize that the environmental problems they face, like the Denver radium sites, threaten not only their quality of life but also the long-term survival of life itself.

In essence, citizens must come to terms with environmental degradation in the West, and make the short-term sacrifices necessary to relieve the growing problems of pollution. Trends in public policy are moving cautiously closer to encouraging life-style changes. Recycling, conservation, slower growth and increased energy efficiency are all essential policy goals. In effect, westerners will have to become pioneers again, but this time the frontier they must explore and tame is one that they have created themselves.

Notes

1. Robert C. Paehlke, *Environmentalism and the Future of Progressive Politics* (New Haven, Conn.: Yale University Press, 1989), 16.

2. *Ibid.*, 17.

3. Bob Sipchen, "The Muir Mystique," *Los Angeles Times*, April 20, 1988, Part V, 1.

4. John Opie, "Environmental History in the West," in Gerald D. Nash and Richard W. Etulain, eds., *The Twentieth Century West: Historical Interpretations* (Albuquerque: University of New Mexico Press, 1989), 210–11.

5. Robert M. O'Brien and Sheldon Kamieniecki, "The Politics of Toxic Waste Management: The Case of the Colorado Radium Sites," a report prepared for the Superfund Division of the U.S. Environmental Protection Agency, 1980; and Robert M. O'Brien, Michael Clarke, and Sheldon Kamieniecki, "Open and Closed Systems of Decision Making: The Case of Toxic Waste Management," *Public Administration Review* 44 (July/August 1984), 334–40.

6. Tamara Jones, "Exxon Suspends Alaska Cleanup; Work Is Left Undone," *Los Angeles Times*, September 15, 1989, Part I, 21.

7. *Ibid.*

8. *Ibid.*

9. *Ibid.*

10. Associated Press, "Alaska Sues Seven Oil Companies," *Los Angeles Times*, August 16, 1989, Part I, 4.

11. Larry Stammer, "EPA Chief Wants Exxon to Honor Pledge," *Los Angeles*

Times, August 5, 1989, Part I, 26; and Jerry Adler, "Alaska After Exxon," *Newsweek* (September 18, 1989), 53.

12. Mitchel Satchell and Betsy Carpenter, "A Disaster That Wasn't," *U.S. News and World Report* (September 18, 1989), 69.

13. Barbara Roberts, *Oregon Bluebook, 1989–1990* (Salem: State of Oregon, 1989), 258–59.

14. Charles McCoy, "Timber Firms Allowed by Court to Fell the Ancient Forests of Western Oregon," *The Wall Street Journal*, September 7, 1989, A6.

15. Mike Francis, "The Owls Are Coming! The Owls Are Coming! Californians Cry," *The Oregonian*, August 25, 1989, Part 4, 1.

16. Times Wire Service, "Conferees OK Compromise on Logging, Spotted Owl Protection," *Los Angeles Times*, September 30, 1989, Part I, 28.

17. *Ibid.*

18. Kevin Roderick, "The Quality of L.A. Life: A Times Poll Special Report," *Los Angeles Times Magazine*, April 2, 1989, 10–11.

19. Robert Gottlieb, "Our Water Agencies' Historic Growth Agenda Needs a New Mission," *Los Angeles Times*, September 14, 1989, Part 3, 2.

20. Emilia Askari, "Bottled Water: Not All Pure and Simple," *Los Angeles Herald Examiner*, Special Reprint Edition on Water, January 1989, 20.

21. *Ibid.*, 11. The contaminants found in the water belonged to a carcinogenic group of chemicals called trihalomethanes or THMs. The Beverly Hills sample registered 46.5 parts per million. While this figures does not exceed current EPA standards for THMs, the EPA does plan to lower maximum allowable levels of THMs to between 50 and 10 parts per million by 1990.

22. City of Los Angeles Department of Water and Power, *The Los Angeles Aqueduct Filtration Plant*, #20M, 1987.

23. Zachary Smith, *Groundwater in the West* (San Diego: Academic Press, 1989), 65.

24. Maura Dolan, "Landmark Plan on Smog Okayed," *Los Angeles Times*, August 16, 1989, Part 1, 1.

25. Erik Eckholm, "Distant Pollution Tied to Acid Rain," *New York Times*, August 23, 1985, A1.

26. Patrick McDonnell, "Border Sewage Treatment Pact Seen as Breakthrough," *Los Angeles Times*, October 9, 1989, Part 1, 3.

27. *Ibid.*

28. Matthew L. Wald, "Nation Looks to California for Guidance on Pollution Laws," *San Francisco Chronicle*, October 10, 1989, Part 1, 11.

29. Associated Press, "Breakthrough Pact on Auto Smog," *San Francisco Chronicle*, October 3, 1989, Part 1, 1.

30. Kathleen Sylvester, "Environmental Report Card Ranks California Tops," *Governing* (May 1989), 17.

20

CONCLUSION: CONTINUITY, CHANGE AND FUTURE DIRECTIONS IN WESTERN POLITICS AND PUBLIC POLICY

Clive S. Thomas

*L*IKE ANY SOCIETY, AND PARTICULARLY A YOUNG one, the West is constantly changing and developing. Such changes and developments have been particularly significant over the past thirty years during which the region has experienced major changes in its social and economic life and thus in its politics, government and public policy. These political changes include a dramatic shift to the Republicans in national elections in the Mountain states, a substantial reduction in some federal aid programs, the rise of political action committees (PACs) and the emergence of the power of minority groups. The rate and extent of these developments make the last thirty years probably the most significant period in western political development. At least one observer views these developments as being almost as profound as those that transformed the South over the same period.[1]

Such apparently profound developments raise several important questions about the changing nature of politics in the West. In this concluding chapter we draw together the various aspects of continuity, change and possible future developments in the region's politics and public policy. We begin by reviewing the major influences that have affected contemporary western politics and the changes that have resulted. Next we link these influences and changes with possible future development and directions in western politics, government and public policy, both in terms of subregional divisions within the West and by identifying likely major developments and issues and the challenges that these will present to the region's policymakers. Then we assess the probable impact of these contemporary and projected changes on the fundamental nature of western politics, linking them with the ten enduring characteristics that were identified in Chapter 1.

Contemporary Western Politics and Public Policy: Major Influences and Their Consequences

If the last thirty years have been the most significant period in the political development of the West, what has been at the root of this development and what have been its major consequences? What major factors have influenced the nature of politics in the region, and therefore may significantly change politics, government and public policy in the near future? In Chapter 2 we explored twelve major categories of influence that have affected western politics over the years. All twelve have helped shape contemporary western politics, but some have been particularly important. In this section we focus on the more significant of these influences and the major changes that they have produced.

EXPANDING POLITICAL PARTICIPATION AND POLITICAL PLURALISM

More people and more groups are participating at all levels of the American political process than ever before, both nationally and in the West. At first glance this appears in contradiction to the well-publicized fact that voter turnout in the nation is on the decline.

Remember, however, that voting is only one of several ways of participating in politics. It is possible that many citizens believe that direct participation in legislative and executive decision-making is a more effective way to get their message across to government than simply by voting.

The result has been an increased number of interests lobbying in state capitals and at city halls and county seats throughout the region. The work of the legislative and executive branches has expanded considerably. Political activity has intensified as a result of these developments, and therefore competition for public office has increased, as has public scrutiny of those who are elected.

THE TREND TOWARD CONSERVATISM

The national trend toward conservatism, which has had a significant impact in the West, may signify the intensification of the long-standing individualistic political culture in the region. But a close examination reveals that this increasing conservatism has been more evident in the Mountain states and particularly in national elections. In this subregion conservatism appears to be linked with a general antipathy to the social programs of the Democrats during the 1960s, combined with the end of substantial federal public works projects such as those for water and electrification. In short, it appeared to voters in the Mountain states that the federal government no longer offered them anything of value. Increased conservatism in the Pacific states appears to be confined mainly to fiscal matters, with the first major manifestation in California through Proposition 13 in 1978. Yet surveys indicate that the Pacific states are still among the most tolerant and liberal in the nation.[2]

DECLINING POLITICAL PARTIES AND THE
INCREASING POWER OF INTEREST GROUPS

The trend toward the declining power of parties and the increasing power of interest groups in the nation as a whole has also had its counterpart in the West. However, because parties have always been less of a political force in the West, the decline in party identification and the role of parties has been less significant than it has, for example, in the Northeast. Nevertheless, the strong and often dominant role of interest groups in the West has been enhanced, filling the power vacuum left by declining parties. The power of groups has been increased by a rise in the use of PACs, by more sophisticated organization and by a general rise in professionalism of group leaders and lobbyists.

INCREASING PROGESSIONALISM IN POLITICS AND GOVERNMENT

The national trend toward increased professionalism has not been confined to the area of interest group activity. It has also affected campaign techniques, legislators, governors and bureaucrats.

California leads the West, and perhaps the nation, in the development and use of sophisticated campaign techniques promoted by an expanding political consulting business. Although other states in the region have not had to adopt such sophisticated and impersonal campaign methods, the sparsely populated western states have always relied on the media, especially for national and statewide campaigns. Furthermore, increasing political pluralism and the rise of the professional politician are forcing candidates in all western states to follow California's lead.

Perhaps the major trend in state legislatures is the rising rate of incumbency: more legislators are being reelected so that we are seeing the rise of the "professional" as opposed to the "citizen" legislator in the West. There are still, however, wide disparities in the region in this trend and in the support services provided to legislators. Once again, the division appears to be between the Mountain states, where the trend is much less pronounced, and the Pacific states led by California.

This subregional division also appears to reflect the extent of the professionalization of state bureaucracies. However, all western states have increased the size of their bureaucracies in recent years. As Raymond Cox points out in Chapter 10, this has had a very important impact on the role of western governors. Because of the increasing size of state government they have been forced to become managers in addition to their longstanding roles of politician, major party figure and formal head of state government. As managers governors must be more active in the budget process and in policymaking. As elsewhere in the nation, western governors are no longer "Good-Time Charlies."[3]

THE EXPANDING ROLE OF GOVERNMENT

The changing role of western governors is just one example of the expanding role of government in the western states. The most significant expansion has been in state government, and to a lesser extent in local and city government. While the federal role is still very important, it has gone through some significant changes since the mid-1960s. The late 1970s saw a sharp decline in funds for large water projects and a decline of funds associated with many of the Great Society programs begun in the mid-1960s. The Reagan presidency (1981–89) further reduced federal funding for many programs.

Yet the Reagan administration did not reduce the impact of the federal government in the West. In fact, a good case can be made that this impact was increased in both a positive and a negative way. Much of the increased defense spending of the Reagan years found its way west. On the other hand, reduced spending for other programs severely affected the financial capability of many state and local governments. And the administration's stance in its early years to utilize federal lands more fully, including allowing some exploration for oil and gas, may have helped quell the Sagebrush Rebellion, but it also raised the ire of a growing number of environmentalists in the region. When we add to this federal impact the increased role of state government—particularly as an employer, promoter of economic development and provider of human services—a good argument can be made that the West is much more dependent on government today than ever before.

One other manifestation of the expanded role of government, and the growing complexity of public policy issues in the West, is the increase in intergovernmental organizations and cooperation. Organizations like the Western Governors' Association and the Western Region of the Council of State Governments (WCSG) bring together elected and appointed officials to discuss common problems and explore new strategies and policies. Of particular note has been Westrends and the Western States' Stragegy Center. Westrends is a working group of elected and appointed officials and prominent individuals from western businesses, nonprofit organizations and universities, created under the auspice of the WCSG. It has been working to identify future economic and social trends in the thirteen western states to prepare public officials for the policy challenges that lie ahead. It issued its first report in 1989.[4] The Western States' Strategy Center is a public-private partnership that seeks to promote economic development in the West, including international trade.

DEMOGRAPHIC CHANGES

The West has had the fastest growing population of any region over the past twenty years and projections indicate that substantial growth will continue through the year 2000. As a result, demand has increased for government services of all types, especially those in urban areas where most new residents settle. Perhaps even more significant is that a large percentage of the increase in population, particularly in the Pacific and Southwestern states, has been ethnic and racial minorities, especially Chicanos, immigrants from Southeast Asia and blacks. The western population is also seeing an increase in those under eighteen years old and those over sixty-five. As we will see later, these and other demographic changes are likely to have important consequences on western politics and public policy in the future.

CHANGES IN THE ECONOMIC ENVIRONMENT

In line with the nation as a whole, the western economy has diversified considerably since World War II, and particularly since the 1960s. In the 1980s the West discovered the potential of trade with Southeast Asia and other Pacific nations and the term *Pacific Rim* entered into discussion on economic policy in all western state capitals. Japan became a major real estate investor in Hawaii and California. With their lack of natural resources at home, the Japanese also purchased pulp and lumber mills in Alaska and mines and tracts of lumber in the Northwest.[5] Taiwan and South Korea also purchased western real estate and signed agreements to receive western resources, such as Montana coal and Idaho lumber.

Economic diversification in the West has been uneven, however, and the extent to which western states are able to take advantage of Pacific Rim trade also varies. California is still a Gulliver among Lilliputians in terms of economic output and a diversified economy. Washington, Arizona, Colorado and Hawaii are making strides in diversification, and so is Oregon to a lesser extent. The other Mountain states and Alaska, however, have made much less significant advances and continue to search for the elusive solution to the boom and bust cycle.

Given the developments and changes in western politics of the recent past, what can we expect in the next twenty to thirty years? In the next two sections we explore some probable developments. First we examine some of the political divisions that may persist in the region and some new ones that may develop. In the following section we explore some of the specific socioeconomic and political issues that may develop and the challenges that these will present to the region's policymakers.

Future Regional Divisions in the West

Of the many subregional divisions that are likely to develop in western politics in the future we consider here five of the most likely ones.

THE WESTERN SUNBELT AND SNOWBELT

Much has been written in recent years about the so-called Sunbelt-Snowbelt (sometimes called the Frostbelt) division in the United States. The division relates primarily to differences in population and economic growth between states in the northern portion of the country and which are associated with colder climates, and those in the south of the nation from the east to the west coast. This division is set out in Map 20.1 Sunbelt states have generally experienced higher population growth rates, and higher rates of income, employment and productivity growth. This growth is often attributed to the relocation of northern industries to these states, resulting from the incentives of lower taxes and lower labor costs because of lower rates of unionization in Sunbelt states. For similar reasons new industries have also tended to establish themselves in the Sunbelt.[6]

THE FIVE FUTURE "NATIONS" OF THE WEST

In his book *The Nine Nations of North America* Joel Garreau argues that the states represent "misleading ideas" that are no longer relevant for understanding social, economic and political trends in North America—if, indeed, they ever were.[7] Developments since World War II, he argues, have divided North America into nine "nations." He goes on to argue that these nations are a valuable means for understanding future developments on the North American subcontinent. Map 20.2 identifies the nine nations, as well as the four of them that constitute the West. These four are dubbed by Garreau "Ectopia," "MexAmerica," "The Breadbasket" and "The Empty Quarter."

Besides being dominated by concerns about the environment, including a strong antinuclear bias, the "nation" Garreau calles Ectopia looks to the twenty-first century and to Asia for its trade and lifestyle.[8] In addition to the strong influence of Spanish culture, the MexAmerica "nation" experienced the biggest population boom through Mexican and Asian immigration and the movement of retirees and others from the Northeast and Midwest. This area is highly dependent on engineers to secure and maintain its scarcest resource—water.[9] According to Garreau, therefore, California falls into two separate

Map 20.1   The Western Sunbelt and Snowbelt

Source: Adapted by the author for the West from Thomas R. Dye, *Politics in States and Communities*, 5th ed. (New York: Prentice Hall, 1985), figure 1.3, p. 14. Reprinted with permission.

nations, with Los Angeles and San Francisco representing two different value systems—the MexAmerican and Ecotopian, respectively.

The Breadbasket "nation" includes the high plains on the eastern boundary of the West. This area has much in common with the Plains states of the Midwest and is dominated by agricultural considerations, even though a majority of its population are not farmers. Garreau sees it as the area most at peace with itself because, despite occasional fluctuations in agricultural prices, it has built an economy on a renewable resource.[10] The Empty Quarter is the "nation" most dependent on natural resource extraction and thus the one most subject to fluctuating world prices for these resources. It is also dominated by problems of transportation and communications resulting from its enormous size.[11] As we noted in Chapter 2, Garreau finds Hawaii hard to classify and does not include it within one of his nine "nations." It is a North American aberration and an Asian aberration as well—a place of Ectopian possibilities, with MexAmerican growth values and limits, run by Asians.[12] We have included it here as a fifth "future 'nation' of the West."

PACIFIC STATES VERSUS MOUNTAIN STATES

The subregional division in the West that has been alluded to most frequently in this book is that between the Pacific and Mountain states. The likely future distinctions between these regions have two dimensions. First, there is an attitudinal difference: Generally the Pacific states tend to be more liberal compared with the conservatism manifested in the Mountain states. Put another way, the individualistic political culture will probably be more prominent in the Mountain region in the years to come. Second is a disparity in economic well-being as seen in per capita incomes. The Pacific states are likely to remain among the highest in the nation in this regard and many of the Mountain states among the lowest nationally.

DIVERSIFIED V. NATURAL-RESOURCE-BASED ECONOMIES

Geographical proximity of states does not necessarily mean that they have major interests in common. In many ways, for example, California has more in common with the so-called megastates (such as New York, Florida and Pennsylvania) than with its western neighbors. Thus, one future division of the West may be between the diversified economies of states like California, Arizona, Washington, Hawaii and Colorado, and the less diversified states of the region which rely mainly on natural resource extraction. The disparities in

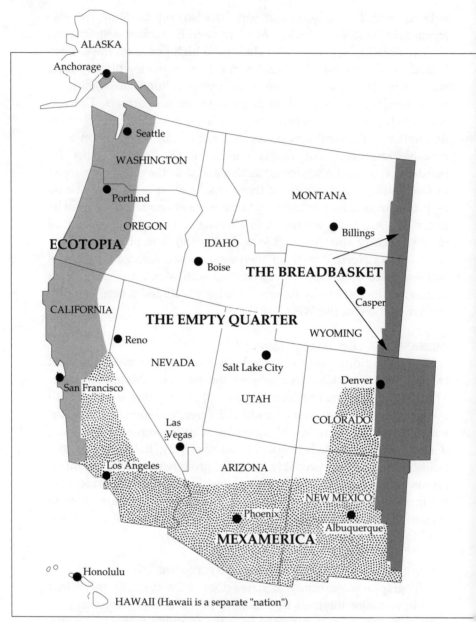

Map 20.2 The Future "Nations" of the American West

Source: Adapted by the author for the West from Joel Garreau, *The Nine Nations of North America*, (New York: Houghton-Mifflin, 1981), following p. 204. Reprinted with permission.

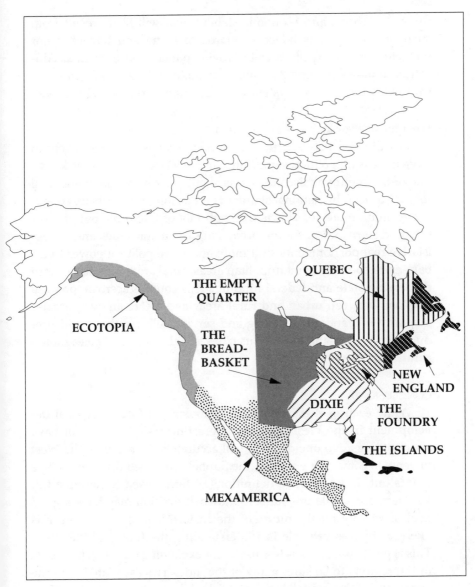

Joel Garreau's Nine Nations of North America

the state income and economic stability that will likely result from such differences may affect standards of living and have a major impact on the ability of states to provide public services such as education. It may also affect their ability to build and maintain infrastructure—water and sewer systems, roads, utility services and the like.

THE URBAN WEST AND THE RURAL WEST

The division between the urban and rural West is also likely to have increasing political significance in the years ahead. As we know, one of the common misconceptions about the West is that it is a rural region. In fact, by national standards it has long been urbanized and is becoming more so. This is true not only of California but of most other western states. As the urbanizing trend continues and as legislative reapportionments shift more and more political power to urban, and especially to metropolitan areas, rural areas may suffer from decreasing state and federal funding. This could exacerbate political tensions between urban and rural areas and create an even greater disparity in standards of living and service delivery that could produce two Wests—the prosperous cities and the poor and beleaguered rural West.

CONCLUSIONS

While each of these five ways of looking at future regional development in the West provides interesting insights, they all have shortcomings. No one division will accurately characterize the West in years to come. For example, the Sunbelt-Snowbelt division, as Dye points out, lacks effective definitions of terms used to describe it.[13] Furthermore, while the Sunbelt-Snowbelt division may have a good deal of validity for the future of the eastern half of the nation, it is likely to be less valuable in understanding the future of the West. This is partly because it is less useful for explaining past developments in the region. To be sure, many of the industries associated with the expansion of the Sunbelt have established themselves in western Sunbelt states. But the big expansion of population of the 1970s affected all western Snowbelt states, and Washington State has benefited from developments in high-tech industries and defense. Oregon has also benefited from high-technology, and Idaho and Alaska from expansion in defense. On the other hand, western Sunbelt states like Utah and New Mexico have benefited less from economic expansion than a northern state like Washington.

Similar problems exist with the other future divisions that we have explored. Nevertheless, taken together they can help us understand likely regional diversities in the West in the years to come.

Future Directions in Western Politics and Public Policy: Developments and Issues and the Challenge to Policymakers

Together with several other factors, these likely developments in western social, economic and political geography in the near future will have an important influence on the day-to-day operations of politics and policymaking in the region, its subregion and its states. We now turn to a consideration of what the specific political developments and issues are likely to be in the West through the first two decades of the twenty-first century. In addition, we assess the challenges to the region's policymakers that these developments and issues will present.

By policymakers we mean all those elected in the West to fill public office at the federal, state and local levels. Of particular importance are those in leadership positions, such as U.S. senators and representatives, governors, legislative leaders and mayors. Also included as policymakers are appointed officials, particularly senior federal civil servants dealing with the West, cabinet members in western state governments and other senior state bureaucrats, city managers, party leaders, and consultants to government, especially those working for so-called "think tanks."

While considering these issues and challenges it is worth bearing in mind the essence of the role of public officials, particularly elected ones, in a liberal democracy. Two of their functions are of particular importance: the resolution of conflict between opposing groups and interests and the provision of public services. These are not the only functions of public officials but their other functions all relate in some way to these two. With these functions in mind we now turn to a consideration of possible future developments, issues and challenges.

Demographic Changes and Their Political Consequences

THE INCREASING IMPORTANCE OF MINORITIES

Minority groups are already important influences on decision-making in many western states. This influence ranges from Alaska where minorities, primarily Alaska Natives, dominated legislative politics for much of the 1980s, to Utah, where minority population and influence is minimal. But because of population projections and an increasing political sophistication among these groups, minority influence is likely to increase in the West in the years ahead.

It is estimated that the percentage of nonwhites in the western population will increase from 20% in 1990 to 25% by the year 2000. Major increases will take place in the numbers of Hispanics and Asians who join the western population, both through natural increase and through immigration. The West is, in fact, becoming the most ethnically diverse region in the nation; and Los Angeles is now the major port of entry for immigrants into the United States.[14]

This expansion in the numbers of minorities will probably lead to greater pressure for low income housing, health services including prenatal and postnatal care, education including bilingual education, and job training and equal employment provisions. The severity of these pressures will depend largely on the extent to which the various minority groups can increase their political participation and sophistication. At first this political action may take the form of increased pressure on policymakers for education, jobs and housing. Depending on whether these demands are met, minority influence may eventually manifest itself in one of two ways. If minority demands are met, this influence may continue to be exerted through voting blocs that cannot be ignored by politicians. If the demands are not met, minority power may develop into more politically aggressive interest groups.

A YOUNGER AND OLDER POPULATION

As indicated earlier, a major demographic change in the West will be the increasing number of those under eighteen and over sixty-five years of age in the population. This will further increase the demand for educational services and for certain types of health care. The West has the highest "dependency ratio" (the number of wage earners compared to non-wage earners) in the nation, meaning that the burden of providing these services will be borne by a relatively smaller portion of the population. This may result in less funds for non-wage earners, like children and the elderly, than in a region with a lower "dependency ratio." This in turn will likely increase the competition between the young and the elderly for scarce resources.[15]

INCREASING URBANIZATION

This trend is likely to bring "quality of life" issues to the fore at both the state and local levels. Of particular importance is the need for improved infrastructure and the continued maintenance of that infrastructure. Increased urbanization will add to the demand for services such as education and health care brought about by the increase in the number of minorities and a larger percentage of children and senior citizens in the population. More and more people concentrated in cities and metropolitan areas also mean bigger environmental problems.[16]

We noted earlier that as urbanization increases and legislative reapportionments allocate more seats to urban and especially metropolitan areas, rural areas, especially in the less populated states, may find their share of services cut considerably. This may be offset somewhat by "back to the country" movements in reaction to the pollution and congestion of big cities and metropolitan areas. But such movements are likely to occur in areas close enough to urban centers to permit commuting employment. They are not likely to occur in the large sparsely populated states like Alaska, Idaho, Montana and Wyoming.[17]

Increased Environmental Consciousness and Its Political Ramifications

Part of the reason people choose to move to the West and continue to reside in the region is to enjoy its unique environment. The Pacific states subregion is already the site of a burgeoning environmental consciousness. There are indications that such a consciousness may also be developing in the Mountain states. As a consequence, of all the issues likely to come to the forefront in western politics, those relating to the environment and the quality of life are likely to be the most significant. At the root of this is a feeling among both westerners and other Americans that "The region that once seemed endlessly bountiful and forever wild has become a land of narrowing limits."[18]

Growing urbanization is likely to increase pressures for controls on pollutants, land use planning and even "no growth" movements in many localities. Environmental interest groups, such as the Sierra Club, Friends of the Earth, and the Audubon Society are likely to grow in size and influence. International pressures for environmental protection articulated by such organizations as Greenpeace, will also likely intensify. Disasters such as the Alaska oil spill in Prince William Sound in March 1989, and the spill off Huntington Beach, California, in February 1990, help to increase demands for environmental protection.

At least at first, these political pressures concerning environmental issues are likely to intensify the existing opposition in many states between those favoring economic development and those advocating environmental concerns. This will be particularly the case in states with less diversified economies where, until now, any form of economic development, environmentally sound or not, has been welcome.

But eventually the situation may become more harmonious, as all major sectors of society come to agree on the importance of the promotion of quality of life policies. Such a breakthrough is likely to occur as the business community comes to realize that it also has a vested interest in supporting environmental quality. This interest will undoubtedly take the form of a combination of economic incentives and political pressures. Business is likely to embrace environmental quality if it can shift the costs to government (that is, to the society as a whole), as has been largely the case in the past with hazardous waste sites and air quality. An example of an economic incentive is the tourism industry which reaps direct benefits from environmental protection. Also, many business leaders, such as those in the high-tech industry, have come to realize that embracing an improved environment is important for attracting higher quality labor to a locality. Political pressures may increase as business more fully realizes the need to create a favorable attitude toward their sector among politicians who will be increasingly forced to deal with environmental questions. Reaching this breakthrough of political consensus on the environment will also require compromises on the part of environmentalists and those who would allow no development at all.[19]

The Changing Role of Government and Its Political Consequences

We noted earlier that a good argument can be made that the West is much more dependent on government at all levels today than ever before. And despite the strongly individualistic political culture of much of the region with its antigovernment rhetoric, this dependence is likely to increase in the years to come. The reason is one of pure necessity. As a result, any change in the role of government—federal, state or local—is likely to send major shock waves through the economy and to have far-reaching social consequences.

Even a state like California may not be immune from the economic impact of changes in government spending. For example, there are consequences for the state in the political transformations that took place in Eastern Europe at the end of 1989. The resultant lessening of East-West tensions led to recommended cuts by the secretary of defense in military spending. This so-called "peace dividend" was to exceed $300 million in fiscal year 1991. In part, the savings were to be achieved by closing military bases, ten of which were located in California. Similar changes were likely in other western states through both base closings and personnel reductions and cuts in defense contracts.

The ability of western states and localities to deal with issues and demands resulting from the changing role of government, changing demographics, and an enhanced environmental consciousness, depends very much on the health of their economies and the skill and foresight of their political leaders. We turn now to consider these two factors.

Economic Factors

A 1986 article in the *Los Angeles Times* summed up the future economic realities in the West this way:

> Decisions made in places like Riyadh and Washington [D.C.] will continue to affect economic outcomes in the West, and the options available to state and local governments to help break these dependencies are limited in the short run.[20]

This, of course, is true mainly of those states dependent on natural resource extraction. And despite what their politicians often claim at election time, these states are also in a much less favorable position to take advantage of economic development opportunities than are the larger and more diversified western states like California and Washington. As in the past, the never-ending search for economic stability is likely to dominate the politics of many western states in the years to come.

There are, however, some important trends in the western economy that offer opportunities to western states capable of taking advantage of them. One is that the West has the fastest growing manufacturing sector of any region, including the rapidly expanding high-technology industry. Another is an increasing service sector, which includes tourism and recreation, transportation and, of course, government employment. At the same time, extractive industries are declining. The western labor force will grow steadily, becoming older, more female, and more ethnically diverse. The West is, in fact, in the midst of an important economic transformation. To be able to take full advantage of these economic changes, states and localities must be prepared to aid economic adjustment with the provision and maintenance of infrastructure, increased vocational and technical education, aid to those dislocated because of changing local economies, and services such as day care.[21]

A NEW ERA OF DEPENDENCE—THE PACIFIC RIM?

Although it may not have become apparent as yet, for the less diversified western states with their natural-resource-based economies, trade with the Pacific Rim countries may be just another in a long string of short-term solutions to their economic woes. They may simply be trading dependence on one set of external forces—Wall Street, capitalists back East, and the federal government—for dependence on another group, foreign investors and customers. This is not to say that such links should not be pursued; many states *must* pursue them out of necessity. But western politicians may want to move with caution, rather than viewing this as an economic panacea.

FILLING THE FEDERAL REVENUE AND SERVICE GAP

Because of federal cutbacks in various forms of aid to states and communities, now and in the immediate future, the states will have to take on more responsibility for water project development and maintenance, power generation and distribution, welfare programs, low income housing, job training, and so on. This, of course, will bring budgetary pressures. This also means that many policy questions will be pushed down from the federal to the state level. Despite increasing bureaucratic professionalism, officials may find themselves dealing with issues and management questions for which they are not prepared. This may cause problems that will only be resolved through increased training or hiring of new technical experts, either of which will add to these budgetary pressures.

The Challenge to Policymakers

INCREASED POLITICAL CONFLICT

Inevitably, many of the future issues identified in this section will exacerbate political differences in the West. Of these the opposition between environmentalists and developers may turn out to be the most difficult of all for politicians to handle. But there is also likely to be a disagreement between the elderly and young over the allocation of scarce resources for the various services that each group demands. Then more conflict may arise between the demands of the majority in each state and those of minorities, as well as political competition among minorities. The causes will be partly economic and partly emotional. Economic struggle may arise over the allocation of funds for social services and special education. The emotional aspect, which has already surfaced in the "English Only Movement" (an antibilingual coalition), will also probably have racist tendencies. The political struggle among minorities will most likely have its roots in economic competition.

Besides these sources of increased political turmoil, there are also the more general differences resulting from the overall increase in political pluralism that will probably continue in the years to come. As interest groups become more politically sophisticated and as more and more of them join the political fray, competition over issues and for budget resources will become increasingly intense. Strong parties would provide some cohesiveness to the resolution of increasing political conflicts. However, the long tradition of weak parties in the West, and the likelihood that they will become even weaker in the years to come, will work to exacerbate the problem of political conflict. For all these reasons conflict-resolution will reach new dimensions in the role of policymakers in the West.

INCREASED DEMANDS FOR SERVICES V. AN ANTITAXES ATTITUDE

When we combine increased budgetary pressures arising from federal cutbacks with projections of a major increase in demand for public services, in the context of western voters' growing reluctance to pay increased taxes, we can see what will be the greatest challenge of all to western policymakers. Some new or increased taxes may be imposed in some states and localities, or some citizens may be willing to accept cuts in services, though this latter alternative is unlikely to work on a large scale. One solution to bridging this financial gap may be to turn to an old source of funds—the federal government. This would involve a certain amount of ideological inconsistency on the part of some of the region's senators and representatives, particularly for those from the Mountain states; but that would be nothing new. It would simply be a new phase in the western tradition of political pragmatism on the part of western representatives in Washington, D.C. In fact, pressure to seek such federal funds may be exerted on these representatives by beleaguered state and local public officials.

While this source of funds may appear unlikely in the present climate of federal retrenchment and may seem to contradict some of our comments above, the anticipated freeing-up of federal funds because of cutbacks in federal defense spending resulting from the lessening of East-West tensions may well make this a possibility as the 1990s progress. Given the choice, western politicians may prefer this type of federal aid to a restoration of a major federal role in infrastructure development.

INCREASED INTERGOVERNMENTAL COOPERATION,
ESPECIALLY AMONG STATES

Concerns such as clean air and water, provision and maintenance of infrastructure and higher education do not neatly confine themselves within state boundaries. Certainly, there may never be common agreement or cooperation on some issues. But, as the past thirty years have demonstrated, western states are coming to realize the value of interstate cooperation and they have just begun to explore the possibility that this may be one way to combat some of the chronic economic and social concerns that will face western states in coming years.

THE NEED FOR PLANNING

Given the projected demographic changes and the resulting demand for public services, the transformation of many state economies with consequences for job training and the crucial role that education at all levels will play in the future of the West, there is an urgent need to develop both short-term and long-term plans to deal with these and other critical issues. Lack of planning would mean a high probability that a mismatch will take place between population growth and service delivery.[22] However, planning is a problematic process in most western states, because of fragmented policy institutions, volatile economies and generally conservative attitudes (which often view planning as socialistic). Nevertheless, some form of planning is the only way to deal with many crucial issues and problems that will confront western states.

A first step along this road may be the improved interstate cooperation mentioned above. If organizations like Westrends and the Western States' Strategy Center can be successful in predicting future developments and helping western policymakers prepare for them, then this may convince state and local officials of the value and necessity of comprehensive planning. Another initial step might be for western governments to use western university public policy units and other "think tanks" to help them in their planning process. Organizations like the Northwest Policy Center (University of Washington), the Rose Institute for State and Local Government (Claremont, Calif.), the Western Rural Development Center (Corvallis, Ore.), and the Institute of the North American West (Albuquerque, N.M.) can aid western governments, in a low-key fashion, in the areas of issue identification and policy planning.

CONCLUSION

The ability of the West's policymakers to meet these challenges over the next twenty to thirty years will very much influence westerners' life-styles. In essence, the key lies in policymakers' understanding the nature of the new frontiers in education, social services, economics and political pluralism. In some of these challenges, like the conflict between developers and environmentalists, the West will be at the forefront. If the region is successful in dealing with this and other issues, its approach and solutions may become models for the rest of the nation.

Reconsidering the Enduring Characteristics of Western Politics

In the light of both recent and possible future developments in the West, will there be major changes in what we have identified in this book as the enduring characertistics of western politics? We will approach this question first by considering the likely future relevance of the ten characteristics identified in Chapter 1. Then we will examine some additional factors that may well become characteristics of western politics in the near future.

The Future Status of the Enduring Characteristics of Western Politics

STRONG EMPHASIS ON POLITICAL PRAGMATISM
AND DE-EMPHASIS OF IDEOLOGY

From what we have said in this chapter, it appears that pragmatism will remain a dominant characteristic of western politics. As in the past, this will be seen in the way that politicians and the public deal with the need for more government assistance. The constant search for economic stability in several of the region's states will also probably reinforce political pragmatism. On the other hand, while it may not reach the form of an integrated ideology, the need to balance the economic and development needs of western states with the need to preserve the environment may well temper the pragmatic approach to politics. Though even here, those with strong environmentalist leanings may take a pragmatic rather than ideological course to achieving their goals.

STRONG STRAIN OF POLITICAL INDIVIDUALISM

With the possible constraints noted above regarding the increasing importance of environmental concerns, political individualism will continue to manifest itself through the lack of strong ideological commitment in the West and an increasing independence on the part of voters. Political individualism is also likely to be the modus operandi of many politicians, especially at the state level. These will most likely continue to place their constituents, district, region or special interests above strong ideological commitment and political party affiliation.[23]

SIGNIFICANT USE OF METHODS OF DIRECT DEMOCRACY

The continued use of methods of direct democracy, particularly the initiative and the referendum, bolsters both political pragmatism and political individualism. This is because these devices enable special interests, politicians and the electorate to circumvent the regular policymaking processes of western states and localities and thus serve to weaken the integrating and coordinating influence of both political parties and the political system as a whole.

Judging by the experience of the past thirty years in the West, it is likely that the use of methods of direct democracy will increase in the years ahead, and not just in California and Oregon, which currently lead the nation in their use. Yet as Hrebenar and Benedict point out in Chapter 6, even today the use of the devices of direct democracy has strayed considerably from what was first intended. The populists and progressives originally viewed these devices as a way for the electorate to become directly involved in the policymaking process and, as a result, to undermine the power of parties and particularly of special interests. But today it is expensive to provide the resources and organization to mount an initiative or referendum drive. Such resources are more likely to be found in the hands of well-organized and politically concerned special interests, rather than in those of some spontaneous grass-roots movement of the unorganized and often politically apathetic public. Furthermore, interest groups have long recognized the value of methods of direct democracy for circumventing an unresponsive legislature or governor. For these reasons the initiative and the referendum have become much less a tool of popular will and more another weapon in the arsenal of special interests.

This situation is likely to intensify as campaign costs rise and interest group and lobbying activity becomes more competitive. This will tend to enhance the power of interest groups, and this in turn will affect some of the other characteristics of western politics, as we shall see.

REGIONALISM AND SECTIONALISM

There are some factors that may work to lessen regional and sectional conflicts in the West and its states over the coming years. At the interstate level such rivalries may be alleviated by improved interstate cooperation and the need to plan solutions to common problems. Within states regional feelings may be lessened by recognition of the need to deal with serious economic problems and the volatility of many western economies.

But in a region so vast and diverse as the West, containing several states larger than New England, regionalism and sectionalism are unlikely to be entirely eliminated from political decision-making. We examined earlier in this chapter five possible future subregional configurations that may come to divide the West. And it is unlikely that major regional divisions within states like Idaho, Alaska and New Mexico will disappear as major factors in policymaking any time soon, especially in the absence of coordinating influences, such as strong political parties and an integrated state policymaking process. As previously noted, perhaps an even more significant factor may be a marked rise in the intensity of conflict between urban and rural areas.

CANDIDATE-ORIENTED ELECTION CAMPAIGNS

The continued weakness of political parties, the power of interest groups bolstered by the increasing use of PACs, and political individualism together are likely to ensure the continuation of candidate-oriented elections, where personality and not party is most important. As populations increase, the personal element of campaigning—one-on-one contact with voters—will give way in western states to greater use of the media for campaigning, especially television.

WEAK POLITICAL PARTIES AND STRONG INTEREST GROUPS

From all we have said so far in this section it should be clear that the power of interest groups is very likely to be enhanced in the years to come and that political parties will become weaker. This, therefore, will remain an important characteristic of western politics.

Two possible, though perhaps unlikely, developments that might change this situation are as follows. One is that the parties at the state level in the West may undergo some revitalization perhaps by better reflecting the needs of voters or by convincing the electorate of the need for better policy planning and coordination. The other is that with the increasing irrelevance of party to many voters and the growing importance of some issues, such as environmental concerns, the present American two party system may break down and other parties may develop in addition to, or take the place of, one of the existing parties. One possibility, especially in states like California and Oregon, is the rise of an environmentalist or "quality of life" party rather like the Green Party in West Germany. While this is very speculative at the present time, it could happen over, say, the next fifty years or so, and as a result constrain some of the power of special interests in the region.

WEAK POLITICAL INSTITUTIONS AND
A FRAGMENTED POLICYMAKING PROCESS

This is also likely to remain a distinguishing characteristic of western politics. The two factors that may help mitigate this to some extent are the increasing professionalism of politicians and bureaucrats, and the increasing need to pursue some type of planning to address the chronic needs of several states, especially their economic and social needs. Together these two factors may help provide some integration and coordination for the policymaking process in western states.

THE DOMINANCE OF THE ISSUE OF ECONOMIC DEVELOPMENT

This is also likely to remain a characteristic of western politics in the coming years, but initially at least for different reasons in different states. In states with chronic economic problems arising from their dependence on natural resource extraction—Alaska, Idaho, Montana and Wyoming, for example—in the immediate future the emphasis is likely to be similar to the past: the need to search out new economic enterprises to help insulate the state from the boom and bust cycle and the vagaries of external influences.

In other western states, primarily those that already have more diversified economies—California in particular, but also Washington, Colorado and Hawaii—the issue of economic development may remain a characteristic of politics for a different reason. This will be because of the increasing consciousness in these states of the importance of the environment and the clash of values that often exists between developers and environmentalists. This clash is particularly intense when development involves natural resource extraction or industrial development that produces pollutants. We believe that this environmental clash will have an important impact on the future developments of western politics.

AN ALL-PERVASIVE DEPENDENCE ON GOVERNMENT

All the likely future characteristics of western politics that we examine here are important determinants of the shape of the political debate in the years to come. Therefore, it is difficult to give any one characteristic primacy over the others. But if we were to single out three, an all-pervasive dependence on government would be among the most important, along with the power of interest groups and political pragmatism. As we have seen, this dependence has probably grown over the past twenty-five years and will likely grow further in the immediate future. As populations increase and electorates become more and more demanding in their desire to improve the quality of their lives, most states in the West will have no other choice than to use government in various ways to meet these needs.

THE WESTERN POLITICAL PARADOX: THE POLITICAL MANIFESTATION
OF THE MYTH AND REALITY OF WESTERN DEVELOPMENT

How, we may ask, will this continuing and increasing dependence on government affect what we have termed the "western political paradox"? Will the western public and its politicians come to terms with this dependence and cease to lambaste the federal government and to complain about the "excessive" size and spending of state governments in the region? This is a difficult question to answer, and the situation will probably vary from subregion to subregion, from state to state and even between regions within states. We provided insights into some possible developments when we discussed the decisions facing policymakers in the West.

In addition, evolving political culture will probably have an important influence in shaping this attitude, as will the extent to which a particular state, or region within a state, is dependent on government or affected by its actions. Past experience suggests that the combination of individualistic political culture and heavy dependence on government produces a strong antipathy toward government at all levels. Several of the Mountain states fall into this category. Politicians need neither be shrewd nor wily to realize that, whether they share their constituents' attitudes in this regard or not, reelection will require that they reflect this attitude. So it will probably be the case that the western political paradox will remain a characteristic of western politics in the immediate future.

Additional Future Characteristics of Western Politics

From our consideration of the ten enduring characteristics of western politics, it appears that all of them will continue to shape the political debate in the West, though in some cases in a modified form from the past. In addition, because of the recent and projected changes, some additional characteristics of western politics are likely to assert themselves over the next twenty or thirty years. We identify four in all of which two, we believe, will be of considerable importance; the other two less so. Listed in their estimated order of significance, these are:

ISSUES RELATING TO THE QUALITY OF LIFE,
PARTICULARLY THE ENVIRONMENT
This has been a major theme of this chapter; and all indications are that it will become a prominent characteristic of western politics.

THE SIGNIFICANCE OF MINORITY GROUPS
Present trends strongly indicate that minorities in the region will move from social movements to political action and will add a new characteristic to western politics.

AN URBAN-RURAL CONFLICT
The dramatic shifts of power and fund allocations from rural to urban areas that are taking place may well produce an increasing urban-rural split that may become a characteristic of politics in many western states.

INCREASED INTERGOVERNMENTAL COOPERATION,
ESPECIALLY AMONG STATES

This may well become a characteristic of western politics as more and more states come to realize the need for dealing with common problems on a regional or subregional basis.

Western Politics and Public Policy: Past, Present and Future

The days are gone in western politics when a few interests, primarily from the business community, dominated state politics, when the governor was a "Good-Time Charlie," when state government bureaucracies were small and when the state policy agenda was so short that it could be dealt with largely behind closed doors in a few weeks each year.

Major changes in western society in recent years have produced an expanding political pluralism that has transformed western politics and will perhaps bring about even greater changes in the years to come. Today the region has much more open and professional government and greater power sharing among groups and interests. The policy agenda at all levels of western government has grown in length and breadth since World War II, and particularly in the last thirty years.

At the beginning of this chapter we noted that some observers have likened this transformation in western politics to the changes taking place in the South during the same period. Yet the changes in these regions differ in two fundamental ways. First, the changes in the West have been gradual and evolutionary. There has been no break with the past that can be traced to a particular event, such as the Montgomery bus boycott in Alabama, the Civil Rights Act of 1964 or the Voting Rights Act of 1965, in the South. The West has had no counterpart to the radical changes that have taken place in southern life and politics resulting from the major expansion in the franchise, which in some states was as much as 500% in a few years. Nor has the West seen a change in the status of any group that can compare with the rapid increased significance of blacks, both socially and politically, that occurred in the southern states.

A second contrast between recent political developments in the West and the South relates to the source of the changes. The revolutionary changes in southern politics since the 1960s were brought about largely by two factors that, until the late 1950s, would not have been seen as *direct* influences on southern politics. One was the *active* political significance of blacks (as opposed to their *latent* political significance, which had been a determining factor in the region's politics since the end of Reconstruction). The other new influence was the active role of the federal government, especially the federal courts but also the Congress and the president, in promoting civil rights and political participation in the South. No such new and powerful influences have developed in western politics. The transformation of western politics can be explained largely in terms of variations in the longstanding influences that were identified in Chapter 2, or by reference to national trends, such as the increased professionalization of government and growth of public awareness.

This, however, is not to understate the importance of the political changes that are transforming the West; it is simply to put them in perspective and say that the impetus and magnitude of these changes have, in some major ways, been different from those taking place in the South. Judging by recent experience, it appears that the likely changes in the next twenty to thirty years in the West will also be primarily the result of variations in these longstanding influences— especially demographic factors, the influence of minority populations and the search for economic diversification and stability in many parts of the region. An added influence, partly the result of the increasing impact of traditional attitudes, may well be an increased sensitivity to the environment and a perceived need to preserve much of the uniqueness of the western landscape and life-style.

In turn these influences will probably modify the characteristics of western politics, but in a gradual and rather imperceptible way that seems to be the hallmark of political developments in the region. While the relative importance of the ten characteristics identified in Chapter 1 are changing, they still appear relevant as fundamental attributes of politics in the West, and will probably remain so in the near future. In addition, we have identified four other characteristics that may well become a part of western politics as the twenty-first century approaches: (1) a deep-rooted political battle between developers and environmentalists that may eventually mature into a primary concern in the western political debate over the environment; (2) the place of minorities, particularly racial and ethnic minorities; (3) development of severe urban-rural tensions; and (4) increasing intergovernmental cooperation, particularly between the states of the region but also among local governments within and between states.

To what extent will the changes in western politics of both the recent past and the near future have the effect of making the West more or less a distinct political region? Based on the belief that regionalism is on the increase in North America, Joel Garreau would argue that the West will become more of a distinct region.[24] The reality of the future of the West in this regard, however, is probably best gauged from past experience. The various influences on western politics affect states differently, and this makes some factors more important in some states than others. This situation will continue and will prevent cohesion on many policies and concerns. On the other hand, there will continue to be common bonds on other issues: federal land ownership and transportation concerns, for example. These bonds may well be nurtured by increased cooperation between states and localities.

Whether or not the West extends its distinctiveness in politics and public policy in the coming years, one truism is likely to persist: the image of the West in the American mind will continue to be one of a latter-day frontier society characterized by opportunity and a free life-style, and of a region that incorporates the hopes and future of the nation. Nonwesterners, at least, are likely to continue to view the West as different and distinct. The extent to which any of these perceptions are true is debatable. Nevertheless, like the distorted images and romance of the Old West, the perception is often more important than the reality. Consequently, these perceptions will likely determine how the rest of the nation views and treats the West in the years to come.

Notes

1. Leonard Ritt, "The Changing Face of Western Politics," paper presented at the annual meeting of the Western Political Science Association, March 1985.

2. George Skelton, "Poll Finds Pacific States Tolerant, Less Alienated," *Los Angeles Times*, November 11, 1987, 28.

3. Larry Sabato, *Goodbye to Good-Time Charlie*, 2nd ed. (Washington, D.C.: Congressional Quarterly Press, 1983).

4. Katherine M. Albert, William B. Hull and Daniel M. Sprague, *The Dynamic West: A Region in Transition* (Lexington, Ky.: Council of State Governments, 1989).

5. Greg Wiles, "Japanese Still Bullish on Hawaii," *Honolulu Advertiser*,

December 30, 1989, C1. This article reported that the three most favored U.S. states for Japanese investment as of late 1989 were California, New York and Hawaii, in that order.

6. Thomas R. Dye, *Politics in States and Communities*, 6th ed. (Englewood Cliffs, N.J.: Prentice Hall, 1988), 11–15.

7. Joel Garreau, *The Nine Nations of North America* (Boston: Houghton Mifflin, 1981), 3.

8. *Ibid.*, 2 and 245–86.

9. *Ibid.*, 4–5 and 207–44.

10. *Ibid.*, 328–61.

11. *Ibid.*, 287–327.

12. *Ibid.*, 117–18.

13. Dye, *Politics in States and Communities*, 11.

14. Albert, Hull and Sprague, *The Dynamic West*, 14–17.

15. *Ibid.*, 5–13 for further amplification of western population trends.

16. *Ibid.*, 18–21.

17. For further analysis of the economic, social and political consequences of increasing urbanization in the West, see Albert, Hull and Sprague, 18–21. For perspectives on the past, present and future of the rural West, see the various contributions in Ed Marston, ed., *Reopening the Western Frontier* (Washington, D.C.: Island Press, 1989).

18. Elliott West, Foreword to Richard G. Athearn, *The Mythic West in Twentieth-Century America* (Lawrence: University Press of Kansas, 1986), ix.

19. For a perspective on the developing environmental consciousness of the 1990s and its likely impact on public policy see Norman J. Vig and Michael E. Kraft, eds., *Environmental Policy in the 1990s* (Washington, D.C.: C. Q. Press, 1990).

20. Bernard L. Weinstein and Harold T. Gross, "West Needs New Economic Foundation," *Los Angeles Times*, December 14, 1986, II, 5.

21. For further perspectives on the changing western economy see Albert, Hull and Sprague, *The Dynamic West*, 22–46.

22. *Ibid.*, 9.

23. For a perspective that questions the claim that western voters exhibit political individualism, see Ritt, "The Changing Face of Western Politics," 16–18.

24. Garreau, *The Nine Nations of North America*, 8, 13.

SELECT
BIBLIOGRAPHY

John Lepore and
Clive S. Thomas

THIS SELECT BIBLIOGRAPHY OF SOURCES ON WESTERN POLITICS, government and public policy includes both academic and popular books and articles. It does not include unpublished materials, such as dissertations, theses, conference papers and in-house reports and documents.

The references cited are of three types: those concerned solely with one or more aspects of politics, government and public policy in the West; those having a significant western content; and those providing essential background for understanding the region's politics. The bibliography is divided into fifteen sections, some of which are further divided into subsections. These divisions are by type of material (*e.g.*, reference works, journals, etc.) and by subject. They are as follows:

1. Reference and Statistical Sources
2. Bibliographies on Western Politics and Related Subjects
3. Regionalism
4. Federalism and Intergovernmental Relations
5. General Works on the Contemporary West and Its Subregions
6. General Treatments of the Poliltics of the West and Its Subregions
7. Politics, Government and Public Policy of Individual Western States
8. Political and Governmental Institutions and Processes
9. Urban and Local Politics and Government
10. Political Ideas and Political Movements
11. Political Culture
12. Minorities and Minority Politics
13. Western Political Issues and Public Policies

14. Historical Perspectives on the West and Its Politics
15. Journal, Magazine and Newspaper Sources on Western Politics and Public Policy

There is some inevitable overlap between sections. For this reason some references are listed more than once; while some others, which include more than one of these section topics in their content, are placed in the section of the major subject covered in that particular book or article.

1. Reference and Statistical Sources

Austin, Erik W. *Political Facts of the United States Since 1789*. New York: Columbia University Press, 1986.

Barone, Michael, and Grant Ujifusa. *The Almanac of American Politics 1988* [and previous editions]. Washington, D.C.: National Journal, 1989 [and previous years].

Beck, Warren A., and Ynes D. Haase. *Historical Atlas of the American West*. Norman: University of Oklahoma Press, 1989.

Burgess, Philip M., Jack A. Brizius and Susan E. Foster, eds. *Profile of the West*. Denver: Western States' Strategy Center, 1987.

COGEL [Council on Governmental Ethics Laws]. *Campaign Finance, Ethics & Lobby Law Blue Book 1988–89: Special Report*. Lexington, Ky.: COGEL through Council of State Governments, 1988.

Council of State Governments. *The Book of the States, 1988–89* [and previous editions]. Lexington, Ky.: Council of State Governments, 1988 [and previous years].

Hornor, Edith R., ed. *Almanac of the Fifty States: Basic Data Profiles with Comparative Tables*. 1989 ed. [and previous editions]. Palo Alto, Calif.: Information Publications, 1989 [and previous years].

Stanley, Harold W., and Richard G. Neimi. *Vital Statistics of American Politics*. Washington, D.C.: CQ Press, 1988.

State Policy Data Book. McConnellsburg, Pa.: Brizius and Foster, 1988 [and previous editions].

U.S. Department of Commerce, Bureau of the Census. *Statistical Abstract of the United States, 1988*. 108th ed. [and previous editions]. Washington, D.C.: U.S. Government Printing Office, 1987 [and previous years].

2. Bibliographies on Western Politics and Related Subjects

Coombs, Allan F. "Twentieth Century Politics." In Michael P. Malone, ed., *Historians and the American West*. Lincoln: University of Nebraska Press, 1983. Pp. 300–322.

Etulain, Richard W. *A Bibliographical Guide to the Study of Western American Literature*. Lincoln: University of Nebraska Press, 1982.

Jonas, Frank H., ed. *Bibliography on Western Politics*. Supplement to *Western Political Quarterly*, 11 (December 1958).

Jonas, Frank H., ed. *Politics in the American West*. Salt Lake City: University of Utah Press, 1969. Pp. 499–528.

Jonas, Frank H., ed. *Western Politics*. Salt Lake City: University of Utah Press, 1961. Pp. 379–92.

Limerick, Patricia Nelson. *Legacy of Conquest: The Unbroken Past of the American West*. New York: W. W. Norton, 1987. Pp. 369–84.

Malone, Michael P., and Richard W. Etulain. *The American West: A Twentieth Century History*. Lincoln: University of Nebraska Press, 1989. Pp. 295–330.

Morgan, Neil. *Westward Tilt: The American West Today*. New York: Random House, 1963. Pp. 388–95.

Nash, Gerald D., and Richard W. Etulain, eds. *The Twentieth Century West: Historical Interpretations*. Albuquerque: University of New Mexico Press, 1989. Pp. 421–46.

Tyson, Carl. *Politics in the American West: A Bibliographical Essay. Journal of the West*, Special Issue, 13(4) (October 1974).

Wilkinson, Charles F. *The American West: A Narrative Bibliography and a Study in Regionalism*. Niwot: University Press of Colorado, 1989.

3. Regionalism

Bensel, Richard Franklin. *Sectionalism and American Political Development, 1880–1980*. Madison: University of Wisconsin Press, 1984.

Garreau, Joel. *The Nine Nations of North America*. Boston: Houghton Mifflin, 1981.

Gastil, Raymond D. *Cultural Regions of the United States*. Seattle: University of Washington Press, 1975.

Gressley, Gene M. "Regionalism and the Twentieth-Century West." In Jerome O. Steffen, ed., *The American West: New Perspectives, New Dimensions*. (Norman: University of Oklahoma Press, 1979). Pp. 197–234.

Jensen, Merrill, ed. *Regionalism in America*. Madison: University of Wisconsin Press, 1965.

Markusen, Ann R. *Regions: The Economics and Politics of Territory*. Totowa, N.J.: Rowman and Littlefield, 1987.

Maxwell, Neal A. *Regionalism in the United States Senate: The West*. Salt Lake City: University of Utah, 1961. Institute of Government Research Monograph No. 5.

Odum, Howard W., and Harry E. Moore. *American Regionalism: A Cultural Historical Approach to National Integration*. New York: H. Holt, 1938.

Price, Kent A., ed. *Regional Conflict and National Policy.* Washington, D.C.: Resources for the Future, 1982.

Sale, Kirkpatrick. *Power Shift: The Rise of the Southern Rim and Its Challenge to the Eastern Establishment.* New York: Random House, 1975.

Sharkansky, Ira. *Regionalism in American Politics.* Indianapolis: Bobbs-Merrill, 1970.

Steiner, Michael, and Clarence Mondale, eds. *Region and Regionalism in the United States: A Sourcebook for the Humanities and Social Sciences.* New York: Garland, 1988.

4. Federalism and Intergovernmental Relations

Council of State Governments. *Interstate Compacts and Agencies.* Lexington, Ky.: Council of State Governments, 1983.

Dilger, Robert Jay, ed. *American Intergovernmental Relations Today: Perspectives and Controversies.* Englewood Cliffs, N.J.: Prentice Hall, 1986.

Elazar, Daniel J. *American Federalism: A View from the States.* 3rd ed. New York: Harper & Row, 1984.

Grodzins, Martin. "Centralization and Decentralization in the American Federal System." In Robert A. Goldwin, ed., *A Nation of States: Essays on the American Federal System.* Chicago: Rand McNally, 1965. Pp. 1–23.

Hanson, Russell L. "Intergovernmental Relations." In Virginia Gray, Herbert Jacob and Robert Albritton, eds., *Politics in the American States.* 5th ed. Glenview, Ill.: Scott Foresman/Little, Brown, 1990. Pp. 38–82.

Henig, Jeffrey R. *Public Policy and Federalism: Issues in State and Local Politics.* New York: St. Martin's Press, 1985.

Peterson, George E. "Federalism and the States: An Experiment in Decentralization." In John L. Palmer and Isabel Sawhill, eds., *The Reagan Record: An Assessment of America's Changing Priorities.* Cambridge, Mass.: Ballinger, 1984. Pp. 217–59.

Peterson, Paul E., Barry Rabe and Kenneth Wong. *When Federalism Works.* Washington, D.C.: Brookings Institution, 1986.

Reagan, Michael, and John Sanzone. *The New Federalism.* 2nd ed. New York: Oxford University Press, 1981.

Sanford, Terry. *Storm over the States.* New York: McGraw-Hill, 1967.

Walker, David. *Toward a Functioning Federalism.* Cambridge, Mass.: Winthrop, 1981.

Western Governors' Association. *Western Multistate Organization Directory.* Denver: Western Governors' Association, 1987.

Wright, Deil S. *Understanding Intergovernmental Relations.* 3rd ed. Pacific Grove, Calif.: Brooks/Cole, 1988.

5. General Works on the Contemporary West and Its Subregions

Albert, Katherine M., William B. Hull and Daniel M. Sprague. *The Dynamic West: A Region in Transition*. Lexington, Ky.: Council of State Governments, 1989.

Athearn, Richard G. *High Country Empire: The High Plains and the Rockies*. New York: McGraw-Hill, 1960.

Bingham, Edwin R., and Glen A. Love, eds. *Northwest Perspectives: Essays on the Culture of the Pacific Northwest*. Seattle: University of Washington Press, 1979.

Broder, Patricia Janis. *The American West: The Modern Vision*. Boston: Little, Brown, 1984.

DeGrazia, Alfred. *The Western Public, 1952 and Beyond*. Stanford, Calif.: Stanford University Press, 1954.

De Voto, Bernard, "The West: A Plundered Province." *Harper's Magazine*, 159 (August 1934), 355–64.

De Voto, Bernard. "The West Against Itself." *Harper's Magazine*, 194 (January 1947), 1–13.

Gates, Paul W. "The Intermountain West Against Itself." *Arizona and the West*, 27 (Autumn 1985), 205–36.

Gressley, Gene M. "Colonialism: A Western Complaint." *Pacific Northwest Quarterly*, 54 (January 1963), 1–8.

Gressley, Gene M. "The West: Past, Present, and Future." *Western Historical Quarterly*, 17 (January 1986), 5–23.

Lamm, Richard D., and Michael McCarthy. *The Angry West: A Vulnerable Land and Its Future*. Boston: Houghton Mifflin, 1982.

Marston, E., ed. *Reopening the Western Frontier*. Washington, D.C.: Island Press, 1989.

Morgan, Neil. *Westward Tilt: The American West Today*. New York: Random House, 1963.

Nugent, Walter. "The People of the West Since 1890." In Gerald D. Nash and Richard W. Etulain, eds., *The Twentieth Century West*. Albuquerque: University of New Mexico Press, 1989. Pp. 35–70.

Peirce, Neal R. *The Mountain States of America: People, Politics and Power in the Five Rocky Mountain States*. New York: W. W. Norton, 1972.

Peirce, Neal R. *The Pacific States of America: People, Politics and Power in the Five Pacific Basin States*. New York: W. W. Norton, 1972.

Perrigo, Lynn I. *The American Southwest: Its People and Cultures*. Albuquerque: University of New Mexico Press, 1975.

Robbins, William G., Robert J. Frank and Richard E. Ross, eds. *Regionalism and the Pacific Northwest*. Corvallis: Oregon State University Press, 1983.

Steffen, Jerome O., ed. *The American West: New Perspectives, New Dimensions.* Norman: University of Oklahoma Press, 1979.

Stegner, Wallace. *The American West as Living Space.* Ann Arbor: University of Michigan Press, 1987.

Stegner, Wallace, and Page Stegner. "Rocky Mountain Country." *Atlantic* (April 1978), 44–64.

Steiner, Stan. *The Waning of the West.* New York: St. Martin's Press, 1989.

Wiley, Peter, and Robert Gottlieb. *Empires in the Sun: The Rise of the New American West.* Tucson: University of Arizona Press, 1982.

Young, Mary. "The West and American Cultural Identity: Old Themes and New Variations." *Western Historical Quarterly,* 1 (April 1970), 137–60.

6. General Treatments of the Politics of the West and Its Subregions

Anderson, Totton J. "The Political West in 1960." *Western Political Quarterly,* 14 (March 1961).

Bell, Charles G. "Politics in the West." *Western Political Quarterly,* 28 (June 1975).

Donnelly, Thomas C., ed. *Rocky Mountain Politics.* Albuquerque: University of New Mexico Press, 1940.

Emenhiser, JeDon A. *Rocky Mountain Urban Politics.* Logan: Utah State University Press, 1971.

Goodall, Leonard, ed. *Urban Politics in the Southwest.* Tempe: Institute of Public Administration, Arizona State University, 1967.

Jonas, Frank H. "The Spirit of Contemporary Politics in the American West." *Western Political Quarterly,* 18 (September 1965), 5–20.

Jonas, Frank H., ed. *Politics in the American West.* Salt Lake City: University of Utah Press, 1969.

Jonas, Frank H., ed. *Western Politics.* Salt Lake City: University of Utah Press, 1961.

"Politics in the West." *Journal of the West,* Special Issue, 13(4) (October 1974).

7. Politics, Government and Public Policy of Individual Western States

Gunther, John. *Inside USA.* New York: Harper & Brothers, 1947.

Hrebenar, Ronald J., and Clive S. Thomas, eds. *Interest Group Politics in the American West.* Salt Lake City: University of Utah Press, 1987.

Jonas, Frank H., ed. *Politics in the American West.* Salt Lake City: University of Utah Press, 1969.

Jonas, Frank H., ed. *Western Politics*. Salt Lake City: University of Utah Press, 1961.

Morgan, Neil. *Westward Tilt: The American West Today*. New York: Random House, 1963.

Peirce, Neal R. *The Mountain States of America*. New York: W. W. Norton, 1972.

Peirce, Neal R. *The Pacific States of America*. New York: W. W. Norton, 1972.

Peirce, Neal R., and Jerry Hagstrom. *The Book of America*. New York: Warner Books, 1983.

ALASKA

Fischer, Victor. *Alaska's Constitutional Convention*. Fairbanks: Institute of Social, Economic and Government Research, University of Alaska, 1975.

Harrison, Gordon S. *Alaska's Constitution: A Citizen's Guide*. 2nd ed. Anchorage: Institute of Social and Economic Research, University of Alaska, 1986.

Hunt, William R. *Alaska: A Bicentennial History*. New York: W. W. Norton, 1976.

McBeath, Gerald A., and Thomas A. Morehouse, eds. *Alaska State Government and Politics*. Fairbanks: University of Alaska Press, 1987.

Morehouse, Thomas A., Gerald A. McBeath and Linda Leask. *Alaska's Urban and Rural Governments*. Lanham, Md.: University Press of America, 1984.

Naske, Clause-M., and Herman E. Slotnick. *Alaska: A History of the 49th State*. Grand Rapids, Mich.: William D. Eerdmans, 1979.

Thomas, Clive S. *"The Thing* That Shook Alaska: The Events, the Fallout and the Lessons of Alaska's Gubernatorial Impeachment Proceedings." *State Legislatures*, 13, 2 (February 1987), 22–25.

ARIZONA

Berman, David R. "Political Culture: Change and Continuity." In *Culture and Values in Arizona Life*. Phoenix, Ariz.: Arizona Academy, 1987. Pp. 115–30.

Everett, Ray. *Arizona History and Government*. Phoenix: Arizona Board of Regents, 1977.

Goldwater, Barry M. *With No Apologies: The Personal and Political Memoirs of United States Senator Barry M. Goldwater*. New York: William Morrow, 1979.

Hansen, Gerald E., and Douglas A. Brown. *Arizona: Its Constitution and Government*. 2nd ed. Lanham, Md.: University Press of America, 1987.

Luey, Beth, and Noel J. Stowe, eds. *Arizona at Seventy-Five: The Next Twenty-Five Years*. Tempe and Tucson: Arizona State University Public History Program and the Arizona Historical Society, 1987.

Mann, Dean E. *The Politics of Water in Arizona*. Tucson: University of Arizona Press, 1963.

Mason, Bruce B., and Heinz R. Hink. *Constitutional Government in Arizona*. 7th ed. Tempe: Cleber Publishing, 1987.

Powell, Lawrence Clark. *Arizona: A Bicentennial History.* New York: W. W. Norton, 1976.

Shadegg, Stephen C. *Arizona Politics: The Struggle to End One-Party Rule.* Tempe: Arizona State University Press, 1986.

CALIFORNIA

Beck, Warren A., and David A. Williams. *California: A History of the Golden State.* Garden City, N.Y.: Doubleday, 1972.

Bell, Charles G. "California." In Alan Rosenthal and Maureen Moakley, eds., *The Political Life of the American States.* New York: Praeger, 1984. Pp. 31–59.

"California: American Dream, American Nightmare." *Newsweek* (July 31, 1989), 21–29.

Christensen, Terry, and Larry N. Gerston. *The California Connection: Politics in the Golden State.* Boston: Little, Brown, 1984.

Culver, John H., and John C. Syer. *Politics and Power in California.* 3rd ed. New York: Macmillan, 1988.

Driscoll, James D. *California's Legislature.* Sacramento: Center for California Studies, California State University, 1986.

Englebert, Ernest A., ed. *California Water: Planning and Policy.* Davis: California Water Resources Center, 1979.

Hamilton, Gary, and Nicole Woolsey Biggart. *Governor Reagan, Governor Brown: A Sociology of Executive Power.* New York: Columbia University Press, 1984.

Hart, John. *The New Book of California Tomorrow: Reflections and Projections from the Golden State.* Los Altos, Calif.: William Kaufman, 1984.

Kotkin, Joel, and Paul Grabowicz. *California, Inc.* New York: Rowson Mack, 1982.

Lavender, David. *California: A Bicentennial History.* New York: W. W. Norton, 1976.

McWilliams, Carey. *California: The Great Exception.* New York: Current Books, 1949. Rpt. Santa Barbara, Calif.: Peregrine Smith, 1976.

Medsger, Betty. *Framed: The New Right Attack on Chief Justice Rose Bird and the Courts.* New York: Pilgrim Press, 1983.

Mowry, George E. *The California Progressives.* Berkeley and Los Angeles: University of California Press, 1951.

Muir, William K., Jr. *Legislature: California's Schools for Politics.* Chicago: University of Chicago Press, 1982.

Quinn, T. Anthony, and Ed Salzman, eds. *California Public Administration: Text and Readings on Decision-Making in State Government.* Sacramento: California Journal Press, 1982.

Putnam, Jackson K. *Modern California Politics 1917–1980.* San Francisco: Boyd and Fraser, 1980.

Putnam, Jackson K. *Old-Age Politics in California: From Richardson to Reagan.* Stanford: Stanford University Press, 1970.

Rapoport, Roger. *California Political Odyssey of Pat and Jerry Brown.* Berkeley: Nolo Press, 1982.

Rogin, Michael Paul, and John L. Shover. *Political Change in California: Critical Elections and Social Movements, 1890–1966.* Westport: Conn.: Greenwood, 1970.

Rolle, Andrew F. *California: A History.* 4th ed. Arlington Heights, Ill.: Harlan Davidson, 1987.

Ross, Michael J. *California: Its Government and Politics.* 3rd ed. Pacific Grove, Calif.: Brooks/Cole, 1987.

Starr, Kevin. *Inventing the Dream: California Through the Progressive Era.* New York: Oxford University Press, 1985.

Walters, Dan. *The New California Facing the 21st Century.* Sacramento: California Journal Press, 1986.

COLORADO

Abbott, Carl, Stephen J. Leonard and David McComb. *Colorado: A History of the Centennial State.* Rev. ed. Boulder: Colorado Associated University Press, 1982.

Athearn, Robert G. *The Coloradans.* Albuquerque: University of New Mexico Press, 1976.

Curtis, Martin. *Colorado Government and Politics.* 3rd ed. Boulder: Pruett Press, 1972.

Lorch, Robert S. *Colorado Government.* 4th ed. Boulder: Colorado Associated University Press, 1987.

Shockley, John S. *The Initiative Process in Colorado Politics: An Assessment.* Boulder: Bureau of Governmental Research and Service, University of Colorado, 1980.

Simmons, Thomas H. "Colorado." In Alan Rosenthal and Maureen Moakley, eds., *The Political Life of the American States.* New York: Praeger, 1984. Pp. 61–81.

Straayer, John A. *The Colorado General Assembly.* Niwot: University Press of Colorado, 1990.

Walton, Roger. *Colorado: A Practical Guide to Its Government and Politics.* Fort Collins, Colo.: Shields, 1973.

Wright, James E. *The Politics of Populism: Dissent in Colorado.* New Haven, Conn.: Yale University Press, 1974.

HAWAII

Callies, David L. *Regulating Paradise: Land Use Controls in Hawaii.* Honolulu: University of Hawaii Press, 1984.

Coffman, Tom. *Catch a Wave: A Case Study of Hawaii's New Politics.* Honolulu: University of Hawaii Press, 1972.

Cooper, George, and Gavan Daws. *Land and Power in Hawaii: The Democratic Years.* Honolulu: Benchmark Books, 1985.

Daws, Gavan. *Shoal of Time: A History of the Hawaiian Islands.* Honolulu: University of Hawaii Press, 1968.

Fuchs, Lawrence H. *Hawaii Pono: A Social History.* New York: Harcourt, Brace and World, 1961.

Kent, Noel J. *Hawaii: Islands Under the Influence.* New York: Monthly Review Press, 1983.

Lind, Andrew W. *Hawaii's People.* 4th ed. Honolulu: University of Hawaii Press, 1980.

Phillips, Paul C. *Hawaii's Democrats: Chasing the American Dream.* Washington, D.C.: University Press of America, 1982.

Rapson, Richard L. *Fairly Lucky You Live in Hawaii! Cultural Pluralism in the Fiftieth State.* Washington, D.C.: University Press of America, 1980.

Reporter at Large. "Islands of Disenchantment—I." *The New Yorker* (August 30, 1982).

Reporter at Large. "Islands of Disenchantment—II." *The New Yorker* (September 5, 1982).

State and Local Government Relationships in the State of Hawaii. Chicago: Public Administration Service, 1962.

Tabrah, Ruth M. *Hawaii: A Bicentennial History.* New York: W. W. Norton, 1980.

Wang, Jim. *Hawaii State and Local Politics.* Hilo, Haw.: Wang Associates, 1982.

Zalburg, Stanford. *A Spark Is Struck: Jack Hall and the ILWU in Hawaii.* Honolulu: University of Hawaii Press, 1979.

IDAHO

Barton, Rayburn, ed. *Idaho Government Manual.* Boise: School of Social Science and Public Affairs, Boise State University, 1983.

Barton, Rayburn, ed. *Idaho Legislative Manual.* Boise: School of Social Science and Public Affairs, Boise State University, 1984.

Blank, Robert H. *Individualism in Idaho: The Territorial Foundations.* Pullman: Washington State University Press, 1988.

Blank, Robert H. *Regional Diversity of Political Values: Idaho Political Culture.* Washington, D.C.: University Press of America, 1978.

Martin, Boyd A. *Idaho Voting Trends: Party Realignment and Percentage of Votes for Candidates, Parties and Elections, 1890–1974.* Moscow: Idaho Research Foundation, 1975.

Martin, Boyd A., Ray C. Jolly and Glenn W. Nichols, eds. *State and Local Government in Idaho.* Moscow: Bureau of Public Affairs Research, University of Idaho, 1970.

Peterson, F. Ross. *Idaho: A Bicentennial History.* New York: W. W. Norton, 1976.

Rusco, Elmer R. *Voting Behavior in Idaho.* Reno: University of Nevada, Bureau of Governmental Research, 1966.

Stapilus, Randy. *Paradox Politics: People and Power in Idaho.* Boise: Ridenbaugh Press, 1988.

MONTANA

Bryan, Frank. *Politics in the Rural States: People, Parties and Processes*. Boulder, Colo.: Westview Press, 1981.

Lopach, James J. *A State Mandates Local Government Review: The Montana Experience*. Davis: University of California Institute of Governmental Affairs, 1979. California Studies in Community Policy and Change, No. 5.

Lopach, James J., ed. *We the People of Montana . . . The Workings of a Popular Government*. Missoula: Mountain Press Publishing, 1983.

Lynch, Neil J. *Montana's Legislature Through the Years: An Historical Analysis of the Legislature from Territorial Days Through the Present*. Butte: n.d.

Malone, Michael P., and Richard R. Roeder. *Montana: A History of Two Centuries*. Seattle: University of Washington Press, 1976.

McCrory, John P. "Administrative Procedures in Montana: A View after Four Years with the Montana Administrative Procedure Act." *Montana Law Review*, 38 (Winter 1977).

Montana Constitutional Convention Studies. Helena: Montana Constitutional Convention, 1971.

Montana Legislators 1864–1979: Profiles and Biographical Directory. Missoula: University of Montana Bureau of Governmental Research, 1980.

Neely, Gerald J. *The Montana Legislature: Its Structure and Procedure*. Billings: Western Litho, 1969.

Renne, R. R. *The Government and Administration of Montana*. New York: Thomas Y. Crowell, 1958.

Toole, K. Ross. *Twentieth Century Montana: A State of Extremes*. Norman: University of Oklahoma Press, 1972.

Transcript of Proceeding of the Montana Constitutional Convention. Helena: Constitutional Convention, 1972.

Waldron, Ellis, and Paul B. Wilson. *Atlas of Montana Elections, 1889–1976*. Missoula: University of Montana Publications in History, 1978.

NEVADA

Bushnell, Eleanor, and Don W. Driggs. *The Nevada Constitution: Origin and Growth*. 6th ed. Reno: University of Nevada Press, 1984.

Edwards, Jerome E. *Pat McCarran: Political Boss of Nevada*. Reno: University of Nevada Press, 1982.

Elliott, Russell R. *History of Nevada*. 2nd ed., rev. Lincoln: University of Nebraska Press, 1987.

Glass, Mary Ellen. *Nevada's Turbulent 50's*. Reno: University of Nevada Press, 1981.

Johns, Albert C. *Nevada Government and Politics*. Dubuque, Iowa: Kendall/Hunt, 1971.

Laxalt, Robert. *Nevada: A Bicentennial History*. New York: W. W. Norton, 1977.

Ostrander, Gilman M. *Nevada, the Great Rotten Borough*. New York: Alfred A. Knopf, 1966.

Richardson, James T. "The 'Old Right' in Action: Mormon and Catholic Involvement in an Equal Rights Amendment Referendum." In David G. Bromley and Anson Shupe, eds., *New Christian Politics*. Macon, Ga.: Mercer University Press, 1984.

Rusco, Elmer R. *Voting Behavior in Nevada*. Reno: University of Nevada Press, 1966.

NEW MEXICO

Beck, Warren A. *New Mexico: A History of Four Centuries*. Norman: University of Oklahoma Press, 1962.

Donnelly, Thomas C. *The Government of New Mexico*. Albuquerque: University of New Mexico Press, 1953.

Folmar, Richard H. *Legislative Apportionment in New Mexico, 1844–1966*. Santa Fe: New Mexico Legislative Council Service, 1966.

Garcia, F. Chris. "Manitos and Chicanos in New Mexico Politics." In F. Chris Garcia, ed., *La Causa Politica: A Chicano Political Reader*. Notre Dame, Ind.: University of Notre Dame Press, 1974.

Garcia, F. Chris, and Paul L. Hain, eds. *New Mexico Government*. Albuquerque: University of New Mexico Press, 1976, revised edition 1981.

Holmes, Jack E. *Politics in New Mexico*. Albuquerque: University of New Mexico Press, 1967.

Larson, Robert W. *New Mexico Populism: A Study of Radical Protest in a Western Territory*. Boulder: Colorado Associated University Press, 1974.

Simmons, Marc. *New Mexico: A Bicentennial History*. New York: W. W. Norton, 1976.

Vigil, Maurilio. "Hispanos and the Governorship in New Mexico." *New Mexico Highlands University Journal*, 1, 1 (May 1979).

OREGON

Baker, Gordon E. "Reapportionment by Initiative in Oregon." *Western Political Quarterly*, 13 (June 1960), 508–19.

Burton, Robert E. *Democrats of Oregon: The Pattern of Minority Politics, 1900–1956*. Eugene: University of Oregon Books, 1970.

Dodds, Gordon B. *Oregon: A Bicentennial History*. New York: W. W. Norton, 1976.

Harmon, Robert B. *Government and Politics in Oregon: An Information Source*. Monticello, Ill.: Vance Bibliographies, 1979.

McCall, Tom, with Steve Neal. *Tom McCall, Maverick: An Autobiography*. Portland, Ore.: Binford & Mort, 1977.

McCann, Lluana, ed. *Oregon Policy Choices, 1989*. Eugene: Bureau of Governmental Research and Service, University of Oregon, 1989.

Neuberger, Richard Lewis. *Adventures in Politics: We Go to the Legislature.* New York: Oxford University Press, 1954.

Oregon Board of Education. *Government in Oregon: Teachers' Resource Handbook of State and Local Government.* Salem: Division of Instructional Services, Oregon Board of Education, 1971.

Oregon 2000 Commission. *The Challenges and Costs of Rapid Population Growth: The Report.* Salem, Ore.: The Commission, 1979.

Seligman, Lester, *et al. Patterns of Recruitment: A State Chooses Its Lawmakers.* Chicago: Rand McNally, 1974.

UTAH

Arrington, Leonard J., and George Jensen. *The Defense Industry of Utah.* Logan: Utah State University Press, 1965.

Durkham, Homer. *State and Local Government in Utah.* Salt Lake City: Utah Foundation, 1954.

Gottlieb, Robert, and Peter Wiley. *America's Saints: The Rise of Mormon Power.* New York: G. P. Putnam, 1984.

Heineman, John, and Anson Shupe. *The Mormon Corporate Empire.* Boston: Beacon Press, 1985.

Local Government Modernization Study. 5 vols. Salt Lake City: Center for Economic and Community Development, University of Utah, 1973.

Peterson, Charles S. *Utah: A Bicentennial History.* New York: W. W. Norton, 1977.

Utah Foundation. *State and Local Government in Utah.* Salt Lake City: Utah Foundation, 1962.

Williams, J. D. "Separation of Church and State in Mormon Theory and Practice." *Dialogue: A Journal of Mormon Thought,* 1 (Summer 1966).

WASHINGTON

Avery, Mary W. *Government of Washington State.* Rev. ed. Seattle: University of Washington Press, 1974.

Bone, Hugh A., and Robert C. Benedict. "Perspectives on Direct Legislation: Washington State's Experience, 1914–1973." *Western Political Quarterly,* 28 (June 1975), 330–51.

Bone, Hugh A., and Cindy M. Fey. *People's Right to Know: An Analysis of the Washington State Disclosure Law.* Seattle: University of Washington, Institute of Governmental Research, 1978.

Clark, Norman H. *Washington: A Bicentennial History.* New York: W. W. Norton, 1976.

Jackson, David H. *The Administrative Reorganization Experience in the State of Washington.* Seattle: University of Washington, Institute of Governmental Research, 1971.

Ogden, Daniel M., Jr., and Hugh A. Bone. *Washington Politics.* New York: New York University Press, 1960.

Simmons, Robert. "The Washington State Plural Executive: An Initial Effort in Interaction Analysis." *Western Political Quarterly*, 17 (June 1965), 369–81.

Swanson, Thor, *et al.*, eds. *Political Life in Washington: Governing the Evergreen State*. Pullman: Washington State University Press, 1985.

Washington, State of. *A History of Washington's Local Governments*. Volume I of the Final Report of the Washington State Local Governance Study Commission. Olympia, 1988.

Washington, State of. *The Quiet Crisis of Local Governance in Washington*. Volume II of the Final Report of the Washington State Local Governance Study Commission. Olympia, 1988.

WYOMING

Building a Stronger Wyoming. Stanford, Calif.: SRI International, 1985.

Cawley, Gregg, *et al. The Equality State: Government and Politics in Wyoming*. Dubuque, Iowa: Eddie Bowers, 1988.

Griffin, Kenyon, ed. *Politics and Policies in Wyoming*. Laramie: Wyoming Government Research Bureau, 1984.

Griffin, Kenyon N., and Michael J. Horan. "Judicial Merit Retention in Wyoming: An Analysis and Some Suggestions for Reform." *Land and Water Law Review*, 15 (1980), 567–91.

Larson, T. A. *History of Wyoming*. 2nd ed. Lincoln: University of Nebraska Press, 1978.

Miller, Tim R. *State Government: Politics in Wyoming*. Dubuque, Iowa: Kendall/Hunt, 1981.

Peterson, Henry J. *The Constitutional Convention of Wyoming*. Laramie: University of Wyoming Press, 1940.

Richard, John B. *Government and Politics of Wyoming*. Dubuque, Iowa: W. C. Brown, 1966.

Schilling, Bill. *State Expenditures: How Wyoming Compares to the Region*. Cody: Wyoming Heritage Foundation, 1988.

Sodaro, Craig, and Randy Adams. *Frontier Spirit: The Story of Wyoming*. Boulder, Colo.: Johnson Books, 1986.

Trachsel, Herman H., and Ralph M. Wade. *The Government and Administration of Wyoming*. New York: Thomas Y. Crowell, 1956.

Walter, Oliver B. "Wyoming Conservative But Not Always So." *Social Science Journal*, 21 (1984).

8. Political and Governmental Institutions and Processes

GENERAL

Conway, M. Margaret. *Political Participation in the United States*. 2nd ed. Washington, D.C.: CQ Press, 1990.

Cornwell, Elmer E., Jr., Jay Goodman and Wayne Swanson. *State Constitutional Conventions*. New York: Praeger, 1975.

Drucker, Peter E. *The New Realities: In Government and Politics, in Economics and Business, in Society and World View*. New York: Harper & Row, 1989.

Erikson, Robert S., Norman R. Luttbeg and Kent L. Tedin. *American Public Opinion: Its Origin, Content and Impact*. 3rd ed. New York: Macmillan, 1988.

Gray, Virginia, Herbert Jacob and Robert Albritton, eds. *Politics in the American States: A Comparative Analysis*. 5th ed. Glenview, Ill.: Scott Foresman/Little, Brown, 1990.

Hagstrom, Jerry. *The New Landscape of American Politics*. New York: W. W. Norton, 1988.

Sorauf, Frank J. *Money in American Politics*. Glenview, Ill.: Scott Foresman, 1988.

Verba, Sidney, and Norman H. Nie. *Participation in America: Political Democracy and Social Equality*. New York: Harper & Row, 1972.

ELECTIONS, CAMPAIGNS AND VOTING BEHAVIOR

Abramson, Paul, *et al*. *Change and Continuity in the 1988 Elections*. Washington, D.C.: Congressional Quarterly Press, 1990.

Alexander, Herbert, and Mike Eberts. *Public Financing of State Elections: A Data Book on Tax-Assisted Funding of Political Parties and Candidates in Twenty States*. Los Angeles: Citizens' Research Foundation, 1986.

Beck, Paul A. "A Socialization Theory of Partisan Realignment." In Richard G. Niemi and Herbert F. Weisberg, eds., *Controversies in American Voting Behavior*. San Francisco: Freeman, 1976.

Benedict, Robert C., *et al*. "The Voters and Attitudes Toward Nuclear Moratorium Initiatives." *Western Political Quarterly*, 33 (March 1980).

Burnham, Walter Dean. *Critical Elections and the Mainspring of American Politics*. New York: W. W. Norton, 1970.

Carmines, Edward G., and James A. Stimson. "The Two Faces of Issue Voting." *American Political Science Review*, 74 (March 1980).

Chambers, William N., and Walter Dean Burnham, eds. *The American Party Systems*. 2nd ed. New York: Oxford University Press, 1975.

Clark, Cal, and B. Oliver Walter, eds. "A Symposium on Politics in the West: The 1980 Election." *Social Science Journal*, 18 (October 1981).

Cronin, Thomas E. *Direct Democracy: The Politics of Initiative, Referendum and Recall*. Cambridge, Mass.: Harvard University Press, 1989.

Everson, David H. "The Effects of Initiatives on Voter Turnout: A Comparative State Analysis." *Western Political Quarterly*, 34 (September 1981), 415–25.

Groth, Alexander J., and Howard G. Schultz. *Voter Attitudes on the 1976 California Nuclear Initiative*. Davis: University of California, 1976. Institute of Governmental Affairs Environmental Quality Series, No. 25.

Hensler, Deborah R., and Carl Hensler. *Evaluating Nuclear Power: Voter Choice on the California Nuclear Initiative.* Santa Monica, Calif.: Rand Corporation, 1979.

Key, V. O., Jr. "Secular Realignment and the Party System." *Journal of Politics,* 21 (1959), 198–210.

Key, V. O., Jr. "A Theory of Critical Elections." *Journal of Politics,* 17 (February 1955), 3–18.

Magleby, David. *Direct Legislation: Voting on Ballot Propositions in the United States.* Baltimore: Johns Hopkins University Press, 1984.

Niemi, Richard G., and Herbert Weisberg. *Controversies in Voting Behavior.* 2nd ed. Washington, D.C.: Congressional Quarterly Press, 1984.

Price, Charles M. "The Initiative: A Comparative State Analysis and Reassessment of a Western Phenomenon." *Western Political Quarterly,* 28 (June 1975).

Ranney, Austin, ed. *The Referendum Device.* Washington, D.C.: American Enterprise Institute, 1981.

Sheldon, Charles H., and Nicholas P. Lovrich. "Knowledge and Judicial Voting: The Washington and Oregon Experience." *Judicature* (November 1983).

Sheldon, Charles H., and Nicholas P. Lovrich. "Voters in Contested, Nonpartisan Judicial Elections: A Responsible Electorate or a Problematic Public?" *Western Political Quarterly* (June 1983).

Walter, B. Oliver, ed. *Politics in the West: The 1978 Elections.* Laramie: Wyoming Government Research Bureau, University of Wyoming, 1979.

Webster, Gerald R. "Presidential Voting in the West." *The Social Science Journal,* 25, 2 (1988), 211–32.

Western Political Quarterly. Vols. 2–24 (1948–70). [Includes a round-up of elections in western states during election years.]

Wolfinger, Raymond E., and Steven J. Rosenstone. *Who Votes?* New Haven, Conn.: Yale University Press, 1980.

POLITICAL PARTIES AND INTEREST GROUPS

Bibby, John F., Cornelius P. Cotter, James L. Gibson and Robert J. Huckshorn. "Parties in State Politics." In Virginia Gray, Herbert Jacob and Robert Albritton, eds., *Politics in the American States.* 5th ed. Glenview, Ill.: Scott Foresman/Little, Brown, 1990. Pp. 82–122.

Campbell, Bruce A., and Richard J. Trilling, eds. *Realignment in American Politics.* Austin: University of Texas Press, 1980.

Galderisi, Peter F., Michael S. Lyons, Randy T. Simmons and John G. Francis, eds. *The Politics of Realignment: Party Change in the Mountain West.* Boulder, Colo.: Westview Press, 1987.

Gibson, James L., *et al.* "Whither the Local Parties?" *American Journal of Political Science,* 29 (February 1985).

Hrebenar, Ronald J., and Ruth K. Scott. *Interest Group Politics in America.* 2nd ed. Englewood Cliffs, N.J.: Prentice Hall, 1990.

Hrebenar, Ronald J., and Clive S. Thomas, eds. *Interest Group Politics in the American West.* Salt Lake City: University of Utah Press, 1987.

Jewell, Malcolm E., and David M. Olson. *Political Parties and Elections in American States.* 3rd ed. Chicago: Dorsey Press, 1988.

Kleppner, Paul. "Politics without Parties: The Western States, 1900–1984." In Gerald D. Nash and Richard W. Etulain, eds., *The Twentieth-Century West.* Albuquerque: University of New Mexico Press, 1989. Pp. 295–338.

Kleppner, Paul. "Voters and Parties in the Western States, 1876–1900." *Western Historical Quarterly,* 14 (January 1983), 49–68.

Mayhew, David R. "The Parties and the West." In *Party Loyalty Among Congressmen.* Cambridge, Mass.: Harvard University Press, 1966.

Mayhew, David R. *Placing Parties in American Politics: Organization, Electoral Settings, and Government Activity in the Twentieth Century.* Princeton, N.J.: Princeton University Press, 1986.

Sorauf, Frank J., and Paul Allen Beck. *Party Politics in America.* 6th ed. Glenview, Ill.: Scott Foresman, 1988.

Thomas, Clive S., and Ronald J. Hrebenar. "Interest Groups in the States." In Virginia Gray, Herbert Jacob and Robert Albritton, eds., *Politics in the American States.* 5th ed. Glenview, Ill.: Scott Foresman/Little, Brown, 1990. Pp. 123–58.

FINANCE AND BUDGETING

Adams, James Ring. *Secrets of the Tax Revolt.* New York: Harcourt, Brace, Jovanovich, 1984.

Bahl, Roy. *Financing State and Local Governments in the 1980's.* New York: Oxford University Press, 1984.

Clark, Cal, and Janet Clark. "Federal Aid to Local Governments in the West: An Irony of the Reagan Revolution." *Policy Studies Review,* 9 (1990).

Clark, Terry Nichols, and Lorna Crowley Fergusson. *City Money: Political Processes, Fiscal Strain, and Retrenchment.* New York: Columbia University Press, 1983.

Duncombe, Sydney, and Richard Kinney. "The Politics of State Appropriation Increases." *State Government* (September/October 1986), 113–23.

Fairfax, Sally K. "Interstate Bargaining over Revenue Sharing and Payments in Lieu of Taxes: Federalism as if States Mattered." In Phillip O. Foss, ed., *Federal Lands Policy.* Westport, Conn.: Greenwood Press, 1987.

Fairfax, Sally K., and Carolyn E. Yale. *The Federal Lands: A Guide to Planning, Management, and State Revenues.* Covelo, Calif.: Island Press, 1987.

Hansen, Susan B. "The Politics of State Taxing and Spending." In Virginia Gray, Herbert Jacob and Robert Albritton, eds., *Politics in the American States.* 5th ed. Glenview, Ill.: Scott Foresman/Little, Brown, 1990). Pp. 333–77.

Herzik, Eric B. "Projecting the Fiscal Impact of Municipal Annexation." *Municipal Management,* 7, 2 (Fall 1984), 47–53.

Magleby, David B. "The Movement to Limit Government Spending in American States and Localities, 1970–1979." *National Civic Review* (May 1981).

Schwadron, T., ed. *California and the American Tax Revolt.* Berkeley: University of California Press, 1984.

Sears, John O., and Jack Citrin. *Tax Revolt: Something for Nothing in California.* Cambridge, Mass.: Harvard University Press, 1982.

Walzer, Norman, and David L. Chicoine, eds. *Financing State and Local Governments in the 1980's: Issues and Trends.* Cambridge, Mass.: Oelgeschlager, Gunn & Hain, 1981.

LEGISLATURES

Bushnell, Eleanore, ed. *Impact of Reapportionment on the Politics of the Thirteen Western States.* Salt Lake City: University of Utah Press, 1970.

Campbell, Ernest H., ed. *The State Legislatures of Alaska, Washington and Oregon.* Union, Wash.: Northwest Regional American Assembly for Alaska, Oregon and Washington, 1966.

Dixon, Robert G. *Democratic Representation: Reapportionment in Law and Politics.* New York: Oxford University Press, 1968.

Francis, Wayne L. "Leadership, Party Caucuses and Committees in the U.S. State Legislatures." *Legislative Studies Quarterly,* 10 (1985), 243–57.

LeBlanc, Hugh. "Voting in State Senates: Party and Constituency Influences." *Midwest Journal of Political Science,* 13 (February 1969).

Patterson, Samuel C. "State Legislators and the Legislatures." In Virginia Gray, Herbert Jacob and Robert Albritton, eds., *Politics in the American States.* 5th ed. Glenview, Ill.: Scott Foresman/Little, Brown, 1990). Pp. 161–200.

Rosenthal, Alan. *Legislative Life: People, Process and Performance in the States.* New York: Harper & Row, 1981.

Stoiber, Susanne A., ed. *Legislative Politics in the Rocky Mountain West: Colorado, New Mexico, Utah and Wyoming.* Boulder: Colorado Bureau of Governmental Research and Service, University of Colorado, 1967.

Weberg, Brian, and Beth Bazar. *Legislative Staff Services: 50 State Profiles.* Denver: National Council of State Legislatures, 1988.

GOVERNORS AND THE EXECUTIVE BRANCH

Beyle, Thad L. "Governors." In Virginia Gray, Herbert Jacob and Robert Albritton, eds., *Politics in the American States.* 5th ed. Glenview, Ill.: Scott Foresman/Little, Brown, 1990). Pp. 201–51.

Beyle, Thad L., ed., *Gubernatorial Transitions: The 1982 Election.* Durham, N.C.: Duke University Press, 1985.

Beyle, Thad L., and Lynn Muchmore. *Being Governor.* Durham, N.C.: Duke University Press, 1983.

Center for Policy Research. *Reflections on Being Governor.* Washington, D.C.: National Governors' Association, 1981.

Cox, Raymond W. "The Expanding Role of the Western Governor as a Manager." *The Western Governmental Researcher*, 4, 3 (Winter 1989).

Elling, Richard C. "Bureaucracy." In Virginia Gray, Herbert Jacob and Robert Albritton, eds., *Politics in the American States*. 5th ed. Glenview, Ill.: Scott Foresman/Little, Brown, 1990). Pp. 287–330.

Glashan, Roy R., comp. *American Governors and Gubernatorial Elections, 1775–1978*. Westport, Conn.: Meckler Books, 1979.

Ransome, Coleman B., Jr. *The Office of the Governor in the United States*. University, Ala.: University of Alabama Press, 1956.

Rosenthal, Alan. *Governors and Legislatures: Contending Powers*. Washington, D.C.: CQ Press, 1990.

Sabato, Larry. *Goodbye to Good-Time Charlie*. 2nd ed. Washington, D.C.: Congressional Quarterly Press, 1983.

JUDICIARIES

Dubois, Philip L. *From Ballot to Bench*. Austin: University of Texas Press, 1980.

Glick, Henry R. *Courts, Politics and Justice*. New York: McGraw-Hill, 1983.

Hall, William K., and Larry T. Aspin. "What Twenty Years of Judicial Retention Election Have Told Us." *Judicature*, 70 (April–May 1987).

Jacob, Herbert. "Courts: The Least Visible Branch." In Virginia Gray, Herbert Jacob and Robert Albritton, eds., *Politics in the American States*. 5th ed. Glenview, Ill.: Scott Foresman/Little, Brown, 1990). Pp. 252–86.

Neely, Richard. *How Courts Govern America*. New Haven, Conn.: Yale University Press, 1981.

Porter, Mary Cornelia, and G. Alan Tarr, eds. *State Supreme Courts*. Westport, Conn.: Greenwood Press, 1982.

Stolz, Preble. *Judging Judges*. New York: Free Press, 1981.

Stumpf, Harry P. *American Judicial Politics*. San Diego: Harcourt, Brace, Jovanovich, 1988.

Wold, John T., and John H. Culver. "The Defeat of the California Justices: The Campaign, the Electorate, and the Issue of Judicial Accountability." *Judicature*, 70 (April–May 1987).

9. Urban and Local Politics and Government

GENERAL

Bollens, John C., and Henry J. Schmandt. *The Metropolis: Its People, Politics, and Economic Life*. 4th ed. New York: Harper & Row, 1982.

Buenker, John D. *Urban Liberalism and Progressive Reform*. New York: Charles Scribner's Sons, 1973.

Carruthers, Garrey E., Eugene C. Erickson and Kathryn N. Renner. *Delivery of Rural Community Services: Some Implications and Problems*. Las Cruces, N.M.: New Mexico State University Agricultural Experiment Station, 1975.

Fox, William F. *Size Economies in Local Government Services: A Review.* Washington, D.C.: U.S. Department of Agriculture, 1980.

Hahn, Harlan, and Charles H. Levine, eds. *Readings in Urban Politics: Past, Present and Future.* 2nd ed. New York: Longman, 1984.

Jones, Bryan D. *Governing Urban America: A Policy Focus.* Boston: Little, Brown, 1983.

Judd, Dennis R. *The Politics of American Cities: Private Power and Public Policy.* 3rd ed. Glenview, Ill.: Scott Foresman/Little, Brown, 1988.

Ladd, Helen F., and John Yinger. *America's Ailing Cities: Fiscal Health and the Design of Urban Policies.* Baltimore: Johns Hopkins University Press, 1989.

Peterson, Paul E. *City Limits.* Chicago: University of Chicago Press, 1981.

Seroka, Jim, ed. *Rural Public Administration: Problems and Prospects.* Westport, Conn.: Greenwood Press, 1986.

Waste, Robert J. *The Ecology of City Policymaking.* New York: Oxford University Press, 1989.

THE WEST AND ITS REGIONS

Abbott, Carl. "The Metropolitan Region: Western Cities in the New Urban Era." In Gerald D. Nash and Richard W. Etulain, eds., *The Twentieth-Century West.* Albuquerque: University of New Mexico Press, 1989.

Abbott, Carl. *The New Urban America: Growth and Politics in Sunbelt Cities.* Chapel Hill: University of North Carolina Press, 1981.

Bernard, Richard M., and Bradley R. Rice, eds. *Sunbelt Cities: Politics and Growth Since World War II.* Austin: University of Texas Press, 1983.

Davis, Ronald L. F. "Western Urban Development: A Critical Analysis." In Jerome O. Steffen, ed., *The American West: New Perspectives, New Dimensions.* Norman: University of Oklahoma Press, 1979. Pp. 175–96.

Emenhiser, JeDon A., ed. *Rocky Mountain Urban Politics.* Logan: Utah State University Press, 1971.

Goodall, Leonard, ed. *Urban Politics in the Southwest.* Tempe: Institute of Public Administration, Arizona State University, 1967.

Luckingham, Bradford. "The American Southwest: An Urban View." *Western Historical Quarterly,* 15 (July 1984), 261–80.

Luckingham, Bradford. "The Urban Dimension of Western History." In Michael P. Malone, ed., *Historians and the American West.* Lincoln: University of Nebraska Press, 1983. Pp. 323–43.

West, Roy B., ed. *Rocky Mountain Cities.* New York: W. W. Norton, 1949.

INDIVIDUAL WESTERN CITIES AND LOCALITIES

Abbott, Carl. *Portland: Planning, Politics and Growth in a Twentieth Century City.* Lincoln: University of Nebraska Press, 1983.

Barth, Gunther P. *Instant Cities: Urbanization and the Rise of San Francisco and Denver.* New York: Oxford University Press, 1975; Rpt. Albuquerque: University of New Mexico Press, 1988.

Bean, Walton. *Boss Ruef's San Francisco.* Berkeley and Los Angeles: University of California Press, 1952.

Bish, Robert L. *Governing Puget Sound.* Seattle: Puget Sound Books, 1982.

Bridge, Franklin N. *Metro Denver: Mile High Government.* Boulder: University of Colorado Publications, 1963.

Chute, Charlton F. "The Honolulu Metropolitan Area: A Challenge to Traditional Thinking." *Public Administration Review,* 18 (Winter 1958).

Luckingham, Bradford. *The Urban Southwest: A Profile History of Albuquerque, El Paso, Phoenix and Tucson.* El Paso: Texas Western Press, 1982.

Melnick, Rob, and Deborah Roepke, eds. *Urban Growth in Arizona.* Tempe: Morrison Institute, 1988.

Sale, Roger. *Seattle, Past and Present.* Seattle: University of Washington Press, 1976.

Scott, Mel. *The San Francisco Bay Area: A Metropolis in Perspective.* 2nd ed. Berkeley: University of California Press, 1985.

Simmons, Marc. *Albuquerque: A Narrative History.* Albuquerque: University of New Mexico Press, 1982.

Wirt, Fred. *Power in the City: Decision Making in San Francisco.* Berkeley: University of California Press, 1974.

10. Political Ideas and Political Movements

Beitzinger, A. J. *A History of American Political Thought.* New York: Dodd, Mead, 1972.

Bellah, Robert N. *Habits of the Heart: Individualism and Commitment in American Life.* Berkeley: University of California Press, 1985.

Buck, Solon Justus. *The Granger Movement.* Cambridge, Mass.: Harvard University Press, 1913. Rpt. Lincoln: University of Nebraska Press, 1963.

Edelman, Murray. *The Symbolic Uses of Politics.* Urbana: University of Illinois Press, 1964.

Goldman, Eric F. *Rendezvous with Destiny: A History of Modern American Reform.* New York: Alfred A. Knopf, 1952.

Green, James R. *Grass-Roots Socialism: Radical Movements in the Southwest, 1895–1943.* Baton Rouge: Louisiana State University Press, 1978.

Hofstadter, Richard. *The Age of Reform: From Bryan to F.D.R.* New York: Alfred A. Knopf, 1955.

Ionescu, Ghita, and Ernest Gellner, eds. *Populism: Its Meaning and National Characteristics.* London: Weidenfeld and Nicolson, 1970.

McKenna, George, ed. *American Populism.* New York: G. P. Putnam's Sons, 1974.

Minar, David W. *Ideas and Politics: The American Experience.* Homewood, Ill.: The Dorsey Press, 1964.

Pollock, Norman: *The Populist Response to Industrial America.* New York: W. W. Norton, 1962.

Rowley, William D. "The West as Laboratory and Mirror of Reform." In Gerald
    D. Nash and Richard W. Etulain, eds., *The Twentieth Century West*. Al-
    buquerque: University of New Mexico Press, 1989.

11. Political Culture

Almond, Gabriel, and Sidney Verba. *The Civic Culture: Political Attitudes and
    Democracy in Five Nations*. Princeton, N.J.: Princeton University Press,
    1963.
Almond, Gabriel, and Sidney Verba, eds. *The Civic Culture Revisited: An An-
    alytical Study*. Boston: Little, Brown, 1980.
Elazar, Daniel J. *American Federalism: A View from the States*. 3rd ed. New York:
    Harper & Row, 1984. Chap. 5, "The States and the Political Setting."
Elazar, Daniel J., and Joseph Zikmund II, eds. *The American Cultural Matrix*.
    New York: Thomas Y. Crowell, 1975.
Elazar, Daniel J., and Joseph Zikmund II, eds. *The Ecology of American Political
    Culture*. New York: Thomas Y. Crowell, 1975.
Elkins, David J., and Richard E. B. Simeon. "A Cause in Search of Its Effect
    or Does Political Culture Explain?" *Comparative Politics* (January 1979),
    127–65.
Inglehart, Ronald. "The Renaissance of Political Culture." *American Political
    Science Review*, 82, 4 (December 1988), 1203–30.
Kincaid, John, ed. *Political Culture, Public Policy and the American States*. Phil-
    adelphia: Institute for the Study of Human Issues, 1982.
Patterson, Samuel C. "The Political Cultures of the American States." In
    Daniel J. Elazar and Joseph Zikmund II, eds., *The Ecology of American
    Political Culture*. New York: Thomas Y. Crowell, 1975.
Pye, Lucian, and Sidney Verba, eds. *Political Culture and Political Development*.
    Princeton, N.J.: Princeton University Press, 1963.
Ritt, Leonard G. "Political Culture and Political Reform." *Publius*, 4 (Winter
    1974).
Rosenbaum, Walter A. *Political Culture*. New York: Praeger, 1975.
Sharkansky, Ira. "The Utility of Elazar's Political Culture: A Research Note."
    In Daniel J. Elazar and Joseph Zikmund II, eds., *The American Cultural
    Matrix*. New York: Thomas Y. Crowell, 1975.

12. Minorities and Minority Politics

GENERAL
Barrera, Mario. *Race and Class in the Southwest: A Theory of Racial Inequality*.
    Notre Dame, Ind.: University of Notre Dame Press, 1979.
Cain, Bruce E., and D. Roderick Kiewiet. *Minorites in California: A Report*.
    Pasadena: California Institute of Technology, 1986.

de la Garza, Rodolfo O., Anthony Kruszewski and Tomas A. Arciniega, eds. *Chicanos and Native Americans: The Territorial Minorities.* Englewood Cliffs, N.J.: Prentice Hall, 1973.

Harris, Louis. *The Anguish of Change.* New York: W. W. Norton, 1973.

Lamm, Richard D., and Gary Imhoff. *The Immigration Time Bomb: The Fragmenting of America.* New York: E. P. Dutton, 1985.

Luebke, Frederick C. "Ethnic Minority Groups in the American West." In Michael P. Malone, ed. *Historians and the American West.* Lincoln: University of Nebraska Press, 1983. Pp. 387–413.

Makielski, S. J., Jr. *Beleaguered Minorities: Cultural Politics in America.* San Francisco: W. H. Freeman, 1973.

Nelson, Dale C. "Ethnicity and Socioeconomic Status as Sources of Participation: The Case for Ethnic Political Culture." *American Political Science Review,* 73 (December 1979), 1024–38.

Piatt, Bill ¿*Only English? Law and Language Policy in the United States.* Albuquerque: University of New Mexico Press, 1990.

White, Richard. "Race Relations in the American West." *American Quarterly,* 38(3) (1986), 396–416.

Yzaguirre, Raul. "The Perils of Pandora: An Examination of the English-Only Movement." *Journal of Hispanic Policy,* 2 (1986–87).

ASIANS AND PACIFIC ISLANDERS

Chen, Jack. *The Chinese of America.* New York: Harper & Row, 1980.

Daniels, Roger, Sandra C. Taylor and Harry H. L. Kitano. *Japanese Americans: From Relocation to Redress.* Salt Lake City: University of Utah Press, 1986.

Gardner, Robert W., Bryant Robey and Peter C. Smith. "Asian Americans: Growth, Change, and Diversity." *Population Bulletin,* 40 (October 1985).

Irons, Peter. *Justice at War: The Story of the Japanese American Internment Cases.* New York: Oxford University Press, 1983.

Kitano, Harry H. L. *Japanese American: The Evolution of a Subculture.* 2nd ed. Englewood Cliffs, N.J.: Prentice Hall, 1976.

Knoll, Tricia. *Becoming Americans: Asian Sojourners, Immigrants, and Refugees in the Western United States.* Portland, Ore.: Coast to Coast Books, 1982.

Lyman, Stanford. *The Asian in the West.* Reno: University of Nevada, 1970.

Melendy, H. Brett. *Asians in America: Filipinos, Koreans and East Indians.* Boston: Twayne, 1977.

Melendy, Howard Brett. *The Oriental Americans.* Boston: Twayne, 1972.

Wu, Cheng-Tsu, ed. *"Chink!" Anti-Chinese Prejudice in America.* New York: Harcourt, Brace and World, 1972.

BLACKS

Abramson, Paul. *The Political Socialization of Black Americans: A Critical Evaluation of Research on Efficacy and Trust.* New York: Free Press, 1977.

Bullock, Charles S., and Harrel R. Rodgers, Jr., eds. *Black Political Attitudes: Implications for Political Support*. Chicago: Markham Publishing, 1972.

Greenberg, Edward S. "Black Children and the Political System." *Public Opinion Quarterly*, 34 (Fall 1970), 333–45.

Katz, William. *The Black West*. Garden City, N.Y.: Anchor Press, 1973.

Savage, William Sherman. *Blacks in the West*. Westport, Conn.: Greenwood Press, 1976.

Walton, Hanes, Jr. *Black Politics: A Theoretical and Structural Analysis*. Philadelphia: Lippincott, 1972.

Walton, Hanes, Jr. *Invisible Politics: Black Political Behavior*. Albany: State University of New York Press, 1985.

Walton, Hanes, Jr. "The Recent Literature on Black Politics." *PS*, 18 (Fall 1985), 769–80.

HISPANICS

Acuna, Rodolfo. *Occupied America: A History of Chicanos*. 3rd ed. New York: Harper & Row, 1988.

Brischetto, Robert R., and Rodolfo O. de la Garza. *The Mexican American Electorate: Political Participation and Ideology*. Austin: Joint Publications of the Southwest Voter Registration Education Project, San Antonio, Texas, and the Hispanic Population Studies Program of the Center for Mexican American Studies, University of Texas at Austin, 1983.

Browning, Harley L., and Rodolfo O. de la Garza, eds. *Mexican Immigrants and Mexican Americans: An Evolving Relation*. Austin: Center for Mexican American Studies, University of Texas at Austin, 1986.

Camarillo, Albert, ed. *Latinos in the United States: A Historical Bibliography*. Santa Barbara, Calif.: ABC-CLIO, 1986.

de la Garza, Rodolfo O., ed. *Ignored Voices: Public Opinion Polls and the Latino Community*. Austin: Center for Mexican American Studies, University of Texas at Austin, 1987.

de la Garza, Rodolfo O., and Robert R. Brischetto. *The Mexican American Electorate: Information Sources and Policy Orientations*. Austin: Southwest Voter Registration Education Project, San Antonio, Texas, and the Hispanic Population Studies Program of the Center for Mexican American Studies, University of Texas at Austin, 1983. Occasional Paper No. 2.

Garcia, F. Chris, ed. *Latinos and the Political System*. Notre Dame, Ind.: University of Notre Dame Press, 1988.

Garcia, F. Chris. *Political Socialization of Chicano Children: A Comparative Study with Anglos in California Schools*. New York: Praeger, 1973.

Garcia, F. Chris, and Rodolfo O. de la Garza. *The Chicano Political Experience: Three Perspectives*. North Scituate, Mass.: Duxbury Press, 1977.

Moore, Joan, and Harry Pachon. *Hispanics in the United States*. Englewood Cliffs, N.J.: Prentice Hall, 1985.

Romo, Ricardo. "Mexican Americans in the New West." In Gerald D. Nash and Richard W. Etulain, eds., *The Twentieth Century West*. Albuquerque: University of New Mexico Press, 1989. Pp. 123–46.

Santillan, Richard. *The Hispanic Community and Redistricting, Volume II*. Claremont, Calif.: Rose Institute of State and Local Government, Claremont McKenna College, 1984.

Santillan, Richard. "The Latino Community in State and Congressional Redistricting: 1961–1985." *Journal of Hispanic Politics*, 1 (1985).

Vigil, Maurilio. *Hispanics in American Politics: The Search for Political Power*. Lanham, Md.: University Press of America, 1987.

NATIVE AMERICANS

Barsh, Russell Lawrence, and James Youngblood Henderson. *The Road: Indian Tribes and Political Liberty*. Berkeley: University of California Press, 1980.

Deloria, Vine, Jr., ed. *American Indian Policy in the Twentieth Century*. Norman: University of Oklahoma Press, 1985.

Deloria, Vine, Jr., and Clifford M. Lytle. *American Indians, American Justice*. Austin: University of Texas Press, 1983.

Deloria, Vine, Jr., and Clifford M. Lytle. *The Nations Within: The Past and Future of American Indian Sovereignty*. New York: Pantheon, 1984.

Dippie, Brian W. *The Vanishing American: White Attitudes and U.S. Indian Policy*. Middletown, Conn.: Wesleyan University Press, 1982.

Murdock, Margaret Maier. "Political Attachment Among Native Americans: Arapahoe and Shoshoni Children and the National Political System." *Social Science Journal*, 20 (April 1983), 41–58.

National Indian Youth Council. *American Indian Political Attitudes and Behavior Survey: Data Report*. Albuquerque: N.M.: The National Indian Youth Council, 1983, 1984, 1985 and 1986.

Olson, James S., and Raymond Wilson. *Native Americans in the Twentieth Century*. Urbana: Illinois University Press, 1984.

Parman, Donald R. "Indians of the Modern West." In Gerald D. Nash and Richard W. Etulain, eds., *The Twentieth Century West*. Albuquerque: University of New Mexico Press, 1989. Pp. 147–72.

Prucha, Francis Paul. *A Bibliographical Guide to the History of Indian-White Relations in the U.S.* Chicago: University of Chicago Press, 1977.

Taylor, Theodore W. *American Indian Policy*. Mt. Airy, Md.: Lomond Publications, 1983.

U.S. Indian Policy: A Critical Bibliography. Bloomington, Ind.: Published for the Newberry Library by Indiana University Press, 1977.

Wax, Murray. *Indian Americans: Unity and Diversity*. Englewood Cliffs, N.J.: Prentice Hall, 1971.

Weyler, Rex. *Blood of the Land: The Government and Corporate War Against the American Indian Movement*. New York: Vintage, 1982.

WOMEN

Anderson, Karen. "Western Women: The Twentieth-Century Experience." In Gerald D. Nash and Richard W. Etulain, eds., *The Twentieth Century West*. Albuquerque: University of New Mexico Press, 1989. Pp. 99–122.

Armitage, Susan H., and Elizabeth Jamison, eds. *The Women's West*. Norman: University of Oklahoma Press, 1987.

Darcy, R., Susan Welch and Janet Clark. *Women, Elections and Representation*. New York: Longman, 1987.

Poole, Keith T., and L. Harmon Zeigler. *Women, Public Opinion, and Politics: The Changing Political Attitudes of American Women*. New York: Longman, 1985.

13. Western Political Issues and Public Policies

GENERAL

Baaklini, Abdo I., ed. *Linking Science and Technology to Public Policy*. Albany: State University of New York, 1979.

Branch, Melville C. *Regional Planning: Introduction and Explanation*. New York: Praeger, 1988.

Ingram, Helen M., Nancy K. Laney and John R. McCain. *A Policy Approach to Political Representation: Lessons from the Four Corners States*. Baltimore: Resources for the Future, Johns Hopkins University Press, 1980.

Romer, Roy, and Philip M. Burgess. *Regional Policy Management: The Task Ahead*. Denver: Federation of Rocky Mountain States, 1976.

Walker, Jack. "The Diffusion of Innovations Among American States." *American Political Science Review*, 63, 3 (1969), 880–99.

ECONOMICS AND ECONOMIC POLICY

Arrington, Leonard J. *The Changing Economic Structure of the Mountain West, 1850–1950*. Logan: Utah State University, 1963.

Berge, Wendell. *Economic Freedom for the West*. Lincoln: University of Nebraska Press, 1946.

Burgess, Philip M. *Balancing Growth and Economic Development: A Western White Paper*. Denver: Western Governors' Policy Office, 1976.

Burgess, Philip M., and Craig Liske. *Managing Resource Scarcity: Lessons from the Mid-Seventies Drought*. Denver: WESTPO Institute for Policy Research, 1978.

Clarke, M. K. *Revitalizing State Economies: A Review of State Economic Development Policies and Programs*. Washington, D.C.: National Governors' Association, 1986.

DeVoto, Bernard. "The West: Boom or Bust?" *Colliers* (December 25, 1953).

Dubnick, M. "American States in the Industrial Policy Debate." *Policy Studies Review*, 4, 1 (1984).

Hayes, Lynton R. *Energy, Economic Growth and Regionalism in the American West.* Albuquerque: University of New Mexico Press, 1980.

Siegel, Lenny, and John Markoff. *The High Cost of High Tech.* New York: Harper & Row, 1985.

White, William Allen. *The Changing West: An Economic Theory About Our Changing Age.* New York: Macmillan, 1939.

Williams, Bruce A. "Regulation and Economic Development." In Virginia Gray, Herbert Jacob and Robert Albritton, eds., *Politics in the American States.* 5th ed. Glenview, Ill.: Scott Foresman/Little, Brown, 1990). Pp. 479–526.

EDUCATION POLICY

Cambron-McCabe, Nelda, and Allan Odden, eds. *The Changing Politics of School Finance.* Cambridge, Mass.: Ballinger, 1982.

Campbell, Roald, and Tim Mazzoni, Jr., eds. *State Policy Making for the Public Schools: A Comparative Analysis.* Berkeley, Calif.: McCutchan, 1976.

Fuhrman, Susan, and Alan Rosenthal, eds. *Shaping Education Policy in the States.* Washington, D.C.: Institute for Educational Leadership, 1981.

Iannaccone, Laurence. *Politics in Education.* New York: Center for Applied Research in Education, 1967.

Lieberman, Ann, and Milbrey W. McLaughlin, eds. *Policy Making in Education.* Chicago: University of Chicago Press, 1982.

Mueller, Van, and Mary McKeown, eds. *The Fiscal, Legal, and Political Aspects of State Reform of Elementary and Secondary Education.* Cambridge, Mass.: Ballinger, 1986.

Odden, Allan, and L. Dean Webb, eds. *School Finance and School Improvement.* Cambridge, Mass.: Ballinger, 1983.

Pearson, Jim B., and Edgar Fuller, eds. *Education in the States: Historical Development and Outlook.* Washington, D.C.: National Education Association, 1969.

Richards, Allan R. *Some Aspects of Higher Education: Arizona, Colorado and New Mexico.* Albuquerque: Division of Government Research, University of New Mexico, 1961.

Scribner, Jay D., ed. *The Politics of Education.* Chicago: University of Chicago Press, 1977.

"A Special Issue: Rethinking the Federal Role in Education," *Harvard Educational Review*, 52, 4 (November 1982).

U.S. Department of Education. *A Nation at Risk: The Imperative for Educational Reform: A Report to the Nation and the Secretary of Education.* Washington, D.C.: United States National Commission on Excellence in Education, 1983.

Wirt, Frederick, and Samuel Gove. "Education." In Virginia Gray, Herbert Jacob and Robert Albritton, eds., *Politics in the American States*. 5th ed. Glenview, Ill.: Scott Foresman/Little, Brown, 1990). Pp. 447–78.

ENVIRONMENTAL POLICY

Allin, Craig. *The Politics of Wilderness Preservation*. Westport, Conn.: Greenwood Press, 1982.

Hays, Samuel. *Beauty, Health, and Permanence: Environmental Politics in the United States, 1955–1985*. New York: Cambridge University Press, 1987.

Jessup, Deborah Hitchcock. *Guide to State Environmental Programs*. Covela, Calif.: Island Press, 1988.

Medler, Jerry. "Governors and Environmental Policy." *Policy Studies Journal*, 17, 4 (June 1989).

Nash, Roderick. *The American Environment: Readings in the History of Conservation*. 2nd ed. Reading, Mass.: Addison-Wesley, 1976.

Nash, Roderick. *Wilderness and the American Mind*. 3rd ed. New Haven, Conn.: Yale University Press, 1982.

Neal, Homer A., and J. R. Schubel. *Solid Waste Management and the Environment: The Mounting Garbage and Trash Crisis*. Covela, Calif.: Island Press, 1987.

O'Brien, Robert M., Michael Clarke and Sheldon Kamieniecki. "Open and Closed Systems of Decision Making: The Case of Toxic Waste Management." *Public Administration Review*, 44 (July/August 1984), 334–40.

Opie, John. "Environmental History in the West." In Gerald D. Nash and Richard W. Etulain, eds., *The Twentieth Century West*. Albuquerque: University of New Mexico Press, 1989. Pp. 207–32.

Paehlke, Robert C. *Environmentalism and the Future of Progressive Politics*. New Haven, Conn.: Yale University Press, 1989.

Pinchot, Gifford. *The Fight for Conservation*. Seattle: University of Washington Press, 1967.

Richardson, Elm R. *The Politics of Conservation: Crusades and Controversies, 1879–1913*. Berkeley: University of California Press, 1962.

Roderick, Kevin. "The Quality of L.A. Life: A Times Poll Special Report." *Los Angeles Times Magazine* (April 2, 1989), 10–11.

Schmandt, Jurgen, Judith Clarkson and Hilliard Roderick, eds. *Acid Rain and Friendly Neighbors: The Policy Dispute Between Canada and the United States*. Covela, Calif.: Island Press, 1988.

Tucker, William. *Progress and Privilege: America in the Age of Environmentalism*. Garden City, N.Y.: Anchor Press/Doubleday, 1982.

Vig, Norman J., and Michael E. Kraft, eds. *Environmental Policy in the 1900s*. Washington, D.C.: CQ Press, 1990.

LAND AND NATURAL RESOURCES POLICY

Burgess, Philip M. "Rebels with a Cause: The Sagebrush Movement and the Future of Federalism." In *Agenda for the '80's: A New Federal Land Policy*. Salt Lake City: League for the Advancement of States' Equal Rights, 1981.

Dana, Samuel T., and Sally K. Fairfax. *Forest and Range Policy.* 2nd ed. New York: McGraw-Hill, 1980.

Foss, Phillip O., ed. *Federal Lands Policy.* Westport, Conn.: Greenwood Press, 1987.

Francis, John G., and Richard Ganzel, eds. *Western Public Lands: The Management of Natural Resources in a Time of Declining Federalism.* Totowa, N.J.: Rowman and Allanheld, 1984.

Ganzel, Richard, ed. *Resource Conflicts in the West.* Reno: Nevada Public Affairs Institute, 1983.

Hays, Samuel P. *Conservation and the Gospel of Efficiency: The Progressive Conservation Movement, 1890–1920.* Cambridge, Mass.: Harvard University Press, 1959.

Kneese, Allen, and F. Lee Brown. *The Southwest Under Stress: Natural Resource Development Issues in a Regional Setting.* Baltimore: Published for Resources for the Future by Johns Hopkins University Press, 1981.

Nienaber, Jeanne, and Daniel McCool. *Staking Out the Terrain: Power Differentials Among Natural Resource Management Agencies.* Albany: State University of New York Press, 1985.

Peffer, E. Louise. *The Closing of the Public Domain.* Stanford, Calif.: Stanford University Press, 1951.

Popper, Frank J. "The Timely End of the Sagebrush Rebellion." *The Public Intrest*, 76 (Summer 1984), 61–73.

Robison, Ken. *The Sagebrush Rebellion: A Bid for Control.* Blackfoot, Idaho: Save Our Public Lands, 1981.

Voight, William, Jr. *Public Grazing Lands.* New Brunswick, N.J.: Rutgers University Press, 1976.

Welch, Susan, and Robert Meiwald, eds. *Scarce Natural Resources: The Challenge to Public Policy Making.* Beverly Hills: Sage, 1983.

WATER POLICY

Benson, Lenni Beth. "Desert Survival: The Evolving Western Irrigation District." *Arizona State Law Journal*, (2) (1982), 377–417.

Brown, F. Lee, and Helen M. Ingram. *Water and Poverty in the Southwest.* Tucson: University of Arizona Press, 1987.

Cooper, Erwin. *Aqueduct Empire.* Glendale, Calif.: Arthur H. Clarke, 1968.

Corbridge, James, ed. *Special Water Districts: Challenge for the Future.* Boulder: University of Colorado Natural Resources Law Center, 1983.

Englebert, Ernest A., ed. *Water Scarcity: Impacts on Western Agriculture.* Berkeley: University of California Press, 1984.

Folk-Williams, John A. *What Indian Water Means to the West.* Santa Fe, N.M.: Western Network, 1982.

Folk-Williams, John A., Susan Fry and Lucy Hilgendorf. *Western Water Flows to the Cities.* Santa Fe, N.M.: Western Network and Covelo, Calif.: Island Press, 1985.

Fradkin, Philip L. *A River No More: The Colorado River and the West.* New York: Alfred A. Knopf, 1981.

Gardner, Delworth. "Institutional Impediments to Efficient Water Allocation." *Policy Studies Review,* 5, 2 (1985), 353–63.

High Country News. Western Water Made Simple. Washington, D.C.: Island Press, 1987.

Hundley, Norris, Jr. *Water and the West: The Colorado River Compact and the Politics of Water in the American West.* Berkeley: University of California Press, 1975.

Ingram, Helen M. *Patterns of Politics in Water Resources Development: A Case Study of New Mexico's Role in the Colorado River Basin Bill.* Albuquerque: University of New Mexico Division of Government Research, 1969.

Ingram, Helen M. *Water Politics: Continuity and Change.* Albuquerque: University of New Mexico Press, 1990.

Kahrl, William L. *Power and Water: The Conflict over Los Angeles' Water Supply in the Owens Valley.* Berkeley: University of California Press, 1982.

Leshy, John. "Irrigation Districts in a Changing West—An Overview." *Arizona State Law Journal,* (2) (1982), 345–76.

Ostrom, Vincent. *Water and Politics.* Los Angeles: Haynes Foundation Press, 1953.

Pisani, Donald J. "The Irrigation District and the Federal Relationship: Neglected Aspects of Water History." In Gerald D. Nash and Richard W. Etulain, eds. *The Twentieth Century West.* Albuquerque: University of New Mexico Press, 1989. Pp. 257–92.

Reisner, Marc. *Cadillac Desert: The American West and Its Disappearing Water.* New York: Penguin Books, 1986.

Smith, Zachary. *Groundwater in the West.* San Diego: Academic Press, 1989.

Smith, Zachary A., ed. *Water and the Future of the Southwest.* Albuquerque: University of New Mexico Press, 1989.

Worster, Donald. *Rivers of Empire: Water, Aridity, and the Growth of the American West.* New York: Pantheon, 1986.

OTHER POLICIES AND ISSUES

Albritton, Robert. "Social Services: Welfare and Health." In Virginia Gray, Herbert Jacob and Robert Albritton, eds., *Politics in the American States.* 5th ed. Glenview, Ill.: Scott Foresman/Little, Brown, 1990. Pp. 411–46.

Friedman, Robert. "The Politics of Transportation." In Virginia Gray, Herbert Jacob and Robert Albritton, eds., *Politics in the American States.* 5th ed. Glenview, Ill.: Scott Foresman/Little, Brown, 1990. Pp. 527–59.

"MX Fallout in Zion." *Sunstone Rview* (July–August 1981).

Skogan, Wesley G. "Crime and Punishment." In Virginia Gray, Herbert Jacob and Robert Albritton, eds., *Politics in the American States.* 5th ed. Glenview, Ill.: Scott Foresman/Little, Brown, 1990. Pp. 378–410.

Titus, Costandina A. *Bombs in the Backyard: Atomic Testing and American Politics.* Reno: University of Nevada Press, 1986.

14. Historical Perspectives on the West and Its Politics

Athearn, Richard G. *The Mythic West in Twentieth-Century America.* Lawrence: University Press of Kansas, 1986.

Billington, Ray Allen. *America's Frontier Heritage.* New York: Holt, Rinehart and Winston, 1966.

Billington, Ray Allen, and Martin Ridge. *Westward Expansion.* 5th ed. New York: Macmillan, 1982.

Faulk, Odie B. *Land of Many Frontiers—A History of the American Southwest.* New York: Oxford University Press, 1970.

Haystead, Ladd. *If the Prospect Pleases: The West the Guidebooks Never Mention.* Norman: University of Oklahoma Press, 1946.

Hine, Robert V. *The American West: An Interpretive History.* 2nd ed. Boston: Little, Brown, 1984.

Johansen, Dorothy O., and Charles M. Gates. *Empire of the Columbia: A History of the Pacific Northwest.* 2nd ed. New York: Harper & Row, 1967.

Lamar, Howard R. *The Far Southwest, 1846–1912: A Territorial History.* New Haven, Conn.: Yale University Press, 1966.

Limerick, Patricia Nelson. *Legacy of Conquest: The Unbroken Past of the American West.* New York: W. W. Norton, 1987.

Lowitt, Richard. *The New Deal and the West.* Bloomington: Indiana University Press, 1984.

Malone, Michael P., ed. *Historians and the American West.* Lincoln: University of Nebraska Press, 1983.

Malone, Michael P., and Richard W. Etulain. *The American West: A Twentieth-Century History.* Lincoln: University of Nebraska Press, 1989.

Mezerik, A. G. *Revolt of the South and West.* New York: Duell, Sloan and Pearce, 1946.

Nash, Gerald D. *The American West in the Twentieth Century: A Short History of an Urban Oasis.* Englewood Cliffs, N.J.: Prentice Hall, 1973; and Albuquerque: University of New Mexico Press, 1977.

Nash, Gerald D. *The American West Transformed: The Impact of the Second World War.* Bloomington: Indiana University Press, 1985.

Nash, Gerald D., and Richard W. Etulain, eds. *The Twentieth Century West: Historical Interpretations.* Albuquerque: University of New Mexico Press, 1989.

Nichols, Roger L., ed. *American Frontier and Western Issues: An Historiographical Review.* Westport, Conn.: Greenwood Press, 1986.

Owens, Kenneth N. "Government and Politics in the Nineteenth-Century West." In Michael P. Malone, ed., *Historians and the American West.* Lincoln: University of Nebraska Press, 1983. Pp. 148–76.

Pomeroy, Earl S. *The Pacific Slope: A History of California, Oregon, Washington, Idaho, Utah, and Nevada.* New York: Alfred A. Knopf, 1965.

Schwantes, Carlos A. *The Pacific Northwest: An Interpretative History.* Lincoln: University of Nebraska Press, 1989.

Smith, Henry Nash. *Virgin Land: The American West as Symbol and Myth.* Cambridge, Mass.: Harvard University Press, 1950.

Webb, Walter P. *Divided We Stand: The Crisis of a Frontierless Democracy.* New York: Farrar & Rinehart, 1937.

15. Journal, Magazine and Newspaper Sources on Western Politics and Public Policy

California Journal. Sacramento, Calif.: California Journal Press. *Monthly review of California politics.*

Comparative State Politics. Springfield, Ill.: Sangamon State University. *Bimonthly review of all aspects of state politics including the western states.*

Governing. Washington, D.C.: Congressional Quarterly Press. *Monthly magazine of trends and developments in state and local government.*

High Country News. Paonia, Colorado. *Monthly newspaper dealing with the West focusing mainly on environmental issues.*

Journal of the West. Manhattan, Kansas. *Quarterly journal of western history and culture; sometimes includes articles on western politics.*

Intergovernmental Perspective. Washington, D.C.: U.S. Government Advisory Commission on Intergovernmental Relations (ACIR). *Quarterly magazine featuring articles on intergovernmental relations and the federal system.*

National Civic Review. New York, N.Y.: National Municipal League. *Published eleven times a year. Focuses on state, local and regional government, intergovernmental relations, citizen action and organization.*

The Social Science Journal. Department of Sociology, Colorado State University. *Quarterly journal of the Western Social Science Association. Often publishes articles on western politics, policy and political economy.*

State Government. Lexington, Ky.: Council of State Governments. *Bimonthly journal focusing on all aspects of state government.*

State Government News. Lexington, Ky.: Council of State Governments. *Monthly review of innovations in programs, services and legislation in the states.*

State Legislatures. Denver, Colo.: National Conference of State Legislatures. *Published ten times a year. Focuses on developments and trends in state legislatures.*

The Western Governmental Researcher. Graduate Center for Public Policy and Administration, California State University at Long Beach. *Published twice yearly by the Western Governmental Research Association. Includes articles on various aspects of government in the West with a focus on management and administration.*

Western Historical Quarterly. Department of History, Utah State University. *Quarterly journal of the Western History Association. Includes articles on the development of various aspects of western politics and policy.*

Western Political Quarterly. Department of Political Science, University of Utah. *Quarterly journal of the Western Political Science Association. Until the early 1970s it devoted space to articles relating to the West. In recent years, however, it has become more of a general political science journal.*

CONTRIBUTORS

ROBERT C. BENEDICT is associate professor of political science at the University of Utah. Many of his scholarly writings have focused on the West, energy and environmental policy and the use of the initiative and referendum process. Currently he is examining the role of political party activists in western states.

DAVID R. BERMAN is professor of political science at Arizona State University where he specializes in state and local politics. He is the author of *State and Local Politics*, now in its sixth edition, and numerous articles in professional journals.

MATTHEW A. CAHN is a Ph.D. candidate in the Department of Political Science at the University of Southern California. His reserach interests include public policy, environmental policy, and political theory. His current work focuses on political theory and environmental policy.

R. MCGREGGOR CAWLEY is associate professor of political science, University of Wyoming. He has published several articles in the areas of public land policy and environmental politics.

CAL CLARK is professor of political science at the University of Wyoming. His major areas of interest are comparative public policy and international political economy. He is the author most recently of *Taiwan's Development* (1989).

JANET CLARK is professor of political science at the University of Wyoming. Her major areas of interest are state and local government, American politics, and women in politics. She is the co-author of *Women, Elections and Representation* (1987) and *Government and Politics in Wyoming* (1988).

RAYMOND W. COX III is director of the Master of Public Administration program and associate professor in the Department of Government at New Mexico State University. He is the author of a book on dispute resolution for the International Personnel Management Association and is currently preparing a text on public administration.

JOHN H. CULVER is professor of political science at California Polytechnic State University in San Luis Obispo. He is the co-author of *Power and Politics in California* and author of several articles on judicial politics, capital punishment, and California politics.

TIM DE YOUNG is an attorney with Modrall, Sperling, Roehl, Harris & Sisk in Albuquerque. He is co-author of *California Water: A New Political Economy* (1978) and several articles on natural resources law, special water districts and state water policy and management.

SALLY K. FAIRFAX teaches at the University of California at Berkeley and writes about legal aspects of public resource administration. Her work includes *The Federal Lands* (with Carolyn Yale) and numerous articles and papers on federal-state relations.

RICHARD H. FOSTER is professor of political science and chair of the Political Science Department at Idaho State University. He maintains a lifelong professional and personal interest in politics and government in the West.

JOHN G. FRANCIS is professor and chair of the Department of Political Science at the University of Utah. He is the author of a number of articles on natural resources and political parties in the western states. He is the contributing co-editor of two books on western issues: *Western Public Lands,* and *The Politics of Realignment: Party Change in the Intermountain West.*

F. CHRIS GARCIA has been a professor of political science at the University of New Mexico since 1970. He is the author or editor of six books, the latest being *Latinos and the Political System,* and more than thirty articles, reviews, and book chapters in the area of voting behavior and public opinion, ethnic politics, socialization, and education. He is currently a co-principal investigator on a Ford Foundation–sponsored national survey of Latino political attitudes.

EUGENE R. GOSS is a Ph.D. candidate in the Department of Political Science at the University of Southern California. His research interests include public policy, environmental policy, and political theory. His current research centers on water policy in California.

PAUL L. HAIN is dean of the College of Arts and Humanities at Corpus Christi State University in Texas. He served eighteen years in the Political Science Department at the University of New Mexico and was chair of the department from 1984 to 1989. He is author of numerous articles about state legislatures, co-author of *America's Legislative Processes: Congress and the States* (1983) and co-editor (with F. Chris Garcia) of *New Mexico Government* (1976, 1981).

ERIC B. HERZIK is associate professor in the Department of Political Science at the University of Nevada, Reno. He has published articles on various aspects of state and local politics, policy analysis and executives. His most recent book is *Gubernatorial Leadership and State Policymaking.* Current research interests include analyses of nuclear waste transfer and storage.

RONALD J. HREBENAR is professor of political science at the University of Utah. He is the principal co-author of *Parties in Crisis: Party Politics in America* and the author of *The Japanese Party System* as well as other articles on Japanese party politics in American and Japanese journals.

SHELDON KAMIENIECKI is vice-chair and associate professor in the Department of Political Science at the University of

Southern California. He has authored numerous book chapters and journal articles on environmental policy and political behavior. His books include: *Public Representation in Environmental Policymaking, Party Identification, Political Behavior and the American Electorate, Referendum Voting* (co-author), and *Controversies in Environmental Policy* (co-editor).

JOHN LEPORE is a graduate student in public administration at the University of Alaska Southeast. He holds a B.A. in government from the University of Alaska and worked for four years as a paralegal assistant for the State of Alaska Limited Entry Fishing Commission.

MARGARET MAIER MURDOCK is associate professor of political science at the University of Wyoming. In addition to minority political issues, Murdock is interested in Indian studies, childhood political socialization and constitutional law.

CHRISTINE MARIE SIERRA is assistant professor of political science at the University of New Mexico. She specializes in the study of American race and ethnic relations, interest groups and social movements. Her publications include articles on Mexican American political behavior and Latino interest group advocacy on U.S. immigration policy.

CLIVE S. THOMAS dates his interest in the American West to the age of four when his grandmother took him to see his first western movie in his home town in the west of England. He is now professor of political science at the University of Alaska Southeast. His publications include several authored and co-authored chapters and articles on interest groups, legislative politics and Alaska politics. He has acted as an advisor to several interest groups and to the Western Office of the Council of State Governments.

ROBERT J. WASTE is associate professor of political science at California State University at Chico. His publications include: *The Ecology of City Policymaking* (1989), *Power and Pluralism in American Cities* (1987), and *Community Power: Future Directions in Urban Research* (1986), which he edited.

KENNETH K. WONG is assistant professor in the Department of Education at the University of Chicago. He is author of *City Choices* (1990) and co-author of *When Federalism Works* (1986). In 1989–90 he held a Spencer Fellowship to study the state fiscal role in public education.

INDEX

567